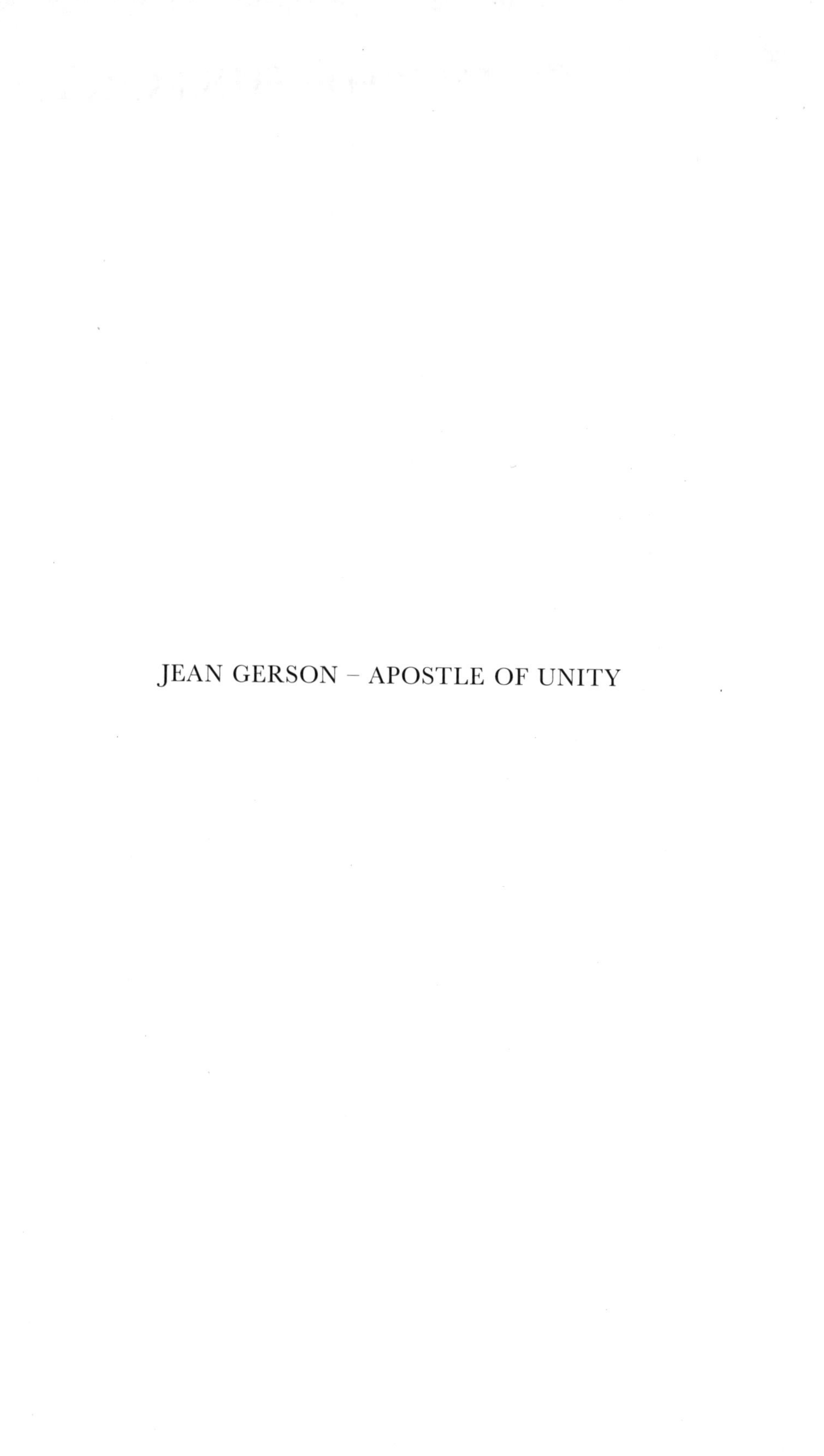

JEAN GERSON – APOSTLE OF UNITY

STUDIES IN THE HISTORY OF CHRISTIAN THOUGHT

VOLUME XCIV

G.H.M. POSTHUMUS MEYJES

JEAN GERSON – APOSTLE OF UNITY

Gerson as ecclesiastical doctor (*pulpit in the Convent-Church at Urach, Germany*)

JEAN GERSON APOSTLE OF UNITY

HIS CHURCH POLITICS AND ECCLESIOLOGY

BY

G. H. M. POSTHUMUS MEYJES

TRANSLATED BY

J. C. GRAYSON

BRILL
LEIDEN · BOSTON · KÖLN
1999

This book is printed on acid-free paper.

Library of Congress Cataloging-in-Publication Data

Posthumus Meyjes, G. H. M. (Guillaume Henri Marie)
Jean Gerson – apostle of unity : his church politics and ecclesiology / by G. H. M. Posthumus Meyjes.
p. cm. — (Studies in the history of Christian thought, ISSN 0081-8607 ; v. 94)
Includes bibliographical references and indexes.
ISBN 9004112960 (alk. paper)
1. Gerson, Jean, 1363-1429. 2. Church—History of doctrines—Middle Ages, 600-1500. I. Title. II. Series.
BX4705.G45P57 1999
262'.02'092—dc21 99-29699
CIP

Die Deutsche Bibliothek - CIP-Einheitsaufnahme

Posthumus Meyjes, Guillaume H. M.:
Jean Gerson – Apostle of Unity : his church politics and ecclesiology / by G. H. M. Posthumus Meyjes. – Leiden ; Boston ; Köln : Brill, 1999
(Studies in the history of Christian thought ; Vol. 94)
ISBN 90-04-11296-0

ISSN 0081-8607
ISBN 90 04 11296 0

PRINTED IN THE NETHERLANDS

To Engelien

CONTENTS

PREFACE

'*Habent sua fata libelli.*' In this case that is especially true. With the first version of this book I made my entrance into the scholarly world in 1963, when I gained the degree of Doctor of Divinity at the University of Leiden.[1] The dissertation was written in Dutch and thus only accessible to a limited public. It was my friend Heiko Oberman who strongly encouraged me to publish it in English as well. He did not leave it at that, for he also arranged a subsidy for the translation, which remained practically untouched for many years; only a few chapters were translated in the 1970's, but the further revision remained in suspense. That was partly the result of my appointment as professor of Church history and the history of dogma at Leiden (1967), which led me to pursue my research and teaching outside the middle ages so that, apart from a second more modest study of Gerson[2] – a direct spin-off from my dissertation – I went on to tackle quite different themes. Time passed, and it was not until my retirement that I again found the time and the opportunity to go back to my first love and take the necessary revision in hand. Thus this revised version of my first work now appears thirty six years later.

In preparing the new edition I have made grateful use of critical remarks, queries and suggestions put forward in the reviews of my dissertation. Above all the discussions which the well known 'gersonisant' Mgr. A. Combes, the Nijmegen professor R.R. Post, both alas now no longer with us, and the latter's successor, my former colleague emeritus professor A.G. Weiler, devoted to my book in the sixties, have set me thinking and their influence will be detected on several points. Mgr. Combes, who to my astonishment – because of his studies of Ruusbroec? – proved to know Dutch, sur-

---

[1] *Jean Gerson. Zijn kerkpolitiek en ecclesiologie*, thesis, Leiden, 's-Gravenhage 1963, appeared, under the same title, as commercial edition in the series: Kerkhistorische Studiën behorende bij het Nederlands Archief voor Kerkgeschiedenis, 10, 's-Gravenhage 1963.

[2] *Jean Gerson et l'Assemblée de Vincennes (1329). Sa conception de la juridiction temporelle de l'Eglise.* Accompagné d'une édition critique du De jurisdictione spirituali et temporali. Préface de Marcel Pacaut, Leiden 1978 (Studies in Medieval and Reformation Thought, vol. XXVI).

prised me within a year of the publication of my dissertation with a detailed and in general agreeably positive verdict on the first part.[3] He did not fail to point out my errors and omissions, which I was grateful to acknowledge, and made criticisms of a question of attribution. In this, however, I was unable to follow him; indeed I found it a new example of the hypercriticism with which, in my youthful boldness, I had reproached him in my dissertation. The medievalist Post found my account of Gerson's idea of the hierarchy insufficiently clear and posed the difficult question of how one was to explain why a conciliarist such as Gerson should have been so remarkably critical of canonists, when recent work (Brian Tierney) had shown just what an important contribution canonistic legal discussions had made to conciliarism.[4] Finally, my colleague Weiler suggested that I had been very summary in my treatment of Gerson's views on the Church as a mystical body.[5] A very just criticism, which can be directly traced to my membership of the Reformed tradition.

In this revised version I have tried to satisfy my critics. Errors have been corrected, omissions filled in and new insights taken into account as far as possible. I have added a new chapter, expanded the text and documentation on many points, and of course have done my best to include the literature which has appeared in the meantime as well as the fruits of my own continued research. I am conscious that the notes have sometimes swollen to an extent which borders on the excessive. But that was hard to avoid, since the interpretation of Gerson, particularly the themes with which this book is concerned, is still contentious, which made more detailed documentation inevitable.

I must thank first the Faculty of Divinity at the University of Groningen, which made me very proud by awarding the original version of this book the prestigious Mallinckrodt prize in 1965. I also voice my thanks to Professor Heiko A. Oberman, for the great loyalty and encouragement I have received from him over the years and above all for his unwearing patience. I had not been aware of

---

3 André Combes, *La théologie mystique de Gerson. Profil de son évolution*, I, Romae [etc.] 1963, Appendice II: 'Gerson et l'Eglise d'après G.H.M. Posthumus Meyjes', 403-17.

4 *Nederlands Archief voor Kerkgeschiedenis*, N.S. XLVI (1965), 237-41.

5 *Tijdschrift voor Theologie* (5) 1965, 95-7.

this quality in him before, but I have come to realise its existence over many years of putting it to the test, which, however, did not put any noticeable strain on our relationship. I also express my thanks to the directors of the 'Gravin van Bylandt Fonds' in The Hague for the award of a generous subsidy to meet the costs of translation. In this context I also thank the translator Mr J.C. Grayson (Southport, United Kingdom) for the energy with which he has worked and for the particular care that he has been willing to devote to my intellectual progeny. Finally I thank my publishers, Koninklijke Brill, for the agreeable collaboration which I once again received from them and for the very handsome style in which, loyal to a long tradition, they have produced this book.

Like the first, this revised version is dedicated to my wife. There is quite a difference between forty-eight years of marriage or twelve. There too, many things have been revised, but not fundamentally, just as little as in this book.

G.H.M. Posthumus Meyjes
Willem de Zwijgerlaan 20
2341 EK Oegstgeest
The Netherlands

December 1998

LIST OF ILLUSTRATIONS

The illustrations 2-5 are taken from O. Feder [ed.], *Ulrich Richental. Das Konzil zu Konstanz, 1414-1418: Kommentar und Text*, Starnberg-Konstanz 1964, 2 vols., a facsimile ed. (*Rosgarten Museum*, Constance)

ILLUSTRATIONS
1-5

1. The papal palace at Avignon (*17th century drawing – Private collection*)

2. A session of the Council in the cathedral of Constance

2. A session of the Council in the cathedral of Constance

3. Pope John XXIII's secret flight from Constance with the Duke of Austria as his companion

4. The Cardinals leave the conclave after the election of a new Pope

5. The coronation of Martin V

INTRODUCTION

It has been Gerson's misfortune, especially for the interpretation of his ecclesiology, that the Gallicans claimed him as one of their own very soon after his death. The eagerness with which his authority was invoked by such men as Jacques Almain and Jean Mair in the sixteenth century, and later by Richer, Bossuet and Dupin, had the result that he earned the reputation of an early champion of Gallican liberties. Although it has now been realised for some time that the relationship between Gerson and these later theologians was not in fact very deep, and it has long been known that the Gallican appeal to him rested largely on a misunderstanding, if it was not wholly illegitimate – as if he had wished to replace the traditional form of the Church by a conciliar system – one cannot say that the interpretation of his ecclesiology has taken these facts sufficiently into account.

This Gallican misrepresentation, which distorted the picture of his ecclesiology for many years, was gradually transformed in the nineteenth century into an Ockhamist or Marsilianist misrepresentation, not a little helped by the ultramontanism and neothomism in vogue at the time. But it was the First Vatican Council, with its definition of papal infallibility, that had a negative effect on historical research. The decrees of this council laid a heavy burden on the minds of many scholars, Roman Catholics of course,[1] and certainly did not encourage them, in fact they hindered them, in taking an unprejudiced and more objective approach to the conciliar period in general and its principal characters in particular.

It seems undeniable to us that these authors formed a very facile view of the crisis into which the Church had fallen as a result of the schism. True, they did not fail to depict this crisis, often with great vigour, when they set the scene; but when they came to describe and evaluate the specific cases of the attitudes of Gerson, d'Ailly and many others, it seems as if they had completely lost sight of the crisis, and pronounced verdicts which bore witness to their own orthodoxy rather than to their historical fairness and objectivity.

---

[1] Other historians, whether or not they were protestants, were much less concerned at that time with the later middle ages.

Gerson's ecclesiology, in particular, was a victim of this attitude. In virtually all the publications of the end of the last century and the first half of this, he is described as a radical revolutionary, a daring innovator, the defender of 'multitudinism', as an Ockhamist or, even worse, as a Marsilian. One of our aims in this book is to demonstrate that such verdicts are unjust; we wish to show that Gerson's views of the Church must be regarded as those of a cautious and conservative theologian.

The possibility of winning understanding for a new interpretation greatly increased as the climate in the R.C. Church altered since Vatican I. One can see Vatican II as the symbol and expression of this wind of change. A. Franzen described the transition from Vatican I to Vatican II in these words: 'the joint responsibility of the world episcopacy for the whole Church, which had declined so greatly since Trent, and had been too obscured by the definitions of the First Vatican Council, became more and more prominent. This not only raised once again the question of the principle behind the relationship of papal primacy and episcopacy, but at the same time allowed the ecumenical council an important function in the life of the Church.' Franzen coupled with this remark an observation of Yves Congar. Comparing the decrees of the Council of Constance with those of Vatican I, Congar spoke of a pendulum swinging between two extremes. Just as Constance had overemphasised the superiority of the council above the Pope, so Vatican I had laid the stress too exclusively on papal primacy, to the detriment of the voice of the council.[2]

The change of climate to which these statements testify was linked with a renewed interest in conciliar questions and hence in that period of the history of the Church in which councils had been most prominent: the fifteenth century, with the controversial Councils of Pisa, Constance and Basle. In the nineteenth century, under the heavy hand of Vatican I, this period of Church history had remained in comparative darkness; but now there was a new interest in it, aroused by the renewed relevance of the questions with which the Church had then been confronted.

In recent decades, whether or not they were inspired by Vatican II, numerous new publications, both historical and dogmatic, have

---

[2] Foreword (viii-ix) to *Das Konzil von Konstanz. Beiträge zu seiner Geschichte und Theologie* (ed. August Franzen & Wolfgang Müller) Freiburg [etc.] 1964.

taken as their theme 'la vie conciliaire de l'église' in the broadest sense. The fifteenth century councils were studied with renewed zeal, and great attention was paid to the legitimacy of these assemblies of the Church and to the meaning and scope of their decrees and decisions. The phenomenon of conciliarism in particular was again of interest to scholars. Giuseppe Alberigo, Walter Brandmüller, August Franzen, Hubert Jedin, Hans Küng, T.M. Parker, Brian Tierney, and many others devoted monographs and articles to it, so that a much more nuanced and objective picture of conciliarism was gained.[3] These and related studies helped enormously to give us a clearer and better picture of the age in which Gerson lived and worked and the solutions that he proposed.

Quite apart from the greatly increased interest in the conciliar period itself since the 1950's, research into Gerson himself had revived two decades earlier. The initiator was Mgr. E. Vansteenberghe. In the 1930's he produced a number of thorough new studies of Gerson and edited several of his previously unpublished French works. These heralded his intention to prepare a new edition of Gerson's complete works, which was however prevented by his premature death in 1943.[4] The realisation of Mgr. Vansteenberghe's plans fell to his old pupil Mgr. Palémon Glorieux, thanks to whom a new edition of Gerson's collected works appeared between 1960 and 1973.[5]

This edition can certainly not be regarded as definitive. It suffers from a great many instances of carelessness and inaccuracy and was clearly published too soon. The chief objection to it is that the very rich manuscript tradition of Gerson's works–certainly of his Latin treatises and sermons–was very inadequately incorporated. In most cases the editor contented himself with collating a single manuscript with Dupin's text,[6] which frequently if not always remained decisive. In the case of doubtful or puzzling readings one is thus compelled to go back to the manuscripts and prepare a better colla-

---

[3] A good survey is given in the collection of articles, edited under the title *Die Entwicklung des Konziliarismus. Werden und Nachwirken der konziliaren Idee*, ed. Remigius Bäumer, Darmstadt 1976 (with extensive bibliographie).

[4] See *DThC* tables générales III, s.v. 'Vansteenberghe Edmond (1881-1943)' (E. Javelet), and P. Glorieux in the introduction to his ed. of Gerson's works (Gl. 1, 9 n. 3).

[5] Jean Gerson, *Oeuvres complètes*, ed. Mgr. P. Glorieux, I-X, Paris [etc.] 1960-73.

[6] Johannes Gerson, *Opera Omnia*, opere et studio Lud. Ellies Dupin, I-V, Antwerpiae [= Amsterdam] 1706.

tion oneself. Another shortcoming of this edition is that the annotations leave a great deal to be desired, and that Gerson's references to the fathers, commentators on the sentences and sources of Church law, or the works of his contemporaries in many cases are not traced or only very inadequately. There too this edition makes a heavy demand on the researcher's own efforts.

On the other hand, this edition is a great advance on its predecessors, especially that of Dupin; and not only because of its handy format but above all because Mgr. Glorieux included the many recently discovered French texts of Gerson in the original and not in Latin translation as Dupin had done. It is another important virtue of this edition that it is the first to contain Gerson's oeuvre purged from the many works wrongly attributed to him. Mgr. Glorieux also supplied very useful bibliographical and historical surveys in each volume, lists of important manuscripts and their dissemination, as well as the necessary indices. Thus this edition, although it falls disappointingly short in textual criticism, has become a very useful working tool, for which it is appropriate to give posthumous thanks to the editor.

Apart from the contribution of Mgr. Vansteenberghe and Mgr. Glorieux to research on Gerson, there were others, as always chiefly French scholars, who were involved in its recent revival. Among them Mgr. André Combes deserves pride of place. He published a very solid body of work on Gerson, which in its extent many times exceeds the works of Gerson himself. We may also name Max Lieberman – an unusually acute and critical scholar, who was known for that reason as the enfant terrible of Gerson studies –, the palaeographer Gilbert Ouy and the French-speaking Belgian scholar Louis Mourin. One may say that it is thanks above all to the publications of all these scholars that research on Gerson has been raised to a previously unknown level of refinement and precision, and that their work brought into being a whole new specialism: that of the 'gersonisants'. It has rightly been said that thanks to their activities the world of Gerson has become 'a building site where everything is up for discussion.'[7]

[7] Cited in the work of Delaruelle (e.a.), mentioned on the next page (865).

This book attempts to pursue the renewal of research we have described and to restore Gerson to himself, to his own age and to the tradition he belonged to, by allowing him to be his own interpreter in a study of his ideas of the Church. The best approach to this problem appeared to be not to turn immediately to his ecclesiology, but first to examine his attitude to the time and his position in the politics of the Church. This was not because his Church politics and ecclesiology were two different fields but because the concrete choices he made in matters of Church policy gave a more solid basis on which to identify the ideas he found decisive, than more abstract theories would have done. In addition, he incorporated his experiences in Church politics and the lessons he had learned from his age into his ecclesiology. Thus old and new were combined in his theory of the Church. The better to recognise both elements, it seemed advisable to distinguish his Church politics from his ecclesiology and to deal with them separately.

A disadvantage of such an approach is that some repetition is unavoidable. We realise this and are well aware that it may be irritating. But we have chosen to accept these objections, because we know of too many studies, including more recent ones, which drew mistaken conclusions on Gerson's views and intentions from a couple of statements taken out of their historical context or tradition. To demonstrate this, we have had to return more than once in the second part to subjects that had already been discussed in the historical chapters.

Given the important role that Gerson played in his time, he is of course regularly mentioned in histories of the conciliar period, for example the classic work of Noël Valois, now more than a century old, *La France et le Grand Schisme d'Occident* (1896-1902). Valois' work was constantly by our side when writing the first part of this book. We also made grateful use of O. Martin, *Les origines du Gallicanisme* (1939) and of the more recent work of E. Delaruelle, E.-R. Labande and P. Ourliac, *L'Eglise au temps du Grand Schisme et de la crise conciliaire* (1962-4), in which Gerson is given a very central role.[8]

---

[8] One will find in this work a very good survey of the state of research, chiefly French, on Gerson. ('Etat actuel des études gersoniennes, II, 861-9). For more recent studies see Giovanni Matteo Roccati, 'Forschungsbericht: Gersoniana', *Wolfenbütteler Renaissance Mitteilungen*, IX (1985) 40-6.

As for the monographic studies of Gerson, we may name first the book of Schwab, written a century and a half ago (1858).[9] The only objection one can make to this extremely thorough study is that it makes constant reference to Gerson's works, which does not make its accessibility easier. Less critical but agreeably readable is the book of James L. Connolly, *John Gerson, Reformer and Mystic* (1928), which however is now largely superseded, in particular by the unusually penetrating but sometimes rather wilful studies of Gerson by André Combes.

Of the more recent monographs we may name first Louis B. Pascoe, *Jean Gerson: Principles of Church Reform* (1973); further Christoph Burger, *Aedificatio, Fructus, Utilitas. Johannes Gerson als Professor der Theologie und Kanzler der Universität Paris* (1986); D. Catharine Brown, *Pastor and Laity in the Theology of Jean Gerson* (1987) and finally Mark S. Burrows, *Jean Gerson and De consolatione Theologiae* (1991). All these works touched on the theme which is the subject of this book. Because the first version, although difficult of access because it was in Dutch, was consulted by all these authors, – in some cases it appears chiefly through the notes –, there had already been some exchange of ideas, which is continued where necessary in this new version.

The only recent monograph which deals with Gerson's ecclesiology in the strict sense is that of the Irish scholar John B. Morrall, *Gerson and the Great Schism* (1960). This gives a brief chronological account of the main points of Gerson's ecclesiology. As such it is a very successful book. The author attempted to free himself from the traditional picture but in our opinion with only partial success.

For our own research two works of André Combes were of particular importance, in which Gerson's ecclesiology was discussed in passing. Firstly, his famous study of early humanism in France, *Jean de Montreuil et le Chancelier Gerson* (1942); and secondly his two volume work *La théologie mystique de Gerson*, which is more recent (1963-5).

Because even recent studies of Gerson frequently cite Dupin's edition, we always give a double reference in our notes: first to the edition of Mgr. Glorieux and then to that of Dupin.[10] In the cita-

---

[9] Johann Baptist Schwab, *Johannes Gerson. Professor der Theologie und Kanzler der Universität Paris. Eine Monographie*, Würzburg 1858.

[10] We name first the title of the work of Gerson and then refer, in brackets, to the relevant passage in the edition of Glorieux (in Arabic numerals) followed by that of

tions themselves we have often modified the punctuation and spelling, and restricted the use of capitals for the sake of readability.

Dupin (in Roman numerals), e.g.: *Vade in pace* (Gl. 7*, 1094-5; Dupin IV, 566D-7C).

PART ONE

GERSON'S CHURCH POLITICS

plurima dixi quae ad ecclesiasticam pacem utilia videbantur... Nec ignoro posse ea a tot capitibus in varias facile traduci sententias, et forsan adversas; quae tamen omnia, si cum distinctione temporum circumstantiarum quoque se offerentium multiplicate pensari digna fuerint, arbitror ea inventuris nexu concordi veritatis inter se iunctas esse, utpote quae circa idem centrum eumdemque cardinem pii desiderii volvebantur.

Gerson in a letter to the Duke of Orléans (5. January 1404) inc. *Multa hactenus* (Gl. 2, 71; Dupin II, 74)

CHAPTER ONE

GERSON AND THE ECCLESIASTICAL POLICY OF THE UNIVERSITY OF PARIS UNTIL 1395

> *... videtur sequi, sine temeraria assertione, quod in praesenti schismate quilibet contendens de papatu et cardinales tenentur secundum animi praeparationem dimittere status suos pro sedando illud et scandalo subditorum removendo.*
>
> Gerson, *De iurisdictione spirituali* (Gl. 3,7; Dupin II, 265D)

The greater part of the life of Jean Gerson (1363-1429) was marked by the tragic events which have come to be known as the Western Schism. This Schism which kept Christendom divided for nearly forty years (1378-1417) in two so-called 'obediences'–the obedience to the Pope of Rome and that to the Pope of Avignon–formed the background of his life and work, on which it had a decisive impact. Without the Schism his life would have taken a different course. His nature, inclined to contemplation and mysticism, would have found a broader field for its development. The Schism is to blame for the fact that ecclesiology and Church politics became so important in his thought and action.

Historians have stressed, above all, that the Western Schism revealed a crisis in the relationship of Church and State, a crisis which is alleged to have gone hand in hand with the growing discrepancy, in the thirteenth and fourteenth centuries, between the universal claims of the Church on the one hand and the awakening nationalism of the European states on the other. Although we must acknowledge that this factor was of importance,–and we need only think of the enormous opportunities which the Schism gave to what later came to be called 'Gallicanism',–we believe that it was not so much a controversy between Church and State, as one within the Church itself, which brought about the Schism, and that the actual crisis was thus of an ecclesiological nature. The internal structure of the Church, notably the relationship between its head and its members, Pope and hierarchy, had become problematical, and the effects of this became manifest in the Schism.[1] No wonder, therefore, that the Council of Constance (1414-18), which succeeded in restoring the unity of the Church, put the *reformatio in capite et membris* as one of the main themes on its agenda.

If the Schism provided the background of Gerson's life and work, the University of Paris was its centre. In his day, this institution enjoyed immense prestige and was regarded as the nursery of learning in general and of theology in particular. For Christians of the time, simple believers as well as for the princes and the clergy, Paris was the highest authority in matters of doctrine, the guarantee of orthodoxy.[2] It was assumed that the University of Paris was infallible on points of faith and morals.[3] Its position was described in the most exalted terms. John XXII, whose views on the Beatific Vision were censured by the University,[4] praised it as of divine institution, intended to enlighten the peoples; its wisdom and the knowledge of its teachers were of benefit to all Christendom; Urban V called it a star in the heavens, spreading its rays over the darkness of heresy and schism, while Gerson, following a current

---

[1] See W. Ullmann, *The origins of the Great Schism*, London 1948, 7ff.

[2] For the role of the university of Paris in this time, see E. Delaruelle, E.-R. Labande, P. Ourliac, *L'Eglise au temps du Grand Schisme et la crise conciliaire (1378-1449)*, [Paris] 1964, 468-76.

[3] For some examples, see Denifle, *CUP* III, no.s 1557-83; IV, no. 1781, and Pearl Kibre, *Scholarly Privileges in the Middle Ages. The Rights, Privileges and Immunities of Scholars and Universities at Bologna, Padua, Paris, and Oxford*, London 1961, 260.–Gerson, *Ecce Rex* (Gl. 5, 251; Dupin V, 337A): '[Theologica facultas Parisiensis] non facile erret in his quae sunt fidei.' In his sermon *Suscepimus* (Gl. 5, 545; Dupin II, 285D) (the theological faculty of) the University of Paris is called: 'cathedra ubi veritas sedet.' Cf. also *Nova positio* (Gl. 6, 153; Dupin V, 411C; 613D): 'Placet tandem attendere quod in curia romana plerumque minor est abundantia theologorum quam consuevit esse Parisiis exempli gratia. Et dum inde trahitur causa fidei per appellationem ad curiam romanam, solet remitti ad universitatem Parisiensem, sicut visum est pluries temporibus nostris.' *Octo regulae* (Gl. 10, 256-260 (257): '... quanta fuerit reputatio praedictarum universitatis et theologicae facultatis Parisiensis apud summos pontifices et curiam romanam in damnandis erroribus ex hoc pluries innotuit, quod ab eisdem universitate et theologica facultate consilium super errorum damnatione dum imminebat facienda, reperiuntur quaesivisse et ab eisdem remisisse. Non immerito, cum iura scripta testentur ibi apicem sapientiae et theologicae fore ibique fidem catholicam circumcinctam, numero inexpugnabili bellatorum.'

[4] On the controversy concerning the Beatific Vision, see Ockham, 'Tractatus contra Ioannem,' in: *Guillelmi de Ockham Opera Politica* III, ed. H.S. Offler, 20-156, and Ludwig Ott & Erich Naab, *Handbuch der Dogmengeschichte*, IV, fasc. 7b, Freiburg 1990, 242-53.

image of his time,[5] compared it with Paradise, where the throne of knowledge was to be found, and from which the fount of learning flowed in four streams – the faculties – spreading life over the whole face of the earth.[6]

These eulogies illustrate the enormous authority and prestige which the University of Paris enjoyed in the Church in general, as well as its central position in the ecclesiastical system. The University, however, was also very closely associated with the royal court. As 'the King's daughter' ('fille du Roy') it enjoyed the special protection of the kings of France. It was not unusual for them to ask its advice in affairs of state, and on occasion it also acted as mediator in controversies between king and people. Its representatives were frequently members of the royal council, and its theologians were often appointed confessors to the princes. Pierre d'Ailly, for example, was for several years chaplain to the King, while from 1393 Gerson performed the same function for Philip the Bold, Duke of Burgundy.[7] It has been rightly said that there were no important questions, even in the field of politics, in the fourteenth and fifteenth centuries, which were decided without the intervention of the University of Paris.[8] Its double relationship, with the Church on the one hand and the court on the other, involved the University in far-reaching consequences when the Schism broke out. Its independence was threatened by the Pope as well as by the King, who both tried to make it subservient to their respective political aims.[9]

Jean Gerson was born on 13 December 1363, the first child of Arnoul le Charlier and Elisabeth la Chardinière, at Gerson-les-Barbey, not far from Rethel in the diocese of Rheims. He probably

---

[5] See George H. Williams, *Wilderness and Paradise in Christian Thought. The Biblical Theme of the Desert in the History of Christianity and the Paradise Theme in the Theological Idea of the University*, New York 1962, 158ff.

[6] Gerson in a letter to his Navarrist friends (1400), inc. *Ecce pareo* (Gl. 2, 36; Dupin I, 110B): '[Universitas Parisiensis] videtur insuper quasi fluvius ille paradisi [in] quatuor partes divisus, irrigans universam superficiem terrae.'

[7] For Gerson's relationship with Philip the Bold, see M. Lieberman, 'Autour de l'iconographie gersonienne (2)', *Rom.* 85 (1964), 49-100 (65-72).

[8] J.B. Schwab, *Johannes Gerson. Professor der Theologie und Kanzler der Universität Paris*, Würzburg 1858, 58ff.; P. Viollet, *Histoire des institutions politiques et administratives de la France* II, Paris 1898, 323.

[9] Cf. E. Delaruelle, *L'Eglise au temps du Grand Schisme*, 471-2: 'Obsédé par le Grand Schisme le pape ne voit plus dans l'université qu'un instrument politique du règne... Au sortir du Grand Schisme, elle ne sera plus que l'université du roi de France.'

received his first education at the Benedictine priory of Rethel, and went afterwards to the school attached to the mother house, the monastery school of Saint-Rémy at Rheims.[10] In 1377, at the age of 14, he left this town in order to study in Paris. He matriculated in the faculty of arts, and was awarded a bursary to the College of Navarre, which at this time became the centre of French humanism.[11] With Nicolas of Clémanges, a fellow Navarrist, and with Pierre d'Ailly, one of its teachers – and soon its regent –, he struck up close friendships, which would endure throughout his life. After four years he attained the degree of licentiate in arts.[12]

In 1381, still holding his bursary at the College of Navarre, Gerson began his study of theology. Pierre d'Ailly and Gilles Deschamps were his teachers. They introduced him to the secrets of scholastic thought, according to the principles of the *via moderna*. He completed the course in the usual time, was meanwhile proctor of the French nation and in 1387 became *baccalaureus biblicus*. In 1388, as a member of the University's embassy, headed by Pierre d'Ailly, he went to Avignon in order to present to the Pope the University's case in favour of the condemnation of the dominican Jean de Monzon, who had argued against the doctrine of the immaculate conception. After proceeding to the degree of *sententiarius* in 1390, followed in 1392 by that of *baccalaureus formatus*, he received his *licentia docendi* from the hands of the Chancellor of the University, Pierre d'Ailly, at 29 years of age, on 18 December 1392.[13]

Apart from a treatise written in connection with the Monzon-affair,[14] few other works are preserved from Gerson's years of study. In particular we do not possess his commentaries on the senten-

[10] For his early years, see H. Jadart, *Jean Gerson, 1363-1429, recherches sur son origine, son village natal et sa famille*, Rheims 1882, and G. Marlot, *Histoire de la ville cité, et université de Rheims*, IV, Rheims 1846, 151ff. For his biography in general, see the lit. mentioned in *TRE* 12, 532-38 s.v. 'Gerson, Jean' (Christoph-Peter Burger).

[11] G. Ouy, 'Le Collège de Navarre, berceau de l'humanisme français,' in: *Actes du 95e Congrès National des Sociétés Savantes. Section de philologie et d'histoire jusqu'à 1610*, I, Bibliothèque Nationale, Paris 1975, 275-99.

[12] P. Glorieux, 'La vie et les oeuvres de Gerson', *AHDLM* 38 (1951) 149-92 (150).

[13] P. Glorieux, 'L'année universitaire 1392-93 à la Sorbonne à travers les notes d'un étudiant', *RSR* 19 (1939) 429-82 (470).

[14] In 1389 he wrote against Jean de Monzon. See G. Ouy, 'La plus ancienne oeuvre retrouvée de Jean Gerson', *Rom.* 83 (1962), 433-92. The work is incorporated in Gl. 10, 7-24.

ces,[15] and only dispose of a number of sermons, almost all preached before the court. It was certainly through his teacher Pierre d'Ailly, who must soon have discovered his pupil's intellectual and rhetorical talents, that Gerson was chosen to preach before such an august audience while still so young. Besides these sermons we still possess one of his disputations given during the ceremonies marking the conferment of his doctorate.

In order to bring out the importance of these few pieces from his early life,–and the much greater mass of work from his later years, –we shall dwell a little longer on the historical circumstances in which he uttered his words, and will relate the history of the Schism during and after his years of study in the first part of this book. As far as possible, we shall focus our attention on the University of Paris and the ecclesiastical policy which it followed. This is for two reasons. In the first place because Gerson was educated in the tradition of this institution, and secondly because the University of Paris remained of central importance for him, as a result of the fact that he was soon appointed its Chancellor (1395), a position he retained until 1415, when he left Paris in order to attend the Council of Constance.[16]

***

A year after Gerson had begun his University studies, Pope Gregory XI, who had returned from Avignon to the eternal city a couple of months before, died on 27 March 1378. Western Christendom had rejoiced at the Pope's return to Rome, for it seemed that with it the period of what Petrarch called 'the Babylonian Captivity', the exile of the papacy in its enclave at Avignon, belonged to the past. However, not long after the death of Gregory, the Church was to experience a disaster still greater than this exile.

On 8 April 1378, the sixteen cardinals who were present in Rome chose as the new Pope the Archbishop of Bari, Bartolomeo Prignano, who took the name of Urban VI. The election was held amid tumultuous scenes. Before and during the conclave, the

---

[15] P. Glorieux, 'Le Commentaire sur les Sentences attribué à Jean Gerson', *RTAM* 18 (1951), 128-39.

[16] See James L. Connolly, *John Gerson, Reformer and Mystic*, Louvain 1928, 191 n. 3.

Roman populace made clear its preference for an Italian Pope, in a noisy and often threatening way. For some, this popular agitation would later form a reason to impugn the validity of Urban's election, but there is no evidence to suggest that the cardinals had any doubts about their choice during the first weeks of his pontificate. On the contrary, they all recognised him, to begin with, as a rightful Pope. They accepted benefices from his hands and informed the Christian princes, as well as the cardinals who were still in Avignon, of their choice. This general acceptance which Urban VI received from the cardinals was, however, to be short-lived.[17]

Urban had been chosen because the cardinals were divided into parties and none of the respective candidates could count on enough votes. Therefore, they had looked to someone outside the sacred college. The humble Neapolitan, Bartolomeo Prignano, owed his election to the fact that he was known for his integrity, was familiar with Avignon, and had won his spurs as a ruler of the Church. Gregory XI had made him vice-chancellor of the Italian provinces, a task which he had fulfilled with loyalty.[18] But alongside these positive qualities, Urban also had some less attractive traits, which became evident once the tiara had been placed upon his brow. His ascetic way of life often degenerated into an impulsive and petulant rigorism. He rashly and unthinkingly criticised the cardinals for their worldly conduct. These spoilt princes of the Church, who were accustomed to be treated quite differently at Avignon, and had expected to receive the same treatment from the simple Prignano, were violently criticised by him on the very first day after his coronation. These rebukes, in which the Pope was liable to forget himself, continued, and once even threatened to come to blows. Every day cardinals were accused of simony or worse crimes. In a short time Urban VI had alienated nearly the entire sacred college.

Is it any wonder that the cardinals sought, one by one, to leave Rome on the pretext of the bad climate? Towards the end of June, barely three months after the election, all but the Italian cardinals had gathered at Anagni.[19] From there they sought contact with var-

[17] For the history of Urban's election, see, besides N. Valois, *La France et le grand schisme d'Occident* I, Paris 1896, 20ff, in particular Ullmann, *Origins*, 13ff.

[18] Ullmann, *Origins*, 16.

[19] Valois, *Schisme* I, 74ff.

ious European rulers, and on 9 August 1378 ventured to declare Urban's election null and void, on the grounds that it had been held under duress from the Roman populace.[20] The princes were informed that the holy see was vacant, while Urban himself was summoned to appear at Anagni, to answer for himself as a usurper. Naturally, he did not comply with this request, but proposed that the validity of his election should be decided by a council, a suggestion which was rejected by his opponents. Several Italian cardinals, including the Aragonese Peter de Luna, – the later Benedict XIII – , who had at first remained loyal to him, also released themselves from their obedience and joined their colleagues who had fled earlier, at Fondi. There, in a short conclave held on 20 September 1378 they elected Cardinal Robert of Geneva as Pope.[21] He took the name of Clement VII and established his seat at Avignon in 1379. As a result of this election, the Schism in the Western Church had become a fact.

Clement VII found himself in a more favourable position than his rival, especially in the earlier period of his pontificate. He was in full vigour, belonged to a rich and powerful family – distantly related to the King of France[22] – and he could not fail to come off best in comparison with Urban, whose unpredictable and hot-tempered behaviour often made it difficult for his own subjects to recognise in him the true vicar of Christ. The majority of the cardinals had rallied to his side, while he also received, sooner or later, the support of John of Naples, France, the most powerful nation in Christendom at the time, Scotland, Savoy, Castile, Aragon, Navarre and Lorraine.[23] Urban VI was not deterred by this formidable block of adherents. He created many new cardinals, and found his supporters in England, Flanders, Portugal, the German territories, Hungary and Scandinavia.[24]

What were the reactions in France, and especially at the royal court, to the double election? When Urban VI had been chosen on

---

20 Referring to Gratian D. 79 c. 9.

21 Valois, *Schisme* I, 79ff.

22 Valois, *Schisme* I, 81; 109.

23 Ullmann, *Origins*, 115.

24 L. Salembier, *Le grand schisme*, [5] Paris 1921, 71. For a detailed survey of the rival obediences, see the maps in R.N. Swanson, *Universities, Academics and the Great Schism*, London [etc.] [1979], xiii & xiv.

8 April 1378, and the report of his election had reached Paris, he was at first – and certainly until the month of July, – recognised as the rightful Pope by the King and the University. A later report even states that the entire University went in solemn procession to Notre Dame to celebrate the election of the new Pope.[25] When the cardinals arrived at Anagni, they soon made contact with Charles V of France, and with the University, in the hope of enlisting their support to declare the election of Urban null and void.[26]

On the instructions of the King, a national synod was held in Paris (11 September 1378), to determine the French standpoint on the election of Urban VI. In this assembly, which was attended by a large number of ecclesiastical and University dignitaries, two envoys of the dissident cardinals were allowed to speak. They informed the gathering that the election of Pope Urban had been brought about by threats from the Roman populace. The King withdrew from the debates and left the decision in the hands of the assembled clergy. Not inclined to support the cardinals in their objections against Urban, the clergy advised the King to take a cautious attitude in such a 'high, dangerous and dubious' affair.[27]

To the outside world at least, Charles began by adhering strictly to this advice for neutrality, and took no steps to the disadvantage of Urban. Meanwhile, however, new reports about the conduct of the election were arriving, by which Charles became more and more convinced that the dissident cardinals were right. He let them know that he would guarantee their personal safety. Presumably the King had made his choice in favour of the cardinals at an early stage – Valois says in October 1378.[28]

A second assembly, again convened by the King, took place on 16 November 1378 in the royal palace at Bois-de-Vincennes. This time the King had invited many of the magnates of the realm as well as theologians and canonists, and they advised, almost unanimously, that Clement VII should be recognised as Pope.[29] The King followed the advice of the meeting, which was entirely in accordance with his personal conviction.

---

[25] This notice, however, stems only from Urban. See Valois, *Schisme* I, 96 n. 1.

[26] Denifle-Chatelain, *CUP* III no. 1609.

[27] Denifle-Chatelain, *CUP* III no. 1613.

[28] Valois, *Schisme* I, 111.

[29] Denifle-Chatelain, *CUP* III no. 1614.

A couple of months earlier, the University had welcomed the election of Urban, and therefore found some difficulty in following the King in his open adherence to Clement.[30] Moreover, there were internal divisions. At the beginning of January 1379 the University addressed itself to Charles. Referring to its vocation to seek the truth, and warning that it would not be prepared to jeopardise its international reputation at the will of a prince, it requested the King to respect its freedom, and not to compel it to take decisions on matters which were still insufficiently clear. It would be better, so some judged, if the King exerted himself to move both Popes to resign, and to settle the grievous conflict.[31] Moreover, they felt that the University could only take a decision if all the faculties and the nations were unanimous.

The King seems to have allowed the University its freedom to begin with, but it was not permitted to remain neutral for very long. At about Eastertime, several cardinals appeared in person in Paris to plead Clement's case. The King gave them ample opportunity to make a report before a large and impressive audience, on their experiences with Urban. These assemblies, for several were held, proved to be effective.[32] The King was strengthened in his adherence to Clement, while the more hesitant allowed themselves to be won over by the reports of these eye-witnesses. The cardinals could be satisfied with the success of their mission: on 15 May 1379, amid processions, prayers and the ringing of bells, Clement was proclaimed to be the true Pope. Everyone who did not obey him was to be regarded as a heretic.

The relative peace in which the members of the University had been left, was now over. In a letter sent in late May, the King pressed them to give an early declaration in favour of Clement.[33] Meanwhile, the divisions within the University had continued unchanged. Not only were the four faculties at odds with each other, but within the faculty of arts the four nations could not reach any agreement. The faculties of law and medicine had been for Clem-

---

30 Denifle-Chatelain, *CUP* III no. 1605. By sending a *rotulus* to Clement the University had already shown that it acknowledged him as the true pope. See Denifle-Chatelain, *CUP* III no.s 1606 and 1620.

31 Fr. Bliemetzrieder, *Das Generalkonzil im grossen abendländischen Schisma*, Paderborn 1904; Denifle-Chatelain, *CUP* III, nr. 1616.

32 Denifle-Chatelain, *CUP* III no. 1618; Valois, *Schisme* I, 130.

33 Denifle-Chatelain, *CUP* III no. 1623; Valois, *Schisme* I, 137.

ent virtually from the beginning. The French and Norman nations joined them, having already shown, by sending a *rotulus*, that they considered Clement the rightful Pope. The Picard and English nations on the other hand, even if the majority of them were in favour of Clement, desired further discussion. The rector proposed new debates: the matters which the King had raised in his letter were issues of principle, so that the fullest discussion was necessary, in which, more than had hitherto been the case, the masters should also be involved. A new meeting was accordingly fixed. Although some of the Picard and English nations continued to stand by their neutral position, the greater part of the theologians proved to have been won for Clement. Thus, a unanimous decision had not been reached. Nonetheless, on 26 May, ten delegates from the faculties, led by the rector, appeared before the King, and the theologian Simon Freron informed him in the most humble terms that the University had chosen for Clement.[34]

This choice had thus been made largely under pressure from the King. Yet Charles did leave some room for the other opinion, as appears from his last words, recorded by Philippe de Mezières: 'I have followed the advice of the cardinals, and as far as possible I have chosen the safest course. I was thus of the opinion, and I am still entirely convinced, that Clement VII is the true shepherd of the Church... If it should ever be said that I erred, – which I cannot accept – then know that I have always tried to serve and to follow our holy mother Church; but I am prepared on this point to submit to a general council or another competent assembly. May God not count against me whatever I have done, without my knowledge, against this future decision of the Church.'[35]

After Charles' death on 16 September 1380 the actual power in France fell into the hands of the Dukes of Anjou, Bourbon, Burgundy and Berry, all uncles of the new King Charles VI, who was only 12 years old. For a short time Louis of Anjou exercised an almost sovereign power as regent. He had particular motives for supporting Pope Clement VII. His aspirations were directed towards founding a kingdom which he dreamt of establishing within the

[34] Denifle-Chatelain, *CUP* III no. 1624.

[35] Valois, *Schisme* I, 326ff. Many years later Gerson refers to these words in his *De auferibilitate* (Gl. 3, 312; Dupin II, 224B).

papal territories on the Adriatic sea, and which was to include the Kingdom of Naples. These plans had the full blessing of Clement who hoped that the founding of the 'Adriatic kingdom' would allow the whole of Italy to be rapidly brought under his control. But matters did not turn out as planned. At the beginning of 1382 Louis appeared in Italy with an admirably equipped army, paid for from papal funds, but his successes were meagre. There was no decisive battle and the expedition soon petered out, while its leader met an inglorious end in the autumn of 1384.[36]

The friendly relations between the regent Louis of Anjou and Pope Clement augured little good for the more neutrally inclined spirits at the University of Paris. Doubtless, they were in the minority, but a minority which included several of the leading figures. Among them could be reckoned Conrad of Gelnhausen, whose *Epistola concordiae* of 1380 was one of the earliest conciliar manifestoes to appear in France.[37] One year earlier, his compatriot Henry of Langenstein, the Vice-chancellor of the University,[38] had also been won over to a conciliar solution, while Pierre d'Ailly, Gerson's mentor and intimate friend, can be mentioned as the third of those who were now thinking along these lines.[39] It is impossible to trace the steps by which the idea propagated by this minority conquered the University so rapidly, but it is a fact that within two years after declaring its adherence to Pope Clement, the University had completely altered its opinion.[40]

On 20 May 1381 the University met in solemn assembly to deliberate what it should do in order to bring the pernicious Schism to an end. Its opinion was that there was no more suitable means than the calling of a general council. The faculties, which two years before had chosen virtually unanimously for Clement, were now

---

36 Salembier, *Le grand schisme*, 105-6.

37 A critical ed. of this letter is provided by F. Bliemetzrieder in his *Literarische Polemik zu Beginn des grossen abendländischen Schismas*, Wien–Leipzig 1909, 111-40.

38 Henry's *Epistola concilii pacis* is incorporated in Dupin's ed. of Gerson's *Opera Omnia*, II 809-40. The first chapters, which are lacking here, were provided by O. Hartwig, *Leben und Schriften Heinrichs von Langenstein*, Marburg 1858, 28ff. Cf. Georg Kreuzer, *Heinrich von Langenstein. Studien zur Biographie und zu den Schismatraktaten unter besonderer Berücksichtigung der Epistola pacis und der Epistola concilii pacis*, Paderborn [etc.] 1987 (Quellen und Forschungen aus dem Gebiet der Geschichte, NF 6).

39 Valois, *Schisme* I, 340-1.

40 Possibly Charles V's last words had contributed to this effect. Cf. Bliemetzrieder, *Generalkonzil*, 77.

agreed that the *via concilii* must be followed, and the University—provided that the court gave leave to discuss the issue—should make every effort to win over the princes and prelates to this solution.[41]

When the University's spokesman, the theologian Jean Rousse, informed the Duke of Anjou of the new plans, the latter replied that he would have Rousse arrested. This brutal measure was entirely in accordance with the Duke's Clementine policy. Perhaps his anger had been especially aroused by a decision which had been taken in the University circle at about this time (15 June 1381) and which had laid down that, given the abnormal situation in which the Church found itself, a certain difference of opinion had to be regarded as admissible, and in particular that none was to be considered a heretic or schismatic for refusing to believe in the legitimacy of Pope Clement.[42] But be that as it may, the Duke was only willing to release Jean Rousse after the Rector and the faculties had repeatedly requested it, and then only on condition that the University should give its unreserved support to Pope Clement, with whom the court maintained such close and friendly relations. Furthermore, it was in future to desist categorically from disputing questions concerning the papal election or a general council.[43]

These measures, by which the University's freedom was cynically sacrificed to the demands of politics, were the occasion for many professors and students, particularly foreigners, to quit Paris, either for Rome where they put themselves under the protection of Pope Urban, or to the east where many of them gained important positions at the young German universities. Jean Rousse and a numerous company withdrew to Rome. In the months which followed Henry of Langenstein, Conrad of Gelnhausen and Henry of Oyta, to name only those who were later to be of importance for Gerson, successively left the French capital and found refuge in the German states. Henry of Langenstein retired first to the Eberbach monastery near Mainz. Then, until his death in 1397, he held a professorship at the University of Vienna, where he was esteemed as an ora-

---

[41] Bliemetzrieder, *Generalkonzil*, 83ff.

[42] Valois, *Schisme* I, 343; Henry of Langenstein, *Epistola concilii pacis*, cap. 13 (Dupin II, 823A): '... mota fuit nuper quaestio in universitate Parisiensi, 15. die Iunii: Utrum stante controversia, quae nunc est in ecclesia Dei de papatu, haereticum sit, seu schismaticum, aliquem electorum negare esse papam? Et fuit super hoc magna doctorum altercatio et congregatio.'

[43] Rel. de Saint-Denys, *Chronique* I, 86.

cle. Henry of Oyta obtained a similar appointment at the University of Prague. Conrad of Gelnhausen became Vice-chancellor of the new University of Heidelberg, the first Rector of which was the Dutchman Marsilius of Inghen, another fugitive from Paris.[44]

In the years following the exodus of the foreign scholars, the University of Paris remained exposed to great political pressure. It was now no longer possible to take any standpoint which smacked of neutralism. It is thus hardly astonishing to learn that at a university meeting on 3 February 1383, the faculties unanimously decided to renew the declaration in favour of Clement which they had issued in 1379. No source of information had been neglected, so they said, and taking everything into consideration they were forced to conclude that Bartolomeo Prignano – Urban VI – had no right whatsoever to the papal tiara.[45]

Urban VI died on 15 October 1389, the end of a sad and unedifying pontificate.[46] It may be imagined that the news of his death would have revived hopes of a speedy restoration of unity, especially at the court of Avignon. At any rate, it might be expected that Urban's cardinals would declare the Holy See vacant, and that before proceeding to an election they would seek contact with Clement's sacred college, as this was senior in its composition. Moreover, many of Urban's cardinals, if they had not already been reduced to silence by his callous behaviour, had been on poor terms with him, so that it was to be expected that they would now look for a rapprochement with Clement. All these speculations, however, proved completely unfounded, for on 2 November, scarcely two weeks after Urban's death, the sacred college at Rome, without discussing the matter with anyone, elected the young and highly

[44] A.L. Gabriel, '"Via antiqua" and "Via moderna" and the Migration of Paris Students and Masters to the German Universities in the 15th Century', in: *Antiqui et Moderni*, Berlin 1974, 439-83.

[45] Denifle-Chatelain, *Chartularium* III, no. 1650.

[46] Cf. Valois' judgement (*Schism* IV, 480): 'Urbain VI: un réformateur maladroit et fantasque, mais aussi un ombrageux et cruel; un ambitieux, un opiniâtre, qui à force d'emportements, et nullement de son plein gré, eût fini peut-être par faire le vide autour de lui.'

immature Cardinal of Naples as Pope. He took the name of Boniface IX. The Schism had not moved a step nearer to solution.[47]

The French King had recently outgrown his tutelage and wished to show what he was capable of. He now returned to the old plan of compelling the Church to unite by force, which had been in abeyance since the death of Louis of Anjou. This idea of a crusade in a new style, invoked with the aim of liberating Italy from the grip of the 'intruder', was well received by Pope Clement, who until his death supported no other ecclesiastical policy except that of violence, then called the *via facti* or *via rigoris.* Charles planned to appear in Avignon at Easter 1391 and then to proceed, as the Pope's humble guide and protector, to the 'holy land', Italy. Clement would be placed on the throne of Peter, and Charles would receive the imperial crown as reward.[48]

This is the background against which we must place the sermon *Adorabunt eum*, which Gerson gave before the King and the other magnates of the realm at Epiphany 1391.[49] At this date he had not yet completed his studies – he was still a bachelor – and this was the first occasion on which he appeared, so to speak, as the effective spokesman of the University. The sermon shows that in University circles, and especially in the faculty of theology, the King's bellicose plans were watched with a critical eye.

In this respect the last part of the sermon is particularly important. Here, Gerson turns to speak of the King's spiritual responsibilities. The welfare of ruler and realm, he claims, is intimately related to the place which is allotted to faith. That the King possesses this faith is obvious, and apparent above all from the fact that he constantly lavishes his care and love on his most humble and devoted daughter, the University of Paris, where the throne of faith is established.[50] The King was always glad to listen patiently to it, when

---

[47] Valois, *Schisme* II, 158-60.

[48] Valois, *Schisme* II, 174ff.

[49] *Adorabunt eum* (Gl. 7*, 519-38; Dupin III, 980-94). Cf. Valois, *Schisme* II, 394-5, and Combes, *La théologie mystique* I, 218ff. Combes' interpretation, however, – 'solitude de Gerson' – seems rather speculative. For a very comprehensive survey of Gerson as preacher, we refer to D. Catherine Brown, *Pastor and Laity in the Theology of Jean Gerson*, Cambridge [1987], 17-35.

[50] *Adorabunt eum* (Gl. 7*, 530; Dupin III, 988B): '... que vostre tres humble et tres devote fille, l'Universite de Paris, avez garde en tous tans et chierement amée, en laquelle la charite et le trone de la foy, c'est assavoir science et la saincte escripture et

ever matters of faith were concerned, and from early morning to late at night he gave audience to innumerable suitors in the Louvre, 'without his attention ever wandering, or lapsing into boredom.'[51]

Gerson then brings to the King's attention, with much display of humility, the evil consequences of the Schism from which Christendom had already been suffering for twelve years. 'O King, your faith is so firm, and your love for the Christian commonwealth so unfeigned that you would not be able to sleep until you have found an adequate remedy. If you had been informed previously of the plans of the University of Paris, you would certainly have listened to them.' Some say, however, that it is not possible to indicate a suitable way to return to unity, because one would then offend the King and Clement.[52] But is there then any law or decretal which can forbid the restoration of unity? That is unthinkable, he exclaims rhetorically, for in such a case a law established for the benefit of the Church would operate to its detriment.

History, he believes, can supply an answer to the question, why God has not put an end to the Schism. The people of Israel, who had also known dissension, were freed from it whenever they addressed themselves to God in prayer and fasting. 'Where, in our day, has there been any recourse to these means and to general processions? Christ speaks of sins from which none may be freed but by prayer and fasting (Mark 2: 9). Perhaps the Schism must be seen as one of these sins. Then it cannot be resolved by human means. We must resort to prayer and fasting, and not on a limited scale, but generally, not only in France but in all the countries of Christendom. God will surely lead us out of our sin, for the prayers of multitudes do not fail.'[53]

---

divine sapience, que on nomme theologie, est sur toutes autres universites plus habundamment et plus vrayment trouvée...'

[51] *Adorabunt eum* (Gl. 7*, 531; Dupin III, 988D).

[52] *Adorabunt eum* (Gl. 7*, 533; Dupin III, 990B): 'Mais aucuns pourroient dire, et pleust à Dieu sans male intention, que on ne peut trouver voye, remede ou maniere qui soit convenable et qui ne soit moult preiudiciable à vostre vray partie et à nostre saint pere le pape Clement, que je croy, et qui de sa grace m'a beneficie de son propre mouvement.' For the last part of this sentence, see Denifle-Chatelain, *CUP* III no. 1563: 'Item motu proprio Johanni Arnaudi de Gersonio.'

[53] Gerson reminds the King that he was 'a son of prayer.' *Adorabunt eum* (Gl. 7* 537; Dupin III, 993A): 'Mais aussi, sire, j'ay oy devant vous et ailleurs publiquement annuntier que par oroison fut [impetrée] votre noble personne à Dieu par le bon pape Urbain [V], et que ainsi vostre pere le tenoit et creoit. Vous estez doncques filz d'oroison la devote'. For the background of this story, see Valois, *Schisme* III, 224 n. 2,

The sermon shows clearly that Gerson felt deeply attached to the University as such. In this respect his words attest to an attitude of independence, which seems difficult to reconcile with his age and the position he had at the time. Here, for the first time, we touch upon the phenomenon of his well-developed self-awareness; not in any personal sense, but a self-awareness based upon the firm conviction that he was acting as a member of the University. Time and again he shows himself deeply convinced that the University, the *studium*, had to play its role as guardian in respect to the *regnum*, as well as to the *sacerdotium*.[54] The University, he felt, was called upon to watch over the boundaries which were drawn in society from on high. When these boundaries were threatened, it had to ring the warning bells. This explains why the University, although 'fille du Roy', – and as such intimately connected with the interests of the crown, – nevertheless, from time to time, asserted its independence by formulating opinions and advice which could be anything but agreeable to the King.

Soon after this sermon a plenary session of the University was held, where the subject of the evil Schism was raised once again.[55] It was attended by 300 masters, and they unanimously decided to ask for another audience with the King. A theologian – according

---

where one reads: 'D'après un ouvrage composé peu après l'année 1400, probablement en Angleterre, c'est en célébrant la messe à Saint-Jean-de-Latran qu'Urbain V aurait obtenu que Dieu exauçât le voeu du roi de France: «Et tuus genitor, o Rex, probavit in te. Quoniam, cum uxorem sterilem annis quatuor, ut dicitur, habuisset, dubitans ob id regnum ad heredem extraneum devenire, Urbani pape V, [sancte] memorie, interpellati orare provide Rome, ad altare sancte sanctorum Laterane basilice celebrantis, piis intercessionibus, in te heredem promeruit exaudiri.» (*Responsiva Unitatis fidelium ad processum regis Francie*; Bibl. Bodléienne, ms. Digby 188, fol. 13 ro). Effectivement, la messe que célébra Urbain V, au Latran, le 2 mars 1368 (Baluze, *Vitae paparum*..., t. I, c. 381), put précéder de peu la conception de l'enfant qui naquit le 3 décembre suivant et devint Charles VI.'

54 H. Grundmann, 'Sacerdotium-Regnum-Studium. Zur Wertung der Wissenschaft im 13 Jhdt.', *AKG* 34 (1952) 5-21; Delaruelle [e.a.], *L'Eglise au temps du grand schisme*, 468; 'La fin du XIVe siècle et le début du XVe furent donc pour Paris un temps d'apogée: l'université traite de puissance à puissance avec le Saint-Siège et s'égale à l'Empire: *Sacerdotium, Regnum, Studium.*' Cf. Gerson in his sermon *Dominus regnavit* (Gl. 5, 229-243 (239); Dupin III, 1457-1467 (1465A), held on St. Louis commemoration-day, 25 August 1392. Here he states that St. Louis had held the University of Paris in the highest esteem: 'Nam et fontem illum scientiae praeclarissimum, Parisiensem universitatem fovit semper, et magnis privilegiis usque nunc manentibus dotavit. Haec est per quam bene Francorum Reges regnant, per quam stabiliuntur in veritate, et per quam de christianis christianissimi sunt effecti...'

55 Rel. de St.-Denys, *Chronique* I, 692-6.

to Denifle, Gilles Deschamps[56]–was deputed as spokesman of the delegation. He earnestly requested the King to devote his attention to the restoration of the Church's unity. The Schism was the cause of countless disasters, and it must be considered one of the primary duties of the secular rulers to seek a way out. The rest of Christendom was called upon to share in this task. Finally, the University of Paris was under the special obligation to further the cause of unity. After a speech on these lines the whole delegation went on its knees to implore the King to lead the Church along the path back to unity and to be mindful of the services which his illustrious predecessors had rendered to the faith. But alas, following hints from an unknown quarter–according to the Monk of St Denys–Charles decided against the plea, and even expressly forbade similar matters to be raised in future.[57]

The decretist faculty complied with the royal ban. It was also the only one to send a *rotulus* to Clement in 1392.[58] The theologians, on the other hand, stood their ground for a while. An anonymous member of their faculty–perhaps Gilles Deschamps again, but in any case not Gerson[59]–published, about this time, a tract in which the prelates, the doctors and all believers are reminded of their duty to strive for unity. The Pope was criticised for sending only his supporters as legates, and for doing as little as the prelates to further

---

56 Denifle-Chatelain, *CUP* III no. 1661.

57 The King received more than one delegation from the University at this time. (Rel. de St.-Denys, *Chronique* I, 694: 'Ob sedacionem huius horrendi schismatis maiestatem regiam iampridem et vicibus reiteratis adierant.') Since it must be excluded that Gerson would have ignored the royal prohibition, we assume that he referred in his sermon *Adorabunt eum* of Epiphany 1391 to an audience which was probably held at the end of December 1390 in the Louvre, and that after Epiphany there was another audience, which resulted in the strict ban on the treatment of questions of Church unity. In March 1391 Charles abandoned his war plans (Valois, *Schisme* II, 179), so that the audience where Gilles Deschamps was spokesman must have taken place between Epiphany and March 1391.

58 Denifle-Chatelain, *CUP* III no. 1597, cf. no. 1662.

59 Denifle-Chatelain, *CUP* III no. 1663, suggests as author either Gilles Deschamps or Gerson, which drove Mgr. Glorieux to incorporate this treatise in his edition of Gerson's works (Gl. 6, 1-21). We agree with Mgr. Combes (*La théologie mystique* I, 229), who rejects this ascription, and add to his argumentation that, in contradistinction to the anonymous author of the treatise who pleads for following the *via concilii* (see in particular, Gl. 6, 10) Gerson at this stage of his life knew of no other remedy for the schism than renunciation. Misled by the false ascription to Gerson, Pascoe's survey of Gerson's ideas about the role of theological doctors in church matters, is to be read with caution. (Pascoe, *Jean Gerson*, 95-7).

reunion. It was also unjust that far reaching decisions had been taken without the doctors being consulted. Every doubtful case ought to have been referred for thorough investigation by the doctors before the prelates pronounced *sententialiter* upon it.

The tract also speaks of the various ways in which unity might be reached. Above all it recommends the way of the general council, recommended in 1381 by the University of Paris. It describes as less suitable the suggestion that the matter should be put in the hands of a commission made up of representatives of both parties. Some of Clement's followers were in favour of this proposal. Referring to the third possibility, resignation, the author claims that the Pope should have surrendered his position as soon as he realised that by remaining in office he was prolonging the Schism.

The tract ends with a forceful appeal to the University to awaken the *negligentes*, those who fail to seek means of restoring unity. As the secular power is only indirectly interested in the unity of the Church, the advice of the King and his council is of secondary importance. Finally, if the decretist faculty persists in standing aside, objections against its orthodoxy will have to be raised.[60]

We do not know whether these words found any echo, nor the exact date when they were written.[61] We have introduced them since they can be regarded, up to a point, as an example of the prevailing mood in the faculty of theology at the time on the issue of ecclesiastical policy. In virtually all the proposals made in these years, one detects an enhanced self-awareness, coupled with a certain resentment against the unwillingness and lack of zeal of the secular and many of the spiritual authorities in France to do anything for the cause of Church unity.

This tendency can also be observed in Gerson. More than once he had the honour of speaking before a highly placed audience, and on occasion he could be very critical about the Church leaders because of their thirst for benefices, which made them forget their care for the welfare of the Church, or about the princes because they failed to search for a remedy for the confusion.[62] In a sermon

60 Denifle-Chatelain, *CUP* III no. 1663.

61 Bliemetzrieder, *Generalkonzil*, 115ff.

62 See for instance his sermons *Misit illos in vineam suam* (Gl. 5, 362-76; Dupin III, 1021-30), given before the University, and *Dominus regnavit* (Gl. 5, 229-43, 241; Dupin III, 1457-67, 1466CD).

given before the King on 2 June 1392 – attended by Philip the Bold, Duke of Burgundy, who would nominate him, shortly afterwards, as his chaplain –, Gerson happens to speak of the war with England, and urges above all that peace should be consolidated, that the poor people should be pitied, and that the Church should be cherished and freed from its tormenting schism. He thinks that if the princes could reach an agreement, it should also be possible to agree about the Pope.

> Neantmoins quant à present il pourroit sembler que ce seroit par faire une bonne entreprise de commun assentiment des Français et des Anglais, et aura on bien matiere de la trouver, et s'il n'y auroit que faire l'unité de saincte esglise ce est ce une matiere tres saincte et tres necessaire.[63]

Noble words, but whether they made much impression on the King is to be doubted. It is certain, on the other hand, that Charles was not deterred from following the *via facti* by the pleas of the University but by political pressure from England. Furthermore, the mental illness which began to reveal itself in March 1392, also helped to push his warlike schemes into the background.[64]

More important for our purpose than the scanty details supplied by his earliest sermons is Gerson's treatise *De iurisdictione spirituali*.[65] – When a student of theology had gained his *licentia docendi* – as Gerson did on 18 December 1392 – he was expected to deliver three addresses, which were not so much in the nature of an examination as intended to give expression to the civil effect and social responsibility bound up with the degree of licentiate.[66] The various ceremonies and scholastic disputations associated with them were entitled: *vesperiae, aulica* and *resumpta*. In the *resumpta* the theme of the preced-

---

[63] *Accipietis virtutem* (Gl. 7*, 448; Dupin III, 1259D). See J. Mourin, *Jean Gerson prédicateur français*, Brugge 1952, 77-83.

[64] Valois, *Schisme* II, 397ff.

[65] *De iur. spir.* (Gl. 3, 1-9; Dupin II, 261-7).

[66] Cf. Pierre d'Ailly in his second treatise against the Chancellor of the University of Paris (ed. Bernstein, 281^{11-17}; Dupin I, 769B): '...licentia docendi in theologia, a cancellario data, est potestas seu auctoritas spiritualis... Sed magisterium, eciam in theologia, non est, ultra licentiam predictam, aliqua auctoritas spiritualis, sed solum quidam honor, seu quidam honoris gradus politicus seu civilis. Unde magisterium huiusmodi se habet ad licentiam, sicut nuptie ad sacramentum matrimonii. Et licet huiusmodi sacramentum sit spirituale, non tamen huiusmodi nuptie, sed sunt quedam sollempnitas ad honorem et decorem sacramenti...'

ing disputations was taken up again.[67] In the treatise *De iurisdictione spirituali* we possess Gerson's *resumpta*, which he delivered soon after 18 December 1392.[68]

In this disputation he speaks of the limits of the ministry of the Church, a theme which had become highly relevant as a result of the Schism. He starts from the following premise: if he who exercises spiritual jurisdiction knows, or ought to know, that his exercise of it endangers the religious life of others or religion in general, he is obliged to surrender his powers. Thus we are not concerned here with the question of whether a spiritual leader should step down if he has neglected his task or fallen short in any other way, but with the much more paradoxical case, that he must resign his jurisdiction for the simple reason that its exercise is to the disadvantage of others. Canon law had provided for the eventuality.[69]

The proof is adduced in a reference to pastoral leadership (*praesidentia pastoralis*), brotherly love (*fraterna caritas*), and due service (*debita servitus*). Just as the first of these, by virtue of John 10: 11, assumes that the pastor will not flee if danger threatens the faith, so he ought to quit if his presence gives any reason to this danger.– Brotherly love compels us sometimes to give up that which is not in itself forbidden (1 Cor. 8: 13). This implies that the surrender of ecclesiastical jurisdiction is allowed, if its maintenance creates a scandal. Moreover, Boniface VIII had established the possibility of renunciation in one of his decretals,[70] while Celestine V had given the example of such a surrender of the papal dignity.[71] – The third proof of the thesis is derived from the well-known adage: '*beneficium datur propter officium*.'[72] This saying makes clear that a benefice is a means and not an end. If the possession of it comes into conflict

[67] P. Féret, *La faculté de théologie de Paris et ses docteurs les plus célèbres* III, Paris 1896, 79ff.

[68] Glorieux, 'L'année universitaire 1392-93 à la Sorbonne, à travers les notes d'un étudiant', *RSR* 19 (1939) 429-82 (470).

[69] X 1.9.10. Here, with reference to I Cor. 8: 13, the well-known hexameter: 'Debilis, ignarus, male conscius, irregularis / quem mala plebs odit, dans scandala, cedere possit.'

[70] VI I.7.1.

[71] Gerson refers to Alexander of St Elpidio, *De ecclesiastica potestate* III, cap. 6 (ed. Rocaberti 37a).–Cf. J. Leclercq, 'La rénonciation de Célestin V et l'opinion théologique en France du vivant de Boniface VIII', *RHF* 25 (1939) 173-92. At the request of the Paris Celestines, Pierre d'Ailly wrote in 1408 his *Vita beatissimi Petri Celestini quinti*. Cf. L. Salembier, *Petrus de Alliaco*, Insulis 1886, XL-XLI, 322-6.

[72] VI I 3. 15.

with the goal for which it was established, then it should be given up. The same holds for the ministry, for '*quod pro caritate institutum est, contra hanc militare non debet*,'[73] or, in more Aristotelian terms: '*cessante fine et causa institutionis, cessare debet institutio.*'[74]

Taken literally, these are poorly chosen rules, for they could give the impression that Gerson wished to attack the hierarchy as an institution, while in fact nothing could have been further from his mind. He never attacked the structure of the hierarchy as such, either here or anywhere else. He wished only to defend the thesis that the subject, the holder of an ecclesiastical office, had to give way in certain cases. In no way did he attack the office itself.

He then relates the thesis which he has thus proven to the actual circumstances of the time, and raises three questions: 1. Is it an article of faith, that there is a Pope? 2. Do the followers of the Pope of Rome stand by him from misplaced loyalty? 3. Is there a better way to attain unity than by a voluntary or enforced resignation (*via cessionis*)?

1. For Gerson it was beyond dispute that the Roman Church possessed the principate, and that there was a single primate. It is entirely in accordance with natural and divine law, he says, that the Church is under the rule of one head. If all are obliged to follow one faith, then there must also be one person who guards that faith. Many passages from scripture and from the decretals could be cited to prove this. Gerson leaves them to one side and claims: even if it were not a catholic truth that there is but one Pope, the *consuetudo* followed since the apostles would make it a rule.[75]

But the problem of the Schism is precisely that there are two claimants to this dignity, both of whom are regarded within their respective obediences as the only true Pope. Whoever chooses one Pope, excludes the other entirely. A follower of the Pope of Rome will for example say: 'Clement is no Pope'. But if someone within the obedience of Clement himself were to say something like this, how would it have to be regarded? As heresy? No, replies Gerson, and he argues that although it is true that the statement: 'Clement

---

[73] Bonaventura, *Comm. in libr. sent.* IV d. 17 p. 3 a. 1 q. 2 (ed. Quaracci IV, 452, 56) refers for this formula to Bernard of Clairvaux. *De praecepto et dispensatione*, c. 2, 5 (*PL* 182, 864).

[74] Roman legal rule. Cf. Thomas Aquinas *S.th.* I q. 96 a. 3 obiect. 3.

[75] *De iur. spir.* (Gl. 3, 5; Dupin II, 263C-4B). With reference to Thomas Aquinas *S.th.* II^{a} II^{ae} q. 39 a. 4; and C. 23 q.5 c.44.

is no Pope' smells of heresy (*sapere haeresim*), it cannot be unconditionally qualified as heretical.[76] There is no doubt that he is following Ockham in this thesis, which is also wholly in the spirit if the University's decision of 15 June 1381.

> In his *Dialogus* Ockham compiled a list in which he ranked the various catholic truths in a hierarchic order.[77] In this hierarchy, he includes, among others, certain truths which cannot be clearly proved from scripture or tradition, nor logically deduced from them, but derive from an historical-contingent, rational truth, connected with one or more catholic truths from Scripture or tradition. As examples of this sort of truths Ockham names the monastic rules, the certainty that Augustine confessed the faith, the catholicity of the creed of Athanasius and the ecumenicity of the first four councils. These truths are not catholic in the strict sense of the word, although they approach the catholic truths very closely, and 'smell of the catholic truth' (*sapere catholicam veritatem*).
> Gerson, formulating in a negative sense, follows this argument when he claims that the statement: '*Clemens non est papa*', can be formally equated with the proposition: '*Symbolum Athanasii est falsum*'. Both statements smell of heresy but they cannot strictly be called heretical, because they are concerned with matters which are largely historical-contingent in their nature, and about which no absolute certainty can be achieved. This certainty cannot be provided by a council either, because such a body could only make an infallible pronouncement on whether there should be a Pope or not, but not on the question of whether Clement is Pope. This would involve a decision on facts, while a council can err in things of such nature ('*in illis quae facti sunt errare possit*').[78]

Gerson thus put the question, whether Clement was Pope or not, outside the proper sphere of catholic truths, thereby leaving a margin for doubt on the legitimacy of his papacy. The attractive feature of this view was that it took the phenomenon of schism out of the rather narrow confines of the strictly juridical way of looking at it, and set it in a much broader context. Since Gerson did not allow salvation to depend on the first place on the recognition of Pope Clement, matters of a purely juridical nature, especially the validity

---

[76] *De iur. spir.* (Gl. 3, 5; Dupin II, 263C).

[77] Ockham, *Dialogus* I 2, 2 (ed. Goldast, 411[55]-12[48]).

[78] *De iur. spir.* (Gl. 3, 6; Dupin II, 265A): 'Iuxta hoc facile est videre quomodo in ista materia concilium potest errare et quomodo non. Quia si proponeretur ista propositio: an deberet esse unus papa, concilium circa illa errare non posset. Si autem proponeretur ista: an Clemens sit papa, cum includat unum quod est facti, et etiam in illis quae facti sunt, errare possit, sicut in moralibus, in scibilibus, *ut bene deducit Ockham.* non oportet dicere quin errare possit...'

of his election, were relegated to a secondary position, thus allowing the quest for unity to be raised to a higher plane.

On the other hand, the juridical aspects of the affair could not be entirely neglected. If it was permissible to doubt the legitimacy of Clement's papacy, what was to be thought of the validity of the sacraments administered in his obedience? What was the worth of the sacrament if it was administered by a priest who had been instituted by a dubious Pope? Gerson, referring to Robert Holcot, dispelled these doubts with the remark that the sacraments are at all times administered and received under the tacit assumption that nothing is lacking in the *intentio* of the minister, and that everything is performed *rite*.[79]

2. The question follows, whether we may ascribe any malice to the followers of the other Pope. Do they hold fast to the Pope of Rome out of bad faith? In Gerson's argument, this is a very important question, for if the answer is yes, the solution he proposed would be completely impossible. His starting point was that the Pope must resign if his remaining in office causes offence (*scandalum*). In one case only was he not obliged to do this, namely if the believers caused a scandal deliberately—*ex malitia*. The Pope was not bound to yield to such rebellion. Is there any evidence of this among the supporters of the Pope of Rome? The answer is no. Gerson feels that in general they have chosen his part in ignorance of the facts of his election. The majority is thus in error, but in good faith, not out of malice. Consequently, there is no obstacle to resignation.[80]

In this connexion he raises indirectly the question of who must be held responsible for the outbreak of the Schism. Like many others, and notably his pupil, Nicolas of Clémanges, he points to the cardinals.[81] By their unlucky words and deeds they caused a

---

[79] He refers to 'Olkoth in IV' (Gl. 3, 6; Dupin II, 261A), by which he probably meant Robert Holcot, *Comm. in libr. sent.* IV q. 3 ad 7um (cf. q. 3 pr. 5), where one reads: 'Ad septimum cum dicitur non requiritur intentio, quia tunc haberet dubitare quilibet in elevatione an debeat adorare vel non. Dico quod non debet dubitare dintinguendo dubitare contra credere, sed credere debet quod sacerdos bona fide facit, et adorare secure. In illa tamen adoratione subintellegitur conditio puta si consecratum est, et ideo nullum periculum est etiam hostiam non consecratam adorare, quia non adoret nisi sub conditione tacita ibi subintellecta.' Gerson often adapted this reasoning to the case of the schism.

[80] *De iur. spir.* (Gl. 3, 6; Dupin II, 261B).

[81] In his *De corrupto statu ecclesiae*, cap. IX-XI (ed. Lydius I, 10a-12b; modern ed.: A.

completely unique schism to arise, thus making it possible for the anti-Pope to ruin the Church. Therefore the prime responsibility for restoring order is theirs too.[82] But others have this duty as well. If they omit to perform it, then it is to them, rather than to those who follow the Pope of Rome – literally to 'those who keep to the false party' –, that the term schismatic is applicable.[83]

3. It is clear from all these considerations that there can be no better means to solve the present Schism than resignation. Both Popes and their cardinals should give up their office voluntarily, for they are clearly in conflict with the interest of the faithful.[84]

> The objections which might be urged against this proposal are refuted at the end of the disputation. In the first place, there is the objection that the resignation of one of both Popes would remove the consequences of error but not its cause. In other words, the legal question would be left unanswered. Gerson believes that this objection applies more to the supporters of the *via facti*, for waging war would certainly not remove the cause of error. Furthermore, he regards it as unhelpful to raise the ques-

---

Coville, *Le traité de la ruine de l'église de Nicolas de Clamanges*, Paris 1936, 121-3) Nicolas bitterly attacked the cardinals for their lust for power and goods. He held them chiefly responsible for the outbreak and continuation of the schism. Pierre d'Ailly also expressed himself in these years in very negative and sarcastic terms about the cardinals in his *Epistola diaboli Leviathan*. Cf. P. Tschackert, *Peter von Ailli*, Gotha 1877, [5]-[21], and I.W. Raymond, 'D'Ailly's «Epistola Diaboli Leviathan»', *CH* 22 (1953) 181-91.

[82] *De iur. spir.* (Gl. 3, 6; Dupin II, 265B): 'factum cardinalium fuit scandalosum. Probatio: quia fuit factum vel dictum minus rectum praebens alteri occasionem ruinae. Et qui bene volet profundare illud punctum videbit quomodo cardinales super omnes qui in mundo sunt tenentur remediare schismati, etc. Et multa similia. Unde non est simile de isto schismate et aliis, quia illud est totum mirabiliter propter facta cardinalium tribus mensibus post electionem qualemcumque primi.'

[83] Gerson again rejects the *via facti*. Cf. *De iur. spir.* (Gl. 3, 7; Dupin II, 265D): 'falsissima... est opinio illorum qui dicunt procedendum esse per bella contra partem adversam; et haec alias deduxi in sermone *De angelis* et coram rege.' By *De angelis* the sermon *Factum est proelium* is meant, which he held a couple of months before at St. Michel (29th sept. 1392) (Gl. 5, 292-324 (303-5); Dupin III, 1468-80). This sermon, however, was certainly *not* preached before the King, as Mgr. Glorieux thought possible (Gl. 5, xii, 228, 'Sermon devant le roi?'), for in that case Gerson would have expressed himself in French, not in Latin. Moreover, he addresses his audience in this sermon at least three times with: 'reverendi patres', which points to an audience of prelats. The statement 'coram rege', therefore, should be understood as a reference to the sermon *Adorabunt eum* (Epiphany 1391), which was actually held before the King. See above n. 49.

[84] Cf. *De iur. spir.* (cited above, epigraph). The often used expression 'secundum animi praeparationem', means 'prompte', as appears from *Libellus articulorum* (Gl. 6, 265; Dupin II, 293C): '... quilibet catholicus debet habere promptitudinem seu praeparationem animi ad obediendum...' We fail to grasp why Mgr. Combes (*La théologie mystique* I, 213 n. 109) qualified this expression as 'une réstriction si lourde de sens.'

tion of law, for it only arouses the hatred of the opposite party to describe it as heretical or schismatic. That might indeed only cause a new dissension.

The second objection: the case may be imagined in which the true Pope might resign, while the false one does not. Does that not create a real danger? No, for there are other cases known in history, of Popes who exercised their office well, without having been chosen in the proper way. Moreover, the united cardinals could always legalise such a Pope's election.

In the third place it may be objected that resignation indicates weakness, and that this renders the matter suspect. Here Gerson refers once more to Celestine V. When he resigned, he was far from putting himself under any such suspicion, on the contrary he was praised for his humility, which had led him to give up his own rights for the sake of the greater good.

Finally, a practical question. What is to be done with the priests who have been ordained within the jurisdiction of the schismatic party? Must they be ordained again, or will their first ordination suffice? Gerson appeals to history to justify the latter course. Moreover, we may be confident that God, in his mercy, adds whatever is missing to the sacramental acts of invalidly ordained priests.[85]

De iurisdictione spirituali shows that at the time he had completed his university studies, Gerson was an outspoken supporter of the solution of the Schism by means of resignation. He made an unequivocal choice for the *via cessionis*, and showed himself again a strong opponent of the military solution (*via facti*). He saw no hope in the summoning of a general council either, since this could only pass judgement in cases of heresy, not of schism.[86] The objections of a juridical nature which could be raised against the proposal of resignation, made little impression on him, as the unity of the Church was for him a greater good than the maintenance of the positive legal order. Whenever his thoughts on ecclesiastical policy were later to change, the unity of the Church remained their guiding light.

During the early months of 1393, processions and prayers were held everywhere in France to plead for unity. The court, the University and the clergy took part in this official display of piety, and for his

[85] *De iur. spir.* (Gl. 3, 8-9; Dupin II, 267BC).

[86] *De iur. spir.* (Gl. 3, 5; Dupin II 264B): '...et non celebrabitur etiam concilium quod haereses expellit et non schismata.'

part Clement furthered this path to unity by introducing a special mass *pro sedacione schismatis.*[87] It may be doubted whether all members of the University took part in these processions enthusiastically, especially given the sermon Gilles Deschamps preached before the King at this time on behalf of the University, and in which he spoke sharply of the duty to strive for unity. Whoever obstinately asserts that it is not necessary to advance the unity of the Church, must be regarded as a heretic, and whoever actually opposes this effort, as a schismatic. The attempt to bring unity closer by means of prayer is held to be insufficient, even an affront to God. With reference to the two papal pretenders, he remarks that they must be driven out, if they refuse to make any effort for unity.[88] We can hear in this address the same anger at the unwillingness to come to the aid of the Church in its hour of need, which we already observed in University circles, and particularly in the faculty of theology.

Meanwhile it seemed as if the King was more inclined to meet the University's desires. In June 1393 his mental illness had again returned, so that he was unable to take decisions on matters of Church and State. When the news of the King's recovery reached the University in January 1394, it immediately led the University to request an audience. A deputation went to St Germain-en-Laye, where in the presence of Charles, the Dukes of Orleans, Berry, Burgundy and Bourbon, the theological doctor Etienne de Chaumont argued that God had healed the King so that he might come to the aid of the Church. If Charles failed to fulfil this duty, he would forfeit his title of *rex christianissimus.*[89] The Duke of Berry, as the eldest prince of the blood, answered in the name of the King. This eager supporter of Pope Clement gave quite a different answer from that expected of him. He told the deputation that the godless Schism had lasted long enough, and was a scandal for the King and for the whole court of France. 'Search for means of ending it, to the honour of the kingdom. If you indicate a way which can find support of the royal council, you may be assured that it will be followed closely.' The deputation, pleasantly surprised by

---

[87] Valois, *Schisme* II, 403ff.

[88] Denifle-Chatelain, *CUP* III no. 1666.

[89] Rel. de St.-Denys, *Chronique* II, 94; Valois, *Schisme* II, 407; Bliemetzrieder, *Generalkonzil*, 119ff.

the changed sympathies of the court, which had rarely shown any real interest in the unity of the Church before, returned to Paris and celebrated the decision with a great procession.

The King appointed a commission made up of members of the royal council to discuss with the representatives of the University the means to restore the unity of the Church. The University delegation threw itself into frenzied activity. It had a ballot box placed in the monastery of the Mathurins in which everyone was invited to put his suggestion for the ending of the Schism. The box later proved to contain ten thousand suggestions, a large number explained by the fact that–as Gerson reveals to us–many had tried to add weight to their proposals by depositing more than one schedule in the box.[90] The committee went through the papers and compiled a *schedula communis.*

Three main means for the restoration of peace appeared to have been proposed: consulting the universal Church, setting up an arbitration committee, or the simultaneous resignation of both the Popes: *via concilii, via compromissi* and *via cessionis.* It proved difficult to reach any agreement with the King's commission, so that the representatives of the University proceeded to take independent measures. A great assembly of the University was held on 26 February 1394 and gave its approval to the proposals, declaring itself ready to defend them against all comers. The faculty of divinity appointed Guillaume Barrault as its spokesman to inform the King of these plans.[91]

At the same time, Gerson gave an Easter sermon before the court (19 April 1394).[92] In it he tactfully reminded the King of the role which the University had played in the condemnation of Pope John XXII in the matter of the Beatific Vision, clearly intending to make the King look on 'his daughter', the University, with more respect.[93] He also rebuked the passionate ambition which had divided the Church in its head and members, causing persecution and chaos in the wordly sphere. Ambition had not even been afraid

---

[90] *De substractione schismatis* (Gl. 6, 23 : Dupin II, 8D): '...stat quod idem homo ponet centum schedulas ad opinionem suam tamquam diversi posuerint, ut secundum pluralitatem schedularum iudicetur.' Cf. Bliemetzrieder, *Generalkonzil*, 120 n. 1.

[91] Denifle-Chatelain, *CUP* III no.s. 1678-80.

[92] *Pax vobis* (Gl. 7*, 779-93; Dupin III, 1204-14).

[93] *Pax vobis* (Gl. 7*, 779-93; Dupin III, 1205A). See above n. 4, and *Ecce Rex* (Gl. 5, 250; Dupin V, 336D-7A).

to reach out her grasp to the highest ecclesiastical dignity, the papacy; and as a result, that which had been established to serve the common good of the Holy Church, had become instead the source of evil and dissension.[94] 'Where are we to turn for support in these circumstances except to the princes?' In earlier times it was they who came to the aid of the Church when it was in need, or suffering persecution. Now their support was more necessary than ever, for it concerned a schism of unprecedented nature and scope. Alas, to their shame, many prelates, along with many others, refused to do anything to bring about unity. Some of them even tried to fend it off by false means, and to work against peace. The princes ought to have realised that they should have supported those who sought for peace. If they failed to do so, they would have been guilty before God. It would of course have been desirable that the '*falsa pars*' should go over to the Avignonese obedience, but now that it was clear that this could not be achieved through the methods proposed, nor by war, other ways had to be sought. If someone acting in bad faith should try to obstruct this, he would be guilty of a mortal sin, and would deserve, as a schismatic, to forfeit his status.[95]

Unfortunately, despite the recent encouraging words of the Duke of Berry, this exhortation of Gerson's was entirely justified. The court's willingness to come to the aid of the Church seemed to have vanished in a very short time. The reason for this was that the partisans of Pope Clement had not been idle. The Pope's chamberlain, François de Conzié, in particular had been involved in doubtful intrigues in Paris, which were still being discussed years later. He wished, at any price, to prevent the University gaining access to the King, while he also tried to ensure that Charles should forbid any further discussion of the Schism. Well provided with gold and silver, he seems to have bribed many of the courtiers. Unfortunately for the University, the prince who was most sympathetic to them, Philip the Bold, Duke of Burgundy, was not at the court during these months. The Dukes of Berry and Orleans, whose unconditional preference for Clement was widely known, thus had every opportunity to push forward their views. [96]

Under these circumstances, the University was unable even to

[94] *Pax vobis* (Gl. 7*, 790-1; Dupin III, 1212B-13A).
[95] *Pax vobis* (Gl. 7, 791-3; Dupin III, 1213AD).
[96] Bliemetzrieder, *Generalkonzil*, 127ff; Valois, *Schisme*, II, 425.

gain access to the King, and it therefore decided to present its plans for peace–*via cessionis, via compromissi* and *via concilii*–to him in writing. Pierre d'Ailly and Gilles Deschamps were closely associated in the preparations for this, while Nicolas of Clémanges, the Cicero of his time, received the task of embellishing the paper with the flowers of his rhetorical skill.[97] The work, which was also intended to be sent to all corners of Europe, was read out and accepted in a plenary session of the University on 6 June 1394, the eve of Pentecost.[98] The Roman obedience congratulated the University on its plans and encouraged it to continue on the path it had begun.[99] The reception given by the court was less welcoming. The Duke of Berry even refused to allow the University delegates access to the King. He called it a scandalous presumption, that they should propose Clement's deposition, and threatened that if the University did not give up its plans, he would have its champions drowned.

At last, on 30 June, after Philip of Burgundy had returned to the court, the University gained the audience it had desired, although in a much more modest form than it had wished. Guillaume Barrault elaborated on the University's proposals, as contained in the letter of 6 June, and offered the King a copy of them, sealed with the great seal of the University.[100]

> Unlike the plans of a couple of months previously, this letter did not recommend the *via concilii* in the first place, but the absolute renunciation of both papal pretenders, that is the *via cessionis*. The University felt that no method was simpler or more acceptable than this, for it would completely eliminate the bone of contention. Once the way had been completely cleared by resignation, the cardinals–either the older ones only, or the full college–could proceed to elect a new Pope.
>
> In the event of the Popes refusing, as they had up till then, to give up their real or supposed rights, the University proposed the *via compromissi*. They described this way as simpler than a general council, and also more agreeable for both parties. In this case, arbiters would have to be chosen, to whose decisions the Popes would be obliged to submit. These arbiters would have the duty of investigating the disputed points, and

97 Rel. de St.-Denys, *Chronique* II, 130.

98 Valois, *Schisme* II, 413 n. 3.

99 Bliemetzrieder, *Generalkonzil*, 126ff.

100 Text of the letter in Rel. de St.-Denys, *Chronique* II, 136-82, and Denifle-Chatelain, *CUP* III no. 1683, 617-25. See also G. Ouy, 'Le recueil épistolaire autographe de Pierre d'Ailly et les notes d'Italie de Jean de Montreuil', in: *Umbrae codicum occidentalium* 9, Amsterdam 1966, xxxix.

> giving a decisive judgement on them. They might also choose a new Pope, if they were authorised to do so by the sacred college.
> If the Popes were unwilling to agree with this method as well,[101] then no other course would be left but to hold a general council. This could be made up of prelates only or–because, alas, so many of them were unlettered–partly of prelates and partly of theological and canonist doctors, chosen from among the members of the senior universities of both parties. This number might also be increased to include representatives of the chapters and the monastic orders.
> To these proposals, which were expressly intended not to exclude other paths to the restoration of unity, they added the remark that a Pope who rejected all three ways and was unwilling to make any other suggestion to reach the desired goal, must be regarded as an obstinate schismatic and consequently as a heretic. His followers would be obliged to withdraw their obedience from him, and he would have to be deprived of his government of the Church and the apostolic attributes. Such a vicar of Christ would no longer be a shepherd but a tyrant, to be severely punished, and deserving to share the lot of Dathan and Abiram, far from all the living (Num. 16).
> After a detailed and eloquent lament on the degeneration of the Church –in which Nicolas of Clémanges displayed his great skill–the letter concluded with an urgent appeal to the King to continue to further the unity of the Church, and above all not to listen to those who tried to derive advantage for themselves from confusion.

After listening graciously to this long speech, the King received the letter and commanded it to be translated in order to weigh up its contents more thoroughly. The University delegation, now convinced that their case was won, were told when they could return to hear the King's response.

The result, however, was not what they had expected. The chamberlain François de Conzié and other followers of Pope Clement showed that they had not worked in vain to deter the King from his plans for peace. When the deputation from the University returned to the court (10 August) they were informed by the Chancellor that the King was not prepared to go any deeper into the matter, and

[101] Rel. de St.-Denys, *Chronique* II, 148: 'Frivolum est quod sumitur papam non posse seipsum in alterius dicionem submittere... Numquid Petrum anteibit, cui non ad evangelii veritatem ambulanti Paulus in faciem libere resistit [Gal. 2: 11], quam Pauli correctionem summisse et humiliter sustinuit? Numquid et papatus noster a fraterne correctionis eximitur lege, ut eidem omnium malorum agendorum licentiam impune donemus? De Deo solo Job sanctus id loquitur: Non est qui dicat tibi: «Cur ita facis» [Job 9: 12]? Caveant qui hunc titulum soli omnipotencie debitum et sacris litteris ascriptum in seipsos usurpando transtulerunt.'

was also unwilling for the University to persist in it. If the University should receive letters from elsewhere, or feel the need to address the King in writing, the Chancellor was to be informed of this, on pain of punishment for *lèse-majesté*. The University's repeated and urgent requests for this rigorous decision to be moderated, fell on deaf ears. The Duke of Berry, absent at that moment, had made his decision, and any possible revocation would have to await his return. The University, deeply shocked by this flat refusal, turned to the only weapon at its disposal: a strike. Lectures, public sermons and all further activities were suspended until its rightful demands were met.[102]

Since Pope Clement knew only one way to restore ecclesiastical unity, the *via facti*, one can imagine that he was far from happy with the recent proposals which had emerged in University circles, and he made every effort to wreck these schemes. We have already seen how the chamberlain François de Conzié was sent to Paris to drive a wedge between the court and the University. Clement now summoned the Chancellor of the University, Pierre d'Ailly, and Gilles Deschamps to appear before him in Avignon, ostensibly because he needed them in the administration of the Church. They found it wiser, however, not to respond to this honourable invitation, for fear of the Pope's vengeance.[103]

On 17 July, that is shortly before silence was imposed on the University, they made a written protest to the Pope against the activities of his chamberlain and tried to induce Clement to cooperate with the King, who, so they still believed, had taken upon himself the task of restoring the unity of the Church. Clement was almost enraged when he read this letter, which he called a satire on the Holy See. He was even more embittered when it became clear to him that his cardinals had largely been won over to the plans of the University. They had assembled on their own initiative, and had declared their agreement with the proposals. When Clement learned that the court was not at all in favour of the University's policy, he regained his courage and again took up his old plans of military intervention in Italy. But it was too late. After a short illness he died on the morning of 16 September 1394.[104]

---

102 Rel. de St.Denys, *Chronique* II, 182-84.
103 Valois, *Schisme* II, 421.
104 Valois, *Schisme* II, 426ff.

Almost a week later, on 22 September, the news of Clement's death reached the King. The new situation created was discussed on the same day in the royal council. At the suggestion of Simon de Cramaud, the Patriarch of Alexandria and as such the head of the French clergy, it decided to urge the cardinals not to proceed to a new election but to await further messages from the court.[105] As soon as the news of Clement's death had reached it, the University broke the silence it had observed for more than a month, and sent a delegation to the palace to make the following request to the King: first, that no new election should be held before the cardinals had discussed the question of unity. In connexion with this the University pointed to the ways to unity which it had proposed, and particularly recommended the *via cessionis.* In the second place it requested that an assembly of the Church should be summoned, in order to establish the guidelines to be followed. Furthermore, it felt that it was desirable to make contact with the Roman Pope, Boniface IX, and the princes who supported him. Finally, it urged the holding of prayers and processions, while also requesting permission to exchange ideas on Church policy freely with other universities. The King gave a favourable reply to all these requests, although mildly rebuking the long duration of the University's strike and calling on them to end it, to which they agreed. The University wrote to the cardinals optimistically: 'the unity which is so much desired is almost restored; in any event you have it in your hands!'[106]

In a letter to the cardinals (24 September), the King repeated, with greater urgency, his request that the vacancy of the see should be continued until further reports were received from him. As legates, his council appointed the Patriarch Simon de Cramaud and the royal confessor and Chancellor of the University, Pierre d'Ailly. The Duke of Berry, however, declared that he was well aware of the views of the cardinals, and that they would be less pleased to welcome Church dignitaries than laymen. He also stated that Pierre d'Ailly was *persona non grata* at the court of Avignon, where he was considered to be one of those who had taken the initiative in all the

[105] Valois, *Schisme* III, 6ff.
[106] Valois, *Schisme* III, 7.

University's *démarches*. This advice was followed, and the council composed another delegation.[107]

All the decisions taken so energetically and so unanimously by the court and the University turned out, alas, to be in vain. When the messenger with the King's first letter reached Avignon, the cardinals were on the point of going into the conclave. They did receive the letter, but felt it more fitting to delay opening it until after the election. To escape suspicion that they wished to prolong the Schism by electing a new Pope, they also composed a declaration, which was to acquire great importance in the course of events. They declared: 'If we become Pope, we shall loyally follow all ways which can lead to unity, including the *via cessionis*, if the majority of the sacred college should decide in favour of it.' Eighteen of the twenty one cardinals present signed this declaration, among them, though under protest, Petrus de Luna. It was he who on 28 September 1394, received all the votes but one. He accepted the nomination and took the name Benedict XIII. His coronation took place on 11 October.[108]

Petrus de Luna belonged to an old, aristocratic, Aragonese family. As a ruler of the Church, he was firm in character, penetrating in mind and enjoyed great respect as a canonist, having held a chair in this subject at the University of Montpellier. He had been created a cardinal in 1375 and had been concerned in the tumultuous election of Urban VI and in that of Clement VII. As a diplomat he had done the latter good service. To the University of Paris he was known as a worker for the unity of the Church.[109]

Since this Pope was to make such a mark on the history of the Schism, it is appropriate to say something more of him. History's judgement of Benedict XIII has generally been particularly unflattering. He has been accused of tyrannical ambition and wilful obstinacy, while the key to his conduct has largely been found in his fear of losing his high dignity. It may, however, be very much doubted whether this psychological explanation does full justice to the phenomenon of Petrus de Luna. It is much more likely that it was not primarily subjective factors which determined his attitude, but objective ones. In our opinion, Petrus de Luna, the canonist, was a

107 Valois, *Schisme* III, 8-9.
108 Valois, *Schisme* III, 14.
109 Valois, *Schisme* III, 15; Salembier, *Le grand schisme*, 147ff.

typical representative of the juridical-absolutist papacy, and there is a great deal more to be said for the view that his fatal stubborness was fed by an absolutist ideology than for the view that it grew from subjective roots.[110]

As soon as the election of Benedict had been settled, he and his cardinals informed the King. On 9 October, during a service in St Denis, Charles received a letter from Benedict, who expressed his warm feelings towards the King and promised that very important news was to come. Soon, new legates from Avignon appeared and claimed to the court and the University that Benedict was inspired by the best intentions, was firmly resolved to end the execrable Schism, and would be glad to be assured of the King's support in this. Benedict, so the envoys concluded, had only accepted the papal title at the insistence of the cardinals. He had repeatedly assured them that he would rather spend his life in the wilderness or in a monastery, than assist in prolonging the Schism.[111]

The King was well pleased with this news, of which he also informed the University. The University was equally optimistic and wrote Benedict a detailed letter in this spirit, encouraging him to seize the favourable opportunity, to make use of the good intentions of the princes and to resign. However the anti-pope in Rome might act, Benedict's resignation would in any case restore peace. For even in the worst case, if the anti-pope should refuse to resign, he would be isolated and the whole world would condemn him for his obstinacy. The University, for its part, offered its humble services in the cause of the struggle for the unity of the Church, and pointed once more to the fatal role which François de Conzié, the chamberlain had played. Finally, it requested permission to present a *rotulus* to Benedict in the near future.

Benedict received the University's letter with the greatest sympa-

---

[110] Cf. *DThC* 12, c. 2028, s.v.'Pierre de Lune' (E. Amann). Alluding to Benedict's treatise *De schismate*, Amann says: '... il est très facile de voir le sens dans lequel s'orientait la pensée de l'ancien professeur de Montpellier. Elle n'allait à rien de moins qu'à incarner toute l'Eglise dans le pape, source exclusive de tout pouvoir, de tout droit, de toute juridiction.' Combes, *Jean de Montreuil,* 509: 'Plus on étudie Benoît XIII, plus il est difficile de lutter contre la conviction que sa résistance était, pour une très grosse part, d'essence juridique.' Haller (*Papsttum* I, 219-20; 524-35), formulated a pronounced positive judgement about Benedict, as did Valois (*Schisme* IV, 480-1).

[111] Rel. de St.-Denys, *Chronique* II, 206.

thy. On an earlier occasion, he had already declared to the legates of the University that he was willing to resign. Taking off his skull-cap, he had said that he would lay down the papacy as promptly as he laid down his headgear! He would be glad to sign the *rotulus*. He asked the King to continue to work for unity in collaboration with the French clergy and, above all, the University of Paris. Benedict was glad to learn which way they felt to be the most suitable. The King, for his part, received the Pope's legates in a very friendly fashion, and sent his confessor, Pierre d'Ailly, to Avignon ahead of a royal delegation.[112]

D'Ailly's sermon to the new Pope, even if we make allowances for its rhetorical style, again reveals the high expectations which Benedict's person and his wish for peace had aroused in the King and also in the University. He dreamed not only of a restoration of the Church's unity but even saw a *reformatio*–indeed, even a golden age, in the offing.[113]

If one compares this bold optimism with the mood which prevailed in the court and the University soon after Clement's death, when all had unanimously urged the prolonging of the vacancy, it seems that much had changed. But one must not forget that Benedict was known in both court and University as an outspoken advocate of unity. In this respect he seemed to stand head and shoulders above his predecessor, of whom the University had rightly expected very little for the sake of Church unity. Clement had not spoiled them in that respect, and things could quite easily improve. Moreover, as we saw, the cardinals had been far from unsympathetic towards the University's proposals to escape from the Church's difficulties by means of either resignation, compromise or a council. Furthermore, before they went into the conclave they had signed an undertaking which–although its contents were not then known to anyone outside the circle of the sacred college–could only arouse hopes for something good. All this seemed guarantee enough that the Schism was about to be ended, and it explains the mood of optimism which prevailed at the court and in the University, despite the fact that their original wish, for the election to be postponed, had not been met.

In accordance with the desire of the Pope, Charles began discus-

---

112 Valois, *Schisme* III, 18ff.

113 P. Tschackert, *Peter von Ailli*, Gotha 1877, 353; L. Salembier, *Petrus de Alliaco*, 39.

sions with the clergy and the University on the policy to be followed in the Church. On 3 February 1395 he summoned a council (National Synod I) in Paris, attended by the two Patriarchs of Alexandria and Jerusalem, as well as the archbishops, bishops, abbots, doctors and representatives of the monastic orders and the universities – an honourable company, more than a hundred strong.

The leadership of the synod, which lasted more than two weeks, was in the hands of Simon de Cramaud, the Patriarch of Alexandria.[114] Before the official discussions began the Chancellor, Pierre d'Ailly, gave a detailed speech, at the request of the University, in which he returned to the three proposals made by the University, and once again commended the *via cessionis* as the most suitable. It was this solution which was recommended, at the very beginning of the synod, by a great majority: 87 of the 109 prelates present expressed themselves in favour of it.

In the following two weeks the discussions concentrated on the question of the instructions which were to be given to the delegates whom the King was to send to Avignon. They grew to a detailed memorandum, in which the *via cessionis* was recommended in very guarded terms.[115] If the Pope should declare himself ready to accept this, the princes of the other party were to be informed at once so that they might induce the intruder of Rome to follow the same path. If he should refuse to resign, he would only prove that he was serving a false cause,and it would be justified in taking action against him, withdrawing from obedience to him, or applying other means of compulsion.[116]

The delegation which was to present Benedict with this advice consisted of the Dukes of Berry, Burgundy and Orleans, and also of the King's advisers and representatives of the University. The company arrived at Avignon on 22 May 1395, where Benedict received them in the grandest style. It cost them some effort to induce the Pope to allow them to see the declaration which had been signed by him and the cardinals on the eve of the conclave, but after prolonged urging Benedict permitted a copy to be made. The delegation urged him to resign but the Pope saw more hope in the so-called *via conventionis*, that is a conference between the two Popes

114 Valois, *Schisme* III, 33-4.
115 Rel. de St.-Denys, *Chronique* II, 226-42.
116 Valois, *Schisme* III, 27ff.

and their respective cardinals. Such a meeting was to be held under the protection of the King of France, at a place not far outside the French territory, in order to exchange ideas on the restoration of unity. Everyone would be given ample opportunity to make his standpoint known, without coercion. The royal delegation feared—and probably not without reason—that such a 'summit-conference' would degenerate into an endless dispute on the juridical competence of the two rivals, and that the cause of unity would not advance one step further as a result.[117]

Gilles Deschamps acted as the spokesman of the delegation and urgently implored the Pope to accept the method proposed: resignation. Benedict replied that the unity of the Church was very close to his heart, and that he was ready to give all he had, even his life, for it. Now that the King had made this proposal, he would gladly consider it, but he wished to have a written statement with reasons showing why resignation was in fact the best way to achieve unity. Once again it was Gilles Deschamps who stated on behalf of the delegation that they felt it entirely unnecessary to put their proposal in writing. That would only cause delay and new complications. Moreover, such a piece of paper would contain only one two-syllable word: *ces-sio*! The Pope, piqued by this reply, expressed his astonishment that people who were accustomed to discuss even the smallest questions of secular importance in great detail, should apparently not consider such discussions necessary in a matter of the highest spiritual importance. He needed time to think it over, and warned that nothing would be achieved by threatening him with force.[118]

At the suggestion of the Duke of Burgundy it was then decided to invite the cardinals to make their personal opinions known. With the exception of the cardinal of Pamplona who showed himself a faithful partisan of Benedict, it seemed that they were all more or less enthusiastic about a solution by means of resignation. Benedict, understandably, objected strongly to his cardinals' independent action. He continued to oppose the *via cessionis*, and persisted in prefering a conference with the Pope of Rome. His argument was always that in past cases of schism the *via cessionis* had never been followed. It was not prescribed by law, and had not been practised

117 Valois, *Schisme* III, 44ff.
118 Rel. de St.-Denys, *Chronique* II, 264.

by the Fathers. Rather, it had always been rejected as unsuitable. If it were to be applied, a novelty would be introduced 'which could insult God, bring harm upon the Church, and bring the power of the keys into discredit', to say nothing of other disadvantages.[119] He added that although he was obliged to justify himself to God alone, he did not wish to give the King the impression that he was holding on to his dignity out of vanity. He therefore declared himself prepared, in the event of a meeting with his rival coming to nothing, to hand the matter to an arbitration committee chosen from both parties; in other words to go over to the *via compromissi*. This promise was repeated in later bulls.

During the last audience he made his meaning clear in drastic terms: 'I should rather be burned alive than follow the *via cessionis*, for that would only strengthen the intruder's position.'[120] Since the members of the royal delegation were equally unwilling to deviate from their position, and saw hope only in the Pope's resignation, the two standpoints remained irreconcilable, and the only result of the discussions was that misunderstanding of the respective positions was henceforth ruled out. Against the Pope's will, his cardinals assured the King that they were willing to offer their help in effecting the *via cessionis*.[121]

In these ominous circumstances, the responsibility for the welfare of the University of Paris was placed on Gerson's shoulders.

---

[119] Rel. de St.-Denys, *Chronique* II, 288-90.
[120] Valois, *Schisme* III, 63.
[121] Schwab, *Gerson*, 138 n. 2.

CHAPTER TWO

FIRST YEARS AS CHANCELLOR OF THE UNIVERSITY, 1395-1398

Quamvis via cessionis secundum se considerata sit optima, tamen potest fieri prorsus inutilis si principes et clerus alterius obedientiae nullo modo isti viae velint consentire.

Gerson, *De substractione* (Gl. 6, 24; Dupin II, 8C).

In the period which we have just described Gerson's role in ecclesiastical politics had to remain limited–after all, these were his prentice years–but in April 1395 this was to change. For in that year he was raised to a dignity[1] which placed him in a very exposed position and forced him to intervene more directly in Church politics, indeed to help to determine them. On 2 April 1395 Pierre d'Ailly was appointed Bishop of Le Puy-en-Velay, a see which he soon (15 November 1396) exchanged for the much more lucrative diocese of Cambrai.[2] Since the Chancellorship of the University could not be held in conjunction with the bishopric, he was obliged to resign the first dignity. Not without d'Ailly's intervention,[3] his pupil Gerson was chosen as his successor on 13 April 1395. Gerson was glad to accept the new post to escape from life at court.[4]

The University of Paris had developed, inter alia, from the cathedral school of Notre-Dame, which explains why the Chancellor of the cathedral enjoyed great authority over the University. It is true that papal intervention had placed limits on this power, but in Gerson's day the Chancellor of the University still enjoyed great

---

1 See Chapter VI n. 1.

2 Tschackert, *Peter von Ailli*, 84ff.; Burger, *Aedificatio*, 31 n. 19.

3 Gerson in a letter to d'Ailly (1402) inc. *Postulare dignata est* (Gl. 2, 63; Dupin III, 304): '... te [Petro de Alliaco] insuper promotore in cancellariatus officium tibi successi, quamquam non meritis aequis.' For the background of his nomination, see G. Ouy, 'La plus ancienne oeuvre retrouvée de Jean Gerson: Le brouillon inachevé d'un traité contre Juan de Monzon (1389-90)', *Rom.* 83 (1962), 433-71 (454-62).

4 Gerson in a letter to an unknown intimate (Feb. 1400), inc. *Ista est pars angustiarum* (Gl. 2, 18: Dupin IV, 725D): 'Cogor rursus fluctibus, etsi non semper, immergi, vel ingratus iudicabor; a quibus, ut emigrarem, sola haec fuit occasio cancellariam postulandi, et contulit hoc Deus, aliter tamen quam sperabam.'

prestige. The Chancellorship was in the gift of the Bishop of Paris, but was often 'reserved',[5] as in the case of Gerson, who owed his nomination to Benedict XIII.[6]

The primary task of the Chancellor was to make sure that the University's scholarly activities respected the bounds of orthodoxy. It was he who granted the *licentia docendi* on apostolic authority.[7] He took the chair at University discussions, spoke in its name, represented it at court, in the curia and at councils, while finally, unlike the Rector, he also held a chair in the faculty of theology.[8]

It will be clear that particularly in the complicated circumstances produced by the Schism, a very heavy burden of responsibility rested on the shoulders of the Chancellor. This burden was made heavier still because the actual authority that he could exert at this time was no longer commensurate with the prestige he enjoyed. A man such as Gerson, who was driven by a sense of responsibility and not chiefly by ambition, might well despair to find that his authority often counted for very little, and that the University over whose spiritual welfare he was supposed to watch, sometimes appeared not only willing but also able to go its own way.

Gerson was appointed a month before the royal delegation left for Avignon to induce Pope Benedict to resign. As we have seen, the Pope was totally unwilling to accept the King's advice. In spite of his earlier promises on the point, he did not contemplate resignation; on the contrary he tried to strengthen his following, with some success: the University of Toulouse, for example, rallied to his side. Resentment at the obstinacy of Pope Benedict increased day by day, especially in University circles, where such a man as d'Ailly, who was regarded as an adherent of Benedict, was therefore excluded from the discussions on unity by the faculty of arts.[9]

---

[5] Hastings Rashdall, *The Universities of Europe in the Middle Ages*, (ed. F.M. Powicke & A.B. Emden), I, [Oxford 1969], 401 n. 1.

[6] Benedict XIII in a letter to Gerson (13 April 1395), inc. *Dilecto filio ... Litterarum scientia* (Gl. 2, 5-6). See the art. mentioned above, n. 3, (457-60).

[7] For more details concerning the role of the Chancellor in Paris see Alan B. Bernstein, *Pierre d'Ailly and the Blanchard affair*, Leiden 1978, 6-12, and Burger, *Aedificatio*, 28-35. For the formula used by the Chancellor when conferring the *licentia docendi*, see Chapter XI n. 72.

[8] Glorieux, 'l'Enseignement', 88.

[9] Denifle-Chatelain, *Auctarium Chartularii* I, c. 707; J. Haller, *Papsttum und Kirchenreform* I, Berlin 1903, 225 n. 3.

Very soon Gerson found himself forced to take a stand against a strong current of opinion in the University, which was considering freeing itself from its obedience to Benedict – *substractio oboedientiae* – in order to force him to yield. In about August 1395[10] the University addressed a number of questions to the Pope, which, for all their ironical submissiveness, left little doubt of their meaning. 'Is the Pope obliged to follow the *via cessionis* and can he fall into mortal sin if he refuses? Can he still plead ignorance after the steps taken by the cardinals, the court and the clergy? Is it true that the oath he took during the conclave and the decisions of his cardinals now confront him with a choice between resigning and incurring the guilt of perjury? Is his conduct schismatic? Are the cardinals released from their obligation to obey him? Can he and must he be compelled to follow the *via cessionis*? And if he refuses, may he be condemned by a council of his own obedience and would it be permissible to depose him? Are the sentences which he has pronounced against those who concern themselves with this matter valid?'[11]

Gerson set out his views on these questions in a brief work, *De substractione schismatis*,[12] in which he urged that such questions should be allowed to lie, as long as there was no information about the intentions of the princes of the other obedience. If the University of Paris were to issue a binding ruling, for example if it were to state that Benedict had in fact committed perjury, he feared that the Pope and his following would feel forced to decide the contrary, which would result in an almost unhealable schism *in iis quae sunt fidei*. In other words, a heresy would be created, which could only be eliminated if one of the two parties were explicitly to revoke its decision. He thinks it possible to imagine – and further developments were to prove him right on this point – that other universities, especially the English, would take up the argument against any pronouncement from the University of Paris.[13]

He explains his viewpoint by referring to the Schism with the

---

[10] Not February 1396 as Connolly, *John Gerson*, 63, asserted, following Hefele-Leclercq, *Histoire des conciles*, VI 2, Paris 1915, 1184. Cf. Valois, *Schisme* III, 71 n. 4.

[11] C.E. DuBoulay, *Historia Universitatis Parisiensis* IV, Paris. 1668, 752, 753, 755.

[12] (Gl. 6, 22-4; Dupin II, 7-9). Because of the uncertainty which it reveals about the view of the English universities (cf. Gl. 6, 22; Dupin II, 7 A), it seems to us that the work must have been written in 1396 rather than in February 1395, as is suggested by Mgr. Combes (*La théologie mystique* I, 212 n. 107).

[13] *De substractione* (Gl. 6, 22; Dupin II, 7CD).

Greeks. In his opinion, this had originated above all from the fact that the Latin side had proceeded to fix the controversial points in dogma. If it had been left as a controversy on the powers of the Pope, agreement would certainly have been possible in the end. Agreement had not, however, been achieved, and doctrinal decisions had been taken which made the Schism between East and West almost unbridgeable. There was simply no middle way when it came to pronouncements on the faith, and this made it regrettably necessary to force people to confess heresy.[14] A typical example of his irenical cast of mind.

Gerson therefore felt that no decisions ought to be taken in haste, for as long as it was uncertain either that the Pope would resign or that the princes and clergy of his obedience would come out in support of such a policy, there was no point at all in declaring Benedict a schismatic.[15] It would not promote the unity of the Church, while – to say nothing of other disadvantages – the only result would be that their own party would lose ground to the opposite party, which was already stronger and more intransigent. He made it clear to the faculty of theology that the entire responsibility would be on its head if it took doctrinal decisions when it did not need to do so. It would be more sensible to proceed much more cautiously, to raise the matter in the presence of the *baccalaurei*, and not simply to work from *schedulae*, but to deal with the questions *viva voce* in open and closed discussions. Great weight would have to be given to the views of the theological doctors in these discussions.[16]

He still supported the *via cessionis*, which he called, in itself, the most just, but which he did not (yet) consider practicable, as long as the intentions of the opposite party were unknown.

> quamvis via cessionis secundum se considerata sit optima, tamen potest fieri prorsus inutilis si principes et clerus alterius obedientiae nullo modo isti viae velint consentire.[17]

---

[14] *De substractione* (Gl. 6, 22; Dupin II, 8A): '... notetur materia de confirmatione schismatis inter Latinos et Graecos. Haec enim confirmatio praecipue et principaliter venit postquam Latini propositiones in fide determinaverunt, de quibus prius erat controversia; quia si solum de iuribus papalibus fuisset dissensio, sicut erat ab initio, faciliter fuissent Graeci reducti per bonos mediatores. Sed quia in articulis fidei sive determinationibus non cadit medium, schisma irreparabile constitutum est; non enim facile est homines ad revocandum vel confitendum se fuisse haereticos inducere.'

[15] *De substractione* (Gl. 6, 23; Dupin II, 8B).

[16] *De substractione* (Gl. 6, 23; Dupin II, 8C).

[17] *De substractione* (Gl. 6, 24; Dupin II, 9A): 'adhuc ignoratur opinio et voluntas alio-

A very wise and reasonable point of view, which in no way justifies the qualification of Gerson as an 'esprit hardi'.[18] The example which he cited to warn against precipitate action – the Great Schism – was instructive, in so far as it reveals that in his eyes the unity of the Church represented the greatest good. We may regard it as further evidence of his non-legalistic cast of mind.

If the questions that the University ventured to put to Benedict had shown that its patience was largely exhausted, this was made even clearer in a programme which it offered to the King on 25 August in the same year.[19] It urged Charles VI to take the defenders of the *via cessionis* under his protection and to punish its opponents severely. It also asked him to summon a national synod to discuss the new situation and in particular to consider depriving Benedict of the right of collation, because this continued to assure him of supporters. A boycott of the apostolic taxes would be another means of bringing the Pope to submission. The programme took great pains to show that these measures were not revolutionary, but were merely intended to return to the old-established rights of the French Church – that is, their tone was Gallican. Finally the University pressed for envoys to be sent to all quarters to inform foreign princes of the King's intentions and to sound their views on the matter.

The court had already decided to send envoys,[20] so it was able to comply with the University's wish at once. At the end of 1395 two delegations were sent to England, one in the King's name and the other in that of the University of Paris. The Patriarch of Alexandria, Simon de Cramaud, was at the head of the royal delegation, while the University appointed, among others, Pierre LeRoy, Abbot of Mont St. Michel, and Jean Courtecuisse, the later Bishop of Paris.[21] Richard II of England, who was then seeking the hand of Charles's daughter, the young Isabella of France, received both delegations extremely courteously. Personally, Richard was well-disposed to the French plans but he was unwilling to do anything

---

rum alterius obedientiae, ex quorum consensu vel dissensu pendet utilitas et sufficientia viae cessionis...'

[18] Hefele-Leclercq, *Histoire des Conciles* VI 2, 1187.

[19] F. Ehrle, 'Neue Materialien zur Geschichte Peters von Luna', *ALKGM* VI (1892) 139-302 (200); Valois, *Schisme* III, 74-5.

[20] The letter of instruction for the royal envoys is dated 24 August 1395, cf. Ehrle, 'Neue Materialien', 201.

[21] Ehrle, 'Neue Materialien', 201.

without the support of his clergy. When the legates suggested that they should approach the University of Oxford, the King of England did his best to dissuade them. There would be little point, he remarked, because most of the professors and students were on vacation. But it was generally known that the University of Oxford had ranged itself very decidedly on the side of the Pope of Rome, and it is therefore more probable that Richard advised against an approach because he feared disagreeable discussions.[22] The preferences of this University in ecclesiastical politics are revealed very clearly in its answer to the proposal from Paris, which it sent to Richard some months later. It emphatically rejected the *via cessionis* and saw the only prospect of a solution in French submission to the Pope of Rome or the calling of a general council.[23]

Charles VI, who was then at Compiègne, was informed of this reply from the University of Oxford on 1 July 1396. He passed it on to the University of Paris to answer, which, as might be expected, was not at all happy with it, and described it as an empty display of learning.[24] Gerson, who was at Compiègne when the English delegation was received, wholeheartedly shared the opinion of his University.[25] In later years, however, when circumstances were very different, he came back to the English proposal for the calling of a council and spoke of it in a very positive sense.[26] At this date, however, he was not yet thinking along these lines.

The hope that England could be won for the policy of cession was thus proved vain. Delegations, again from both court and University, which were sent to Germany around Easter 1396, had as little success. King Wenceslas refused even to receive the University members of the mission, no doubt moved by suitable presents from Pope Benedict. On the other hand the royal legates were received, but were able to achieve no more than a promise from Wenceslas

---

[22] Rel. de St.-Denys, *Chronique* II, 326.

[23] Valois, *Schisme* III, 76-7.

[24] Rel. de St.-Denys, *Chronique* II, 432: 'tot argumentorum abyssus et racionum multiplicatio non nisi ostentacionem et apparenciam concludebant (sc. those of the University of Paris).'

[25] See his often caustic marginal comments on the letter of the University of Oxford (printed in italics in Gl. 10, 324-45), and cf. G. Ouy, 'Gerson et l'Angleterre. A propos d'un texte polémique retrouvé du Chancelier de Paris contre l'Université d'Oxford 1396', in: *Humanism in France at the end of the middle ages and in early renaissance*, ed. A.H.T. Levi, Manchester 1970, 43-81.

[26] *Propositio coram Anglicis* (Gl. 6, 130; Dupin II 126D). See below, 54-9.

to discuss the proposals with the clergy of his empire. King Sigismund of Hungary was more positive and approved the *via cessionis*. The Archbishops of Trier and Cologne as well as the Dukes of Bavaria and Austria also welcomed the French plans.[27]

Within the obedience of Avignon Charles found support for his plans from the King of Aragon above all. But unfortunately the King died on 13 May 1396 before the envoys, Simon de Cramaud and Gilles Deschamps, had left his kingdom. The struggle for the throne which now burst out in Aragon diverted attention from the French plans.[28] Charles's proposal found a less enthusiastic welcome from the King of Castile. Here, and in the other Spanish kingdoms, there was even a certain resistance to the policy of Paris, because it was suspected – certainly not without reason – that Benedict's Spanish origin irritated French national pride and was one of the reasons why they wished to be rid of him.[29] Gerson did not omit to point out this circumstance.[30]

Although the time-consuming and expensive delegations had in fact achieved little, some satisfaction was felt in Paris at the vague agreement with French policy expressed by some foreign princes, and it was decided to call a national synod, finally to take the decisions on the practical implementation of the *via cessionis*.[31] As we have seen, the plan for such a synod had already been put forward by the University in late August 1395, but the date had had to be put back repeatedly because of a variety of circumstances, chiefly the time-consuming missions to foreign courts. It was August 1396 before the synod met (National Synod II). The discussions were held in Paris from 16 August to 14 September.[32]

---

[27] Rel. de St.-Denys, *Chronique* II, 414-20; Salembier, *Le grand schisme*, 158.

[28] Valois, *Schisme* III, 83, 114ff.

[29] Valois, *Schisme* III, 83-4.

[30] *De papatu contendentibus* (Gl. 6, 26; Dupin II, 15C): '... notetur quod etiam de parte nostra rex Hispaniae et rex Aragonum et praesertim eius populus non sunt adhuc determinati ad istam viam cessionis, immo dicunt multi vidisse multas litteras quibus oppositum clare pependitur. Et istis sic perdurantibus constat quod cessio non esset via totaliter sufficiens; immo multi formidant ne iam sit formatus unus rancor et quoddam seminarium discordiae inter illos Hispanos et Arragonenses ex una parte, contra Gallicos; et interpretatur quod in odium eorum volunt papam deponere quia de patria.' Cf. Valois, *Schisme* III, 84 n. 2.

[31] The objective of the synod had been laid down by the King; Ehrle, 'Neue Materialien', 218.

[32] Ehrle, 'Neue Materialien', 203ff.; Valois, *Schisme* III, 104-7; Victor Martin, *Les origines du Gallicanisme* I, [Paris] 1939, 270-2.

The result of the debates was influenced by the absence of both Gerson's protector Philip the Bold and the Duke of Berry. They were in England preparing for the approaching marriage of Richard II to Isabella of France. Simon de Cramaud was also absent; he had not yet returned from Spain. In the absence of these three men, all of them pronounced supporters of a policy of substraction, the leadership of the assembly fell to the Duke of Orléans, who needed Benedict's support for his plans of conquest in Italy, and was therefore averse to the rigorous measure of substraction.

Supporters and opponents of this policy were given every opportunity to state their case. For the University substraction was defended by, among others, the theologian Pierre Plaoul, one of the envoys to Germany.[33] The influential Abbot of Mont St. Michel, Pierre LeRoy, also pleaded for it. The argument of this 'greatest canonist in France', as a contemporary called him,[34] was unmistakeably Gallican in tone. Appealing to old legal texts and conciliar *canones*, he regarded the withdrawal of the right of collation from the Pope and resistance to certain fiscal measures of the curia as justified, because they would restore the ancient sacred order of the Church. Substraction was allowed, because it did not introduce anything new but on the contrary restored the old state of affairs.[35]

The pleas of the opponents of substraction were less surprising, but certainly just as acutely argued. Naturally, like Gerson, they held out the threat of excommunication against all those who dared to violate the rights of the Holy See. The representative of the University of Toulouse, the dominican Sanche Mulier, developed the thesis that it was not permitted to sin in any circumstances whatever, and therefore not even if a great good were to be acquired. Recognising that the unity of the Church had to be regarded as a very great good, he argued that the guilt of mortal sin would be incurred, if an attempt were made to achieve that unity by denying the Pope his rights.[36]

After the problem of substraction had been illuminated from many sides, each member of the assembly was invited to make his

---

33 Ehrle, 'Neue Materialien', 220-1.

34 This was the verdict of Guillaume Fillastre; cited by Martin, *Gallicanisme* I, 271 n. 2.

35 Martin, *Gallicanisme* I, 271-2.

36 Ehrle, 'Neue Materialien', 213.

opinion known in writing, after which the synod proceeded to vote. The *schedulae* were collected in three bags and handed to the Duke of Orléans, who, for reasons which are not entirely clear, kept silent on the result of the vote. Not until some time later did it become known that the majority had proposed one more attempt to urge the Pope to abdicate, before withdrawing obedience to him; a sizeable minority had been ready to take this step immediately.[37]

Thanks to the Duke of Orléans the moderate tendency triumphed at the synod, and the drastic measure of substraction was put off for a time. This result was certainly to Gerson's liking, for although he must certainly have been invited to attend as Chancellor of the University, he was not present at the assembly.[38] It is clear from his *De papatu contendentibus*[39] that his views had not changed in the meantime. In it he again warned against substraction, urging the same arguments as in his earlier *De substractione schismatis*. He again pointed out, for example, that it made no sense at all to urge the Pope to resign until the other party's intentions were known. Even if resignation in itself could be regarded as the best solution, the Pope would only be obliged to take that course if unity could not be achieved by any other human means, and it was also certain that no even more mortal evil would result from it.[40]

Although they agree in their arguments, the two works differ slightly in their tendency, for in the *De papatu contendentibus* Gerson rejects substraction more decisively, and tries to show that there was no ground in law for action against Benedict. The Pope cannot be accused of perjury, because he has expressly proclaimed that he would give up his life for the sake of unity, which implies a willingness to yield in principle.[41] On the other hand, Gerson can fully understand why the Pope does not proceed to resign, as long as he does not know what steps the other party is planning to take. Bene-

---

37 Valois, *Schisme* III, 107; Haller, *Papsttum* I, 223; Martin, *Gallicanisme* I, 272 n.3.

38 The list of university delegates is in Ehrle, 'Neue Materialien', 213, 219-20.

39 Gl. 6, 24-8; Dupin II, 14-17. Gerson mentions an apostolic nuncio who had 'novissime 'appeared in Paris, (Gl. 6, 25; Dupin II, 14D). This could allude to Pierre Ravat or Elie de Lestrange; cf. Valois, *Schisme* III, 101, and Ehrle, 'Neue Materialien', 229[33-7].

40 *De papatu contendentibus* (Gl. 6, 24-6 (25); Dupin II, 15AB): '... notetur quod via cessionis est inefficax et insufficiens si alii de alia obedientia nolint illam recipere; et ideo mirum videretur quod ad talem viam, quae ex hypothesi possibili esset efficax, aliquis obligaretur...'

41 *De papatu contendentibus* (Gl. 6, 24-5; Dupin II, 14BC).

dict, he argues, is shrewd enough not to reveal his personal intentions on this point; if he did so, he would only incite or strengthen ambition for the papal dignity in others. Not until the plans of the other party are known, and Benedict's reaction to them has been seen, was there any point in taking up a position. Until then every step was premature.[42]

He cannot understand those who, with a good conscience, feel that they can release themselves from their obedience to the Pope, even though he has not been accused, let alone condemned, as a heretic or schismatic. Do the proponents of substraction, he asks, realise the penalties that will be imposed on them if they carry out their plans? Not everyone is free to pass judgement on the Pope, and those who venture to scorn his sentences or violate his jurisdiction invite serious suspicion of being schismatics. If the princes regard substraction as permissible on these grounds, they ought to be aware that they will have little right to object when their subjects rise in revolt against them on the pretext that they are ruled by tyrants.[43]

Just as Gerson regards the argument for substraction as inadequate, so he can find little positive in the situation that would be the result of substraction. In particular, he doubts whether it would be to the advantage of the Church if the clergy were to allocate benefices. Would good prelates really be preferred, and would the students be remembered? And is it sound and justified to incite the princes to encroach on the Church's power of jurisdiction?[44] The

---

[42] *De papatu contendentibus* (Gl. 6, 25-6; Dupin II, 15C): 'Nono notetur quod papa non potest teneri ad cessionem secluso iuramento, nisi istae tres conditiones ponantur: 1° quod per cessionem habeatur unio; 2° quod aliter non posset humanitus haberi; 3° quod malum illud propter quod sit cessio facienda, sit mortiferum animabus et quod per cessionem non augeatur.'

[43] *De papatu contendentibus* (Gl. 6, 26-7; Dupin II, 16A): 'Tertiodecimo notetur quomodo potest requiri salva conscientia a papa qui non est iudicatus schismaticus aut haereticus, posset removeri obedientia circà illa quae ad eum semper spectare confessa sunt. Et advertere debent talia agentes super poenis expressis... Si dicatur quod papa ostendit se schismaticum, hoc non est clarum per praecedentia. Item non est talis iudicatus ab habentibus potestatem; et non est in potestate libera cuiuslibet sic iudicare de papa et ab eius obedientia removere, aut contemnere sententias suas vel iurisdictionem diminuere; et videatur si tales sint suspecti de schismate contra papam. Item notent principes quid tales facerent contra eos si impune auderent, et quam fidelitatem servarent, quia sic dicere possent quod essent tyranni, etc.'. The same argument was urged by Raoul d'Oulmont in February 1397; cf. Valois, *Schisme* III, 139ff.

[44] *De papatu contendentibus* (Gl. 6, 27; Dupin II, 16B).

future was to prove him right on all counts. He had serious objections to the bitterness with which the University, above all, insisted on a forced *via cessionis*. It made it appear as if resignation was the only possibility, and therefore tried to push through a revolutionary policy at all costs. He reminds the University of its programme of ecclesiastical policy, now two years old, in which, as we know, it had referred not only to the *via cessionis* but also to the *via concilii* and *via compromissi*.[45]

Which of these possibilities was his own preference at this time? He says nothing of the *via compromissi*–not entirely rejected by Benedict–and his remarks on the *via concilii* do not give the impression that he expected a great deal from it.[46] May we infer from this that, in spite of everything, he still hoped that Benedict would resign voluntarily? Or did he feel that the other Pope was preparing for a more positive solution? We cannot say for certain, but it seems most probable that he expected an early change in the ecclesiastical situation, which would bring either voluntary resignation or another responsible solution within the bounds of possibility. In other words, time would bring relief.

We are in the dark about the reason for Gerson's absence from the synod of Paris in 1396. Perhaps, after attending the reception of the English delegation at Compiègne on 1 July, he had not returned to Paris but headed directly northwest for Bruges. Be that as it may, there is no evidence of any activity in Paris during the summer of this year, while it is certain that he was in Bruges on 12

---

[45] *De papatu contendentes* (Gl. 6, 27-8; Dupin II, 16C): 'Decimo octavo notetur et advertat Universitas quomodo aliqui de suppositis improbant simpliciter et de plano vias quas ipsa reputavit utiles, bonas et convenientes et per quarum quamlibet posset haberi pax; et rationes ad hoc dedit et se obtulit in litteris patentibus quamlibet illarum contra quemlibet sustinere. Et videatur ergo si circumstantiae sic sunt immutatae vel ex persona vel tempore quod omnes viae aliae praeter cessionem sint factae ineptae et insufficientes.'

[46] *De papatu contendentibus* (Gl. 6, 28; Dupin II, 16D-17A): 'Decimo nono notetur specialiter probatio concilii generalis quod tamen necessario fiendum quidam bene apparenter persuadent propter electionem novi papae; et haec est radix in summa brevi, quia magna pars catholicorum est neutra, sic quod credit quod neuter sit papa, aut in dubio suspensam se tenet. Isti vero consequenter habent credere aut dubitare de cardinalibus utriusque partis quod non possint etiam simul eligere papam novum, quia si neuter sit papa maxima pars eorum nec habet nec habere potest potestatem creandi novum papam, nec alii quicumque a cardinalibus nisi per concilium generale, supposito quod omnes catholici particulariter consentirent in aliquos certos pro eligendo novo papa; si non fieret collegialiter nihil esset, alioquin Urbanus intrusus habuisset maximam apparentiam.'

October 1396 to take possession in person of the deanery of the chapter of St Donatian.[47] He owed this benefice – a foundation of the Counts of Flanders – to the Duke of Burgundy, Philip the Bold, who had become Count of Flanders through his marriage to Margaret of Mâle, on the death of her father in 1384. We shall see that an important episode in Gerson's life took place in Bruges. But first let us return to France.

There the last months of 1396 were dominated by the marriage of Richard II of England to Isabella, the daughter of Charles VI. This event was significant for the relations of the two countries and for ecclesiastical policy, in so far as new steps were taken to reach a definitive truce and the two Kings – Richard against the feeling of his clergy – agreed to send joint delegations to Avignon and Rome to urge the Popes once again to consider abdication.[48]

The French ambassadors, among them Gilles Deschamps and Jean Courtecuisse, appeared in Avignon in mid-July 1397, accompanied by ambassadors from England and Castile. Gilles Deschamps begged the Pope to accept the *via cessionis*, a plea which Benedict rejected – could he have done otherwise? Only the *via conventionis* and possibly the *via compromissi* were eligible. When one of the ambassadors received this reply from the Pope, he could not control himself any longer and added the threat: 'If the unity of the Church has not been achieved by Candlemas, Charles VI will see to it that the reasons why this Schism has continued for so long are removed', an unmistakeable hint of the possibility of withholding the Pope's apostolic revenues and depriving him of the right to appoint to benefices.[49]

Undiscouraged by their experiences in Avignon, the envoys then turned their steps towards Rome, where their welcome was hardly any different. They found themselves opposed on all sides, and it was apparent that special hostility was felt for the University of Paris. The best course, the Romans felt, would be for the King of France to use his endeavours to bring the followers of Benedict to submit to the Pope of Rome. In any case, that was better than res-

[47] Vansteenberghe, 'Gerson à Bruges', 10. See Gl. 10, 430: 'Actes et Documents' doc. 12b.
[48] Valois, *Schisme* III, 108.
[49] Valois, *Schisme* III, 117-19.

ignation. Boniface himself put it thus: 'I shall never cede my rights to anyone ... I swear that if I do otherwise, I shall never eat or drink again, never do anything pleasing to God. I shall give up my hope of heaven.'[50]

At the same time King Wenceslas of Germany felt obliged to do something for the Church and opened discussions with Charles. The two princes met at Rheims on 23 March 1398, and decided to issue one more call on both Popes to resign. It was Pierre d'Ailly who was appointed to inform the Pope of Avignon of the wishes of the two kings. Accompanied by a large and distinguished delegation, he begged Benedict to restore peace to the Church and to realise the noble intentions – of resignation – which he had long cherished. But – the narrative begins to grow monotonous – the Pope again refused. 'I should think', he said, 'I had committed a mortal sin, if I took such a step.'[51]

The University of Paris, it seems, had already dismissed the possibility of a settlement with Benedict. Pursuing the policy it had adopted at the synod of 1396, it held several meetings for discussions and finally decided, almost unanimously, that the Church in France should prepare for a so-called partial substraction.[52] Early in 1397 Jean Courtecuisse informed the King of the University's decision. The result was that new discussions were arranged, attended by the King, the princes and other members of the royal council. Here too, there was no lack of voices to warn against the revolutionary plan, but the supporters of substraction proved to be in the majority. Some of them were even bold enough to submit a proposal to bind the members of the University by oath to follow the policy of substraction and cession. This motion caused great indignation and forced the King to intervene. Following his intervention, it was decided in December 1397 to leave the question of substraction in abeyance for a year.[53]

This decision was not very significant, for four months earlier, on 12 September 1397, Charles VI had already declared that France had chosen the *via cessionis*. A decree was proclaimed expressly for-

---

50 Valois, *Schisme* III, 119-23.
51 Valois, *Schisme* III, 124ff; Salembier, *Le grand schisme*, 161.
52 Ehrle, 'Neue Materialien', 281; Valois, *Schisme* III, 139ff.
53 Valois, *Schisme* III, 140-1; Rel. de St.-Denys, *Chronique* II, 526.

bidding 'de prêcher, dogmatizer, faire, ne écrire épistres ne autres quelconques écritures ou choses qui puissent donner, faire ou porter aucun préjudice ou empeschement à ladite voye de cession.'[54] A month later he went a step further; considering that the Pope was abusing his right of nomination to appoint his partisans, he warned Benedict that he would no longer recognise any prelate who was not regularly elected by the chapter or whom he himself had not proposed for appointment. Charles's measure had fewer consequences than one might expect. Established custom above all, but also the respect that was still felt for Benedict, in spite of everything, proved more powerful than the King's attempts at authoritarian reform.[55]

It scarcely needs to be said that Benedict was not the man to be impressed by such measures. On 8 August 1397 he answered the threat of substraction by explicitly confirming that the right of awarding benefices was his. Earlier, in November 1396, he had already forbidden appeals against pontifical decisions, on pain of loss of ecclesiastical dignity. When the *magister sacri palatii* dared to suggest to him in a sermon that rejection of the *via cessionis* would cause the Pope to be suspected of disregarding the welfare of the Church and would be taken as a sign that he was hardening his heart, he had to pay for his words by imprisonment, which was to last two years.[56]

These threats and measures, which both sides regarded as provocative, only exacerbated the existing intransigence and brought an open breach between Paris and Avignon closer. The King felt impelled to take the step, in order, as he believed, to rescue the Church. For his part Benedict showed that he was prepared for the worst. He recruited troops and had his palace put in a state of defence.

On 7 March 1398 Charles VI issued a circular letter summoning the prelates, chapters and universities of the country to assemble in a national synod (National Synod III) at Paris thirty days after Easter,

---

54 Martène & Durand, *Thesaurus novus anecdotorum* II, Paris. 717, c. 1151.
55 Martin, *Gallicanisme* I, 274.
56 Valois, *Schisme* III, 142ff.

to discuss the question of total or partial substraction of obedience to Benedict.[57]

The meeting, which was opened on 22 May, far surpassed those of 1395 and 1396, both in the number of delegates and in their prestige. Eleven archbishops, 60 bishops, 30 abbots, numerous lower clergy and many members of the universities, in all 300 delegates with the right to vote, gathered in the royal palace, where the synod was held. There was great interest from the court too. This time the Duke of Orléans did not preside alone, but shared the task with the King of Navarre and the Dukes of Burgundy and Berry, who were assisted by the royal Chancellor, Arnauld de Corbie, and a great many members of the royal council. Once again the debates were organised to allow equal numbers of speakers for and against the policy of substraction.[58]

Simon de Cramaud was the first speaker. He gave a survey of the various steps taken by the court to bring about unity in the Church since the election of Benedict XIII. On the King's instructions he then informed the synod that it was not to discuss the *via cessionis*, since that had already been decided on because of Benedict's obstinacy. The only point at issue was to decide whether the Church in France should withdraw wholly from its obedience to the Pope, or if partial substraction would be enough to make the Pope reconsider.[59]

We shall not repeat the arguments of the supporters and opponents of substraction *in extenso* but merely cite the most important, those of the papalist or Gallican sides respectively. Pierre Ravat, Bishop of St Pons, defended Benedict, as whose spokesman he acted. Ravat, although he faced tough opposition, and to that extent was not lacking in personal courage, had an easier task than his opponents since his point of view was far closer to the prevailing opinions on Church and hierarchy than the thesis of the Gallicans, whose interpretation of tradition cannot be absolved from one-sidedness. But what we wish to stress is that one must not imagine that

---

57 The letter summoning the synod in Ehrle, 'Neue Materialien', 273-87.

58 The proceedings of this synod and the most important speeches were published by Bourgeois du Chastenet, *Nouvelle Histoire du Concile de Constance*, Paris 1728, Preuves, 3-84. A good account of the synod's deliberations, from a Gallican point of view, was given by Martin (*Gallicanisme* I, 275-90); from a canonistic point of view, by Buisson (*Potestas und Caritas*, 196-206).

59 Bourgeois du Chastenet, Preuves, 4; Ehrle, 'Neue Materialien', 276.

Ravat was one of a few who were unwilling to bow the knee to Baal at this time. For he too was one-sided, in so far as he said nothing in his speech about the essential point of the crisis in the Church. By reducing the problem of the Schism to the simple question: is it lawful to rebel against a Pope? he made it seem as if there was no other obedience and as if the problems would disappear by themselves, if loyalty to the Pope of Avignon were demonstrated. We cannot regard that as anything but a negation or belittlement of the crisis in which the Church found itself. Ravat revealed his inferiority to Gerson, whose virtue, in our view, was that he always involved the other party in his reasoning, and from the outset made the unity of the Church the starting point and the goal of his thought and work.

In Ravat's opinion obedience was owed to the Pope as long as he did not demand anything in conflict with natural law, divine law or the general structure of the Church. The Pope is free, he said, to deviate from the positive ordinances of the Church – the decisions of his predecessors or of councils – because he is exalted above human law, and can in fact be regarded as its creator. When, in the past, he has granted permission for chapters and monastic houses to choose their spiritual leaders for themselves that does not mean that he has definitively given away his right of nomination. As head of the community he continues to possess the right to levy taxes, in the interest of the Church as a whole, while he can also lay claim to the taxes of procuration.[60] This was Ravat's reply to the specifically Gallican theses.

Ravat painted a detailed picture of the consequences of substraction. In the first place he pointed out that anyone who dared to rebel against the Pope would be excommunicated; he went on to make it clear that substraction would lead to chaos. The legal order, which rested on papal authority right down to its most remote ramifications, would not merely totter but would collapse, if men were so rash as to take the law into their own hands. And what advantage would they gain in return? A right of free collation? But they should be aware how pressure would be exerted by the laity and how favouritism would decide. Those who urged substraction claimed to wish to bring the Schism to an end, but they could be

---

60 Buisson (*Potestas und Caritas*, 196-7) showed that Ravat by stating that the Pope was exalted above human law, remained in the tradition of Innocent IV.

certain that substraction would merely add to the confusion, for there would always be people who would recognise only Benedict, so that the Avignon obedience would be divided into two camps. Does the King not have a duty to strive for unity, they will ask? Without doubt, but in questions which touch the Church, only the Church has the right to decide. The King should stay out of it, and confine himself to sending embassies, organising conferences and preparing for the holding of a council.[61]

Those who pleaded the case for substraction included, besides Pierre LeRoy the Abbot of Mont St Michel, Simon de Cramaud and the two theologians Gilles Deschamps and Pierre Plaoul. Simon de Cramaud devoted an important part of his argument to the thesis that the duty to obey the Pope ceases when his conduct causes harm to the Church. Only as long as he does not act in conflict with the status of the universal Church is he owed obedience. And if, for example, he should wish to alienate the patrimony of the Church, resistance would be lawful on the grounds of the consideration that his power is granted him to build up and not to break down (2 Cor. 13:10). Hence it was tolerable to resist Benedict because his behaviour had widened the Schism. Even without a prior judicial condemnation, he was to be regarded as a heretic and schismatic, and so it was lawful to withdraw obedience from him. Circumstances compelled this step all the more, since Benedict lived off France. The incomes that he drew from that country explained his refusal to yield and it was a reasonable assumption that once he ceased to receive any funds, his followers would desert him. 'Everything that he receives from here merely nourishes the Schism.'[62]

Pierre LeRoy also pointed out that the Pope's authority could not be regarded as absolute, but that it was to be guided by the purpose for which it was created. Christ, he observed, had given Peter the power to protect his flock, to lead the faithful in the path of salvation. That meant that they were obliged to obey the Pope because and in so far as he issued the legal edicts which directly served the cause of that salvation. The faithful were only bound to do the will of the Pope when it reflected God's will, when the ordinances of the curia served the welfare of the Church. Now it is said that

---

[61] Martin, *Gallicanisme* I, 277ff.

[62] Rel. de St.-Denys, *Chronique* II, 578, 580; Buisson, *Potestas und Caritas*, 197-9.

one may not do evil to acquire good, and that is correct, but if the argument is urged against substraction, it is not correct, for substraction was not an evil; on the contrary it was a good, since by it the Pope could be led back to the path from which he had strayed. Benedict would resist substraction and proceed to excommunications, but one need not fear this. For in the opinion of the doctors the exercise of the power of the keys was always subject to the reservation of error, and thus the reservation that God's will is not violated; but it was as clear as day that Benedict would commit such a violation if he were to excommunicate those who released themselves from their obedience to him, for no other reason than to promote the unity of the Church. Therefore it was not necessary to be absolved from such an excommunication.[63]

The theologians Gilles Deschamps and Pierre Plaoul spoke in the same spirit, but laid even greater stress on the right and duty of the King to intervene in ecclesiastical affairs, as had been done several times in the past. Deschamps pointed out that the King had sworn an oath to defend the frontiers of his kingdom, which also bound him to ensure that the Church in his dominions was not subject to the Pope absolutely, but only to a reasonable extent. Precisely because it was undeniable that there was no higher instance than the Pope himself, when the Pope abused his power, one ought to arm oneself against usurpation in advance and be vigilant, so that the Pope did not acquire excessive authority in the kingdom. Deschamps defended substraction with the well known argument that if a prelate gave offence to the people and there was no hope of his mending his ways, he could not be maintained in office any longer, for he had been instituted for the sake of the faithful and not for his own sake.[64]

Pierre Plaoul went even further. He regarded substraction as not only permissible or useful but as a sacred duty *de necessitate salutis*! Whoever resisted it was promoting the Schism and must therefore be shunned as if he had been excommunicated. The current objection, which we know from Gerson and Ravat, that substraction endangered not only papal authority but the secular power as well, because the same weapon might be turned against the prince, made no impression on Plaoul. The Pope's authority was not at all to be

---

[63] Bourgeois du Chastenet, Preuves, 21-8; Martin, *Gallicanisme* I, 280-2.

[64] Bourgeois du Chastenet, Preuves, 37-40; Martin, *Gallicanisme* I, 282.

compared with that of a King. There was an essential difference between them, since the princes had received power from God to rule and exert their authority, but the spiritual leaders had to be guided by the words of Jesus: 'Among you, whoever wants to be great must be your servant' (Matt. 20:26). The consequences of a possible abuse of power by the princes would therefore always remain limited, for they could only harm the bodies or wealth of their subjects. But if the Pope exceeded his powers, that was a very different matter; there was much more at stake and it was not an exaggeration to say that a Pope who abused his power could corrupt the whole of Christendom.[65] Plaoul's intention is clear: by making secular power relative and spiritual power absolute, he aimed to show that substraction would not easily be turned against a prince.

After the various speakers had been given the opportunity to reply to their opponents – in many cases making their own intentions clearer – a vote was taken (11 June – 2 July). This was arranged in such a way that each delegate with the right to vote made his opinion known *viva voce* in the presence of the Dukes and some of the King's advisors, before casting his vote in a signed *schedula*.[66] While the vote was in full swing, the Rector appeared, accompanied by other University representatives, to announce that the University of Paris had decided in its last meeting to release itself wholly from obedience to Benedict. The universities of Montpellier and Orléans expressed themselves in the same way.[67]

On 28 July the Chancellor Arnauld de Corbie was able to announce that the great majority of the votes had been cast in favour of total substraction, so that Benedict was deprived not only of the right to appoint to benefices but also of his spiritual suzerainty. As long as the Pope of Avignon refused to follow the *via cessionis* in fact, the French Church would persist in this policy.[68]

The ordinance, which was dated 27 July but must have been composed later,[69] justified this decision in detail. It gave as the primary motives: the abominable egotism of both Popes, their excessive ambition for the tiara, by which the Church was torn apart and

[65] Bourgeois du Chastenet, Preuves, 73-4; Martin, *Schisme* I, 283.
[66] Valois, *Schisme* III, 161; Haller, *Papsttum* I, 234.
[67] Valois, *Schisme* III, 170.
[68] Rel. de St.-Denys, *Chronique* II, 582; Martin, *Gallicanisme* I, 287.
[69] Text of the ordinance in Rel. de St.-Denys, *Chronique* II, 598ff.; cf. Valois, *Schisme* III, 183 n. 2.

the emergence of stubborn errors was promoted. All the fruitless negotiations between the court and Benedict were summarised in this document, which did not put forward any new points of view. It is noticeable that the ordinance made an explicit protest against the view, propagated by Benedict himself, that the revolt against him was intended to put a Frenchman on the papal throne. 'Following Christ, who made no distinction between Jews and Greeks, we too regard as equally good ... and excellent an African, an Arab, and an Indian, provided at least that he is a true Catholic and not blinded by passion, that he does not dishonour the Church nor lead her into error.'[70]

The vote showed that the Duke of Orléans was the only one of the princes to have voted against substraction. He and thirty others wished to give the Pope one last chance to resign voluntarily. The Dukes of Burgundy and Berry, on the other hand, had been glad to join the majority and did not omit to point out that their decision had been influenced by the straitened financial situation of the kingdom.

The decision in favour of complete substraction was only a beginning; many arrangements had to be made to put it into practice. Obviously this posed complicated problems, if we bear in mind how strongly monarchical the Church was in its structure and how substraction now suddenly cut off the links with the top. Passing over the short term ecclesiastical measures,[71] most of which transferred the specific powers of the Pope to the bishops and archbishops, we turn to the sacred college. How did Benedict's cardinals react to substraction?

As early as 17 September the great majority of them – 18 of the 23 – had already informed Charles that they agreed with the recent decision, and had also released themselves from their obedience to the Pope.[72] They immediately began to launch verbal and written polemics against their former master from Villeneuve, on the other side of the Rhône, where they had withdrawn for safety. They de-

---

[70] Rel. de St.-Denys, *Chronique* II, 628.

[71] Besides Valois, *Schisme* III, 184-7, see Haller, *Papsttum* I, 239-42, and, in particular, G. Mollat, 'L'application en France de la soustraction d'obédience à Benoît XIII jusqu'au concile de Pise', *Revue du Moyen Age Latin* I (1945) 149-63.

[72] Rel. de St.-Denys, *Chronique* II, 652.

picted him as a schismatic and heretic, as Julian the Apostate, even as Simon Magus.[73] Nor was this all. Whether or not it was at their direct instigation – which seems likely – the bellicose Geoffroy de Boucicaut[74] appeared on the scene, attracted by the favourable opportunity to enrich himself at no great risk, and offered his services to recall the citizens of Avignon, the cardinals who had remained loyal to Benedict, and finally the Pope himself to order. Boucicaut, accompanied by a number of so-called *routiers* or irregular troops, laid siege to Avignon at the end of 1398. This siege was to last, with varying intensity, for three years.[75]

***

Gerson, as we saw, was not merely absent from the national synod of 1396, but also, as he tells us himself,[76] from that held two years later. Presumably he stayed away from Paris when the synod of 1398 was held and was apparently unable, or thought it unnecessary or inadvisable to interrupt his mission in order to cast his vote in Paris.[77] When we remember his distaste for the policy of substraction, we shall be inclined to assume that he avoided both synods deliberately. Perhaps he feared that if the Chancellor of the University came out openly against substraction, he would be deposed and replaced by an adherent of the new policy, thereby driving the University, which he already believed to be on the wrong path, directly into the arms of heresy. It would therefore be better to stay away from the synod, and thus avoid the risk of being compelled to hand over the reins of authority altogether. We should not forget that he owed his appointment as Chancellor to the Pope. If he were to speak out against substraction, he would naturally be suspected of being the Pope's advocate rather than praised as the advocate of the truth. But in the circumstances, an advocate of the Pope was identified with an advocate of heresy. Was it purely imaginary to fear that such a person would be treated as harshly as the

73 Valois, *Schisme* III, 193.
74 Salembier, *Le grand schisme*, 167 n. 1.
75 Valois, *Schisme* III, 196ff.
76 Gerson in a letter to the Duke of Orleans. See Chapter III, epigraph.
77 Cf. Combes, *Jean de Montreuil*, 359 n. 3.

heretic himself? We do not think so. There was a serious danger that Gerson would have been persecuted if he had openly voiced his objections to the Gallican policy of substraction at the synod.

CHAPTER THREE

ON THE BASIS OF SUBSTRACTION, 1398-1403

Porro in conclusione substractionis non affui, quam tamen conclusam impugnare pertinaci animositate non praesumpsi. Sed postquam dominus noster Benedictus viam cessionis et alia quae petebantur accomoda pro pace et reformatione ecclesiae dictus est acceptasse, opposuit se parvitas mea cum discriminibus non modicis, ut ipse neque papatum de facto irreversibiliter amisisse neque haereticus aut schismaticus iudicandus esse causaretur.

Gerson in a letter to the Duke of Orleans (5. Jan. 1404) inc. *Multa hactenus* (Gl.2, 71; Dupin II, 74B)

The development of church policy in France after the decision for substraction of 1398 was even more dominated–in fact crippled–by the controversy between the Dukes of Burgundy and Orléans, the uncle and the brother of the powerless King Charles VI, who both tried to sway the royal council. Philip of Burgundy wished at all costs to persist in the policy of substraction, because this left his hands free to realise his dream of founding a Burgundian kingdom. That kingdom was already beginning to take shape, for he had acquired Flanders in 1384, Brabant followed in 1390 and three years later Limburg fell into his hands.[1]

The ambitions of his nephew Louis of Orléans lay elsewhere; they were aimed at the conquest of territory in northern and central Italy, and were directly descended from Louis of Anjou's plans to found an Adriatic kingdom. Just as Anjou, who died in 1384, had enjoyed the support of the warlike Pope Clement VII, so the Duke of Orléans could count on a helping hand from Benedict XIII. The close relationship between Benedict and the Duke of Orléans explains why the latter was so zealous to reverse the substraction and return to obedience to the Pope.

Gerson spent more than a year–at any rate from 4 June 1399 to 20 September 1400–without interruption in Bruges, where he car-

---

[1] A good survey in Burger, *Aedificatio*, 26-8 ('Gersons Position im Spannungsfeld Burgund-Orléans').

ried out reforms in his chapter and also devoted himself to the contemplative life.[2] We learn much about his personal life from a memorandum written at this time, entitled *Causae propter quas cancellariam dimittere volebat*[3] in which he describes how the Chancellorship had become a burden to him, which he wished to give up so that he could remain in Bruges. The courtly life in which he had been forced to take part, unexpectedly and against his will, placed him in a situation for which he could no longer accept responsibility. Tossed back and forth between the favours of the feuding princes, Burgundy and Orléans, both of whom he was obliged to please,[4] he felt that resignation was justified and not just a flight from responsibility.[5] The University had forced him to follow decisions of the majority – substraction – which were against his convictions, while he would do better to be silent about dangerous opinions, because it would achieve nothing if he were to oppose them.[6] As chancellor he had to submit to the proposals of the faculties and grant degrees to students who, in his eyes, were intellectually and morally unfit to receive them. He had to spend all his valuable time preparing official speeches, which left him no time for his devotions.[7] If he resigned his position as Chancellor and remained in Bruges, he would exchange his bitter poverty in Paris – the Chancellor still lived in the College of Navarre – his beggary, for a *mediocritas aurea*.[8] Moreover, he would be able to devote himself wholly to the contemplative life to which he was naturally inclined and for which his talents fitted him. The active life was in conflict with his natural bent, it confused and oppressed him.[9] Why then should he not lay down his office? Had not Gregory of Nazianzus and Celestine V resigned for the same reasons? There were *magistri*

---

[2] Vansteenberghe, 'Gerson à Bruges', 15ff.; Schwab, *Gerson*, 264.

[3] Gl. 2, 17-23; Dupin IV, 725-8.

[4] *Causae* (Gl. II, 18; Dupin IV, 725A): 'Cogor enim pluribus dominis magnis valde qui adversissimi sunt, complacere vel obsequi; nomina non explico illa scientibus.'

[5] *Causae* (Gl. 2, 18; Dupin IV, 725 A).

[6] *Causae* (Gl. 2 19-20; Dupin IV, 726C): 'Cogor multitudinem insequi ad agendum quod non placet aut licet vel ut hostis ac suspectus ambitione haberi.'

[7] *Causae* (Gl. 2, 18-19; Dupin IV, 725D-6A).

[8] *Causae* (Gl. 2, 19; Dupin IV, 726A): 'Cogor etiam in temporali vita quasi mendicare et despectus vivere, cum mediocritas aurea non amara paupertas sit tutissima, secundum exigentiam status.'

[9] *Causae* (Gl. 2, 21; Dupin IV, 727B): 'Est autem natura mea et consuetudo ad agibilia prorsus inepta, scrupulọsa, iners, formidolosa, levissime perturbata, ut plus millies experior jugiter.'

enough whose talents lay in the practical sphere rather than contemplation, and who, because they were bolder and more adroit, would be much better able to fill his position.[10]

The point that interests us in this connection is his reference to Benedict. Gerson says that he has formed the impression that Benedict was unwilling to resign because he had been misled by his friends, who have made it appear as if his resignation would cause the Church to cease to exist, and as if no one else could be found to rule it.

> Aestimo per audita et facta Benedictum ne cederet ab amicis hoc superbiae fuco fuisse deceptum, quasi videlicet ecclesia recederet cum sua cessione, nec alius talis ad regimen ipsi debitum posse reperiri. Haec vero plane tentatio demonii meridiani.[11]

This statement is important because it appears in such a personal work as the *Causae*, and thus removes any doubt one might have about his private feelings towards Benedict. We will shortly see further evidence that Gerson regarded Benedict as misled, and therefore that his objections to substraction were not the result of blind loyalty to Petrus de Luna, as is sometimes assumed and as seemed to be the case with d'Ailly. Gerson certainly had serious reservations about the Pope's refusal to resign, but by no means felt that they were a reason to force him to resign.[12]

Following his memorandum Gerson informed the faculty of theology that he wished to lay down his office as Chancellor, and asked them to invest Dominique Petit with this office. The faculty granted his wish and on 3 March 1400 it requested the chapter of Notre Dame and the Bishop of Paris to appoint Dominique Petit as Chancellor and at the same time to allow Gerson to succeed Petit as pastor, in exchange for his Chancellorship. The request was delayed and in the meantime the Duke of Burgundy intervened and

---

[10] *Causae* (Gl. 2, 21-2; Dupin IV, 727C-8A).

[11] *Causae* (Gl. 2, 21-2; Dupin IV, 728A). Cf. his sermon *Apparuit gratia Dei*, where he openly warned Benedict for the *daemonium meridianum* (Gl. 5, 79; Dupin II, 65A): 'Sic ambitio retentiove dignitatum in pernicie ecclesiae subtili malo fingit se vellet multis proficere nec ecclesiam exponere discrimini perversorum. Et hoc est plane *daemonium meridianum* quod facit quandoque esse martyrem diaboli dum esse gloriatur quis in persequentibus martyr Dei.' To warn somebody for the seduction of the *daemonium meridianum* means to admonish him to resist the danger of mortal sin (*acedia*)! Cf. *DThC* 11, 2027 s.v. - 'paresse' (E. Vansteenberghe).

[12] See below n. 34.

persuaded Gerson to reconsider his decision.[13] He could not resist the pressure of Philip of Burgundy, to whom, after God, he said that he owed everything.[14] He remained Chancellor but was unable to return to Paris, since an illness kept him in Bruges. We may almost be grateful for the enforced leisure which this illness caused, for we owe to it a number of letters and treatises which must be numbered among his most personal utterances and which reveal Gerson to us in his simplicity, his conservatism and his deep concern for the state of the University and the Church.

It was presumably during this stay in Bruges that he composed his *De modo se habendi tempore schismatis.*[15] Reading this work one must recall that Flanders–which was in the English sphere of influence –had originally chosen for the Pope of Rome at the outbreak of the Schism. The Duke of Mâle had never recognised any Pope but Urban VI.[16] But when, after his death, Flanders fell to Philip of Burgundy, Philip tried to win it for the obedience of Avignon. He had only very partial success, and Gerson's work confirms that the adherents of the two Popes in Flanders were locked in bitter conflict. They excluded one another from the sacraments and denied the validity of sacraments performed by priests who recognised the other Pope. Gerson, whose deanery in Bruges led him to regard Flanders as his second homeland, tried to act as peacemaker, putt-

[13] Vansteenberghe, 'Gerson à Bruges', 23; Denifle-Chatelain, *CUP* IV, no. 1761.

[14] Letter to his friends (27 April 1400), inc. *Attulerunt eximiae* (Gl. 2, 29; Dupin IV, 723B): 'Mandatus sum quippe ab illo cui, post Deum, me et omnes operas meas debeo, dominum meum, dominum Burgundiae loquor, cuius utinam aliud circa me et pro me modestius, humilius, salubriusque consilium exstitisset, ignoscat Deus, idipsum consulentibus.' See also what he says about Philip of Burgundy (1342-1404), born on St. Anthony's day (17 January), in his sermon *Nuptiae factae sunt* (Gl. 5, 387; Dupin II, 357B), where he refers to his other sermons held on St. Anthony's day. See also Chapter I n. 7.

[15] Gl. 6, 29-34; Dupin, II 3-7. Date uncertain; cf. Schwab, *Gerson*, 154 n. 4; also Valois, *Schisme* IV, 496 n. 6. In any case it was by Gerson, according to the list of his works compiled by his brother, (Gl. I. *Introduction Générale*, 24 no. [33]). This fact escaped Mgr. Combes, *La théologie mystique* I, 213-5.

[16] For the situation in Flanders see: N. de Pauw, 'L'Adhésion du clergé de Flandre au pape Urbain VI et les évêques de Gand. 1379-1395', *Bulletin de la Commission Royale d'Histoire* II, Bruxelles 1904, 692-702; L. Salembier, 'Deux conciles inconnus de Cambrai et de Lille durant le Grand Schisme', added as 'Appendice III' to Hefele-Leclercq, *Histoire des Conciles* VI 2, 1481-1544 (notably 1540-4); G. van Asseldonk, *De Nederlanden en het Westers Schisma (tot 1398)*, Utrecht / Nijmegen 1955, 90, 94ff.; Delaruelle, *L'Église au temps du grand schisme*, 40-2.

ing forward a number of theses, some of which were directly related to his *De iurisdictione spirituali* of 1392.

In these theses he sought to prove that, in spite of the Schism, it was still possible to live in peace and community with one another. He attacked a number of *a priori* opinions, remarking, for instance, that the stubbornness with which some had chosen one of the two rival Popes, could entail the risk of heresy, in so far as it could involve *pertinacia*. In questions of the election of a Pope, in which so many human and contingent factors played a part, absolute certainty was unattainable. Hence, instead of excommunicating those who took a different view, it was essential in principle to leave room for an opposite and for a neutral opinion.[17]

Very consistently, he then goes on to point out that it is not only permissible, but even to be recommended, in the present Schism, to make the obedience shown to one or other party depend on a tacit or explicit condition. Because it is impossible to know for certain who is the true Pope, it is only reasonable to make one's obedience subject to such a reservation, as one does in the case of a celebrant who is thought to have performed the consecration improperly.[18]

Typical of Gerson's non-legalistic approach, and a further proof that solidarity and humility mattered more to him than the letter of the law, was his assertion that some adherents of the rightful Pope might well have to be counted among the schismatics, and conversely some followers of the wrongful obedience among the true members of the Church.[19] Why? Because one can be right a hundred times, but for the wrong motives. Ultimately, it was not legal right but brotherly love that was decisive.

> Stat aliquem verae parti assentientem sic pertinacem esse quod vel propter quaestum vel propter vanam gloriam vel aliam causam non habet animum paratum ad obediendum veritati agnitae si vel per ecclesiam vel aliter ostenderetur errare, vel si etiam in tanto dubiorum involucro pro sua assertione sustinenda, separaret se a membris veris et vivis ipsius

[17] *De modo se habendi* (Gl. 6, 30; Dupin II, 4B). This thesis follows from the University's decision of 21 June 1381.

[18] *De modo se habendi* (Gl. 6, 31; Dupin II, 5A). He used already the same reasoning in his *Resumpta* (see Chapter I n. 79).

[19] *De modo se habendi* (Gl. 6, 29; Dupin II, 4A): 'Possibile est aliquos verae parti assentientis esse veraciter schismaticos, et aliquos falsae parti modo praedicto assetientis schismaticos non existere...'

> ecclesiae; non est enim schisma tantum in separatione membrorum a capite, sed etiam in separatione pertinaci membrorum ab invicem.[20]

He raises a problem in his eighth conclusion, in which he states that it is more sensible to promote the unity of the Church by troubling its leaders – who, after all, were the cause of the dissension[21] – than by breaking communion with one another, and tormenting one another with excommunications. The difficulty is that Gerson, whom we know to have been strongly opposed to substraction, now suddenly refers to this method of bringing the Popes to reason.

> Salubrius, iustius et tutius est quaerere unitatem ecclesiae insistendo contra contendentes de papatu, et hoc per viam cessionis utriusque vel substractionis oboedientiae vel alterius licitae coactionis, quam subditos per excommunicationes aut aliter vexari seu turbari.[22]

How are we to explain this change of front? It seems most plausible to us that once France had gone over to substraction, Gerson felt that if the other obedience were to decide on a similar measure, the chance of restoring the unity of the Church would be increased. This assumes that his theses were primarily directed against the followers of the Pope of Rome; that they were the ones who had broken the bonds of brotherhood and had denied the validity of the sacraments administered by the priests of the Avignon obedience. This assumption is by no means rash, in view of the conditions in Flanders; on the contrary. Be that as it may, Gerson's advice was not very principled, but in the light of his love for the unity of the Church, it was not entirely incomprehensible.

At the end of September 1400, his health fully restored, Gerson returned to Paris. In the following months he produced several moral theological tracts in French, and resumed his activities as a

---

[20] *De modo se habendi* (Gl. 6, 32; Dupin II, 5D-6A).

[21] *De modo se habendi* (Gl. 6, 32; Dupin II, 6A): 'quoniam ubi radix et origo totalis vel principalis istius schismatis consistit, ibi eradicatio eiusdem fieri debet et antidotum assumi pro unitatis adeptione. Ipsi enim sunt qui peccaverunt, alii autem qui oves sunt quid meruerunt?'

[22] *De modo se habendi* (Gl. 6, 29; Dupin II, 4A). In 1402 Gerson had given a more detailed reflection on papal power and, in this connection, on the legitimacy of substraction, in his *De vita spirituali animae*, lectio 3 (Gl. 3, 153-5; Dupin III, 26AC). The passage ends as follows: 'Diutius spe nostra tenuit nos sermo de hac potestate summi pontificis, quoniam tempestas praesens ad hoc impulit, pro qua magis necesse est potestatem hanc ad clarum dignoscere atque secernere quam olim antea, praesertim ad videndum substractionis factae iustificandae vel cassandae rationem, praesuppositis eis quae facta sunt.'

preacher and university lecturer. Well known works, such as *Lectiones duae super Marcum*, *De distinctione verarum visionum a falsis*, and *Lectio de duplici logica*, all of which formed part of the same course of lectures, date from this period, October 1401 to January 1402. The comprehensive *De vita spirituali animae*, which we shall study in more detail in another context, belonged to the same cycle of lectures on the gospel of Mark and, as Mgr. Glorieux showed, must have been composed in these months, around April 1402.[23]

The discussion of Schism and substraction, which continued in all the branches of the Church, State and University, flared up again in the spring of 1402, when the University of Toulouse addressed a manifesto to the King and the *parlement*, rejecting the decision for substraction and pleading for a return to obedience. Shortly before this, the University of Orléans had ventured to declare that it had voted against substraction at the time. The Toulouse scholars repeated the old arguments against the rebellious measure, listed the punishments that had been incurred, and painted a sombre picture of the evils that substraction had already brought about. This was not all, for contrary to official policy, which sought to induce both rival Popes to resign, the University openly declared that it wished to recognise Benedict as Pope and ranged itself openly behind the policy he had followed from the start, the *via conventionis*.[24]

The letter from Toulouse and the explanation of it which the delegates of the University gave to the *parlement*, aroused great indignation in Paris, especially among some princes and members of the University. Considering that they had chosen the party of Benedict without his consent, the duke of Berry—who was governor of Languedoc—had the delegates arrested at once, while also giving orders to have the decision for substraction proclaimed again in his province. Philip of Burgundy ordered a refutation of the memorandum to be composed.[25] His adversary, the duke of Orléans, who was doing his utmost to have the decision of 1398 reversed, and who therefore welcomed the démarches of the universities of Toulouse and Orléans, had managed to induce the King to appoint

---

[23] Glorieux, 'L'Enseignement universitaire de Gerson', 88-113. See also below, Appendix II.

[24] Valois, *Schisme* III, 257ff.

[25] Valois, *Schisme* III, 265ff.

him as guardian of the prisoner of Avignon. That was to have important consequences.

In university circles in Paris there was still vigorous opposition to Benedict, and when the University of Toulouse was bold enough to issue its memorandum, that provoked Paris to petition for an audience with the King. On 14 and 15 April he received two spokesmen. One of them defended the thesis that anyone who opposed substraction proved himself a schismatic, while the other, Jean Courtecuisse, attempted to prove that Benedict had committed perjury and was therefore no longer worthy of the pontificate. He continued that it was desirable to call a council of the Avignon obedience to investigate this question more fully.[26]

In all probability these drastic schemes formed the background to Gerson's *Protestatio super statum ecclesiae*,[27] a brief explanation intended for the faculty of theology. In his capacity as Chancellor, he stated in very positive terms that he would continue to work for the benefit of unity in the Church, but refused to allow the University to discuss: questions concerning the lawfulness of adhesion to Benedict, the justness of the *via cessionis* or of substraction. He announced that he would resist *ex officio* any attempt by the University to realise the aim of many to brand Benedict as the really guilty party, to declare him a heretic or to proceed to persecute his present or future adherents.

> Si fiat accusatio praedicta nomine Universitatis vel facultatis theologiae, ego minimus inter eos sed fidelis filius et zelator sui honoris, quia obligor ex officio providere ne errores in Universitate pullulent, protestor quod hoc neque fuit neque est de consensu meo, quia etiam nunquam fui praesens ubi haec materia pro facultate tractaretur.[28]

---

[26] Valois, *Schisme* III, 261.

[27] Gl. 6, 34-5; Dupin II, 1-3. Dating uncertain. Schwab, *Gerson*, 178 n. 1, placed it in 1402; B. Bess (*Johannes Gerson und die kirchenpolitischen Parteien Frankreichs vor dem Konzil zu Pisa*, Marburg 1890, 48), in 1406 on the grounds of Gerson's statement: 'deliberationem generalis concilii huius obedientiae ... exspectando' (Gl. 6, 34; Dupin II, 1A), which would be inappropriate in 1402. Valois, *Schisme* III, 269 n. 4, was convinced by Bess, while Combes, *Jean de Montreuil*, 359 n. 5 (cf. also 567, 572ff.), followed Schwab but was unable to advance any proper arguments against Bess. That Bess's consideration is not decisive is indicated by *De restitutione obedientiae* of 1402 (Gl. 6, 65; Dupin II, 31C), where Gerson does not show himself completely averse to a council of one obedience. There is therefore no reason to reject Schwab's dating.

[28] *Protestatio* (Gl. 6, 35; Dupin II, 20C).

The only result of such a policy, Gerson argued, would be to confirm the Schism rather than to resolve it – one need only think of the Schism with the Greeks.[29]

In this explanation, which clearly reflects a greater consciousness of his office since his return from Bruges, Gerson declared that he would produce a more detailed reply to the followers of Benedict.[30] It is not entirely certain, but it is probable that we have this reply in the form of his *Replicationes* .[31] In this treatise excerpts appear taken from an older and highly venomous polemic against Benedict XIII, a work that is usually ascribed to Jean Courtecuisse. Be that as it may, Gerson takes Benedict under his protection in his reply, turns the arguments of the anonymous author on their head and tries to show that it is not the Pope by his conduct but the author by his tone who comes so objectionably close to falling into heresy.[32] Throughout the work he tries to show Benedict's attitude in a more positive light, while also criticising the monomaniac obstinacy with which the Pope's enemies urged the panacea of the *via cessionis* as the only possibility. He regards this as a sign of their lack of imagination and difficult to reconcile with the fact that the University, in its famous letter to the King (1394), had pointed out three ways to compose the Schism: the *via cessionis*, the *via compromissi* and the *via concilii*.[33]

Why did Gerson feel the need to take the captive of Avignon under his protection? We already know that he was unenthusiastic about the official policy of substraction, and that this was not the result of blind loyalty to Benedict. Had he not described him as 'misled'? Gerson had not changed his verdict, as we see from the closing words of his reply:

> Non dicuntur ista ad excusationem Benedicti, quem pro certo apparens est, captiose et per malum consilium egisse, aut bono consilio nequaquam credidisse ... dicantur ista non ad iustificandum dominum Benedictum, sed ad videndum quid suis opponentibus respondere posset, ne de pertinacia convinci posset a quibusdam.[34]

---

[29] *Protestatio* (Gl. 6, 35, Dupin II, 2A).

[30] *Protestatio* (Gl. 6, 35; Dupin II, 2A): 'accusatio multiplex odiosissima, turpissima et infamis... ut haec latius offero me deducturum.'

[31] Gl. 6, 35-42; Dupin II, 9-14.

[32] *Replicationes* (Gl. 6, 37, 39; Dupin II, 10B, 12A).

[33] *Replicationes* (Gl. 6, 38; Dupin II, 11B).

[34] *Replicationes* (Gl. 6, 42; Dupin II, 13D). *De restitutione obedientiae considerationes* (Gl.

In other words, he felt that, if one looked at the case objectively, there were not enough grounds to accuse Benedict of *pertinacia*, and therefore to condemn him as a heretic. To make this clearer, he interprets Benedict's conduct as far as possible in a positive light, without rushing to his defence or excusing him. He was not uncritical of Benedict, but this is far from saying that he had doubted the legitimacy of his election. André Combes suggested that Gerson was neutral towards Benedict, and defended this suggestion by arguing that Gerson would have tried harder to expel the other Pope and his adherents if he had really been convinced that Benedict was the true Pope.[35] The error of this thesis is plain from the fact that as early as 1392, in his *Resumpta*, Gerson had described the followers of the other obedience as belonging to the *pars falsa*,[36] in later works he speaks, for example, of the 'pretended' rights of the Pope of Rome.[37] We infer from this that for him Benedict was certainly the true governor of the Church, but–and this is the point–Gerson could not allow his church policy to be guided by this conviction, because that would inevitably have continued the Schism, and a greater horror than a divided Church was unimaginable to him.

Precisely because the unity of the Church was the supreme good, he had tried to avert substraction. We now see that as soon as he received reports that Benedict was showing himself more amenable to resignation, he made efforts to bring about a restitution, a return to obedience.[38] Thanks to Jean de Montreuil–and to André Com-

---

6, 59; Dupin II, 33C): 'Nonne dominus Benedictus sperabatur ab omnibus promptissimus ad cedendum? Quid tamen post assumptionem fecerit scimus omnes et dolentes experimur.' Cf. also Valois, *Schisme* III, 269 n. 2: 'Un adversaire de Benoît XIII constatait encore, vers 1401: «Et cancelllarius dixit saepissime quod nesciret nec vellet eum [Benedictum] defendere.»'

35 Combes, *Jean de Montreuil*, 389.

36 *De iurisdictione spirituali*, (Gl. 3, 6-7; Dupin II, 265C). In the same treatise pope Clement VII is distinguished from Urban VI, who is qualified as the *'iniustus'* pope of Rome (Gl. 6, 28; Dupin II, 265C).

37 See Gerson's comments on the letter from the University of Oxford (1395) (Gl. 10, 325). The University had stated that the late Urban VI had been deprived–*spoliatus*–of a part of his papal possessions, which provoked Gerson to write: 'non debet dici spoliatus, quia *nulla fuit eius electio*.' And (Gl. 10, 339): 'Notorie per vim et metum fuit intrusus; quare, cum nunquam in papatu ius habuit statim ad aliam electionem est processum'. *Disputatio de schismate*, (Gl. 6, 101; Dupin II, 79B): 'et per consequens poterit convenienter dominus Benedictus in *praetensum ius* alterius substitui.'

38 Gerson in his letter inc. *Multa hactenus* to the Duke of Orleans (5. January 1404), (Gl. 2, 71; Dupin II, 74), cited above Chapter III device.

bes who fished this important fact out of one of Montreuil's letters —we know that it was a very courageous deed on Gerson's part to enter the lists for Benedict at this moment, and that his intervention was by no means agreeable to his *dominus naturalis*, the Duke of Burgundy. Referring to Gerson's efforts to avert substraction, and after the return to obedience, Jean de Montreuil wrote:

> In quo tam magnanimiter quam fortiter ad disciplicentiam omnium, potentissimi domini sui naturalis, et eorum maxime qui rerum tum fungebantur habenis, sese idem cancellarius viriliter opposuit, ut de quadraginta quattuor sacre theologie professoribus triginta tres efficacibus suis rationibus actutum converteret, et induceret demum saniorem universitatis portionem secum esse...[39]

Before we examine how he sought to bring about a return to obedience, we must mention that at about this time, the end of 1401 and the beginning of 1402, a plan surfaced which aimed to break through the impasse by calling a council representing all the countries of the Avignon obedience. So far as this plan originated, as in the case of Jean de Courtecuisse, in a desire to condemn Benedict as a heretic and then depose him, Gerson was vehemently opposed to it; naturally, for it ran clean contrary to his policy of restitution. But so far as such a council was desired to restore order within their own obedience as a first step to bring about a return to unity, he had fewer objections. This is clear from the following works, all written around Easter 1402: *De schismate*,[40] *Considerationes de restitutione oboedientiae Benedicto*[41] and *De concilio generali unius oboedientiae*.[42]

In the first of these tracts Gerson starts from the desire of many in the Church to bring proceedings against Benedict and to call a council (of one obedience) in order to remove the existing uncer-

---

[39] Jean de Montreuil in his letter inc. *Etsi nil prosit* to Nicolas of Clémanges (ed. Combes, *Jean de Montreuil*, 562-4, 562). Cf. Valois, *Schisme* IV, 524 (additions et corrections, III, 269 n. 4).

[40] (Gl. 6, 42-51; Dupin II, 17-24. This treatise is referred to in *De vita spir. animae*, lectio 4, cor. 13 (Gl. 3, 169; Dupin III, 47B): '... scripsisse memini quod etiam ubi via cessionis fuisset minus bona, tamen acceptare eam debebat dominus Benedictus, attenta deliberatione regni Franciae et aliorum subditorum suae obedientiae.' Cf. *De schismate* (Gl. 6, 44; Dupin II, 18B): '... causa praecisa et praecipua substractionis fuit negatio cessionis, sicut multi tenent quod sic fuit pronunciatum per Cancellarium Franciae ex deliberatione concilii praelatorum.'

[41] Gl. 6, 58-61; Dupin II, 32-5.

[42] Gl. 6, 51-8; *De restitutione obedientiae*, Gl. 6, 62-6; Dupin II, 24-32.

tainty in the Church; he examines in *De schismate*, one of his more fundamental treatises, whether it is right to hold such a council. After urging a number of arguments in favour, he then rejects it on four grounds.

1. It is generally accepted that a general council can only be called by the Pope and that this rule may only be deviated from if the Pope refuses *pertinaciter* to call a council. But this is not the case, since Benedict has not yet been deprived of the papal dignity and has not even been accused of heresy, still less condemned; hence there can be no question of *pertinacia* or heresy. True, there are some who believe that such a condemnation is superfluous, since he can be deposed on the grounds of notorious errors, and thus–*ipso iure*–be regarded as *minor quolibet catholico*, but such a reasoning is wholly inappropriate, for one should always await a judicial pronouncement. If one fails to do so, the whole legal order is overthrown. In other words, only after a verdict can the Pope be said to be *minor quolibet catholico*. All this is in tune with the assertion of (pseudo-)Isidore in his *Liber conciliorum*, where we also find the legal rule: *ante omnia spoliatus debet restitui*.[43] Applied to the present impasse

[43] Pierre d'Ailly often referred to the ps. Isidorian *Liber conciliorum*, which he held in very high esteem; in this he was sometimes followed by his former pupil. See e.g. Gerson's *De schismate* (Gl. 6, 45-6; Dupin II, 19AC): 'Supponimus insuper quod Benedictus nondum depositus est de papatu, quia nec fuit iuridice accusatus nec auditus et per consequens non convictus; nam et si haereticus et schismaticus sit de iure deponendus et apud Deum sic mereatur, non est tamen depositus de facto ante sententiam, ut notatur V quaest. 4 c. Novae [here, we fear, Mgr. Glorieux simply copied Dupin's wrong reading. The reference should be: C.8 q. 4 c. Nonne, = c.1] et Glossa super hoc verbo 'pro dubia' [Dupin omits 'pro dubia']... Dicentes quod papa haereticus minor est quocumque catholico et iurisdictioni ecclesiae subest, intelligunt quod ab aliis potest ut inferior iudicari; sed ante iudicium debet semper reputari maior... Iura ad haec non allego, quia totus textus *libri conciliorum* ab Isidoro plenus est, quod concilium nullum robur habet nec potest convocari nisi auctoritate papae, et quod *ante omnia spoliatus debet restitui* (cf. Isidori praefatio, in: P. Hinschius, *Decretales ps.-Isidorianae*, 19 §. VIII, and 18 §. VI. See also Gratian C.3 qq. 1 and 2, and Glossa; X 2, 13 c. 5-7).' In the passage above cited, we think, Gerson directly followed Pierre d'Ailly. Cf. the latter's *De materia concilii generalis* (ed. Oakley, 271 and 285), where he refers to the same Glossa ad C.3 q.1 tit. Quod restitutio): '... quod clerici non debent a papa etiam suspecto de haeresi ante definitionem concilii discedere, et quod hoc est schisma facere, et quod hoc facientes, si misericordiam consequi debeant, satisfacere tenentur. Alioquin officiis ecclesiasticis privantur, ut 8 q.4 cap. Nonne. Et haec plenius patent in *Libro conciliorum*...' He continues: 'Unde pro casu praesenti et eius dependenciis valde expedit videre *Librum conciliorum*, ubi ad plenum legitur quod a Gratiano truncate diversis in locis recitatur. Ideo Johannes Faventinus, Laurentius et Archidiaconus in hac materia ad *Librum conciliorum* remittunt.' – A.M. Stickler (*Historia Iuris Canonici Latini* I, Augustae Taurinorum 1950, 140-2) stresses the fact that in ps.-Isidore's work the rule *spoliatus ante*

this rule means that there is only one way to arrive at a lawful council, and that is by returning to the status quo of 1398, by reversing the decision for substraction, for it can cannot be expected that Benedict will be ready to call a council, as long as he is a captive; he must first be restored to his liberty.

2. The proposal to call a council in the existing circumstances is made more difficult by the fact that the various representatives who would attend it hold very different views on Benedict and on the lawfulness of substraction. Sometimes the attitude of the princes to Benedict is not even certain. If the question were to be put – is Benedict to be regarded as the true Pope or as a heretic? – one would have to be prepared to find that for many this was not in question, and that they would withdraw from the discussion, so that no progress would have been made.[44]

3. But if it is assumed that all parties would be ready to hold an inquiry into Benedict's attitude, then he himself and his friends would have to be heard. And if not all the charges brought against him were completely convincing, the University of Paris, which wished to persist in the policy of substraction, would not only achieve nothing, but would risk a humiliating condemnation, for the opponents of substraction were in the majority. Nor could one rely on the infallibility of a council, for that applies only to questions of faith and not to questions of fact and positive law, which was precisely what was at stake in substraction.[45] Also, it was to be expected that if Benedict were accused, he would bring a counter-

---

omnia debet restitui was fundamental. For some details on d'Ailly's use of the Liber conciliorum, see Oakley, *Political Thought*, index s.v. 'Liber conciliorum' & 'Isidore of Seville'. – J.F. von Schulte (*Die Geschichte der Quellen und Literatur des canonischen Rechts* I, Stuttgart 1875, 41) identifies this work with the socalled 'collectio Dionysio-Hadriana', in which, however, he was not followed by P. Landau, 'Vorgratianische Kanonessammlungen bei Dekretisten und in frühen Dekretalensammlungen', in: *Proceedings of the Eight Internat. Congress of Med. Canon Law*, Città del Vaticano 1992, 93-116 (109 n. 86 & n. 87). See also Stump, *The Reforms of the Council of Constance*, 228-31 (228 n. 86). – In Henry of Langenstein's *Epistola concilii pacis* (cap. 5-10) there are also abundant references to ps.-Isidore.

[44] *De schismate* (Gl. 6, 46; Dupin II, 19D-20A).

[45] *De schismate* (Gl. 6, 47; Dupin II, 20B): 'Nec valet hoc dicere quod Dominus non permittet errare concilium, quoniam in eis quae sunt facti aut iuris positivi, et breviter in omnibus aliis praeterquam in materiis quae sunt pure de fide, ecclesia fallit et fallitur, servata caritate... Istae vero propositiones: substractio fuit bene facta, vel male facta, non sunt propositiones pure de fide sed praesupponunt alias innumeras quae sunt pure de facto.' Cf. Chapter I n. 78.

charge of rebellion against the cardinals and bishops. Some of them have also been led astray into openly heretical statements in their polemics, so that they have played into the Pope's hands. If it were assumed that Benedict would submit to the verdict of the council, then his accusers would have to reckon with the possibility of being repaid in their own coin.[46]

4. The proposal to call a council of one obedience was objectionable in every respect for it would either be unable to take any decision – and therefore pointless – or it would take a decision but lack the power to put it into effect. That would be highly undesirable and prejudicial for a later council, and contain the seeds of new Schisms, which could only be ruinous for France. Therefore, rather than pressing for a one-sided council, let the Church look to the princes and their impartial advisers for rescue.[47]

The *Considerationes de restitutione obedientiae*, which Gerson wrote at the same time, show even more clearly that his rejection of a unilateral conciliar solution, was accompanied by a preference for the restoration of obedience, albeit not unconditionally. Those who opposed restitution, he remarks, argue that in all probability, after obedience had been restored, Benedict would still persecute those who had once forsaken him, causing new clashes between the clergy and the princes or the Pope and his cardinals. They also doubted that the Pope, if released, would in fact keep the promise to resign he had given in captivity. They feared that instead he would use his freedom to strengthen his position by creating new cardinals. Finally, they thought it very doubtful that Benedict would in fact be willing to ratify decisions taken during substraction – the granting of benefices, the appointment of prelates etc.[48]

Gerson took an attitude of tempered optimism to this sceptical prognosis, which unfortunately was to prove all too accurate. He does not disguise the difficulty of burying the hatchet and allaying all the rancour and animosities, but counts on the magnanimity of

---

[46] *De schismate* (Gl. 6, 46-8; Dupin II, 20A-1B). The reference (Gl. 6, 47; Dupin II, 20C) to '*Quaedam scripta*' with heretical theses appears to relate to the attack on them in this treatise (Gl. 6, 36-8, 39-40; Dupin II, 10 and 12A).

[47] *De schismate* (Gl. 6, 48-51; Dupin II, 21B-2C; 22D-3) contains the all too true statement: 'nulla sit implacabilior et irremediabilior divisio quam illa quae sit sub religionis praetextu.'

[48] *Considerationes de restitutione* (Gl. 6, 58-60; Dupin II, 32C-3D).

Benedict, who will have learned in captivity how unreasonable it was to ignore good advice.[49]

The restoration of obedience could not be unconditional, since there had to be security in advance about Benedict's readiness to grant a general pardon, especially to the cardinals, but also to all others who had rebelled against him by withdrawing their obedience. Nor would it be possible, after restitution, to deviate from the line followed during the period of substraction with regard to the granting of benefices. These proposals would have to be worked out in more detail by a small number of representatives of the clergy and the princes. Gerson felt that this *via media* was to be preferred in every respect to the *via rigoris* urged by some, in which Benedict was to be eliminated in the figurative and perhaps even in the literal sense. He thought he could assume that the princes of his own obedience would agree to the plans he had worked out, and he speculated that once unity had been restored in the Avignon camp, peace proposals could be put to the Roman obedience, which could then be realised either by a council or in some other way.[50]

The most interesting point of the whole work is the conviction with which Gerson takes it for granted that he could stipulate that Benedict should respect the decisions on Church organisation taken during the substraction. Of course the Church had gone through the inevitable changes of personnel during substraction, changes which had been largely effected on the authority of the bishops. Gerson wished to see this practice confirmed and made grateful use of substraction to the extent that he tried to maintain the practical consequences attached to it, even after obedience and a more normal procedure had been restored. This implies a certain criticism of the centralised, curialist organisation of the Church, or, to put it another way, a demand for a *reformatio ecclesiae*.

---

[49] *Considerationes de restitutione* (Gl. 6, 60; Dupin II, 34 AB): 'vexatio dabit aut dedit intellectum [sc. Benedicto] ad cognoscendum qualiter inexpediens non credere consilio.'

[50] *Considerationes de restitutione* (Gl. 6, 60-61; Dupin II, 34B-5A): 'Postremo si fuerit haec obedientia resarcita et unita, poterimus cum communi consensu offerre alteri obedientiae omnem viam ponendi pacem in Ecclesia, sive concilium generale sive aliter.'

In his *De concilio unius oboedientiae*[51] Gerson reveals a little more about the nature of such a reformation. This work, which is made up of seven theses, dates from the same period as the two tracts we have just discussed, and again contains a plea against a one-sided council. Most of its arguments are already familiar. What is new, however, is his attack on the argument that it would be an opportune moment to call a council for the sake of a *reformatio ecclesiae in moribus per modum determinationis*, i.e. to make binding pronouncements on religious and moral life. Reformation, he says, means that certain decisions and Church traditions which cause confusion, are abolished or revised. But this cannot be done unilaterally, because the questions concerned the status of the Church as a whole, and therefore the whole Church had to be consulted.[52] Hence there cannot be any generally binding decisions, but that does not mean that certain abuses in particular regions or churches could not be very properly abolished by provincial and diocesan synods. Some opinions urging this had already been given.[53]

In this connection he gives an account of the historical growth and development of the temporal power of Church and the Pope, an account to which he attaches important consequences.[54] He distinguishes three stages in this historical development: first, that of the primitive Church, when the Church and the Pope possessed no temporal property at all. Then the period after Constantine, when the clergy began to acquire temporal jurisdiction and property; and finally the period in which the Popes demanded and accumulated ever more temporal powers, rights and possessions.

The point of this distinction is in its assertion that temporal power was unknown to the primitive Church and that although Christ was rightfully entitled to *dominium universale* in spiritual and temporal matters, he had refrained from exercising temporal jurisdiction, clearly in order to avoid damaging his spiritual jurisdiction.

---

[51] On the authorship of this treatise, see Appendix I.

[52] *De concilio unius oboedientiae* (Gl. 6, 53; Dupin II, 26A): '... reformatio ecclesiae universalis non potest fieri in moribus sine abolutione multorum statutorum super excommunicationibus et ceteris traditionibus nimis multiplicatis, quae nec observantur nec observari possunt rationaliter ubique propter varietatem morum et temporum. Et tamen tales remotiones statutorum et canonum antiquorum aut additiones novorum fieri nequeunt rationabiliter pro tota ecclesia sine consensu communi.'

[53] *De concilio unius oboedientiae* (Gl. 6, 53; Dupin II, 26B).

[54] *De concilio unius oboedientiae* (Gl. 6, 54-7; Dupin II, 27A-8). For more details, see the present author's *Jean Gerson et l'Assemblée de Vincennes*, 80ff.

But, asks Gerson, does this mean that Christ was not a Pope in the fullest sense? Or Peter? Of course they were. Therefore it cannot be regarded as an attack on the papal dignity if the administration of the *temporalia* by God's vicarius is taken from him.[55] There is no doubt whatever that the Church ought to be governed by one supreme head in spiritual matters,

> sed de traditionibus humanis pro regimine temporalium ecclesiae, totaliter oppositum invenitur, quoniam secundum varietatem temporum, locorum et gentium et rituum, variandae sunt decretales et ordinationes super collationibus et regimine talium temporalium.[56]

This theory, with its strict distinction between the temporal and the spiritual in the Church, explains why Gerson could strongly oppose total substraction, but have fewer objections to partial substraction.[57]

This line of thought had been developed from within Gerson's

---

55 *De concilio unius oboedientiae* (Gl.6, 55; Dupin II, 28): '... latissima est differentia in spiritualibus et temporalibus quoad hoc; et utinam fuisset bene semper intellecta a prioribus et modernis forte quod adhuc starent Graeci cum Latinis. Patet enim ... quod papa potest manere papa universalis in perfectione magna, immo maiori quam erat Sylvester, et tamen nullum habebit exercitium actuale circa temporalia ecclesiae universalis per dioceses, quantumcumque habeat dominium vel plenitudinem potestatis in habitu.' Previously (Gl. 6, 54; Dupin II, 27A), he had already argued that the Pope–like Christ–possessed under divine law the 'dominium universale spiritualium et temporalium respectu omnium.'

56 *De concilio unius oboedientiae* (Gl. 6, 56; Dupin II, 28A). Cf. *De restitutione obedientiae* (Gl. 6, 64; Dupin II, 31B): 'Porro de istis temporalibus administrationibus ecclesiarum, possessionum, iurium, beneficiorum et similium, Christus per seipsum immediate nullatenus se intromisit nec ordinare curavit, sciens et volens talia esse variabilia secundum exigentiam temporum, personarum et locorum, ad communem Ecclesiae utilitatem, non ad unius aut paucorum singularem pompam aut inutilem vanitatem sive voluntatem. Ratio postulat, nec negamus, ut domino papae et suis cardinalibus fiat sufficiens provisio de bonis ecclesiasticis, sicut olim summo sacerdoti inferiores suas decimas offerebant; *sed haec provisio nonne poterit adimpleri absque hoc quod necesse sit ex toto ius ordinariorum cassari vel suspendi?* Profecto sic.'

57 He considered such a partial substraction to be permissible even without the Schism. Cf. *De concilio unius oboedientiae* (Gl. 6, 56; Dupin II, 28C): '... etiam stante unitate ecclesiae talis substractio vel in toto vel in parte fieri fortassis debuisset; et hoc si absque graviori scissura in spiritualibus potuisset contingere; et ita sapientissima lucet in hac parte Dei providentia quae ex malo schismatis alia bona sciet elicere'. This statement is to be seen, we think, against the background of the conviction he shared with the Franciscans, that poverty and spirituality went hand in hand, and that the spiritual force of a poor Church was far greater than that of a rich one. See Chapter VIII n. 69.

own camp and was inspired by his wish to see the early restoration of unity in it. But he would not have been true to himself if he had left it at that, if he had not also looked beyond the bounds he had set and brought the other obedience into his reflections. What did he think ought to be done, at that moment, to restore unity in his own camp? Should the goal be resignation, compromise or conciliation? Or a combination of the three? He did not make a clear choice, for he did not regard himself as competent to do so, and therefore only repeated the views of certain anonymous authors, who tended towards a combination of the three ways. Resignation, these unknown writers believed, would not be enough to bring about unity, for there would have to be a council, which in turn assumed the *via compromissi*–so that the Church would not be entirely dependent on the consensus of the two pretenders, and would have an authoritative body which, if one of the rivals was unwilling to resign, could declare him a schismatic and depose him.[58]

Up to this time Gerson had always resisted a conciliar solution to the conflict of the two obediences. He considered that the case of the Schism did not lend itself to such a solution, because it was a case of facts and not of faith; and a general council could not make infallible pronouncements on facts. Now, however, in this work of 1402, his point of view appears to have slightly changed, to the extent that he no longer rejects the *via concilii* out of hand, but is willing to include it, albeit with some hesitation, in his consideration of Church policy. He hesitated because he foresaw the difficulties of calling such a council: by whom and on what authority was it to be summoned if the Pope was unwilling to do so? He was also reluctant to set a bad example to posterity. For that reason he withheld judgement and preferred to leave the question to specialists.[59] At this point, then, he was still a long way from the conciliar solution of the Schism which he was later to champion, but these brief and cautious remarks are significant as the first steps on his path to that position.

We shall pass over the discussions at this time, so important for literary history, of the *Roman de la Rose*, a work which Gerson despised, for its sensual mysticism seemed to him to be the source of

---

58 *De concilio unius oboedientiae* (Gl. 6, 57-8; Dupin II, 29B).

59 *De concilio unius oboedientiae* (Gl. 6, 57-8; Dupin II, 29B).

all immorality. Instead we shall turn our attention to the *Trilogus in materia schismatis* which he composed in the winter of 1402/3,[60] a work which has been rightly described as the most attractive and liveliest illustration of his conciliatory position between the parties.[61] It shows us how mysticism had sharpened his insight so that he was able to achieve an unusual objectivity.

'Frequently', so the author begins, 'I have climbed the lofty citadel of reason, above the clouds of sinful passions, to gaze out over the raging sea of conflict and to contemplate ways of stilling the storm which buffets the ship of the Church. But alas, I see the helmsmen of the Church furiously fighting each other, as if with drawn swords, hurling fiery scorn at each other in their polemics. Their struggle is so bitter that they have altogether lost sight of the common enemy and their proper task, and think only of how they can throw each other off the ship. 'Schismatics, brood of serpents, betrayers' cries one party; 'perjurers, heretics' retorts the other. In the midst of this slander and invective, I stand trembling with fear, for grave as the situation is already, I see even greater disasters ahead, now that heresy has raised its head! The truths of the faith are already being presented as *dubia*, and who can guarantee that passion will leave the truth unharmed. Many are struggling as if in darkness, striking out blindly, not caring whom they hit, friend or foe. They suspect one another on the grounds of general rules of law, while the question is: do those rules apply to this particular situation? The language of the Church is a babel of confusion, and the builders, or those who think themselves such, no longer understand one another. What is to be done? To offer resistance is beyond my powers, but to remain idle is impossible.'[62]

While he lamented the misery of the Church and the confusion of spirits, so he pursues his allegorical description, three figures appeared to him, indistinguishable from one another, *zelus*, *benevolentia* and *discretio*, who began to exchange their ideas in secret chambers of his house. It turned into a lengthy discussion, which ended in a decision that *zelus* should try to bring the conflicting parties together

[60] *Trilogus* (Gl. 6, 69-96; Dupin II, 83-103). Dating etc., Combes, *Jean de Montreuil*, 353ff., and below n. 65. This title is based on BN lat. 14905 fol. 170r. Cf. the lists of Gerson's brother (Gl.I, 24, [34]).

[61] Schwab, *Gerson*, 160.

[62] *Trilogus* (Gl. 6, 69-71; Dupin II, 83A-4).

in the hope of at least preventing the controversy becoming even more acute, and Schism turning into heresy. *Zelus* felt that he could best perform his task by composing three – naturally fictitious[63] – letters, the first in the name of the University of Paris to the King, in reply to the letter of the University of Toulouse, and containing a proposal to restore obedience; then a letter from the captive Benedict to King Charles, and finally a letter from the King to Benedict.

Zelus addresses his own obedience and asks if it is not a proof of worldliness when one calls: 'I choose Benedict', while another says 'I am for substraction', and a third would prefer to remain neutral? Like a flock of sheep frightened by a wolf which creeps up on them in the night, no one knows where he must turn. Only a few are prepared to obey the truth and be guided solely by what is edifying; they hate nobody whom they believe to be sincere in the search for truth, because they know that Paul and Barnabas were once unable to agree but did not hate and persecute each other because of it. 'This has been forgotten by those who recently composed that painful letter on behalf of the University of Toulouse. Let them now learn what the supporters of substraction, especially at the University of Paris, have to say in reply, putting aside all passion.'[64]

'Letter' of the University of Paris

'If the charges which you, Toulouse, have brought against us were well founded, then it would be very much to the discredit of your zeal that you had let us and the court remain in error for four years. It seems as if you wanted first to await the outcome of substraction[65] and thus determine the right by the result. Or perhaps you needed so much time to polish the style of your letter to perfection?

---

[63] *Trilogus* (Gl. 6, 74; Dupin II, 87C): 'Multa tamen, id advertite, locuturus sum nominatim sub modo triplicis epistola, qualia loqui vel posse vel debere personas introductas, non me, licentia oratoria coniecturat.'

[64] *Trilogus* (Gl. 6, 74-6; Dupin II, 87B-8D). The letter of the university of Toulouse had been presented to the king on 16. April 1402 (Valois, *Schisme* III, 265). Gerson referred to the letter in very negative terms in his sermon *Fulcite me* (Gl. 5, 337; Dupin III, 1426B): '... hostes a domesticis non secernunt, quod evenire solet pugnantibus in tenebris. Cuius rei praebet argumentum epistola quaedam grandis nuper edita, quae tota probris, tota contumeliis scatet, tota vitiosissimo prorsus confutationis genere confundit.'

[65] On the grounds of this statement we are inclined to place the *Trilogus* about the end of substraction, i.e. around February 1403.

Well, I must let you know that you would have done better to choose another language, for this does you no honour. You say, it is true, that you wish to bring the University back from the misguided path of substraction, but overlooking the presumption of trying to teach the University of Paris, which excels all others in age and prestige, you ought at least to have put forward arguments that could not be turned against yourself. Disobedience is the sword with which you wish to smite us. We turn it against you, for must one not obey God rather than man (Acts 5:29), and is it not therefore necessary to shun the company of a notorious schismatic and heretic? You accuse us of bringing about substraction, but has it escaped you that the King, the princes, the prelates and the clergy of France and Spain were all in favour of it? You argue that they were all misled by us. Well, we shall persist in substraction '*donec interim nobis, paratis corrigi si erramus, clarius aliquid commodiusque pro ecclesia dilucescat.*'[66] You must therefore pass the same verdict on us as on the others. But you dare not do so. You ask why we do not give up substraction if we assert that we do not persist in it *pertinaciter.* Ask the King, we follow our conscience. Just as one is free to doubt whether Benedict is the true Pope, and if obedience to him is to the benefit of the Church, so it is permissible to release oneself from obedience to him.[67] You will be aware, after all, that if he falls into heresy or Schism the Pope is *inferior quolibet christiano*, as you will know that papal power was granted to build up the Church and not to destroy it. Paul resisted Peter (Gal. 2: 11). That one may ask a Pope: 'Cur ita facis?' is proven by the case of Pope Anastasius.[68] Why then, brethren, have you torn yourselves away from the common decision of the King and the State? What can be the result except disorder, if you do not abide by the will of the majority? The impure motives which may have led some to support substraction, do not excuse your separatism, for in public affairs this is unavoidable; moroever, God does not operate by morally unimpeachable

---

[66] *Trilogus* (Gl. 6, 80; Dupin II, 92A).

[67] *Trilogus* (Gl. 6, 81; Dupin II, 92A): 'Nam quantum licet dubitare de domino Benedicto an perdiderit ius in papatu... tantumdem fas est ab eius obedientia recedere.' Cf. *De vita spir. animae* (Gl. 3, 139; Dupin III, 24 B): 'unde quantum licet dubitare de iure alicuius in papatu vel episcopatu, tantumdem licet suas constitutiones in dubium revocare.'

[68] *Trilogus* (Gl. 6, 63; Dupin II, 92B). On Anastasius, see Tierney, *Foundations*, 88, 89.

methods alone. How often have impious and tyrannical princes not issued the best laws?'[69]

If even a modern reader is impressed by the power of this elaborate rhetoric, he must be well aware that it does not reflect Gerson's own conviction without qualification. Personally, he still had serious objections to the stubbornness with which the University upheld the policy of substraction. Knowing this, one might assume that the words put into the mouth of *zelus* express his own convictions more purely.[70] For after his eloquent defence of the policy of substraction *zelus*, encouraged by *benevolentia*, proceeds to warn its most vehement defenders, reminding them that they had withdrawn from obedience very lightly.

'Exposed as the princes are to continual temptation, they deserve pity rather than disdain. And just as one must often bear evil in ordinary life and leave its punishment to God's justice, so it is necessary to show oneself lenient to the faults and mistakes of the rulers. Christ enjoined obedience to the hypocritical Pharisees, while, as Aristotle remarked, the prince is above vengeance. If this is true in the secular sphere, would a similar humility towards the highest dignitaries of the Church not be appropriate also? Even if Benedict had in fact erred by refusing to resign for so long, one should bear in mind the misleading flatteries he was exposed to from his followers, the weakness of the human heart, which loves to seek honour. Is he to have no forgiveness? Is the prison cell, the loss of honour and fortune, the great misery which he has suffered for more than four years, not enough to outweigh his guilt? It would be well if his opponents were to ask themselves if they were inspired by feelings of hatred rather than zeal for the common good.'[71]

'Letter' of Benedict to Charles

Benedict bemoans his misery to Charles at length, calling God as his witness to his upright zeal for the unity of the Church. 'I need not trouble you long to prove my good will. Originally—on the ad-

[69] *Trilogus* (Gl. 6, 76-84; Dupin II, 89-94C).

[70] Cf. his remark in *De duplici logica* (Gl. 3, 62-3; Dupin IV, 217C): 'Sed verum est illud Bernardi: «zelus sine discretione praecipitat» (Bernard of Clairvaux, *In Cant. hom.* 49, ML 183, 1018). Discretio autem esse non potest absque humilitate, nec humilitas in complacentia sui et innitendo propriae prudentiae conservatur.'

[71] *Trilogus* (Gl. 6, 84-6; Dupin II, 94D-5D).

vice of my cardinals – I stuck to the *via conventionis*, and then to the *via compromissi* and finally I have openly declared for the *via cessionis*. I remain faithful to my promise but I shall only resign if it can be foreseen that this will truly restore unity in the Church. At the moment I consider the *via conventionis* the most appropriate.' The letter closes with a passionate and eloquent appeal to the King to release the Pope from his distressed state.[72]

'Letter' of Charles to Benedict

In Charles' reply to Benedict the *via conventionis* is rejected and the King again falls back on resignation, urging the Pope to regard this demand as motivated solely by a yearning for peace and unity. 'Your offer to resign, you felt, must be made in general terms, because otherwise there was a danger that your opponent would abuse your promise and fail to resign himself. But what then? Why do you fear that others will profit from your promise? That is their responsibility, not yours. You, however, can be sure that you will win great fame if you disregard the intentions of the other Pope and give up your own position at any rate. It would be a splendid example of humility and love, and you would rightly be called 'benedictus' by everyone.'[73]

After these pleas, *zelus*, *benevolentia* and *discretio* resume their discussion and ask what can be done. For which party must the Church choose? Whom must it support? Or must there be a repetition of the struggle between Pompey and Caesar, when the Roman Republic stood between them with Cato, who was unable to support either of them?[74] They agree with *zelus* that in the existing crisis, only God can offer a solution, but *discretio* adds that they must not simply wait for one, for that would be the same as tempting fate. No, to put a stop to the confusion, human effort is also required, and the old points in dispute cannot be ignored at the assemblies of the people, the University and the court.[75]

That was Gerson's conclusion. The assemblies to which he refers may perhaps be connected with the national synod called by the

---

[72] *Trilogus* (Gl. 6, 86-91; Dupin II, 96-9C).
[73] *Trilogus* (Gl. 6, 91-5; Dupin II, 99C-102D).
[74] *Trilogus* (Gl. 6, 95-6; Dupin II, 103A).
[75] *Trilogus* (Gl. 6, 95-6; Dupin II, 103AB).

King at the end of February 1403, just after his recovery from a long illness, for 15 May that year, and intended to determine France's attitude to Benedict once again.

That many were no longer as enthusiastic for substraction had been clear enough from the letter of the University of Toulouse, referred to in detail in the *Trilogus*. The decision of 1398 was regarded with growing scepticism in various circles. One reason for this was that, exactly as Gerson and others had predicted, the reality had turned out to be lamentably different from the dream. The dream was of an autonomous French Church which, freed from the yoke of the curia and foreign exploitation, would be master in it own house, as it had been in earlier times. But the reality since 1398 had been largely that matters were decided by the favour of the princes, the fiscal burden remained the same or increased and it was by no means the best candidates who were given the best opportunities. The University of Paris, which had gained less for its masters from the new regime than it was accustomed to, had even been forced to suspend its lectures and public preaching in 1400 to attend to this problem.[76]

The ground was therefore well prepared for a change of policy, which, however, came about sooner than anyone could have suspected: with the help of the Duke of Orléans Benedict succeeded in escaping from captivity in Avignon on 12 March 1403 and reached Provence, the territory of Louis II of Anjou, with whom he could feel completely safe. Once he was free again, new friends rallied round him. The citizens of Avignon were the first to return to obedience, rapidly followed by the cardinals who, kneeling and loudly lamenting, begged the Pope for forgiveness and promised strict obedience to him in future. Several bishops also returned to obedience to Benedict.

All this took place before 15 May, when the synod had been summoned to meet in Paris.[77] There was hardly any question of calm deliberation at this assembly, because of the continual efforts of the Duke of Orléans to frustrate the debates by attempts to force through his own policy. On 25 May two envoys from the sacred college arrived in Paris, and told the King that the cardinals had

---

[76] Valois, *Schisme* III, 257ff; Martin, *Gallicanisme* I, 292ff.

[77] Martin, *Gallicanisme* I, 294ff.

already returned to obedience four weeks earlier because they had come to realise that substraction had achieved nothing; on the contrary, it had increased the confusion. The Pope, they claimed, was ready to follow the advice of the princes and was waiting for their peace proposals. They concluded with an urgent plea for the King to do everything he could to return to obedience. Charles replied, referring to the synod, that the decision was not for him to take but for the clergy.[78]

The Duke of Orléans, however, was intent at all costs on preventing the decision being discussed at length in the synod; this was quite probable, for the advocates of substraction had already prepared a detailed memorandum. Orléans therefore caused the archbishops, whom he had approached earlier, to take secret soundings on the attitude of their suffragans to restitution. When it emerged that the majority were in favour, on 28 May, accompanied by several prelates, he hastened to see the King. Charles immediately complied with the wishes of his brother, and confirmed on oath that he personally was willing to render due obedience to Benedict, and would ensure that his whole kingdom did the same. The King's promise was recorded in writing by notaries and he himself was the first to begin a *Te Deum* before the altar to express his joy.[79] All the bells of Paris began to ring, as a sign that France had returned to obedience. The decree of restitution, in Latin, was dated 28 May.[80]

The Dukes of Burgundy and Berry were furious at the King's decision, taken entirely without their knowledge and very far from welcome to them. But Louis of Orléans had also foreseen their reaction and managed to calm his uncles with the following statement by Benedict (which later events showed to be worthless): the Pope would accept the *via cessionis* in three cases: if the *intrusus* were to declare himself willing to do so; if he should die or be deposed. Benedict also revoked all his former declarations against the *via cessionis* and promised not to accuse anyone because of the substraction, not even at a council of his own obedience to be held within a year to discuss the unity, reform and liberties of the Church. The Pope would conform to the decisions of this council. Finally, he

78 Rel. de St.-Denys, *Chronique* III, 84-6.
79 Valois, *Schisme* III, 337ff.
80 Rel. de St.-Denys, *Chronique* III, 92.

would not cast doubt on the validity of appointments to benefices made during substraction.[81]

One may doubt whether they were entirely assured by these papal promises; the fact is that the Dukes of Burgundy and Berry had little alternative but to resign themselves to this *fait accompli*, and they did so without delay. The same is true of the University of Paris, the faculties and nations of which debated restitution on 29 and 30 May. The faculties of theology and medicine voted unanimously in favour, as did the Picard and French nations. The English nation wished to remain neutral while the Normans at first argued for the continuance of substraction but soon came round to the majority view.[82] The verdict of the faculty of law is not known, but in view of the numerous links between its members and the court and *parlement*, one may assume that it too must have set aside its former objections and agreed to restitution.[83]

On the express wish of the King, it was Pierre d'Ailly who announced the decision for restitution. He did so on 30 Mai in a sermon in Notre Dame, in the presence of the King, the princes, numerous prelates and a great multitude of people.[84] At the end of his sermon d'Ailly read out the promises which Benedict had declared himself willing to make. Is further argument necessary to show how high expectations were, and that virtually all the wind had been taken out of the sails of the opponents of restitution? The end of a dark time seemed to be in sight, and all France was celebrating. The University did so in August, in a way befitting its dignity, by resolving the dispute with the dominicans and restoring them to their former rights, to the regret of the other mendicant orders, who found that this was a threat to their traffic in confessions.[85]

On Whit Monday (4 June), at the close of a procession, Gerson preached a sermon full of high hopes, in which he connected the recent decision with the events of the first Pentecost.[86] 'By the resto-

---

[81] Valois, *Schisme* III, 336, 339ff. The promises were given orally by Benedict to an envoy of the Duke of Orléans. Text of the declaration in DuBoulay, *Historia* V, 64.

[82] Schwab, *Gerson*, 168.

[83] Valois, *Schisme* III, 341.

[84] Cf. Gl. 10, 462 (Actes et Documents 28): '30 mai [1403]. Hodie reddita est solemniter obediencia domino nostro Benedicto pape decimo tertio et publicata in ecclesia Parisiensi et fuit factus sermo solemnis per magistrum Petrum de Aliaco episcopum Cameracensem.'

[85] Schwab, *Gerson*, 168; Denifle-Chatelain, *CUP* IV, no. 1781.

[86] *Emitte Spiritum Tuum* (Gl. 5, 255-65; Dupin II, 35-43). Gerson refers to D'Ailly's

ration of obedience we have, as it were, been recreated, reunited and reborn through the outpouring of the Holy Ghost with the Pope and he with us, the members with the head and the head with the members.'[87] He says that submission to God, humility and prayer are the most important, if not the only, conditions in the mystical body of the Church, to receive perfect life, and he sees the continuance of the Schism as proof that pride has not been sufficiently humbled.[88] He instances Benedict as an example, saying 'if the Pope has learned his lesson well enough in the school of oppression, God will undoubtedly free him through the lesson of humility; and not only to his own advantage but to the advantage of the whole Church, unless the sins of his subjects stand too much against this.'[89]

---

recent sermon (Gl. 5, 259; Dupin II, 38C): '... thema sumptum a reverendo patre et praeceptore meo domino Cameracensi pridie in ecclesia Parisiensi.'

87 *Emitte Spiritum Tuum* (Gl. 5, 256; Dupin II, 36A).

88 *Emitte Spiritum Tuum* (Gl. 5, 258; Dupin II, 37C): 'Praecipua et si non unica dispositio in corpore mystico ecclesiae ad suscipiendam in suis membris perfectam vitam, est humiliatio sub Deo per orationem veram et devotam; propterea duratio schismatis iam ferme quinque lustris nostram ostendit superbiam nondum satis humiliatam...'

89 *Emitte Spiritum Tuum* (Gl. 5, 258-259; Dupin II, 38A): 'Si dominus noster papa positus in schola tribulationis sufficienter didicit lectionem humilitatis,... Deus absque dubitatione eripiet eum et glorificabit eum, non tantummodo pro se sed et pro Ecclesia, nisi fortisan subditorum peccata nimis obstiterint.'

CHAPTER FOUR

OBEDIENCE RESTORED, 1403-1406

... schisma praesens cuius sedationem invenire non sufficerent leges humanas iam conditae, nisi superior lex divina viva et architectonica consulatur.

Gerson, *Apparuit gratia Dei* (Gl. 5, 73; Dupin II, 61B)

After the restitution of obedience Gerson and many others were at first convinced that Benedict would have learned the value of humility through the bitter trials he had undergone during his captivity, and would therefore prove more accommodating to the wishes of the Church and willing to resign.[1] After all, his promises, of which the Duke of Orléans and later d'Ailly had spoken, seemed to point in this direction. And had he not shown himself inclined to forgive by welcoming back the disloyal cardinals? But it soon became very clear that – once again – the sceptics were right, for Benedict showed that he had not changed, and was very far from willing to redeem his promises generously.

Now, after the restitution, he interpreted his promise to abdicate in the event of the death, deposition or resignation of the *intrusus* of Rome, to mean that he was willing – as he had always argued before – to give up his pontificate spontaneously, if that would in fact be to the advantage of the unity of the Church. Fine words, but in fact the proviso made his promise worthless, for he could always argue that unity was not served by his abdication; and who was entitled to convince him otherwise?

The second promise, to call a council within a year, also turned out differently from expectation. Though Benedict did claim that a council would fulfil his long cherished desire, he did nothing to call one.[2] And although he had promised to conform to its decisions, he now declared that if his honour, his rights or his freedom

---

[1] See Chapter III, epigraph.

[2] Bliemetzrieder, *Generalkonzil*, 182.

were attacked by a council, he would use every means at his command to defend himself.[3]

He showed that he was just as unwilling to ratify the elections and collations which had taken place during the substraction (his third promise) in the case of the Abbot of St. Denis, whose appointment had in fact been confirmed by the Archbishop of Paris. When the Abbot appeared before Benedict, he was not only treated as an *intrusus*, but also had to submit to a painfully searching and humiliating investigation of his clerical and moral qualities; while he was also forced to see himself described not as an Abbot but as a monk in the bulls issued to him. He was given to understand that his only chance of retaining his benefice was to renounce it first; he might then receive it back from the Pope's hands. But even that was not certain, for Benedict had repeatedly left previous appointees *in puris et nudis*, transferring their dignities to others.[4]

In September 1403, when envoys from Charles VI, including Pierre d'Ailly, asked the Pope to make good his promises swiftly, they were given the vaguest of answers, as were other deputations, all of whom returned empty handed.[5] A delegation from the University of Paris also waited on the Pope, to offer him a *rotulus*.[6] Gerson was a member of this delegation, and acted as its spokesman on 9 November in Marseilles, where the Pope was at the time, since he had not yet returned to Avignon, thinking it unsafe.[7]

Taking Ps. 27:9, *Benedic haereditati tuae*, as his text for this sermon, which was adorned with numerous classical citations, Gerson invoked the blessing of the Pope on his whole obedience, and in particular on the University of Paris, in whose name he presented the *rotulus* at the end of his speech. He called on Benedict to consider the desolation of his inheritance and to gather his stray sheep.[8] He does not deny that this would be a difficult task, but for that very reason he thought it vital that the Pope's attention should be turned

---

[3] Valois, *Schisme* III, 356-7.

[4] Rel. de St.-Denys, *Chronique* III, 100; Martin, *Gallicanisme* I, 296-7.

[5] Valois, *Schisme* III, 345-9.

[6] That this was a delicate matter and that the University had prepared its measures with great care, is well shown by Mgr. Combes, *Jean de Montreuil*, 438, 439.

[7] Gl. 5, 107-22; Dupin II, 43-54. See Combes, *Jean de Montreuil*, 490-504.

[8] *Benedic* (Gl. 5, 109; Dupin II, 44B).

to the most important point, and the side-issues left to others.[9] Furthermore – and this concerned everybody – animosities should be buried. For its part the University had already shown its goodwill, when it returned to obedience, by explicitly forbidding the discussion of past wrongs, while its desire for peace was also revealed by the way in which it had complied with Benedict's wish and restored unity with the dominican order.[10] With a reference to the sermon he had given at the time, he recalls the universal joy that the decision for restitution had brought.

It was a noble picture of Benedict which Gerson drew in this sermon. He depicted him as naturally mild and forgiving, and claimed that these qualities had allowed the Pope to withstand the temptations of the Devil, who had sought to lead him into despair and vengeance. 'God did not forsake you when, like a second Jonah, you were thrown into the raging storms, when you had to suffer oppression and bitterness. Protected in the holy bowels of the holy citadel, he led you to the coast of freedom, and peace came.'[11]

Is this mere flattery? Was Gerson simply conforming unthinkingly to the courtly style of the curia, and how are these eulogies to be interpreted otherwise? We feel that they must be seen as typically rhetorical productions, that is as a means of convincing an audience, as attempts to guide Benedict's ethos in a particular direction. Gerson held up a mirror to the Pope and the image that appeared in it was dominated by humility and long-suffering. In this way he attempted to call him to show forgiveness and meekness, in short to adopt an attitude that was the opposite of his previous behaviour. The exalted picture of the Pope's conduct during the substraction sought to achieve this aim. His attitude then was, so to speak, intended to act as an example for the attitude he should follow now and later. It did not matter whether this example was solidly based; the main point was that it should be followed.

We arrived at this interpretation because we could not accept that Gerson, who had twice shown that he regarded Benedict as

---

[9] *Benedic* (Gl. 5, 109; Dupin II, 44D-6A): 'alioquin... rediret illa inculpatio Jethro ad Moysen: «Stulto labore consumeris» ' [Exod. 18: 18]; sic Petrus Clementem, sic Bernardus Eugenium, immo sic apostolus discipulum suum charissimum monuerunt [2 Tim. 2:4; 1 Cor. 6:2, 4].'

[10] *Benedic* (Gl. 5, 111; Dupin II, 45D-6A). Cf. also Denifle-Chatelain, *CUP* IV no. 1781.

[11] *Benedic* (Gl. 5, 112-13; Dupin II, 46C-7A).

'misled', should have found any occasion to withdraw this judgement in the Pope's attitude since restitution. Moreover, he later claimed that he had acted as the *legatus coactus* of the University in this mission to Marseille.[12] He had to overcome his reluctance; and what can be more plausible than to assume that this reluctance was the result of his distrust of Benedict, a distrust which caused him even greater difficulties now that it was his task to ask a favour of the Pope, namely the approval of the University's requests in the *rotulus*?[13]

Before he presented the *rotulus*, Gerson gave a pious description of the Pope's special inheritance: the University of Paris. Traditional comparisons – the University as a paradise, surrounded by the four rivers of the faculties – were varied by a mild, contemplative passage which ended in a prayer that Benedict might bless the University and, instead of listening to the slander and flattery of those who wished to estrange him from it, might embrace it with love and relieve the distress from which several *doctores* and *magistri* had so long been suffering.[14]

We do not know if it is to be seen as a sign of his agreement with these words or as the result of a separate approach, but the fact is that in a bull of 18 November 1403 the parish of St. Jean de Grève, not far from St. Germain, was perpetually associated with the office of chancellor.[15] A month later, on 24 December, Gerson also ac-

---

[12] Letter to the Duke of Orléans, inc. *Multa hactenus* (Gl. 2, 72; Dupin II, 74D): 'Denique non tam missus quam coactus legatus ad dominum nostrum super hac materia pro parte Universitatis praeclarissimae studiosorum... proposui primo Massiliae, dehinc Tarascone sermonem...'

[13] Valois, *Schism* III, 348, remarked on this sermon that Gerson flattered the pope 'de la façon la plus hyperbolique' but did not venture to propose a remedy for the Schism. But he did not need to go that far, for peace in his own camp had to be restored before there could be a peace with the other obedience. That this is what he thought, is clear from his letter to the Duke of Orléans of two months later inc. *Multa hactenus* (Gl. 2, 71; Dupin II, 74D): 'Placuit quoque restitutio, quam et praedicavi coram celeberrimo coetu populorum (i.e. the sermon *Emitte Spiritum tuum* (Gl. 5, 255-65; Dupin II, 35-43). Per hanc itaque oboedientia secum unita, portum generalis attingere facilius sperabatur.' Morrall, *Gerson*, 65, takes the same line as Valois. Cf. also Combes, *Jean de Montreuil*, 376, 493.

[14] *Benedic* (Gl. 5, 118-22; Dupin II, 51-4). Gerson spoke of 'XVII' (Dupin II, 52C) years, during which the *magistri* and *doctores* had been in distressed circumstances. This means that the last *rotulus* was presented to the pope in 1386.

[15] Denifle-Chatelain, *CUP* IV no. 1801; Valois, *Schisme* IV, 82 n. 3; N. Valois, 'Gerson curé de Saint-Jean en Grève', in: *Bulletin de la Société de l'histoire de Paris*, 28 (1901), 49-57. The perpetuity came to an end in 1409 (Cf. Gl. 10, document 44).

quired the canonry of the prebend of Notre-Dame which had fallen vacant through the appointment of Gérard de Montaigu as Bishop of Poitiers.[16] If the Pope thought that this would make Gerson a willing tool in his hands, he was mistaken, for though Gerson was loyal, he could not be bought, as was to become clear soon enough.

After his sermon at Marseille Gerson remained at the papal court for a time and had more than one meeting with Benedict. In these conversations he pressed the Pope to resign.[17] He also saw his former pupil Nicolas of Clémanges, who had been Benedict's secretary since 1397.[18] With Clémanges and a certain Muretus he decided not to forward the letter *Altitudinem tuam,* which Jean de Montreuil had composed for Benedict and had submitted for their judgement. They felt that the letter contained much of value but was in some respects too coarse and satirical, and in a sense insulting to the Pope.[19] We mention this because it proves that although he had his suspicions of Benedict, Gerson was not inclined to go to extremes. And this is something to be borne in mind in interpreting the famous sermon *Apparuit gratia Dei* (Titus 2:11, 12) which he preached on behalf of the University in Benedict's presence at Tarascon on New Year's Day 1404.[20]

'Niemals war in ähnlicher Weise vor einem Papste gepredigt worden',[21] said Schwab of this sermon, reflecting a general feeling, for other authors have made similar comments.[22] So far as this verdict could give the impression that Gerson went too far in Tarascon – which according to Salembier,[23] Connolly[24] and Ehrle[25] was in

[16] P. Glorieux, 'La vie et les oeuvres de Gerson', 167.

[17] See Appendix IV.

[18] Valois, *Schisme* III, 270 n. 4.

[19] Valois, *Schisme* III, 350 n. 1; Combes, *Jean de Montreuil*, 525-41.

[20] Gl. 5, 64-90; Dupin II, 54-73. Combes, *Jean de Montreuil*, 552-61; Schwab, *Gerson*, 171-9. Important for those who seek his autograph are the words with which Gerson offered the manuscript to the Duke of Orléans: letter inc. *Multa hactenus* (Gl. 2, 72; Dupin II, 74D): 'En accipite itaque sermonem qualiscumque ille est, ubi aliqua sed pauca ex dictatis in margine posita sunt quae brevitas praeceps eripuit ne proferrem.'

[21] Schwab, *Gerson*, 178 & 171.

[22] Valois, *Schisme* III, 417-18; Morrall, *Gerson*, 66: 'The sermon could hardly have been couched in stronger terms.'

[23] In *DThC* VI 1, 1315, s.v. 'Gerson': 'Le 1er janvier 1404... l'éloquent orateur avait prêché devant Benoît à Tarascon, et ne lui avait point ménagé les avertissements les plus

fact the case, although they omitted to say how far and on what points,—we cannot share it, for the freedom to which the sermon bears witness is by no means too blunt, but rather befits the priestly character; it is directly comparable with the way in which the prophet Nathan had addressed King David (2 Sam. 12: 1-15). That was the feeling of a contemporary, Jean de Montreuil, who, alluding to the benefices that Gerson had just received, said of this sermon:

> Sed quis e regione—et id postquam idem summus pontifex grandia sibi beneficia in spe et de facto contulerat—ad suam sanctitatem audentius, sanctius, planius, pleniusque locutus est?[26]

Gerson himself did not feel that he had gone too far;[27] on the contrary he was to refer to this sermon more than once afterwards.[28]

For a better understanding of Gerson's position at that moment, we repeat that he had long been convinced that Benedict was misled and surrounded by a court of flatterers who continued to dissuade him from resignation and concealed from him the disastrous state of the Church. It is a natural assumption that his sermon was intended to break through the paralysis in which the policy of the Church found itself as a result, and that—perhaps naively, in view of Benedict's characteristic stubbornness, but at least with laudable intentions—he wanted once again to depict to Benedict the distress brought by the Schism, in the hope of persuading him to take

---

graves. Son discours où, comme assez souvent chez lui, le vrai se mêle au faux, avait eu un très grand retentissement.'

[24] Connolly, *John Gerson*, 60: 'For his [Gerson's] expression was not always careful, and in the heat of the controversy he was known more than once to make extreme statements of which in sober moments he would disapprove!' This is in flagrant contradiction of the fact that Gerson referred to his sermon at Tarascon more than once. Moreover, the important responsibility of preaching before a Pope would rule out any thought of improvisation.

[25] Ehrle, *Martin de Alpartils Chronica*, 495: 'Dieser Gefahr trat Gerson am I. Januar 1404 in seiner... Rede mit seltenem Freimut, leider auch mit manchen irrigen Anschauungen entgegen.'

[26] Jean de Montreuil in a letter, inc. *Etsi nihil prosit*, to Nicolas of Clémanges (ed. Combes, *Jean de Montreuil*, 562-3).

[27] Gerson in a letter to d'Ailly (1405), inc. *Decreveram* (Gl. 2, 79; Dupin II, 74B): 'Porro mihi conscius sum nihil protulisse tunc quod non esset sacrae fidei monitisque salubribus accommodum et examinata veritate stabilitum. Nihilominus quot, o bone Jesu, super eodem sermone mihi relata sunt quae nedum non dixeram sed nec cogitaveram!'

[28] See e.g. *Pro convocatione Concilii Pisani* (Gl.6, 124; Dupin II, 122C).

action to restore unity. He already felt called to make such an appeal as a priest but, more important, he was conscious of his role as Chancellor of the University of Paris, that is as spokesman for the institution which, in the opinion of the time, was the supreme guardian and watchdog of the well being of all Christendom. In his sermon he remained loyal to this institution, in so far as the points he offered for Benedict's consideration reflected the proposals for the healing of the Schism put forward by the University in its famous letter to the King ten years earlier.[29]

The sermon consists of two sections. The first includes a sermon on the text for the day, the circumcision of the Lord, which was treated in four points, which concern both the Schism and the reformation of the Church. The second section consists of four *considerationes de pace*, i.e. as many suggestions to end the Schism.

Gerson holds up to his audience as an example the humility of the Son of God, shown by his willingness to submit to the Jewish law of circumcision; he calls on them to give up all pedantry and imagination, carnal appetites and vanity, and to live a pious and sober life, serving God alone.[30] The circumcision brings him to the controversy between Peter and Paul described in Galatians 2: 11-15.

> At the time Augustine and Jerome had corresponded on the meaning of this passage of scripture. Augustine defended the thesis that Paul's correction of Peter was seriously meant, while Jerome–fearful of attacking the authority of Peter–interpreted the controversy as purely shadow fencing. In the early middle ages Jerome's interpretation prevailed. This changed in the 13th century with Thomas Aquinas, who brought forward Augustine's interpretation and regarded the correction as real, but on the other hand he did not omit to state that Peter had only been guilty of a venial sin. Nicolas of Lyra, however, although he restated both points of view more fully, observed the same limits as Thomas.[31] The views of Gal. 2 that Augustine and Jerome had defended were not only handed down in the *Glossa ordinaria* but also appeared in Gratian's Decree, so that the controversy between Peter and Paul gave the canonists food for thought as well.
>
> The canonists were accustomed to refer to Gal. 2 in the context of dis-

---

[29] See Chapter I n. 100.

[30] *Apparuit* (Gl. 5, 69-70; Dupin II, 58AD).

[31] Karl Holl, 'Der Streit zwischen Petrus und Paulus zu Antiochien in seiner Bedeutung für Luthers innere Entwicklung', in: *Gesammelte Aufsätze* III, 134-45, and the present author's *De controverse tussen Petrus en Paulus. Galaten 2:11 in de historie*, 's-Gravenhage 1967.

cussions on the boundaries of papal power. The starting points for their discussions of this point were in particular D. 40 c. 6, and C. 9 q. 3 c. 13 of the decree. These canons determined that no one – neither emperor, nor clergy, nor king, nor people – had the right to judge the Pope. He was answerable to God alone and only God could pass judgement on his actions.[32]

In practice, however, as history had shown, it was sometimes necessary to answer such questions as: how to act if the Pope abused his power, if he defended heretical opinions, committed immoral acts or harmed the Church. The Schism had made this last question painfully relevant for many people, with the result that the canonists' explanations of this kind of delicate point were consulted even more avidly.

In their proposals for a solution, one canonist would naturally go further than another. Some considered that only passive resistance to the Pope was justified, others argued for more active forms of opposition. Without exception – and this is the point that concerns us – they defended the right of resistance to the Pope in certain cases by referring to Gal. 2:11, the reproof that Peter had received from Paul in Antioch. It was therefore by no means rash and certainly not revolutionary for Gerson to attempt to induce Benedict to take positive steps by reminding him of this case. It was less rash, in fact, because as a priest, in the general opinion of the scholastics, Gerson was explicitly entitled to administer fraternal correction, even to his superiors, if there was a threat to the faith. Here too the incident at Antioch provided the argument.[33]

The controversy between Peter and Paul gave Gerson occasion to put a number of questions to Benedict which, he claimed – for he was fond of personification – had been inspired by *studiositas*.

'Tell me', *studiositas* had once said to him, 'if Peter was not in error in his faith, how could Paul have asked him «Cur ita facis»'? Paul did so on the authority of the *lex divina*, which commands us to point an erring brother back on to the right path. If Peter had resisted Paul, would not Paul have been able to withdraw from obedience and appeal to a council of the Church? Would this council have stood above Peter or vice versa? If Paul had been excommunicated because of his attitude, would he have taken any notice? And if Peter had persisted in his view, would he then have forfeited the papal dignity *eo facto*? If not, could he have been deposed, and how and by whom? If he had tried to defend his error by force, would it have been lawful to resist him by force, even to imprison

[32] See Brian Tierney, 'Ockham's Conciliar Theory', *JHI* XV (1954) 40-70.
[33] See d.p. C. 2 q. 7 c. 39. Cf. Gerson's treatise *An liceat* (Gl. 6, 284; Dupin II, 304B).

him and put him to death? Jerome and Augustine did not agree on this point; must one of them therefore be judged a heretic? And finally, what should we think of the fact that the decision not to apply circumcision any more was taken by James and not by Peter (cf. Gal. 2: 9)?'[34]

Gerson tried to silence *studiositas*, but she protested, exclaiming: 'Is it inappropriate to raise such questions, which can make the great ones of the earth realise how far their power extends, where its boundaries lie and what rights they enjoy under divine, natural and human law? For if they do not know this, error will soon gain the upper hand. And why should it be unlawful to discuss the power of Peter while questions of the omnipotence of God were raised every day?'[35]

These questions, which Gerson was to answer in the second section of his sermon, are broken off abruptly here, and he returns to the theme of the day: the circumcision of the Lord. All the questions concern the papal dignity, and in their rhetorical nature they already reveal something of the direction his thoughts were taking and the point of his criticism of Benedict. He works this out in more detail under four headings and brings the decisive points more clearly to the fore.

1. The circumcision teaches us that every prince and prelate, even if he is raised above the law, is subject to his own law, and this both to serve as an example to his subjects and to show his reverence for God, whose grace must be revealed in him. Christ submitted to the law to teach the leaders of Church and State. But many of them pay no attention and cling to the letter of dead human laws. These slaves of the letter fail to see the spirit of the law – love – and do not realise that positive law must yield to the *lex aeterna*, *aequitas* and epikie.[36]

Though Gerson had used it earlier, this is the first time we have

---

[34] *Apparuit* (Gl. 5, 71-2; Dupin II, 59D-60B). See Chapter I n. 101.

[35] *Apparuit* (Gl. 5, 72; Dupin II, 60B). For more details, see Ockham, *Breviloquium* I, c. 1 & 2 (ed. Scholz, 40-3).

[36] *Apparuit* (Gl. 5, 73; Dupin II, 61AB): 'Ubi nihilominus notandum occurrit contra eos qui tanta obstinatione legibus mortuis adhaerent, legem vivam fundatam in lege aeterna et in aequitate seu epikeia penitus ignorantes vel spernentes, quod lex perficitur et impletur dum vel in finem meliorem vel salubrioribus mediis ordinatur, qui finis est caritas secundum apostolum (Rom. 13: 10); alioquin Christus legem antiquam non iam implesset quam solvisset (cf. Matt. 5: 17).'

come across the concept of 'epikie' (ἐπιείκεια) or fairness, which we shall discuss at length elsewhere. It derives from Aristotle and is to be regarded as a principle of interpretation; that means that judgements must be passed according to a norm of fairness, when a case arises for which the law makes no provision. In this sermon Gerson applies it openly for the first time to the Schism, which he appears to regard as such a *casus novus*, for which positive law did not provide and which therefore had to be resolved by epikie.

> Et hoc ... non mediocriter spectat ad schisma praesens, cuius sedationem invenire non sufficerent leges humanae iam conditae, nisi superior lex divina viva et architectonica consulatur.[37]

Because human, positive law is unable to find a solution, one must go back to its roots, the *lex divina*.[38]

2. From the humility shown by Jesus in allowing himself to be circumcised, the prelates can learn that, the higher they are placed, the more they must display humility. It is as if we are listening to Bernard when Gerson adds:

> Quamobrem summus pontifex non ficta verborum humilitate sed veritatis attentione profunda nominatur 'servus servorum'; et certe ita servus, ut secundum praeparationem cordis, etsi non semper secundum exhibitionem operis, ipse vitam suam, quanto magis statum suum, exponere pro cuiuslibet subditi sui salute nedum pro toto grege teneatur.[39]

We may be sure that these words made a disagreeable impression on Benedict. But what exactly did Gerson mean by them? He attacked Benedict's autocratic way of thinking and acting, and tried to make him more accessible to the voice and yearnings of the Church as a whole. The Pope must not wish to do everything himself, nor must he think that as long as he stood at the head of the Church, everything was satisfactory, for were there not many abuses which cried out for reformation, and how long had the Schism already lasted? In other words, he protested against the autocratic behaviour of Petrus de Luna, holding up to him the warning example of an anonymous Pope, in whom we can recognise Urban VI.

---

37 *Apparuit* (Gl. 5, 73; Dupin II, 61B).

38 *Apparuit* (Gl. 5, 74; Dupin II, 61C): 'ad legis divinae radicem et interpretationem consultatio referatur...'

39 *Apparuit* (Gl. 5, 75; Dupin II, 62B).

Urban, blinded as he was, had never been willing to listen to good advice, and in spite of countless proofs to the contrary he always maintained that he had been elected unanimously. When it was pointed out to him that he had to listen to the advice of others, he rejected this, saying 'what happened to me is of such a nature that no one but I myself can judge it.'[40]

It was a shrewd move of Gerson's to bring this man forward, for he could be quite certain firstly that Benedict would understand his allusion, and secondly that he would warmly agree with his opinion of Urban. Why? Because Petrus de Luna had been present as a cardinal at the confused election of that Pope, and since he had been Urban's confessor, he had known him very well. So well, in fact, that he and others had felt themselves forced to flee to Anagni and declare the election invalid!

A fine illustration, moreover, of Benedict's resentment of Urban is given by the fact that the former had ordered a painter to make a picture of Urban, representing him as an intruder in the Church. The painting decorated the wall of Benedict's study – situated not far from the famous 'Chambre du Cerf' – in the papal palace, and so, when contemplating how to restore the unity of the Church, he had its malefactor constantly before his eyes![41]

3. Jesus' submission to circumcision tells the prelates that they must not overburden the faithful with laws and regulations. Gerson feels that they are too quick to resort to excommunication, while he also believes that they put too much pressure on the conscience of their flocks, through their provincial laws and rules. He also deplores the way in which they abuse the right of reservation, especially *in foro confessionis*. Gerson uses these examples to show that the power of legalistic thinking in the Church of his day is excessive. Against this, he urges that Christ had deliberately refrained from extending the law, in order not to obscure the main point, salvation. The Lord also knew:

> quod nisi lex viva evangelica et aeterna dominetur, leges scriptae non solum supervacuae sed crebro perniciosae redduntur.[42]

---

[40] *Apparuit* (Gl. 5, 76; Dupin II, 63A); see Appendix III.

[41] Valois, *Schism* IV, 481 n. 1.

[42] *Apparuit* (Gl. 5, 76-7; Dupin II, 63A).

Gerson now applies his opinion to a practical case: if a bishop wishes to rule his diocese for the good of his subjects' souls, he must not add to the burden of laws, but rather appoint as leaders pious men whose merits have qualified them for the post. This is the point on which all reformation hinges. For if the pillars that must support the Church are decayed, how can the other parts of the fabric remain standing? One can go on and on extending the *humanae traditiones*, but as long as the prelates allow themselves to be guided by vanity and covetousness rather than by humility the Church will suffer. Nor will this state of affairs be altered by depriving bishops of the right to collate to benefices and transferring it to the Pope, for that both overburdens him and disturbs the hierarchy of the Church.

> Nonne monstruosum erit videre caput usurpans membrorum omnia inferiorum officia et quasi sit gladius delphicus ad omnia se coaptans?[43] Sed et curia sua, curia romana, quae ad similitudinem primae hierarchiae angelicae ordinanda erat et replenda viris charitate fervidis et contemplatione suspensis ut seraphim, viris sapientia divina splendidis ut cherubim, viris aequitate firmissimis ut throni, nonne mutabitur in curiam peccantium?[44]

This passage is a fine illustration of how Gerson's programme of reformation is closely connected with his views on the nature of the hierarchy, which had been formed by pseudo-Dionysius. We may put it this way: he rejects an absolutist, legal supremacism and pleads, here and elsewhere, for a harmonious division and distribution of ecclesiastical responsibilities throughout the whole hierarchy. It was axiomatic to him that the Pope was the highest hierarch, but that did not mean that he was the only hierarch. He must not claim all power for himself and draw it into his hands, for there were other hierarchs – especially the bishops and pastors – who, even if they worked at a lower level, had still received their own task directly from God, and therefore had to be given the fullest opportunity to perform it. That was in fact the general tendency of Gerson's programme for reformation, a programme which had far-reaching consequences in the practical life of the Church in his day.

4. Finally Jesus' example can teach us that a prelate must display his mercy and not his power to his subjects. Why should he be

---

43 'Gladius Delphicus', cf. Aristotle, *Pol.* 1252*b*2.

44 *Apparuit* (Gl. 5, 77; Dupin II, 64A).

merely strict? Is he too not weak, and can he manage without God's grace? Let the prelates beware of hypocrisy, for there is nothing more pernicious for a people than leaders who are guilty of this vice. A good pastor is always intent on avoiding offence, and will be inclined to say with David 'I am the one who has sinned' (2 Sam. 24:17) or with Jonah 'cast me into the sea' (Jonah 1:16) rather than to regard himself as righteous and to wash his hands of guilt. Gregory of Nazianzus appealed to these words of Jonah when he gave up his position in Constantinople, where he was doing very good work. And it would be good if every prelate, even those who were completely unconscious of any fault, were to ponder these words. All the more so since there appeared to be many who did not share his opinion.[45]

Benedict can rarely have heard a more urgent or more evangelical call to resign, for it is crystal clear that this was the message of Gerson's sermon.

The second part of the sermon is introduced by a request from Gerson to *studiositas* to supply him with means, drawn from divine law, *ad sedandum pestiferum schisma.* For that was where the reformation of the Church had to start. Four considerations were elaborated by *studiositas* and offered to the Pope for his judgment.

1. The goal of ecclesiastical *politia* and of every law that maintains it, is the peace that brings salvation, *pax salutifera.* That was why the apostle named sometimes love, sometimes Christ as the goal of the law, referring in the first case to peace, in the second to salvation. Dionysius, Augustine and Boëthius had argued that everything sought to attain this peace as its goal and destination. And because this goal was the highest, every term of the law which was in conflict with it, must disappear; for otherwise the highest justice would degenerate into the greatest injustice.

The new laws which were to resolve the Schism must also be drawn from the infallible rules of divine law.[46] Here, as in the first

---

45 *Apparuit* (Gl. 5, 78; Dupin II, 64C).

46 *Apparuit* (Gl. 5, 85; Dupin II, 69C): 'Et quoniam huius schismatis tam extranea videtur esse pestis ut tale numquam visum fuerit minus habens provisionis humanae remedium, docente hoc sua in dies radicatione, expedit ad eius expulsionem institutio novorum canonum, cum ea quae de novo emergunt novo egeant auxilio vel iam conditorum necessaria est moderatio... nulla via proficiens ad sedationem schismatis repudianda est, quantumcumque iura vel leges humanae videantur opponi, ut de

section of this sermon, Gerson vigorously condemns the slaves of the letter, who have no idea of the spirit of the law or of epikie. Their rigid adherence to human law alone will be the ruin of the Church. It was they—and here he answers the questions he had put at the beginning—who proclaimed the foolish views that there could be no disputing of papal power, that even if a Pope were *peccabilis*, one could not ask him: 'Cur ita facis?' and that in no case could a council be called without his authority. They regard the statement that '*Benedictus est papa*' as an article of faith, and maintain that a Pope can never be summoned before a council.[47] All these theses fail to see the fundamental point that the good of the Church, in absolute terms, is founded on God and Christ alone and only secondarily on the Pope. Otherwise there could be no assurance of salvation during a vacancy.[48] There are some who think that the Pope is without sin, others think him all-powerful, while yet others believe that those who do not obey him are excluded from salvation in all cases, '*quod quanta temeritate dicatur, ipsi viderint assertores.*'[49]

2. All the authority of the hierarchy exists for the sake of the peace that brings salvation. Whoever opposes the misuse of authority therefore is not resisting an ordinance of God, but is obeying his command to remove the one who gives offence, just as it is permitted by the law of nature to oppose force with force. It follows from this that obedience is not always praiseworthy nor disobedience punishable, as some (members of the University of Toulouse?) assert. If, for example, peace were to be disturbed because someone possessed great power over the Church, and it was certain that

---

electione summi pontificis sic ac sic celebranda et similes, dummodo ius divinum maneat inviolatum.'

47 *Apparuit* (Gl. 5, 85; Dupin II, 69C): 'Ex his denique quis non videat quam impium est, praesertim apud eos qui se ecclesiasticos dici volunt, si peritos in evangelica lege vel non consulere vel abiicere vel maiori sacrilegio habere probro cognoscantur. Hinc errores, hinc praesumptuosae assertiones, hinc perplexitates inextricabiles, hinc obstinatae defensiones adinventionum humanarum in perniciem ecclesiae et pacis salutiferae finis sui, ut quod non licet disputare de potentia papae, quod non potest sibi dici: «cur ita facis?» cum tamen sit peccabilis; quod non potest in aliquo casu ecclesia sine eo convocari vel congregari; quod hic est fidei articulus: Benedictus est papa, exempli gratia; quod absque eo non stat salus...'

48 *Apparuit* (Gl. 5, 85; Dupin II, 70A): '... salus ecclesiae in solum Deum ordinetur absolute et essentialiter, et in hominem Christum de ordinata lege, sed accidentaliter ordinatur in papam mortalem; alioquin dum vacat sedes per mortem papae, vel naturalem vel civilem, ut puta si sit haereticus depositus, quis hominum salvus esset?'

49 *Apparuit* (Gl. 5, 86; Dupin II, 70A).

peace would be restored if he were to give up that power, then he would be obliged to do so. In this case, giving up his power would be the same as *bene uti*, while remaining in power would be to misuse it. This idea is the basis of the memorable and true words which Gerson claims to have heard more than once from Benedict's lips: 'I am ready to give up my life, if that should be necessary for the unity of the Church.' But, so Gerson continues, if a man is willing to give up his life itself, how much more ought he to be willing to give up his status?[50]

3. Every reasonable being is obliged to work for the peace of the Church, in accordance with his vocation. This is plain from the obligation to follow the Church, to love one's neighbour and to serve God. And even though it may be true that human, all too human, factors sometimes play a role in this work for peace, yet activity is always to be preferred to lethargy which makes no attempt. Hence it would be possible to defend the thesis that someone who adheres to the true party but does nothing, is much more guilty than an adherent of the *pars falsa* who does make an effort for the unity of the Church.[51]

The issue at stake in the Schism is of such a nature that it is possible to have doubts about it without endangering one's own salvation. For the Church itself is fallible when it comes to the interpretation of facts, as it showed by honouring a woman–Joan!–as Pope for so long. And this explains how one can be certain that there is a Schism, but unable to explain who are the actual schismatics.[52]

This was not the first time Gerson had defended this view for, as we saw, he had already used similar expressions in his *Sententia de modo se habendi tempore schismatis* and even in his *Resumpta* of 1392. And just as he had already cited the Great Schism as a warning and an example, so he again refers to it, arguing that its lesson was that all hope flew out of the window if no one would make an effort.

---

[50] *Apparuit* (Gl. 5, 86-7; Dupin II, 70CD). The reference to the letter of Dionysius to Novatus (not 'Donatus' as Dupin wrote), is from Eusebius, *h.e.*, VI, c. 45 (ed. Schwartz, 267); the same reference in d'Ailly's *Tractatus brevis de varietate viarum ad unionem ecclesiae* of 1403 (see Ehrle, *Martin de Alpartils Chronica*, 501).

[51] *Apparuit* (Gl. 5, 87; Dupin II, 71B): 'Propterea stat aliquem adhaerentem iustae parti plus esse de schismate culpabilem quam alterum parti falsae...'

[52] *Apparuit* (Gl. 5, 87-8; Dupin II, 71BD). 'Johanna' was already mentioned in *De iurisdictione* (Gl. 3, 9; Dupin II, 267C).

> Docet nos schisma Graecorum, quod iam nemo non curat, nemo non desperat.[53]

The University of Paris, however, forms a happy exception to this rule, for it is working zealously for unity. Though others might cry *Pax, fiat pax*, that meant little, for they strove to bring about this good object for unworthy motives or by means, such as war, excommunication or separation, which could not possibly bring about the desired goal. What then will bring it about? Resignation. But is that responsible? Yes, for every pastor has a duty to seek his sheep who have gone astray, as well as to watch over the faithful ones. He must do everything in his power to reunite his flock, which can even mean that he must leave the faithful sheep. That cannot be called flight, rather an act of rescue. But would not such a resignation form a bad example for posterity? Possibly, but an uncertain disadvantage in the future weighs little in the balance against a certain peace today, which would be achieved by resignation.[54]

4. Salutary peace is such a lofty good that no one may abstain from seeking it for reasons of prestige, status or his own advantage. Those who assert that they must uphold the honour of their own party are therefore in the wrong. What scorn did the high priest, Christ, not have to suffer, to reconcile heaven and earth? His honour was irrelevant; for him a pure conscience was enough. And therefore, as long as divine law is not violated, no path which may lead to peace can be neglected; not even that path which means ceding one's rights to the other party.

> Propterea rursus non improbabile videtur, attentis circumstantiis offerentibus se in praesenti schismate, si pars iusta possit a iuris sui prosecutione desistere, ut ad iniustam ius suum transferret et fieret iusta, seu per novam electionem intrusi, seu per aliam viam in iure scripto non habitam, dummodo ius divinum utrobique inviolatum maneret.[55]

At the close of his sermon he speaks of the calling of a council, to which he no longer appears to have any objections. First of all he states that the fear of being put in the wrong at a council is not an argument to oppose it. He advances on his position of 1403 and no

---

[53] *Apparuit* (Gl. 5, 88; Dupin II, 71C). He had already referred to the Great Schism in 1395 in his sermon *Ante diem festum* (Gl. 5, 52-3; Dupin III, 1144A). See also Mourin, *Gerson prédicateur*, 73 n. 4.

[54] *Apparuit* (Gl. 5, 88; Dupin II, 71D-2A).

[55] *Apparuit* (Gl. 5, 89; Dupin II, 72C).

longer mentions the impediments of positive law, while he seems to have given up his other old objection, that the case of the Schism did not lend itself to a conciliar solution because it was a matter of the interpretation of facts, on which a council could not reach an infallible decision. He now remarks:

> Nunc autem schisma praesens, quamquam in his quae facti sunt plurimum haereat, eius nihilominus terminatio tam perplexa cernitur tamque difficilis, ut supra hominum vires, ingenia, inventiones et consilia videatur. Ubi vero deest humanum, potest et debet absque temeritate divinum auxilium etiam miraculosum exspectari.[56]

Because the problems of the Schism so far exceeded human capacity to resolve them, one could be confident that the Holy Spirit would not be absent at a general council, and would lead the meeting to the right decision, even though it was a decision on facts.[57]

We can therefore conclude that while the 'facticity' of the Schism had at first been a reason to argue against a council and to seek a solution within the field of positive law, Gerson now found himself compelled to revise his opinions, when this policy failed. The long continuance and the distress of the Schism forced him to seek a remedy outside positive law, and he was willing to consider a conciliar solution, though not exclusively.

The question of the significance of this sermon and what we can deduce from it with regard to the development of Gerson's ecclesiastical policy, is much more difficult to answer than might be thought at first. For on the one hand the sermon certainly marks a turning point in his policy, but on the other it contains hardly a single idea which cannot be found somewhere in his earlier writings.

To begin with the most important: the fundamental distinction between divine and natural law on the one hand and positive or human law on the other had already been applied in 1402, and he had developed it in detail in his *De vita spirituali animae*, where he first

---

56 *Apparuit* (Gl. 5, 89-90; Dupin II, 73A).

57 *Apparuit* (Gl. 5, 89; Dupin II, 73A): '... pium est credere quod in tractatione praesentis materiae [concilium] non erraret. Audiamus rationem. Constat itaque quod in materiis fidei terminandis error non cadit in generali concilio; rationem dant doctores ex speciali assistentia Spiritus Sancti et Christi regentis Ecclesiam nec permittentis errare in his ad quae humana investigatio pervenire non potest.'

made use of the concept of 'epikie'.[58] The distinction of three kinds of law, and the related idea that the Schism could not be resolved within the positive legal order and that a solution must therefore be sought in divine and natural law, were not new either. Nor was the idea of reformation broached for the first time in this sermon; and his suggestions for ecclesiastical policy in the stricter sense had been heard before. For example, Gerson now argued strongly for resignation, but he had already pleaded the case for it in his earliest years. Nor is there a lack of parallels in his earlier writings for the still rather undeveloped proposal to resolve the conflict by calling a council.[59]

Thus, in spite of the fact that the essential points of his argument cannot be regarded as 'new', in our opinion the sermon did mark a caesura in the development of Gerson's thinking on ecclesiastical policy. Why? Because the various strands from which it was composed were interwoven and related to one another more than they had been previously; this greater integration resulted in a more conscious and decisive line on ecclesiastical policy. To put it in rather 'loaded' terms, one might say that Gerson originally regarded the Schism as a more or less casual disaster that had befallen the Church, a disaster which could be averted by relatively modest, i.e. devotional, measures. But the long continuance of the Schism and his painful experiences with Benedict awoke Gerson to a realisation that the Schism was not just a fortuitous event, but much rather a sign that there was something wrong with the structure of the Church. This put the phenomenon of the Schism in a new perspective; it was impossible to detach it from the need for a reformation, and the old cry for reformation in head and members was heard again, with new urgency, in the current distress of the Church. At this time Gerson came to see that if the responsible leaders of the Church had heeded earlier calls for a reformation,

---

58 In so far as many elements from this sermon had been prepared in *De vita spirituali animae*, this shows once more how theory preceded practice for Gerson, and how his ecclesiastical policy followed from his ecclesiological reflections.

59 The view of Schwab (*Gerson*, 178), that Gerson was closely following Henry of Langenstein in this sermon, is one we cannot share. In any case, one cannot draw any conclusions from the fact that both of them invoked the legend of Pope Joan, for that was very widely believed at the time; cf. J.J.I. Döllinger, *Papstfabeln des Mittelalters*, Munich 1863. Ludwig von Pastor, *Geschichte der Päpste* I, Freiburg 1886, 143, saw Gerson's plea for a conciliar solution as proof of the influence of Henry of Langenstein. That too seems too facile a conclusion. See Chapters X and XII.

the Schism would never have come about; or to put it another way, the origin and continuance of the Schism showed that they had paid too little attention to the call for a reformation.[60]

It is obvious that this broader perspective enormously expanded his arsenal of arguments, for old insights could now be applied to the new situation, and the current criticism of the state of the Church could be strengthened with traditional elements. As we shall show, the theologians' criticism of the growing influence of the law, the excessive power of absolutist legal thinking, culminating in grotesque speculations on the papal plenitude of power, was traditional. We now see that Gerson put this criticism to Benedict, in his rhetorical questions on the controversy between Peter and Paul, in the first place to impress on him the need for a reformation of the Church, but also to free him from his absolutist delusions and to persuade him to take a more evangelical attitude. The idea of 'l'Église, c'est moi', by which Benedict, like many of his predecessors, had allowed himself to be inspired, simply could not be reconciled with the submissive humility which, Gerson was convinced, was the essential condition for the ending of the Schism. For the sake of the Church, the Pope should renounce his rights. *Humilitas* was opposed to *potestas*. The changed ecclesiastical policy we have summarised was to remain Gerson's starting point in later years.

That Gerson's proposals were far from agreeable to the Pope and that Benedict must have listened to him with feelings of distaste and irritation, is easy to imagine. Valois even assumed that the sermon cost Gerson his recently acquired benefice.[61] The Duke of Orléans, who was attending the curia in these months, also heard the sermon,[62] and one might assume that the Pope let him know of his displeasure and astonishment. A couple of days later the Duke asked for the manuscript of the sermon, and we can see from Gerson's brief but important covering letter that there must have been complaints and reproaches. Gerson, at least, felt obliged to defend his sermon and also his ecclesiastical policy to the Duke. It is in this letter, *Multa hactenus*, that we find the fine phrase which we have

[60] See J. Miethke in the introduction to *Quellen zur Kirchenreform im Zeitalter der grossen Konzilien des 15. Jahrhunderts* I, 14-18; Hubert Jedin, *Geschichte des Konzils von Trient* I, Freiburg 1951, 1-22.

[61] Valois, *Schisme* IV, 82 n. 3.

[62] Letter inc. *Multa hactenus* (5 Jan. 1404) (Gl. 2, 72; Dupin II, 74C). Cf. Valois, *Schisme* III, 418 n. 2.

quoted as the epigraph to the first part of this book. In a later letter, addressed to d'Ailly, Gerson asked his friend to support him by contradicting the false rumours which were circulating about his sermon at Tarascon.[63] This too shows that his words had made an impression.

Let us turn to Benedict. What were his intentions? He was as unwilling as ever to resign; autocrat as he was, and as convinced of his own rightness as of his superior training in canon law, he saw the only solution in a summit conference with his Roman rival, Boniface IX. In other words, he revived his old plan for the *via conventionis*. In May 1404 he sent envoys to Rome with instructions to prepare for such a meeting. After a long wait, they were finally received in audience on 22 September. Boniface told them that he yearned to do something for unity but that his state of health unfortunately would not permit him to think of travelling, so that there could be no meeting with Benedict. He was wholly unenthusiastic about the *via compromissi* which the legates then proposed, and equally averse from their suggestion that, in the event of his death, he should bind his cardinals to suspend a new election so that agreement could be reached with the other party on the way in which unity could be restored.[64]

Shortly after this unsuccessful interview, Boniface IX died, on 1 October 1404. The opportunity that now arose to end the Schism, which, as one should not forget, had already lasted a quarter of a century, was lost through considerations of prestige and through the mutual distrust of the parties. In the hope of emerging from the struggle triumphant, the Roman party demanded Benedict's abdication; but he and his supporters were not willing to capitulate unconditionally, and demanded a guarantee that if their master should step down, a new Pope should be elected by both groups of cardinals jointly. That was not to the taste of the nine Roman cardinals; on 17 October 1404 they chose one of their number, Cosimo de Migliorati, cardinal of Bologna, as Pope. He took the name of

[63] Letter inc. *Decreveram* (1404) (Gl. 2, 80; Dupin II, 75D): 'Tu praeceptor sapientissime, coram cuius oculis totus palam sum, tibi intus et in cute notus, digneris accipere baculum defensionis meae in hoc articulo quo apprehenso voces oppositas, si ita dignum visum fuerit, valeas compescere.'

[64] Valois, *Schisme* III, 373-81.

Innocent VII. Innocent had held influential positions under his predecessor, and it was obvious that there would be little change in the policy of the curia. During his brief reign–1404-6–partly from unwillingness, partly from impotence, Innocent VII did nothing to end the Schism.[65]

In the meantime Benedict had seen a chance to strengthen his following in France and elsewhere. His relationship with the French court was better than ever, while his envoys had also achieved some successes in Aragon, England and Hungary. He now made plans for an armed assault on Rome in order to bring his rival to see reason, as he put it.[66] The enterprise had the full support of the King of France and, of course, of his brother, the Duke of Orléans. At the end of 1404 Benedict set out. He took ship at Marseille and reached Nice on 21 December. Five months later he made a glorious entry into Genoa, where Pierre d'Ailly had prepared his reception,[67] and proclaimed his intention to hold a summit conference with Innocent VII. Innocent told him that this was inconvenient, and Benedict found this a welcome occasion to stigmatise his rival's behaviour. He wrote to the King of France that since the *intrusus* and his 'anticardinals' were systematically thwarting every attempt to restore unity, the whole of Christendom ought to take up arms to expel him. That was in fact a declaration of war and a return to the policy of the *via facti*, always upheld by his predecessor Clement VII. But, just as Clement had failed to carry out his warlike plans, so Benedict also failed. In spite of encouraging reports that the rival Pope in Rome was in great difficulties–he only just managed to escape from his besieged palace–and in spite of the diplomatic successes of his envoys in several Italian cities, and the certainty that the French court was behind him, a war in Tuscany hampered the progress of the expedition and in 1405 Benedict was forced by an epidemic to withdraw from Genoa. His funds were no longer sufficient to cover this delay, and this meant the definitive end of his Italian adventure.[68]

---

65 Valois, *Schisme* III, 380-4.
66 Valois, *Schisme* III, 401.
67 Valois, *Schisme* III, 405; Tschackert, *Peter von Ailli*, 120.
68 Valois, *Schisme* III, 398-416.

What was happening at the University of Paris in these years? What did it think of Benedict and his aspirations? According to Valois Gerson's sermon at Tarascon well expressed the University's feelings about the Pope.[69] He found the proof of this in a letter which Benedict sent to the University exactly a month later – 1 February 1404 – and which appears to answer the concerns and objections voiced by Gerson.[70] The Pope thanked the University for its good wishes, but thought them quite superfluous, since the cause of unity was never out of his thoughts for a moment, and he was ready to give his life for the Church. Urging the *magistri* to remain of one mind with him and with one another, he did not fail to point out that they had nothing to complain of about his favours. If they followed his advice loyally and devoted themselves wholly to study, as their predecessors had done, they could be sure of his good will in the future.

The fact that the University made efforts at the end of 1404 to form direct relations with the new Pope in Rome, shows that it was not entirely reassured about Benedict's intentions. When Benedict was preparing to travel from Nice to Genoa, a delegation from the University, including Pierre Plaoul and the professor of theology Jean Arnaud, as the personal representative of the Duke of Berry, went to Rome to urge Innocent to resign. As was to be expected this came to nothing, but the University claimed to be satisfied, even speaking of good news which it had received from the antipope, and tried to interest the royal council and the *parlement* in a combined attempt. Nothing came of this for the time being.[71]

Though the court might welcome Benedict's forceful plans, the clergy and the University gave them very little support. And that was easy to explain, for besides the idealistic motives for opposition that had to be overcome, these groups were very discontented with the financial sacrifices which the Pope demanded. To raise money for his war preparations Benedict had levied special taxes, which he also imposed on certain categories of the clergy – especially the monastic orders – and on the members of the universities, who were traditionally exempt from such special taxes. They did not fail to

---

69 Valois, *Schisme* III, 418 n. 3.

70 The letter is edited by Combes, *Jean de Montreuil*, 439 n.3, with reference to Appendice II (623-4).

71 Valois, *Schisme* III, 422 n. 5, 423-6.

protest against this breach of their privileges, but Benedict refused to be moved. In the end feeling ran so high that in November 1405 the University was forced to suspend its lectures. Because it was the custom in advent for the preachers in the churches of Paris to be provided by members of the University, and these members declared their solidarity with the strike, a great scandal was caused. The Duke of Orléans tried to mediate the day before Christmas; in vain, for he was no longer trusted. Not until the end of January 1406 did the University persuade the King to rule that there should be no more talk of fiscal measures until the end of the year.[72]

On 27 April 1404 Gerson had lost his protector, Philip the Bold, Duke of Burgundy. His much less intelligent and more turbulent son John the Fearless had inherited his father's animosity towards the Duke of Orléans. That was a sign that there was little to be expected from him, and indeed an explosion was not long delayed. When John was in France in August 1405 to pay homage to the King for Flanders, he used the opportunity to build up a power base opposed to that of his uncle, the Duke of Orléans. Falling on Paris with his army, he carried away the dauphin and protested openly in the royal council against the way in which the country was being misgoverned. The Duke of Orléans rightly regarded these actions as directed against him. He prepared for a trial of strength and civil war seemed imminent, but at the last moment a reconciliation was contrived.[73]

It was Gerson who preached the famous sermon *Vivat rex* to celebrate this reconciliation in the Louvre on 7 November 1405, in the presence of a distinguished audience which included the King of Navarre, the Dukes of Berry, Orléans, Burgundy and Bourbon, members of the royal council and many prelates.[74] The sermon, delivered in French, is mainly of importance for those who are interested in Gerson's view of the State, and those who have dealt with this subject have paid much attention to it.[75] For our purpose

---

[72] Valois, *Schisme* III, 425-6. Gerson pleads for the abolition of these taxes in *Vivat Rex*. See below, n. 76.

[73] Valois, *Schisme* III, 419, 426.

[74] Gl. 7*, 1137-85; Dupin IV, 583-621 (in Latin).

[75] There is a good summary in Schwab, *Gerson*, 416-26; 428. Besides Schwab we also name E. Guillon, *De Johanne Gersonio quatenus in arte politica valuerit*, Parisiis 1888, and, in particular, Carl Schäfer, *Die Staatslehre des Johannes Gerson*, (Diss. Cologne), Bielefeld

it is sufficient to point out that the sermon had many points of resemblance to the one he had given a year earlier before Benedict at Tarascon. If he had then taken the peace of the Church as his theme, now, before the princes, he placed the peace of the State in the forefront. In full awareness of his dignity as Chancellor, he presented an impressive list of measures to be taken in order to restore peace in the temporal as well as in the spiritual sphere.[76] And just as he had begun to address the Pope on the need for a reformation of the Church, so he now allowed himself to make similar proposals for the government of the State. He spoke as frankly, especially to the Duke of Orléans, as he had to Benedict. Valois even speaks of Gerson's 'audace étrange'.[77] Be that as it may, the sermon *Vivat rex* is a fine illustration of Gerson's political independence.

1935. We have not seen M.C. Batts, *The Political Ideas of Jean Gerson*, (Ph. Dissertation), University of Ottawa 1976.

[76] *Vivat Rex* (Gl. 7*, 1182-4; Dupin IV, 620AB; 621B). In very exalted terms he speaks of the University as 'la fille du Roy'. Since the well-being of the State depends on the place which is allotted to faith, this institution, being 'maistresse de la foy', should be listened to eagerly. He states that if the University of Paris had been as great and populous in the time of Mohammed as it is now, Islam would have been less powerful. 'Et par aventure se du temps de Mahommet elle eust esté si grande et si peuplé comme maintenant... ceste maudite secte n'eust pas tant dominé.' One should also remember how important a role the University had played in finding a solution to the Schism: 'à peine nul autre pais a parlé de le faire cesser se non aucunement a l'esmouvement de l'université.' Therefore, it should be exempt from fiscal charges. 'Par ces choses appert qu'elle doit estre franche et quitte de tous subsidez..., soient dismez ou ou aultrez subvencions, tant pour ce qu'elle est fille du roy, franche et noble, comme par ce que singulierement elle labeure pour tout le royaume et toute l'eglise.' He ends his sermon with a cautious recommendation of the *via cessionis*.

[77] Valois, *Schisme* III, 426 n. 3.

CHAPTER FIVE

ON THE WAY TO THE COUNCIL OF PISA, 1406-1408

Non repugnat iuri divino et ex consequenti nec iuribus humanis debite interpretatis, quin ex duobus collegiis amborum contendentium possit fieri unum collegium ab utraque parte receptum pro dando ecclesiae verum et indubitatum Christi vicarium, aut nunc aut suo tempore et loco opportunis.

Gerson, *Acta quaedam de schismate* (Gl. 6, 98; Dupin II, 77AB).

At the end of 1405 envoys from the King of Castile arrived in Paris. As in 1397, they proposed to Charles VI that both Popes should again be urged to resign and declared schismatics if they refused.[1] The Religieux de St Denys says that this plan was welcomed by the princes,[2] but Benedict tried to frustrate it by sending one of his newly appointed cardinals, Antoine de Chalant, to Paris, with instructions to convince the court that unity could only be served by showing loyalty to the Pope of Avignon.[3]

The cardinal was not admitted to an audience without some difficulty; when he finally managed to penetrate to the King's presence, the University also announced its opinion. At a plenary session on 15 May 1406 it had come to the conclusion that substraction could not be regarded as ended, and that the Church was still 'en tel estat comme nous estions devant la restitution.' It argued that the decision for restitution taken in 1403 had been dependent on the three conditions mentioned by the Duke of Orléans: resignation, a council within one year and ratification of the appointments made during the substraction. Since the Pope had shown his bad faith by not complying with any of the three, the decision of 1403 could be declared null and void, and that of 1398 remained valid.[4]

---

1 Rel. de St.-Denys, *Chronique* III, 358; Valois, *Schisme* III, 427.

2 Rel. de St.-Denys, *Chronique* III, 360.

3 Valois, *Schisme* III, 429ff. Antoine de Chalant who attended Benedict's Council at Perpignan, remained faithful to him till the beginning of 1408. Cf. Valois, *Schisme* IV, 103 n. 2, and reg. s.v.

4 Martin, *Gallicanisme* I, 302ff.

The theologian Jean Petit was appointed to explain the University's decision to the princes. He appeared before them on 18 May but the sight of such exalted company unnerved him. Instead of speaking of the 'decision' of the University, he confined himself to pleading for the necessity of 'maintaining' the substraction, while also pressing for the condemnation of the letter from the University of Toulouse, by now four years old. He also protested against the fiscal measures of the curia. The University was indignant that Petit had not performed his instructions to the letter, and compelled him to inform the princes of its conclusion again, but this time in precise terms.[5]

The princes did not comply with the University's wishes immediately, but handed the responsibility to the *parlement*. The University was issued with letters of credence from the royal council and permitted to explain its point of view to the *parlement*. Its spokesmen were Pierre Plaoul, Jean Petit and the King's advocate Jean Juvenel des Ursins. Each of them in his own way, but all equally clearly, they stigmatised the letter of Toulouse as a slander and a *lèse-majesté*. They wanted its author severely punished, and also urged that all copies of the letter should be destroyed.[6]

The intention behind all this is clear: by procuring an official condemnation of the Toulouse letter the University sought to persuade the secular authorities to go back to substraction. As for the fiscal proposals, the University spokesmen did not fail to point out that they were in line with past practice, when the King, and not the Pope, had had authority over the Church in France. In spite of the objections from some members, the *parlement* decided on 2 July to take the University's proposals under consideration over the following days.[7]

To be brief, on 17 July a decree was issued condemning the letter from the University of Toulouse as slanderous and insulting to the King, the princes, the clergy and the University of Paris. Everyone who possessed a copy of the letter was obliged to hand it in to be destroyed, on pain of a heavy fine. On 11 September the University had the pleasure of seeing its fiscal proposals ratified by the *parlement* as well. Its third wish, for the continuation of substraction, was to

---

5 Martin, *Gallicanisme* I, 303.
6 Valois, *Schisme* III, 431.
7 Valois, *Schisme* III, 439ff.

be discussed at a national synod, which, although summoned for All Saints' day, was not opened until 17 November.[8]

To prepare itself for this synod the University held a number of meetings. The faculty of theology, for example, met on 16 November to discuss its policy: back to substraction, or a neutral line. Pierre d'Ailly tried in vain to row against the tide at this meeting. Averse to substraction as he was, he pleaded for a council of the Avignon obedience to discuss its internal difficulties, and a general council to deal with the questions of the reformation of the Church. D'Ailly admitted that resignation was an excellent idea, but not the only way; there were other means of achieving the desired goal. To ensure freedom of discussion, he pointed out that a prelate who had subscribed to substraction in 1398 but who now wished to take a different line in 1406, ought not to be regarded as a schismatic on these grounds. D'Ailly was able to enlist the support of only 27 of the 69 masters present for his reasonable arguments. We are not surprised to find Gerson among them.[9]

It was probably at about this time that Gerson composed his *Acta de schismate tollendo*,[10] a brief work in nine theses, which makes no mention of substraction but again establishes that in the existing circumstances it was entirely justified to pass over positive law and to take one's stand exclusively on the basis of natural and divine

---

[8] Schwab, *Gerson*, 184ff.

[9] Bourgeois du Chastenet, *Nouvelle histoire*, Preuves, 152; Tschackert, *Peter von Ailli*, 124; Valois, *Schisme* III, 457. In his sermon of 7 November: *Memento finis* (Gl. 7* 698; Dupin III, 1573) Gerson had already spoken about a council of the Avignonese obedience in these terms: 'Si conclus pour ung remede general; en ce concil de France on avise de pourveoir à tous inconveniens; et Dieu les doint bien aviser et mieux exequter à la fin qui doit regarder chascun à l'onneur de Dieu, à la reformacion de l'esglise et de crestienté, à l'edificacion des vivens et à la delivrance des trespasses, prestante eo qui est alpha et omega, principium et finis.'

[10] Gl. 6, 97-8; Dupin II, 76-7. The work is difficult to date. Dupin thought that it had been composed, like the *Disputatio de schismate* (Gl. 99-105; Dupin II, 77-82), after the death of Innocent VII. Schwab (*Gerson*, 190), and Glorieux agreed. Morrall (*Gerson*, 70) without stating his reasons, put it a little earlier, in our opinion rightly, for it makes no mention of the death of the pope of Rome; on the contrary proposition 7, which speaks of *contendentes*, gives the impression that the two rivals were still alive. When reading this work one must free oneself from the idea that it was intended for (the cardinals of) the other obedience, like the *Disputatio*. In *Acta quaedam* Gerson is addressing his own party. The fact that propositions 1, 2 and 4 recur in the first conclusion of the *Disputatio* (Gl. 6, 101-2; Dupin II, 79A-80C), need not argue against this; it merely proves that the two works were composed at about the same time.

law.[11] This would greatly increase the number of possible ways out of the impasse. Gerson names several of them, but without recommending one in particular.

Besides the thesis that it would not be in conflict with divine law if one obedience were to transfer its right to the other party—a thesis which he had already defended in his sermon at Tarascon[12]—he comes back, in passing and without any special emphasis, to the conciliar solution.

> Concilium generale utriusque partis, non obstante contentione de papatu, potest celebrari *pro dando ecclesiae suam unionem* per viam cessionis vel alterius provisionis. Nec obstare debent iura quaecumque positiva, ut quod 'spoliatus ante omnia debet restitui' vel quod papa debet praesidere, aut quod debeat esse aequalitas in vocibus et similia.[13]

Proposition 7 is important in connection with later developments. In it he makes a proposal that anticipates the procedure adopted at the Council of Pisa in 1409: restoration of unity through the appointment of a *vicarius Christi* by the combined colleges of cardinals.

> Non repugnat iuri divino et ex consequenti nec iuribus humanis debite interpretatis, quin ex duobus collegiis amborum contendentium possit fieri unum collegium ab utraque parte receptum, *pro dando ecclesiae verum et indubitatum Christi vicarium*, aut nunc aut suo tempore et loco opportunis.[14]

Hence, although Gerson did not speak at the national synod of 1406 (National Synod IV), we know his opinions on the subjects discussed. There is some uncertainty about the number of high ecclesiastical dignitaries who attended, but in any event there were significantly fewer than at the assemblies of previous years.[15] At the first session, held in Paris on 17 November, two representatives of the University spoke, among them Jean Petit. In a bitter catalogue of complaints against Benedict, depicting him as a perjurer, a schismatic and suspected of heresy, Petit again argued that the decision for restitution of 1403 was invalid, because the Pope had not kept

[11] *Acta* (Gl. 6, 97; Dupin II, 76AB).
[12] *Apparuit* (Gl. 5, 89; Dupin II, 72C).
[13] *Acta* (Gl. 6, 98; Dupin II 77A). For the adage 'spoliatus...' see Chapter III n. 43.
[14] *Acta* (Gl.6, 98; Dupin II, 77AB).
[15] Valois, *Schisme* III, 456.

his promises. Since there was just as little to be expected from Benedict's rival, both Popes ought to be urged to resign.[16]

After the topic had been stated, it was decided to follow the pattern of the synods of 1396 and 1398, and allow equal numbers of speakers to put the case for and against substraction. The Archbishop of Tours, Ameilh de Breuil, Pierre d'Ailly, Bishop of Cambrai and Guillaume Fillastre, Dean of Rheims, were appointed to plead the case for Benedict, while the defence of the University's thesis was entrusted to Simon de Cramaud, Patriarch of Alexandria, Pierre LeRoy, Abbot of Mont St Michel, and the theologian Pierre Plaoul. The King's advocate, Jean Juvenel des Ursins, was to sum up as the final speaker.[17]

The advocates of substraction urged more or less the same arguments as those put forward at the synod of 1398. The scholar Pierre LeRoy again went to great lengths to show that the Popes had encroached on the prerogatives of the French crown by drawing to themselves the right of appointment to benefices, and that it was necessary to revert to the time-honoured order, and go back to the *droit commun.* Only the King could undo these usurpations of the curia. The Abbot thought substraction lawful on the grounds that the Pope had abused his power, which in canon law was only effective '*clave non errante*'. When he remarked that it had never been Christ's intention that the Popes should suck the Church dry, because He had only commanded Peter to feed his sheep and not to shear them, he was rudely interrupted by Fillastre. Quite in the spirit of these synods, Fillastre cried: 'I do not know how things are done where Pierre Le Roy comes from, but in my country sheep are always shorn. And because the flock is entrusted to the Pope, he has the right to do both, to feed them and to shear them'.[18]

Pierre Plaoul regarded both Popes as stubborn schismatics, and consequently as heretics; all those who continued to adhere to one of them put themselves under the same suspicion. Invoking the distressed state of the Church, he felt that the King had a right and a duty to summon a council and take all the necessary measures to

---

16 The speeches of the various speakers at this synod are in Bourgeois du Chastenet, *Nouvelle Histoire*, Preuves, 94-234; a summary in *Chroniques* III, 465-73. Cf. Buisson, *Potestas und Caritas*, 201ff.

17 Bourgeois du Chastenet, *Nouvelle Histoire*, Preuves, 117.

18 Bourgeois du Chastenet, *Nouvelle Histoire*, Preuves, 164-76. A good summary of Le Roy's arguments in Martin, *Gallicanisme* I, 315ff.

resolve the schism. Arguments from positive law must yield to the duty to serve peace, which was based on natural and divine law. This argument reminds us of Gerson, but Plaoul went further. He could not find a single positive thing to say of Benedict or his rival, and asserted that the Church was being prostituted by them. 'Ces deux contendents veulent charnellement *concumbere cum ea*, come à une épouse charnelle. Et pour ce nous departions d'eux.'[19]

Simon de Cramaud felt that the University's wish must be granted, and that neither the King nor his subjects ought to show obedience to either of the rival Popes, 'these two foxes', because they were both clearly schismatics. In his opinion the French Church could retain the papal right of appointment in its own hands, nor was it dependent on the Vicar of Christ for appeals. For there were primates in France – the Archbishops of Bourges, Vienne and Lyons. Moreover, would it not be much simpler to settle French cases in France, instead of Italy?[20]

The first speaker to put the case against substraction was Ameilh de Breuil, Archbishop of Tours, who began by reminding the synod that no previous schism had been resolved by resignation, but that in such cases the Church had always resorted to a general council. Like his colleagues, de Breuil also argued that the recent experience of substraction had been no argument for its resumption. At any rate, they ought not to think that it would wring any concessions from Benedict, whom he described, in rather unsubtle but not unpleasing terms: 'Il est du pays des bonnes mulles; quant elles ont pris un chemin, l'on les escorcheroit plus tost que l'on les feroit retourner, que elles ne fassent à leur teste.'[21] Substraction also had the great disadvantage that it blocked all other avenues – the *via cessionis*, *via compromissi* and *via concilii*.[22] A very important objection.

Guillaume Fillastre countered the undisguised Gallicanism of such men as Simon de Cramaud. He not only voiced his amazement that the synod should venture to attack the Pope, but even dared to assert in the presence of the princes that a King could be deposed by a Pope but not a Pope by a King. This remark caused

---

19 Bourgeois du Chastenet, *Nouvelle Histoire*, Preuves, 177-99 (188).

20 Bourgeois du Chastenet, *Nouvelle Histoire*, Preuves, 123.

21 Bourgeois du Chastenet, *Nouvelle Histoire*, Preuves, 148.

22 Bourgeois du Chastenet, *Nouvelle Histoire*, Preuves, 141; cf. Valois, *Schisme* III, 465ff.

great indignation, and Fillastre was quickly obliged to take back his words. 'Sire, je say bien que vostre Seignourie n'est mie comme aux autres. L'impereur tient son imperance du pape, mais vostre royaume est par heritage. Je say bien que vous n'occupés pas tant seulement le lieu de par homme, mais estes une personne moyenne entre spirituelle et temporelle ..., vostre royaume n'est pas comme les autres. Il est hereditaire, ne le tenés d'aucun. Vous estes empereur en vostre royaume, en terre vous ne connustes nul souverain *in temporalibus*.'[23]

Pierre d'Ailly complained in his speech of the bitterness with which some speakers had attacked Benedict, even though he had not yet been condemned as a heretic. As for substraction, he thought it more proper for the decision to be taken by the faculty of theology alone and not by the University as a whole. To avoid endangering the unity of the University, d'Ailly advised the prelates not to cast a decisive vote but merely an advisory one, for a split between the University and the prelates was more to be feared than the Schism itself. As a practical policy, he again suggested a council of the Avignon party, which would not only have to restore order in its own obedience, but could prepare the way for a later general council. D'Ailly called substraction an illegitimate weapon, since under canon law obedience could not be refused to a Pope even if he were suspected of heresy. Benedict's refusal to resign was not a proof of his *pertinacia*. That charge could only be laid against him if he were to resist the calling of a council, but there was no sign of that. 'Il est prest de faire conseil general et de poursuivir la conclusion du conseil.'[24]

After the King's advocate had summed up the arguments of the various speakers, it was time for the members of the synod to cast their votes for or against substraction. A minority urged that one more attempt should be made to bring Benedict to reason. Others, more radically, wished to break off all ties with him, while a third group put forward a compromise solution: obedience should be maintained in spiritual matters but withheld in temporal affairs, the right of appointment to benefices, taxes etc. The majority of the

---

[23] Bourgeois du Chastenet, *Nouvelle Histoire*, Preuves, 163; cf. Martin, *Gallicanisme* I, 319ff.

[24] Bourgeois du Chastenet, *Nouvelle Histoire*, Preuves, 149-61; Valois, *Schisme* III, 467 n. 1.

assembly inclined to this compromise, technically known as 'partial substraction', and this was the decision taken on 4 January 1407. A month later this decision became law through the issue of two royal ordinances.[25] We may wonder if d'Ailly and Gerson regretted the decision for partial substraction, even if their hopes of a council had been disappointed. For had they not put this forward as a lawful solution for years?[26]

On 6 November, that is before the national synod had met, Innocent VII, the Pope of Rome, breathed his last. This news took an improbably long time to reach Paris, for although Benedict had heard it in mid-November, it was the end of December before it was known in Paris.[27] The synod's discussions were already over and it was preparing to vote, unaware of the fact that the Roman college had elected the elderly and ascetic Venetian Angelo Corrario, cardinal of Constantinople, as Pope.[28] He took the name of Gregory XII. As soon as Innocent's death was announced, as on previous occasions, France made immediate attempts to induce the cardinals to suspend the election. It was likely, said the letter to Rome, that Benedict would now speedily resign. If he did not fulfil this hope, France intended to restore peace without him, and counted on the good will of the other party in doing so. Perhaps a meeting of the two sacred colleges would be the quickest way to reach the desired goal.[29]

If we may assume that the news of Gregory's election reached Paris a couple of days after that of the death of his predecessor, Gerson's *Disputatio de schismate tollendo*[30] can be dated very precisely. It must have been written in the last days of December, for it begins by asking if the recent death of the Pope of Rome has created an opportunity for the cardinals of that obedience to proceed to a new election, *ad tollendam tandem funditus per cessionem suam schisma praesens.* The answer is negative. New elections, argues Gerson, would only prolong the Schism, unless the person elected were to declare himself ready to resign immediately. But previous experience has

---

[25] Valois, *Schisme* III, 472ff.; Salembier, *Le grand schisme*, 221.
[26] See Chapter III n. 57.
[27] Valois, *Schisme* III, 477 n. 1; 484; 489 n. 5.
[28] Valois, *Schisme* III, 487.
[29] Valois, *Schisme* III, 477.
[30] Gl. 6, 99-105; Dupin II, 77-82.

shown how little trust one could place in such promises. He thinks it certain that the Schism would long since have been resolved if those in high and low positions in the Church had sought Jesus Christ and not their own benefit. They have not done so, and that explains why it is so difficult to find a practical solution. Of course, resignation would be the best remedy, but just as a doctor who knows an excellent cure for his patient will nevertheless prescribe another medicine, once he finds that his patient cannot bear the drug, he who seeks a remedy for the Schism must take the circumstances into account and in this case propose another way forward instead of the best course, resignation.[31] Only if it were beyond doubt that all parties, in both obediences, would argue for resignation, would it make sense to demand Benedict's abdication.[32] Gerson had already defended this point of view, while d'Ailly too had taken up the cudgels for it at the recent synod.

After going on to prove in detail that it would not be a violation of divine law if the Roman cardinals were to recognise Benedict as Pope, or 'introduce him into the pretended rights of the other', as he puts it literally,[33] his disputation concludes that in any case a new election must be avoided. The University ought to incite the King and the princes to send legates to Rome, to inform the cardinals of France's view. No detailed proposals should be put forward, for they would only anticipate the results of future decisions. Because the case demanded urgency, couriers should be sent ahead to announce the arrival of the official delegation. Finally, it was not necessary to wait for the opinion of Benedict or any other Church dignitaries on all this, although it would be as well to inform them of the plan and to encourage them to give their support.[34]

Gerson's proposals were overtaken by events, for when he wrote Gregory had not only been elected but crowned as well. We know today that this was to prolong the Schism, but contemporaries, despite the experiences to which Gerson referred, seem to have found cause for optimism in this election, on the grounds that, before go-

[31] *Disputatio* (Gl. 6, 99-100; Dupin II, 78B-9A): 'Puto autem quod in principio prosecutionis unitatis ecclesiae per viam cessionis, consideratio ista fuisset valde utilis et valde ponderanda, sicut et nunc; non enim semper illud quod absolute melius est in se, est melius ex circumstantiis omnibus simul positis et attentis.'

[32] *Disputatio* (Gl. 6, 103; Dupin II, 81AB).

[33] *Disputatio* (Gl. 6, 101; Dupin II, 79B).

[34] *Disputatio* (Gl. 6, 103-4; Dupin II, 81BD).

ing into the conclave, the cardinals had sworn a solemn oath that if one of their number were to be elected to the highest office, he would step down if his rival were to resign or die, and if the 'anti-cardinals' were to agree to unite with them to hold a joint election for a new Pope. Within a month of his enthronement the Pope would inform the secular rulers of his own obedience and the other, as well as the antipope and the anticardinals, of his intention to abdicate, while within three months he would send embassies to discuss a meeting place with the other party. No new cardinals would be appointed during those negotiations, unless it appeared necessary to make up his college to the same number as that of his rival. Finally, the cardinals decided that the Pope was to renew all these promises immediately after his election.[35]

After his election on 30 November Pope Gregory confirmed the promises he had made as cardinal. In fact it seemed as if he intended to keep them, for on 11 December, he announced his election to Benedict, pointing out that the time for wrangling about the law was past. 'A true mother always gives up her rights rather than see her child cut in two. I am ready to give up my tiara if you declare yourself willing to do the same.' At the same time, letters in equally generous terms were sent to the King of France, in which Gregory did not conceal his love for that country or omit to praise the University of Paris for its zeal in the cause of Church unity. He and his college also made overtures to the Avignon cardinals, while he also informed the world of his intentions in an encyclical.[36]

Is it surprising that these generous intentions of Gregory XII revived Gerson's hopes of an early end to the Schism? We can imagine the feelings that must have overcome him when the good news arrived from Rome. For had he not always pleaded for just such a solution as that which Gregory now put forward: renunciation of his own rights in favour of the whole Church? Nor was Gerson alone in his enthusiasm; all over France the reports from Rome were received with joy. Bells were rung to celebrate the imminent reunion and even the greatest sceptics, such as the Religieux de St

---

[35] Valois, *Schisme* III, 485ff.

[36] Valois, Schisme III, 486; the encyclica in Martène & Durand, *Thesaurus novus* II, 730-3.

Denys, dropped their objections when the messengers from the new Pope arrived in Paris.[37]

The assembled clergy, who were still in Paris for the synod, decided on 21 January that if Benedict were to accept the proposals of his rival and both Popes were to step down, a new election should be held by the cardinals acting jointly. In that case, Benedict was promised a peaceful retirement. But if he should refuse to resign, he would no longer be a member of the mystical body of the Church, and he could be sure that his cardinals would join their Roman colleagues.[38]

Benedict's first reaction to his rival's initiative roused some hopes. In a letter to Gregory he thanked God, who had finally found the man who was inspired by the same zeal for unity as he himself, and he expressed his joy that he and Gregory could now complete what he had always failed to achieve with Gregory's predecessors. He had been astonished by the remark in Angelo's letter in which the *via conventionis* was dismissed as impracticable. As if Benedict could be held responsible for that! Far from it. He had always proposed this path to Gregory's predecessors and wished to continue in it. But to eliminate all uncertainty about his good intentions, he and his cardinals were ready to meet Angelo and his anticardinals at a place to be agreed. After all the necessary measures to restore unity had been taken, he would renounce his rights, on condition that Gregory did likewise, and both colleges would then jointly elect a new Pope. Petrus de Luna had many copies of this letter to Gregory made for circulation.[39]

The letter did not receive a uniformly favourable welcome in Paris. The University deduced from the sentence about the *via conventionis* that the Pope was still not quite serious in his intention to resign, nor was the court completely reassured.[40] To remove all uncertainty and to find out how far their intentions were honest, the royal council and the clergy decided to send an embassy to both Popes. There were no fewer than 36 legates, many famous names among them. Besides those who took a nationalist line, such as Simon de Cramaud, Pierre LeRoy, Gilles Deschamps, Pierre Plaoul

---

37 Rel. de St.-Denys, *Chronique* III, 496, 502.

38 Martène & Durand, *Thesaurus novus* II, 1312.

39 Valois, *Schisme* III, 493; Rel. de St.-Denys, *Chroniques* III, 504.

40 Rel. de St.-Denys, *Chronique* III, 512; Valois, *Schisme* III, 496.

and Jean Petit, there were more conservative members, such as Ameilh de Breuil, Guillaume Fillastre, Pierre d'Ailly and Gerson. A special tax was levied to meet the cost of the mission. The legates were given their instructions in a letter from the King dated 13 March 1407. They were to demand a bull from Benedict, stating his unconditional willingness to resign. This bull was to be provided within ten days of their arrival, on pain of substraction. The delegates were not to stay longer than three weeks in Marseille, where the Pope was still living; after that they were to go on to Rome, to put similar proposals to Gregory XII. If the two rivals could not agree on a meeting place – Lucca, Florence, Genoa or Pisa were mentioned – the legates were to press them to appoint procurators or empower their cardinals to proceed to a new election.[41]

We know from his sermon *Vade in pace*,[42] delivered on 18 March 1407, shortly before he and the other members of the solemn embassy set off that Gerson still had high hopes. Fully confident that Gregory's promise to resign was seriously meant, he exclaims:

> Graces à Dieu, louenge et gloire, quant il nous ha donné victoire. Victoire voirement nous ha donné Dieu, quant à la voye de paix, tant quise et demandée, la voye de cession, il ha encliné les cuers des deux contendents... Et d'où vient ceste victoire, je vous pri, si non par l'especial don et inspiration du Dieu de paix, et de toute consolation, sinon par l'abundant grace de celuy sans lequel nous ne pouvons ne paix ne bien avoir? ... Quantes foys par quans desirs, depuis près de trente ans, avons nous demandé pais, huchié pais, souspiré pais: Veniat pax, reveingne pais. Quantes processions en ont esté faites, quantes legacions par toute crestienté! Et jusques à cy nous n'avons eu nulle si certaine nouvelle d'aprochement de paix comme de present. Nous n'avons nulle si belle victoire contre schismatique division comme maintenant quant la voye plus briefve et convenable pour la debouter hors et faire trebuchier est ouverte, prise et acceptée, au moins par parole et par escrips: Dieu veuille que par effet.[43]

Emphatically he warned his hearers not to make light of resignation. It was no simple matter, he argued, to give up one's office, and whoever declared his willingness to do so displayed an unusual degree of perfection.[44]

---

41 Valois, *Schisme* III, 499ff.
42 Gl. VII*, 1093-1100; Dupin IV, 565-71. See Appendix IV.
43 *Vade in pace* (Gl. 7*, 1094-5; Dupin IV, 566D-7C).
44 *Vade in pace* (Gl. 7*, 1096; Dupin IV, 568A); cf. Valois, *Schisme* III, 478ff.

Before the solemn embassy from Paris had arrived in Marseilles, legates from Pope Gregory had already attended on Benedict and, after long deliberations, had reached an agreement on the meeting place of the two rivals. They chose the north Italian city of Savona, where the meeting was to be held not later than All Saints' Day. This was a concession on the part of Pope Gregory, for Savona had belonged to the obedience of Avignon since 1404.[45]

After conferring with Gregory's envoys in Avignon, the impressive train of royal delegates arrived in Marseille on 9 May to a warm and cordial welcome from Benedict. First of all, they fulfilled their instructions by enquiring about Benedict's attitude to resignation. He declared that he was willing to resign, but refused to put this down in writing. He also refused to exact an undertaking from his cardinals not to elect a new Pope, if he or his rival were to die, until an agreement had been reached with the sacred college of the other obedience. The legates tried to put pressure on him through his cardinals but with no more success than the two delegates from the Duke of Orléans.[46] A last attempt by d'Ailly and Gerson also came to nothing. 'My deeds', said Benedict, 'rather than my words will show you that I am concerned only with the honour of God and the interest of the Church, and that I yearn for nothing more than to comply with the demands of the King, his people and all Christendom.'[47]

On their return to Aix, empty handed, on 21 May, the legates deliberated: now that Benedict again seemed to want to go his own way, should they renounce obedience to him in conformity with their instructions from Charles VI?[48] There was no lack of votes for this course, but the majority thought differently and felt it advisable to delay substraction since in the first place it would prevent the conference in Savona; and secondly the envoys from Gregory had emphatically warned them against any act that could be regarded as intimidation. D'Ailly and Gerson in particular pointed to the

45 Valois, *Schisme* III, 502. A report of the journey in Rel. de St.-Denys, *Chronique* III, 528ff.

46 Gerson's sermon *Rogate quae ad pacem sunt Jerusalem*, which he gave before the cardinals, has been lost. For a summary of the sermon, see Rel. de St.-Denis, *Chronique* III, 605-7.

47 Rel. de St.-Denys, *Chronique* III, 612ff; Valois, *Schisme* III, 514.

48 Valois, *Schisme* III, 516ff.

dangers of substraction in their *Rationes ad differendam substractionem*.[49] Their arguments carried conviction, for the final assembly unanimously decided to reject this policy.

In Aix the embassy split up; several envoys returned to Paris to inform the court and the University of the latest developments; these roused furious reactions, above all in the University. Ameilh de Breuil and some others were left in Marseilles to keep an eye on Benedict while the remainder, Gerson among them, set off via Genoa, Lucca, Florence and Viterbo for Rome, where they arrived on 5 July.[50]

Bitter disillusionment awaited the legates in the eternal city, for Pope Gregory's attitude had changed completely. His generous and dynamic actions of only six months ago had given way to hesitancy, indecision and suspicion of his rival, Benedict. Political and personal factors may have contributed to this change of course. In the first place Ladislas of Naples, who found in Gregory a devoted defender of his interests, persuaded him not to resign, while in the second place the threatening attitude of the King of France towards Benedict did not encourage Gregory to put himself under the King's protection in Savona. 'There are in France,' he said later, 'so many rival princes that the word of one is no guarantee against the anger of another.' Finally, the decisive factor was that the aged Pope was unable to distinguish between the interests of God's family and those of his own. His nephews, to whom he was very close – he had sent one of them as his envoy to Benedict – continually reminded him that giving up his position would also spell the end of their family's prestige. Gregory, or as Dietrich of Niem was accustomed to call him 'Errorius', was too weak and too senile to be able to resist these evil counsels.[51]

The numerous negotiations between the legates and the Pope came to nothing. Constantly changing his point of view, constantly raising new objections, now willing to go to Savona and now refusing, Gregory tried the patience of the delegates. The discussions

---

49 Besides d'Ailly and Gerson the *Rationes* (Martène & Durand, *Thesaurus novus* II, 1329B-30F, and Gl. 6, 105-7) were signed by 'Philippus abbas b. Dionysii in Francia' (Philippe de Vilette) and 'Jacobus de Noviniano' (Jacques de Nouvion, the King's secretary). Cf. Valois, *Schisme* III, 517.

50 Valois, *Schisme* III, 518ff. Fragments of Jacques de Nouvion's report of the embassy to Rome are to be found in 'Actes et Documents', doc. 41, in Gl. 10, 480-91.

51 Valois, *Schisme* III, 520ff; 534.

were endless, but so was the ingenuity of the legates in finding new ways to disarm every new objection. But all to no avail, for when the mind is made up, reasoned argument is futile. Gregory too let the delegates leave empty handed.[52]

They began their return journey in early August. On 21 August Gerson reached Genoa, where he was to remain until the beginning of the following year. From Genoa he and d'Ailly wrote a moving letter to Gregory, telling him of the intense joy they had felt at his earlier proposal to resign, and urging him in the strongest terms to go to Savona after all. He could put his trust in the protection guaranteed by the King of France, while he must also understand the scandal that would be caused by his refusal to go, and the damage it would do to the apostolic throne.[53]

The more Gregory hesitated to go to Savona, the more haste Benedict made. He reached the city, after a short stay in Nice, on 24 September. Gregory had also set off by then, but made very slow progress, and was no farther than Viterbo, where he spent several weeks. In spite of the urgent pleas of his cardinals and the French delegates to make haste to join Benedict, he only agreed to continue his journey as far as Siena. He reached that city in early September and stayed there four months. He spent his time in writing letters, so that the date fixed for his meeting with his rival was passed time after time. Time and again he suggested another meeting place, to which Benedict replied with objections. In the end both Popes advanced a few miles, Benedict to Porto Venere, Gregory to Lucca, so that the distance between them was no more than a day's journey, but they went no further. There was to be no meeting between them.[54]

When Gerson returned to Paris at the beginning of February 1408,[55] he found the political situation completely changed: just over two months earlier, on 23 November 1407, the Duke of Orléans had been assassinated at the instigation of John the Fearless, Duke of Burgundy. This outrage found an apologist in the

[52] Schwab, *Gerson*, 200ff; Valois, *Schisme* III, 529ff.

[53] Letter to Pope Gregory (15 Sept. 1407), inc. *Grandem universo populo* (Gl. 2, 84-6).

[54] Valois, *Schisme* III, 543ff.

[55] Cf. M. Lieberman, 'Chronologie Gersonienne V', *Rom.* 78 (1957) 450 n. 4, with reference to 438 n. 3.

theologian Jean Petit, with whom Gerson was to become entangled, as a result, in a long and bitter conflict. In the end this was to lead to his never seeing Paris again after 1415.

With the Duke of Orléans, Benedict lost his most powerful supporter, and there was no one else who could resist the pressure from the University to revert to total substraction. On 12 January 1408 the King had already told Benedict that France would go over to neutrality if the unity of the Church had not been restored by Ascension Day, 24 May.[56] In his reply Benedict pointed out that it was really no fault of his that unity had not been restored. Nevertheless, the right of collation had been withheld from him for many years and the French Church had felt entitled to trample on his decisions and on canon law in general. Now it even intended to proclaim its neutrality. But was it the function of the King to set a time limit for a work that lay in the hands of divine providence? A unilateral decision to adopt neutrality violated divine law and the respect that ought to be shown to the Pope, and could not go unpunished. Benedict summoned the King to renounce his intention and threatened him with a bull excommunicating all those who were to be guilty of substraction or appealing against pontifical decisions.[57]

On 14 May the letter and bull from Benedict were delivered to Charles by Sanche Lopez, who wisely withdrew speedily.[58] The princes and the University were furious at the Pope's threats and on 21 May they held an open air conference in the Louvre to discuss their next steps. Numerous high dignitaries attended and speeches were made by Jean Courtecuisse and others.[59] To the old arguments against Petrus de Luna he added a number of new ones, declaring that the recent bull had insulted the dignity of the King and the sovereignty of the kingdom. Benedict was accused of wishing to perpetuate the Schism, and so was no longer to be regarded as the shepherd but as the enemy of the Church, fit to be deposed not only from the papacy but from every other ecclesiastical office. His threats need not be taken seriously.

The University gave its full support to these complaints and also

---

56 The letter, inc. *Pax ecclesiastica* (Dupin II, 103D-5C).

57 DuBoulay, *Historia* V, 152-4; Valois, *Schisme* III, 606-16.

58 Valois, *Schisme* III, 607ff.

59 Jean Courtecuisse's speech in DuBoulay, *Historia* V, 158.

demanded that the bull be destroyed and the Pope's collaborators hunted down and punished. It got its way, for after the bull had been ceremonially torn into shreds before the whole assembly, the King's men dragged the aged and venerable dean of St Germain l'Auxerre from the pulpit and threw him into the dungeon on a charge of *lèse-majesté*. The terror against Benedict's supporters or those who were believed to support him, continued into the following weeks. Guy de Roye, Archbishop of Rheims, and Pierre d'Ailly thought it prudent to lie low.[60] Others, including the Abbot of St Denis and some of the canons of Notre Dame, were unable to escape arrest. The fury of the University was directed in particular against Gerson's pupil and friend Nicolas of Clémanges, until recently Benedict's secretary, who was suspected, if not of being the author of the bull, at least of having known of its contents. Nicolas was unable to clear himself of suspicion but managed to escape arrest. Gerson was not troubled.[61]

Four days after the open air meeting in the Louvre, on 25 May, the King had the neutrality of France proclaimed. He invited foreign princes to join him in this decision. The princes of Germany and Bohemia, as well as those of Hungary and Navarre, acceded to his request. Charles pressed the cardinals to shun the two rival Popes, who 'had been unable to find a suitable place in the whole world to fulfil their sworn promises', and to join forces to take action.[62] The University of Paris wrote to the two sacred colleges in the same spirit.

On 11 August a synod (National Synod V) was opened in Paris which was to lay down guidelines for the organisation of the Church, now that neutrality was a fact. It decided that all Benedict's decisions taken before 19 May 1407, the date when he had signed his bull, should remain in force, while points in dispute should be decided by common law. Anyone who still recognised Benedict was to lose his benefice.[63]

Even before this synod was held, the French commander in Genoa had been ordered to place Benedict under arrest.[64] The

---

60 Lieberman, 'Chronologie Gersonienne V', *Rom.* 78 (1957) 452-3.
61 Valois, *Schisme* III, 610.
62 Schwab, *Gerson*, 211.
63 Valois, *Schisme* IV, 21ff.
64 Rel. de St.-Denys, *Chronique* IV, 614.

Pope managed to escape in his galley to Perpignan. After blaming Gregory for the failure of the conference in Savona, on the day of his departure, 15 June, Benedict called a council, which was to be held at Perpignan on All Saints' Day, and was to have as its theme the unity and reformation of the Church.[65]

Pope Gregory was not to be outdone, and also summoned a council to be held somewhere in Northern Italy. If possible, he was in an even more difficult position than his rival. He had already shocked his cardinals by causing the failure of the conference at Savona, and now he alienated them even more by appointing his nephews to the sacred college. That was the last straw for most of them. They deserted him, left Lucca and went to Pisa, from where they loaded their former master with accusations and reproaches. In the meantime they also sought contact with the other party.[66]

On 29 June the cardinals who had deserted the two Popes met in Livorno. They unanimously declared that they wished to promote the unity of the Church by a policy of resignation and the holding of a council, and promised that they would never return to their former masters except as negotiators. If Benedict or Gregory died, they would not choose a successor, while they declared in advance that any election by those cardinals who had remained loyal would be null and void.[67]

The cardinals informed the princes and prelates of both obediences of their decisions. They also advised them that a general council would be held at Pisa next year, on the authority of the combined sacred colleges. The universities of Paris, Oxford and Bologna approved this plan, on the grounds of the urgency of the circumstances and the right of the Church under divine and natural law to seek within itself the means to maintain itself and restore its unity.[68] The Council of Pisa was to be opened on 25 March 1409.

Of the numerous events described above the murder of the Duke of Orléans was the most shocking, the calling of the Council of Pisa

[65] On this almost exclusively Spanish council see F. Ehrle, 'Aus den Acten des Afterconcils von Perpignan', *ALKGM*, V (1892) 387-465; VII (1900) 576-693.

[66] Valois, *Schisme* IV, 3ff.

[67] Valois, *Schisme* IV, 14-15.

[68] Salembier, *Le grand schisme*, 243. On the prehistory of the Council of Pisa see especially Bliemetzrieder, *Generalkonzil*, 221-94.

the most welcome. As for the first, on 8 March 1408 the theologian Jean Petit, who was attached to the house of Burgundy, had defended the outrage committed by his master. He portrayed the Duke of Orléans as the cause of all the dangers that harassed the country and declared that since Orléans was a tyrant, the Duke of Burgundy had been entitled to take judgement into his own hands. Other meetings followed in September, at which the murder was condemned in the bitterest terms and reparation demanded for the crime. The King let it be known through the Dauphin that justice would be done and threatened that if John the Fearless did not submit to him, war would be declared.[69]

Amid these threats of civil war France, as we saw, had decided to go over to neutrality in Church matters. Shortly afterwards this was followed by the positive news that the cardinals of both parties had reached agreement and called a council to be held at Pisa. The announcement of France's neutrality implied not only that the King was bringing excommunication on himself, but that the Church of France was again faced with the need to provide for the 'acephalous' situation in which its neutrality had placed it.[70] For that purpose, as we saw, a national council had been called for 11 August. It continued into the beginning of November, and culminated in a solemn procession of the clergy to the royal palace. In all probability it was on this occasion, Sunday 4 November 1408, that Gerson preached on behalf of the University before the court, that is before the princes, for the King was absent, and gave his sermon *Veniat pax*.[71]

> The most recent interpretation of this sermon is that of Mgr. Combes. He devoted several pages to it, in which, in his trenchant style – that is by dealing blows right and left, in text and notes, at previous authors, because they had failed to see what he thought he could see – he tried to persuade his readers that this sermon was evidence of a remarkable change ('inflexion') in Gerson's point of view on ecclesiastical policy, especially with regard to his verdict on Benedict XIII. That change was supposed to have meant that Gerson, who had previously taken Benedict under his protection, who had rejected substraction and wel-

---

69 For a detailed review of all the events which took place between the assassination and the peace of Chartres (9 April 1409), see A. Coville, *Jean Petit. La question du tyrannicide au commencement du XVe siècle*, Paris 1932, 225-57.

70 Cf. Valois, *Schisme* IV, 24-37.

71 Mourin, *Gerson prédicateur*, 187-96. *Veniat pax* (Gl. 7*, 1100-23; Dupin IV, 625-42).

comed restitution, who had never accepted a conciliar solution but always waited for the Pope to take the initiative, had now suddenly dropped Benedict and shown himself entirely won over to the cause of the council.[72]

We consider this account wholly inaccurate and the result of the fact that Mgr. Combes was tempted to trace a line of development in Gerson's ideas on Church policy, which in this case is based on too few relevant texts. Had Mgr. Combes studied the chronology of Gerson's thought on Church policy more acutely, more thoroughly, he would not have described him as an 'obstiné défenseur de Benoît XIII'.[73] If Mgr. Combes had included more of Gerson's writings in his study, he would also have realised that Gerson had not been completely dismissive of any form of substraction since 1402, and he would not have failed to discover that Gerson had long regarded the *via concilii* as a legitimate, albeit temporarily impassable, way forward to the restoration of unity.

The sermon *Veniat pax* is a passionate plea for peace and reflection addressed to the princes of France, in the first place to use all their efforts to come to the aid of the Church, being in grave danger; and secondly to avert a civil war. The desperate situation of the Church had become even more acute, because the consensus which the two colleges of cardinals had reached on the way to restore unity threatened to be thwarted by the machinations of 'the enemy of the human race'. Both Gregory and Benedict, each on his own way, had listened to the evil whisperings of the Devil, and the result was that the yearned-for restoration of unity now seemed out of sight again. To prevent that, France ought immediately to go on to a devotional offensive, using processions and other spiritual means to ward off the Devil's temptations. That was the message which Gerson laid before his exalted audience.[74] And to convince them that this mes-

[72] Combes, *La théologie mystique* I, 243-51.

[73] Combes, *La théologie mystique* I, 241 n. 200.

[74] That this was the main theme of the sermon is shown by its conclusion, in which he again repeated what ought to be done: *Veniat pax* (Gl. 7*, 1123; Dupin IV, 642B): '... toulte l'eglise de France, qui est comme la mere du roy, et sa fille l'Université de Paris, font trois devotes oblations. Se offrent premierement de faire oroisons et prieres, car aultres armeurez ils n'ont pour ceste paix [et] union. S'offrent d'exhorter le peuple partout à faire le pareil, et à correction de vie, par bonne predicacion. Se offrent en toultes aultres manieres que le roy et vous, nosseigneurs, enseignerez, en particulier et en universal, à y obeir en toute diligence et entiere affection.'

sage came directly from the University of Paris,[75] which watched over the welfare of State and Church alike, he again put his words into the mouth of 'la fille du roy' herself, and introduced her speaking in oracular terms.

> Reveingne paix... prie maintenant avecques le saint prophete Ysaie [57:2] la fille du roy, l'enseigneresse de verité, la mere et la fontaine de toutes estudes, la belle lumiere et clere du très noble et très chrestien royaulme de France, comme de toute chrestienté. Reveingne paix, dit elle; et à bon droit demande paix, et huche paix. Paix espirituelle et paix temporelle; paix espirituelle en saincte eglise contre scismatique et division; et paix temporelle ou noble royaulme de France contre doubteuse affliction.[76]

'Peace within this noble realm', the daughter of the King cries, 'seems to be lost. It seems as if peace is in hiding or in exile. How often have we not turned to God with lamenting, with weeping and with sighs, to implore him to grant us peace? With the prophet we cry out: 'Hast thou spurned Judah utterly? Dost thou loathe Zion?' (cf. Jer. 14: 19). Can God's mercy of former times have deserted us? Division, fear and violence raise their heads everywhere and tear poor Christendom asunder. May God give us peace and end the violence.'

Gerson asserts with great diffidence that he would never have dared to address such an illustrious company if so many things were not at stake at the same time: the honour of God and his Church, the salvation of the King and his kingdom, and the authority of the University. Addressing the princes,[77] he implores them not to doubt his good intentions. If they should nevertheless take offence at his words, then he begs them to accept that this was

---

[75] He remarks that because of peace the university had been transferred from Athens to Rome and so on to Paris (*Veniat pax*, Gl. 7*, 1115; Dupin IV, 636B): 'Pour quoy se transporta l'université d'Athenes à Romme et de Romme à Paris si non par deffault de paix?' Cf. *Vivat rex* (Gl. 7*, 1138; Dupin IV, 584A). For more details of this socalled *translatio studii*, see Rashdall, *Universities* I, 273, and G. Ouy, 'La plus ancienne oeuvre de Jean Gerson', *Rom.* 83 (1962) 446-8.

[76] *Veniat pax* (Gl. 7*, 1100; Dupin IV, 626C).

[77] *Veniat pax* (Gl. 7*, 1102; Dupin IV, 626D-7A): 'Et james ne me fusse enhardis ne consenti, moy de tres petite et pauvre condicion, et en si petit temps comme de trois ou de quatre jours, que je eusse osé telle charge entreprendre, se quatre choses en especial ne m'y eussent induit et comme astraint.'

the result of ignorance alone and not of ill will or partisan feeling for one person or another.

Looking back, he recalls the recent efforts of the King and the University for the sake of peace. They had sent a long letter with many recommendations 'to those of Rome', as he describes them. But what had become of it? The enemy of the human race, realising that the *kairos* was at hand and peace was within reach, had stiffened his resistance and ensured that Gregory, who had first shown good will and even taken an oath to resign, later changed his mind and rejected this course as unrealistic and unlawful.[78]

Once again without mentioning his name or dignity Gerson turns the attention of his audience to Benedict, and asks 'what good can be said of our man? For who could ever have thought that such a senseless, frivolous and dishonest intention would lie so deep in his heart that he would seek to excommunicate the King? *O Dieu, la personne du roy, tant innocent et sans coulpe quelconque en ceste matière!*' He continues: 'Is this not a clear proof of temptation by the Devil, of the inspirations of evil angels?' He had found at least twelve errors and intolerable wrongs in the letter of excommunication, but he would pass over them, knowing that everyone is convinced of the scandal of this damnable deed.[79]

To console his audience he closes this section of his sermon with the words of Paul, '*Nihil possumus contra veritatem*' (2 Cor. 13: 8),[80] and states that the remedy is to return to God with even more submission than before, until the Council of Pisa. All the impurities and errors must be done away with, for peace is granted only to those who are of good will. Just as he had argued in previous years, now he repeated his view that the cause of the lamentable Schism was

---

[78] *Veniat pax*, cons. 1 (Gl. 7*, 1103; Dupin IV, 627BD): '... l'ennemy de l'umain lignage ... de tant plus s'efforcera par soy... d'empescher ceste paix comme il sent que elle approche plus: *insidiatur calcaneo* [cf. Gen. 3:15].'

[79] *Veniat pax*, cons. 1 (Gl. 7*, 1103; Dupin IV, 627CD): 'Et de celuy de par de ça, que en pourrons nous de bien dire? Qui eust pansé par avant que une telle folle entreprise, plaine de temerité detescande et de faulseté se fust en son cueur tant crueusement embatue comme de vouloir excommunier la personne du roy? ... Et n'est ce mie temptacion certainne de l'ennemy? immissiones per angelos malos? Je diroie plus avant se je cuidoie que fust besoing, et se ne savois bien que qui[conque] aperçoit l'indignité de ceste damnable besoigne. Et y ai trouvé par compte fait douze erreurs ou defaux intollerables ou plus.'

[80] What he actually meant by citing this text becomes clear from a comparison of this statement with the citation given in Chapter VIII n. 47!

the moral decay of Christendom.[81] Those who wanted peace, therefore, must work to remove that cause. The Bishop of Paris and the chapter of Notre Dame had already taken some initiatives for the holding of processions throughout the kingdom, fasting and days of prayer and other devotions, on the model of those in Rome.[82] Gerson thought the Schism so deeply rooted that it could not be eradicated without special divine intervention. In this case it would not be tempting God to ask Him for a miracle.[83]

The second section of the sermon was considerably fuller, and contained an urgent plea to the princes to preserve peace in the temporal sphere and to refrain from all violence among themselves.[84] Warning that war would only harm the public cause and the poor, he tried to win the princes for peace by telling them of the advice which 'la bonne pensée' had given him in a meditation. It would take us too far to go into this and we shall merely remark that he did not hesitate to honour the memory of the Duke of Orléans, but at the same time pleaded for forgiveness towards his murderer.[85]

In view of the grimness with which he was to work for the condemnation of Jean Petit's proposition in defence of tyrannicide, five years later, this plea for forgiveness is surprising. Yet one should remember what it would have meant if he had pleaded for justice when France was on the brink of civil war. The effect would have

---

[81] See above, p. 25. *Veniat pax*, cons. 2 (Gl. 7*, 1104; Dupin IV, 628B): 'C'est certain que la cause de ce douloureux scisme est la corruption des meurs du peuple crestien, si comme les mauvaises humeurs engendrent discort de maladie au corps humain. Si fault que la cause soit ostée qui veult que le bon effet de paix viengne.'

[82] *Veniat pax*, cons. 2 (Gl. 7*, 1104; Dupin IV, 628AB): 'Monseigneur l'evesque de Paris et le doyen et chapitre de la mere esglise Nostre Dame y ont pieça commencé entre eulx, et n'actendent fors la bonne ordonnance du roy et de vous, nosseigneurs, et des aultres, prelas et gens d'esglise, et plus avant y proceder tant et instituer jeusnes comme processions, et aultres oeuvres d'oroison et de devote religion... Soient faictes doncques telles oeuvres de religion par tout ce royaulme, plus que par avant, à l'exemple de ceulx de Romme.'

[83] *Veniat pax*, cons. 2 (Gl. 7*, 1104; Dupin IV, 628B): 'Et en bonne foy c'est bien de necessité, veu que ce maudit scisme est tant enraciné que jamais ne se ostera du tout sans l'especiale ayde de Dieu et comme par miracle. Et tiens que en ce cas present on pueut raisonnablement demander miracle sans tempter Dieu, *quia opus est supra vires humanas.*'

[84] *Veniat pax* (Gl. 7*, 1105-23; Dupin IV, 629A-42B).

[85] See M. Lieberman, 'Chronologie Gersonienne X. Le sermon *Memento Finis*', *Rom.* 83 (1962) 83-89, with (85 n. 1) more details about the Celestine Peter of Burgundy (Pierre Pocquet), mentioned by Gerson.

been the opposite of what he was seeking to achieve. He would have thrown oil on the flames and played into the hands of those who wanted war, thus making his plea for peace futile. No wonder, therefore, that he was so guarded about the crime of John the Fearless: the preservation of peace was a greater good than the restoration of justice at that moment.[86] It was at the same time in the interest of the council to come, that every cause of discord should be avoided.

> Soit aussy bien advisé yci que riens ne ce face ou conclue ou determiné absolument, qui puisse estre cause en ce concile avenir d'empeschement de la matiere principale et de division entre les aultres qui y viendront.[87]

[86] We agree entirely with Mourin (*Gerson prédicateur*, 194) who, pointing to the difference between the situations in 1408 and 1413, remarks: 'Le peuple et l'Université ont évolué, comme le chancelier, en raison de la guerre civile. Et lorsque en 1413, le procès s'ouvrira, ce ne sera plus un procès de la justice civile: ce sera un procès de doctrine porté devant la Faculté de théologie, puis devant l'évêque de Paris. Le plan en est différent. Et Gerson, qui ne devra plus défendre alors le peuple de Paris et de France, parlera avec une hardiesse qui lui vaudra à lui-même l'exil.' As early as the *De auferibilitate* Gerson had forcefully refuted, on theological grounds, one of Jean Petit's central theses (see Chapter VI n. 107). We cannot discover whether this pronouncement dates from 1409, or—as appears more probable—was not added to the treatise until the time of the Council of Constance.

[87] *Veniat pax*, cons. 3 (Gl. 7*, 1105; Dupin IV, 628D-9A).

CHAPTER SIX

GERSON AND THE COUNCIL OF PISA, 1409

Non enim habet corpus ecclesiae mysticum, a Christo perfectissime stabilitum, minus ius nec robur ad procurationem suae unionis quam corpus aliud, civile mysticum vel naturale tantum.
Gerson, *De unitate* (Gl. 6, 137; Dupin II, 114D).

Although Gerson did not attend the Council of Pisa, for reasons which are not clear,[1] he still helped to prepare for it. The evidence is that we possess no fewer than four works by him in which he defended the unusual manner of the assembly's convocation – by the cardinals rather than by the Pope – and also tried to establish in advance that the decisions taken by the council would be valid in law. Both arguments were coupled with a penetrating statement of the case for the *via concilii.*

To understand his point of view we may recall that it was many

[1] Speaking about himself in the third person, Gerson says in the addition to his sermon *Ambulate* (Gl. 5, 45; Dupin II, 206B): 'Joannes cancellarius Parisiensis... tempore concilii Pisani dumque absens ab eo legebat Parisius...'. Cf. *De unitate ecclesiae* (Gl. 6, 136; Dupin II, 113D): '... ne pergat ad sacrum concilium Pisis...' It is not clear what occupations prevented Gerson from attending the Council. Valois (*Schisme* IV, 82) assumed that he was kept in Paris by his work as Chancellor, professor and pastor. Mgr. Combes (*La théologie mystique* I, 275-8) rejected this assumption and suggested another explanation, which was too speculative, however, even to mention. Risking speculation in our turn, we wonder if it may have been the problems at his deanery of St Donatian in Bruges which prevented him from travelling to Pisa. It is clear at any rate 1. that these problems had been facing him for some time, and 2. that they forced him to leave for Bruges, where certain he was in the first week of August 1409. See Vansteenberghe, 'Gerson à Bruges', 38-41; Lieberman, 'Chronologie Gersonienne VIII', *Rom.* 81 (1960), 47; Gl. 10, 500-2. – In the records of the chapter of Notre-Dame (10. Sept. 1408) one reads: 'De supplicatione domini Cancellarii [= Gerson] quod habeat litteram testimonialem quod cancellaria *non est dignitas sed officium simplex* cum litteris recommandatoriis.' (Gl. 10, 492). We must confess that we do not understand exactly what this means. Was it his wish that the Chancellor's authority should be reinforced from a moral into a juridical one? According to M.-D. Chenu ('Officium. Théologiens et canonistes', in: *Etudes d'Histoire du Droit Canonique, dédiées à Gabriel Le Bras*, II, Paris 1965, 835-9 (837)) the notion of an *officium* concerns 'l'action effective imposée par le rôle qu'on tient, ou le métier qu'on pratique dans la collectivité.' What, then, might have been the reason that he asked for changing his 'dignity' into an 'office' at this moment? Is it to be seen in relation to the problems at his deanery of St Donatian, to the Petit affair, to the Council of Pisa, or to what else? *Non liquet.*

years since he had come to the conclusion that no solution was to be found on the basis of positive law, so that to that extent he certainly had no difficulty in defending the unaccustomed way of convocation. As far as the *via concilii* itself was concerned, there again the transition was easy, for, as we have shown, he had long since overcome his initial reluctance to consider this solution.[2]

The difference from his earlier position is that in the works written in preparation for Pisa, he presented a much more detailed case, and moreover committed himself exclusively to the *via concilii*. Whereas previously he had been willing to accept every way which was not in conflict with divine or natural law, from now on he pinned his hopes solely on a conciliar solution to the Schism. This was, no doubt, because, after so many years of discord and disagreement, now at last both parties had found each other, and had decided *jointly* to restore unity by following the *via concilii*. The fact that this decision was taken in common, Gerson considered as a clear sign that the mightmare of a divided Church now was nearing its end, and that therefore all Christians had to make a supreme effort to its realisation.[3] It is no coincidence that we find in these works the first clear references to Henry of Langenstein and Conrad of Gelnhausen, the earliest advocates of a conciliar solution in France.

The works in question were: first a short sketch, half extract, half reply;[4] secondly a work not printed until modern times, entitled *De*

[2] Gerson himself reveals the connection with the opinions he had defended earlier by referring to his sermon before the pope at Tarascon. See below n. 6 and *Pro convocatione concilii Pisani* (Gl. 6, 124; Dupin II, 122C): 'Notetur factum Scipionis. Allegavi et fundavi in sermone circumcisionis Tarascone', a reference to *Apparuit gratia Dei* (Gl. 5, 84-5), where one reads: 'Nasica Scipio: cum consul, inquit, iuris ordinem sequitur id agit ut cum omnibus legibus Romanorum corruat imperium.' Cf. also *Conversi estis* (Gl. 5, 177; Dupin IV, 702A); *De auferibilitate* (Gl. 3, 313; Dupin II, 224D) and *De unitate ecclesiae* (Gl. 6, 143; Dupin II, 119C). The example stems from Valerius Maximus, *Facta et dicta memorabilia*, III 2, 17. Cf. Combes, *Jean de Montreuil*, 558ff. See also below n. 58.

[3] We prefer this solution to the flat and rather tautological explanation of his 'conversion', as proposed by Mgr. Combes (*La théologie mystique* I, 262): 'Si Gerson consent enfin à accepter ... la thèse conciliaire, c'est pour la raison qu'il se sent maintenant d'accord avec ceux qui ont démontré que la convocation du concile était opportune et convenable.' In the last resort, we think, his 'conversion' depended directly on his deep-rooted, Augustinian and pseudo-Dionysian ideas about 'unity'. Cf. ps.-Dionysius Areopagita, *De divinis nominibus*, cap. 13 (*MG* 3, col. 987): 'Quae enim multa sunt partibus sunt unum toto, ut corpus... *Unum dico illud quod omnia participant...*' See further below notes 28, 49 & 102, and Chapter IX n. 44.

[4] *Pro convocatione concilii Pisani* (Gl. 6, 123-125; Dupin II, 121-3). We wonder if this

auctoritate concilii,[5] wrongly characterised by its first editor as 'un plan plutôt que'un traité, dans sa forme définitive.' The concluding words make it clear that it certainly was a finished piece of work.[6] In the third place there is the *Propositio facta coram Anglicis*, the sermon *Congratulatur*[7] which Gerson delivered before an English delegation in Paris en route to Pisa, on 29 January 1409. On the same day – and this is the fourth work – he had put his *De unitate ecclesiastica*[8] on paper, adding to it four *Considerationes*.[9] This completes the list, for the *Propositiones utiles* are not by him but by d'Ailly.[10]

Since all these works were written at the same time and with one and the same purpose, it is obvious that they duplicate one another occasionally, nor can this repetition be totally avoided in our exposition. Passing over the draft which we mentioned first, we shall

---

tract may be considered as a reply to the anonymous document, printed by Mansi (*Amplissima collectio* XXVII, 223-6), and translated by Crowder (*Unity, Heresy and Reform*, 55), who qualified it as 'an objective forecast of legal difficulties which the council might meet, as it claims to be, prepared for the advice of the cardinals.' We dare not decide the question, but it seems very likely. In passing we note that in this tract (Gl. 6, 124; Dupin II 122C) Gerson referred for the first time to Conrad of Gelnhausen and Henry of Langenstein. 'Videatur tractatus praepositi Wormacensis et tres considerationes suae. Item tractatus magistri Henrici de Hassia.'

[5] This treatise was edited for the first time by Miss Z. Rueger, 'Le "De auctoritate concilii" de Gerson', *RHE* LIII (1958) 775-95. It was reedited by Mgr Glorieux (Gl. 6, 114-23). Mrs. Rueger's edition lacks art. 9 concl. 2 and art. 12 concl. 3; Gl. lacks only art. 12. concl. 3, in all cases without comment. – Mgr. Combes (*La théologie mystique* I, 241, n. 199) casts doubt on Gerson's authorship of this work. We do not share his doubt, for the following reasons: 1. nearly all the theses defended in *De auctoritate* recur in Gerson's works written at the same time. (We refer in particular to art. 1 concl. 6: the refutation of an assertion of Henry of Langenstein.) 2. the closing sentence of the work must be regarded as typically 'Gersonian' (see next note); 3. the verse (Hosea 1: 11) named in the same art. 14. forms the text for his sermon *Propositio facta coram Anglicis*.

[6] *De auctoritate concilii*, art. 14 (ed. Rueger, 777, 795; Gl. 6, 133) reads: 'Et comprehenduntur sub numero XXXI quia duravit schisma per XXXI annos completos.' A 'plan' would not conclude with such a formula. Cf. also the last words of *De auferibilitate* (Gl. 3, 313; Dupin II, 224D): 'Ecce ergo viginti considerationes quodam ordine geometrico se sequentes, quae iunctis aliis sedecim in quarum qualibet initium est *Unitas ecclesiastica* (Gl. 6, 136-45; Dupin II, 113-18). Additis quoque aliis quattuor dudum Tarascone praedicatis (*Apparuit gratia Dei*, Gl. 5, 64-90; Dupin II, 54-73), redduntur XL considerationes.'

[7] Gl. 6, 125-35; Dupin II, 123-30. See Combes, *La théologie mystique* I, 259.

[8] *De unitate ecclesiae* (Gl. 6, 136-42; Dupin II, 113-18).

[9] Gl. 6, 142-5; Dupin II, 118-21.

[10] See Tschackert, *Peter von Ailli*, Appendix, [34] n. 1. Morrall (*Gerson*, 86 n. 3; 112 n. 2) ascribed this work both to Gerson and to d'Ailly! A modern ed. was provided by F. Oakley, 'The *Propositiones utiles* of Pierre d'Ailly: an epitome of conciliar theory', *CH* 29 (1960), 399-403.

begin by considering the *De auctoritate concilii*, a work in 14 articles, most of them in turn divided into *conclusiones.*

Gerson starts from the assumption that not only the *corpus mysticum* but also its hierarchical structure is founded on institution by Christ and must therefore be regarded as a *congregatio authentica*, which does not lose its unity during a vacancy.[11] He then summarises a number of cases in which the Church has the right to call a council without the intervention of the Pope. He states, for example, that whenever the Pope is either unable or unwilling to summon a council – and this failure would be harmful to the Church – then the cardinals may assume the responsibility. If they too fail to act – *per mortem vel aliter* – the right of summons falls to the bishops acting together. Here, highly characteristically, and clearly correcting a pronouncement of Henry of Langenstein,[12] Gerson asserts that – *lege stante*[13] – they will never disappear entirely or fall into heresy.

> stante christiana lege universitas episcoporum est inobliquabilis secundum affectum et intellectum, nec est compossibile Christi lege eos omnes collective desinere per mortem vel haereticare.[14]

In other words he believes it is unthinkable that a situation should ever occur in which the whole episcopacy should disappear. At most, the Church might have to do without a Pope and the cardinals for a time, but no more far-reaching threat to the hierarchy could ever exist. However great a catastrophe befell the Church,

---

[11] *De auctoritate concilii*, art. 1 concl. 1-7 (Gl. 6, 114). For the meaning of 'authenticus' see Chapter XI n. 24.

[12] *De auctoritate concilii*, art. 3 concl. 1-6 (Gl. 6, 115). Cf. Henry of Langenstein, *Epistola consilii pacis*, c. 14 (Dupin II, 826BC). Cf. Kreuzer, *Heinrich von Langenstein*, 227.

[13] The often used formula 'lege stante' (cf. below, notes 62, 86, 87, 88 etc.) refers to the nominalistic distinction between God's *potentia ordinata* and *potentia absoluta*, for the meaning of which, see H.A. Oberman, *The Harvest of Medieval Theology*, Cambridge (Mass.) 1963, Index of subjects s.v. 'Potentia dei absoluta' & 'Potentia dei ordinata' (492), and Glossary (473): '*Potentia dei ordinata (stante lege; de facto; secundum leges ordinatas et institutas a deo)* The ordained power of God – This is the order established by God and the way in which God has chosen to act in his *opera ad extra*, i.e., over against the contingent order outside him. It is the power which is regulated by the revealed and natural laws established by God. Between the absolute and ordained power of God there is no real distinction but a merely rational distinction.' See also J. Altensteig, *Lexicon Theologicum*, Cologne 1619 (reprint 1974), s.v. 'potentia Dei' (715-16).

[14] *De auctoritate concilii*, art. 3 concl. 4 (Gl. 6, 115).

the community of the bishops would never disappear altogether.[15] And it ought to be regarded as certain *de fide* that the same body formed the guarantee that the Church would never err in matters of faith nor be attacked by schism.[16]

When he then proceeds to claim that the *multitudo fidelium* is unerring, and explicitly says that not only laymen are to be included in it,[17] he is once more disagreeing with Henry of Langenstein, or, if one prefers, with Ockham, for whom infallibility was, in the final analysis, not attached to the hierarchy. He also distinguishes himself from Ockham in his thesis that a general council, in contrast to an individual Pope, cannot err in decisions concerning matters of faith and the organisation of the Church. The council is infallible on the grounds of a special privilege from Christ: the promise of the aid of the Holy Spirit. This means that the decisions on faith taken by a council are accepted by the *multitudo fidelium* through the working of the same Spirit.[18] The corollary is that in matters which concern the status of the whole Church, the Pope is obliged to call on the aid and advice of the *ecclesia universalis*, i.e. the totality of all the local Churches.[19]

If the statements cited above might have been imagined without the Council of Pisa, the same cannot be said of what follows. Articles 6 and 7 refer unmistakeably to the actual situation. In article 6 Gerson shows that the *ecclesia congregata* possesses authority over both pretenders to the papal throne, who, like all believers, are obliged *de necessitate salutis* to follow the guidelines issued by the

---

[15] *De auctoritate concilii*, art. 3 concl. 3 (Gl. 6, 115): 'deficientibus papa et cardinalibus per mortem vel aliter, aut neglegentibus damnabiliter, auctoritas congregandi christianam religionem devolvitur ad episcopos catholicos.'

[16] *De auctoritate concilii*, art. 3 concl. 5 (Gl. 6, 115): 'collegium omnium episcoporum christianorum non posse errare in fide et schismate maculari, est certa fide credendum.'

[17] *De auctoritate concilii*, art. 3 concl. 6 (Gl. 6, 115): 'multitudo quae non potest errare, non est tantum multitudo fidelium complectans viros et mulieres, parvulos et adultos.'

[18] *De auctoritate concilii*, art. 5 concl. 10 (Gl. 6, 116).

[19] *De auctoritate concilii*, art. 5 concl. 1, 4, 6 (Gl. 6, 115-116); '[1] Non est possibile, stante lege Christi, concilium generale aut universalem Ecclesiam congregatam debite, in determinando veritates fidei aut necessarias vel utiles pro regimine Ecclesiae errare. [4] Ecclesiae consilium quo papa in definiendo magistraliter et obligative veritates fidei aut necessarias pro regimine Ecclesiae tenetur uti, est universalis Ecclesiae et ecclesiae Romanae et ecclesiae Parisiensis et omnium singularium Christi vere ecclesiarum consilium, coniunctim et divisim. [6] Ecclesia congregata vices universalis Ecclesiae gerens, non solum quia universalem Ecclesiam repraesentat sed quia hoc habet speciale a Christo privilegium, est inobliquabilis secundum legem.' – For Gerson's use of the term *ecclesia universalis*, see Chapter X n. 23, and Chapter XII n. 67.

Council.[20] Why? Because the assembled Church possesses full power to interpret the Scriptures and more particularly to deduce from them the paths it must follow to achieve unity. On pain of losing eternal bliss, both pretenders are obliged to conform to the interpretation of the assembled Church. As long as the Church is assembled in council, obedience to the two pretenders should be suspended;[21] and if, for any reason, it should prove difficult for the two parties to reach a unanimous decision, they should allow themselves to be guided by *epikie*. The assembled Church would thus perform the function of the *vicarius Christi*.[22] After all, it was possible that the Council might decide to depose both Popes.[23]

Following his first thesis, Gerson goes on to argue that the *sufficientia ecclesiae*, founded on the fact that it was Christ who instituted the Church and its offices, justifies the conclusion that there shall exist until the end of time a body to receive instructions from above for the benefit of the welfare of the Church:

> usque ad consummatione saeculi erit aliquis vel aliqua communitas divina deputatione officiata ad recipiendum a Deo illustrationes speciales pro utilitate ecclesiae generalis.[24]

Thus the Church will never lack leadership, for Christ himself stands as guarantor of the regular exercise of the hierarchical functions. It is he, and not the Pope, who gives the Church life in the hierarchical sense. The background to this thesis is the idea that all offices in the Church receive their inspiration directly from Christ; and that as such the assembled Church is sufficiently endowed with the power to lead Christendom.[25] In other words, office-holders attending the council, to which ordinary believers might also have

---

20 *De auctoritate concilii*, art. 6 concl. 1, 3 (Gl. 6, 117).

21 *De auctoritate concilii*, art. 7 concl. 1, 2 (Gl. 6, 118).

22 *De auctoritate concilii*, art. 7 concl. 7, 8 (Gl. 6, 118): 'non tantum suspensio obedientiae respectu summi pontificis est facienda, consulente ecclesia universali legitime congregata, sed etiam ea epikeiante divinas leges et humanas, verus ipso desinente esse Christi vicarius.'

23 *De auctoritate concilii*, art. 8 (Gl. 6, 118): 'Si in facto recenti de papis ecclesia universaliter congregata reperiret se perplexam collegialiter dissentiendo ex causa iusta et rationabili, perderet ius suum et alius ius praetensum.'

24 *De auctoritate concilii*, art. 9 concl. 2 (Gl. 6, 119). Cf. concl. 1: 'usque ad saeculi consummationem durabunt in christiana religione officia et gratiae de quibus Apostolus, I ad Cor. xii, sub sensu qui ibi explicatur.'

25 *De auctoritate concilii*, art. 9 concl. 6 (Gl. 6, 119).

access[26]—which is not the same as to have the right to vote!—need not fear that they will be deprived of divine inspiration.[27]

As we have seen, apart from the Council of Pisa, Benedict and Gregory both summoned assemblies of the Church at virtually the same time, respectively on All Saints' Day 1408 and Pentecost 1409. Gerson asks which of the three assemblies is to be regarded as authentic, that is, lawful and authoritative. His answer is: the Council of Pisa. Why? In the first place, because neither Pope had won the consent of the universal Church for his assembly. In the second place, because the whole of Christendom has adhered to the view, for as long as the Schism had endured, that a council called jointly by both parties might be regarded as representative by the entire Church.[28] He adds that every believer is obliged to consider the assembly at Pisa 'valid', 'sufficient' and 'authentic'.[29]

The whole of the eleventh article is devoted to proving the legitimacy of the Council and demonstrating that the *ecclesia congregata* has the right to compel the two pretenders to attend.[30] Those who do not know Gerson will be surprised to discover how cautiously he expresses himself, how carefully he respects the fundamental hierarchical structure of the Church. For example, he does not admit that the assembled Church has the power of jurisdiction over the Pope.[31] He only believes that the Church, and more specifically the

---

26 *De auctoritate concilii*, art. 9 concl. 9 (Gl. 6, 119): 'in sacratissima illa conventione in Martio celebranda, in qua tractabitur de fide aut statu universalis ecclesiae, debent recipi omnes christiani catholici volentes interesse.'

27 *De auctoritate concilii*, art. 9 concl. 7 (Gl. 6, 119): 'officiarii [concilii] in exercitio sui officii percipiunt Deum inspirantem aut operantem per eos.'

28 *De auctoritate concilii*, a. 10 concl. 2 (Gl. 6, 120): 'tota christianitas asseruit et tenuit per xxxi annos quod vocatio solemnis fidelium generaliter, ad faciendum aliquid universalem Ecclesiam tangens, *facta concorditer per ambos contendentes* aut aliquem amborum, gerit vices totius Ecclesiae catholicae.'—concl. 7: 'Quilibet christianus adultus habens usum rationis tenetur credere de necessitate salutis quod *universalis Ecclesia ex ambabus obedientiis* potest rite et canonice congregari, duobus contendentibus ex malitia se opponentibus aut negligentibus.'

29 *De auctoritate concilii*, art. 10, especially concl. 9 (Gl. 6, 121): 'tenetur quilibet fidelis... assentire sub poenae aeternae damnationis, quod conventio in Martio celebranda... est valida, sufficiens et authentica ad terminandum hoc pestiferum schisma.'

30 *De auctoritate concilii*, art. 11 concl. 3 (Gl. 6, 121): 'licet verus Christi vicarius inter mortales homines non habeat aliquos vel aliquem superiorem, citatus tamen per ecclesiam catholicam aut aliquos vice eius, tenetur comparere.'

31 *De auctoritate concilii*, art. 11 concl. 4 (Gl. 6, 121): 'Ecclesia congregata non per modum praelationis aut ordinaris iurisdictionis supra papam inquirit de eo an sit intrusus sive non.'

cardinals, has a right to subject the legal title of the two rivals to closer scrutiny.[32] Its full powers in this respect may be compared with those which it possesses with regard to an heretical Pope, whom it may call to account and compel to resign. On the same grounds, the two contenders, suspected of *intrusio* as they were, ought to appear before the forum of the Church and resign their authority into its hands.[33] As far as this resignation is concerned, he warns (for he had learned from recent history) that the council must not be content merely to extract a declaration from the Popes that they are willing to resign; they must actually do so, and that was what France had been trying to bring about by her declaration of neutrality. If the Popes refuse to resign they prove themselves schismatics.[34]

Finally Gerson goes briefly into the question of why both Popes must in fact be considered heretics, even if they do not proclaim any opinions at odds with the dogma of the Church. This last was the criterion employed by some canonists, who would not declare a Pope a heretic until he had shown himself a follower of a previously condemned heresy, for example by preaching Arianism.[35] In the context of these canonist debates on the case of an heretical Pope, the question had soon been posed: what was the Church to do if the actions or omissions of a Vicar of Christ threatened its welfare; and what was to be done if he was guilty of immorality or *pertinacia*? Many canonists, especially Johannes Teutonicus in his *Glossa ordinaria*, defended the view that in cases of this sort a Pope could be condemned.[36] Gerson certainly will have had arguments of this nature in mind when he formulated the following thesis:

---

[32] *De auctoritate concilii*, art. 11 concl. 8 (Gl. 6, 121): 'sine iurisdictione super duos contendentes, saltem super illum ex eis qui est Christi vicarius, domini cardinales utriusque partis potuerunt ambos contendentes citare ad videndum de titulo eorum.'

[33] *De auctoritate concilii*, art. 11 concl. 2, 6 (Gl. 6, 121).

[34] *De auctoritate concilii*, art. 11, concl. 1-5 (Gl. 6, 122).

[35] See Tierney, 'Ockham, the Conciliar Theory and the Canonists', in *JHI* XV (1954) 40-71.

[36] Johannes Teutonicus, *Glossa* ad D. 40 c. 6 (ed. Romae 1584, 185): 'Sed quare [papa] non potest accusari de alio crimine? Ponamus quod notorium sit crimen eius vel per confessionem vel facti evidentiam. Quare non accusatur vel de crimine simoniae, vel adulterii, etiam cum admonetur, incorrigibilis est et scandalizatur ecclesia per factum eius? Certe credo quod si notorium est crimen eius quandocumque, et inde scandalizatur ecclesia, et incorrigibilis sit, quod inde potest accusari. Nam contumacia dicitur haeresis.'

> Sancte et iuste ex actibus exterioribus potest [sc. papa] convinci et condemnari in foro publico ecclesiae tamquam haereticus, sine hoc quod mentaliter sit talis aut vocaliter se esse talem confiteatur.[37]

He could feel confident of support from Pierre d'Ailly, who had defended the same thesis in a balanced exposition years earlier.[38]

Much of what Gerson had defended in such lapidary theses in the *De auctoritate concilii* was to be elaborated in his *Propositio coram Anglicis*, given on behalf of the University of Paris before the English delegation on 29 January 1409.[39] The fourth consideration of this sermon is of special interest to us, because it offers a fine example, more detailed than in any of his other writings, of his deep rooted conviction of the hierarchical structure of the *corpus mysticum*.[40]

Gerson aptly chose as his text Hosea, 1:11, 'Then the people of Judah and of Israel shall be reunited and withdraw from the land; for great shall be the day of Jezreel.' Applying the Aristotelian division into four causes to these words of the prophet, he argued that the causes of unity were: the *perfectibilitas* of the Church – *causa materialis*; its *ordinabilitas*, by virtue of which it desires to be placed under a single head – *causa finalis*; its *intelligibilitas*, which leads it to interpret laws according to the standard of fairness – *causa efficiens*; and finally its innate *foecunditas*, which makes it strive for self-preservation – *causa formalis*. These distinctions are illustrated in more detail in four *considerationes*.

1. Just as *materia* seeks form, as the imperfect strives for perfection, as a woman yearns for a man, so the Church longs for unity – pseudo-Dionysus, Boëthius and Augustine made it clear how every-

---

37 *De auctoritate concilii*, art. 12 concl. 6 (Gl. 6, 122).

38 Pierre d'Ailly, *De materia concilii generalis* (ed. Oakley, 310): '... considerandum est quod licet Petrus a Paulo fuerit reprehensus et rationabiliter reprehensus [Gal. 2: 11], quia scilicet non recte ambulat ad veritatem evangelii, tamen nec ex textu vel ex Glossa apparet quod fuerit haereticus, nec erraverit errore haeresis. *Quare similiter papa in aliquibus casibus, ubi non est haeresis, potest reprehendi et corrigi.*'

39 Gl. 6, 125-35; Dupin II, 123-30.

40 For an analysis of the concept of the Church as mystical body, we refer to our Chapter X § 4.

thing in its being strove for unity.[41] Thus the Church, the kingdom of God, the *hierarchia subcelestis*, abhors division as being in conflict with its essential character. Its perfection and beauty are founded upon unity, for which Christ died, a unity which for more than thirty years has fallen into its opposite, under the rule of the two-headed monster of schism, to the scorn and the joy of the godless.[42]

2. The purpose of the Council of Pisa, is that the Church should place itself under one head and thus obey the command of Christ, who being Himself the *caput primarium* from whom all momentum, power and grace in the Church derive, after His Ascension gave all power in the Church to the Pope, the *caput secundarium*.[43] But now there are two rivals for the papal dignity, thereby bringing scandal on the first head of the Church. As in the days of Paul, the cry is heard: '*Ego sum Gregorii, ego Benedicti*' (cf. 1 Cor. 1:12). To bring this grievous situation to an end, *caritas* compels us to elect a third party to the papal dignity. This course is not open to objection from positive law, since the proposal meets all the requirements of morality.[44]

---

41 *Propositio facta coram Anglicis* (Gl. 6, 127); Dupin II, 124C). As apostles of unity Dionysius, Boëthius and Augustine are also named together in *Apparuit gratia Dei* (Gl. 5, 84; Dupin II, 69A), and in *Vivat Rex* (Gl. 7*, 1149; Dupin IV, 592D): 'Rien ne peust durer sans unité, comme declaire sainct Denis de France, ultimo cap. [XIII] De divinis nominibus; et Boecius De consolatione [cf. ed. Loeb, *De consolatione* III, 11^28-41; 104-108].'

42 *Propositio facta coram Anglicis* (Gl. 6, 127-8; Dupin II 125AB).

43 *Propositio facta coram Anglicis* (Gl. 6, 128-129; Dupin II, 125CD). Gerson had already made use of the distinction between *caput primarium* and *caput secundarium* in *De vita spirituali animae* (Gl. 3, 155; Dupin III, 36B); 'Porro ubi persona papae mortua esset aut morte corporali aut morte civili, quam pertinacia notoria et convicta in suo crimine destruente ecclesiam manifestat, concilium generale robur haberet ex sede apostolica et Christi approbatione qui in necessitate tali vellet nobis non deesse. Hoc forte intelligunt qui dicunt connexionem membrorum ecclesiae ad unum caput Christum essentialem esse et non ad eius vicarium papam, qui est caput secundarium, quoniam ipso destituto nihilominus manet unitas ecclesiae.' The distinction, which can also be found in Conrad of Gelnhausen (*Epistola concordiae*, ed. Bliemetzrieder, 129^10-41: *caput principale –caput secundarium*), was traditional; see Congar ('Aspects ecclésiologiques de la querelle entre mendiants et séculiers', *AHDLM* 36 (1961) 35-151 (42 n. 17), who refers to Innocent III, Gregory IX and Innocent V.

44 *Propositio coram Anglicis* (Gl. 6, 129; Dupin II, 126AB). Gerson informed his audience, as he often did–see his sermons *Omnia dedit* (Gl. 5, 411; Dupin III, 202); *Bonus pastor* (Gl. 5, 127; Dupin II 545A) and *Ambulate* (Gl. 5, 48; Dupin II, 208B)–that an *animalis homo* (1 Cor. 2:14) had appeared to him in meditation and asserted that the calling of a council '*non licebat, non decebat, non expediebat.*' The *animalis homo* was using almost the same Bernardine terminology–cf. Bernard of Clairvaux, *De consideratione* III. iv. 15: '*quid liceat,*

3. Gerson elaborates this argument and claims that by interpreting the laws according to their spirit, rather than their letter, the Church will be restored to unity. For how long has it suffered without a council, although men of wisdom have been pleading for one for years? Had not the University of Oxford proposed a council as long ago as 1395?[45] Even earlier, at the beginning of the Schism, Pierre d'Ailly had recommended this solution.[46] At the same time, Henry of Langenstein and Conrad of Gelnhausen made their pleas for such a meeting, while the University of Paris had urged the *via concilii* as a solution in its letter to the King.[47] In earlier times, there had been many who pressed for an assembly of 'Israel and Judah'. And now that two such famous universities as Paris and Oxford have joined forces to support it, does not the *via concilii* deserve our fullest confidence?

4. The great detail of the last consideration, which takes up almost half of the treatise, proves that it was the most important. Gerson chose as the starting point of his exposition of the *foecunditas* of the Church Paul's epistle to the Ephesians, 4: 1-6 and 11-16. From these texts he concluded that the unity of the Church and the richness of its hierarchy are founded upon a *semen divinum*, which is indissolubly linked with it and which, like blood in the human body, gives life to the parts that compose it.[48] The bonds between the Church and

---

quid deceat, quid expediat' – as Conrad of Gelnhausen, who in his *Epistola concordiae* (ed. Bliemetzrieder, 117) stated as his first conclusion 'quod pro remediando et de medio auferendo scismate moderno *expedit, potest et debeat* concilium generale convocari.' For the background of this distinction, see in particular Buisson, *Potestas und Caritas*, 72-3 , and index s.v. 'Massstäbe sittlichen Handelns'.

45 *Propositio facta coram Anglicis* (Gl. 6, 130; Dupin II, 126D): 'Ecce quid praeclara universitas Oxoniensis, unde sibi nequit satis congratulari, pridem ad hoc concilium petendum determinavit se et misit in Franciam, scio quia interfui dum proponeretur haec conclusio Compendii, sub hoc themate Joelis I: 14: «Vocate coetum, coadunate senes.» ' It concerns the meeting at Compiègne of 1th. July 1396, where the answer of the University of Oxford on the proposition of the University of Paris to settle the Schism by propagating the *via cessionis*, by William Scroop was presented to the King. See Valois, *Schisme* III, 78-9, and above Chapter II n. 24.

46 This, d'Ailly's *Oratio coram duce Andegavensi de dissidiis inter Urbanum et Clementem componendis*, given on 20 May 1381, has not yet been found. See Salembier, *Petrus de Alliaco*, XXIX; Denifle-Chatelain, *CUP* III, XVIII and 340; Valois, *Schisme* I, 340-2 and Bliemetzrieder, *Generalkonzil*, 86ff.

47 See Chapter I notes 37, 38 & 101.

48 *Propositio facta coram Anglicis* (Gl. 6, 131, Dupin II, 127B): 'Congregatio filiorum Israel et Juda pariter sumit suam efficaciam et virtutem a divino semine, quod per ecclesiasticum corpus tamquam sanguis vivificus diffusum est et radicaliter seu inseparabiliter insertum.'

Christ are formed by the Holy Spirit, which through the sacraments and other means of grace brings about harmony in the *corpus mysticum*. Compared with the Old Testament community, which had to do without the enormous power of the sacraments, the unity of the Church is both richer and closer, and also more manifold than that of the State; for unlike the latter it is founded not only on the law of nature but also on the law of God. That is also the reason why the Church has more legislation than the State.[49]

As in the *De auctoritate concilii* Gerson stresses once again that the Church does not derive its power to create the degrees of the hierarchy from within itself. Rather, the hierarchy is God-given. Once again he cites Henry of Langenstein in this context, though this time he gives a more moderate interpretation of Henry's view that the Church could have instituted the primacy if it had not already been instituted by Christ Himself.[50] Why? Probably, we think, because as Chancellor of the University of Paris he did not wish to attack Henry, who had been Vice-chancellor of the same *alma mater*, before an audience of Englishmen. Be this as it may, there was no alteration in the trend of Gerson's own argument, nor in his thesis that the Church could at all times be assured of the presence of the hierarchical functionaries and that consequently it will never be reduced to laymen or even to a woman.[51]

He makes a distinction between changing and permanent elements in the structure of the hierarchy, *partes fluentes* and *partes essentiales*, between office-holders and offices. *Papa fluit, papatus stabilis est.* In its changing parts the Church is composed of people,

---

[49] *Propositio facta coram Anglicis*, ver. 1, 2, 3 (Gl. 6, 131-3; Dupin II, 127C-8): 'congregatio ecclesiastica ad unum corpus Christum fit et agglutinatur per vinculum amorosum Spiritus Sancti, mediantibus qualitativis dispositionibus reddentibus in corpore mystico complexionalem harmoniam vivificam et decentem. Haec autem dona sunt virtutes theologicae, fides, spes et caritas; sunt etiam sacramenta ecclesiastica; sunt diversae divisiones gratiarum prout unicuique concessum est. *Hoc est semen in quo conveniunt ambae obedientiae.*'

[50] *Propositio facta coram Anglicis*, ver. 4 (Gl. 6, 132, Dupin II, 128AB): 'nec, ut opinor, voluisset unquam oppositum sentire... Henricus de Hassia, dum ponit quod Ecclesia posset sibi instituere summum pontificem, si non fuisset immediate constitutus a Christo. Addit enim quod hoc potuisset Ecclesia a Spiritu Sancto edocta et autorisata, quod est probabiliter sentiendum.' Cf. Kreuzer, *Heinrich von Langenstein*, 227-8.

[51] *Propositio facta coram Anglicis*, ver. 6 (Gl. 6, 132; Dupin II, 128B): 'Congregatio ecclesiastica ad unum caput Christum lege stante non remanebit in sola muliere, nec in solis laicis, sed erunt usque ad consummationem saeculi episcopi et sacerdotes aliqui fideles.'

who administer it in accordance with the laws which were given to it to ensure its continued existence.[52] Because this plenitude of power of the Church is of supernatural origin, nobody, not even the Pope, may make substantial alterations to the hierarchy, for example by abolishing the episcopate or the cardinalate.

The meaning of the distinction between Pope and papacy appears from what follows. Gerson goes on to explain that the *congregatio ecclesiastica* does not have the power to institute or abolish the papal dignity, *papatus*,[53] but that it can adopt a new method of electing the Pope, either by itself or through a council. It is also free to depose a regularly elected Pope, if it believes that will best serve its welfare. The implicit assumption is that a Pope is elected to protect the welfare of the Church (*causa finalis*) and that he must therefore be removed if his acts are in conflict with it.

> Ipse enim pastor instituitur pro utilitate gregis et dum praesidentia sua cedit in grave detrimentum, mercenarius reputandus est, immo latro, immo lupus rapax, si quaerit in praesidentia tam damnosa remanere.[54]

It cannot be claimed that this represents a completely new point of view, for Gerson had already written in a similar vein in his *Resumpta* of 1392 and other passages in his works make it clear that he allowed the welfare of the whole to prevail over the *potestas* of one. At most, we may notice two differences: firstly, his formulation had become sharper; and secondly, he names the general council as the institution which is to decide whether the exercise of his office by the Pope is in harmony with the welfare of the Church.

At the end he shows that a council may assemble without papal authority in certain cases. In this connection, he refers not only to the practice of the early Church but also to an argument drawn from corporative law.

---

[52] *Propositio facta coram Anglicis*, ver. 7 (Gl. 6, 132; Dupin II, 128C): 'congregatio ecclesiastica constituitur in suis partibus fluentibus... ministerio hominum, secundum legem primitus inditam et insitam ipsi corpore ecclesiastico, et prout ipsum habet in se semen vivum et efficax seipsum multiplicandi atque conservandi in successione specifica quantum ad partes fluentes, et in successione materiali quantum ad essentiales.'

[53] When Morrall (*Gerson*, 81) writes: 'The *corpus ecclesiasticum* cannot appoint or depose a *Pope*,' he shows that he has missed the point of Gerson's distinction.

[54] *Propositio facta coram Anglicis*, ver. 10 (Gl. 6, 133; Dupin II, 129A).

> Quaelibet congregatio libera, non subjecta tyrannidi, habet hanc facultatem seipsam congregandi. Patet in confraternitatibus et aliis multis conventionibus caritativis.[55]

There is thus no obstacle to an actual assembly. But can a council without the Pope act with authority? Gerson's answer is remarkably cautious but still affirmative. In an emergency, when the Pope falls into heresy, loses his reason, offends against morality or, as now, refuses to summon a council and thereby proves that he does not listen to the Church (Matt. 18: 15-17), then a council has the right to meet on its own initiative.

> In talibus et similibus casibus congregatio ecclesiastica sumit auctoritatem et virtutem seipsam uniendi ex divino semine per universum corpus suum diffuso.[56]

In his *De unitate ecclesiae*[57] as well, Gerson hoped to disarm the objections from positive law that might be raised against the summoning of the Council of Pisa. The treatise contains twelve considerations, with four more added to round off the case. It seems certain to us that the draft to which we referred above may be seen as a preparatory study for this work, and the considerations appended to it. These considerations are crammed with an avalanche of adages and rules, borrowed from the Scriptures, from philosophy, from canon and civil law, to which he refers with one and the same effect, i.e. to prove the insufficiency of positive law.[58]

> Unitas ecclesiae essentialis semper manet ad Christum sponsum suum.[59]

---

55 *Propositio facta coram Anglicis*, ver. 12 (Gl. 6, 133-4; Dupin II, 129C).

56 *Propositio facta coram Anglicis*, ver. 12 (Gl. 6, 134; Dupin II, 129D).

57 Gl. 6, 136-42; Dupin II, 113-18.

58 *Considerationes quattuor*, cons. 1 (Gl. 6, 142-5; Dupin II, 118-21): 'Unitas ecclesiae ligatur quadruplici lege, divina scilicet vel evangelica, naturali, canonica et civile, quarum duas extremas regulare necesse est per primas secundum epikeiam, id est bonam aequitatem. Hoc itaque ex traditionibus earumdem legum ultimarum convincitur, quarum annotationes aliquas pro minus eruditis et illiteratis placet adducere.' This is followed by 5 annotations, two concerning canon law, three concerning civil law, in which he refers to: (1) X. 4.14.8.; (2) Clem. preface; (3) Dig. 1.3.12.; (4) VI. reg. iuris 88, and Dig. 1.3.29.; (5) Dig. 1.3.25; VI. reg. iuris 61, and–with some pride, we feel, since it proved that for long he had had his doubts about a solution according to the rules of positive law–the very frequently cited example from Valerius Maximus *Facta et dicta memorabilia* (see Chapter VI n. 2). In cons. 2, he cites a long list of scriptural and philosophical rules to the same effect.

59 *De unitate* (Gl. 6, 137; Dupin II, 114C).

Gerson develops this thesis to claim that whenever the Church does not possess a vicar, either *de iure* or *de facto*, it is entitled by divine and natural law to gather together on its own initiative, in a council, to choose a new and undisputed head. The authoritative institution in this case is the college of cardinals, while the princes or any other Christians may lend their aid in the summoning of a council.[60]

The first argument for this thesis is drawn from natural law.

> Non enim habet corpus ecclesiae a Christo perfectissime stabilitum minus ius et robur ad procurationem suae unionis quam corpus aliud, civile mysticum vel naturale verum.[61]

He explains and asks: does not natural law say that a part must give itself for the whole? Well then, that means that the Popes must be guided by the advice of the council and must resign their position in the interest of their flock.[62]

As in his other works of this time, he again asserts that the Church is not so bound to the positive legal order that a general council can never assemble without a Pope. For the council disposes of sufficient authority to interpret the positive law by the standard of *epikie*.[63] Moreover, positive law was given to aid in building up the Church, and so whenever it is at odds with this purpose it must be abandoned. The right to judge such cases belongs in the first place to the theologians and in the second to the canonists.

---

[60] *De unitate* (Gl. 6. 137; Dupin II, 114D): 'et hoc non solum auctoritate dominorum cardinalium, sed etiam adiutorio et auxilio cuiuscumque principis vel alterius christiani.' Morrall (*Gerson*, 83) gives the following incorrect translation: 'It [i.e. the General Council] can do so not only without the authority of the Cardinals but even with the aid and help of any prince or any other Christian.' Cf. d'Ailly, *Propositiones utiles* (Dupin II, 113B): 'Pro sedando praesenti schismate absque auctoritate papae, immo ipso contradicente, potest auctoritate universalis ecclesiae generale concilium congregari; et non solum per dominos cardinales convocari, sed etiam in casu per quoscumque fideles, specialiter maiores et potentiores, qui vel auctoritativa potestate, vel charitativa admonitione scirent et possent ad executionem cooperari.'

[61] *De unitate* (Gl. 6, 137; Dupin II, 114D). Cf. *De vita spirituali animae*, cited above n. 43.

[62] *De unitate* (Gl. 6, 137-8; Dupin II 115AB): 'Unitas ecclesiae ad unum certum vicarium Christi... quodammodo accidentalis atque mutabilis est.' Cf. *Apparuit* (Gl. 5, 85; Dupin II, 70A): 'salus ecclesiae in solum Deum ordinatur absolute et essentialiter, et in hominem Christum de ordinata lege, sed accidentaliter ordinatur in papam mortalem.'

[63] Cf. Henry of Langenstein, *Epistola concilii pacis*, cap. 15 (Dupin II, 829A-35A, notably 831D-2A).

> Auctoritas vero doctrinaliter utendi epikeia residet principaliter apud peritos in theologia, quae est architectoria respectu aliarum [sc. scientiarum], et consequenter apud peritos in scientia iuris canonici et civilis.[64]

If both the rival Popes should refuse to appear at Pisa or should be unwilling to resign, the council must still proceed to elect a new Pope. Whoever rejects this rule of conduct – which the King too wishes to follow, as he had shown by his declaration of neutrality of 25 May 1407 – acts against the will of God.[65] And whoever believes, on the grounds of the legal maxim *spoliatus ante omnia debet restitui*, that no steps can be taken against either Pope until there has been a return to obedience, forgets that this maxim belongs to positive law rather than to divine or natural law.[66] Moreover, this rule is not unconditionally valid, for it is as inapplicable to heretics or schismatics as it is to *intrusi* or *furiosi*.[67]

As for the means to act against a recalcitrant Pope placed at the disposal of the Church by divine or natural law, they are many. The Church may, for example, declare its neutrality, suspend its obedience to him or deprive him of his administrative duties. If it does so it need not fear his sentences, for a Pope who will not submit to fraternal correction shows himself a heretic or schismatic. It is self-evident that in such cases the Church may assemble against his will, while it is also clear that, if necessary, it is justified in compelling him to resign or even taking his life. Whether the present Schism justifies such drastic measures is quite a different question. Gerson's intention was merely to summarise a number of possible methods of defence in general terms.[68]

---

64 *De unitate* (Gl. 6, 138; Dupin II, 115CD).

65 *De unitate* (Gl. 6, 139; Dupin II, 116B). Cf. Valois, *Schisme* III, 614.

66 *De unitate*, cons. 8 (Gl. 6, 39; Dupin II, 116C). Since both parties in common had decided to restore unity by the convocation of a council, he retracts what he had said in earlier years, i.e. that the *status quo ante* had to be restored (substraction had to be repared) before the convocation of a council could be envisaged. Cf. Chapter III n. 43, and Chapter V n. 13.

67 *De unitate* (Gl. 6, 139: Dupin II, 116CD). Cf. Conrad of Gelnhausen, *Epistola concordiae* (ed. Bliemetzrieder, 132^{20-6}), and Henry of Langenstein, *Epistola concilii pacis*, cap. 15 (Dupin II, 831A-2A).

68 A comparison of this statement with *De vita spir. animae*, lect. 4, corr. 14 (Gl. 3, 171-2; Dupin III, 48BD) shows that Gerson's reflection on the problem of excommunication did not proceed primarily from canon law but from theology, i.e. in discussion with the commentaries on *l.s.* IV d. 25.

The concluding passage of *De unitate* again makes clear how, for Gerson, the origin of the Schism was connected with the inadequate attention paid in the past to the reform of the Church. In a sense he regarded the Schism as God's punishment for this omission and vigorously urged that a start be made on this reformation, as soon as the Church once more possessed a single undisputed head, '*ne iusto Dei iudicio deterius quid contingat.*'[69]

***

Since Gerson was not present at the Council of Pisa, we may pass over its history briefly.[70] Convened at a rather late stage,[71] the Council opened on 25 March 1409, with a procession to the cathedral, where the discussions were to take place. Conforming to the rules for the representation of the universal Church in ecumenical councils observed since the IVth Lateran Council (1215), the participants at this assembly were numbered in the hundreds.[72] Besides the cardinals of both obediences, ten from Avignon and fourteen from Rome, on whose authority the Council had been summoned,

---

[69] *De unitate* (Gl. 6, 141-2; Dupin II, 118BC). Cf. the proposals by which the *Propositio facta coram Anglicis* is concluded (Gl. 6, 125; Dupin II, 122D): '9° fiat statim post electionem reformatio ecclesiae; notentur avisata', a reference to the *Avisata* of the University of Paris (cf. Valois, *Schisme* IV, 31, and *Quellen zur Kirchenreform* (ed. Miethke), 26) – See also the marginal annotation in ms. E (= BN lat. 14907) of *De unitate* (Gl. 6, 141 n. 4): 'Notentur avisata per dominum Cameracen[sem], et alia in concilio provincie R[emensis] ultimate celebrato', a reference to Gerson's sermon *Bonus pastor* (Gl. 5, 123-44; Dupin II, 542-58), which was held at the provincial synod of Rheims (29 April 1408). For a summary of this sermon and its effects, see Connolly, *John Gerson*, 95ff., and Jadart, *Jean de Gerson*, 180-8. Without good reason, M. Lieberman had some doubts about the historicity of the synod of Rheims ('Chronologie Gersonienne V', *Rom.* 79 (1958) 451 n. 1).

[70] The writer who has shown the greatest understanding of the council, in our opinion, was Bliemetzrieder, *Generalkonzil*, 294ff. and 306ff. – There is a selection from the *Acta* of the Council of Pisa in translation in Crowder, *Unity, Heresy, and Reform*, 58ff. See also Josef Lenzenweger, 'Von Pisa nach Konstanz', in: *Das Konzil von Konstanz*, 36-54.

[71] The letter of convocation dated 14 June 1408 is in Mansi, *Amplissima collectio* 27, 1161-75.

[72] A. Hauck, 'Die Rezeption und Umbildung der allgemeinen Synode im Mittelalter', *HV*, 10 (1907), 465-82; J. Gill, 'The Representation of the "universitas fidelium" in the Councils of the Conciliar Period', in: *Councils and Assemblies* (ed. G.J. Cuming & D. Baker), Studies in Church History 7), Leiden 1971, 167-95. List of participants in Mansi, *Amplissima collectio* 26, 1236-56.

they included a great many archbishops, bishops and abbots as well as innumerable doctors of theology and law. A great variety of nationalities was represented, but on this occasion this did not prevent unanimity. On the contrary, there was broad agreement between the various nations at the Council and little sign of partisan feeling.[73]

The chairmanship of the Council was entrusted to the elderly Guy de Malesec, former Bishop of Poitiers, to whom this honour fell as the only one of the higher prelates who owed his dignity to Pope Gregory XI, the last undisputed Pope before the Schism.

The council saw it as its first and most important task to remove Gregory and Benedict, unable and unwilling as they appeared to restore the unity of the Church. Steps to prepare for this were taken on the day after the opening of the Council and an impressive procedure was adopted. To be able to establish with certainty that both Popes had deliberately failed to attend, two cardinals, two archbishops, several doctors and a notary went to the doors of the cathedral, had them opened and in a loud voice summoned both rivals to come forward. When no answer came and no emissaries appeared, the procession returned and informed the Council of its findings. In the following weeks this formality was repeated several times, always without result, and during the fourth session, on 31 March, both Popes were accordingly pronounced obdurate.[74]

The activities of the Council were interrupted for the celebration of Easter, while the condemnation of the two rival Popes had to be postponed because of the appearance of ambassadors from Rupert of Bavaria, who – in a very circumstantial speech – challenged the legitimacy of the Council and proposed that Pope Gregory should be requested to suggest another place of assembly. These envoys were given such an unfriendly reception that they thought it wise to leave Pisa in haste. Petrus of Ancorano, a professor at Bologna, was instructed to refute the German accusations and acquitted himself of this task brilliantly.[75]

Charles Malatesta, prince of Rimini and a loyal protector of

---

[73] Valois, *Schisme* IV, 77: 'Ce qui frappe dans l'histoire de ce concile, c'est avant tout, l'unanimité de ses membres.'

[74] Valois, *Schisme* IV, 90; Salembier, *Le grand schisme*, 254.

[75] This refutation was read out at the 7th session on 4 May. It is printed in Mansi, *Amplissima collectio* 26, 367-94. Schwab (*Gerson*, 235-8) gave a good summary.

Gregory, was the next to come to the aid of his master. He too attempted to reconcile the cardinals with Gregory and induce them to hold the Council elsewhere, but they resisted this, appealing to the fact that both Benedict and Gregory had at the time appointed Pisa as the place of the meeting. It was also the city to which they had been summoned and it was not possible to change the convocation. Pierre d'Ailly and others were appointed by the Council to bring Malatesta over to their way of thinking, but did not manage to persuade him that instead of supporting Gregory, he should encourage and if necessary compel him to resign. On the contrary, Malatesta advised Gregory to go to Pistoia, while the Pope himself declared that he would never go to a city dependent on Florence. And how could he leave his loyal allies Rupert of Bavaria and Ladislas of Naples in the lurch?[76]

Meanwhile, on 24 April, the fifth session had heard the act of accusation, a document of 37 articles, in which the obstinacy, bad faith and refusal of the two Popes to honour their solemn promises, were listed in detail. The common initiative of the cardinals was further described as a deed legitimately undertaken in the interest of sacred unity. In the eighth session, the Council affirmed its title to be a regularly summoned and assembled gathering of the Church: it represented the universal Church and had the authority to pass judgement on both Popes.[77]

To verify the complaints made against Gregory and Benedict, the Council appointed a committee, which heard a great many witnesses in numerous sessions.[78] At the tenth and eleventh sessions, 22 and 23 May, the points of the accusation were read out once more, each time with a reference to the number of witnesses who confirmed them.[79] On the same day, a bull arrived from Pope Benedict, forbidding his cardinals to elect a new Pope. The Council felt that this bull was worth more than many statements from witnesses, for what more telling proof of obduracy could be imagined?[80]

At a special assembly on 28 May the doctors of theology present,

---

76 Bliemetzrieder, *Generalkonzil*, 297ff.
77 Mansi, *Amplissima collectio* 26, 1195-229.
78 Valois, *Schisme* IV, 91ff.
79 Mansi, *Amplissima collectio* 26, 398.
80 Salembier, *Le grand schisme*, 261.

at the request of the cardinals, were asked if Benedict and Gregory might be regarded as schismatics and heretics on the basis of the charges laid against them, and if so, whether they should be excommunicated. They answered this question in the affirmative.[81] Finally, the fifteenth session on 5 June proclaimed the definitive condemnation of Petrus de Luna and Angelo Corrario. Simon de Cramaud pronounced the sentence and declared that the holy and general council had found the charges against both Popes well founded. As notorious schismatics and obdurate heretics, who had scandalised the Church by their perjury and broken promises, they had shown themselves unworthy of their high dignity and were declared *ipso facto* deposed from their office and excluded from the Church by the will of God and in accordance with the holy *canones*. It was forbidden to show them any obedience or to support them in any way.[82]

On 15 June the twenty four cardinals withdrew to the archbishop's palace to elect a new Pope. On 26 June, after a conclave of ten days, at the instigation of Balthasar Cossa, they unanimously elected the Cardinal of Milan, Petrus Philarghi of Candia, who took the name of Alexander V. A Cretan of humble birth and already seventy years old, he belonged to the Franciscan order. He had begun his theological studies in Oxford and completed them in Paris (1378-81) where he had earned a high reputation as a professor and preacher. On his return to Lombardy, through his loyal support of Urban VI, he had won the confidence of the Duke of Milan, who had appointed him his son's tutor. In 1386 he was named Bishop of Piacenza, and later became Archbishop of Milan; as such he had been created a cardinal by Innocent VII. Under Gregory XII he had chosen the side of the dissident cardinals and had been zealous in working for the cause of the Council of Pisa. It must be said that the two sacred colleges could hardly have made a better choice than Petrus Philarghi, who was a man of the most amiable and generous character.[83]

After Alexander had been crowned on 7 July, he sent ambassadors to all the Christian princes to announce his election. In

---

81 Schwab, *Gerson*, 239 n. 2.

82 Hefele-Leclerq, *Histoire des Conciles* VII 1, 46ff.

83 Salembier, *Le grand schisme*, 264. On Alexander's theology: F. Ehrle, *Der Sentenzkommentar Peters von Candia des Pisaner Papstes Alexander V*, Münster i.W. 1925.

France, above all, the news was welcomed enthusiastically and was celebrated everywhere with processions of thanksgiving and ringing of bells. The final sessions of the council were presided over by the new Pope, whose first act was to ratify the decisions taken by the cardinals since they had released themselves from their obedience to their former masters. He combined the two sacred colleges and also announced that to continue the work of the Council of Pisa, there would be another assembly in 1412, which would make the reform of the Church its theme. The Council was closed on 7 August.

***

We return to Gerson. In the week before the coronation of Alexander V his course of lectures on the gospel of Mark had reached Mark 2:20: '*Venient autem dies cum auferetur ab eis sponsus*', a text which once more gave him the occasion to concern himself with ecclesiology. When they were expanded in later years these lectures developed into a treatise which, under the title *De auferibilitate sponsi ab ecclesia*,[84] was widely disseminated after 1415 and is still among the most famous, or for some the most notorious, works of Gerson. It consists of twenty 'geometrically arranged' considerations, which, as the author himself observed, should be read in conjunction with the *De unitate* and the *Considerationes* attached to that work.[85]

With reference to his text from Mark, Gerson establishes that the Bridegroom, Christ, will never be taken away from the Church in

---

[84] Gl. 3, 294-313; Dupin II, 209-24. Mgr. Glorieux in his 'L'Enseignement', 95ff., pointed out that this is the correct title, and not *De auferibilitate p a p a e ab ecclesia*. Glorieux' view is supported by the manuscripts. Cf. Combes, *La théologie mystique* I, 414 n. 36. Yet Gerson himself spoke in his *De pot. eccl.* (Gl. 6, 223; Dupin II, 236C) of *De auferibilitate papae*! For the dating see Schwab, *Gerson*, 231 n. 1, and Gl. 3, Introduction, xii 102: 'Date: 15 juin–8 juillet 1409. Sans doute retouché au Concile de Constance (20 avril 1415); ce jour-là, en effet, on le voit reporté par Franz de Dachau "in loco conventionis Gallice, hoc fuit ad Predicatores".' Cf. Chapter IX n. 137.–Nowhere in his writings did Gerson explicitly refer to Giles of Rome's *De renunciatione papae*, but one might rightly suppose with Scholz (*Publizistik*, 64 n. 17), that he knew it quite well and made a good use of it, in particular when he composed his *De auferibilitate*. We therefore consider it appropriate to make occasional references to this work.

[85] *De auferibilitate*, cons. 20 (Gl. 3, 313; Dupin II, 224D). See above n. 6.

the present dispensation. Christ is not *auferibilis*, and the mystical body of the Church will continue to exist until the end of time, by virtue of the lifegiving influence which is radiated upon it by its Head.[86] True, in the absolute sense a separation between Christ and the Church can be imagined, but only in so far as it would affect the created aspect of both.[87] Of more importance than this purely speculative consideration is the thesis that Christ, as the Bridegroom of the *ecclesia militans*, can free himself from an individual *viator*, whenever the latter dies or falls into sin, but that there can never be any suggestion of a collective separation.[88] The bond of grace that links Christ to the Church will never be broken, and it is unthinkable that the *influxus* from above can be blocked, for the Church possesses the promise of the Spirit, which is the Spirit of Christ, and which gives the mystical body life and form. How does he give the Church form? By exerting an influence on it through the various hierarchical offices and dignities, which he established at the same time as his Church. For if the Church is to endure until the end of time, it must, as a work of God, exist in a perfect form, for *Dei perfecta sunt opera* (Deut. 32:4). But 'perfect' means 'with all its parts'.

> Manebit ergo semper ecclesia cum suorum integritate et perfectione membrorum.[89]

---

[86] *De auferibilitate*, cons. 1 (Gl. 3, 294; Dupin II, 210AC): '... nemo concesserit quod absque capite valeat permanere corpus aliquod, vere vel mysticum. Sed ecclesiae corpus mysticum manere semper usque ad consummationem saeculi necesse est, lege stante. Mt. ultimo [28:20]. Hoc ergo fiet per vivificum influxum capitis in ipsum.' Cf. Conrad of Gelnhausen, *Epistola concordiae* (ed. Bliemetzrieder, 129$^{14-32}$): '[Ecclesia] acephala esse non potest, eo quod promisit se nobiscum fore omnibus diebus usque in consummationem seculi. Mt. ultimo [28: 20]... Christus dicitur caput ecclesiae, in quantum gracia persone singularis exuberans in eo... influit sensum... in ipsam ecclesiam... et in quantum Deus influit talem graciam capitis auctoritative. Racione cuius indefectibilis influxus huius capitis habet ecclesia privilegium indeviabilitatis.'

[87] *De auferibilitate*, cons. 2 (Gl. 3, 295; Dupin II, 210CD). Morrall (*Gerson*, 88) did not realise that the second consideration was of a speculative tendency, and that Gerson was reasoning 'de potestate absoluta' here, unlike cons. 1 , where he argued from the existing order, 'lege stante'.

[88] *De auferibilitate*, cons. 3 (Gl. 3, 295; Dupin II, 211A): 'haec omnis collectio nihil aliud est quam ecclesiastici corporis indissolublilis compago, quemadmodum dici solet totum nihil aliud esse quam suae partes simul sumptae. Sed haec compago manet in aeternum, lege stante.'

[89] *De auferibilitate*, cons. 5 (Gl. 3, 296; Dupin II, 211D).

From this thesis, which is highly characteristic of his ecclesiology, Gerson draws the conclusion that there will always remain in the Church a certain quantum of the gift of grace, sufficient for its edification and continued existence. Neither the hierarchical order nor the papal office, the episcopal dignity or the status of the priesthood shall ever be abandoned or disappear. As a good Aristotelian Gerson describes this hierarchical principle as a potential, a seed:

> Fuerunt [sc. status papalis etc.] enim primitus velut in quodam seminario vivifico positi in ecclesia per Christum, et postmodum crescente ecclesia, discretio talium magis innotuit, velut si stipes vineae se in folia et flores et ramos explicuerit.[90]

Thanks to this living seed the Church can continue from generation to generation and above all maintain its hierarchical order.[91] Likewise, this means that the Church, or a council as its representative, can choose a Pope and also establish the manner in which this is to be done. The Pope is thus not exclusively competent in this matter; if that were the case it could be imagined that through his death or unwillingness to take steps to choose a successor, the Church might be left without a *summus pontifex*, but this is not permitted, at least in this dispensation. It is undeniable that in fact the Popes themselves had consistently laid down the rules for their succession, but it was always rightly the custom for the Church to ratify these rules, either implicitly or explicitly.[92]

A division between Bridegroom and bride, in the sense that the Church might be reduced to a single woman, to all women, or only to laymen, is unthinkable, except in a new divine dispensation. For this would mean that the Church could do without the hierarchy and consequently the sacraments.

---

[90] *De auferibilitate*, cons. 5 (Gl. 3, 297; Dupin II, 212A).

[91] *De auferibilitate*, cons. 6 (Gl. 3, 297; Dupin II, 212A): 'Hoc autem semen quid aliud debet intellegi quam vis insita spiritualis et ars quaedam vivifica per universum corpus ecclesiae, per quam hierarchicus ordo potest usque in finem subsistere. Et ex his protinus infertur quod ecclesia vel concilium eam repraesentans potest instituere vel eligere vel designare summum pontificem in sacra sede Petri.'

[92] *De auferibilitate*, cons. 6 (Gl. 3, 297-8; Dupin II, 212BD): 'Quod si quis dixerit modos qui nunc observantur pro electione summi pontificis determinatos esse per summos pontificos, placet; sed ecclesia *consensu suo vero vel interpretativo* approbavit; aut in defectu qualem praediximus fas haberet immutare, et ita fas ut in contrarium nullius posset cuiuscumque pontificis auctoritas legem dare.'

> Patet hoc praesupponere quod sacerdos a non sacerdote, et episcopus a non episcopo nequit constituti; immo nec a tota multitudine laicorum aut mulierum simul congregata si per casum mortui essent omnes sacerdotes.[93]

Gerson believes that no one will disagree with this although in a certain letter – by which he again means the *Epistola concilii pacis* of Henry of Langenstein – the contrary seems to be asserted, if one interprets it in a disobliging sense. Also, Jerome's statement that the apostles chose Peter as head of the Church must not be interpreted to mean that the primacy was set up on their initiative, for in electing Peter as Pope they were merely obeying a command of Christ.[94]

This discussion of the origins of the primacy brings Gerson to the papal dignity; the focus of his treatise passes from the Head of the Church, Christ, to his Vicar, the Pope. First of all, he states that unlike the political order, which may be changed to suit time and place, the order of the Church, instituted by Christ, remains unalterably monarchical. He is very decided on this point, and claims for example that anyone who proclaims the opinion that there should be more Popes, or that every bishop is Pope in his own diocese, is guilty of a serious error; and if he should persist in it would deserve to be reckoned among the heretics, like Marsilius of Padua and others.[95] From the fact that the organisation of the State, as a human community, is subject to change, it follows that the Pope may not demand the maintenance of the positive legal order in the Church, in the same absolute way as the maintenance of the divine legal order. The Schism with the Greeks had originated in the neglect of this distinction.[96]

With his ninth consideration, in which he claims that a Pope may legitimately resign, Gerson confronts his readers with the central problem of the Western Schism.

---

93 *De auferibilitate*, cons. 7 (Gl. 3, 298; Dupin II, 213).

94 *De auferibilitate*, cons. 7 (Gl. 3, 298; Dupin II, 213AB).

95 *De auferibilitate*, cons. 8 (Gl. 3, 298-9; Dupin II, 213BC).

96 Cf. this whole passage with *De vita spir. animae* (Gl. 3, 153-4; Dupin III, 35C), where he gives a description of the different powers which can be distinguished in the papal office, and elucidates his thought by referring to the same examples (the thesis that 'every bishop is Pope in his own diocese', and the example of the Schism with the Greeks).

> Auferibilis est vicarius sponsus ecclesiae per voluntariam eius cessionem aut renunciationem a papatu.[97]

In earlier times, he continues, some had doubted whether the resignation of Pope Celestine V (1294) was lawful, on the grounds that the Pope had bound himself to the Church by an oath which might be called a spiritual marriage bond; and that he was, after all, instituted into his office by divine law. These doubts had been removed by the issue of the decretal which ruled that Celestine's resignation was lawful.[98] And that was the right decision, for it is clear 1. that an obligation under oath ceases whenever it comes into conflict with *salus*; and 2. that the bond of spiritual marriage between Pope and Church is not sacramental and therefore not unbreakable; and 3. that the actual Bridegroom of the Church can only be Christ, and others are merely his Vicars, who owe their office to human election, and may therefore be released from it by human intervention.[99]

If Christ's Vicar may separate himself from the Church, the reverse is also permissible: in certain cases the Church may free itself from the Pope and even deprive him of his office. The Church has the right to defend its interest; and if the Vicar of Christ should try to degrade or tyrannise over it, the Church may withdraw its obedience, for God gave it no office except for the sake of its strengthening and common advantage. The goal of the law is love (1 Tim. 1:5) and on this Christ founded the office of Pope, as is plain from John 21:17 'If you love me, tend my sheep.' Who will deny that it is possible to imagine cases in which, if the properly elected Vicar is not removed, this love will not be served, and instead of being built up the Church will be pulled down, torn apart instead of being bound

---

97 *De auferibilitate*, cons. 9 (Gl. 3, 299; Dupin II, 214A).

98 VI. I. 7. 1. He had already referred to this decretal in his early years, see Chapter I n. 70. Before explaining the decretal, he referred to a number of cases of legitimate resignation which were summed up by the jurists, probably having VI. I. 7. 1 in mind.

99 *De auferibilitate*, cons. 9 (Gl. 3, 299-300; Dupin II, 214AC). Cf. Giles of Rome, *De renunciatione*, cap. X pars 7 (ed. Rocaberti, 29a-30b) and cap. XIV (ed. Rocaberti, 38a): 'sed emittens votum, quod habebit curam de tam universali bono sicut est tota universalis ecclesia, si videat se insufficientem et manifeste cernat bonum publicum sub ipso languere, malefaceret si tale votum servaret. (With ref. to C. 22 q.4. c. 1.).' *Ibidem*, cap. XI (ed. Rocaberti, 34b): 'potestas enim papalis est in ecclesia a Deo, et ideo non potest unquam tolli potestas papalis secundum se... sed fit tamen opere creaturae, quia fit opere humano [sc. per electionem, PM], quod papalis potestas sit in hoc homine. Ideo ex opere humano fieri potest, quod talis potestas desinat esse in hoc homine.'

together? And why should the right of self-defence not belong to the Church as a whole, when every individual has the right to resist by force, and even to throw into the sea, any Pope who should dare to assault someone's life or chastity?[100]

These considerations bring Gerson to the thesis which we have already heard him defend, that a Pope may be deposed by a general council even when the latter has assembled against his will. As a rule, he argues, councils do indeed assemble on the authority of the Pope but in emergencies, when positive law fails to meet the case, it is justified to deviate from this rule and be guided by the principle of *epikie* and γνώμη. On whose authority is such an 'acephalous' council founded? On the authority of Christ, the Head of the Church, and also on the divine and natural law revealed by him, according to which–see Mark 2:23 and 1 Sam. 21:4-7–it is lawful to deviate from the rule in emergencies.[101]

In certain circumstances a council is justified in deposing a Pope, not merely *conciliative* but also *iudicialiter*, i.e. by its own authority, judicially. Gerson's evidence to support this thesis is again drawn from natural law, but this time he buttresses his argument using Aristotelian principles. Without denying that the Pope possesses *potestas auctoritativa* over all believers, he claims that the Vicar ought to exercise his power for the good of the Church and not for his own benefit. If he does not do so, he automatically forfeits his authority to the Church; and to that extent we may agree with Augustine when he says that the power of the keys is not given to the 'one' but to the 'unity'.[102] Moreover, according to Aristotle, every

---

[100] *De auferibilitate*, cons. 10 (Gl. 3, 300; Dupin II, 214C-15A). Cf. *De vita spir. animae*, lect. 3 (Gl. 3, 152-3; Dupin III, 34AB): '... papa de quo minus videretur si via facti vellet ignes spargere per domos christianorum..., aut mulieres violare, non per hoc desineret esse papa; attamen nulli dubium esse debet quin huic via facti ecclesia vel eius pars posset via facti demolitioni suorum bonorum et violationi uxorum resistere, etiam per incarcerationem realem papae ubi tunc aliter neque via iuris neque via facti obstare relictum est.' Much crasser examples of papal misconduct were summarised by Huguccio in his gloss on D. 40 c. 6 'nisi deprehendatur a fide devius', cited by Tierney, *Foundations*, Appendix I, 248-50.

[101] *De auferibilitate*, cons. 11 (Gl. 3, 300-1; Dupin II, 215BC). With many examples, probably borrowed from Conrad of Gelnhausen, *Epistola concordiae* (ed. Bliemetzrieder, 130[5]-31[11]), or Henry of Langenstein, *Epistola consilii pacis*, cap. 15 (Dupin II, 831A-2A).

[102] *De auferibilitate*, cons. 12 (Gl. 3, 301; Dupin II, 215D-16A): 'Nolumus tamen impugnare quin summus pontifex habeat potestatem regitivam et auctoritativam respectu omnium hominum quantum Christus voluit et cognovit expediens sibi dare pro exercendo eam, non pro se tantummodo, sed magis ad utilitatem ecclesiae, qualem aucto-

community has the right to warn an erring ruler and, if he proves incorrigible, to depose him.

> Et haec potestas inabdicabilis est a communitate libera... quanto magis hoc habebit ecclesia.[103]

Furthermore, history shows that the vicegerents of Christ have often been called on to justify their conduct to the Church. Nor was it out of humility, as some allege, that Symmachus or Marcellinus submitted to the judgement of the council, but because they were obliged to do so. The council, as representative of the Church, cannot meddle in the plenitude of power itself, but it can intervene in the way in which it is exercised, just as, in more general terms, the final verdict on faith and morals belongs to the Church. Hence also Augustine's statement: '*Ego evangelio non crederem, nisi me auctoritas ecclesiae commoveret*'.[104] Whoever decries the council, which represents the Church, therefore decries God, by whom it is led.[105]

If a council decides to depose a Pope, obviously it cannot deprive him of the power of consecration, for this is of a sacramental nature and as such is indestructible. But the council judges merely the *usus* and *exercitium* of a Pope's power of consecration, and derives its right to do so from the fact that the Pope received this power for the benefit of the Church. If he abuses his power of consecration, the council can take action against him, for example by withdrawing obedience. But are others apart from the Church or the council competent to make a decision on this matter? No, and certainly not when it is a question of general substraction. Even a more limited substraction may only be resolved upon in the most extreme cases, and then only when the entire Church has given its consent.[106] Caution is necessary, for as Aristotle pointed out, there is great danger in allowing subjects to grow accustomed to the idea of disobeying their ruler.[107]

---

ritatem non habet totum ecclesiae residuum nisi *unitive* quodammodo vel elective. Et ex ista verum est quod claves datae sunt nedum uni sed unitati.' Cf. Chapter IX n. 44.

103 *De auferibilitate*, cons. 12 (Gl. 3, 302; Dupin II, 216A). Probably Gerson refers to Arist., *Pol.* V 8 (1308b 31).

104 Cf. Augustine, *Contra ep. Manicheï*, 5, 6 (*ML* 42, 176).

105 *De auferibilitate*, cons. 12 (Gl. 3, 302; Dupin II, 216C).

106 Here Gerson seems to resume what he had defended in his *De concilio unius obedientiae*. See Chapter III n. 57.

107 *De auferibilitate*, cons. 14 (Gl. 3, 304-5; Dupin II, 217D-18C): 'Sed utrum haec obedientiae substractio ... valeat per alium quam per ecclesiam vel generale concilium?

In consideration 16 Gerson goes into detail on the question on which he had touched earlier:[108] should the deposition of the Pope by the Church or a council be regarded as a declarative or an authoritative act? In the first case the role allotted to the Church is more passive; the deposition is based on the conviction that a Pope who falls into a heresy which has already been condemned, be it avowed or secret, must be regarded *eo facto* as deposed. In the second case, it takes action via a legal procedure, which results in an authoritative decision that he is deposed.

The background of this problem lies in the canonist discussion of the case of an heretical Pope. Since we have already touched on this, we shall say no more here, but merely observe that Gerson showed himself an outspoken adherent of the authoritative view on the question of the deposition of a Pope. He was undoubtedly influenced in this by the misuse which many had made of the declarative view. Without naming the Gallicans, who, as we saw, repeatedly employed the declarative argument, he attacks in particular Wyclif and his spokesman Richard Fitzralph, better known as the Bishop of Armagh, *dominus Armacanus*.[109]

Forte videretur respondendum negative, praesertim si fiat sermo de substractione generali et auctoritativa, et quae liget omnes de ecclesia in hoc stare; secus est de substractione particulari quoad hos vel illos et quae non fertur auctoritative, sed vel doctrinaliter et insinuative, vel necessitatis quadam inductione.' This consideration is concluded by an implicit reference to the Petit affair, (which, one might suppose, Gerson added to his text in the years of Constance): 'Quanto magis erronea et damnanda est assertio quod licet unicuique subditorum mox ut aliquis est tyrannus, ipsum viis omnibus fraudulentis et dolosis sine quavis auctoritate vel declaratione iudiciaria morti tradere; praesertim si addat haec assertio quod tyrannus ille omnis est, qui non praeest ad utilitatem subditorum. Sed de hac re alibi, de qua viderint assertores.'

108 Cf. Chapter III n. 43. As early as 1397 he had defended the view that a prelate who fell into heresy might not be regarded as deposed *eo facto* (*Tradidit Jesum*, Gl. 5, 558; Dupin II, 593BC): 'etsi praelatus haereticus dignus est deponi, nihilominus non est eo facto depositus, sicut aliquis quantumcumque sit dignus episcopari non est eo facto episcopus, nisi per electionem divinam vel humanam manifestam.' Used as an argument against Wyclifites and Waldensians, e.g. in *An liceat* (Gl. 3, 286; Dupin II, 305D-6A).

109 See Katharine Walsh, *A fourteenth century Scholar and Primate. Richard FitzRalph, Avignon and Armagh*, Oxford 1981. We regret that the author of this very thorough work hardly discussed the reception given to Richard's oeuvre in France. When one reads the other passages in which Gerson referred to Richard–*Pax vobis* (Gl. 7*, 783; Dupin III, 1207B); *Vade in domum* (Gl. 5, 568, 570; Dupin III, 1296A, 1297B); *De vita contemplativa* (Gl. 3, 66; Dupin IV, 219D); *De vita spir. animae* (Gl. 3, 145; Dupin III, 28C); *Quomodo stabit regnum* (Gl. 7*, 989; Dupin II, 440B); *De nuptiis* (Gl. 6, 204; Dupin II, 375D)–it appears that he only had objections to his views on *dominium*, but thought highly of him as author of the *Summa de quaestionibus Armenorum*, and as defender of the rights of the secular clergy. (See Chapter X, n. 24.) The same seems to apply to Pierre d'Ailly, who attacked

For Fitzralph and Wyclif, who despite their extreme Augustinianism were rather more inclined to the Donatist way of thinking on this point, the legal title to the exercise of office lay in the personal holiness of the office-holder. The same might be said of lay rulers, whose *dominium* they held to be founded on *iustitia caritatis.* Gerson considers this doctrine highly undesirable in both Church and State. The whole hierarchical structure of the Church, he claims, would be undermined if an office were to be founded on the personal holiness of its holder or on his predestination. For then subjects would never know if they were to obey their leaders, as it is impossible to say whether anyone is holy or predestined. In fact, the contrary is truer, and we should act on the assumption that even a sinner may be a rightful king, bishop or priest. If the lawful tenure of an office is not based on the personal holiness of its holder, the lack of it forms no reason *eo facto* to resolve that he must be stripped of it. Hence it follows too that a minister of the Church, even if he is a heretic or a schismatic, cannot forfeit his office except by an authoritative decision of the Church.

> Dicamus ergo concludentes probabiliter quod sicut humana electio dat ius et titulum ad papalem dignitatem ... sic per humanam destitutionem perdit illam praesidentiam et non aliter, eo invito, sive sit haereticus sive sit schismaticus.[110]

Even though he never says so in so many words, Gerson in fact wanted the rules that applied to the deposition of bishops and priests to apply to the Pope as well.[111] The paradoxical thesis–previously only defended with reference to kings[112]–that the Church is

---

Richard's view of *dominium* in *Utrum Christi dono gerens* (Dupin I, 643A) and *Utrum indoctus* (Dupin I, 650A). For more details, see Oakley, *Political Thought*, index s.v. 'FitzRalph, Richard.'

110 *De auferibilitate*, cons. 16 (Gl. 3, 308; Dupin II, 221A).

111 Cf. *De auferibilitate*, cons. 15 (Gl. 3, 307; Dupin II, 219C): 'Advertamus tamen in hac materia [sc. renunciationis] quod oportet nos concedere consequenter... ad factum Celestini qui cessit papatum, quod papatus non dicat ordinem super sacerdotium vel episcopatum.' This is followed by a reference to Bonaventura *Comm. in l. s.* IV d. 26. See also *An liceat* (Gl. 6, 286; Dupin II, 305CD): '... non est verum quod papa eo facto quod cadit in haeresim praesertim latentem, sit depositus a papatu, sicut non est verum de aliis episcopis; peccatum haeresis, licet reddat unum praelatum dignum depositione, iuncta pertinacia, non tamen reddit eum depositum eo facto, sed requiritur humana dispositio.'

112 Cf. for example Petrus de Palude, *De causa immediata ecclesiasticae potestatis* (ed. Paris. 1506, fol. 22[vo a]): '[papa] potest deponere omnem [regem] non solum propter heresim aut schisma aut aliud crimen intolerabile in populo, sed etiam propter insuf-

justified in deposing a Pope as a heretic and schismatic even if he is not so in fact, – *etiam ubi, in casu ipse non est veraciter et mentaliter talis,*[113] – is not so much a sign of its author's radicalism as of the seriousness of the impasse from which he sought to escape. On this occasion, unlike his argument in the *De auctoritate concilii,*[114] Gerson tries to make his thesis acceptable by citing analogous cases from canon law. They include the case of a man who, knowing that excommunication is in store for him, refuses to answer charges made against him or to swear the oath demanded of him. In neither case must one rule out the possibility that he is a true Christian. Nonetheless, he is rightly to be condemned as a heretic, for the Church cannot see into his heart and must therefore rely on external evidence – his attitude – and on the statements of witnesses.[115]

A Pope may thus be deposed even if he is guiltless, but never without the most compelling reasons.

> Auferibilis est vicarius sponsus ecclesiae per ecclesiam, etiam sine culpa sua, quamvis non sine causa.[116]

This thesis too is defended by an appeal to several possible cases.[117]

> 1. We may envisage a case in which witnesses report the death of a Pope who has fallen into the hands of the Saracens. On the basis of this information preparations are made to elect a new Pope. But what if it should later prove that the report was false and the first Pope is released from captivity? Then there would be no alternative but to depose him.
> 2. Deposition is also justified in the event that Christ's vicar, for whatever cause, loses his reason.
> 3. Also if, after the election of a new Pope, all the cardinals should be struck down by death, so that the election cannot be proclaimed, then the Church is entitled to proceed to elect a new Pope.
> 4. It has a right to do so if the cardinals do not appear to be in a position to make their choice sufficiently credible.
> 5. If through malice, error or for some other reason, a rightly elected

---

ficientiam, utpote si quis ydiota sensu vel impotens viribus in regno praeesset et propter cuius insufficientiam regnum fidelium periclitaretur. Talis certum est quod mereretur deponi, quia bonum commune praeferendum est privato.'

[113] *De auferibilitate,* cons. 18 (Gl. 3, 310; Dupin II, 222A). Cf. above n. 38.

[114] See above n. 37 & 38.

[115] *De auferibilitate,* cons. 18 (Gl. 3, 310; Dupin II, 222AC).

[116] *De auferibilitate,* cons. 19 (Gl. 3, 310; Dupin II, 222D). Cf. *regula iuris* 23 at the end of VI: 'Sine culpa, nisi subsit causa, non est aliquis puniendus.'

[117] Cf. Conrad of Gelnhausen, *Epistola concordiae* (ed. Bliemetzrieder, 131^{12}-4^{1}; 136^{29}-7^{5}).

> Pope is not obeyed by his subjects and if it is certain that they will give obedience to another vicarius, then a new Pope should be elected. Gerson continues and gives as example: ut forte si Graeci vellent redire ad unitatem Ecclesiae dummodo tolleretur papa iam existens et novus rite canonice crearetur.
> 6. Finally the Church may depose a Pope who has given his oath to resign but will not abide by it, to the scandal of Christendom.[118]

Gerson does not deny that most of these cases occur very rarely but still he feels it right to list them, even if only to 'confound those who think they can decide everything by their written laws,'[119] – a clear hit at the canonists.

To round off this summary we will merely point out that one does Gerson a grievous injustice and shows one's ignorance of him if one ascribes his increasing radicalism in ecclesiastical policy to his supposed revolutionary nature. There is only one explanation for Gerson's growing radicalism and that is, that the unity of the Church was at stake. Now that all the signs suggested that the deplorable and scandalous Schism was nearing its end, every consideration that delayed or threatened this consummation had to be suppressed. The two-headed monster had raged long enough; it was high time for the Church to have a single head again. Once again we cite the 'revolutionary' Gerson, who concluded his *De auferibilitate* thus:

> Nec sufficit dicere: 'habemus papam Christum, sufficit ut credamus in eum'. Nam talis unio ad Christum etsi sit necessaria, non tamen usquequaque sufficit, ut in ea stemus, non procurando quantum in nobis est unionem alteram ad unum vicarium suum in terris, de quo constet Ecclesia.[120]

---

[118] *De auferibilitate*, cons. 19 (Gl. 3, 311; Dupin II, 222AB). Cf. Henry of Langenstein, *Epistola concilii pacis*, cap. 15 (Dupin II 830D-31A). – For a vigorous attack on Gerson's thesis and the cases cited by him in that connection, see Caietanus, *De comparatione*, cap. 28 (ed. Pollet, 190-4).

[119] *De auferibilitate*, cons. 19 (Gl. 3, 311; Dupin II, 223C).

[120] *De auferibilitate*, cons. 20 (Gl. 3, 312; Dupin II, 224). Probably a reminiscence of Jean de Varennes, Wyclif and Hus. The former, trying to comfort the people, had exclaimed in a sermon (Dupin I, 914A): 'Bonnes gens, ne vous desconfortez pas, car a pape ne poons faillir, car le doubs Jesus est nostre vraye Pape et Chief de l'Eglise.' Cf. Schwab, *Gerson*, 672, and Valois, *Schisme* IV, index s.v. 'Varennes (Jean de).' – Gerson denounced Hus, who, following Wyclif, had written: 'Quod solus Christus, et non papa, est caput Ecclesiae.' Cf. Gerson's letter (24 Sept. 1414) to Conrad de Vechte, Archbishop of Prague, inc. *Ceterum recepimus* (Gl. 2, 164, 11), to which he added a list of censured articles taken from Hus' *De ecclesia*.

CHAPTER SEVEN

FROM PISA TO THE COUNCIL OF CONSTANCE, 1409-1418

Ecclesia vel generale concilium eam repraesentans est regula qua Spiritu Sancto directa, tradita a Christo, ut quilibet cuiuscumque status etiam papalis existat, eam audire ac eidem obedire teneatur; alioquin habendus est ut ethnicus et publicanus (Mt. 18:17).

Gerson, *Ambulate* (Gl. 5, 44; Dupin II, 205A)

Most authors who have cast doubt on the legitimacy of the Council of Pisa have been unable to find anything to praise in its achievements. The tree was rotten, they argued, and must bear fruit after its kind. This explains the emphasis and rhetorical vehemence with which they have argued that the Council of Pisa only made the Schism even more complicated, since the Church now had to deal with three Popes who challenged one another's authority, instead of two.

We do not share this view, because it completely fails to do justice to the positive fact that after more than 30 years of pernicious Schism, the parties at Pisa at least managed to talk to each other again. Certainly they failed to achieve unity; Gregory XII and Benedict XIII could still count on supporters but compared to the much greater support given to Alexander V, and after his sudden death to John XXIII, this twofold fact grew less important and appeared to be no more than a residual problem.

One should realise that the Pope of Pisa was not recognised only by France, then the central nation of Christendom, but by England, Portugal, Bohemia, Prussia and several other territories in Germany and Italy. Only Naples, Poland, Bavaria and a few other states in Germany and Italy remained loyal to Gregory, while the obedience of Benedict after 1409 was reduced largely to Spain, Aragon and Scotland. The great majority had sided with Alexander V and for that reason alone, though still admitting the fact of the Schism, it seems to us that he had a better claim to represent the way forward for the Church than Pope Gregory XII and his much smaller following. Be this as it may, the rotten tree of Pisa bore fruit in the shape of the Council of Constance, and whatever else may be said of that, at least it managed to restore the unity of the Church in 1417.

***

Gerson's enthusiastic welcome for the election of the Pope of Pisa, Alexander V, is evident in the sermon, *Pax hominibus,*[1] which he gave on behalf of the University before the King and the magnates on 18 December 1409. He used the occasion to make a passionate plea for peace, not just peace in western christendom but peace with the Greeks as well. The Cretan origin of Pope Alexander seemed to augur well for this,[2] while hope also appeared to be justified by the intentions of the Byzantine Emperor Manuel Palaeologus, who had called on the western princes for aid in his struggle against the Turks a few years earlier.[3]

Gerson dilates at length on the need for reunion, starting from the axiom that the whole of humanity, in God's plan, forms a single body whose members ought to work together in unity to share in

---

[1] Gl. 7*, 763-78; Dupin II, 141-53. Cf. L. Mourin, 'L'Oeuvre oratoire de Jean Gerson et les manuscrits qui la contiennent', *ADHLMA* XV (1946) 225-61, and by the same author, *Gerson. Prédicateur français*, 196-202. – Mgr. Combes repeatedly denied Gerson's authorship of the sermon *Domine si in tempore hoc* (Gl. 5, 204-17; Dupin II, 131-41), first in *Jean de Montreuil*, 397 n. 1, and then, in more detail, in *La théologie mystique* I, 207-11, 412 B. We entirely agree with Combes's argument, and add that there must have been a good reason for the sermon to be omitted from the lists of Gerson's works made by Jean le Célestin and Jacques de Cérizy (Gl. 1, 22-33). The discrepancy which Buisson (*Potestas und Caritas*, 209) rightly detected between *Domine, si in tempore hoc* and the authentic sermon *Ambulate* (Gl. 5, 39-50; Dupin II, 201-9) is thus simply explained.

[2] *Pax hominibus* (Gl. 7*, 766, 773; Dupin II, 141A, 149D): 'Nous avons de present Pape un et certain, Pape qui est docteur excellent en theologie, par quoy il scet mieux que c'est de ceste division des Grecs et en quelz points elle gist. Il est Grec de nation; il est de grande experience et qui desja y a commise legacion. En oultre concil general se doit celebrer dedans trois ans ou pourront estre les Grecs. En surplus l'empereur des Grecs et les siens desirent tous cette union et ceste paix avec plusieurs autres bonnes circonstances qui pourront estre cy apres declarées ... Et ycy je forme et prens la premiere supposition et requeste que fait la fille du Roy. C'est que l'union ja commencée se parfait du tout tellement que les Latins obeissent à nostre vraye Pape Alexandre le Quint, car autrement ceste union des Grecs de laquelle nous parlons ne se pourroit si convenablement faire.'

[3] See Valois, *Schisme* IV, 111; John W. Barker, *Manuel II Palaeologus (1391-1425). A Study on late Byzantine Statesmanship.* New Brunswick 1969; Delaruelle, *L'Eglise au temps du Grand Schisme*, 160.

the good things of nature and the Spirit. He follows in the footsteps of Boëthius and pseudo-Dionysius by distinguishing between a natural, a civil and a theological goodness and unity, which refer respectively to natural human capacities, the political order and the ecclesiastical order; and points out that the last is brought into being by the Holy Spirit alone, whose gifts of grace are distributed by the Church. That Church includes all those who acknowledge the primacy of Peter. True, Christ is its actual Head, but he saw fit to appoint a second Head to preserve and distribute that grace. For that reason everyone must strive to ensure that obedience is shown to the Pope, by the Greeks as well, who wrongly assert that the Patriarch of Constantinople is the head of the Church.[4]

Clearly fearing that the Orthodox would demand that the western Church should recognise their Emperor as the universal lord of the world, Gerson goes on to argue that in temporal matters national diversity is legitimate.

> ce n'est point ainsy expedient que tous les hommes soient gouvernés et unis par samblables loys civiles et politiques commes ilz doivent estre gouvernés par une meisme foy et uns meismes articles et sacremens. Dit par exemple Aristote que selon la varieté des gens y convient varier les loys.[5]

One who wished to transfer this doctrine to the Church and claim that her laws too need to be adapted to the exigencies of time and place, would only be right so far as he spoke of the laws that regulated the worldly side of the government of the Church. For this side of the Church is not essential; only the evangelical law, which is one and unchangeable, is essential. Whoever denies this falls into the error of believing that each individual can gain salvation in his own sect.[6]

Gerson was no less offended by the view that to recognise the Pope as sovereign lord must necessarily do the princes an injustice.

---

[4] *Pax hominibus*, cons. 1-3 (Gl. 7*, 766-9; Dupin II, 144B-6B).

[5] *Pax hominibus*, cons. 4 (Gl. VII*, 769; Dupin II, 146B), with a reference to Aristotle, *Nic. Eth.* V, 10.

[6] *Pax hominibus*, cons. 4 (Gl. 7*, 769; Dupin II, 146C): '... qui n'auroit regart au gouvernement de saincte Esglise fors es decrez et decretales qui sont pour gouverner la juridiction ez possessions de l'Esglise et sa temperance, ceste objection auroit apparence. Mais ce n'est pas le principal que de ces droits, mais le principal est de la loy evangelique qui ne peut estre que une, sans variation pour quelconque variété de gens ou de païs.'

For the obedience shown to the princes can be freely given, albeit subject to the reservation that they do not transgress against the divine or natural order. Only when the princes abuse their power can their subjects withdraw their obedience.[7] Gerson is here defending what was later to be called the doctrine of *potestas indirecta papalis in temporalibus.*[8]

If the Pope takes decisions on the faith through a general council, everyone must obey them as decisions of the one, holy Catholic Church, led by the Holy Spirit and incapable of error.[9] The Greeks are therefore bound by the *filioque* clause. But if they wish to appeal to a general council on this question of dogma, they must not be branded as dogmatic heretics for that reason. It would be better to seek common ground for discussion without insisting on *filioque*, and for example to return to the state of things as it was before that doctrinal decision was taken. He gives as an example the bull *Unam sanctam* of Boniface VIII, which had been made a dead letter by his successor.[10]

Unlike the doctrinal pronouncements of the Church, papal decisions which do not concern matters of divine law in the strict sense are not universally valid. Those who realise this properly possess the key to reunion with the Greeks, for their separation grew out of certain usages which are not in conflict with divine law. And just as differences are permissible in the secular sphere, within the bounds of natural law, so there must be room for diversity in the Church. The key to success in attempts at reunion is to take the Scriptures as the basis on which to distinguish between the essential and the

---

[7] *Pax hominibus*, cons. 4 (Gl. 7*, 769-70; Dupin II, 146C-7). Gerson refers to Petrus Aureoli, by which he probably means his *Comm. in l.s.* II d. 44 a. 3: 'Utrum omnis potestas et principatus secularis sit a Deo' (ed. Romae 1605, 328-30, 330B): '... impeditur pax in vita communitatis hominum, quoniam ex modica causa imo iniusta conspicitur saepe principem insurgere contra pontificem, maxime ubi non est superior communis ambobus. Videmus etiam quod ex hoc potest principes in principatu suo tyrannizare, quia non est superior ad quem fieri possit appellatio. Unde ubi in civitate vel communitate secundum rectam rationem tota communitas potest consurgere ad eius correptionem vel, si incorruptibilis est, ad perpetuam depositionem.' Cf. the present author's *Jean Gerson et l'Assemblée de Vincennes*, 135-210.

[8] See Chapter IX n. 109.

[9] *Pax hominibus*, cons. 6 (Gl. 7*. 770-1; Dupin II, 147C-8).

[10] *Pax hominibus*, cons. 5 and 6 (Gl. 7*, 770, 771; Dupin II, 147B, 148A). In 1306 Pope Clement V rectified the bull *Unam sanctam* by issuing the breve *Meruit* (X 5.7.2). Cf. J.-F. Lemarignier, J. Gaudemet et Mgr. Guillaume Mollat, *Histoire des Institutions Françaises au Moyen Age III, Institutions Ecclésiastiques*, Paris 1962, 324-35 (335).

inessential. This is all the more necessary, since the Church has acquired a settled position in the world and has been endowed with countless temporal possessions and jurisdictions.

> ... qui ne scet discerner et congnoistre qui est droit divin ou seulement droit positif, il erre legierement en jugeant de l'un comme de l'autre, et nescit separare preciosum a vili (Jer. 15:19). Et encores est plus de necessité depuis la dotation de l'Esglise que par avant. Car n'est chose qui plus trouble la police de toute crestienté que de vouloir gouverner par une meisme maniere l'espirituauté des hommes et la temporalité, et reputer que temporalité soit proprement espirituauté. Je diz proprement, car tout ce qui est donné à saincte Eglise est aucunement espirituel par dedicacion et appropriacion ou attribucion.[11]

Gerson constantly emphasised the need to keep these spheres in the Church distinct and to realise what is central and what is secondary, spiritual and temporal in it, not only when it concerned the Western Schism but also, as here, when the Schism of East and West was at issue. For him the two schisms were related because he was convinced that it was ultimately one and the same enemy which had fomented the Western Schism and threatened reunion with the Greeks: the excessive power of positive law in the Church and the misplaced preoccupation with its temporal power and jurisdiction.[12]

All these considerations lead to four practical suggestions, which are offered to the King in the name of the University. First of all Gerson urged that embassies be sent to Spain, Aragon, Scotland and Hainault, the followers of Benedict XIII, to confirm and expand the unity of the western Church. This assumed that the internal strife in France would be composed.[13] The University was ready to prepare the ins and outs of this diplomatic mission with representatives of the royal council. The peace process ought also to be promoted by causing processions and sermons to be held in all parts of the kingdom, following the example set by the University.

---

[11] *Pax hominibus*, cons. 8 (Gl. 7*, 772; Dupin II, 149A). Cf. the present author's *Jean Gerson et l'assemblée de Vincennes*, 107-10.

[12] In *Dominus his opus*, cons. 19 (Gl. 5, 228; Dupin IV, 694C) he refers to this passage.

[13] *Pax hominibus*, cons. 9 (Gl. 7*, 774; Dupin II,150A): 'Si samble expedient que premierement en ce royaume tant entre seigneurs que entre chevaliers, bourgeois et clers, soit faicte union plus que faire se porra en oubliant les divisions passées, soit qu'elles soient venues à cause des deux dampnés contendens du papat, soit autrement.'

Finally, the preparation of the coming council ought to be vigorously taken in hand.[14]

> ... la quart et darniere supplication de la fille du Roy: c'est que tant envers nostre sainct Pere et tout le college des cardinalz, comme envers les Grecs, comme envers tous autres crestiens, on labeure que le besoignes principales et accessoires qui seront requises à celebrer ce concil soient telement disposées par avant que quant venra au fait n'y aist aucune division, debat ou confusion. Soit avisé bon ordre de celebrer ce concil et du lieu et du temps et des choses qui y seront à traitier, soit des libertés des esglises particulieres, soit de ce fait principal de la paix des Grecs, soit de la manière de soy avoir contre tous les mécréans à l'augmentation de crestienté et à l'honneur de Dieu et la salvation des ames.[15]

Apart from this sermon and apart from Gerson's forceful intervention in the Gorrell affair and the associated attack on Alexander's bull *Regnans in excelsis*,[16] which we shall discuss in another context, there is not much to report of his ecclesiastical policy in the years between Pisa and Constance. Much of his attention in these years was taken up by the disastrous struggle between the Burgundians, who had popular support and later chose the side of England, on the one hand, and the Armagnacs on the other, who found their supporters among the nobles and the higher clergy. Although not a typical Armagnac, Gerson was pursued with bitter hatred by the Burgundians until his death, because he never ceased to attack Jean Petit, the apologist of the murder of the Duke of Orléans, in his sermons and writings.[17] Even after Petit's death he did all he could to have Petit's theses condemned, because he thought them fatal to Christian morality and the political order. He had the satisfaction of seeing his zeal rewarded: on 23 February 1414 the Bishop of Paris issued a decree condemning Petit's theses.[18] Because the Duke of Burgundy did not submit to this decision and appealed first to the Pope and later to the Council of Constance, the struggle was

[14] *Pax hominibus*, cons. 9-12 (Gl. 7* , 773-7; Dupin II, 149C-53A).

[15] *Pax hominibus*, cons. 12 (Gl. 7*, 777; Dupin II, 153A). The council to which Gerson refers is not that of Constance, for that was not convoked until 1413, but that which had been decided on at Pisa.

[16] See the dossier 'Contre le pouvoir des mendiants' in Gl. 10, 30-9.

[17] Cf. Gl. 10, 164-284, 'Autour du tyrannicide'.

[18] Denifle-Chatelain, *Chartularium* IV, no. 2015, cf. 2033.

continued with great bitterness on both sides.[19] But this is to run ahead of events. Let us turn to the Council of Constance.

After Alexander V died at Bologna on 3 May 1410, less than a year after his election, the cardinals went into conclave and chose as his successor Balthasar Cossa, who took the name of John XXIII (1410-15). The newly elected Pope had had a chequered career. He came from a family that had prospered through its maritime activities, which were sometimes difficult to distinguish from piracy. In his youth Balthasar had been employed in the family business. Later he entered the service of the curia and rose rapidly under Boniface IX. His talents and interests lay in the field of administration rather than the spiritual sphere.[20]

One of the first acts of the new Pope was to implement a decision of the Council of Pisa and call a new Council in Rome in 1412, which was to devote itself to the reformation of the Church. This assembly was not very important; it had to be put off repeatedly and did not really get under way until 1413. Apart from condemning Wyclif, it took virtually no decisions, partly because of lack of interest, partly because of political circumstances, and partly too because of John's reluctance to set about reformation seriously.[21]

A more important event was the unanimous election of Sigismund of Hungary (1367-1437) as King of the Romans on 2 June 1411. (He did not become Holy Roman Emperor until 1434.) Although his personal inclination was to regard Gregory XII as the true Vicar of Christ, he soon sought contact with John XXIII, not only because John's obedience was so much greater than that of his rivals, but also because he needed the Pope's cooperation to realise his ambitious plans: to reunite the Church through a great council and thus reestablish peace in western Europe.[22] When Sigismund approached John, the Pope was no longer in Rome but at Rimini, where he had had to flee in haste because Ladislas of Naples, the protector of Gregory, had succeeded in making himself master of the Eternal City. In this predicament, aggravated by the lack of

[19] See now Walter Brandmüller, *Das Konzil von Konstanz 1414-1418* II, Paderborn 1997, 95-114.

[20] Josef Lenzenweger, 'Von Pisa nach Konstanz', in: *Das Konzil von Konstanz*, 45.

[21] Salembier, *Le grand schisme*, 281-90.

[22] Valois, *Schisme* IV, 229.

confidence in him shown by his cardinals, who now also included Pierre d'Ailly, Gilles Deschamps, Guillaume Fillastre and François Zabarella,[23] he was left with no choice but to agree to Sigismund's proposal and call a general council in his territory, at Constance. Not long after Sigismund himself had informed the Kings of France and England of these plans, Pope John issued the convocation bull *Ad pacem et exaltationem ecclesiae* on 9 December 1413.[24] In it he called on Christendom to appear at Constance on 1 November 1414 to reach a solution to three problems: 1. the restoration of the unity of the Church (*causa unionis*); 2. the condemnation of the errors of Wyclif and Hus (*causa fidei*); and 3. the reform of the Church in head and members (*causa reformationis*). In what follows we shall confine ourselves to the history of the *causa unionis*.[25]

John XXIII had been reluctant to come to Constance. He felt unsafe there and only decided to attend once he had assured himself of the support of a number of princes of the surrounding territories. For example, he appointed Frederick of Austria protector of the Roman Church, at an annual salary of 6,000 guilders; in return Frederick undertook to provide him with protection and military assistance in Constance. Well-furnished with funds from the curia, to help the decisions go his way, the Pope made a splendid entrance into Constance, accompanied by nine cardinals, a large number of prelates and secular lords, almost 600 in all and mostly from Italy.

In the weeks and months that followed, other high dignitaries flocked to Constance and it was not long before the imperial city had three patriarchs within its wall, twenty nine cardinals, thirty three archbishops, many bishops, abbots and doctors, and a multitude of lower clergy, secretaries etc. from all the domains of the western Church. When the Council was at full strength, the total number of persons who had poured into the city, according to the

---

[23] *DThC* I, 645 s.v. 'Ailly, (d') Pierre' (L. Salembier)

[24] Ulrich von Richental, *Chronik des Constanzer Concils 1414 bis 1418*, [ed.] Michael Richard Buck, Stuttgart 1882, 20-3.

[25] For the *causa reformationis* we refer to two important recent publications: *Quellen zur Kirchenreform im Zeitalter der grossen Konzilien des 15. Jahrhunderts.* I. Die Konzilien von Pisa (1409) und Konstanz (1414-1418) [ed.] Jürgen Miethke und Lorenz Weinrich, Darmstadt (1995), and Phillip H. Stump, *The Reforms of the Council of Constance (1414-1418)*, Leiden/New York/Cologne 1994. See also Brandmüller, *Das Konzil von Konstanz* II, 67-94.

chronicler Ulrich von Richental, was more than 72,000, about ten times its normal population, but that was a clear exaggeration.[26] Because the delegates from France were not appointed until November[27] and the Council was unwilling to take any decision without the French and King Sigismund, little happened in the last months of the year and it was spring before the important decisions were taken.

On the appointed day, 1 November 1414, Pope John celebrated a solemn mass in the cathedral of Constance. In his sermon he announced that the official opening of the Council would take place shortly, and so it did on 5 November. On that occasion he let it be known that the Council must be regarded as the continuation and confirmation of the work of the Council of Pisa. By that he meant that the two other pretenders to the papal throne, Benedict and Gregory, must be brought to resign and submit to him, preferably by argument but if necessary by force. In other words, he thought himself the true Vicar of Christ and felt that even to question the legitimacy of his papal dignity was a sign of godlessness. Before Pisa his supporters had reproached both contenders with upholding extremist '*potestas*' ideas and had argued for the Council as a protest against this; but now, after Pisa, they made use of the same absolutist argument to defend the legitimacy of John's papacy.[28]

As long as his supporters were in the majority John's efforts were successful but this was not to last for long, for a serious controversy soon arose. In mid-November legates of Gregory XII arrived in Constance and demanded the respect due to representatives of a Pope. They were vigorously opposed by the largely Italian supporters of John, who regarded him as the only true Pope. But by now numerous non-Italian delegates had arrived in Constance, who were less convinced of this and did not share the Italians' radicalism. Finally a compromise was found: although Gregory's representatives were forbidden to display the papal coat of arms above their lodgings, Gregory was promised that he would receive due honour as Pope if he chose to attend the Council.

---

[26] Hermann Tüchle, 'Die Stadt des Konzils und ihr Bischof,' in: *Das Konzil von Konstanz*, 55-66 (56).

[27] Martène et Durand, *Thesaurus* II, 1538.

[28] A. Franzen, 'Das Konzil der Einheit', in: *Das Konzil von Konstanz*, 79. We have made grateful use of this excellent essay in what follows.

This compromise solution was thanks largely to the work of Pierre d'Ailly. He had arrived with a large retinue of followers on 17 November, and as soon as he heard of the Italian plans, he, cardinal Guillaume Fillastre and other French prelates and doctors had submitted a counter-proposal. This stated that the Council of Constance formed the continuation of the Council of Pisa and that the two assemblies of the Church were therefore to be regarded as one. There could be no question of simply ratifying the decisions of 1409, as John wished, certainly not before real efforts had been made to achieve the reunification and reformation of the Church. For according to the decisions of Pisa, and by their oaths, the Pope and cardinals were bound to work for those goals.[29]

On 14 December d'Ailly presented a written submission to the Council, pressing for the rivals of John XXIII to be encouraged to resign voluntarily, instead of being threatened with force. If they should be willing to do so, then the Council could offer them honourable positions. But if they stubbornly continued to refuse, pressure should be put on their obediences to ensure that no successors were elected on their death.[30] Taken literally, the decrees of Pisa granted Pope John and his supporters the right to enforce unity with the sword. D'Ailly, however, had grave objections to such a course, and tried to weaken the decisions of 1409 by arguing that even a general council could err, not merely on facts but on points of law, because only the universal Church enjoyed the privilege of infallibility.[31] Gerson could never have brought himself to utter such an Ockhamist view, though he would have agreed with the eirenical intentions which had led d'Ailly to this much maligned thesis.

Meanwhile the discussion of the *causa fidei* had gone ahead. An

---

[29] Tschackert, *Peter von Ailli*, 186.

[30] Mansi, *Amplissima collectio* 27, 544sq.; Tschackert, *Peter von Alli*, 187.

[31] Mansi, *Amplissima collectio* 27, 547: 'Licet concilium Pisanum probabiliter credatur repraesentasse universalem ecclesiam et vices eius gessisse, quae a Spiritu Sancto regitur et errare non poterit, tamen propter hoc non est necessario concludendum, quod a quocumque fideli sit firmiter credendum, quod illud concilium errare non potuit, quum plura priora concilia fuerint generalia reputata, quae errasse leguntur. Nam secundum quosdam magnos doctores generale concilium potest errare non solum in facto sed etiam in iure et, quod magis est, in fide quia sola universalis ecclesia hoc habet privilegium, quod in fide errare non potest, iuxta illud Christi dictum Petro, non pro se nec personali sua fide, se pro fide universae ecclesiae: Petre, non deficiet fides tua [Luke 22:32].'

important question was: which body ought to condemn the heretical opinions of Wyclif? Who possessed the highest authority in matters of faith, the Pope or the general council? The supporters of John XXIII upheld the former's claim; d'Ailly the latter's. The cardinal argued that the Pope formed only a part of the Council and therefore could not take decisions in the name of the whole. A vigorous discussion broke out when d'Ailly asserted that the Council was above the Pope in this matter and might even have the right to depose him. John was told of these claims, and d'Ailly proposed to defend his thesis in writing in the presence of the assembled cardinals and doctors. He cited biblical arguments and also pointed out that the absolutist opinions of his opponents undermined the authority of the Council of Pisa and thus John's own position, for his election had been the result of a decision taken by that Council. Finally d'Ailly observed that one council possessed just as much power as another, so that if a Pope had been appointed by the Council of Pisa, he could be deposed by the Council of Constance.[32] This was too much for John and he decided in future to censor all motions submitted by the cardinals. As for d'Ailly himself, there was already a rumour that the Pope would try to bridle him.[33] D'Ailly escaped these threats thanks to the arrival of King Sigismund.

From Aachen, where he had just been crowned King of the Romans, and accompanied by his Queen and a very numerous retinue, Sigismund arrived by ship in Constance on Christmas Eve 1414. During the splendid midnight mass in the cathedral on 25 December, in which Sigismund took part with his entire train, the Pope handed him the dagger as a sign of his role as *advocatus ecclesiae* and adjured him to perform his high office for the good of the Church. D'Ailly too reminded him of his responsibility as *defensor fidei* and urged him to come to the aid of the Church like a new Constantine.

The King immediately took the initiative and demanded that the Council should first pronounce on the outstanding question of admitting the legates of Popes Gregory and Benedict to its deliberations. Opinions were divided, but with d'Ailly's support and thanks to the authority of Sigismund the Council decided on 4 January

---

[32] Tschackert, *Peter von Ailli* 190-3; d'Ailly, *De ecclesiae auctoritate* (Dupin II, 952A-3C).
[33] Valois, *Schisme* IV, 265.

1415 that they ought to be received with all the honour due to their dignity.[34] This decision clearly abandoned the foundations laid at Pisa and gave a sign that Constance was going to take a completely new look at the problem of the three Popes. That put an end to the precedence enjoyed up to that time by John XXIII, and in fact it decided that all three pretenders to the papacy were equally entitled and consequently ought to be treated equally. There were now, in theory, three ways to arrive at an undisputed head of the Church: either to allow fate to decide, or to force two Popes to step down, or to depose all three and unanimously elect a new one.[35]

In the meantime delegates of the two Popes had arrived in Constance. Gregory's legates paid their respects to King Sigismund on 25 January 1415 and used the occasion to declare that their master was ready to resign at a council summoned by the King and at a session over which he presided, provided that the other pretenders followed the same line. They protested vehemently against the pretensions of 'a certain person who is called John XXIII by some; who imagined that he was the chairman of the Council'.[36] The legates of Benedict, on the other hand, demanded a personal interview between King Sigismund and their master, whom they called one of the most notable personalities of his age,[37] and suggested Nice as the place for this meeting.

This was a critical moment, for now that the Council had been informed of the intentions of two of the three rivals, a decision on the future of John XXIII could not be put off. Given the tension between John and Sigismund, however, at first no one dared to make more than the most guarded proposals. Finally Cardinal Fillastre, after discussions with Pierre d'Ailly and the intervention of King Sigismund, ventured to make the following suggestion.[38] The only certain chance of peace, said the cardinal, was for John XXIII to abdicate voluntarily, as he was obliged to do if he wished to be regarded as the true shepherd of the Church. This was not an original idea, but it was inevitable. The Pope took it very badly and, as

---

34 Mansi, *Amplissima collectio* 27, 548-9.

35 Franzen, 'Das Konzil der Einheit', 81-2.

36 Delaruelle, *L'Eglise au temps du grand schisme*, 173.

37 Mansi, *Amplissima collectio* 27, 551.

38 A translation of Cardinal Fillastre's proposal was provided by Crowder (*Unity, Heresy and Reform*, 69-74).

one might expect, showed his bitterness towards Fillastre. Naturally, the Pope's numerous supporters also sharply rejected the proposal.[39]

Once the word 'resignation' had been mentioned, it continued to dominate the discussions. D'Ailly openly ranged himself behind this policy and used every effort to rebut the arguments of John's Italian followers. John himself, as soon as he realised that opinion was moving in favour of his resignation, tried to escape it by suggesting that the right to vote in the Council should be restricted to the higher prelates and abbots, who were to cast their votes individually. Since the number of non-Italian bishops and prelates at that moment was still quite small, this would be to his advantage, for he could be perfectly sure of his own following, which he was still reinforcing by liberal grants of benefices. The long-awaited arrival (31 January 1415) of the delegation from England made hardly any difference to this, for although this delegation made a spectacular entrance into Constance with no fewer than 800 horses in its train, there were only three prelates among it.[40]

Circumstances forced the abandonment of the system of individual voting in favour of that of voting by nations, as had been the practice at Pisa. It is not clear exactly how this came about. Valois remarked that 'le groupement par nations se fit, pour ainsi dire, de lui-même.'[41] According to Finke it was the result of an initiative of the Bishop of Salisbury, Robert Hallum, who had just arrived,[42] while John XXIII believed it was the outcome of Sigismund's machinations.[43] Whatever the reason, the fact is that when the second session of the Council began on 6 February the German and English nations jointly announced that they would not appear at the next session unless the system of individual voting was replaced by voting by nations. A day later the two French representatives present joined this camp.

John XXIII did everything he could to thwart the new system of

---

[39] Mansi, *Amplissima collectio* 27, 558; Valois, *Schisme* IV, 268ff.

[40] Franzen, 'Das Konzil der Einheit', 84; Delaruelle, *L'Eglise au temps du grand schisme*, 174-5.

[41] Valois, *Schisme* IV, 271.

[42] Finke, *Forschungen* ,29.

[43] Franzen, 'Das Konzil der Einheit', 84 n. 30 with reference to H.G. Peter, *Die Information Papst Johannes XXIII. und dessen Flucht aus Konstanz bis Schaffhausen*, Freiburg 1926, 77ff.

voting, for he realised that it would reduce the comfortable majority of votes on which he could count up to then to not more than a quarter of the total. Voting by nations, a system which originated in the universities, especially the faculty of letters, meant that the participants in the Council were now grouped in four, later five, nations (French, German, English, Italian, and later Spanish), which in the first instance met in their own assemblies to deliberate on the questions on the agenda. The national decisions were then submitted to plenary sessions of the Council for joint decisions to be taken.[44]

With the exception of the Italians, the other nations soon agreed to the proposal to urge John to abdicate. The Pope seemed to agree and on 16 February he had Cardinal Zabarella read out a declaration that he was ready to give up his rights in the interest of the peace of the Church if at least the notorious heretics Petrus de Luna (Benedict XIII) and Angelo Corrario (Gregory XII) in their turn abandoned their alleged claims to the papal tiara. At the same time he invited King Sigismund, the princes and all the participants in the Council to unite with him against the two *intrusi*, if they should refuse to resign.[45]

The champions of a policy of resignation by all three Popes gained significant reinforcements with the arrival on 21 February 1415 of thirteen delegates from the University of Paris,[46] Gerson among them; he acted as representative of the King, the University and the ecclesiastical province of Sens.[47] But before making known

[44] Contrary to what is stated by Morrall (*Gerson*, 96), d'Ailly was no supporter of the system of voting by nations. To avoid majority decisions being taken by the Italian delegates, he suggested that in the first instance votes should be taken by provinces of the Church, but did not win enough support for this. See his *De reformatione* (Dupin II 915C-16A). Cf. Tschackert, *Peter von Ailli*, 205ff., and Oakley, *Political Thought*, 152 n. 46, and Appendix VI, 348-9.

[45] Mansi, *Amplissima collectio* 27, 564.

[46] For accurate details of the date of arrival in Constance and the composition of the delegation see Combes, *La théologie mystique* I, 280 n. 8 and 9.

[47] Valois, *Schisme* IV, 273 n. 5 argues, referring to the register of the chapter of Notre-Dame for 8 January 1414 (last printed in Gl. 10, 517), that Gerson was not sent to Constance in this triple capacity. But see how he subscribed his *Responsio ad quaestionem* (Gl. 10, 253; Dupin V, 937B); 'Joannes etc., ... tamquam ambassiator christianissimi regis Francorum ac Universitatis Parisiensis et Ecclesiae Gallicanae pro provincia Senonensi ad hoc sacrum Concilium Constantiense.' In *Oportet haereses esse* (Gl. 5, 434; Dupin II, 348A) he calls himself an envoy of the King, and in *Dialogus apologeticus* (Gl. 6, 299; Dupin II, 388A) he makes Volucer say, with the agreement of Monicus: 'Scis nihilominus quod a christianissimo rege Francorum et a praeclarissima filia sua Universitate Pari-

their views the delegates first took their bearings. Two days after their arrival they were very courteously received by John XXIII, who declared that he had awaited them with impatience and spoke in very laudatory terms of the King of France and his 'daughter', the University of Paris. After their call on the Pope, they paid their respects to Sigismund. The King personally introduced them to the delegates of the German nation and pressed them to join in the efforts of the German and English nations, which they said they were willing to do.[48] Now that the delegates of the University of Paris agreed to the policy of abdication, the fate of John XXIII was sealed.

The French, German and English nations jointly drew up a formula of abdication. John accepted it at the second session of the Council (2 March 1415), for which King Sigismund thanked him on his knees.[49] The Pope issued a bull announcing his intention to the whole of Christendom.[50] But that was by no means enough, for when it came to deciding exactly how the triple abdication was to be effected, the difficulties began to accumulate. Sigismund proposed to go to Nice to open negotiations with Benedict and the King of Aragon. Because this would mean that Benedict would have to abdicate by proxy, John opposed this suggestion and offered to visit his rival in person. The Council in its turn was very unenthusiastic about this, because it feared that if John left the whole Council would fall apart.[51]

A completely new situation arose when John, disguised as a stable boy, left Constance secretly in the night of 20/21 March, and fled to Schaffhausen, which lay in the sphere of influence of the Duke of Austria, who was well-disposed to him and was waiting for him half way. In a letter to the King of France John announced that the pressure put on him by the Council of Constance, the unusual voting procedure, the plots against him and the way in which he had to submit to being watched by Sigismund's spies had led

---

siensi, immo et ab Ecclesia Gallicana pro provincia Senonensi delegatus extitit ad generale concilium ...' That Gerson acted as a delegate of the province of Sens is explained by the fact that, from Merovingian times till 1622, Paris was a suffragan diocese of Sens.

48 Valois, *Schisme* IV, 273ff.

49 Mansi, *Amplissima collectio* 27, 566.

50 Mansi, *Amplissima collectio* 27, 568.

51 Von der Hardt, *Constantiniense concilium* II, 389.

him to this deed. He told Sigismund that he had fled to Schaffhausen to be free to perform his promises there.[52]

When the bird had flown, the confusion in Constance was naturally enormous. It was not imagination to fear that the Council, deprived of its helmsman, would run aground. Many were overcome by confusion and panic. Merchants began to pack their bags and leave the city; some clerics followed their example.[53] Cardinals and lay dignitaries travelled to Schaffhausen to negotiate with John. Without waiting for their return, the representatives of the University of Paris decided to address a call to the Council, and entrusted this task to Gerson as their Chancellor. It was he, therefore, who addressed the Council on 23 March 1415 in his sermon *Ambulate dum lucem habetis*.[54] The short time he had had to prepare his sermon forced him to go back to theses he had previously developed in his works in defence of the Council of Pisa, especially *De auferibilitate sponsi* and *Propositio facta coram Anglicis*.[55]

The sermon *Ambulate* is to be regarded as a great attempt to maintain confidence in the good cause of the Council. He does not mention the confusion caused by John's flight, but argues all the more emphatically that the Council is a sacred assembly of the Church, willed by God and led by the Spirit; as such it is entitled to do everything necessary for the restoration of unity within the Church.

With the psalmist (Ps. 89: 7; Vg. 88:8) Gerson exclaims 'God is he who is greatly to be feared in the assembly of saints, and to be had in reverence of all them that are round about him'. And he continues:

> Let us fix our mind on that text for fear we stray too far afield. If I am not mistaken, we see there the fourfold cause of this holy synod, that is the efficient, formal, final and material cause. If anyone wants to know the efficient cause, that is clear enough. God, greatly to be feared. It is

---

52 Valois, *Schisme* IV, 285ff.

53 Connolly, *John Gerson*, 176.

54 Gl. 5, 39-50; Dupin II, 202-9. For this sermon see especially Buisson, *Potestas und Caritas*, 207-8 and Combes, *La théologie mystique* I, 282-92. Crowder (*Unity, Heresy and Reform*, 76-82) provided a fine translation of this sermon which we made use of in our text without further acknowledgement.

55 In a communication, probably added to the sermon later, Gerson refers to these works, which had become available in the meantime (*Ambulate*, Gl. 5, 45; Dupin II, 206AB): 'qui tractatus et propositio prodierunt in publicum, ut habeat qui voluerit fas est.'

by his impulse, mercy inspiration and influence that the Church is now brought together... Next, the formal cause is this very bringing together or association of the Council of holy men and modelled in the Holy Spirit, the form and *exemplar* of our acts, who is the bond and connection linking separate members of the saints, making them one ... If anyone goes further to ask for the final cause of this holy assembly, that surely is that God, greatly to be feared, should be glorified ... Finally, all those who are round about God can be taken as the material cause, of itself unformed. For just as men by falling into schism, as a result, deform in some way or other God's creation, since, according to Plato and Aristotle, man is the end of all things, so it is necessary that all things are modified according to the requirements of their end.[56]

After thus recalling the exalted foundation on which the Council rests, he returns to the *causa formalis*, the Holy Spirit, which leads him naturally to the Church. For it is the Spirit which gives life to the one, holy, Catholic and apostolic Church, of which the Creed speaks. To illustrate the nature and essence of the Church as a *corpus mysticum*, he continues with a lengthy citation from the fourth chapter of Paul's epistle to the Ephesians, and goes on to formulate twelve considerations which, as he says, are directly derived from the Creed and the teaching of the apostle.[57] With reference to the Church, he develops the following theses:

1. The unity of the Church consists in one head, Christ. It is bound fast together by the loving bond of the Holy Spirit by means of divine gifts, which render the constitution of the mystical body harmonious, lively and seemly, so as to undertake effectively the exercise of the spiritual aspects of life. 2. The unity of the Church consists in one secondary head, who is called Pontiff, Vicar of Christ. 3 By the life-giving seed (*semen*) instilled into it by the Holy Spirit the Church has the power and capacity to preserve itself in the integrity and unity of its parts. 4. The Church has in Christ a bridegroom who will never fail. Thus as the law stands, neither can Christ give the bride, his Church, a bill of divorce, nor the other way round. 5. The Church is not bound by the bond of marriage to the vicar of her indefectible bridegroom that they are unable to agree on a dissolution of the tie and give a bill of divorce.

On the authority, composition and conduct of a general council, his argument is as follows:

56 *Ambulate* (Gl. 5, 41-2; Dupin II, 203BC).
57 *Ambulate* (Gl. 5, 43; Dupin II, 204C).

> 6. The Church, or a general council representing it, is so regulated by the direction of the Holy Spirit under authority from Christ, that everyone of whatsoever rank, even papal, is obliged to hearken to it and obey it. If anyone does not, he is to be reckoned a gentile and a publican (Matt. 18:17). A general council can be described in this way: a general council is an assembly called under lawful authority at any place, drawn from every hierarchical rank of the whole catholic Church, none of the faithful who requires to be heard being excluded, for the wholesome discussion and ordering of those things which affect the proper regulation of the same Church in faith and morals. 7. When the Church or general council lays anything down concerning the regulation of the Church, the Pope is not superior to those laws, even positive laws. 8. Although the Church and general council cannot take away the Pope's plenitude of power, which has been granted by Christ supernaturally and of his mercy, however it can limit his use (*usus*) of it by known rules and laws for the edification of the Church. For it was on the Church's behalf that papal and other human authority was granted. 9. In many circumstances the Church or general council is able to assemble without the explicit consent or mandate of a Pope, even duly elected and alive... 10. If the Church or general council agrees on any other way or lays down that one way is to be accepted by the Pope to end schism, he is obliged to accept it. Thus he is obliged to resign, if that is the prevailing opinion ... 11. The Church or general council ought to be particularly dedicated to the prosecution of perfect unity, the eradication of errors and the correction of the erring, without acceptance of persons. Likewise to this: that the Church's hierarchical order of prelates and curates should be reformed from its seriously disturbed state to a likeness of God's heavenly hierarchy, and in conformity to rules instituted in early times.[58] 12. The Church has no more effective means to its own general reformation than to establish a continuous sequence of general councils, not forgetting the holding of provincial councils.[59]

The sermon *Ambulate*–full of reminiscences not only of the works to which he explicitly refers, but also of his earlier writings on the reformation of the Church,–contained all the elements needed to break through the impasse caused by the Pope's flight and to restore the Council's confidence in itself. While the cardinals went back and forth between Constance and Schaffhausen to negotiate with John on the procedure for his abdication, the Council held its third session on 26 March under the chairmanship of d'Ailly. It

---

[58] *Ambulate* (Gl. 5, 45; Dupin II, 206A): 'quod hierarchicus ordo ecclesiasticus praelatorum et curatorum multipliciter turbatus, reformetur ad similitudinem coelestis hierarchiae et conformiter ad regulas primitus institutas.'

[59] *Ambulate* (Gl. 5, 44-5; Dupin II, 205A-6B).

declared that the Council had not been terminated by the Pope's departure but had retained its 'integrity and authority'. It would not disperse before the Schism had been resolved and reformation in head and members completed, while it would only meet in another place if it itself judged that there was a solid reason to do so. Finally it decided that the participants might not leave Constance without the Council's permission.[60]

On the same day the cardinals returned from Schaffhausen with what they claimed was good news. John was willing to abdicate by proxy, although he had attached some conditions to this. In the first place, that his own personal safety should be guaranteed and King Sigismund should leave the Duke of Austria undisturbed; secondly that his cardinals should be free to visit him; thirdly that all members of the curia should rally to him. This last condition above all roused fury in Constance; all the more so when notices were fixed to the doors of the cathedral, summoning the members of the curia to leave for Schaffhausen within six days on pain of excommunication. This was seen as a sign that the Pope wished to break the Council and was demanding new discussions. In the meantime John did not wait for the arrival of royal troops, but withdrew to the castle of Laufenburg, not far from Basle.[61]

In these confused circumstances the Council held its fourth session on 31 March in the presence of Sigismund, the princes and the majority of the cardinals. It issued the decrees which were to raise such a storm in later times. In their amended and expanded versions, after the fifth session of 6 April, the most important were:

> Haec sancta synodus Constantiniensis generale concilium faciens, pro exstirpatione praesentis schismatis, et unione ac reformatione ecclesiae Dei in capite et membris fienda, ad laudem omnipotentis Dei in Spiritus sancto legitime congregata, ad consequendum facilius, securius, uberius et liberius unionem ac reformationem ecclesiae Dei ordinat, diffinit, statuit, decernit, et declarat, ut sequetur.
> Et primo declarat, quod ipsa in Spiritu sancto legitime congregata, generale concilium faciens, et ecclesiam catholicam militantem repraesentans, potestatem a Christo immediate habet, cui quilibet cuiuscumque status vel dignitatis, etiam si papalis exsistat, obedire tenetur in his quae pertinent ad fidem et exstirpationem dicti schismatis, ac generale reformationem dictae ecclesiae Dei in capite et in membris.

[60] *COD*, 383; Rel. de St.-Denys, *Chronique* V, 485.
[61] Valois, *Schisme* IV, 291ff.

> Item, declarat, quod quicumque cuiuscumque conditionis, status, dignitatis, etiam si papalis exsistat, qui mandatis, statutis seu ordinationibus, aut praeceptis huius sacrae synodi et cuiuscumque alterius concilii generalis legitime congregati, super praemissis, seu ad ea pertinentibus, factis, vel faciendis, obedire contumaciter contempserit, nisi respuerit, condignae poenitentiae subiiciatur, et debite puniatur, etiam ad alia iuris subsidia, si opus fuerit, recurrendo...[62]

While John fled again from Laufenburg to Breisach, close to the frontier with Burgundy, where he knew that he would be safe, the Council held its sixth session, devoted to determining the proxy procedure. John was to be invited to agree to this procedure within two days of the arrival of the delegates from the Council, and then to leave for Constance or for Ulm, Ravensburg or Basle, for further negotiations. On 19 April the envoys arrived at Breisach. After receiving them in audience five days later, the Pope tried to escape across the Rhine to Burgundy, and when he was prevented, to the castle of Neufchâteau which belonged to his protector, the Duke of Austria. The latter, however, now beginning to realise what it meant to be under a royal ban and to be attacked by powerful armies, withdrew his protection and not only prevented John from reaching Alsace but also refused to allow him to remain at Neufchâteau, on the pretext that the castle was under threat from the people of Basle. He had John escorted back to Breisach and from there, on 27 April, to Freiburg, a city which was under Sigismund's control.[63]

In the circumstances there was nothing left for the hunted and harassed Pope but to capitulate. He agreed to the procedure proposed but was unwilling to abdicate in fact until he was offered the chance to leave for Burgundy, Savoy or Venice, that is for a place where he could be sure of his freedom.[64] The Council, however, would not hear of this and prepared to take tough measures. At its seventh session (2 May) it decided to summon John before the

---

[62] The decree *Haec sancta* (sometimes referred to as *Sacrosancta)* in *COD*, 385-6 (385[15-34]). A translation can be found in Crowder (*Unity, Heresy and Reform*, 83). For the meaning of this decree we refer to two excellent articles, one by Brian Tierney, 'Hermeneutics and History. The Problem of Haec Sancta' (1969), the other by Walter Brandmüller, 'Besitzt das Konstanzer Dekret «Haec sancta» dogmatische Verbindlichkeit?' (1969).

[63] Valois, *Schisme* IV, 301-5.

[64] Valois, *Schisme* IV, 307.

Council on charges of heresy and simony.[65] The cardinals who had been kept out of the decision protested vehemently but in vain. Zabarella, Fillastre and d'Ailly were not even allowed to defend the Pope. After a committee had been named to hear the witnesses against John, the tenth session (14 May) deprived him of his power over the Church. In its first draft the charge contained no fewer than seventy four points, for even the sins of his youth were included in a spiteful attempt at completeness.[66] After a number of the accusations had been rejected as too fanciful, the twelfth session (29 May) heard judgment pronounced by the chairman of the sacred college, the Cardinal-Bishop of Ostia. John XXIII had lost the pontifical dignity forever and was once again Balthasar Cossa.[67] Two days later the accused was informed of the verdict and accepted it not only with resignation but with total submission.[68]

As for the two remaining pretenders, Benedict XIII and Gregory XII, the latter realised that it was time to abandon his dignity, of which hardly more than the name was left. At the fourteenth session (4 July) his procurator Malatesta informed the Council that Pope Gregory renounced his claims to the Holy See and confirmed the decisions of the Council of Constance. The Council declared the two obediences perpetually united and closed all the proceedings and censures pending against Gregory.[69] It allowed his clergy to retain their rights and dignities, while incorporating his cardinals into the same college as the others.[70] Now that this obstacle on the path to unity had been removed, every effort was concentrated on bringing Benedict XIII to submssion. King Sigismund himself was to conduct the negotiations with him and the King of Aragon, and set off on 18 July via Savoy for Perpignan, where he arrived on 19 September.[71]

As part of the accompanying festivities, on 21 July 1415, three days after Sigismund's departure, Gerson preached his famous sermon

---

65 Mansi, *Amplissima collectio* 27, 625.
66 Mansi, *Amplissima collectio* 27, 662-73; 684-96.
67 *COD*, 393-394.
68 Valois, *Schisme*, IV 311ff.
69 *COD*, 396-7.
70 Mansi, *Amplissima collectio* 27, 730ff.
71 Valois, *Schisme* IV, 333.

Prosperum iter faciat nobis.[72] In it he depicted the King's journey allegorically as the Church's path to unity and reformation. These noble goals, he argued, could only be reached by three ways: the way of peace, the way of truth and the way of virtue.

In his exposition of the way of peace he rests his case entirely on the decrees proclaimed during the fifth session. He declares that the Pope must conform to the decisions of the Council in all matters that concern faith, the Schism and reformation.[73] As in his *De auferibilitate sponsi*,[74] he also points out that the Council can depose a rightful Pope *etiam sine culpa sed non sine causa*.[75] Linking his argument to earlier pronouncements, he states that the Council can declare papal decisions void and in general is entitled to interpret, revise or even suspend positive legal rules, regardless of whether they have been issued by Popes or by councils, if it is in the interest of the unity of the Church.[76] In his opinion all these theses were wholly in accordance with the decree *Haec sancta*.

Just as the way of peace concerned the *causa unionis*, so the way of truth concerned the *causa fidei*. Again appealing to recent decrees, Gerson devotes this second part of his sermon to the powers of the Council to condemn heresies, referring in this context both to John XXIII and to Huss. In the third and most detailed section he turns to the *causa reformationis* and in particular defends the full power of the Council to abolish abuses in the Church. The Council's investigations into John's conduct had revealed not only that he was guilty of simony but that a Pope could not adopt such practices with impunity.

> Ex quo confunditur illa quorundam temeritas qui papam in collatione beneficiorum non posse committere simoniam vel disputabant vel definiebant.[77]

Just as in his sermon *Ambulate* a few months earlier, here again Gerson emphasises that a council, though it cannot assume the Pope's plenitude of power as such, certainly has the right to inter-

---

72 Gl. 5 , 471-80; Dupin II, 273-80.

73 *Prosperum iter* (Gl. 5, 474; Dupin II, 275C-6A).

74 See Chapter VI n. 114.

75 *Prosperum iter* (Gl. 5, 474-5; Dupin II, 276AB). Cf. Chapter VI notes 37 and 38.

76 *Prosperum iter* (Gl. 5, 475; Dupin II 276C).

77 *Prosperum iter* (Gl. 5, 477; Dupin II, 278C).

vene in the use (*usus*) he makes of it. If, for example, Popes refuse to hold general councils or if they deny lower prelates the opportunity to exercise their hierarchical functions, or if they trample on the decisions of earlier assemblies of the Church, a council has the right to take action against them; papal power must not, however, be so limited that the whole Church has to be consulted for each decision to be taken. 'General councils are less easy to organise nowadays than they were in ancient times, when everything was decided in common.'[78]

As for the structure of a general council, Gerson appeals to Aristotle, who in his *Politica* claimed that the best form of government was that which combined monarchy, aristocracy and democracy.[79] Now a general council is made up in this way,[80] and therefore possesses the authority of the Pope, albeit not in the same way as the Pope himself.

> ... in concilio papalis potestas includitur quamvis aliter haec potestas in papa, aliter in concilio; sicut aliter claves Petro traditae sunt, aliter ecclesiae. Unde concilium in multis quae papam respiciunt, habet auctoritatem conciliativam et dictativam, papa exercitativam et executivam.[81]

This does not mean that the council may assume all the hierarchical functions of the Church, that it may ordain and absolve, but that the guidelines it issues are binding. In other words, whoever resists the general council resists the Holy Spirit by which it is led.[82]

The powers of the council are not confined to the Church but extend to the State also. When wars rage and endanger Christendom, a council can legitimately intervene between the belligerents and compel them to seek a peaceful solution. Gerson says how delighted he was when he heard from King Sigismund himself of the King's intention, after ending the Schism, to attempt to mediate

---

[78] *Prosperum iter* (Gl. 5, 477-8; Dupin II, 278D-9A).

[79] Aristotle, *Pol.* IV, 11-12 (1295a25-1297a6).

[80] *Prosperum iter* (Gl. 5, 478-9; Dupin II, 279B): 'Esset vero omnium optima et saluberrima politia quae triplicem hanc bonam complecteretur, regalem, aristocratiam et timocratiam. Est autem concilium generale politia talis composita, habens suam directionem magis ex assistentia speciali Spiritus Sancti et promissione Iesu Christi quam ex natura vel humana sola industria. Hinc est illud quod praediximus, quod ipsum est saluberrima et efficacissima regula ad regimen totius ecclesiae tranquillum vel conservandum vel reformandum vel inveniendum, tamquam supremus et sufficiens legislator universalis et potens epiekes.' Cf. Chapter XII notes 83-5.

[81] *Prosperum iter* (Gl. 5, 479; Dupin II, 279C).

[82] *Prosperum iter* (Gl. 5, 479; Dupin II, 279D).

between the Kings of France and England and to negotiate a peace between Poland and the Teutonic Order.[83]

The sermon closes with a proposal for a general council to be called regularly every ten years:

> quoniam si tot et tam enormia discrimina provenerunt ecclesiae Dei dum cessatum est a conciliis generalibus, quanta demum erit salutaris utilitas ex frequentiori celebratione perspicuum est.[84]

That Benedict XIII was by no means inclined to accede to the request of Sigismund and to give up his papacy spontaneously, will not surprise those who recall his previous attitude. On the contrary, the Pope drew new courage from the abdication of his two rivals, for he could now be sure for the first time that he was the true Vicar of Christ not only *de iure* but also *de facto.* All he had to do was to bring nine tenths of Christendom back under his obedience! As a condition of his abdication he demanded: rejection of the decisions of Pisa, the closing of the Council of Constance and its reopening at a 'free' place, and finally his recognition as the legitimate Pope.[85]

It goes without saying that Sigismund rejected all these conditions. He and the envoys of the Council withdrew to Narbonne, where at the end of 1415, after all the efforts of the Spanish princes to bring Benedict to reason had proved fruitless, a treaty was negotiated which prepared the way for the reunion of Benedict's obedience with the Council. While all the censures imposed on him by John XXIII and Gregory XII were lifted, it was decided to leave Benedict's appointments in favour of his obedience in being. If his cardinals detached themselves from him, they would be regarded as true members of the sacred college. Finally it was agreed that the criminal proceedings against Benedict would be instituted before a new Pope was elected. This treaty was later to be confirmed by the Council.[86]

On 6 January 1416 King Ferdinand of Aragon withdrew from his obedience to Benedict, and was soon followed by the princes of Castile and Navarre. After the envoys of these rulers, the former

---

83 *Prosperum iter* (Gl. 5, 479; Dupin II, 279D).

84 *Prosperum iter* (Gl. 5, 480; Dupin II, 280B). The Council took further decisions on this in its thirty ninth session (9 October 1417). Cf. *COD*, 414-15. For earlier advocates of regular council meetings, see Brandmüller, *Das Konzil von Konstanz* II, 339ff.

85 Valois, *Schisme* IV, 332ff.

86 Mansi, *Amplissima collectio* 27, 827ff.; Schwab, *Gerson*, 524.

protectors of Benedict, had appeared in Constance, the proceedings for heresy were begun on 5 November 1416. The accusation was much shorter than that against John XXIII, only comprising twenty seven points, all of which concerned Benedict's refusal to abdicate.[87] On 28 November the stubborn old man was summoned to appear in person at Constance within 100 days, which he refused to do. In order to find grounds to condemn him as a heretic, the Council cited his bull of 1406, in which he had forbidden substraction on pain of excommunication. Gerson took on the sad task of proving the charge of heresy. In his *Libellus articulorum contra Petrum de Luna*[88] he drew both on this bull and on Benedict's treatise *De schismate*, written many years earlier.[89] Gerson's *Libellus* contains nothing new from the point of view of his ecclesiology.

On 26 July 1416 Cardinal Guillaume Fillastre was at long last able to tell the Council that Pope Benedict XIII, alias Petrus de Luna, had been condemned as a heretic and deposed. The Church had found him to be a perjurer, schismatic and heretic, for which reason he had *ipso iure* forfeited all his rights and dignities.[90] While heralds proclaimed the decision to the people of Constance, the participants in the Council sang a *Te Deum* at the close of the session to give thanks for the liberation of the Church.[91]

The deposition of Benedict XIII brought the Western Schism to an end; it remained only to seal the restoration of unity by electing a new Pope. Twenty three members of the sacred college took part in the election, reinforced by higher prelates, all representing the nations.[92] On 8 November Sigismund opened the conclave, which promised that it would choose a virtuous man with the necessary capacities to take in hand the reformation of the Church. Once the King had left the prelates alone, and soldiers were posted to guard the conclave chamber, the deliberations began. At first, while national preferences were still prominent, there were six candidates but this number was soon reduced to four. On 11 November, while

---

87 Mansi, *Amplissima collectio* 27, 968ff.

88 Gl. 6, 265-77; Dupin II, 293-302. Cf. Brandmüller, *Das Konzil von Konstanz* II, 259-76 (273).

89 See Chapter I n. 110.

90 *COD*, 413-14.

91 Valois, *Schisme* IV, 350ff.

92 Brandmüller, *Das Konzil von Konstanz* II, 358-70.

the King's procession passed by the windows of the chamber, the members finally agreed to vote for cardinal Otho Colonna. He took the name of Martin V.

The new Pope was forty nine years old and belonged to the famous family of the Colonna, which had already supplied numerous cardinals.[93] He had been appointed to the sacred college by Innocent VII and had detached himself from Innocent's successor Gregory XII in 1408 to join the other cardinals at Pisa in the election of Alexander V, and later in that of John XXIII. In Constance he had acted more than once as an arbiter and by avoiding accusations of partisanship had won the trust of both King Sigismund and his fellow cardinals. He had studied law for a time at Perugia but was not distinguished in the subject.[94]

Immediately after his coronation Martin V was confronted by the problem of reformation. We shall pass over this but briefly mention a controversy which brought him into conflict with Gerson, and which again hinged on the theme of tyrannicide. A German dominican, Johannes von Falkenberg, at the instigation of the Teutonic Order, had written a work against the King of Poland, defending the thesis that in certain circumstances it was lawful to kill a king and make war on his subjects. The case had been brought before the Council and investigated but, although the treatise was condemned to be burned, no further action was taken because the opposition was too strong. The Poles again brought the matter before the Council but the Pope, who was very much under the influence of the Teutonic Order, imposed silence on them.[95] When they then appealed to a future council the reply was that it was prohibited to appeal from a papal decision (10 May 1418).[96] The Poles

93 Salembier, *Le grand schisme*, 380 n.1

94 Valois, *Schisme* IV, 405.

95 Hefele-Leclercq, *Histoire des conciles* VII 1, 505ff., 567ff.

96 In his *Dialogus apologeticus* (Gl. 6, 302-3; Dupin II, 390D-1A) Gerson describes what happened in the consistory meeting where the prohibition was announced: '... pro parte dominorum Polonorum interiecta est tandem appellatio ad futurum Concilium; cui appellatione cum respondendum esset, lecta est, ut dicitur, in consistorio generali et publico quod ultimo Constantiae celebratum est minuta quaedam sub forma bullae, destruens, ut asserunt qui legerunt eam, fundamentale penitus robur nedum Pisani sed Constantiensis Concilii et eorum omnium quae in eis, praesertim super electione Summi Pontificis et intrusorum eiectione, attentata factave sunt. Continebat itaque in nullo casu licere appellationem a Papa facere, nec eius iudicium in causis fidei declinare, plane contra legem Dei decretaque Concilii.'

would not give up and insisted that Falkenberg's doctrine should be condemned, which caused a great uproar. In his *An liceat in causis fidei a papa appellare*[97] Gerson took up the cause of the Poles, for two reasons. First, because the principle for which they were arguing was in fact the same as that which he had championed in the Petit affair. Secondly, because if the Church were to acquiesce in the recent papal prohibition, all the recent gains would be nullified and free rein given to the fatal papal absolutism which, Gerson was convinced, was responsible not only for many of the abuses in the Church but above all for the outbreak and long continuance of the Schism.

***

If we survey Gerson's activities at the Council of Constance, so far as they concerned the *causa unionis*, it appears that in ecclesiastical policy and ecclesiology he had remained largely true to his principles since 1408. His sermons at the Council repeated the arguments he had developed more fully in the works written to prepare for and defend the Council of Pisa. This has allowed us to be brief in our account, the more so since in the second part of this book we shall devote a separate chapter to his most important ecclesiological treatise, *De potestate ecclesiastica et de origine iuris et legum*, which first saw the light during the Council of Constance.

---

[97] Gl. 6, 283-90; Dupin II, 303-8. See the fundamental article by Remigius Bäumer, 'Das Verbot der Konzilsappellation Martins V. in Konstanz', in: *Das Konzil von Konstanz*, 187-213. We remark in passing that Mgr. Combes cast doubt on Gerson's authorship of this work (*La théologie mystique* II, 282-6) in a gratuitous way, for it flew in the face of all the evidence. Gerson himself referred to it in his *De examinatione doctrinarum* (Gl. 9, 459; Dupin I, 8B). Moreover, the work is mentioned in *Annotatio I* (Gl. 1, 25 [45]), as well as in *Annotatio II* (Gl. 1, 31 [39]).

PART TWO

GERSON'S ECCLESIOLOGY

At vero respondent alii vero non ad originem ecclesiasticae potestatis positam a iure divino, tantumdem considerantes quantum respiciunt decretales cum glossis, allegationibus, concordantiis sine numero doctorum unius ad alterum... quod semper intellexit concilium generale auctoritatem summi pontificis exceptam esse in omni constitutione sua qualicumque... Benedictus autem Deus qui per hoc sacrosanctum Constantiense concilium... liberavit ecclesiam suam ab hac pestifera perniciosissimaque doctrina qua semper manente perseverasset semper schisma nutritum ab ea.

Gerson, *De potestate ecclesiastica* (Gl.6, 229; Dupin II, 240BC)

CHAPTER EIGHT

CHURCH AND LAW

> ... *legislatores ecclesiastici et civiles plerumque sua potestate et auctoritate noscuntur abuti, praesertim ecclesiastici illi qui quidquid ordinant, quidquid monent, quidquid praecipiunt, volunt pro divinis legibus haberi, par quoque robur habere per interminationem damnationis aeternae.*
>
> Gerson, *De vita spirituali animae* (Gl. 3, 161; Dupin III, 40CD)

As a rule the ecclesiological conceptions of late medieval theologians were heterogeneous in their composition, for they not only included biblical and theological elements – notably developed by Augustine and pseudo-Dionysius Areopagita –, but were also influenced by canon law, ethics and, not to be forgotten, the political philosophy of Aristotle. When we interpret such an ecclesiology we must be careful to take this peculiar structure into account, and indicate how far the various components fertilised each other, held each other in check, or merely co-existed peacefully.[1] Only in this way is it possible to give a reasonably adequate characterisation.

Without wishing to belittle the other elements in Gerson's ecclesiology, we feel that it is most important to isolate his views on the role of the law within the Church. We feel that his relationship to the law, and especially his discussion with the canonists, are clearly the creative part of his views on the Church, to the extent that it would be difficult to talk about his ecclesiology before he had defined his position with regard to the law, i.e. before the year 1402.

Before we deal with Gerson's legal views in more detail, we wish to remind the reader that the Church which Gerson knew was dominated by its juridical characteristics.[2] Even though the Church's

---

[1] This, for instance, is the case with Alvarez Pelayo's formless compilation *De planctu ecclesiae.*

[2] H.E. Feine, *Kirchliche Rechtsgeschichte* I, [2]Weimar 1954, 266-7: 'Sic [die Kirche] beherrscht alle Lebenden, vom Höchsten bis zum Niedrigsten, die Gesamtheit wie die Einzelnen mit Geboten und Verboten, eine geschlossene, streng geordnete und gegliederte Körperschaft mit eigenem, hochentwickeltem Recht, ein Staat über den Staaten, in dem die Laien die Regierten, die Geistlichen die Regierenden sind.' Cf. also the fine characterisation by Rudolph Sohm, *Das altkatholische Kirchenrecht*, München/-

development into a universal-juridical entity, led by an absolutist Vicar of Christ, had reached its culmination more than a century before Gerson, and although this entity had been under attack from various sides since 1300, the juridical element was still dominant in his day, as can be seen from the reign of Benedict XIII, a man completely obsessed by absolutist ideas. The Church had taken this path in the century and a half which separated the issue of Gratian's decree in 1140 from the completion of the *Corpus iuris canonici* in 1317. The role played by the science of canon law in this process can scarcely be exaggerated. Hardly a single aspect of the life of the Church had remained outside its reach. As Tierney says: 'Without a study of the canonists we can never hope to understand in all its complexity the polity of the medieval Church, for, to sketch in outline the growth of the *Corpus Iuris Canonici* from the appearance of Gratian's *Decretum* to the outbreak of the Great Schism is, in effect, to record the process by which the Church became a body politic, subject to one head and manifesting an external unity of organization.'[3]

One should realise that virtually all the important Popes of the period had been canonists.[4] Innocent III (1198-1216) had sat at the feet of the 'greatest of the decretalists' Huguccio (1210) and was himself a very capable canonist. His collection of the decretals, *Compilatio tertia*, became the basis of legal practice and teaching. Both Innocent's successors, Honorius III (1216-27) and Gregory IX (1227-41) made their reputations by issuing collections of decretals, that of Gregory being included in the *Corpus*. Innocent IV (1243-54) who occupied the papal throne not long afterwards, has been described by a modern author as 'the greatest lawyer that ever sat upon the chair of St. Peter.'[5] Boniface VIII, himself a competent canonist, gave instructions for the collection of his own decretals and those of other Popes, and this collection, under the name of *Liber sextus*, was added to the *Corpus*. His successor, Clement V (1305-14) gave his name to a collection of decretals called the *Clementinae*. Finally, the collection of John XXII (1316-34), even

Leipzig 1908, 582: 'Aus dem Körper Christi hat sich die Kirche in eine Körperschaft Christi verwandelt.'

[3] Tierney, *Foundations*, 14.

[4] For the following and in general for the rôle played by the canonists in the middle ages, see W. Ullmann, *Medieval Papalism*, London [1949].

[5] F.W. Maitland, cited by Tierney, *Foundations*, 259.

though, unlike the previously mentioned collections, it was not part of the *Corpus*, reveals clearly enough the juridical qualities of its compiler.

These few facts illustrate already the enormous opportunities which canonist scholarship enjoyed during this period of the history of the Church. The canonists themselves were well aware of their position. They were all too convinced that without them, the supremacy of the law in the Church could not be attained. In the encyclopaedia of the sciences, they gave pride of place to canon law, higher even than theology. Hostiensis, one of the most important canonists of the thirteenth century, called canon law the 'science of sciences':

> Haec scientia vere potest scientia scientiarum nuncupari. Nam si bene intelligatur, per eam tam temporalia quam spiritualia regi possunt. Ideo ab omnibus recipi debet et teneri.[6]

This statement, which is taken, as is the following, from Pierre d'Ailly, who clearly found it necessary to protest against them, is by no means unique. The canonist Guido de Baysio (d. 1313), author of a widely disseminated compilation called the *Rosarium*,[7] tells us that some canonists held that law originated with the creation of the world, and thus drew the conclusion that the science of law, being older than the other sciences, was to be considered as of higher value, and consequently as the most fitting to the status of a prelate.[8] These opinions of the canonists can be matched by the statements of other scholars on the importance of their subjects. In general, every scholar is inclined to exalt his own discipline as the highest. This is not only true of our days, but was true of the Middle Ages also. The logic textbook of the time, the *Summulae logicales* of Peter of Spain, the later Pope John XXI (1276-7) opens:

> Dialectica est ars artium et scientia scientiarum, ad omnium methodorum principia viam habens.[9]

---

6 Hostiensis, *Summa aurea*, (Lugduni 1588), prooemium (11). D'Ailly, *Utrum indoctus in iure divino possit iuste praeesse in ecclesiae regno*, Dupin I, 646-62 (655AB). See the art. mentioned below, n. 38.

7 Cf. *DDC* V, 1007-8 s.v. 'Guy de Baysio' (G. Mollat).

8 *Utrum indoctus*... (Dupin I, 655AB).

9 Peter of Spain, *Summulae logicales*, ed. I.M. Bochenski, [s.l. 1948], 1.

Theologians, as is well known, held just as exalted a view of their own study. Although, therefore, one can adduce parallels from other fields which seem to put the claims of the canonists in perspective, one must acknowledge that in practice it was the canonists who had the most right on their side. In the twelfth and thirteenth centuries the canonists had the best chance to put into practice the lofty opinions which they had of their science. They did not have to look far to find their influence and importance in the life of the Church confirmed, and their estimate of themselves was entirely in accordance with this.

1. *Theology and canon law*

What did the theologians think of the *de facto* supremacy of the canonists in the ecclesiastical system? How did they regard the relationship of their science, the *doctrina sacra*, with that of the canonists? Gerson's views on this point were quite pronounced, but we shall pass over them for a moment and first investigate how theologians who preceded him had described the relationship of the two sciences, and what opinions they had held of their canonist colleagues.

In the modern textbooks of canon law, for example in the influential *Commentarium Lovaniense in codicem iuris canonici* by the late Professor A. van Hove, the following observation is made concerning the distinction between theology, in the sense of dogmatic theology, and canon law:

> Theology is concerned with *credenda*, canon law with *agenda*. True, canon law can also concern itself with *credenda*, but from another angle. The task of theology is to deduce the Catholic truths from the sources of revelation; the results of theological study are taken over by the canonists, and serve as the starting point of their science. But as the Church is led not only by canon law, but much more by divine and natural law, it is necessary that canonists, in interpreting the decisions of the ecclesiastical law, should be constantly mindful of the results of theological enquiry, even though this is not the actual subject of their study.[10]

---

[10] A. von Hove, *Commentarium Lovaniense in codicem iuris canonici* I, I Prolegomena, Mechliniae/Romae 1928, 26.

This attitude has a long history, indeed it is as old as canon law itself. Originally, canon law was very closely related to theology, and was regarded as part of it. But from the middle of the twelfth century, and particularly under the influence of civil law, it developed into a separate science, and grew increasingly distinct from theology. As a result, the question arose as to how the two sciences were related to each other. The answer which the great scholastics gave to this question was influenced by Aristotle's encyclopaedic doctrine, his so called theory of subalternation, a doctrine which was introduced in theology notably by Thomas, and whose traces are still clearly to be seen in Van Hove's definition.

According to Aristotle, the various sciences stand in a certain order of precedence: there are higher and lower sciences, and what is the conclusion of an enquiry for one is the starting point for another. The physicist, for example, approaches his subject with principles borrowed from mathematics: the principles of physics are the conclusions of mathematics. Even though the physicist does not know the how and why–*propter quid*–of the results arrived at by the mathematician, he is justified in accepting them as the actual starting point–the *quia*–of his researches. On the basis of these considerations, Aristotle developed his encyclopaedic theory, by which a science came to be regarded as higher, in so far as its conclusions formed the starting point of a lower study.[11]

With the aid of this theory, the scholastics determined the relationship of canon law and theology. We shall give an example. Bonaventure states that there was a controversy among jurists over the question of the authority to excommunicate: some maintained that it was reserved for the bishops alone, but according to others, it belonged also to archpriests, archdeacons and abbots, while still others held that it was also within the power of the priests. He continues:

> sed licet in hac questione canonum sit dicere *quia*, tamen theologiae est dicere *propter quid*, tanquam scientiae superioris.[12]

Both his distinction between '*quia*' and '*propter quid*', and his use of the term *scientia superior* make it clear that the Bonaventure consid-

---

[11] M.-D. Chenu, *La théologie au XIII siècle*, ³Paris 1957, 71-5; Léon Baudry, *Lexique philosophique de Guillaume d'Ockham*, Paris [1958], 244-5 s.v. 'scientia subalternans'.

[12] *Comm. in lib. sent.* IV d. 18 p. II a. 1 q. 3 (ed. Quaracchi, IV, 488).

ered the relationship between theology and canon law in the Aristotelian subalternative sense. And so did the other scholastics, as can be seen, for instance, from Augustinus Triumphus, who in his *De potestate ecclesiastica* described most carefully the relationship of the two sciences:

> ... Yet theology and canonical science differ in their method of consideration in five ways. First, in that matters concerning the sacraments and other divine things and the morals of the faithful are determined by theology in a subtle way and *quasi propter quid*, yet also by that method which can be assigned in theology *propter quid*, but in canon law in a gross and positive manner and only *quia*. Second, in that these are determined by the theologian chiefly for the contemplation of truth, by the canonists chiefly on account of a legal case and the solution of the questions involved therein. Third, in that theologians deal chiefly with divine worship and things which concern the integrity of the faith of one God, while canonists are more concerned with the order of ministers and of ecclesiastical business pertaining to that worship. Fourth, in that by theology are determined canons how the pious shall be enriched and defended against the impious, in canon law the pious [actually] are enriched and defended against the impious. Fifth, in that matters are determined by the theologian more universally and in the forum of conscience, in which is tried the case between God and man, but by the canonist more particularly, making application to particular actions in the exterior forum of judgement where cases are tried between man and man.[13]

Now the question is: what did the theologians actually think of the canonists? Did the practice correspond to the harmonious order of the encyclopaedia, and did the canonists in fact confine themselves to the place allotted to them by the guardians of the *doctrina sacra*? In the current handbooks on the history of canon law—as far as the Middle Ages are concerned—these questions are rarely touched upon, and the same is true of general works on Church history. For the actual relationship of the two sciences one is almost entirely thrown back on a small number of articles and a few scattered remarks in the relevant literature.

While in Gratian's age theology and canon law were closely connected, and their practice even combined by the same person—for example, Rolandus Bandinelli, the later Pope Alexander III,

---

[13] We cite from Lynn Thorndike, *University records and life in the middle ages* (Norton paperback ed.) New York [1975], nr. 63, 161.

Omnebene, Gandulphus, Stephan of Tournai – the two disciplines began to go their separate ways in the thirteenth century. Breaking away from the guardianship of theology, canon law in this period underwent a process of emancipation and developed into an independent discipline. Indeed, within the rising universities, canon law came to be studied in its own faculties. The basis of this new development was, on the one hand, the Gregorian reform, with its claims to universal world dominion by the Pope, and, on the other, the rediscovery of Roman law, particularly of Justinian's *Digest*, about 1070. These were the decisive factors which initiated the process of recording and restructuring of the visible Church, resulting in its transformation into a strict juridical body.

Stephan Kuttner, in his Wimmer lectures, *Harmony from Dissonance*, gives an excellent description of how this process began and what its implications were for the canonists.[14] As he explains, it challenged them on three levels: the quest for harmony of the sources of law; the quest for harmony of ecclesiastical institutions; and the quest for harmony of the mystical body. By the latter he means the problem of perfecting in legal terms the interpenetration of spiritual and corporate entities, which he considers to be the essential hallmark distinguishing the Church from all other modes of social existence. In other words, it was the desire to reconstruct the Church into a *societas perfecta* which was the driving force for the canonists.

The means they used to realize their aims were borrowed from Roman imperial law. A new papal law – the *ius novum* – was thus created for the Church, and manifested itself in a rapidly increasing number of decretals, whose authority was declared to transcend the ecclesiastical *canones* of former times, according to the rule: '*decretalis praevalet canoni*.'[15] As we shall see, it was precisely this new development which was deeply resented by many theologians, who protested vehemently against it when they came into contact with the canonists, i.e. with decretal law.

If we now return to the question of the relationship between the

---

[14] Stephan G. Kuttner, *Harmony from Dissonance. An Interpretation of Medieval Canon Law* (Wimmer Lecture, X), Latrobe, Pa., 1960.

[15] G. le Bras, Ch. Lefebvre, J. Rambaud, *Histoire du droit et des institutions de l'église en Occident, VII: L'age classique, 1140-1378, Sources et théorie du droit*, Paris 1965, 133-66 (135); 222-65.

two sciences, we should first recall that both developed along parallel lines during the twelfth century, with the result that they began to behave towards each other as if they were autonomous disciplines. This tendency, as Yves Congar states, was strengthened in a decisive way by the structure of the new universities, with their decretist and theological faculties. And he continues: 'The fatal consequence was that this autonomous development led to a divergence in viewpoints and opinions.'[16] To this verdict we may add that of Grabmann, who remarked in passing that in the thirteenth century there was not only a division between theology and canon law, but even a 'partial opposition.'[17] In the fourteenth century – to say nothing of the later period – this opposition grew even more pronounced, and it seems reasonable to suggest that there were very few theologians in that period who did not criticise the canon lawyers.

Albertus Magnus (d. 1280), who was vehemently opposed to the use of canon law in the doctrine of the sacraments, made the following cutting remark, which illustrates his lack of esteem for the canonists.

> Decretistae nescient unam obiectionem solvere quam facient.[18]

It is said of Albert's pupil, Thomas Aquinas, that he made grateful use of canonist material. True, Thomas borrowed much from Gratian's decree and from the decretals of Gregory IX, but this does not mean that he accepted the work of the canonists uncritically. At one point he rejects a juridical interpretation of a decretal and concludes:

> licet quidam iuristae ignoranter contrarium dicant.[19]

---

[16] Yves M.-J. Congar, 'Un témoignage des désaccords entre canonistes et théologiens', in: *Etudes d'histoire du droit canonique, dédiées à Gabriel le Bras*, II, Paris 1965, 861-84 (862). See also Joseph de Ghellinck, 'Magister Vacarius. Un juriste théologien peu aimable pour les canonistes', *RHE* 44 (1943), 173-8.

[17] M. Grabmann, *Die Geschichte der katholischen Theologie seit dem Ausgang der Väterzeit*, Freiburg i.B. 1933, 34-5. See also Grabmann's 'Die Erörterung der Frage ob die Kirche besser durch einen guten Juristen oder durch einen Theologen regiert werde, bei Gottfried von Fontaines und Augustinus Triumphus von Ancona', in *Festschrift Eduard Eichmann zum 70. Geburtstag*, Paderborn 1940, 1-18. Preachers often blamed jurists for their attachment to profane sciences, as is clearly shown by M.-M. Davy, *Les sermons universitaires Parisiens de 1230-31*, Paris 1931, 82-90.

[18] *Comm. in libr. sent.* IV d. 27, 21, cited by De Lagarde, *La naissance*, II, 333 n. 84. See also index *s.v.* 'Théologiens et juristes'.

[19] *S.th.* II^{a} II^{ae} q. 88 a. 11 c.

Elsewhere he criticises professors of theology for daring to adduce 'glossulas iuristarum' as authorities. Could he be more disparaging?

> inconsonum et derisibile videtur, quod sacrae doctrinae professores iuristarum glossulas in auctoritatem adducunt vel de eis disceptent.[20]

Elsewhere he blames the decretists for following human law rather than divine law.

> opinio decretistarum non est vera, quia ipsi plus assentiunt in his et sequuntur ius humanum quam divinum, cum plus sit assentiendum divino quam humano...[21]

Our next witness is Roger Bacon (d. 1295). This passionate Aristotelian spared nobody in his criticism, least of all the jurists, whom he accused of introducing the pagan *ius civile* into the Church. He laments that 'in the Church of God, a jurist, even if he only has a smattering of civil law and knows nothing of canon law, is more highly praised than a master of theology.'[22] 'Once', he continues, 'the Roman curia was ruled by God's wisdom, but now it is ruined by legal pronouncements derived from heathen emperors.' Roger regards it as monstrous that men should try to subject Christendom to the Italian *ius civile*, and believes that if a national legal system must be maintained, then it would be better to leave the English clergy under English law, and the French clergy under French law, rather than subject both to an Italian system.[23] The ideal of which this Franciscan scholar dreamed, and which determined his entire criticism of the jurists, was a legal system renewed under the twofold inspiration of canon law, i.e. the law derived from the Scriptures and the Fathers, and Aristotelian philosophy.

However scanty these details may be, they make it sufficiently clear that by the thirteenth century, soon after the separation of the two sciences, there was already much amiss with the actual relationship of canon law and theology.

In the fourteenth century this opposition increased. Dante's complaint in the ninth *canto* of his *Paradiso* is well known:

---

20 *Contra pestiferam doctrinam*, c. 13 ad 11 (ed. Mandonnet, *Opuscula* IV, 308).
21 *Quodlib.* XI q. 8 a. 8 (ed. Mandonnet, 419).
22 *Opus tertium* (ed. Brewer, 85-6); cf. De Lagarde, *La naissance*, II, 143-53.
23 *Compendium studii theologiae* (ed. Rashdall, 398, 420).

Per quanto l'Evangelio e i dottor magni
Son derelitti, e sole ai decretali
Si studia, si che pare a'lor vivagni.[24]

Passing over Robert Holkoth, who makes some comments on this subject in the prologue to his commentary on the Wisdom of Solomon,[25] and the bibliophile Bishop Richard of Bury, who expressly states his reasons for possessing so few law books,[26] we may recall that certain orders, especially the Cistercians, were very much opposed to the science of law. Pope Benedict XII (1334-42), a Cistercian himself, issued a constitution in 1335 in which he forbade his former brethren to go into the study of civil law, lest they should endanger theology.[27]

We arrive at Ockham, whose work time and again bears witness to the great controversy between theologians and canonists. He studies the relationship of the two sciences in depth, and in detail. For that reason, and because of his influence on later generations, we shall devote a little more attention to him.

His *Dialogus* opens by asking: to whom does the determination of the Catholic truths, and consequently the judgement of heresies, belong: to the theologians or the canon lawyers?[28] In the exchange of ideas on this subject between the master and the pupil, three arguments in favour of the canonists are advanced but no fewer than eight in favour of the theologians. The answer given is hardly surprising: it is the theologians who determine the truth, and pass judgement on heresy.

The canonists employed, among others, the argument that they were competent to judge questions of faith because their science had been established by the Church, whose authority according to Augustine's famous dictum: '*Ego vero evangelio non crederem, nisi me catholicae ecclesiae commoveret auctoritas*', was greater than that of the

---

[24] *The Divine Comedy of Dante Alighieri*, ed. and tr. J.D. Sinclair, 3 vols, rev. ed., London 1948, 3 Paradiso, canto IX, p. 138, lines 133-5. See also M. Maccarone, 'Teologia e diritto canonico nella Monarchia, III 3', *Rivista di storia della Chiesa in Italia* 5 (1951), 7-42.

[25] Robert Holkoth, *Sapientia Salomonis*, prol. (ed. 1586) fol. 4vo.

[26] Richard of Bury, *Philobiblion*, ed. Ernest C. Thomas, London 1888, chapt. 2, 16. See also the excellent art. by J. de Ghellinck, 'Un évêque bibliophile au XIVe siècle', *RHE* 18 (1922) 271-312; 482-508; 19 (1923) 157-200.

[27] Cf. U. Stutz, *Die Cisterzienser wider Gratians Dekret*, Weimar 1919.

[28] *Dialogus* I, 1, 1-15 (ed. Goldast, 399-400).

Gospel.[29] This thesis was refuted by interpreting the word 'Church', as used by Augustine, in the sense of the sum of all believers in the past and the present. The authority of this (invisible) Church, to which the *auctor evangelii* also belonged, was certainly greater than that of the Gospel. But canon law owed its origin not to the greater authority of this universal Church, but to the lesser authority of the Popes. Augustine's adage was thus regarded as inapplicable.[30]

Ockham supports his claim that the determination of truth and heresy belongs to the province of theology, with the argument, already familiar to us, that theology is a *scientia superior.* Canon law derives its principles from theology and this means that the latter possesses a more certain and deeper comprehension of them.

> Scientia superior de traditis in scientia inferiori subordinata sibi, certius potest et profundius iudicare quam scientia inferior.[31]

Furthermore, theology was credited with a more certain knowledge of the canonists' conclusions:

> ... habentes perfectam notitiam scientiae subalternantis, certius iudicant de conclusionibus scientiae subalternatae.[32]

In other words, from beginning to end, Ockham regards canon law as being placed under the supervision of theology; there is no law which cannot, if necessary, be corrected by theologians in accordance with their deeper insights.

In order to give his pupil, as he wished, the most comprehensive possible survey of all standpoints, opinions and ideas, the master made sure to remind him of the way in which his contemporary theologians thought of their canon lawyer colleagues:

> Imprimis autem volo te scire, quod auctores theologi moderni temporis canonistas, tamquam non intelligentes, praesumptuosos, temerarios, fallaces, deceptores, cavillatores et ignaros in cordibus suis valde despiciunt.[33]

Why this unbridled contempt? The master replies: because modern canonists, although they know all laws, are completely ignorant of

---

[29] Ockham, *Dialogus* I, 1, 3 (ed. Goldast, 399$^{45-51}$); Augustine, *Contra Faustum Manichaeum*, *CSEL* 25 I, 5, 6, 197.

[30] *Dialogus* I, 1, 1 (ed. Goldast, 399$^{44-50}$), and I, 1, 4 (ed. Goldast, 402$^{39-54}$).

[31] *Dialogus* I, 1, 9 (ed. Goldast, 405$^{46-7}$).

[32] *Dialogus* I, 1, 10 (ed. Goldast, 406$^{57-8}$).

[33] *Dialogus* I, 1, 3 (ed. Goldast, 401$^{39-42}$).

natural and moral sciences, and of theology. In this respect they offer a glaring contrast with their earlier predecessors, the compilers of the holy *canones*, who were deeply versed in all these subjects.[34] This reasoning is reminiscent of Roger Bacon, although he had been more concerned to attack the civil lawyers. Canonists do just as they please, says Ockham; they pay no attention to other sciences, and believe theirs to be autonomous.[35] They treat the hierarchy of the encyclopaedia of sciences with contempt, and in fact work without any higher norm, recognising only one legal principle: their own authority. In fact, Ockham accuses them of positivism, legal positivism, and this accusation, which like Roger Bacon he couples with a lament for the better days of old, is one we shall find again in Gerson.

What distinguished Ockham from the other scholastics linked him with Pierre d'Ailly. Both of them were relatively well informed about canon law, which is something one cannot say of the scholastics in general. True, most of them, beginning with Peter Lombard, cite the decree of Gratian. They also appeal to papal decrees and decretals, but very rarely quote the opinions of canonist commentators, the decretists and decretalists. Ockham's case is different. He appears skilled in canon law, conversant with the usual forms of argument in that science, and therefore in a position to meet the canonists on their own ground, and if need be to engage them with their own weapons.[36]

Up to a point, this can also be said of d'Ailly, whose knowledge of canon law is clear from his treatise *De materia concilii generalis*[37] of 1402-3, and also from such works as *Utrum indoctus in iure divino possit iuste praeesse in ecclesiae regno*.[38] It would take us too far from our sub-

---

[34] *Dialogus* I, 1, 3 (ed. Goldast, 401[42-7]).

[35] Cf. also Congar, 'Désaccord', 883: 'Dans les critiques, extrêmement sévères, que les théologiens adressent aux canonistes, et plus encore au juristes, revient surtout le reproche de ne considérer que le dehors des choses: seul le fait les intéresse, non la nature intime des choses, qui pourtant rend compte de leurs propriétés.'

[36] Brian Tierney, 'Ockham, conciliar theory, and the canonists', *JHI* 15 (1954), 40-70.

[37] *De materia concilii generalis* (ed. Oakley).

[38] Dupin I, 646-62. See the present author's 'Pierre d'Ailly's verhandeling «Utrum indoctus in iure divino possit iuste praeesse in ecclesiae regno»', in: *Kerk in Beraad, Opstellen aangeboden aan prof. dr. J.C.P.A. van Laarhoven*, Nijmegen 1991, 87-101. Some remarks on d'Ailly and canon law in Bliemetzrieder, *Generalkonzil*, 86, 92 n. 5, and, in particular, F. Oakley, *The Political Thought of Pierre d'Ailly*, index s.v. 'Canon law and canonists'. – Swanson, *(Universities*, 46) dates d'Ailly's *Utrum indoctus* as being from 1381, which can

ject to dwell on this question, which, by the way, had been treated already many years earlier by Godefroy of Fontaines, Jean of Mont Saint-Eloi, Augustinus Triumphus, and Francis Caraccioli.[39] We shall confine ourselves to the observation that d'Ailly quotes a relatively large number of canonist authorities, and does not limit himself to the more recent ones. As far as the relationship of canon law and theology is concerned, he shares the view of the scholastics and forcefully defends the primacy of theology. In the prologue to his commentary on the sentences he criticises the lawyers, both civil and canon, in a way which is scarcely outdone by Ockham.[40] And just as Ockham pointed to the earlier *auctores legum*, who at least still had realised that there were other sciences, d'Ailly compares the modern canonists to Gratian, calling him '*magnus ille utriusque iuris doctor*'.[41] The nostalgia for the days of yore to which this exhortation testifies, seems to be confirmed by the statement of a modern historian of canon law, Gabriel LeBras: 'Gratien ressuscité au XIVe siècle se fût perdu dans l'immensité du Palais apostolique et n'eût

---

only be true of the first article; art. 2 refers to the Monzon-affair, which brings us to 1388.

39 See Grabmann's art. mentioned above n. 17. The text of Godefroy de Fontaines' *quaestio* was edited by J. Hoffmanns, *Le dixième Quodlibet de Godefroid de Fontaines (texte inédit)* (Les philosophes Belges, IV, fasc. III, Louvain 1931), 395-8. About 1269, John Peckham treated the question: 'Utrum theologia sit prae ceteris scientiis necessaria praelatis ecclesiae', ed. J. Leclercq in: 'Le magistère du prédicateur au XIIIe siècle', *AHDLM* 15 (1946), 139-41. Some years earlier Humbert de Romanis wrote in his *De eruditione praedicatorum* (in: *Maxima Bibliotheca Veterum Patrum*, 25, Lyon, 490b): 'Alii sunt, qui tantum extollunt scientiam [eorum], quod venerunt ad hanc stultitiam, ut dicerent, quod melius regitur ecclesia Dei per ista iura quam per theologiam.'; R. James Long, '«Utrum iurista vel theologus plus proficiat ad regimen ecclesiae». A Quaestio disputata of Francis Caraccioli. Edition and study', *MS* 30 (1968), 134-62 (140 n. 3), and the *a.c.* (n. 38), 92-3.

40 Oakley (*Political Thought*, 22-3 (cf. 163-5), remarks that d'Ailly frequently criticizes 'ignorant jurists', who betray their unfamiliarity with Holy Writ by imagining that God is limited or in any way bound by 'created laws'. (With ref. to d'Ailly, *Comm. in l.s.*, I. q. 12 a. 2. J).

41 *Comm. in libr. sent.*, Prologus (ed. Brussels 1484?, fol. a 4[ro 2]): 'Sed reperio iterum in hac scola quosdam iuriscanonici professores, qui eciam suas decretales epistolas quasi divinas scripturas accipiunt et eas taliter venerantur, ut propter hoc eorum aliqui plerumque in divinarum prorumpant blasphemiam scripturarum. Tales enim reprehendit magnus ille utriusque iuris doctor, dominus Gratianus sui voluminis d. 9, verba recipiens Augustini, epistula VIII[a] ad iheronymum.' Under the title *Principium in cursum bibliae*, the prologue is also printed in Dupin I, 610B-17C (the passage cited is 614B-15C). Besides Gratian, ps.-Isidore's *Liber conciliorum* is also highly recommended by d'Ailly. (See Chapter III n. 43).

point compris le langage de ses disciples, cependant nourris des gloses du *Décret*.'[42]

***

Let us turn to Gerson. What did he think of all this? We can find many of the data we need to answer this question in three sermons from the years 1406[43], 1408[44] and 1410[45], all of them delivered in his capacity as Chancellor of the University to licentiates in canon law. There is also some information in his *De vita spirituali animae*, which we shall later consider more fully.

Like the theologians already mentioned, Gerson regarded the science of canon law with critical reserve, and followed the activities of its practitioners with considerable scepticism. True, in his *De vita spirituali animae* he rarely engages in open polemic with the canonists, but in fact his criticism is constantly directed against them.[46] He accuses them of introducing a purely juridical way of thought into the Church, a way of thought which, without bothering too much about theology, ethics or piety, speculates freely and–literally –'decrees.'[47] In his opinion, this was to a great extent arbitrary, and therefore in a deeper sense lawless. He detected in the canonists an indifference to theology and morals, and an inability to bear in mind the limits of their science. Acting from a position of supreme self-confidence, they multiplied legal decisions to an incredible extent. 'A single human life,' he says,–perhaps in a traditional figure

---

[42] Gabriel le Bras, *Institutions ecclésiastiques de la Chrétienté médiévale*, première partie, livres II à VI, [Paris 1964], 361.

[43] *Conversi estis* (Gl. 5, 168-79; Dupin IV, 695-702).

[44] *Pax vobis* (Gl. 5, 435-47; Dupin IV, 703-11).

[45] *Dominus his opus habet* (Gl. 5, 218-29; Dupin IV, 686-95).

[46] See *lectio* 2 in particular (Gl. 3, 128-41; Dupin III, 16-25), and the end of the treatise (Gl. 3, 198-202; Dupin III, 70-2).

[47] *De vita spir. animae*, lectio 4, cor. 4 (Gl. 3, 161; Dupin III, 40CD): '... praeterea legislatores ecclesiastici et civiles plerumque sua potestate et auctoritate noscuntur abuti, praesertim ecclesiastici illi qui quidquid ordinant, quidquid monent, quidquid praecipiunt, volunt pro divinis legibus haberi, par quoque robur habere per interminationem damnationis aeternae. Neque tamen accusaverim omnes legislatores taliter et talia loquentes; praesumo enim quod ad rectam regulam et divinam sapientiam sermones suos voluerunt glossari, interpretari et recipi; quod si non hoc humiliter intenderunt, pronuntio, non ego sed apostolus, quod «nihil possunt contra veritatem» [cf. 2 Cor. 13: 8] sed neque contra charitatem.'

of rhetorical scorn –, 'would not suffice to read all the laws and regulations which the canonists have compiled, let alone to obey them.'[48]

His criticism is particularly aimed at the fact that the canonists are insufficiently critical in their employment of the concept of *ius divinum*; that is to say, they abuse it in an absolutist sense, thus losing sight of the distinction between essential and accidental, and fatally allowing human traditions (*traditiones hominum*) to overrule the divine commandments, make them powerless and so close the path to salvation. These traditions had gained influence in all areas of the Church and the world; they penetrate not only the papal decrees and the constitutions of provincial and diocesan synods, but also the rules of the monastic orders, of communities and corporations.[49]

The consequences of all this are serious. A fearful confusion is sown in the community, and the souls of the simple believers are needlessly troubled. Augustine had cited against Januarius the words of Peter:[50] 'Now, therefore, why are you putting God to the test by placing on the neck of the disciples a yoke that neither our ancestors nor we have been able to bear (Acts 15: 10)? But what would you have said, Augustine, of our day with the incredible number of burdens laid on it by men in their folly?' None dares to undertake a holy act, for a net of legal regulations has been thrown over reality, and those who infringe it are threatened with the heaviest penalties: excommunication.[51]

---

48 *De vita spir. anim.*, lectio 4, cor. 12 (Gl. 3, 167; Dupin III, 45C).

49 *De vita spir. anim.*, lectio 2 (Gl. 3, 129; Dupin III, 16D): 'Has vero traditiones hominum quis cunctas dinumeret, in canonibus summorum pontificum, in constitutionibus synodalibus provinciarum aut dioecesum, in religionum regulis, in Universitatum, collegiorum et ecclesiarum statutis, in edictis imperatorum et principum, et in plebiscitis communitatum, quarum plures sub excommunicatione latae sententiae, aliae sub interminatione divinae indignationis, aliae sub voto, aliae et fere omnes sub iuramenti aut fidelitatis debito stringunt et obligant.' *Ibidem*, lect. 4 (Gl. 3, 164-5; Dupin III, 43C): 'Miratus sum aliquando qua ratione ipsi ecclesiastici praesertim ordinati et religiosi prohibentur a scientia medicinae, et non removentur de facto a studio traditionis humanae (= canon law), nam corpus longe melius est quam terrena substantia cui traditiones istae deserviunt.'

50 Augustine, *ep.* 55, 19, 35 ad Ianuarium (CSEL 34, 209, 18sq.). Gerson probably borrowed this citation from Henry of Ghent (*Quodlib.* V, q. 36), see below, Chapter XII n. 123.

51 Gerson pleads in particular for the restriction of the excommunication *latae sententiae*, i.e. the provision by which, for certain offences, the legislator provides for the automatic excommunication of the offender, without further intervention on the part

This criticism of the canonists is coupled by Gerson, as it is by Ockham, with a protest against their positivist way of thinking.[52] In one of his sermons to the young canonists he makes it very clear to what absurdities positivism can lead, by citing a statement of an influential supporter of Clement VII, the cardinal and canonist Peter Amelii (d. 1389). The cardinal is said to have remarked once that if he were ever called to the aid of someone who had fallen into a swamp, he would never help him unless sanctioned by some law or canon. 'We are even ashamed to speak without the law, and how much more therefore to act without it,' so the cardinal was supposed to have said.[53]

As far as the encyclopaedic question is concerned, Gerson's view was no different from that of the other scholastics. Far from being a Rudolph Sohm *avant la date*, and regarding all law as in conflict with the Gospel, he was completely at one with the canonists in believing that the Church cannot survive without legal rules, the *canones*, the decrees and the decretals, which fulfilled a legitimate function and could even possess absolute power. By way of comparison he even called the *lex canonica* the *vox Christi*, in so far as it is the *vox sui vicarii* over the Church.[54] The text which is repeatedly cited

---

of the judge or other authority. For the history of this provision, see P. Hinschius, *System des katholischen Kirchenrechts mit besonderer Rücksicht auf Deutschland* V, Berlin 1895, 131ff. Cf. *De vita spir. animae*, lect. 4, corol. 7, 12 & 14 (Gl. 3, 163, 167, 170-4: Dupin III, 42BC, 45B-6A, 48A-55B): '[Corol. 7] ... theologia quae est lex evangelica,—dicam melius, eius doctrix et explicatrix,—debet in omnibus praecedere praelatos ecclesiasticos in suis constitutionibus et decretis, ne vel obsint praeceptis Dei ..., vel ne credantur ligare ad poenam aeternam, ubi poena civilis sola reperitur. Doctrina haec praecipuum locum habet in materia excommunicationum latae sententiae.' See also *De modo excommunicationum* (Gl. 9, 92-4; Dupin II, 403); *Regulae mandatorum* 123-7 (Gl. 9, 125; Dupin III, 101AB), and below n. 72.

52 Cf. *Pax vobis* (Gl. 5, 439; Dupin IV 705D-6A): 'Haec irritatio legis nonne manifesta est in illis qui nullam viam pro sedatione schismatis dicunt iuridicam, nisi quam libri sui scriptam habent, quasi ius divinum non esset ius, neque via sibi consona dici iuridica mereretur.'

53 *Pax vobis* (Gl. 5, 440; Dupin IV, 707A). Gerson failed to grasp that Peter Amelii was citing the juridical adage: 'Erubescimus cum sine lege loquimur' (Bartol. Comm. 1 ad Auth. 3, 5, 5 (= Nov. 18, 5); Comm. 1 ad Cod. Just. 6, 20, 19).—Peter Amelii wrote against a conciliar solution of the schism as proposed by Conrad of Gelnhausen. Cf. Bliemetzrieder, *Generalkonzil*, index s.v.; and the same author's *Literarische Polemik*, 61-70.

54 *Conversi estis* (Gl. 5, 171-2; Dupin IV, 697CD): 'Quamquam vero vox ista legis Christi... sit appropriate et eminenter lex evangelica, ... nihilominus lex canonica per analogiam quamdam et attributionem nominari non irrationabiliter potest vox Christi, pro quanto ipsa est vox sui vicarii insuper Ecclesiae, vox denique illorum ad quos dixit: "qui vos audit, me audit" (Luke 10: 16), ita ut olim pro una voce lex evangelica et cano-

in this connexion is the word of Christ to the disciples, 'Who hears you, hears Me' (Luke 10: 16). This is the basis on which the *lex canonica* and its science rest.

The point at which Gerson becomes critical is where he believes that this text is improperly interpreted and used as a warrant or cover in order to qualify every legal rule emanating from this Vicar or his assistants as a divine law, and thus to put it beyond discussion. The critical test which he suggests to the canonists is, as we shall see, the extent to which a legal rule agrees with the concept of divine law as strictly defined by theology. Only where this agreement can be clearly demonstrated, can an appeal to the text 'Who hears you, hears Me' be legitimate. Other legal rulings, not being divine, cannot be legitimated by this text. In other words, Luke 10: 16 qualifies as divine and absolute only those legal opinions and statements which conform to the concept of divine law determined by theology and dogma.[55]

This already indicates to some extent how Gerson thought of the relationship of theology and canon law. If canon law ought to derive the yardstick for its legal pronouncements from theology, and canonists were thus dependent on what the theologians regarded as belonging to divine law, then this meant that the science of canon law was subordinate to that of theology. Gerson gives a concrete example of this relationship. It is clear, he says, that the *canones* are derived entirely from the principles of theology. Therefore, a canonist who congratulates himself on his complete mastery of his subject, must also congratulate himself on his skill as a theologian and must not imagine that he can arrive at the same conclusions merely by sticking to the letter of his decree or decretal.[56] Do not let the

---

nica haberentur, neque in duas secernebant facultates theologia et decretorum scientia, nam decreta quales alii nisi theologi praecipui condiderunt, tradiderunt, promulgarunt?'

[55] *De nuptiis* (Gl. 6, 193; Dupin II, 366D): 'Dicet aliquis: reprobas ergo decretales et decreta summorum pontificum, constitutiones synodales dioecesanorum et ita de reliquis? Non reprobo; fateor, scio dictum esse per Christum: «qui vos audit me audit» [Luke 10: 16]; scio legem evangelicam stabilitam in supernaturalibus principiis et in regulis universalibus reliquisse particularium agibilium determinationes apostolis et discipulis suisque successoribus. Nunc vero qualis insania est deserere legem regis, deserere fontem vini sapientiae salutaris, ut stabiliatur primitus lex subditorum et antea ministretur non dicam vinum qualemcumque, sed aqua sapientiae animalis et terrenae; unde fit plerumque irritum mandatum Dei prout se conformans Christus Isaiae verbis pharisaeos arguebat [Matt. 15: 6].' See also below n. 65.

[56] *Conversi estis* (Gl. 5, 175; Dupin IV, 700B).

canonists think that their concordances – the famous *Margarita Martiniana* for example,[57] – give them the right to dispense with the support of theologians, for the interpretation of the divine *canones* is a task to be entrusted only to those who are familiar with the principles of theology.[58] Or, more rhetorically, 'to exclude theology from canon law amounts to the same as tearing out one's own eyes.'[59]

In case of doubt whether a particular canon belongs to the divine law or not, it is theology which makes the final decision, for it is theology which is the science of the highest, immutable and eternal laws. From theology, as from a spring, flow all the divine ordinances set down in the holy *canones*, the regulations of the general councils and the papal decretals.[60]

Gerson mentions the origin of the canon law in passing. Originally, he claims, the *lex evangelica* (= *lex divina*) and the *lex canonica* were one, and no distinction was made between the theological and the decretist faculty. In the beginning, it was always the task of theologians to draft and proclaim the laws of the Church. Just as under the Mosaic law, the commandments which laid down the relationship of man to God were indivisible from the rules which regulated the relationship of man and man (*lex canonica*). That remained the position of the early Church, until about the pontificate of Gregory the Great (590-604).[61] By then the Church had spread

---

[57] *Conversi estis* (Gl. 5, 171; Dupin IV, 697B). On this alphabetical repertorium on Gratian's decretum, usually called after its author Martinus Polonus: '*Margarita Martiniana*', see J.F. von Schulte, *Geschichte der Quellen und Literatur des kanonischen Rechts von Gratian bis auf die Gegenwart*, II, Stuttgart 1877, 137.

[58] *Dominus his opus habet* cons. 10 (Gl. 5, 223; Dupin IV, 690D): 'Hi vero canones si bene inspiciamus, non sunt nisi conclusiones elicitae vel illatae ex principiis theologicis, id est ex evangelio et aliis libris canonicis per illos quibus dicit Christus: «Qui vos audit, me audit» (Luke 10: 16).' Cf. *Pax vobis*, cons. 2 (Gl. 5, 443-4; Dupin IV, 708D-9A).

[59] *Conversi estis* (Gl. 5, 178; Dupin IV, 702A): 'Concludimus deinceps quod theologiam a canonibus excludere nihil aliud est quam suos sibi oculos evellere.'

[60] *Pax vobis* (Gl. 5, 443; Dupin IV, 708D): 'Lex itaque canonica numquid non ab evangelica manat, derivatur et vivit sicut membra a capite, venae a corde, corpus ab anima? Alioquin non diceret Sapientia de seipsa: «per me reges regnant et legum conditores iusta decernunt» [Prov. 8: 15]. Quis a philosophia medicinam, quis scientias alias a metaphysica vel logica separaret? Sic nec canones a theologia. Quare? Quia traditae sunt apud eam [theologiam] leges primae invariabiles et aeternae a quibus originantur sicut a fonte fluvii conclusionum particularium in sacris canonibus. in concillis generalibus, in pontificum decretalibus contentarum.' Cf. *Dominus his opus habet* (Gl. 5, 224; Dupin IV, 708D).

[61] *Pax vobis* (Gl. 5, 444; Dupin IV, 709D): 'Dic cur et quando separatio facta est inter

over the whole face of the earth, and all creatures endowed with reason were under one shepherd.[62] To administer this flock, the number of decrees and decretals had to be multiplied, and this was all the more necessary when the Church acquired by gift a great many estates and jurisdictions, and thus gained a position equal to those of the secular powers. Greater wealth brought a greater number of legal matters and a greater number of legal regulations. Laws were added to laws, constitutions to constitutions, and decretals to decretals. New situations naturally demand new solutions. The expansion of legal business made it humanly impossible for one person at the same time to occupy himself with divine law and to give full attention to 'tradition'. That, in Gerson's opinion, was the origin of the separation of the *lex evangelica* from the *lex canonica* and of the theological faculty from the decretist.[63]

Gerson thus relates the origin of canon law to the expansion of the Church's rôle in the world, in power, wealth, esteem and organisation. Without this development it could have been administered by theologians alone, and the separation of canon law from theology would not have been necessary. He describes the object of the canon law as 'tradition', a concept repeatedly met with in his works, and by which, – like the later reformers who often spoke in this context of '*Menschensatzungen*',[64] – he meant a congeries of legal regulations which were to be included under the *ius humanum*, and which, in greater or lesser connexion with divine law, had been framed to bring order to the worldly side of the Church.[65] The

theologiae et decretorum facultates, cum tempore magni Gregorii et antea soli viderentur ecclesiam regere theologi?'

62 *Dominus his opus habet* cons. 10 & 11 (Gl. 5, 223; Dupin IV, 690D-1A): 'sic instituta videtur et gubernata fuisse sufficienter ecclesia primitiva sub apostolis, ac deinde per successiones varias usque ad doctores sanctos inclusive per quadringentos annos et amplius, quibus temporibus non erat distinctio theologorum et canonistarum, licet canones sacri multi essent ultra tenorem expresse traditum in evangeliis et ceteris libris canonicis... Dominus propter multiplicationem hominum sub lege sua evangelica praevaricantium eam, multis modis voluit huiusmodi canones multiplicari; et ita opus habuit canonistis etiam in regimine spirituali quia proprie dicti theologi nequaquam sufficiebant.'

63 *Conversi estis* (Gl. 5, 172-4; Dupin IV, 698AB); *Diligite iustitiam* (Gl. 7*, 609; Dupin IV, 649B-50B); *Pax vobis* (Gl. 5, 443-4; Dupin IV, 709D); *Dominus his opus habet* (Gl. 5, 227; Dupin IV, 710D-11A).

64 See J.N. Bakhuizen van den Brink, 'La tradition dans l'église primitive et au XVIe siècle', *RHPR* 36 (1956), 272.

65 *Considerate lilia* (Gl. 5, 158; Dupin III, 1432C): 'Non secus est de multitudine traditionum humanarum, nominatim excommunicationum. Ad hoc spectat illud Christ,

decisive question, what was Gerson's final view of the relationship of canon law and theology, depended on his opinion of this worldly aspect of the Church.

In his view, power, rights and possessions of a temporal nature were not essential for the Church, for it had been created as a purely spiritual entity by God, and was therefore perfect;[66] neither Christ nor Peter had had any ambition for worldly power.[67] 'Not essential' is not, however, the same as 'incompatible'. There is a difference between saying: the Church *can* do without worldly power, and the Church *must* do without worldly power. Gerson rejected the second statement because of its spiritualist tendency,[68] and

---

Matth. XV [:6]: «irritum fecistis mandatum Dei propter traditiones vestras», etc.'; *De vita spir. animae*, lect. 2 (Gl. 3, 129; Dupin III, 17A): 'Has vero traditiones hominum quis cunctas dinumeret, in canonibus summorum pontificum, in constitutionibus synodalibus provinciarum aut dioecesum, in religionum regulis, in Universitatum, collegiorum et ecclesiarum statutis, in edictis imperatorum et principum, et in plebecitis communitatum, quarum plures sub excommunicatione latae sententiae... stringunt et obligant'; *Apparuit gratia Dei*, cons. 2 (Gl. 5, 76-7; Dupin II, 63C-4A): 'Et esset profecto grandis in hoc loco querelarum materia contra tot et tam leves excommunicationum et irregularitatum fulminationes, contra tot onera statutorum provincialium et synodalium ad lucrum quale, vel animae vel bursae, novit Deus; contra tot reservationes casuum in foro confessionis, praesertim occultorum, quae confessionem supra quam dici potest impediunt... Multiplicentur quantumlibet humanae traditiones...'; *Conversi estis* (Gl. 5, 178; Dupin IV, 702B); *Pax vobis* (Gl. 5, 438-40; Dupin IV, 705D-6D); *Bonus pastor* (Gl. 5, 127; Dupin IV, 545B). Cf. also Chapter X n. 20.

66 In this context he constantly refers to Deut. 32: 4: 'Dei perfecta sunt opera.' See *De auferibilitate* (Gl. 3, 296; Dupin II, 211D); *Conversi estis* (Gl. 5, 172; Dupin IV, 698B); *Pax vobis* (Gl. 5, 441; Dupin IV, 707A): 'Christus postremo suam ecclesiam nonne perfecta stabilitate fundavit, legem statuens evangelicam; quae si ad regimen ecclesiae sufficit, ut sufficit, quia «Dei perfecta sunt opera», quid nisi confusionem superfluam, lites, discordiam, tanta tamque multiplicata iurium legum et canonum discordantium varietas operatur?'; *Dominus his opus habet* (Gl. 5, 220-1; Dupin IV, 687D, 689A).

67 *De concilio unius oboedientiae* (Gl. 6, 54-56; Dupin II, 27B-28A): '...ecclesia tempore Christi et apostolorum nullum habuit exercitium aut executionem iuridicam et civilem circa huiusmodi temporalia. Immo Christus plus videtur facto et verbo tale exercitium iurisdictionis civilis prohibuisse quam permisisse... Nonne Christus fuit papa perfectissimus? Nonne similiter Petrus? Ipsi tamen omne exercitium abdicaverunt a se in talibus.'; *De vita spir. animae*, lect. 4 (Gl. 3, 178; Dupin III, 53C): 'Rursus non est usquaque certum an ius divinum concesserit praelatis iurisdictionem temporalem immediate aut saltem eius exercitium, sicut Christus illud a se abdicavit.'

68 Gerson defends canon law against those who reject it, and mentions the Waldensians, Marsilius of Padua, Wyclif, and others. See *Conversi estis* (Gl. 5, 441-2; Dupin IV, 707D-708A): 'Praecelsa decretorum facultas cum suis professoribus nequaquam debet ex abutentium suis traditionibus pravitate culpari... Fefellit hic zelus Bonaldelses [Waldenses] haereticos...; dum credunt dicere cum apostolo: «nostra conversatio in coelis est» [Phil. 3: 20], volunt omnia [cum] sua basi metiri. Patuit hic nuper in doctore quodam anglicano [= Wiclif]; patuit in Marsilio de Padua...' According to Lewis &

adopted the first as his opinion. He was thus able to approve, up to a point, of the historical development which had led to the enormous concentration of wealth and worldly power in the hands of the Church. Yet this did not prevent him from addressing serious criticism to the holders of the highest offices in the Church, if he suspected them of being concerned solely with the increase of their power and legal pretensions. In such cases he accused them of being occupied entirely with secondary matters, and urged them to realise that the Church could well manage without worldly possessions; indeed it had reached its healthiest state when it had lived in poverty. '*Numquam enim ecclesia fuit melior quam dum vixit in paupertate.*'[69] In this respect Gerson was clearly in tune with the Franciscan theology.

It was from this standpoint of loyal criticism that he judged the science of canon law. Because, and in so far as, its origin and growth were inseparable from the historical development described above, Gerson could appreciate and to a certain extent even welcome this science.[70] But as soon as it forgot its task as servant, and only sought to increase its temporal power and positive-legal pretensions, and to make it appear as if the Church could not do without them, Gerson gave a warning in the strongest terms, not to confuse essential and accidental and to confine itself to the modest

---

Short, *A Latin Dictionary*, s.v. 'basis', the proverbial expression 'aliquem cum basi sua metiri' means: 'to measure a pillar together with its pedestal, i.e. to give false measure, to estimate too high', with ref. to Seneca, ep. 76, 31.

[69] *De vita contemplativa* (Gl. 3, 76; Dupin IV, 227A). He continues: 'Immo, sicut alias memini declarasse (probably a reference to his sermon *Vade in domum*, cons. 3 (Gl. 5, 577; Dupin III, 1302D-3A), nimium studium in multiplicatione temporalium et iurisdictionum in ecclesia non parva causa est suae desolationis, tam in spiritualibus quam temporalibus; et hoc maneducebatur per similitudinem corporis mystici ecclesiae totalis ad corpus verum hominis, nam intendere nimis regimini sensualitatis spreta directione rationis, est utrumque, tam sensualitatem quam rationem extinguere. Hinc est quod multi proborum et contemplativorum... parum curant si depauperetur ecclesia vel conculcetur in temporalibus, vocatis bonis, videntes tot vitia et abusus ex his provenire... Et haec omnia cessarent, aut non ita saltem abundarent, in paupertate modesta.' See also his letter to d'Ailly inc. *Si de temporali* (1409 or 1413) (Gl. 2, 127; Dupin III, 432B): 'Dico amplius quod si in praelatis omnia concordarent statui illi paupertatis Christi et suorum apostolorum, perfectior esset eorum imitatio et utilior quam sit magnificus status praesentium.' For more details, see our *Jean Gerson et l'Assemblée de Vincennes*, 102ff.

[70] The most extensive description Gerson gives of the rôle and the function of the canonists in the Church, is to be found in the sermon *Dominus his opus habet* (Gl. 5, 220-9; Dupin IV, 688B-95A). See also *Pax vobis* (Gl. 5, 441-3; Dupin IV, 707C-8), and *Diligite iustitiam* (Gl. 7*, 608-9; Dupin IV, 649C).

place allotted to it in the encyclopaedia of the sciences. In his criticism of canon law and canon lawyers he followed completely a tradition whose traces we have already indicated in the thirteenth and fourteenth centuries; a tradition, in our opinion, so widely disseminated that it is not necessary to consider Ockham Gerson's only guide in this matter.

The question however is: was Gerson's negative view of canon law and its practitioners appropriate and justified? It is possible to doubt this. It was certainly inappropriate, for there is no evidence to suggest that he was skilled in the science. Gerson was and remained first and foremost a theologian, whose knowledge of canon law was limited. Unlike his teacher and friend, Pierre d'Ailly, and unlike Ockham, the number of references to canonist texts in his works is relativily small. True, he knows how to find his way in Johannes Teutonicus' *Glossa ordinaria*[71] and in other more general works in the field, but it is striking that if he ventures into the territory of the canon lawyers he never does so independently, and in most cases we can identify his companions. At first, Pierre d'Ailly seems to have acted as his tutor in canon law,[72] while in the year immediately preceding the Council of Pisa, when it was necessary to strengthen the argument in favour of the *via concilii*, the canonist and theologian Conrad of Gelnhausen filled that rôle for him.[73] When he had to immerse himself in the problem of the temporal jurisdiction of the Church, we can see the same phenomenon. All the canonist proofs quoted in his *De iurisdictione spirituali* can be found in the documents of the so-called Assembly of Vincennes. Gerson copied them diligently, but there can be hardly any sugges-

---

[71] See Chapter X n. 16.

[72] See, for instance, *De contractibus* (Gl. 9, 409; Dupin III, 186C-7A), where he imparts some of d'Ailly's wise and 'humanistic' advice to his readers: 'Et venit in mentem dictum ... praeclarissimae memoriae praeceptoris mei, domini Petri cardinalis Cameracensis: «Expertus sum, inquit, dum in allegationibus iurium mihi veritas impugnari videbatur, si dismissis glossis super glossa recursus mihi fiebat ad nudam textus literam, mox apertior patebat intellectus, fatentibus hoc idem et mirantibus allegantibus in adversum...»', and *De vita spir. animae* (Gl. 3, 171-3; Dupin III, 49), where he declares that, thanks to his preceptor, he knew the difference between an *excommunicatio latae sententiae* and a canon. Maybe it was for the same reason that he dedicated his *De vita spir. animae* to d'Ailly. This treatise was fundamental precisely in the juridical respect. Cf. his letter inc. *Postulare dignata est* (Gl. 2, 63-4; Dupin III, 1-4), and *De vita spir. animae* (Gl. 3, 202; Dupin III, 72CD). See above n. 51, and Chapter III n. 43.

[73] See Chapter VI *passim*.

tion that he elaborated on them independently. His canonist training was evidently too slight for that.[74] The same holds true for his treatise *De contractibus*, for which he borrowed much from Petrus de Palude and Henry of Langenstein.[75] It is thanks to these man, all of whom had in common that they were both, canonists *and* theologians, that Gerson in some respect was more indebted to canonistic scholarship than he himself probably was aware of.[76]

But, we may ask, was his verdict on the canonists justified?[77] Were they in fact merely mouthpieces of papal absolutism? Thanks to the remarkable studies of Brian Tierney in particular, we now know better. Tierney has convincingly demonstrated the importance of the contribution made by the canonists to the development of conciliar theory, a theory which by definition is the very opposite of absolutism. Gerson, though he too thought along these lines, found no occasion to revise his verdict and to express himself more moderately on canon law, i.e. on decretal law.. He continued to regard the science as a hotbed of absolutism and legal positivism.

This probably reflected the fact that he was a theologian with a pronounced practical and pastoral bias, who was constantly running into the excessive and suffocating mass of legal rules and bureaucratic regulations in the practice of his ecclesiastical duties, and who found their assumptions and their effects at odds with his own, so much more spiritual views on the cure of souls and the religious life in general. He was not wrong, in our opinion, in holding the canonists responsible for this. For was it not primarily due to their meddling in the domain of the sacraments and in so many other fields, excommunication and Church-order, that the everyday life of the Church groaned under the legalistic yoke? And were not the

---

[74] See the present author's *Jean Gerson et l'Assemblée de Vincennes*, 71-9; 104 n. 72.

[75] *De contractibus* (Gl. 9, 385-421; Dupin III, 165-96). For the background of this treatise, see Clemens Bauer, 'Diskussionen um die Zins- und Wucherfrage auf dem Konstanzer Konzil', in: *Das Konzil von Konstanz*, 174-86. Henry Totting of Oyta composed also a treatise *De contractibus*. See Colette Jeudy, 'Trois manuscrits du "De translatione"', *Medioevo. Rivista di storia della filosofia medievale*, VI (1980), 501-522 (518, 521). The ms. investigated in this art. (Marburg 60) also contains Gerson's homonymous work (fol. 122-37), a fact which escaped Mgr. Glorieux (cf. his list of mss. in Gl. 9, xiii-xiv, 452).

[76] Cf. Tierney, *Foundations*, 11 n. 24: 'even a theologian like Gerson, who was exceptional in that he seldom quoted directly from canonistic sources, frequently used arguments derived from fourteenth-century publicists whose views were based on a solid foundation of earlier canonistic work.' See also below, Chapter XII n. 135.

[77] In the following we try to reply to a critical question raised by the late Prof. Post. See Preface, and cf. our *Jean Gerson et l'Assemblée de Vincennes*, 104-106.

canonists, in particular, responsible for the excessive extension of the idea of papal plenitude of power, which had lead to the destruction of a balanced and harmonious hierarchical order?

Gerson's one-sided view was no doubt also reinforced by negative experiences in the politics of the Church. We refer to his activities in searching for a solution to the disastrous Schism. His experiences in dealing with some of his canonist contemporaries, especially Benedict XIII, – a former professor of canon law, and an absolute ruler *par excellence* – , must have convinced him that the Church had taken a dangerous path when it had embraced Roman imperial law, had increased in worldly power and possessions, and had removed the care of them from theologians and entrusted it to a separate body of specialists. The experience of the Schism gave painful proof that once *potestas* was at stake, such central values as *humilitas* and *caritas* were soon overshadowed and forgotten.

***

After these introductory remarks, we turn to a more detailed discussion of Gerson's ideas of law, in so far as they are important for the understanding of his ecclesiology. The first occasion on which he went into any detail on them, was in 1402, in his *De vita spirituali animae.*[78] What sort of work is this?

Gerson collected under this title half a dozen lectures which he had delivered to students in the theological faculty, in his capacity as professor and Chancellor.[79] These lectures are a good starting point for a study of his ideas on the Church and the law, not only because he never approached the subject in as much detail again, but also because it appears that he referred to them repeatedly and, it seems, with some self-satisfaction. We may therefore assume that they became for him a statement of his considered position on the issues. When he gave the regular Easter sermon to licentiates in canon law, in 1406, he also referred to the earlier lectures,[80] as he

[78] *De vita spir. animae*, cons. 13 (Gl. 3, 113-202; Dupin III, 5-72). Cf. A. Combes, *Essai sur la critique de Ruysbroeck par Gerson* III, Paris 1945, 104ff.; David Schmiel, *Via Propria and Via Mystica in the Theology of Jean le Charlier de Gerson*, St. Louis (Missouri) 1969, 17-47; and Burger, *Aedificatio*, 72-95.

[79] Glorieux, 'l'Enseignement', 88-113; Schwab, *Gerson*, 263 n. 2.

[80] *Conversi estis* (Gl. 5, 178; Dupin IV, 702C): 'Rem potius ad scholasticum examen

did on a similar occasion some years later,[81] and once more in 1414, when he also referred back to lectures for the students of canon law.[82] Furthermore, he cited his *lectiones* of 1402 and summarised them up to a point in his most important ecclesiological treatise, *De potestate ecclesiastica* of 1417,[83] and the opinions advanced in the lectures are repeated in many other works.[84] We may, therefore, conclude that his ideas, in so far as they are concerned with the relationship of the Church and the law, remained the same from 1402, and were a constant factor in the development of his ecclesiology from that time.

What is the theme discussed in the lectures of 1402? In the first place, in *lectio* I, one of a mystical nature: the life of the soul as it is placed, by virtue of baptism, under the influence of the Holy Spirit. *Lectio* II raises the question which particularly interests us, of the nature of the *lex divina*, any infraction of which incurs the penalty of exclusion from the grace conferred by baptism. Gerson calls this a fundamental theological question, because it concerns the human soul, *mores* and *beatitudo*. He considers it well worth the effort to immerse himself in this question, since uncertainty as to its answer had repeatedly caused great confusion in the administration of Church and State. He holds the canonists responsible for this confusion because they had, with their 'traditions', obscured men's view of the principal issue, and had no notion of what the *lex divina* really was.[85]

This leads him to define the concept of divine law in theological terms. He devotes much attention to this and includes the concepts

---

referre congruit, quemadmodum pridem in lectionibus non paucis elucidare describendo tractavi; quod qualiter impleverim, aliorum sit iudicium.' In the last words, as well as in those cited in n. 82, one detects a flavour of self-satisfaction.

81 *Pax vobis* (Gl. 5, 443; Dupin IV, 709).

82 *De sensu litterali*, octava (Gl. 3, 336; Dupin I, 4A): '... quidam inveniuntur nolentes vel nescientes distinguere in ipsis decretalibus et decretis ea quae sunt de iure positivo vel de iure proprie naturali vel de mixto iure ex pluribus. Super qua re tam in lectionibus quam in collationibus pro commendatione dominorum iuristarum saepe locutus sum quantum mihi datum erat et utile videbatur.'

83 *De pot. eccl.*, cons. 13 (Gl. 6, 242-9; Dupin II, 250C-6A).

84 E.g. *De nobilitate* III (1423) (Gl. 9, 489-90; Dupin III, 219A): 'Requiritur ut sciamus quid ius proprie divinum, quid ius proprie humanum seu positivum nominetur, cum differentiis suis ad invicem. Scis autem frater, quanto olim studio tam in collationibus quam in lectionibus materiam hanc aperire conati fuerimus.'

85 *De vita spir. animae* (Gl. 3, 128-9; Dupin III, 16B-17B).

of *lex naturalis* and *lex humana* in his exposition, thus dividing the subject into three. This triple division, into divine, natural and human or positive law, was, as is well known, much older than Gerson, but he refined it and made it more suitable for use as a criterion by which to distinguish between essential and non-essential in the jurisprudence of the Church. He applied the triple division not only to the concepts of *lex* and *ius*, but also to those of *politia* and *dominium* (*lectio* IV), so that in fact he was able to consider all the juridical aspects of the Church within the framework of this scheme. *Lectiones* IV, V and VI prove that this was by no means applicable merely to theoretical questions, for they extend the distinction into the practical field and the consequences for the doctrine of sin, excommunication, oaths and monastic rules. We cannot go into all this, and will confine ourselves to a study of the distinction between *lex divina*, *lex naturalis* and *lex humana*.

2. Lex divina–lex naturalis–lex humana

> Lex divina praeceptoria est signum verum revelatum creaturae rationali, quod est notificativum rectae rationis divinae volentis teneri illam creaturam seu ligari ad aliquid agendum vel non agendum , pro dignificatione eius ad aeternam vitam consequendam et damnationem evitandam.[86]

With this definition, Gerson begins his enquiry into the scope and the importance of the divine law. He explains it in detail, laying great emphasis on the supernatural goal of God's law, that is the beatitude of the rational creature. This sense of purpose is the most important characteristic of the law of God; its exclusive concern with the supernatural distinguishes it both from natural law and from positive law. After defining the concept in general terms, Gerson proceeded to define it in particular, and states the following four corollaries:

1. Not every law may be called *de iure divino* because God's will obliges us to obey it. For nothing can happen without God's willing it; no truth, no beauty, no goodness exists without Him, and no *potestas* can be derived except from Him (Rom. 13: 1). This is not to say,

---

[86] *De vita spir. animae* (Gl. 3, 130; Dupin III, 17C).

however, that every *effectus* in the strict sense is brought about by Him, or that every truth is directly connected with faith. Just as little may we say that every obligation is in the strict sense part of the *lex divina* because God wills it.[87]

2. A law may not be called divine because rational beings have received it through revelation. In the old dispensation, God gave laws to his people by revelation which were only intended for the civil administration, the order of the community. Although this was certainly a revelation, the element of direction to a supernatural goal was absent, and therefore these laws cannot be reckoned as part of the *lex divina* in the strict sense.

By way of clarification, Gerson cites Aristotle's twofold division and points out that this – in accordance with the composition of man out of soul and body – spoke of a twofold goal, a supernatural and a natural one. To attain the former, God gave man laws which may be called divine or theological, and which belong in a strict sense to the divine law. To achieve the latter goal, – irrespective of whether it is described as 'human', 'civil' or 'political', – other laws were given to man; and although these laws exist to serve God's law in the same way as a body exists to serve the soul, they are not therefore to be considered as entirely *de iure divino*.[88]

3. From this close relationship between divine law and the supernatural comes an important consequence for ecclesiology, that is, that not all papal *canones*, decrees and decretals are automatically *de lege divina*. Many of these *canones* were issued only in order to bring order to the ecclesiastical community; they had thus no direct supernatural purpose, and therefore lacked absolute validity. 'We thus speak improperly whenever we say that the laws which regulate the life of the Church are «divine» or «spiritual». Some canon-

---

[87] *De vita spir. animae* (Gl. 3, 133; Dupin III, 19D-20A). Gerson refers here to the scholastic conception of the *generalis influentia Dei*. See Oberman, *Harvest*, index of subjects s.v. 'concursus generalis' (486), and Glossary (463): 'Concursus generalis (Influentia generalis)': 'The cooperation of the first cause – God – with the second cause – creature – indispensable for any action by the second cause, irrespective of the presence of grace.' Gerson seems to be in line with Durand of St Pourçain who in his *Comment. in l.s.* II, d. 1 q. 5 opposed Thomas Aquinas and defended the thesis: 'Quae fiunt a Deo mediantibus causis secundis non fiunt ab eo immediate.'

[88] *De vita spir. animae* (Gl. 3, 133-4; Dupin III, 20AC).

ists are insufficiently mindful of this, and include among the *spiritualia* matters which no-one doubts to be material in their nature.'[89]

4. A law is not divine because it can be derived from the principles of the divine order. Every good law, including the *lex humana*, agrees with the divine law, and there is no legal ruling which cannot, in the final analysis, be deduced from divine principles. Gerson here returns partly to his first thesis, providing a more detailed argument in support of what he had merely indicated briefly, but again concentrating on its ecclesiological importance. To give point to his thesis he raises the question of 'faith' and observes that, even in this connexion, it is not correct to say that every truth which can be deduced from the Scriptures is one of the truths of the faith. Only those truths which have been revealed '*ad credendum pro beatitudinis consequendo*' are the genuine truths of the faith. This implies – and here he works out the ecclesiological implications of his thesis, – that not all papal or ecclesiastical legislation belongs to the truths of the faith, and therefore to the divine law. 'Otherwise one would have to believe, as the canonists seem to urge, in the writings of all the holy doctors, because these teachers are approved of by the Church; and that is folly.'[90]

---

89 *De vita spir. animae* (Gl. 3, 134; Dupin III, 20D-21A): 'Et hoc loco falluntur et fallant crebro quidam canonistarum, praesertim in materia quam tractavimus, et de simonia similiter, ubi spiritualia iudicant illa quae esse carnalia et materialia nullus nescit.' He had already defended the same opinion in one of his earliest sermons *Dedit illi gloriam* (Gl. 5, 185; Dupin III, 1453D).

90 *De vita spir. animae* (Gl. 3, 133-5; Dupin III, 20A-1C). For his statement on theological doctors, cf. in the same treatise, lect. 6 (Gl. 3, 201-2; Dupin III, 71A), where one reads: 'Fatemur itaque datam praelatis et principibus potestatem a Deo, sed refert qualiter et qualem. Doceant nos exempla posita: licentiando in theologia et decretis, data a papa auctoritas; qualis auctoritas? exponendi et interpretandi sacram scripturam, non tamen ut expositio illa sit auctoritas apostolica sed est declaratio quaedam magistralis et scholastica. Libros sanctorum approbat ecclesia, non tamen ut robur auctoritatis teneant par ad ecclesiam, sed ut sciantur in multis esse utile ad aedificationem.' See also *De exam. doctrinarum*, cons. 1 (Gl. 9, 459-460; Dupin I, 10C), and *Apparuit gratia Dei* (Gl. 5, 71-2; Dupin II, 60A). Cf. Petrus Aureoli, *De conceptione B. Mariae virgine* (cited by N. Valois, 'Pierre Auriol, Frère Mineur', *Histoire litt. de la France*, XXXIII (Paris 1906), 497): 'Esto quod dicta sanctorum confirmata sint per concilia, nihilominus omnia dicta sanctorum non sunt tenenda pro fide aut praedicatione ecclesiae orthodoxae, tum quia contradictoria oporteret teneri pro fide... tum etiam quia multa absurda ecclesia confirmasset quae hodie non docent doctores...'; Augustinus Triumphus, *De summa potestate eccl.* a. 100 q. 5: 'Utrum illorum doctorum opera quos ecclesia canonisat ex hoc ipso sint per ecclesiam comprobata.'

What did Gerson do in these four theses? Nothing other than indicate certain consequences of the unbreakable tie, assumed in his definition, between *lex divina* and beatitude, divine law and the supernatural. The theses say hardly anything about what belonged to this supernatural or what meaning the concept of *lex divina* was invested with, for they were purely formal and without exception formulated in a negative sense. The meaning of the concept of 'divine law' has therefore to be discussed.

Meanwhile, it is already possible to state that this theory of law strictly limits the scope of divine, absolute law, for since neither the law of nature nor the positive law is directly concerned with the supernatural, the legal rules derived from them are necessarily outside the absolute order. By relating *lex divina* and the supernatural to each other in such an exclusive sense, Gerson was able to open quite a sizeable breach in the absolutist legal system of the canonists. They regarded the Pope as being raised above the positive and often even above the natural legal orders, so that in fact they identified his authority with that of God, and thus held his legislative power to be absolute. Papal decrees and decretals could therefore, in their opinion, claim an absolute validity.[91] Gerson was strongly opposed to this absolutism and constantly urged the same argument against it, saying: only that which concerns the supernatural can be considered as absolute.

Before pursuing the question of *lex divina*, let us first ask what he understood by the law of nature and positive law. Once again we shall begin with a definition:

> Lex naturalis praeceptiva... est signum inditum cuilibet homini non impedito in usu debito rationis, notificativum voluntatis divinae volentis creaturam rationalem humanam teneri vel obligari ad aliquid agendum vel non agendum pro consecutione finis sui naturalis, qui finis est felicitas humana et in multis debita conversatio domestica, et etiam politica. Homo enim natura animal civile est.[92]

It seems from this definition, which is not uninfluenced by Aristotle, that the difference between the *lex divina* and the *lex naturalis* consists primarily in the fact that while the former is based on revelation, the latter relies on the *ratio* given at the creation. Besides this differ-

---

[91] See Ullmann, *Mediaeval papalism*, 50-113; Tierney, *Foundations*, 85-7; Nörr, *Kirche und Konzil*, 76-7.

[92] *De vita spir. animae*, lect. 2, coroll. 5 (Gl. 3, 135; Dupin III, 21C).

ence in origin, the two laws also differ in their purpose, for that of the *lex naturalis* is natural, – the social order both in State and Church, – while the divine law has a supernatural purpose – the eternal life. Passing over the more complicated questions which are raised in this context, we turn to the *lex humana*. What did Gerson understand by it?

> Lex humana sive positiva praeceptiva... est signum verum humana traditione et auctoritate immediate constitutum, aut quod non infertur necessaria deductione ex lege divina et naturali, ligans ad aliquid agendum vel non agendum, pro consecutione finis alicuius humani.[93]

That is, we speak of human or positive law, in the first place whenever we refer to a law which is based on 'tradition' – on history or custom – and in the second place whenever we are concerned with a law which cannot possibly be related to the divine or natural law. As examples Gerson cites the law of royal succession in France, which is not an elective but a hereditary monarchy, and the fiscal system. Just as neither of these examples can be derived from the law of nature or the divine law, so neither is in open conflict with them. Among examples of human law in the Church Gerson includes a number of statutes of provincial synods, and ecclesiastical ceremonies, as well as all rules concerning penalties or exactions.[94] Time and again he criticises the overwhelming mass of human rules and regulations in the Church, and fiercely pleads for their abolition whenever they are not observed.[95]

Let us now return to the concept of *lex divina*. What did Gerson mean by this? From what we have already said it will be clear that he constantly associated divine law with faith. Whenever he had to justify his theses on the nature of divine law, he turned to *fides*, and clarified his views of the law by applying to them the theological

---

93 *De vita spir. animae*, lect. 2, coroll. 5 (Gl. 3, 135; Dupin III, 21CD).

94 *Conversi estis* (Gl. 5, 175; Dupin IV, 700A).

95 See in particular, *De contractibus*, propos. 16 (Gl. 9, 404-5; Dupin III, 182D-3C): '... ubi papa vel ecclesia vel legislator sciunt quod constitutiones suae vel non publicantur sed dantur oblivioni, vel non approbantur moribus utentium sed passim fit in oppositum, constitutiones illae desinunt habere vim obligationis, tanquam abolitae per non usum vel consuetudinem oppositam, quae non est legum omnium sed positivarum optima interpres.' Then follows a long list of constitutions and legal regulations in Church and society, which should be abolished since they are not observed; with reference to *De vita spir. animae*.

distinctions concerning the concept of faith. Just as it was untrue to say that every truth was a truth of the faith, so it was also untrue to call every obligation an obligation of the faith. The characteristic feature of both, the truths of the faith and of the divine law, was their supernatural orientation. We also find that he applied the well known distinction of explicit and implicit faith to the problem of the law.[96] The number of correspondences can be enlarged still further, and the conclusion is obvious that Gerson defined the concept of divine law by identifying it with the truths of the faith. We believe that this may be regarded as an innovation. At any rate, we are not aware of any such attempt to integrate the two concepts by an earlier author. We also have the impression that Gerson himself believed that he was making an original suggestion on this point.[97]

Once this identification had been completed, it was not difficult to describe precisely the limits and scope of the divine law, for all that was required was to list the catholic truths, which was not such a hard task since Ockham had already drawn up a catalogue of Catholic truths sixty years earlier. Gerson could and did follow the *venerabilis inceptor*, as he did not omit to state.[98]

Following the order of this catalogue, Gerson distinguished four hierarchically ordered spheres in divine law:

> 1. The first sphere is the totality of laws which are valid for the entire human community, and are intended to lead it towards beatitude. These laws were revealed directly by God and set down in the Scriptures, especially in the Gospels. Gerson does not answer the question as to which 'laws' we are to include under this heading. Ockham had placed those religious truths on which man's salvation is primarily dependent in the highest category. He names these as: the Oneness of God, the Trinity, Christ as truly God and truly Man, his passion, death, resurrection and ascension.[99] We may assume that Gerson too included these truths in the first category.

---

[96] *De vita spir. animae*, lect. 2, corr. 5 (Gl. 3, 136; Dupin III, 22B): '... sicut potest una propositio dici fidei proprie, quae non spectaret ad fidem explicitam... ita de legibus fatendum est.'

[97] See above n. 80.

[98] *De vita spir. animae*, lect. 2, corr. 4 (Gl. 3, 135; Dupin III, 21A): 'Si vero quaeritur numerus talium veritatum quae appropriate sunt de fide, remitto nunc ad ea quae tractavit Occam in suo Dialogo, libro II, quamvis aliqua pro incidentali declaratione sum dicturus.' He had already referred to this chapter of Ockham's *Dialogus* in his *Resumpta*. (See Chapter I n. 78).

[99] Ockham, *Dialogus* I, 2, 1 (ed. Goldast, 410^{29}-11^{52}).

2. Also part of divine law are those laws which 'in strict reasoning' (*in consequentia evidenti*) can be deduced from the preceding truths of the faith. 'Strict' in this sense means that their premises are derived entirely from these religious truths. Here too, it cannot be precisely determined what Gerson was referring to; probably to the authentic interpretation of the Scriptures by the Church–in other words, to dogma. In any case, this section is closed by a remark, that the Church cannot err on the point of determining the content of the faith.

3. The third sphere of action of the divine law concerns all laws revealed directly by Christ (*a Christo traditae*) or which can be deduced logically from this direct revelation, have been handed down to us by the apostles and others, and possess an authority which is equal to that of the Holy Scriptures. As an example of such a non-scriptural revelation Gerson cites the statement: *universalis ecclesia pontifici romano subiecta sit.* Human reason, basing itself on the highest truths of religion, could not arrive at this statement, yet it is certain that it belongs to divine law, for if this were not the case, the primacy as a human tradition, would be able to fall, '*quod non dicitur*'.

4. Finally there are those laws which have been revealed in a special manner and vouchsafed to particular people, either for their own sakes, or for that of a small number of the elect. Those laws which can be derived from such particular revelations, also belong to this sphere. Gerson refers here to the apostles, in whom he acknowledges a greater authority than in their successors. 'The apostles received their doctrine directly from Christ; they were eyewitnesses of his deeds, and it was to them that Christ said, «Who hears you, hears Me».' (Luke 10: 16; Matt. 10: 27). We know from the direct statement of Christ, recorded in the Scriptures, that Peter was an apostle, that he received the power of the keys, and that at Pentecost he was instructed in all the truths of salvation by the Holy Spirit. Nothing like this may be said of any of Peter's successors, we must at least assume that the succession took place legitimately, but our only knowledge of this is from human tradition. From all this it is clear how far greater the authority of the early Church was than that of the Church of today and also that neither the Pope nor the council nor the Church have the right to alter in any way what has been handed down from the evangelists or from Paul, 'as some have urged in their folly.' The present day Church possesses, with respect to the determination of the truths of the faith, less authority than the *ecclesia primitiva.*[100]

---

[100] *De vita spir. animae*, lect. 2 coroll. 7 (Gl. 3, 137-9; Dupin III, 23B-4C): 'Consequenter deducitur quomodo maior fuit primitivae ecclesiae auctoritas... quam nunc sit, et quod non est in potestate papae aut concilii aut ecclesiae immutare traditiones datas ab evangelistis et a Paulo, sicut quidam delirant. Nec habent quoad hoc, quod est facere

If we summarise the above, it appears that Gerson included among the divine law the laws which belong to 1. the Scriptures, especially the Creed; 2. dogma; 3. tradition, especially that of 4. the apostolic period. We shall return to the question which this hierarchy raises concerning the relationship of Church, scriptures and tradition, in another connexion. For the moment, let us merely establish that Gerson includes all laws in these spheres under the term *leges pure divinae*, which he distinguishes from the *leges non pure divinae*, the latter also being classified in a hierarchy of four grades.[101]

He understands by this laws which, even if they do not belong to the *lex divina* in the strict sense, can still be derived from it with the aid of probable truths which cannot be denied either by piety or reason. It is in other words, a question of logical reasoning, of which one premise is formed by a religious truth and the other by a probable truth. Whether the conclusion of such a train of reasoning is as absolutely valid as the religious truth itself, depends on the nature of the probable truth. Put more concretely, such an argument is like a chain, as strong as its weakest link.[102]

1. The first stage of the *leges non pure divinae*, is, for Gerson, made up of the laws which have been issued by God or by those whom He has directly authorised, but about which our knowledge comes only from history or from revelations which are not actually *de fide* (as, for example: the election of Clement by Peter). It is not to be doubted that Peter received full power from Christ to choose Clement as his successor, but anyone who chose to raise a doubt about the validity of this election, would be able to defend himself up to a point, because it concerned a historical fact, about which absolute certainty is not to be attained.

2. In the second place, there are those laws not issued directly by God, but which serve the purpose of the divine law, because they too are based on considerations which cannot reasonably be denied. An example is the law that, given the historical development of the Church, the election of a Pope during a vacancy belongs to the competence of the cardinals. Here, the rule of divine law, that if the see is vacant a Pope must be chosen, has had something added to it, which can no longer be

---

aliquid esse pure de fide, parem auctoritatis firmatatem.' Cf. *Dominus his opus habet*, cons. 11 (Gl. 5, 224; Dupin IV, 69AC). Cf. Chapter IX n. 66, and XII n. 112.

[101] *De vita spir. animae*, lect. 2, coroll. 7 (Gl. 3, 137, 139; Dupin III, 23B, 24C).

[102] Technically such a reasoning is called a '*propositio copulativa*'. See Peter of Spain, *Summulae logicales* I, 16 (ed. De Rijk, 9): '[Propositio] copulativa est illa in qua coniunguntur due categorie per hanc coniunctionem "et", ut "Socrates currit et Plato disputat."'

reasonably denied at this stage of historical evolution. The addition is, that the elective power of the Church has been entrusted to the cardinals.

3. To the third stage, Gerson assigns those legal rules which have been deduced from the *leges divinae* with the aid of *propositiones dubiae*, but which may still be embraced because they tend rather to piety than to its opposite. He finds numerous examples of this in the canones and decretals, and mentions specifically the date of feasts, admonitions concerning excommunications, many judgements made by bishops and some of the utterances of the saints.

4. Finally there are those laws which can be derived from the *leges divinae* but which lack the element of necessity, because their opposite could just as well be true.[103].

We are at the end of our exposition of Gerson's views on the divine law. The reason why he felt such a detailed study of questions concerning the Church and the law was required, lay mainly in the fact that, in his opinion, the canonists had been insufficiently critical in their treatment of the concept of divine law. They had misused it by mixing it up with positive legal rules and exactments, thus endangering the good order of the Church, and obscuring her essential core, her divine purpose. By distinguishing *lex divina, lex naturalis* and *lex humana*, and associating them respectively with the supernatural, the human community and 'tradition', he tried to indicate what was to be regarded as essential and what as accidental in the juridical structure of the Church.

He answered the question, what was to be included in the supernatural sphere, by reference to the Catholic truths, of which, following Ockham, he drew up a catalogue. In such a way he defined the sphere of competence of the divine law, even into its furthest reaches. He made it clear that it was in the last analysis the (hierarchical) Church as a whole–and not, as in the absolutist ideology of the canonists, the Pope alone,–who decided the scope of the *lex divina*, in accordance with the norm laid down by the *ecclesia primitiva*.

As far as the *leges non pure divinae* were concerned, we feel that Gerson was a victim of a tendency to excessive systematisation, and moreover cast doubt on his own triple division. We feel it is hardly

[103] *De vita spir. animae*, lect. 2 (Gl. 3, 139-41; Dupin III, 24D-5D).

fortuitous that he only applied this concept once, and never returned to it.

How did this triple division of the law, which Gerson called a '*clavis aurea*' to unlock its essence, work in reality?[104] What guidelines for the practice of ecclesiastical politics were derived from it? Since Gerson confined the title of divine law to those laws which were in direct relationship with the Catholic truths, and scarcely acknowledged in this respect any independent role to the concept of natural law,[105] we may assume that his threefold division was primarily aimed at the absolutist abuse of the positive law by the canonists. The '*traditiones humanae*' of the canon lawyers were to be rejected, all the more so as Gerson, during the Schism, came to realise that no agreement could be reached on the basis of positive law.

We have seen that this insight dawned on him in the years following 1400. Theoretically prepared and elaborated in the lectures he gave in 1402 (*De vita spirituali animae*), it is attested above all by the sermon *Apparuit gratia Dei*, given before Benedict at Tarascon on 1 January 1404. It was at that time that he began to recognise the autocrat in Benedict, the man who let himself be guided by the pernicious ideology of absolutism against which Gerson, as a theologian, already had very serious objections, objections which the persistence of the Schism only strengthened. It was for that reason that he insisted so vehemently that nothing was to be hoped for from positive law. The Schism was a *casus novus*, and as such it fell outside the sphere of strict law. The positive legal order had therefore to be regarded – for the moment – as suspended and the Church had to let itself be led by the guidelines offered by divine law and the law of nature. It was in this connexion that he introduced the concept of 'epikie'. What did he mean by this?

---

[104] *Conversi estis* (Gl. 5, 178; Dupin IV, 702C): '... describere tentaremus quid ius pure divinum, quid pure naturale, quid positivum vel humanum... Hoc enim est velut triplex clavis aurea ad reserationem omnium in iuribus contentorum.'

[105] *Diligite iustitiam* (Gl. 7*, 610; Dupin IV, 650C); *De pot. eccl.*, cons. 13 (Gl. 6, 244; Dupin II, 252A): 'Lex enim divina de ratione sua habet primo ut acquiratur per revelationem, deinde quod ordinet de proximo et per se ad felicitatem aeternam. Lex vero naturalis, etsi possit sic acquiri et ordinari, sicut patet in datatione praeceptorum decalogi in utraque lege, veteri et nova, hoc tamen non habet de ratione sua ut naturalis est, sed transit in divinam.'

3. *The concept of epikie*

The concept of epikie derives from Aristotle, who discussed it in, among other works, his Nichomachean Ethics. He understood by it a correction of the strict law, a correction which was appropriate because every law had a general purpose which by its nature could not foresee every particular case.

> When... the law lays down a general rule, and thereafter a case arises which is an exception to the rule, it is then right, where the lawgivers' pronouncement because of its absoluteness is defective and erroneous, to rectify the defect by deciding as the lawgiver would himself decide if he were present on the occasion, and would have enacted if he had been cognizant of the case in question.[106]

'Epikie' is thus primarily a correction of the law in the sense of adding something to the written law, according to the spirit of the lawgiver. When Aristotle speaks of the virtue of epikie he gives the concept a broader meaning. He means by it something like humaneness, generosity, sympathy. A man gives proof of his epikie when he applies the legal means at his disposal in the milder sense rather than the stricter, when he pays heed to the intention of the lawgiver rather than to the letter of the law, or takes more notice of the good which someone had wished to do, than of the evil which he has done.[107]

A concept comparable to epikie in Roman Law is that of *aequitas* or fairness. One could speak of *aequitas* whenever a law agreed with the feeling of justice, whenever it was fair and right. In later Roman Law, as also in canon law, *aequitas* acquired the further meaning of a benevolent, humane interpretation of the law as opposed to a strictly literal reading. In both meanings, *aequitas* is to be distinguished from epikie in so far as the latter concept is concerned with a correction of the law, while the former is a matter of the quality of the law or of its interpretation. On the other hand, *aequitas* and epikie had in common that they both derived from the principle of humaneness.

---

[106] Aristotle, *Eth. Nik.* V, 10, 3.

[107] For more details about the concept of epikie, see Von Hove, *Commentarium Lovaniense,* I, II, 274ff.; *DDC* s.v. 'épikie' (G. LeBras); G. LeBras, Ch. Lefebvre, J. Rambaud, *Histoire du Droit et des Institutions de l'Eglise en Occident,* VII, Paris [1965], 352-66, 406-20. For Gerson and the use he made of the concept, see Combes, *La théologie mystique* I, 268-72.

The concept of epikie was unknown to the early scholastics and found its way into theology in the course of the thirteenth century, as one of the fruits of the rediscovery of Aristotle. Albertus Magnus knew it,[108] while Thomas of Aquinas devoted a few brilliant pages to it in his *Summa*, which we can be sure were not unknown to Gerson.[109] Although Thomas preferred to use the term *aequitas*, it is certain that he was inspired mainly by Aristotle and not by the jurists. This is clear from the fact that his interpretation of the concept of *aequitas* was taken over very early by the canonists, among them Guido de Baysio in his often cited *Rosarium*.[110]

After Thomas, the concept of epikie/*aequitas* was soon naturalised in moral theology and canon law. All theologians and canonists made use of it, and it was thus not unusual for Gerson to appeal to it also, the less so because of his own preference for moral theology. We wish to emphasise this, as some scholars have been tempted by the mere fact that Gerson applied the concept of epikie to draw too confident conclusions about his sources. That Marsilius of Padua, Ockham, Henry of Langenstein, Conrad of Gelnhausen and d'Ailly all used the idea of epikie, in itself says nothing, for they were by no means exceptional in this.[111] No, if we wish to trace Gerson's sources, we have to proceed more carefully and must not begin with such a widely current concept as epikie.

In his *De vita spirituali animae* Gerson made use of the term for the first time. It is noteworthy that he used it–like Thomas Aquinas to whom he refers–in a strictly moral-theological context.[112] Because of the Schism moral theology had taken on an additional importance for him, for it dealt with such questions as dispensations,

[108] Albertus Magnus, *Comm. in eth.* V, tract. 6 cap. 1 (ed. A. Borgnet vol. VII, 383).

[109] Thomas, *S.th.* I^{a} II^{ae} q. 96 a. 6; II^{a} II^{ae} q. 120 a. 1; Van Hove, *Commentarium* I, II, 281-4.

[110] *Rosarium super decreto*, ad. dist. 45 c. 9, as cited by Van Hove, *Commentarium*, I, II, 280 n. 2.

[111] Z. Rueger, 'Le "De auctoritate concilii" de Gerson', *RHE* 53 (1958), 775-95. This author in her article, marred by many inaccuracies, remarks (780 n. 3): 'Gerson emploie pour la première fois le mot *epikeia* en 1404, et probablement sous l'influence de Jean de Montreuil.' For the last statement she refers to André Combes, *Jean de Montreuil*, who in fact asserted the opposite: 'admettre que Gerson pourrait devoir à Jean de Montreuil le mot et la notion d'épikie serait absurde' (556). Moreover, Gerson did not use the term for the first time in 1404 but in 1402 (see next note).

[112] *De vita spir. animae*, lect. 4, coroll. 6 (Gl. 3, 163; Dupin III, 42A, 62A): 'Et non potest universaliter dari regula nisi ut aequitas quae a philosophis dicitur epikeia iudicabit.' Thomas, *S.Th.* I^{a} II^{ae} q. 97 is cited in lect. 4, coroll. 13 (Gl. 3, 170; Dupin III, 47C).

changes in the law, the bounds of obedience and so on, all of which the Schism had given an unusually urgent importance. This explains how the concept of epikie left the sphere of moral theology and entered that of ecclesiastical politics, where it came to be used as an argument in the struggle against the predominance of positive legal rules, by which the disastrous Schism was only prolonged.

Unlike Thomas, Gerson did not apply the concept of epikie very precisely. If we collect his scattered statements on this matter they can be distinguished into four categories: 1. statements of a general nature; 2. statements of a particular nature, on the function of epikie; 3. statements on the virtue of epikie, and finally 4. statements on the deepest meaning of the application of epikie.

1. As far as the general statements are concerned, they are very varied. If Gerson defines it in one case in the Aristotelian sense as the correction of the law,[113] in another instance he equates it with *discretio*, the power of distinction,[114] while in yet another case he identifies it with the power of dispensation and exception.[115] Although these definitions differ, they agree in assuming the insufficiency of the positive law.

2. Gerson generally describes the function of epikie as interpretative.[116] Epikie interprets the laws not according to the letter but according to the spirit.[117] It ensures that the rules of the law are not in conflict with its spirit: *pax*.[118] It reconciles laws with each other[119]

---

[113] *De vita spir. animae*, lect. IV, coroll, 6, and lect. V (Gl. 3, 162-3, 189; Dupin III, 42A, 62A); *Regulae morales* (Dupin III, 78B); *De protestatione* (Gl. 6, 159; Dupin I, 31C).

[114] *Pax vobis* (Gl. 5, 441; Dupin IV, 707B).

[115] *De pot. eccl.*, cons. 12 (Gl. 6, 230; Dupin II, 241B): 'leges humanae quae feruntur generaliter possunt et debent exceptionem recipere dum deficit ratio legis... Haec autem exceptio multipliciter nominatur; quandoque epikeia, sicut ab Aristotele; quandoque iuris interpretatio, sicut a legistis; quandoque dispensatio, sicut a canonistis; quandoque bona fides, sicut a politicis...; quandoque dicitur aequitas...'

[116] *De vita spir. animae*, lect. 5 (Gl. 3, 189; Dupin III, 62A): '.. elicitur evidens necessitas virtutis illius quam Aristoteles epikeiam, hoc est interpretativam legum appellat; cuius est considerare non nudum de se praeceptum sed circumstantias omnes particulariter ipsum vestientes. Ex hoc consequenter habetur modus concordandi rigorem iustitiae atque severitatem disciplinae cum lenitate misericordiae et favorabilis indulgentiae.'

[117] *Conversi estis* (Gl. 7, 177; Dupin IV, 701D).

[118] *Pro convocatione concilii Pisani* (Gl. 6, 125; Dupin II, 122C): 'recurrendum ad epikeiam et finem legis qui est pax...'

[119] *Pax vobis* (Gl. 5, 443; Dupin IV, 709A); *De unitate eccl.* (Gl. 6, 142; Dupin II, 118D):

and interprets them in accordance with the intention of the lawgiver.

3. In agreement with this, the virtue of epikie is denied to the 'literalists', that is to those who are so obsessed with the written law that they are oblivious of its spirit. We give one example:

> Ubi nihilominus notandum occurrit contra eos qui tanta obstinatione legibus mortuis humanis adhaerent, legem vivam fundatam in lege aeterna et in aequitate seu epikeia penitus ignorantes vel spernentes, quod lex perficitur et impletur dum vel in finem meliorem vel salubrioribus mediis ordinatur, qui finis est caritas...[120]

This protest against the literalists is a sharp one, but here too Gerson knew where to draw the line; he could see the danger if the concept of epikie was too hastily applied:

> ... tamen hoc summopere cavendum est iudicibus, ne usus epikeyae passim et absque manifesta ratione fiat, transmutando legem scriptam; alioquin tolleretur protinus a legibus sua stabilitas.[121]

This warning is positively complemented by his statement that the power of applying epikie belongs primarily to the theologians and only in the second place to the canonists.

> Auctoritas vero doctrinaliter utendi epikeia residet principaliter apud peritos in theologia, quae est architectoria respectu aliarum, et consequenter apud peritos in scientia iuris canonici et civilis, prout ex principiis iuris divini et naturalis habet accipere fundamenta.[122]

Here we see how the concept of epikie is closely associated in Gerson with his encyclopaedic views and his opinions on the law in general. He worked this out more carefully in his *De unitate ecclesiae* (1409) in which he argued in greater detail that human law should be judged by the standard of the divine law and the law of nature, in accordance with epikie and *aequitas*. The proof of this argument,

---

'Unitas ecclesiae ligatur quadruplici lege, divina..., naturali, canonica et civili, quarum duas extremas regulare necesse est per primas secundum epikeiam, id est bonam aequitatem.'

[120] *Pax vobis* (Gl. 5, 73, 85; Dupin II, 61B, 69C); *De consol. theol. III* (Gl. 9, 219; Dupin I, 160B).

[121] *De unitate eccl.* (Gl. 6, 145; Dupin II, 121B).

[122] *De unitate eccl.* (Gl. 6, 138; Dupin II, 115CD).

so he claimed, was to be found in both the canon and civil law themselves.[123]

4. The most fundamental reason for his appeal to epikie is always that the maintenance of the positive legal order merely prolongs the impasse of the Schism and blocks the way back to the re-establishment of the unity of the Church. It is Gerson's thesis that in such a case the Church, as the mystical body of Christ, is justified in self defence, in setting aside the positive legal order for a time, in order to regain its unity by giving itself wholly to its Head, Christ, and his sanctifying and unifying Spirit. Epikie opens the way to this and provides the legitimation, for it points to the intention of the lawgiver, and to the highest law which rules the mystical body: love.[124]

---

[123] *De unitate eccl.*, cons. 1 (Gl. 6, 142; Dupin II, 120D). Cf. Chapter VI n. 58.

[124] See in particular, *De unitate eccl.* (Gl. 6, 136-45; Dupin II, 113-18).

CHAPTER NINE

CHURCH, HIERARCHY AND GENERAL COUNCIL I

The treatise *De potestate ecclesiastica et de origine iuris et legum*

> ... *potest occurrere scandalum trahens ad hoc inconveniens quod Ecclesia posset bene regi usque ad finem saeculi sine papa, ut si generale concilium daret licentiam omnibus episcopis, sacerdotibus, cuilibet supra plebem suam, absque ulla iurisdictionis limitatione vel restrictione... Respondemus quod etsi ad tempus aliquod generale concilium posset aliquid tale facere, quoniam habere papam est praeceptum affirmativum, obligans ad semper sed non pro semper,... nihilominus generale concilium neque deberet neque posset talem defectum capitis usque ad finem saeculi tolerare, stante lege.*
>
> Gerson, *De potestate ecclesiastica* (Gl. 6, 235; Dupin II, 245A)

The treatise *De potestate ecclesiastica et de origine iuris et legum*,[1] presented to the Council of Constance on 6 February 1417,[2] will be the basis of our enquiry into the essentials of Gerson's ecclesiology. It is the obvious choice, for in no other work did he develop his ecclesiological ideas in such careful detail, or express and summarise his meaning more clearly.

Although various authors have given more or less adequate summaries of this famous treatise, it is still worth-while, for two reasons, to attempt a new restatement and interpretation. In the first place it seems that the assessment of it – as of Gerson's ecclesiology in general – is still partly dominated by the completely unjustified assumption of a relationship between Gerson and Marsilius of Padua. The direct consequence of this supposed dependence on the author of the *Defensor pacis* is that Gerson's ecclesiology has been interpreted in a far too radical sense.

In the second place, a new interpretation of the *De potestate*

---

[1] Gl. 6, 210-50; Dupin II, 225-56. See also below n. 13.

[2] Gerson completed his treatise somewhat earlier, as is apparent from his sermon *Nuptiae factae sunt* (17 Jan. 1417), where he refers to *de pot. eccl.* as 'nuper editus'. (Gl. 5, 384; Dupin II, 355A). See also below n. 136 & n. 137.

ecclesiastica is justified by the fact that since Schwab's study of the work in 1858,[3] interpretation has in fact remained at a standstill. This may seem to be a rather daring statement, but it is not. For, although authors like Hübler[4] and Von Gierke[5] in the last century, and Hauck,[6] Salembier,[7] Combes,[8] Morrall,[9] Alberigo[10] and others in ours, devoted more or less serious attention to this important treatise, their respective interpretations remained rather limited and vague, in particular because they failed to investigate the tradition in which the treatise must be placed. For that reason, we will first identify the tradition to which *De potestate ecclesiastica* actually belongs, before discussing the treatise itself. For, as long as this point remains uncertain, the interpretation is necessarily doubtful and the question of just how far Gerson was striking out on a new path ecclesiologically, will remain unanswered.

At the beginning of his work Gerson states his intention of dealing with the power of the Church summarily, without laying claim to any originality:

> satis est si ex bene inventis et doctrinis aliorum, ego meis verbis, meo ordine, favum aliquem veritatis instar apum, propria arte compingam.[11]

To what does this statement refer? What findings and doctrines of others are meant? Where did he gather his honey? It is our firm conviction that he was not above all guided nor primarily inspired by Ockham, Conrad of Gelnhausen or d'Ailly, as is constantly repeated, but by a group of authors with whom one would perhaps not immediately associate him. We mean the so-called curialist writers, such as Giles of Rome, Augustinus Triumphus, Alvarez Pelayo, Alexander of St. Elpidio, and others.[12] We are unable to furnish

3 Schwab, *Gerson*, 722-58.

4 H. Hübler, *Die Constanzer Reformation und die Conkordate von 1418*, Leipzig 1867, 385ff.

5 O. von Gierke, *Genossenschaftsrecht* III, (reprint) Darmstadt 1958, 586ff.

6 A. Hauck, 'Gegensätze im Kirchenbegriff des späteren Mittelalters', *L* XLIX (1938) 225-40.

7 *DThC* VI, c. 1318ff *s.v.* 'Gerson, Jean'.

8 Combes, *Jean de Montreuil*, 474-90.

9 Morrall, *Gerson*, 100-7.

10 Giuseppe Alberigo, *Chiesa Conciliare. Identità e significato del conciliarismo*, Brescia 1981, 215-18.

11 *De pot. eccl.* (Gl. 6, 211; Dupin II, 227A).

12 Cf. R. Scholz, *Die Publizistik zur Zeit Philipps des Schönen und Bonifaz VIII*, Stuttgart 1903; J. Rivière, *Le problème de l'Eglise et de l'Etat au temps de Philippe le Bel*, Louvain/Paris

definite proof that he found his honey here, for none of these authors is specifically mentioned in the tract, but the probability can be demonstrated.

In the first place, we may point out that it would have been remarkable if Gerson had neglected the curialist literature completely, or if he had worked out his ecclesiology without any reference to them. The curialists were specialists in precisely that field, and for that reason it is far more likely that Gerson consulted their works than that he did not.

Secondly, the very title of his work, *De potestate ecclesiastica* could be seen as an indication that he chose a starting point among the curialist authors.[13] At any rate, both Giles of Rome and Alexander of St. Elpidio, as well as Petrus de Palude had published works with similar or virtually identical titles.[14] They were alone in this, for such a title had never been used before their time,[15] while their contemporary opponents mostly treated the same theme under a different title.[16] Gerson therefore followed the curialist custom when he called his tract *De potestate ecclesiastica*. That it was not just a chance

---

1926; N. Iung, *Un Franciscain, théologien du pouvoir pontifical au XIVe siècle, Alvaro Pelayo, évêque et pénitencier de Jean XXII*, Paris 1931; X.P.D. Duynstee, *'s Pausen primaat in de latere middeleeuwen en de Aegidiaanse school*, 2 vols., Hilversum/Amsterdam 1935-6; R. Kuiters, *De ecclesiastica sive de summi pontificis potestate secundum Aegidium Romanum*, 1949; M.J. Wilks, 'The idea of the church as "Unus homo perfectus" and its bearing on the medieval theory of sovereignty,' *MHE*, Congrès de Stockholm, Août 1960, Louvain 1961, 32-50; M.J. Wilks, *The problem of sovereignty in the later middle ages. The papal monarchy with Augustinus Triumphus and the publicists*, Cambridge 1963.

[13] The second part of the title *De potestate ecclesiastica et de origine iuris et legum* refers only to the last *consideratio* (13), in which Gerson analyses a number of juridical terms and conceptions, in accordance with what he had done in his *De vita spir. animae*. At the end of *De pot. eccl.*, cons. 12 (Gl. 6, 249; Dupin II, 255A) he refers explicitly to this treatise as well as to a sermon from his hand *Omnia dedit ei Pater in manus* (Gl. 5, 405-19; Dupin III, 1449-57).

[14] Giles of Rome, *De ecclesiastica sive de summi pontificis potestate* [1301], ed. R. Scholz, Weimar 1929; Augustinus Triumphus of Ancona, *Summa de potestate ecclesiastica* [1320], Augsburg [Johann Schüssler] 1473; Alexander of St. Elpidio, *De ecclesiastica potestate* [1325], in: J.Th. de Rocaberti, *Bibliotheca maxima pontificia* II, Roma 1695, 1-40; Petrus de Palude, *De causa immediata ecclesiastice potestatis* [1325?], Paris [Jean Barbier] 1506. We have not seen the modern ed. of this work prepared by William David McGready (*The Theory of Papal Monarchy in the Fourteenth Century*, Toronto 1982).

[15] J.A. Fabricius, *Bibliotheca Latina* I, Florentiae 1858, 59, following J. Pitseus, *Relationum historicarum de rebus Anglicis* I, Paris. 1619, 287, unjustly considers Alexander, Abbot of Canterbury (1157-1217), as the author of a treatise, entitled: *De ecclesiae potestate*. Cf. F.M. Powicke, 'Alexander of St. Albans: A literary Muddle,' in: *Essays presented to Reginald Lane Poole*, Oxford 1927, 246-60.

[16] E.g. Jean de Paris, Marsilius of Padua and Ockham.

resemblance of a purely formal nature but can be regarded as a indication of dependence on curialist literature and doctrine, will become evident later.

In the third place, we know that in his *Resumpta* of 1392 he referred to a certain 'frater Alexander', who can hardly be any other than the curialist author mentioned above, the Augustinian Eremite Alexander of St. Elpidio.[17] Gerson cited him with approval, and was thus already familiar with curialist literature as a young man. That he continued to gather his honey from works of this kind seems to be confirmed by his lectures from 1402/3, which he published afterwards under the title of *De vita spirituali animae.*[18]

It has not proved possible to determine which particular curialist work Gerson must have consulted. Does this negative result destroy our hypothesis? The texts will show, but it should be remembered that the curialist authors were very dependent on each other. Alvarez Pelayo, for example, in his *Planctus ecclesiae*, took over the *De regimine christiano* of James of Viterbo, more or less without alteration.[19] Alexander of St. Elpidio, like James of Viterbo, made intensive use of the writings of his fellow Augustinian Eremite Giles of Rome, in composing his *De potestate ecclesiastica.*[20] Augustinus Triumphus also included in his work whatever he found of value in Giles of Rome.

These examples could be multiplied in order to demonstrate that curialist literature is so much a whole that it may be considered a single corpus. In that case it is not so strange to find that Gerson's tract sometimes seems to refer to Giles of Rome, and sometimes to another curialist, and that it is not possible to discover precisely whom he was following. Nor must we forget that – although the Council of Constance stimulated a lively book-trade[21] – Gerson was

---

[17] Chapter I n. 72.

[18] See in particular lectio 3, the passage where he considers the relationship between Pope and Church (Gl. 3, 153-5; Dupin III, 34D-6C). The distinction he makes here between *esse formale* and *esse materiale* in the papacy, 'office' and 'person', seems to be borrowed from Giles of Rome, *De renunciatione papae* 14 (ed. Rocaberti, 58b). Cf. Wilks, *Sovereignty*, 500 n. 2, and Tierney, *Foundations*, 147.

[19] Cf. Rivière, *Le problème*, 147 n. 3; H.-X. Arquillière, *Le plus ancien traité de l'Eglise. Jacques de Viterbe, De regimine christiano (1301-1302)*, Paris 1926; Jung, *Alvaro Pelayo*, 39-46.

[20] Scholz, *Publizistik*, 145; Alexander also used James of Viterbo's treatise, cf. the former's *De eccl. pot.* III c. 6 (ed. Rocaberti, 36^b).

[21] Paul Lehmann, 'Konstanz und Basel als Büchermärkte während der grossen Kirchenversammlungen', *Zeitschrift des deutschen Vereins für Buchwesen und Schrifttum*, IV (1921) 6-11; 17-27; reprinted in Paul Lehmann, *Erforschung des Mittelalters*, Leipzig 1941, 253-68.

deprived of most of his folios[22] when he prepared his treatise, and therefore will have relied more than once on his memory, with the inevitable consequences.

***

When he presented *De potestate ecclesiastica*, the Council of Constance had already proceeded to the deposition of Pope John XXIII, and was making preparations to take the same line against Benedict XIII. Both measures were accompanied by lengthy and often acrimonious discussions on the relationship between Pope and Church, Pope and cardinals, and the authority of the Council. Gerson took part in these discussions, and was especially concerned to define the relationship of Pope and Church more exactly; this naturally involved raising the question of the authority of the Council.

In his treatise he made a number of distinctions in the usual scholastic manner, with the aid of which he determined the essence, the limits and the scope of ecclesiastical authority. Before considering the treatise in more detail, we shall look at its structure, with reference to a scheme printed in the editions of Glorieux and Dupin under the title '*arbor de potestate ecclesiastica*'.[23] The Roman numerals refer to the *considerationes* into which the work is divided; thirteen in all. In order to deal reasonably clearly with the many and often complicated questions involved, we will divide the subject matter into the following sections:

---

[22] *Nuptiae factae sunt* (Gl. 5, 385; Dupin II, 355C): 'Vidi nuper sanctum Thomam et Bonaventuram, hic reliquorum libros non habeo.'

[23] Gl. 9, 175-7; Dupin II, 259. See also L. Hödl, 'Kirchengewalt und Kirchenverfassung nach dem Liber de ecclesiastica potestate des Laurentius von Arezzo', in: *Theologie in Geschichte und Gegenwart*, (Festschrift Michael Schmaus), edd. J. Auer & H. Volk, München 1957, 255-78. It seems to us an established fact that the anonymous *Liber de ecclesiastica potestate*, on which Laurentius of Arezzo based the first part of his homonymous treatise, can be identified with Gerson's *de pot. eccl.* (Hödl, 260). In fact Laurentius used the same distinctions as Gerson, as can be seen from the scheme given by Hödl, who, however, does not explain from whom it stems – from Hödl himself or from Laurentius (263ff.). The treatise mentioned on 258 n. 6 may be identified with Gerson's *De auferibilitate*, while 'Johannes Alphonsus', whom neither Grabmann nor Hödl could identify, will be no other than Johannes Alphonsi de Segovia.

1. *Ecclesiastical power* A (considerationes 1-5)
   1. power of order
      a. *super corpus Christi verum*
      b. *super corpus Christi mysticum*
   2. power of jurisdiction
      a. *in foro interiori*
      b. *in foro exteriori*

2. *Ecclesiastical power* B (considerationes 6-9)
   1. Ecclesiastical power in the absolute sense
   2. Ecclesiastical power in the material sense
   3. Ecclesiastical power in the executive sense

3. *Plenitude of ecclesiastical power* (considerationes 10-12)
   1. *plenitudo potestatis* in respect to the papal office
   2. *plenitudo potestatis* in respect to the Church
   3. *plenitudo potestatis* in respect to the State and the temporal possessions of the Church

***

1. *Ecclesiastical power A*

> Potestas ecclesiastica est potestas quae a Christo supernaturaliter et specialiter collata est suis apostolis et discipulis ac eorum successoribus legitimis usque in finem saeculi, ad aedificationem ecclesiae militantis, secundum leges evangelicas pro consecutionem felicitatis aeternae.[24]

We recognise in this careful definition the Aristotelian distinction of a fourfold causation: Christ as the *causa efficiens*; the apostles and disciples as the *causa materialis*; the laws of the Gospel as *causa formalis*; the building of the Church militant and the winning of eternal bliss as *causa finalis*. The power of the Church is thus regarded as existing only in the hands of the apostles and disciples, and their legitimate successors. It is fully in accordance with this that Gerson interprets the idea of the 'Church' in connexion with the power it wields, very strictly, indeed exclusively in the sense of the hierarchy,

[24] *De pot. eccl.*, cons. 1 (Gl. 6, 211; Dupin II, 227A).

from high to low, from the Pope to the humblest representative of the hierarchy.[25]

Gerson expressly states that baptism is adequate for the reception of ecclesiastical power. He recognises that it would be desirable if priests were in a state of grace, but he does not feel that this is a necessity for either the reception or the exercise of ecclesiastical power. His argument is aimed at the Waldensians, the Poor Men of Lyons and their modern successors, the Wyclifites, who, in Gerson's opinion, were rightly condemned on the grounds that the entire hierarchic order would be undermined if it were to be based on sanctifying grace or on predestination.[26]

1. *Power of order*

a. super corpus Christi verum

Ecclesiastical power is then sub-divided into power of order and power of jurisdiction. The former, being based on the sacrament of order, gives the priest power over the true body of Christ, and is thus primarily a power of consecration.[27] As such it cannot be extinguished. The general opinion of the doctors is that this power is equal in all priests; in other words the Pope's power with regard to the Eucharist is no more than that of a simple priest. Both possess equally the power of order which was passed on by Christ to all the apostles, including Judas, at the Last Supper, in the words 'Do this in memory of Me' (Luke 22: 19).

b. super corpus Christi mysticum

Although the power of order is primarily a power over the true body of Christ, that is not all; it is also concerned with the mystical body of Christ, that is, with the Church. By virtue of their power of consecration, priests have power over the Church, in particular

[25] *De pot. eccl.*, cons. 1 (Gl. 6, 211; Dupin II, 227B): 'Unde et "Ecclesiae" contracte sumitur dum loquimur hic de ecclesiastica potestate, pro illis videlicet qui speciali quodam signaculo dedicati sunt ad divinum servitium, a clericatura quae infimum tenet gradum usque ad supremum quo papa decoratur.' – For the different meanings of the term 'ecclesia', see Ockham, *Dialogus* I 5, 31 (ed. Goldast, 501[64]-2[26]), and Tierney, *Foundations*, 125 n. 2.

[26] Cf. art. 1, added to Gerson's letter inc. *Ceterum* to Conrad de Vechte (24 Sept. 1414) (Gl. 2, 163).

[27] *De pot. eccl.* cons. 2 (Gl. 6, 212-13; II, 228BC).

the power to administer the sacraments. The two aspects of the power of consecration, one may say, complement each other, in so far as the power of consecration finds its counterpart in the ministry of the sacraments, and in so far as the eucharist exists for the sake of building up the body of Christ. *Corpus Christi verum* and *mysticum* belong together.[28] But, although the two aspects of the power of consecration complement each other, they are not one and the same; there is a clear distinction between them.

As far as consecration is concerned, all priests are equal; but in the ministry of the other sacraments this is by no means so. The power of consecration, as power over the mystical body of Christ, is not equal in all priests. A simple priest may not do, with regard to the Church, what a bishop may do, although both of them are ordained. How is this difference in authority to be explained? Here too, Gerson adds his voice to the majority of the theologians and considers the consecration of a priest and of a bishop to belong to the same order but regards the latter as a completed form of the former. The difference is thus not one of kind but of degree.

> Concedatur cum maiore parte doctorum, quod supra sacerdotium simplex nulla est altera potestas ordinis neque in episcopis neque in papa, sed aliter est in episcopis et in papa, aliter est in simplicibus presbyteris.[29]

To make this clearer he adduces the well known parallel of the boy and the full grown man, who, so far as their humanity is concerned are essentially the same, though this does not prevent the boy from being unable to beget children. This is how one must see the relationship of priest and bishop; they are equal in so far as their priesthood is concerned, but only the bishop possesses the power of ordination, confirmation, etc., because only he has received the full measure of the sacerdotal dignity.

In this way, Gerson concludes, we may also solve the question which has divided theologians and canonists: is the episcopate to be regarded as a separate order or as the highest grade of the priesthood? On the heart of the question, there is agreement; only in the arguments brought forward do scholars differ. The canonists call the episcopate an independent order, because the powers of a

---

[28] For this distinction see Chapter X, § 3.

[29] *De pot. eccl.*, cons. 3 (Gl. 6, 214; Dupin II, 229C): 'Et hoc [sc. potestas ordinis] est par in omnibus episcopis, ab infimo usque ad supremum qui papa dicitur.'

bishop over the mystical body of Christ are wider than those of a priest; while the theologians, though not denying this, prefer not to speak of a new order, on the grounds that the dignity does not extend the powers over the true body of Christ.[30]

2. *Power of jurisdiction*

a. in foro interiori

The analogy of the boy and the man, which Gerson adduced in order to clarify the relationship of priest and bishop, is clear but does not answer the question, what is the ground for a distinction between a higher and a lower grade of priesthood? Why should a bishop enjoy a greater say over the mystical body of Christ, the Church, than an ordinary priest? The word 'say' indicates that priesthood is not to be considered from the sacramental point of view alone but from the juridical side as well. This aspect, which is closely related to the power of order, is called the 'power of jurisdiction'. In the scholastic literature after Thomas Aquinas[31] this is again divided into *potestas iurisdictionis in foro interiori* and that *in foro exteriori*, depending on whether the power of jurisdiction remains restricted to the private sphere (conscience and confession) or enters into the public sphere of the mystical body (excommunication).[32]

> Potestas ecclesiastica iurisdictionis in foro interiori, quae non est proprie coërcitiva sed magis spontanea quoad subjicientes se eidem, est potestas ecclesiastica super corpus Christi mysticum, illuminando et perficiendo ipsum per doctrinam et sacramentorum ministrationem, et purgando per baptismi et poenitentiae sacramenta.[33]

---

[30] Cf. *DThC* XI 2, 1311-12 s.v. 'ordre' (A. Michel); M. Grabmann, 'Die Lehre des Erzbischofs und Augustinertheologen Jakob von Viterbo', 193; and, in particular, Congar, 'Un témoignage de désaccords', 865-6. Gerson follows his favoured authority, Bonaventure. Cf. *De auferib.* cons. 15 (Gl. 3, 305; Dupin II, 219D): 'Notetur Bonaventura in dist. XXV quarti, ubi quaerit si episcopatus sit ordo supra sacerdotium, et ponit quod neque episcopatus neque papatus dicit nisi plenitudinem aliquam vel dignitatem in ordine, et ordinem novum nullum addit.'

[31] *De iurisdictione.* Ein unveröffentliches Traktat des Herveus Natalis O.P. (1323) über die Kirchengewalt, ed. Ludwig Hödl, München 1959, 12.

[32] Cf. Giles of Rome, *De pot. eccl.* II 12 (ed. Scholz, 110): '... sciendum quod Magister IV sententiarum [d. 18, 6 & 7] innuit duplicem modum ligandi et solvendi: unum qui sit in foro penitencie sive in foro consciencie, ubi agitur causa inter hominem et Deum; alium autem modum qui fit per excommunicacionem in foro exterioris iudicii, ubi agitur causa inter hominem et hominem.'

[33] *De pot. eccl.*, cons. 5 (Gl. 6, 218; Dupin II, 232D).

Seen in this light, the power of jurisdiction is founded *radicaliter* on the sacramental power of order, and as such it is wholly directed to the inner building of the mystical body, the community of believers, which must be achieved through the three hierarchical acts of which pseudo-Dionysius speaks: the acts of purification, enlightenment and completion (*purgare, illuminare, perficere*).[34] Purification takes place through baptism and absolution, enlightenment through teaching and preaching, and completion through the ministry of the other sacraments. The Church's power of jurisdiction rests on texts such as Matt. 18: 18. It was granted to Peter (Matt. 16: 19), but after the resurrection was shared by all the apostles, according to John 20: 23.[35]

The power of jurisdiction is distinguished from the power of consecration by the fact that it assumes not only the presence of a *materia* such as bread and wine, but also the subordination of the recipient to the administrator of the sacrament. The only exceptions are the eucharist, which assumes only the power of consecration and not of jurisdiction; and baptism, which in case of need can be administered by any *viator*, and therefore does not require any special power of jurisdiction.

The essential point of this subordination is its spontaneous and voluntary character, for how can one be absolved or confirmed against one's will? Christ wanted this subordination, from which the Pope is not exempt,[36] because only in this way can he preserve his *ecclesiasticum regimen* from chaos. It is in the nature of hierarchy, according to pseudo-Dionyius Areopagita, *ut infima reducantur ad su-*

---

[34] Dionysius, *De coel. hier.*, III 1 (*MG* 3, 165BC).

[35] *De pot. eccl.*, cons. 5 (Gl. 6, 218-19; Dupin II, 233D). Sometimes the curialists deduced the *potestas ordinis* from John 20: 23, and at other times they deduced the *potestas jurisdictionis* from it. Augustinus Triumphus in his *Summa de pot. eccl.*, I 4 (as cited by Wilks, 'Papa est nomen iurisdictionis,' 83 n. 2) based the *pot. ord.* on this text, while Alexander of St. Elpidio (*De pot. eccl.*, I 2 & 6, ed. Rocaberti 4b, 6b) deduced both powers from it.

[36] *De pot. eccl.*, cons. 5 (Gl. 6, 219; Dupin II, 233C): 'papa qui nulli personae particularis subest ut coerceri iuridice possit ex exteriori foro, subest tamen quoad iurisdictionem hanc annexam ordini sacerdotali confessori suo, et ordinatori suo si antea sacerdos non fuerat; unde et ab Ostiensi consecratur episcopo, qui minor est.' In the last lines Gerson refers to the case that someone, who possesses none or only the minor orders, is elected as Pope. The orders he lacks are to be conferred on him by the Cardinal-Bishop of Ostia. See P. Hinschius, *System des katholischen Kirchenrechts mit besonderer Rücksicht auf Deutschland* I, Berlin 1869, 219: 'Das Recht dazu, welches früher der Kardinalbischof von Ostia besass, steht jetzt dem Vorsteher oder Dekan des Kardinal-kollegiums zu.' More details in Wilks, 'Papa est nomen iurisdictionis', 258 n. 2.

prema per media[37] and it is proper that there should be a distinction between higher and lower, for if every priest were to be empowered by virtue of his ordination to grant general absolution, to preach and to administer the sacraments, then order in the Church would be at an end.[38]

b. in foro exteriori

The power of jurisdiction *in foro exteriori* is distinguished from that *in foro interiori*, by its compulsive character and by the fact that it is more concerned with the external authority of the Church than with its inner life, notably in the enforcement of the sacrament of penance. Gerson defines it as 'the compulsive power of the Church, which may be exercised against those subject to it, even against their will, in order to direct them to the primary goal – eternal bliss.'[39] The most important question which arises in this connexion is that of localising this power of jurisdiction. Who, in the final analysis, is to wield the sword of the Church? The Pope or the Church? Appealing to the text of Matthew 18: 15-17, Gerson chose firmly for the latter.[40]

> If your brother sins [against you], go and reprove him...; if he will not listen, take one or two brothers along with you... If he refuses to listen to them, tell the Church (Vg. *dic ecclesiae*), and if he refuses to listen to the Church, treat him as a pagan or a taxgatherer.

1. As he observes, this text is primarily concerned with the power of excommunication, of exclusion from all the sacraments and from the community of the faithful, of which the apostle speaks in Titus 3: 10 and 1 Cor. 5: 11.

---

37 Dionysius, *De coel. hier.*, IV 3 (*MG* 3, 181A).

38 *De pot. eccl.*, cons. 5 (Gl. 6, 219; Dupin II, 233C).

39 *De pot. eccl.*, cons. 4 (Gl. 6, 216; Dupin II, 230D): 'Potestas ecclesiastica jurisdictionis in foro exteriori est potestas ecclesiastica coercitiva, quae valet exerceri in alterum etiam invitum, ad dirigendum subditos in finem beatitudinis aeternae, velut in finem proximum et principaliter intentum.' Cf. *De vita spir. animae*, lect. 3 (Gl. 3, 144; Dupin III, 28A), and *De auferib.*, cons. 12 (Gl. 3, 301; Dupin II, 215D).

40 Cf. *De vita spir. animae*, lect. 4 (Gl. 3, 171; Dupin III, 48B): 'Expediens videretur nullam excommunicationis ferri sententiam, nisi pro manifesta contumacia, qua se monstrat aliquis audire ecclesiam non paratum. Ratio est quoniam dum semper paratus est audire ecclesiam, cur habebitur sicut ethnicus et publicanus. Hoc tenet Scotus in IV sententiarum 25., et allegat ad hoc textum Christi [Matt. 18: 15-17] in quo fundata est auctoritas excommunicandi et correctionis fraternae.'

2. It is also apparent that the plenitude of power of the ecclesiastical sword, and its use in the Church, covers every Christian, even the Pope. The power was given to the Church, for it is written, 'If he shall not listen, *«dic ecclesiae»*. This does not mean *«dic papae»* for Christ was addressing Peter, who could not possibly be relegated to himself.' Moreover, in Matt. 18: 18 (cf. 16: 19) the expression is in the plural, *«quaecumque ligaveritis»*, from which it is also clear that Christ was referring to the Church as a whole and not to Peter alone.

3. Finally, it can be deduced from this text that it is the Church which has received the '*potestas definiendi, determinandi, statuendi, decernendi, constituendi, praecepta, leges et canones*,'[41] that is the full power to state its decisions on doctrine and life in the most far reaching sense.[42]

All this is related to the decrees of the Council of Constance, which expressly laid down that the Council – which had been assembled legitimately, on the inspiration of the Holy Spirit, and which represented the Church militant, – had received its power *directly* from Christ, and was to be obeyed by everyone, of whatever state or dignity, even the Pope himself. Whoever resisted this was to be punished by the Church, if necessary with the aid of the secular arm.[43]

The power of jurisdiction is therefore granted to the – hierarchical – Church as a whole, and thus to a general council. Gerson works this idea out in the Aristotelian manner, and demonstrates that a divided Church can only possess a potential jurisdictional power, which can only be actualised by reunification through a council. The unity of the Church is, in other words, the precondition of the exercise of its power, and this, he says, is what Augustine meant when he said: '*claves ecclesiae datae sunt unitati non uni*.'[44] This

[41] Gerson, apparently, had the decretum *Haec sancta* in mind (*COD* 385[21]): '[Haec sancta synodus] ordinat, diffinit, statuit, decernit, et declarat.' Cf. d'Ailly, *De materia concilii generalis* (ed. Oakley, 268): '... quod auctoritas iudicandi, statuendi, et definiendi pertinet ad episcopos. Et hoc patet ex definitione concilii generalis, per quam differt a conciliis particularibus, sive provincialibus, quam ponit Huguccio, et post eum Bartholomaeus Brixiensis. 17 dist., cap. 1: «Universale», inquit, «est quod a papa vel eius legato cum omnibus episcopis statuitur.»' See also d'Ailly's *De ecclesiae auctoritate* (Dupin II, 941C).

[42] *De pot. eccl.*, cons. 4 (Gl. 6, 216-17; Dupin II, 231AC).

[43] Decree *Haec sancta* (6 April 1415) in *COD* 385[15]1-6[27].

[44] *De pot. eccl.*, cons. 4 (Gl. 6, 217; Dupin II, 231D). Cf. *De auferib.*, cons. 12 (Gl. 3, 301

does not deny that the power of the keys was granted to Peter, but says that it was given in the first place to the Church—*principalius tamen ecclesia*. Why?

First, the Church is unerring (*indeviabilitas*). The gates of Hell shall not prevail against her (Matt. 16: 18) and her faith shall not weaken. This cannot be said of Peter.

In the second place, the Church has legislative authority (*regulabilitas*). It is the Church which lays down the rules for the exercise of papal power and not vice versa.

In the third place, the Church embraces all powers (*multiplicitas*), and therefore includes the power of the Pope.

Finally, the Church has the authority to obligate (*obligabilitas*), and therefore can intervene in the papal power. If the Pope, on the other hand, makes laws, they only acquire force by being recognised by the Church. Gerson is especially concerned to emphasise this point, 'for several Popes and their adherents seem to act on the principle that, in the Church too, «the will of the prince is law»'.[45] Papal legislation, in other words, requires ecclesiastical consensus.[46]

2. *Ecclesiastical power B*

Gerson also approached the problem of ecclesiastical power and the relationship of Church and Pope in a different way, namely

---

& 303; Dupin II, 216A).—Augustine, *s.* 295, 2, 2 (*ML* 38, 1349): 'Has enim claves non homo unus, sed unitas accepit ecclesiae.' In *De schismate* from 1402 Gerson qualified this *dictum* as a 'haeresis manifesta'! (Gl. 6, 47; Dupin II, 20D).

45 'Quod principi placuit legis habet vigorem', Dig. I 4 1. Giles of Rome applied it to the Pope (*De pot. eccl.* III 8, ed. Scholz, 187), as did Augustinus Triumphus (cf. Wilks, 'The idea of the church', 45 n. 44). See also Ullmann, *Medieval papalism*, 154ff., and Le Bras (next note).

46 Cf. *De auctoritate concilii*, a. 5 concl. 2-4 (Gl. 6, 116), and *De vita spir. animae*, lect. 3 (Gl. 3, 153-4; Dupin III, 34D): 'Habet itaque papa primo dominium superioritatis a Christo super totam ecclesiam cum plenitudine potestatis in eis quae spirituale regimen ecclesiae proprie dictum respiciunt... De hac potestate sunt ius convocandi concilia universalia, ius determinandi *cum concilio* quaestiones fidei per modum articulorum omnes generaliter obligantium.' An excellent survey of the limits of papal power, and the problems that arose in discussions about them, can be found in G. LeBras, *Institutions ecclésiastiques*, Paris 1962 (Fliche & Martin, *Histoire de l'Eglise*, 12**) 322-7. See also Buisson, *Potestas und Caritas*, 74-124, and Klaus Ganzer, 'Päpstliche Gesetzgebungsgewalt und kirchlicher Konsens. Zur Verwendung eines Dictum Gratians in der Concordantia Catholica des Nikolaus von Kues, [= d. p. D. 4 c. 6]' in: *Von Konstanz nach Trient*, 171-88 (186).

through the distinction between the power of the Church, 1. in the absolute sense (*formaliter in se*); 2. in its transmission to others (*materialiter*), and finally 3. in its exercise and administration (*exercitum, exercitio, usus*). These distinctions seem complicated but one need only replace the concept 'ecclesiastical power' by the almost identical concept 'office' in order to grasp their meaning at once: the distinction is between the office as such, the office-holder and the way he exercises his office. Gerson regards this triple distinction as very appropriate, as it harmonises the variations of expression between theologians and canonists, and thus removes many misunderstandings about the nature of ecclesiastical office.[47]

Where are these distinctions derived from? We believe they are taken from the commentaries on the Sentences. In the last distinction (44) of the second book of the *libri sententiarum*, Peter Lombard dealt with two questions, of which the first: *An aliquando resistendum sit potestati* caused the scholastics to express their opinions on the nature of authority in general, and on ecclesiastical and civil power and their relationship in particular. Because of the many questions which arose from this problem, the commentators were compelled to subdivide distinction 44 into more articles and questions, and so there emerged a separate *quaestio*, which one can find for example in the commentary of Thomas Aquinas: *utrum omnis praelatio sit a Deo*.[48] In answering this question, Thomas divides it into three parts, in a way which resembles Gerson's distinction. He says: '*est autem in praelatione considerare tria: scilicet praelationis principium, modum et usum*.'[49] Even closer is the similarity between Gerson and Richard of Middletown, who distinguishes within the *potestas praesidendi* between the *essentia potestatis*, the *modus acquirendi* and the *modus utendi*.[50] We find a similar division in Durand of St. Pourçain.[51] From this we may conclude that Gerson adopted a current distinction when he examined the power of the Church from three points of view. It is therefore not surprising that the later Cardinal Cajetan, who was by no means a sympathizer of Gerson, had no objection whatsoever to him on this point. He says: '*distinguit [sc. Gersonius] et bene, potestatem ecclesiasticam tripliciter accipi*.'[52] The fact that this distinction was currently held by the scholastics, invalidates

---

[47] *De pot. eccl.* cons. 6 (Gl.6, 220-1; Dupin II, 234B).

[48] *Comm. in l.s.* II d. 44. q. 1 a. 2 (ed. Mandonnet, II, 1118).

[49] In corp. art. (*l.c.*, 1119)

[50] *Comm. in lib. sent.* II d. 44 a. 2 q. 1, as cited by De Lagarde, *La naissance* II, 157 n. 62.

[51] *Comm, in lib. sent.* II d. 44 q. 2 (ed. Venetiis 1571, fol 206a): '...praelatio est in hominibus ex ordinatione divina quantum ad debitum, non quantum ad eius acquisitionem vel usum malum...'

[52] Caietanus, *De comparatione*, cap. X (ed. Pollet, 78).

> every interpretation which considers it to be characteristic of Gerson' ecclesiastical theory.[53]

The above shows that the distinction between an office as such, the holder of an office and the way he exercises it, was by no means a novelty. The point, however, is – and this, we think, was Gerson's invention – that instead of restricting the use of this distinction to the separate Church-offices, he applied it to the ecclesiastical power as such, i.e. to a concept in which *all* ecclesiastical offices were included.

1. *Ecclesiastical power in the absolute sense* (formaliter in se)

The power of the Church in the absolute sense, as an abstract idea, is unchangeable (*invariabilis*); it remains the same from the beginnings of the Church until its end. It is the power of the Church which is defined as the sum of all the levels of the hierarchy, from the papacy to the lower priesthood.[54] For the Church in this sense, the hierarchic totality is so essential that if ever one of its components – and the *potestas* associated with it – should be lacking, then the Church would remove itself from its origins and would no longer be what it was intended to be, a perfect institution founded by Christ.

> Ablata penitus una tali potestate iam non maneret ecclesia prout a Christo seminaliter et velut in quodam germine suo perfecte fuit instituta.[55]

If, to give an example, the papacy were to be separated from the other *potestates*, then what remained would no longer have any claim to be called the Church.[56]

But, one may well ask, was Gerson unaware that the Church and its hierarchy had been subject to change and development and that

---

53 For the canonistic use of the distinction *potestas – exercitium*, see Nörr, *Kirche und Konzil*, 171ff.

54 *De pot. eccl.*, cons. 7 (Gl. 6, 222; Dupin II, 235B): 'Potestas ecclesiastica si consideretur in se formaliter et absolute, ipsa est *invariabilis* et eadem a principio nascentis ecclesiae usque ad finem perseverat. Ecclesia siquidem dum sic consideratur in suis partibus essentialibus et permanentibus, quae sunt papatus, cardinalatus, patriarchatus, archiepiscopatus, episcopatus, sacerdotium, habet integrari ex his omnibus...'

55 *De pot. eccl.*, cons. 7 (Gl. 6, 222; Dupin II, 235C).

56 *De pot. eccl.*, cons. 7 (Gl. 6, 222; Dupin II, 235B): '... si papatus per imaginationem praescindatur a reliquis potestatibus inferioribus, id quod superest non dicetur Ecclesia.'

some degrees of the hierarchy had not existed in the earliest period of the Church? He knew this, without doubt, just as his contemporaries knew it. In particular, he realised that the cardinalate, which he nevertheless described as an 'essential and permanent part of the Church', had only arisen at a later date. '*Tempus fuit quo non erant cardinales.*'[57] But, if we may reconstruct his train of thought, he saw no contradiction here, for 'being' and 'becoming', divine institution and historical growth, were related to each other as potentiality and act. The hierarchical Church,' the seed (*semen*) sown by Christ, realised itself and differentiated itself in the various offices and degrees, of which the cardinalate was one. Pseudo-Dionysius and Aristotle joined hands in this interpretation, in so far as the Church was seen, on the one hand, as essentially hierarchical, while on the other hand it was not denied that this hierarchy was capable of development.[58]

'Church' and 'hierarchy' are so much one in the relationship which concerns us here, that we are justified in speaking of an identity. But 'Church' and 'papacy' are also very closely connected, for Gerson, as we have seen, claimed that if the papacy were removed, one could no longer speak of the Church. What then did he think of the relationship of the papacy and the hierarchy ought to be? His answer is a typical proof of his adherence to Aristotelian principles in his ecclesiology. He argues that one may no more ask 'is the power of the Pope greater than that of the Church?' than 'is a part greater

---

57 *Replicationes* (Gl. 6, 39-40; Dupin II, 12A): '... includit errorem manifestum et est contra historias, scilicet quod soli cardinales sint successores Apostolorum, et quod ad illos solos et nullos alios possit dari ius eligendi papam... Nam quaeritur: quid erit de episcopis et primatibus? Quorum igitur erunt successores? Iura sunt pro iis. Item tempus fuit quo non erant cardinales.'–For Gerson the function of the cardinals concerned in particular the guardianship of the temporal possessions of the Church, something they had in common with the mendicants (see Chapter X n. 20). Cf. *De statibus ecclesiasticis*, cons. 1 & 2 (Gl. 9, 27; Dupin II, 531BC): (1) 'Status summi pontificis ac sacri collegii dominorum cardinalium sibi collateralium, fundatus est in ecclesiastica hierarchia subcoelesti immediate a Christo, nec humana institutione seu praesumptione potest destitui. Cui statui qui pertinaciter derogat, censendus est iuxta sacros canones, haereticus atque sacrilegus. (2) Status praedictus dotandus est vel fovendus pro debita et honesta sustentatione temporalium sine quibus, in hac vita misera, spiritualia diu non subsistunt.'–For d'Ailly's changing attitude in respect to the cardinalate since he had become a cardinal himself, see Oakley, *Political Thought*, 119 n. 20.

58 *Propositio facta coram Anglicis* (Gl. 6, 131-3; Dupin II, 128C-9A).

than a whole?'[59] This rhetorical question makes it clear that he considers the relationship of the hierarchy and the papacy in a quantitative sense, and, following in the footsteps of Aristotle, acknowledged the priority of the whole over its parts, and the dependence of the parts in comparison to the *totum integrale.* All degrees of the hierarchy together form the *totum integrale* which is 'the Church'; the papal power, the episcopal power etc. form essential parts of it, both the 'essential' and the 'part' being emphasised. This theory, to which we will return, had an important practical consequence.

Since a general council represents the Church, in the sense of the totality of the hierarchy, the power of the Pope is necessarily represented at such a council, no matter whether the papal throne is occupied or vacant, either by the natural or the civil death of the incumbent.[60] By the same argument, derived from the law of corporations, the general council has the right to the power of the *ecclesia romana*, the holy college, the episcopate and the lower clergy. So it appears, on the one hand, that Gerson regarded the general council as a faithful reflection of the hierarchic Church, – and therefore described it, like the latter, as *invariabilis;* [61] yet this does not mean that he wished to transfer these hierarchic powers to the council permanently. It never occurred to him to draw the conclusion from his theory that the papacy could be abolished on the grounds that a general council possessed the papal *potestas.* His theory was born out of urgent necessity, but he never wished to make that into a virtue!

At the end of this exposition, he poses the question as to whether there is any extra-mental reality corresponding to his concept of the Church. To talk of the Church in an absolute sense is to talk about an abstract idea. Does this idea have any reality beyond human reason, or is it purely a mental concept? This question, which lands us in the midst of the controversy between nominalism and realism, is one which Gerson only answers very summarily, but evidently in a nominalistic way.

---

59 *De pot. eccl.*, cons. 7 (Gl. 6, 222; Dupin II, 235C).
60 *De pot. eccl.*, cons. 11 (Gl. 6, 233; Dupin II 235C).
61 See below n. 70.

He starts by saying that an abstraction as such does not necessarily have to be considered false.[62] He continues and argues that, by the action of human reason, things are freed of the confusing accidents which accompany their appearance, and a concept is formed, which can not be thought of as seperate from the *res singulares ad extra*, because it is there that it has its origin.[63] The concept of a Church in an absolute sense originates, when human reason, abstracting from the accidental differences between–let us say–individual bishops, forms an idea of the episcopate as such, an idea in which all bishops are united, just as all priests are merged in the priesthood. The same reasoning allows the development of a concept of the *ecclesia romana* and the doctrine *ubi papa, ibi Roma*.[64]

2. *Ecclesiastical power in the material sense* (materialiter)

Considered in the material sense, as opposed to the absolute sense, the power of the Church is susceptible to change;[65] it grows and decays, as one can see daily, whenever changes take place in the Church, whenever its ministers are appointed, or lay down their tasks. The papal power is no exception to this rule, for it too is *mutabilis* and *auferibilis*. Here Gerson refers to his *De auferibilitate*, which we have already discussed. He continues his exposition with a lament on the increasing worldliness of the Church, which allows us to share his nostalgia for the time of the primitive Church. In this desire, he was not alone but shared the feelings of all scholastics.[66]

In that early period, he says, the Pope could easily consult a general council, and because of the small number of believers it had still been possible for him to appoint the ministers of the Church in remote districts. As the number of believers grew, and legal regula-

---

[62] 'Abstrahentium non est mendacium'. Aristotelian adage, see De Lagarde, *La naissance* II, n. 63bis.

[63] *De pot. eccl.*, cons. 7 (Gl. 6, 222-3; Dupin II, 235D-6A). For Gerson's philosophical ideas, see Gerhard Ritter, *Studien zur Spätscholastik II. Via antiqua und via moderna auf den deutschen Universitäten des XV. Jhdts*, Heidelberg 1922, 24-8, and Oberman, *Harvest*, 60-2; 331-9.

[64] Alvarez Pelayo, *Planctus* I 31 (ed. Venetiis 1560, 5vo): 'Quod ubicunque est papa, ibi est ecclesia romana et sedes apostolica et caput ecclesiae... Ecclesia ibi est, ubi est caput eius, scilicet papa.' See for more details Wilks, 'Papa est nomen iurisdictionis', 262-4, and Ernst H. Kantorowicz, *The King's two bodies. A Study in the Mediaeval Political Theology*, Princeton N.J. 1970, 204ff.

[65] *De pot. eccl.*, cons. 7 (Gl. 6, 222-3; Dupin II, 236AB).

[66] For a rich survey of early Christian and scholastic statements on the normative role of the primitive Church, see Yves M.-J. Congar, *La Tradition et les traditions. Essai historique*, Paris [1960], 271ff. (Excursus C. 'Limites mises au pouvoir ecclésiastique ou à son exercise').

tions were multiplied, this was totally altered,[67] and the Popes were obliged to follow Jethro's advice to Moses (Exod. 18: 13, 18-21), to divide the task of government and occupy themselves only with the most important matters.[68] If Moses, who had spoken to God as friend to friend, had been willing to listen to the advice of a heathen in questions which concerned the leadership of the synagogue, how much more must the Pope be obliged to pay attention to the will of the whole Church or the general council acting in her name? If even Moses were not above reproach, is there then to be no protest against the innumerable unworthy dealings of the curia? Is the Church to be forbidden to protest against the granting of the humblest benefices *manu papae*? Is no one to be allowed to speak out against the levying of annates, and all the other regulations which are a burden on the truly spiritual life, on the faith and religion? Nothing, so Gerson concludes his protest, is more harmful to the Church than the failure to hold general and provincial councils. There must be changes, but it is pointless to press for these while the Popes continue to usurp the functions and rights of the lower clergy. Let them remember that the highest power in the Church is granted them in order to build it up in accordance with the judgement of the wise man—'*prout sapiens iudicabit.*'[69] The 'wise man' is the general council, which, being itself immutable, can form a judgement on the exercise of the power of the Church according to the changing circumstances of time and place.[70]

Here again, Gerson protests against papal absolutism and cen-

---

[67] *De pot. eccl.* cons. 7 (Gl. 6, 222-3; Dupin II, 236D).

[68] Following Bernard of Clairvaux, *De consideratione* IV 3 (*ML* 182, 776ff.), Giles of Rome, *De pot. eccl.*, I 8 (ed. Scholz, 28-30) used this text to prove that the Pope wielded both swords.

[69] Common moral-philosophical sentence, stemming from Aristotle (*Eth. Nik.*, 5, 15) as appears from *De statibus ecclesiasticis* (Gl. 9, 30; Dupin II, 534A): 'Sed in hoc capere medium conveniens non aliter videtur posse determinari quam iuxta Aristotelis sententiam, scilicet «ut sapiens iudicabit». Nihil autem videtur in hoc sapientius quam generale concilium rite et libere celebratum.' See also next note, and *Considerationes quatuor*, cons. 4 (Gl. 6, 145; Dupin II, 120A; 121A), and below n. 100.

[70] *De pot. eccl.*, cons. 8 (Gl. 6, 225; Dupin II, 237BC): 'Meminerit itaque summus pontifex datam sibi a Deo potestatem supremam in ecclesia ad aedificationem eius (2 Cor. 13:10), «prout sapiens iudicabit». Iudicat autem sapiens de potestatis usu variabiliter, *invariabilis existens, sicut est generale concilium*, et hoc pro temporum, locorum, reliquarumque circumstantiarum diversa qualitate.' In the last part of this phrase one recognizes Isidore's definition of a 'lex bona' (D. 4 c. 2); *De vita spir. animae*, lect. 4 (Gl. 3, 167-9; Dupin III, 46AC), and *Pax hominibus* (Gl. 7*, 769; Dupin II, 146BC).

tralism, and opposes to it the idea of a more balanced dispersion of hierarchical responsibility, which one may also call the pseudo-Dionysian idea of the hierarchic order. He appeals to Aristotle's distinction between the three forms of government: monarchy, aristocracy and democracy, and finds traces of it already present in the Old Testament. Moses was the representative of monarchy, the seventy two elders of aristocracy, and the leaders of the people, that is of the tribes, represented democracy.[71]

3. *Ecclesiastical power in the executive sense* (exercitium, usus, exercitio)

This last distinction is concerned with the manner in which the power of the Church is exercised, legally or illegally, validly or invalidly, etc.[72] This third aspect of the power of the Church is an annex of the second; this is in fact obvious, for just as it is impossible to exercise power without possessing it, so it is pointless to possess power without exercising it.

The question which is at the heart of this section is whether the power of the Church is derived *immediate* from God or *mediate* through man.[73] Gerson applies his threefold distinction to answer it as follows. Ecclesiastical power seen in an absolute sense derives *immediate* from the God-man Jesus Christ. The whole community of

[71] Cf. Chapter XII § 4. John of Paris.

[72] *De pot. eccl.*, cons. 6 & 9 (Gl. 6, 221, 225, 250; Dupin II, 234D, 238A, 255D): 'Potestas ecclesiastica, si consideretur quoad usum vel exercitium, illa mutabilis est et multipliciter variabilis.' From the way in which Gerson distinguishes in the exercise of ecclesiastical power between 'licitus' and 'illicitus', 'ratus' and 'irritus', one can recognise his logical training. Cf. the quadrangle which is behind Gerson's distinctions with Peter of Spain, *Summule logicales*, I 12 (ed. De Rijk, 6):

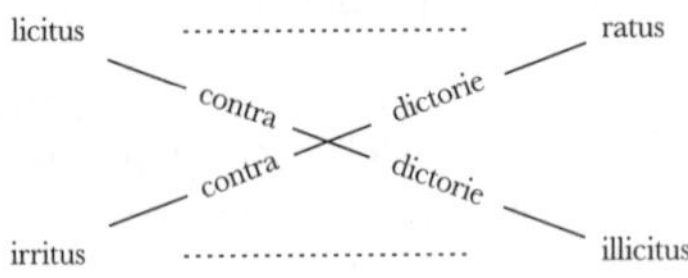

[73] It is mysterious that Morrall (*Gerson*, 104) in this context should refer to Ockham's *Breviloquium* IV 4,—a work which was unknown to Gerson—for the latter, instead of dealing with the origin of the State, examines the origin of ecclesiastical power. Moreover, he does not distinguish, as Ockham did, between 'regulariter' and 'casualiter', but between 'immediate' and 'mediate', which was a very common distinction in ecclesiology. See e.g. Augustinus Triumphus, *De pot. praelatorum* (ed. Duynstee, *'s Pausen primaat* II, 333). In other terms but to the same effect, Giles of Rome, *De renunc. papae*, cap. IX (ed. Rocaberti, p. 34b); for Jean de Paris and Johannes Andreae, see Tierney, *Foundations*, 164ff.; Herveus Natalis, *De iurisdictione* (ed. Hödl, 9, and passim).

men, excluding Christ, could not institute this power as it could and can imperial and other secular powers.

> Nam considerando ecclesiasticam potestatem primo modo, concedendum est absque ulla dubitatione quod illa fuit et est immediate a Deo homine Christo, sic quod a nullo altero fuit instituta. Nec congregatio totius universitatis hominum secluso Christo potuisset sibi potestatem huiusmodi instituere, quemadmodum potuit et posset instituere sibi potestatem imperialem super omnem potestatem regalem, potestatem ducatuum... et ita de reliquis potestatibus pure saecularibus.[74]

But if the power of the Church is considered in the material sense, one must agree that whereas Peter, the apostles and the disciples received it *immediate* from Christ, their successors receive it *mediate* by human intervention. Christ chose the first; their followers received ecclesiastical power by election, consecration or other means of human appointment.

At the same time as the power of the Church, its *usus* or *exercitio* was granted, again *immediate* to Peter, the apostles and disciples, *mediate* to their successors. Perhaps, Gerson speculates, this *usus* was limited by Peter at a later date, when the number of believers had increased, with the agreement of the Church or a general council, in order both to prevent all the apostles or disciples busying themselves with one another's affairs, and thus giving rise to schism, and also to confirm the monarchic organisation of the Church which Christ had willed. This is Gerson's interpretation of the 'Council of the apostles' (Acts 15: 1-21); at least, this seems to be the most obvious interpretation of this otherwise so obscure passage.[75]

At the end of this section he summarises his views on the problem of the direct or indirect transmission of ecclesiastical power, and explains his intention by reference to pseudo-Dionysius. This summary proves, and this remained unnoticed for too long, that he consistently tried to solve the ecclesiological questions with which he found himself confronted in strictly hierarchic terms.[76] The passage will be discussed in our next chapter.

---

[74] *De pot. eccl.*, cons. 9 (Gl. 6, 226, Dupin II, 238A).

[75] *De pot. eccl.*, cons. 9 (Gl. 6, 226-7; Dupin II, 238CD). One might suppose that this passage refers to D. 21 q. 2, where Jerome's famous words are cited: '...Caeteri vero apostoli eodem pari consortio honorem et potestatem acceperunt, ipsumque [sc. Petrum] principem eorum esse voluerunt.' See Hödl, *Kirchengewalt*, 267.

[76] *De pot. eccl.*, cons. 9 (Gl. 6, 227; Dupin II, 239AB).

3. *Plenitude of ecclesiastical power*

In this section Gerson discusses the relationship between Pope and Church from the viewpoint of the concept of *plenitudo potestatis*. Here too, his explanation must be set in the context of theories of the Church, which attached an unduly great importance to this concept. Plenitude of power for the canonists and curialists meant that the entire power of the Church was vested in the office of the papacy, that all order and right in the Church emanated from the papal office.

As the representative of Christ, they argued, the Pope disposed of the same powers as the Son of God. His deeds were to be regarded as if performed by God himself. The curialists derived the idea of plenitude of power directly from the omnipotence of God, while they considered the relationship of Pope and Church as analogous to that between God and creation. Because all power and right flowed from the office of *vicarius Dei*, every legal regulation required papal confirmation. A Pope could not bind his successor, for he too was set above the positive legal order. The Pope owed responsibility to God alone, and no mortal had the right to ask him: 'Cur ita facis?'[77]

It was in the nature of things that this exaltation of the idea of papal plenitude of power, papal absolutism, would be at the expense of the Church, particularly in the sense of the Church as hierarchy. Gerson demonstrates it time and again, when he criticises the canonists so vehemently precisely because they regard the Pope and not the entire hierarchy as the essence of the Church. They even identified the Pope, invested as he was with plenitude of power, with the Church—'*papa qui potest dici ecclesia.*'[78] The result was that the equitable and harmonious division of power through all

[77] For the concept of 'plenitude of power', see Von Gierke, *Genossenschaftsrecht* III, 566ff; Scholz, *Publizistik*, 60ff; Ullmann, *Medieval Papalism*, 76-113; Tierney, *Foundations*, 141-9; Jürgen Miethke, *Ockhams Weg zur Sozialphilosophie*, Berlin 1969, 411; and, notably, Y. M.-J. Congar, *Die Lehre von der Kirche. Von Augustinus bis zum abendländischen Schisma*, § 53. ('Päpste und Kanonisten. Theoretiker der päpstlichen Gewalt als "plenitudo potestatis"'), 164-72.

[78] Giles of Rome, *De pot. eccl.* III c. ult. (ed. Scholz, 209): 'Ecclesia quidem est timenda et mandata eius sunt observanda [cf. Eccles. 12: 13], sive summus pontifex, qui tenet apicem ecclesiae et qui potest dici ecclesia, est timendus et sua mandata sunt observanda, quia potestas eius est spiritualis, celestis et divina, et est sine pondere, numero et mensura [cf. Wisd. 11: 21].'

the organs of the hierarchy was disturbed. We shall now see how Gerson in deviating from, and indeed rejecting, the abolutistic interpretation of the plenitude of papal power, developed a theory which took more account of the rights of the entire hierarchical Church.

1. plenitudo potestatis *in respect to the papal office*

Gerson starts by arguing that whereas ecclesiastical power in a general sense was vouchsafed to all the apostles and disciples, and their successors, the *plenitude* of this power in the absolute sense was entrusted only to Peter and his successors.

> Potestas ecclesiae in sua plenitudine est formaliter et subiective in solo romano pontifice.[79]

Another important point of his exposition is that he strictly rejects tying the papal plenitude of power to the possession of jurisdiction alone, for it is equally based on the sacrament of order. That means: the plenitude of papal power depends on both, election *and* consecration. The latter can precede election but it is in any case just as essential as the power of jurisdiction, which the Pope receives at his election.

By this emphasis on the sacramental basis of papal plenitude of power, Gerson distinguishes himself from the curialists and from the 'jurists', though he only refers specifically to the latter. They held the view that the office of the Pope was purely a matter of jurisdiction. '*Papatus est nomen iurisdictionis et non ordinis.*'[80] That is, papal power depended only on election and not on consecration. True, it was normal for a Pope who did not yet possess the episco-

---

[79] *De pot. eccl.*, cons. 10 (Gl. 6, 227; Dupin II, 239B). Gerson's distinction between the plenitude of power in respect to the papal office and to the Church respectively, was prepared by his exposition of the papal power as given in *De vita spir. animae*, lect. 3 (Gl. 3, 153-4; Dupin III, 35AB): 'Prima potestas (dominium superioritatis a Christo super totam Ecclesiam cum plenitudine potestatis in eis quae spirituale regimen Ecclesiae proprie dictum respiciunt) cognoscitur ex evangeliis et Actibus Apostolorum... De hac potestate sunt ius convocandi concilia universalia, ius determinandi *cum concilio* quaestiones fidei...; correctio insuper praelatorum inferiorum; ... et similia quae ad *universalem Ecclesiae statum* tangunt vel finalem supremamque determinationem respiciunt. Et *haec potestas in Ecclesia immobilis perseverat* quantumcumque persona papae per mortem naturalem vel civilem mutaretur, aut qualemcumque *usus* talis potestatis a papa remanente tolleretur in parte vel in toto (a reference to the practice of substraction).'

[80] See Wilks, 'Papa est nomen iurisdictionis', 257 n. 2.

pal dignity to be ordained, but the power of consecration did not form an essential element of his office. Completely consistently with this, the curialists defended the doctrine that a chosen layman, solely by virtue of his election to the highest office, became 'a true Pope, having all jurisdictional papal power.'[81]

The curialists owed this strictly juridical view of the papal office to the canonists, who in this field as in others had done the preparatory work. Huguccio (d. 1210), to name but one example, had already stated a century earlier that the man chosen became by virtue of election alone 'a true Pope and head of the Church.'[82] Gerson vigorously opposes this doctrine and argues:

> licet aliquis possit elegi in papam non sacerdos... ipse nihilominus appellari non potest aut debet summus pontifex, nisi fuerit in sacerdotem et episcopum consecratus.[83]

For if the papal office were to be based only on the power of jurisdiction, then a layman, or even a woman, would be able to become Pope, which must be considered absurd. The Pope is not so distinct from a bishop that he can achieve his office without ordination.[84]

Although Gerson, in holding this opinion, followed the tradition of the great scholastics,[85] he seems to have been alone among his contemporaries, including Pierre d'Ailly.[86] We can see in this yet

---

[81] Augustinus Triumphus, *Summa* IV 2 (cited by Wilks, 'Papa est nomen iurisdictionis', 258 n. 1): 'puto quod supposito quod esset laicus et non esset constitutus in sacris, electus in papam esset verus papa et haberet omnem potestatem iurisdictionis papalis.' Alexander of St. Elpidio, *De pot. eccl.* III 3, 6 (ed. Rocaberti, 34a; 36b): 'Est etiam diligenter considerandum quod papatus non est nomen ordinis, sed est nomen dignitatis et officium; unde si aliquis eligatur in papam, verus papa est ante consecrationem episcopalem.'

[82] Huguccio, *Summa* ad D. 79 c. 9, cited by Tierney, *Foundations*, 28.

[83] *De pot. eccl.*, cons. 10 (Gl. 6, 227; Dupin II, 239B).

[84] *De pot. eccl.*, cons. 10 (Gl. 6, 227; Dupin II, 239BC): 'Hic autem consurgit aequivocatio non modica propter dominos iuristas, qui loquentes de plenitudine potestatis papalis, solum loqui videntur de potestate iurisdictionis; ex qua locutione videtur haec absurditas sequi, quod pure laicus, immo et femina, posset esse papa et habere plenitudinem ecclesiasticae potestatis.'

[85] Ulrich Horst, 'Das Wesen der "potestas clavium" nach Thomas von Aquin', *MTZ* 11 (1960), 198: 'Leider hat sich Thomas nicht über den Sonderfall ausgesprochen der Eintritt, wenn ein Laie zum Papst gewählt wird, bevor er geweiht ist, aber vermutlich hätte er das Problem so gelöst, dass er Rechtsgewalt überhaupt nur unter Bedingung hat, dass er die Weihe empfängt.'

[86] Cf. d'Ailly, *De ecclesiae auctoritate* (Dupin II, 958D): 'Quia auctoritas sacerdotalis, quae quantum ad potestatem ordinis sacramentalis maior est in ecclesia, non immediate

another proof of how far the sacramental essence of office and Church was beyond doubt for him. A spiritual monarch who did not possess the priestly dignity was for him a purely fictitious juridical monstrosity.

On the other hand, since he did in fact possess this dignity, the Pope fulfilled a highly legitimate function in the Church, for it was the will of Christ that no office should be filled without the mediating authority of the highest hierarch. Only thus could confusion be avoided, only thus could the Church militant be led to follow the example of the Church triumphant. It now becomes clear what Gerson meant by papal plenitude of power. It was the power by virtue of which the monarch of the Church was entitled to exercise his rule, either actually or virtually—*vere vel interpretative*—in the appointment of the hierarchy.[87]

Summarising what he explained earlier Gerson now defines the plenitude of ecclesiastical power in this way:

> plenitudo potestatis ecclesiasticae est potestas ordinis et iurisdictionis quae a Christo [est] collata supernaturaliter Petro sicut vicario suo et monarchae primo pro se et suis successoribus legitimis, usque in finem saeculi ad aedificationem Ecclesiae militantis pro consecutione felicitatis aeternae.'[88]

What does it mean, to say that Christ gave Peter full powers in a supernatural way (*supernaturaliter*)? This qualification limits the plenitude of papal power and distinguishes it from all other authority which may have accrued in the course of time. The power of the successors of Peter had, since the foundation of the Church, been greatly increased by additions of a positive- and natural-legal kind. A good example of this, as far as it concerns the relationship of Church and State, is the donation of Constantine.[89] Within the

---

derivatur a papa, *cum stet aliquem esse papam et non sacerdotem* et per consequens tunc non posset conferre ordinem sacerdotalem.'

[87] *De pot. eccl.*, cons. 10 (Gl. 6, 227-8; Dupin II, 239C): '... ex institutione Christi nullus in ecclesia debet dare vel suscipere gradus hierarchicos, qui sunt purgare, illuminare et perficere, si non interveniat vere vel interpretative auctoritas supremi hierarchae vel monarchae in ecclesia sancta Dei, quatenus in ea vitetur confusio et optimo regimine gubernetur ad exemplar ecclesiae triumphantis.' Cf. Chapter VI n. 92.

[88] *De pot. eccl.* cons. 10 (Gl. 6, 228; Dupin II, 239D).

[89] For more details on Gerson's opinion about the donation of Constantine, see the present author's *Jean Gerson et l'Assemblée de Vincennes*, 83-5, and Louis B. Pascoe., 'Gerson and the donation of Constantine', in: *Growth and development within the Church. Viator. Medieval and Renaissance Studies*, 5, Berkeley / Los Angeles / London 1974, 469-85.

Church, Gerson refers to the expansion of the idea of plenitude of power as a result of the transfer to the Popes of powers which originally belonged to the councils, a transfer which came about as a means of simplification. It is, of course, always easier to be able to appeal to a permanent body such as the curia than to a general council which meets only from time to time. This expansion is also to be explained by the natural inclination of every *communitas perfecta* including the Church, to surround its leader with honour and to grant him privileges and gifts.[90]

These theoretical reflections are then examined in detail, and Gerson appeals to scholars whom he does not name, but who are said to have believed that the Popes of the last century had, without any justification, either declared the decrees of the councils invalid by making reservations in them, or turned them into dead letters by the use of the *non obstante*-clause in their bulls. Alexander V had even gone so far as to lay a *non obstante* on the famous statute of Innocent III, *Omnis utriusque sexus*, which had been accepted at the fourth Lateran Council.[91] This criticism had been answered by others who, 'less well aware of the origin of the power of the Church in the divine law, and relying only on the decretals' had approved such interference. 'They assert that the authority of the Pope should be seen as exempt from all the decisions of the councils, because the Pope is above councils or at least equal to them, and equals cannot bind each other – *'par in parem non habet imperium.*'[92]

'But,' he continues, 'God is to be believed, and He, shedding the light of his law on the Council of Constance, had freed the Church from this pernicious doctrine, which would only have prolonged the Schism.[93] Now it has been established that a council can assemble without the Pope, that in certain cases a Pope can be judged by a

---

[90] *De pot. eccl.* cons. 10 (Gl. 6, 228; Dupin II, 239D-240A).

[91] *De pot. eccl.*, cons. 10 (Gl. 6, 228-9; Dupin II, 240BD). Denifle-Chatelain, *CUP* IV n. 1868: bull dated 12 Oct. 1409, against which Gerson and the masters of the theological faculty protested in their *Contra bullam 'Regnans in excelsis'* (Gl. 10, 34-9). See also *Prosperum iter* (Gl. 5, 478; Dupin II, 280A), and Glorieux's list 'Contre le pouvoir des Mendiants' (Gl. 10, 31).

[92] X 1.6.20. Cf. LeBras, *Institutions*, 322 n. 1: 'Le maxime est dans *Dig.* IV.8.4. Applications dans *Dig.* 36,I.13.4, et dans *Clem.* III.17 c. un. (révocation de la bulle 'Clericis laicos')'; Brian Tierney, *Origins of papal infallibility, 1150-1350*, Leiden 1972, 29ff.

[93] *De pot. eccl.*, cons. 10 (Gl. 6, 229; Dupin II, 240C): 'liberavit ecclesiam suam ab hac pestifera perniciosissimaque doctrina, qua semper manente perseverasset semper schisma nutritum ab ea.'

council, and that moreover a council possesses sufficient power and authority to prescribe laws and rules which limit the papal plenitude of power *non in esse*, sed *in usu suo*.' It is a misconception that the Pope is entitled to issue new constitutions invalidating the decisions which councils have reached with so much care and wisdom. He only has the right to do so when appeal to a council is impossible, and when it is also a question of *occurrens necessitas* and *evidens utilitas*, that is, whenever there is a clear case for a dispensation.[94] In all other cases he is guilty of abusing his power.[95]

Whether all the consequences of such an abuse are to retain their legal force, is a decision which in general Gerson dares not take. It would be best if a council were to lay down the cases in which, and the extent to which, the papal authority in the regulations already embodied in decrees or to be so embodied, is to be regarded as an exception. To annul all earlier legal decisions is a course which he regards as open to practical and juridical objection. To ease the task of the council he sets forward a number of guidelines to reduce the chaos of ecclesiastical law to some order.

2. plenitudo potestatis *in respect to the Church*

> potestas ecclesiastica in sua plenitudine est in ecclesia sicut in fine et sicut in regulatione applicationem et usum huiusmodi plenitudinis ecclesiasticae potestatis per se ipsam vel per generale concilium, ipsam sufficienter et legitime repraesantante.[96]

Previously Gerson had argued that the plenitude of power in the absolute sense (*formaliter*) was given only to the Pope, and was the exclusive prerogative of the papal office. Using his earlier threefold distinction he now defends the doctrine that this power, albeit in a different manner, also lies in the Church, i.e. in so far as the Church embodies the goal of this power and therefore possesses the full right to regulate the way in which the Pope exercises his powers, in accordance with the essence of the Church. To put it more simply, the Church as a whole has the right to concern itself with the way in which the Pope uses his power – *usus* – because he has

---

[94] See *PRE* IV, 708 s.v. 'Dispensation' (P. Hinschius), and Ullmann, *Medieval Papalism*, 50-7.

[95] *De pot. eccl.*, cons. 10 (Gl. 6, 229-30; Dupin II, 240C-1A).

[96] *De pot. eccl.*, cons. 11 (Gl. 6, 232; Dupin II, 243A).

received his power for the sake of the Church (as mystical corps) and its strengthening. This principle opens up the possibility of action against a possible abuse of his power by the Pope, thus defending the Church against the risks of absolutism.

Although Gerson once again calls on Augustine to support his arguments: '*claves datae sunt non uni sed unitati*' – it is clear from his interpretation of these words that he was more inspired by Aristotle than by the Bishop of Hippo.[97] His entire argument that the Church has the right to act against abuse of power by the Pope, is based on the idea of finality, which, as is well known, is central in the philosophy of Aristotle.[98]

> A comparison of Gerson's opinion with the way in which the curialist Giles of Rome approached the relationship of Church and Pope throws light on the problem. From his *De renunciatione papae* it is plain that Giles interpreted the relationship of Pope and Church as a relation of finality: '*Finis autem ad quem ordinatur papatus est commune bonum et regimen totius ecclesiae.*' He elaborates this doctrine syllogistically as follows: '*Illud quod ad hunc finem, videlicet propter bonum publicum institutum est, contra bonum publicum militare non debet. Sed ille qui factus est caput ecclesiae propter bonum publicum factus est. Si ergo est insufficiens ad regendam ecclesiam et renunciare non posset, contra bonum publicum militaret.*'[99] Giles thus appeals to the relation of finality between Pope and Church only in order to defend the right of the Pope to renounce his office freely. The Church has only a passive role here. Gerson went further. He mobilised, as it were, the finality relationship

---

[97] *De pot. eccl.*, cons. 11 (Gl. 6, 232; Dupin II, 243B): 'Propterea loquitur Augustinus cum aliis quibusdam quod claves ecclesiae sunt datae non uni sed unitati, et quod datae sunt ecclesiae. Et hoc convenienter potest intellegi modis quos explicat consideratio [6], quoniam claves datae sunt propter ecclesiam et unitatem eius tamquam propter finem. Potest etiam dici in ecclesia vel in concilio haec plenitudo ecclesiasticae potestatis, nedum in se *finaliter* (according to BN 3126, fol. LXX[rob] and to Richer's ed. of Gerson's works (Paris 1606, I, 136D) this is the correct reading; Dupin and Glorieux incorrectly read 'formaliter') sed aliis duobus modis, videlicet quoad applicationem ad hanc vel illam personam, et quoad usum regulandum, si fortassis in abusum verti quereretur.' – *Morrall* (Gerson, 106) was therefore mistaken when he paraphrased this passage as follows: 'Consideratio 11 urges that the fullness of ecclesiastical power, absolutely speaking, is present in the Church and the Council representing it.' No, absolutely speaking (*formaliter*) the fullness of ecclesiastical power is exclusively present in the Pope (see above n. 79); *finaliter*, however, and in what concerns its *executio* and *usus*, the fullness of power resides also in the Church (cf. n. 96).

[98] In his later years, Gerson wrote a special treatise on this subject, *Centilogium de causa finali* (Gl. 9, 613-25; Dupin II, 704-11). Cf. also Th. Steinbüchel, *Der Zweckgedanke in der Philosophie des Thomas von Aquino nach den Quellen dargestellt*, Münster 1912; and Wilks, *Sovereignty*, Chapter I 'Societas christiana', 54ff.

[99] Giles of Rome, *De renunciatione papae* 24, (ed. Rocaberti, 58b, 62a). Cf. Scholz, *Publizistik*, 64 n. 17.

> to defend the conclusion which he drew from it, that the Church was entitled in cases of need to take an active part against the Pope and to judge him. Thus, while both writers accepted the same relationship between Pope and Church, they differed in that Giles thought exclusively from the viewpoint of the Pope, whose office to him was virtually identical with the Church, while Gerson argued from the viewpoint of the totality of the ecclesiastical hierarchy, whose power, since it was more embracing, was greater than that of the highest hierarch alone.

Gerson finds the reasons why it was sometimes necessary to correct the Pope in the fact that the *summus pontifex*, even though he possesses the plenitude of power, is, as a man, fallible and can therefore turn his power to the disadvantage of the Church. Since the college of cardinals which advises him is just as fallible, it was necessary for the highest lawgiver, Christ, to establish an *indeviabilis regula*, by which abuse of power can be punished, corrected or mitigated. '*Haec autem regula est vel ecclesia vel generale concilium.*' Unshakeable truth is to be found in the Church, and that is the ground on which the decisions of the Council of Constance are based.[100]

Taking up once more the distinction which he made earlier, Gerson defines the relationship of the Pope, the Church and the concept of plenitude of power with the aid of the ideas of *latitudo* and *supremitas*. The first concept recalls us to the notion of ecclesiastical power as the sum of all hierarchical *potestates*–ecclesiastical power in the absolute sense–the second to the concept of the plenitude of ecclesiastical power in the absolute sense.

> Plenitudo ecclesiasticae potestatis si consideratur in sua latitudine, ipsa non est in solo papa, nisi quodam modo *fontaliter*, potestative et originaliter suo modo. Haec enim latitudo potestatis complectitur in se alias potestates ecclesiasticas collective, a summo usque deorsum, et est in eis plenitudo ecclesiasticae potestatis papalis tamquam pars integralis in suo toto; et ita non est maior vel superior ad totam ecclesiam sicut nec pars maior toto.[101]

---

[100] *De pot. eccl.*, cons. 11 (Gl. 6, 233; Dupin II, 243C): 'Haec autem regula est vel ecclesia vel generale concilium. Unde cum medium virtutis aliter non habeatur nisi «prout sapiens judicabit», finalis resolutio ad hanc sapientiam fiet ad ecclesiam, ubi est sapientia indeviabilis, vel ad generale concilium. Hic fundantur ea multa quae per hoc sacrum concilium et constituta et practicata sunt, ut quod papa iudicari potest et deponi per concilium, quod eidem in regulatione potestatis suae quoad usum subjicitur, et sibi potest dici: «cur ita facis?»' Gerson refers to his sermon *Prosperum iter* (Gl. 5, 471-80; Dupin II, 273-80). See also above n. 4 and n. 69.

[101] *De pot. eccl.*, cons. 11 (Gl. 6, 233; Dupin II 243C).

Even though plenitude of power is derived from the papal office, this does not mean to say that it is confined to it. As far as its extension (*latitudo*) is concerned, it is to be seen rather as a collective concept, in which all the power of the Church, from high to low, is included, and of which the power of the Pope is an integrating part –but no more than a part. In this sense, the power of the Pope does not exceed that of the Church, for a part cannot exceed a whole.

If, however, the plenitude of power is considered from the point of view of *supremitas*, then it is beyond doubt that it contains more than all the other powers together. How does this appear? From the fact that all the other powers cannot call a general council, for which papal authority is required as a matter of principle.

> Si vero consideretur haec plenitudo in sua supremitate, tunc absque ulla dubitatione, plenitudo ecclesiasticae potestatis papalis superior et maior est ad reliquas. Sed iam illud quod reliquum est nullo pacto potest constituere generale concilium, iuxta illud quod dictum est prius, quod generale concilium in sua ratione formali includit de necessitate papalem auctoritatem, sive papa sit sive non sit.[102]

The statement that all the *potestates* of the Church, if they do not include the papal authority, cannot constitute a council, and the doctrine that a council, by its nature, includes all the *potestates* of the Church, can be regarded as complementary. The line they take is that without the Pope, the Church cannot begin anything, and in particular that it cannot call a council. In fact, the true state of affairs at Constance was different, for the Church had taken decisions on its own initiative and had even taken action against the Pope. How did Gerson defend this practice? His answer appears in the interpretation which he gives to the words: '*sive papa sit sive non sit*' in the above citation. He shows that whenever the Church has a Pope – '*sive papa sit*' – and the Pope wishes to call a council, then such a decision is most clearly his responsibility, but if he remains obstinate in refusing (*pertinaciter renuit*) to call a council, and this is to the detriment of the Church, then the Church is justified in acting as if there were no Pope – '*sive non sit*.' In such a case, the Church has the full power to assemble, to make regulations for its own welfare and to intervene in the papal power '*quoad applicationem et*

---

[102] *De pot. eccl.*, cons. 11 (Gl. 6, 233; Dupin II, 243D).

usum.'[103] This argument, drawn from the law of corporations, will be discussed in more detail in the next chapter.

The questions of how far the measures could extend, where the frontiers of the exercise of papal power by the Church or a council lay during a vacancy, are discussed at some length.[104] Above all, the council had to ensure that the Church chose a new Pope, either in the regular way (election by the cardinals), or in another fashion, such as by *compromissum*, the intervention of the Holy Spirit, or a miracle. We may note here that Gerson never considered the power of election to belong to the council as such. Further, the council was empowered to exercise the coercive power of the Pope, *iurisdictio coercitiva*, as it had done repeatedly during the Council of Constance; indeed, it had gone so far as to depose the Pope, to pronounce excommunications and to lay cities under interdict. The formulae constantly used in these actions: '*sancta synodus loquens, discernens, definiens*', reflected the language of both the New Testament and the early Church.[105]

But, as he himself objects, is there not a hidden danger in this theory, that people will say, there is nothing to prevent the Church always being ruled without the Pope; let the council appoint bishops and priests, exercise the power of jurisdiction without limits and take on the other functions of the highest hierarch permanently! The answer to this bold suggestion is that while the council is entitled to assume the rights of the Pope for a certain time, it cannot do so permanently. That the Church is ruled by a Pope, is one of the affirmative commandments which apply always, but not in all circumstances – '*ad semper sed non pro semper.*'[106] Therefore, the

---

[103] *De pot. eccl.*, cons. 11 (Gl. 6, 233; Dupin II, 244A).

[104] For a comparison with Ockham's thoughts on this matter, see De Lagarde, *La naissance* V, chap. III, 53-86.

[105] *De pot. eccl.*, cons. 11 (Gl. 6, 234-35; Dupin II, 244B-5A). The decision 'circa Samaytas', referred to in order to prove that the Council was entitled to exercise papal jurisdiction, concerns the foundation of the diocese of Samaitan (Lithuania), with which Archbishop John of Lemberg and Bishop Peter of Wilna were entrusted. See Finke, *Acta concilii Constanciensis* II, 572, and cf. the whole passage with Pierre d'Ailly, *De eccl. auctoritate* (Dupin II, 952C).

[106] 'ad semper sed non pro semper', a current moral-philosophical distinction, stemming from Aristotle. Cf. *De vita spir. animae*, lect. 3, coroll. 6 (Gl. 3. 162; Dupin, III 41D): '... praecepta affirmativa Dei quamvis obligent ad semper non tamen pro semper, ut est communis regula magistrorum; obligant ergo sub quadam disiunctione, ad hoc faciendum vel illud pro isto vel illo tempore, prout casus incidit et sapiens determinavit. Sicut exempli gratia occurentibus duobus in extrema necessitate famis, quorum soli pos-

council cannot tolerate the continued vacancy of the papal throne. Only in cases of *necessitas* or *evidens utilitas* is it empowered to act to fill the gaps; plenitude of power, then, lies in the Church.

Summarising his argument, Gerson states that the undeniable contradictions in canon law on the matter of the plenitude of papal power can only be resolved if a distinction is made between the power of the Church in its absolute, material and executive senses. Only in the first is it unassailable, with neither emperor, nor people nor Church having any right to infringe it in any way.[107] It is because of this '*potestas stupenda et miraculosa*' that emperors and princes kiss the feet of the Pope. As long as the Popes realise that this demonstration of respect is due to their office and not to their person–'*non tibi sed Petro*'–there is no ground for criticism. Seen in this light, there is also no reason why even the most incompetent Pope should not be called *sanctissimus*. Sometimes, however, the Vicars of Christ believe that honour is paid to their person; then human weakness and pride have overcome them, just as when they are concerned only with the extension of their power.[108]

3. plenitudo potestatis *in respect to the State and the temporal possessions of the Church*

In the next section Gerson deals with the question of how far the Pope, by virtue of his plenitude of power, can make claims on the possessions of his subjects, both clerics and ordinary believers, and of heathens. This in turn raises other questions, such as whether the Pope is entitled to become involved in politics, whether there is such a thing as a legitimate heathen *dominium*, and more generally what the relationship of Pope and secular power should be. It cannot be said that all these questions are clearly distinguished, but this does not detract from the complete clarity of Gerson's meaning in

---

sum succurrere, teneor succurrere isti vel illi sub disiunctione et non ambobus simul.' In the same context the distinction is used by Conrad of Gelnhausen (*Epistola concordiae*, ed. Bliemetzrieder, 137[20]).

[107] *De pot. eccl.*, cons. 11 (Gl. 6, 235-36; Dupin II, 245C): 'Hanc enim potestatem formaliter et in se consideratam primo modo nemo iudicare potest, neque Augustus, neque populus, neque totus clerus, immo nec universalis ecclesia.' Cf. C.9 q.3 c.13: 'Nemo iudicabit primam sedem... Neque enim ab Augusto, neque ab omni clero, neque a regibus, neque a populo iudex iudicabitur.'

[108] *De pot. eccl.*, cons. 11 (Gl. 6, 235-6; Dupin II, 245CD).

his main argument. It will become clear that the view which he takes of the relationship of Pope and lay power has many similarities with that defended a century and a half later by the Jesuit Bellarmine,[109] who, curiously enough in the context of our study, had to endure violent criticism from the Gallicans because of it.[110]

> Bellarmine taught, as a conscious reaction against absolutist ideas of the papal power, that the Pope, as Vicar of Christ, could by divine law make no claim on worldly power. This does not mean that he denied that the Pope or the Church could play any role in the secular world; he only denied the papal claim to direct power in the world. His view was that the Pope had only an *indirect* power over the State, that is, he could only intervene in politics when spiritual interests demanded it. Gerson's argument was quite the same.

To make his intention clearer, he introduces two persons, called 'angry refusal' (*detractio livida)* and 'false flattery' (*adulatio subdola)*, who had appeared to him in meditation, and who take it in turns to answer the questions posed, as representatives of the two extreme standpoints. Although he does not reveal who are hidden behind these personifications, it is easy to recognise the defenders of the spiritualist view in 'angry refusal' and those of papal absolutism in 'false flattery'.[111] So far as the former is concerned, one should bear in mind that Gerson included among the spiritualists not only the Cathars or the Poor Men of Lyons, but also Wyclif and Marsilius of Padua.

A closer identification is possible for the absolutist standpoint. The words which are put into the mouth of *adulatio subdola* seem to be largely taken from an anonymous work, most probably to be ascribed to Henry of Cremona, (d. 1312) Bishop of Reggio, and legal adviser to Boniface VIII.[112] Gerson's own thoughts on the

---

[109] As stated already by Gierke, *Genossenschafstrecht* III, 522 n. 13. Other defenders of the Pope's indirect power were Henry of Ghent, Pierre de la Palu and Ockham. For Henry see De Lagarde, *La naissance* II, 200-1, with reference to *Quodlib.* VI q. 23: '...sed iurisdictionis executionem meram habet [papa] in spiritualibus; in temporalibus non nisi in casibus...' For the others see F. Pelster, 'Die indirekte Gewalt der Kirche über den Staat nach Ockham und Petrus de Palude,' *Scholastik* (28) 1953, 78-82.

[110] *PRE* II, 555 s.v. 'Bellarmin' (H. Thiersch, A. Hauck).

[111] *De pot. eccl.*, cons. 12 (Gl. 6, 236-40; Dupin II, 246A-8D). For the tradition of the flattery topos, see Aimé-Georges Martimort, *Le Gallicanisme de Bossuet*, Paris 1953, 112ff. See also the present author's *Jean Gerson et l'Assemblée de Vincennes*, 102-6, and Ganzer, 'Päpstliche Gesetzgebungsgewalt', 186 n. 87.

[112] Scholz, *Publizistik*, 166-72. Editions of Henry's treatises inc. *Non ponant laici os in celum*, and *De potestate papae* are to be found in the same work (Scholz, 471-84, resp. 459-

matter are presented at the end of the dialogue by a third representative, called 'considered opinion' (*discretio moderatrix)*.

Strip the Church of its temporal possessions, cries *detractio livida*, for it is abundantly clear from the word of Christ: 'So with everyone of you who will not part with all his goods, he cannot be a disciple of mine' (Luke 14: 33), that worldly power is not given to the Church and the clergy. If a ruler wishes to endow them with it, then they must refuse it, for no one who fights for God should concern himself with worldly things (2 Tim. 2: 2). Priests should live off alms, and give everything they receive which is not strictly necessary for their own maintenance to the poor.[113] If they deny this, then they are guilty of *sacrilegium*, and the State is entitled to demand it from them.[114]

Adulatio, on the other hand, addresses the priesthood, and particularly the Pope, thus: 'How exalted, O Holy clergy, is your authority. How worthless is all worldly power in comparison with it.' For all the power which Christ received, in heaven and on earth, he passed on to Peter and his successors.[115] For that reason, Constantine could not give anything to Pope Sylvester which did not already belong to him; rather, he merely gave back what had been unjustly withheld.[116] Just as there is no power which is not derived from God (Rom. 13: 1) so there is no power, worldly or ecclesiastical, imperial or royal, which does not belong to the Pope, on whose loins Christ wrote 'King of Kings, Lord of Lords' (Rev. 19: 16)[117] and whose power it is sacrilege to dispute. Even when the Vicar of Christ wastes the temporal possessions of the Church, it is not befitting that anyone should ask: 'Cur ita facis?' Thus, says Gerson, spoke some who were wise in their own eyes, not excluding some of the Popes, so proving once more the adage: '*nihil est quod credere de se non possit, cum laudatur diis aequa potestas.*'[118]

When *adulatio* realises that she has revealed herself too clearly she adopts a more modest tone, and recognises that the State too has its own pos-

---

71). See also J. Miethke, 'Das Konsistorialmemorandum «De potestate pape» des Heinrich von Cremona von 1302 und seine handschriftliche Überlieferung', in: *Studi sul XIV seculo in memoria di Anneliese Maier*, edd. A. Maierù & A. Paravicini Bagliani, Romae 1981 (Storia e Letteratura 151), 421-51.

[113] *De pot. eccl.*, cons. 11 (Gl. 6, 236-7; Dupin II, 246B, cf. 248A); *Super victu et pompa* (Gl. 3, 95-6, 101-2; Dupin II, 635A, 639A); *Bonus pastor* (Gl. 5, 134-5; Dupin II, 551A).Cf. Chapter XII n. 119.

[114] So Wyclif thought. See P. de Vooght, *Les sources de la doctrine chrétienne*, s.l. [1954], 190-1.

[115] Henricus of Cremona, *Non ponant laici* (ed. Scholz, 471).

[116] Henricus of Cremona, *Non ponant laici* (ed. Scholz, 468).

[117] Henricus of Cremona, *Non ponant laici* (ed. Scholz, 471); *De pot. papae* (ed. Scholz, 464).

[118] Juvenal, *Sat.* I, IV 70, 71. Also cited in *Factum est proelium* (Gl. 5, 295-6; Dupin III, 1471A); *Vivat Rex* (Gl. 7* 1161; Dupin IV, 602B).

sessions and jurisdiction, which cannot be abolished at the whim of the Pope. She also acknowledges that Constantine and other rulers had in fact given powers to the Church, which it had not formerly possessed. But, *adulatio* maintains firmly, the Pope is the highest monarch in both the lay and clerical spheres, he receives his power directly from Christ, while worldly rulers only receive their *dominatio* from him, that is only *mediate* from God. Gerson relates this opinion to a decretal of Boniface VIII[119] and states that in recent times some *domini Pruteni*–members of the Prussian Order–had appealed to it to defend their struggle against the unbelievers.[120] Others had found in the same decretal a justification of the deposition of the King of France by Pope Zacharias. [121]

But because this view also seems too hard for many to accept, *adulatio* becomes even more modest. She admits, that just as the heathen before Peter had possessed a true *dominium*, so, after Peter, not all imperial, royal or worldly powers received their force *immediate* from the Pope. The King of France recognised no worldly authority above himself.[122] Being checked in this way in the matter of worldly power induces *adulatio* to turn to the offices, dignities and estates of the Church, which she claims are completely subject to the Pope. He can dispose of them at will, without ever incurring the guilt of simony, for they all belong to him. The Pope is above the law and it is just as impossible for him to be judged by it as for others to abandon their allegiance to him. Only he created the symbol, decided in matters of belief, defined doctrine, rules and laws, while anything decided by others was merely ridiculous and senseless. Moreover, nothing which he had decreed could be repealed by another, while he himself was not bound by any constitution.[123]

This was the view of many, whom Gerson preferred to call 'scholasters' rather than scholars, before the Council of Constance had taken place. 'Whoever asserted the contrary ran the risk of being condemned as a heretic. But even now, after the clearest theological proofs and what is more–after the decisions of the Council, this view is still openly held, so deep rooted is the poison of flattery.'[124]

---

[119] The bull *Clericis laicos* (25 Feb. 1296), in defence of which Henry of Cremona composed his treatises.

[120] Finke, *Acta concilii Constanciensis* IV, 251 n. 1.

[121] *C.* 15 q. 6 c. 3.

[122] *De pot. eccl.*, cons. 12 (Gl. 6, 238; Dupin II, 247B): 'Rex Francorum christianissimus superiorem hoc modo non habet nec recognoscit in terris' (= X 4. 17. 13). Already cited in *Acta de schismate tollendo*, prop. 3 (Gl. 6, 98; Dupin II, 76C). For the meaning of this formula, see Rivière, *Le problème*, 425ff., and Gaines Post, *Studies in Medieval Legal Thought*, Princeton (New-Jersey) 1964, 469ff.

[123] Giles of Rome, *De pot. eccl.*, prol. I (ed. Scholz, 7); for Alvarez Pelayo, see Iung, *Alvaro Pelayo*, 128; Rivière, *Le problème*, 194.

[124] *De pot. eccl.*, cons. 12 (Gl. 6, 237-9; Dupin II, 246D-7D).

'*Discretio moderatrix*', considered opinion, relying on the Gospels, keeps to the *via regia*. 1. She believes that priests may possess temporal property, which becomes theirs by several legal rights, and not merely as alms. This property may not be taken from them by the lay power without the consent of the Church. By possessing them the clergy are able to lead a life different from that of the apostles and more adapted to the changed circumstances of the times. 2. As far as plenitude of power is concerned, it is as great as Christ the lawgiver thought necessary for the building of his Church. Whoever removes himself from this power is guilty of sacrilege. Rather, one should praise God for entrusting such a power to human hands. But the Pope should use this power with wisdom. What on earth can be wiser than a council, guided by the Holy Spirit according to the principle of freedom? 3. When making appointments to offices or benefices, when granting reservations and exemptions etc., the Pope and the cardinals must not accumulate all the power to themselves in such a way that the entire organism of the Church suffers. For if all wish to be the eye and the head, where will the foot remain? (cf. 1 Cor. 12: 15, 21). 4. Finally, the Church must be able to recognise the limits of its authority, and acknowledge that the 'world', even among the heathen, has its own rights, laws and dignities, which cannot simply be usurped by the Church. Only when the secular power abuses its authority and opposes the faith, blasphemes against the Creator, or specifically injures the Church, is the Church entitled to make use of its '*dominium regitivum, directivum, regulativum et ordinativum*' over the State. In this–indirect–sense, one may say that the papal plenitude of power exceeds all other power in the Church or the world, although even in this respect the authority of the entire Church or of a general council, is greater because it is more all-embracing, and comprises the role of infallible leader with the power to carry out a *reformatio in capite et membris*, as well as the exercise of the power of excommunication and the power to decide questions of faith.[125] The council embodies virtu-

---

[125] *De pot. eccl.*, cons. 12 (Gl. 6, 240; Dupin II, 248D): '... potestas universalis ecclesiae vel generalis concilii legitime congregati dici possit maior in amplitudine vel extensione, maior in infallibili directione, maior in morum reformatione in capite et membris, maior in coercitiva potestate, maior in causarum fidei difficilium ultima decisione, maior denique quia copiosior. Complectitur enim saltem virtualiter omnem potestatem et omne politicum regimen, papale, imperiale, regale, aristocraticum et timocraticum...' Cf. the last part of this definition with Giles of Rome, *De pot. eccles.*, II 6 (ed. Scholz, 59-

ally every *potestas* and every *regimen politicum*, as is to be deduced from the definition drawn up by the Council of Constance.

> Concilium generale est congregatio legitima auctoritate facta ad aliquem locum ex omni statu hierarchico totius ecclesiae catholicae nulla fideli persona quae audiri requirat exclusa, ad salubriter tractandum et ordinandum ea quae debitum regimen eiusdem ecclesiae in fide et moribus respiciunt.[126].

This definition gives Gerson the occasion to make the following comments:

1. As appears from numerous decrees and decretals, a council is, as a rule, summoned by the Pope. In three cases, however, it can also legitimately assemble without the Pope:
   a. After the natural, civil or canonical death of the Pope, if he is insane, or if he is captive and cannot be reached.
   b. If the Pope refuses to hold a council, after sufficient requests to do so, and this refusal is harmful to the Church.
   c. If a council, legitimately called by the Pope, fixes the time and place of another council, *sicut infra triennium, vel de decennio in decennium*, a point which was to be settled in the 29th session of the council by the decree *Frequens*.[127]

---

60): 'ecclesia... omnia possidet, quia super omnibus habet auctoritatem, tam super spiritualia quam super temporalia,' and III 10 (ed. Scholz, 197-98): '... in potestate summi pontificis continetur omnis potestas sacerdotalis et regalis, celestis et terrena...' The difference is that Gerson attributes to (the council as representative of) the whole hierarchy, what Giles attributes to the highest hierarch alone.

[126] *De pot. eccl.*, cons. 12 (Gl. 6, 240; Dupin II, 249A); *Ambulate dum lucem habetis* (Gl. 5, 44-5; Dupin II, 205C); *Prosperum iter* (Gl. 5, 479; Dupin II, 279C). Cf. D'Ailly, *De materia concilii generalis*, VIII 6 (ed. Oakley, 268).

[127] *De pot. eccl.*, cons. 12 (Gl. 6, 240; Dupin II, 249A). He concludes this passage by referring to the *Capitula agendorum* (see Miethke, *Quellen zur Kirchenreform*, 222), saying: 'Nihilominus expedit decernere pro futuro modum convocationis, sicut in reformatione salubriter est avisatum, utinam et synodaliter iam esset definitum.' For the background and interpretation of the decree *Frequens*, see Jedin, 'Bischöfliches Konzil oder Kirchenparlement', in: *Die Entwicklung des Konziliarismus*, 220: 'Das Dekret «Frequenz» war der Versuch, eine Art von Parlementarismus in die Kirche einzuführen. Ihm lag die Ueberzeugung zugrunde, dass die Besserung der kirchlichen Zustände, eine Beseitigung der unbestreitbaren schweren Misstände in der Kirche nur durch einen Umbau der bisherigen Kirchenverfassung, vor allem eine Beschneidung des päpstlichen Zentralimus, zu erreichen sei.' See also Stump, *The Reforms of the Council of Constance*, 105-9, and, in particular, Brandmüller, *Das Konzil von Konstanz*, 335-58. Referring to a statement made by Tierney in a very convincing article ('Hermeneutics and History: The Problem of Haec Sancta', in: *Essays in honour of Bertie Wikinson*, Toronto 1969, 355-70 (366)), Brandmüller rightly stresses the fact that 'auch die Periodizität der Konzilien durchaus denkbar [war], ohne dass durch sie die hierarchische Struktur der Kirche und das ordentliche

Because it is not clear in the first two cases who has the right to summon the council, and because this had led to difficulties at Pisa, Gerson recommends that a rule should be drawn up for such cases.[128]

2. According to a *sententia valde probabilis* the hierarchy consists of two *status:* the successors of the twelve apostles (*praelati maiores*), and the successors of the seventy two disciples (*praelati minores*).[129] The former include the bishops and archbishops,[130] the latter the pastors (*curati*). Gerson cites the opinion of the doctors and a pronouncement of the theological faculty of the University of Paris in order to prove that the pastors belong to the hierarchy and that they receive their hierarchic powers *immediate* from Christ. Here he brings in the fruits of the heated discussions which took place at the University of Paris in reply to the theses defended by Jean Gorrel.[131]

3. The essence of a general council is that every *fidelis persona* who wishes to be heard, – by which he means in particular the (higher) representatives of the temporal sphere, – should be given the opportunity.[132] But a distinction is to be made between a *vox consultativa* and a *vox declarativa*. All those who have expertise in a particular field are entitled to an advisory say,[133] but the decisive say belongs

---

Lehramt des Papstes in Frage gestellt wurde.' (Brandmüller, *o.c.*, 352 n. 117). Cf. Chapter XII n. 88.

128 Cf. *Propositio coram Anglicis* (Gl. 6, 133-4; Dupin II, 129CD); *De auferibilitate*, cons. 19 (Gl. 3, 311; Dupin II 223A).

129 The distinction between apostles and disciples is traditional. Gerson refers for it to Isidorus (= d.a. D. 21) and Peter Lombard (= *l.s.* IV d. 24 c. 11), *De pot. eccl.* cons. 3 (Gl. 6, 214; Dupin II, 229C).

130 Peter Lombard (*l.s.* IV d. 24 c. 17) distinguished in the episcopal ordo: patriarchs, archbishops, metropolitans and bishops.

131 For more details, see Chapter X §. 2.

132 *De pot. eccl.*, cons. 12 (Gl. 6, 241; Dupin II, 249D): 'Dicamus tertio naturam generalis concilii talem esse ut nullus fidelis quae audiri voluerit debeat excludi ab audientia, quatenus vel doceatur vel doceat, sicut legitur in principio concilii.' Here he refers to the schedule read and approved at the Council's first session (16 Nov. 1414), and, in particular, to the following passage (*COD*, 382[12-16]): 'Insuper etiam exhortamur omnes catholicos hic congregatos, et alios ad hanc sacram synodum venturos, ut velint diligenter cogitare, et prosequi, et ad nos et eamdem sacram synodum perducere ea per quae possit congregatio catholicorum ad debitam reformationem et optatam tranquillitatem, Deo iuvante, perduci.' Cf. Chapter VI n. 60.

133 *De pot. eccl.*, cons. 12 (Gl. 6, 241; Dupin II, 249D-250A): '[Habentes vocem consultativam] sunt quibus inest notitia talium quae tractantur, etiam usque ad mechanicas artes, ut si quaeratur de modo reparationis ecclesiarum materialium, esse poterit

only to the representatives of the hierarchy, that is – and here Gerson refers to the practice of former councils – above all to the bishops and the higher prelates,[134] but also to the lower clergy, especially the pastors, and further to all those who can be included under both status, such as abbots, deans and provosts. Pastors have the right to vote, not on the grounds of any special privilege but by virtue of their *ordo*.

After devoting a final consideration to the analysis of a number of juridical terms and concepts,[135] Gerson concludes his treatise with the customary formula:

> Finit tractatulus *De potestate ecclesiastica et de origine iuris et legum*; magis ad inquisitionem veritatis quam ad determinationem editus et pronunciatus Constantiae tempore concilii generalis pro parte cancellarii Parisiensis; anno a nativitate Domini 1417, die VI Februarii.[136]

'*Editus*' means that the treatise was finished and available now; '*pronunciatus*' that it was read at dictation speed, either by Gerson him-

in latomis vox consultativa ...; sic dum fit quaestio de philosophicis et moralibus disciplinis, ut sunt praecepta decalogi, possunt saeculares eruditi in philosophiae legibus et moribus dare consilium, et aliquando salubrius quam nonnulli praelatorum vel curatorum vel etiam theologorum; usque adeo quod in generalibus conciliis contra Arium, tempore Athanasii, fuerit interrogatus gentilis philosophus de materia nedum pure morali, sed quae tangebat beatae Trinitatis eamdem essentiam.' Cf. Ockham, *Dialogus* I, 6, 22 (ed. Goldast, 527[55-56]): '...sicut patet in li. *De altercatione Athanasii contra Arrium*, Athanasius et aemuli sui paganum in iudicem pro causa fidei elegerunt.' A reference to ps.-Athanasius = Vigilius of Thapsus, *Altercatio S. Athanasii contra Arium, Sabellium et Photinum haereticos* in *ML* 62, 179-238. Cf. *LThK* 10, 788-9 s.v. 'Vigilius' (J. Martin). Gerson will have had the same legend in mind when he wrote in his *Summaria responsio*, directed against Martin Porée (Gl. 10, 228): 'Unde non est novum vel haereticum quod in materiis fidei, ut de Trinitate, electus sit iudex paganus.' (The phrase is missing in Dupin V, 450B). – Gerson's whole passage should be compared with what was declared in the Council's first session (*COD*, 381[38]-2[5]: 'Praeterea considerantes, quod praecipuum agendum in concilio secundum laudabiles antiquorum conciliorum est de his, quae cernunt catholicam fidem, et attendentes, quod talia propter suam arduitatem exigant diligentiam, tempus sufficiens ac studium, exhortamur *omnes habentes peritiam sacrarum literarum*, ut diligenter secum et *cum aliis* illa cogitent atque tractent, quae eis videbuntur ad hanc rem utilia et opportuna.' By 'experts in the Scriptures', members of the hierarchy in general will be meant, and in particular theological doctors; by 'others', non-theological specialists. Cf. Chapter XI § 4, notably n. 74, and our 'Het gezag van de theologische doctor in de kerk der middeleeuwen', *NAKG* N.S. 63 (1983) 102-28 (118-19).

[134] Cf. this passage with d'Ailly, *De materia concilii generalis* (ed. Oakley, 268-9).

[135] See above n. 13.

[136] *De pot. eccl.*, epilogus (Gl. 6, 250; Dupin II, 255D). See also above n. 2.

self or by others, to those who, for whatever reason, were interested to have a copy of it.[137]

***

Here our summary of *De potestate ecclesiastica* has come to its end. In the next chapter we will investigate, more systematically, what the essentials of his ecclesiological thoughts were. Inevitably this will lead us back, more than once, to what we have discussed in earlier chapters and, in particular, to our paraphrase of his main ecclesiological treatise.

[137] *De pot. eccl.*, epilogus (Gl. 6, 250; Dupin II, 256). For more details concerning the practice of these dictation-sessions, technically called '*pronuntiatio*', see Miethke, 'Die Konzilien als Forum der öffentlichen Meinung,' *DAEM* 37 (1981) 736-73 (753ff.) One might suppose that Gerson's *De pot. eccl.*, like his *De auferibilitate*, was dictated at the Dominican monastery at Constance, where the French delegation was lodged. Cf. Miethke, *a.c.*, 755 n. 61[a], and Gl. 3, Introduction, xiii, 102.

CHAPTER TEN

CHURCH, HIERARCHY AND GENERAL COUNCIL II

The essentials of Gerson's ecclesiology

> *Status papalis obligat papam, tanto amplius quanto maior est in Ecclesia, subjicere se legibus divinis, naturalibus et canonicis, ad utilitatem Ecclesiae. Propterea, cum magis videant oculi quam oculus, videtur quod non sine grandi discrimine salutis, papa possit deliberationes vel instituta generalium conciliorum contemnere, ut non secundum communem sed propriam deliberationem contendat in ecclesiastico regimine praesidere. Propterea bene dictum est quod papa non potest generalem statutum Ecclesiae immutare vel tollere.*
>
> Gerson, *De statibus ecclesiasticis* (Gl. 9, 27; Dupin II, 531A).

The most important question raised by Gerson's treatise *De potestate ecclesiastica* and by his ecclesiological writings in general is this: what is the nature of the Church on which he laid such emphasis? What was the Church whose rights he defended, and what was the *ecclesia* he believed to be represented at the general council? Was it the *ecclesia universalis* which Ockham and his followers had maintained could continue to exist in a single person, even in a woman? Or was it the *congregatio fidelium* in the sense which Marsilius of Padua and Dietrich of Niem had understood? We maintain that, to judge by his *De potestate ecclesiastica* and all his other writings, Gerson never regarded the Church as anything other than a hierarchical organism. This implies that neither the Marsilian idea of the *congregatio fidelium* nor the Ockhamist interpretation of the *ecclesia universalis* played any formative role in his ecclesiology. As this thesis differs from the current interpretation, a rather more detailed proof is desirable.

It is certain that if Gerson had propounded an unhierarchical theory of the Church, he would have strayed from his own intentions, for at the beginning of *De potestate ecclesiastica* he stated quite expressly that he wished to interpret the idea 'Church' in the narrow sense, that is meaning 'hierarchy'. He was thus aware that a different approach was possible, but he intended, at least, to avoid it. Was he consistent in this respect and did he in fact realise his intention? In our opinion, most certainly. What are the arguments for this view?

1. The first part of the work expanded into a broad defence of the rights of the Church as a whole. In this connexion the text Matt. 18: 15-17, in which the words *'dic ecclesiae'* occur, was significant. Gerson deduced from it that the power of the keys had been given *principalius* to the Church and not to the pope, just as he also applied the qualifications *indeviabilitas, regulabilitas, multiplicitas, obligabilitas*, to the Church as a whole and not to the pope alone.
These explanations are placed in the context of consideration 5, dealing with the papal power of jurisdiction, more especially with external jurisdiction. We have seen that for Gerson, the power of consecration and the power of jurisdiction were intimately connected. The power of jurisdiction was founded *radicaliter* on the power of consecrating the sacraments. This was beyond dispute for him and for the same reason he was so opposed to the canonist-curialist theory, which regarded this connection, at least as far as the office of pope was concerned–*papa est nomen iurisdictionis*–as non-essential. He believed that this led to the ridiculous conclusion that the office of pope could be held by a layman, even a woman.
We deduce from this that he can only have meant the hierarchical Church, when he spoke of the 'Church' without any more specific definition, the Church to which Christ had *principalius* entrusted the power of jurisdiction. For if there is no jurisdiction without consecration, no power without the sacrament, then there can be no Church without the hierarchy. By the same reasoning, the qualifications: *indeviabilitas*, etc., can only apply to the hierarchic Church.

2. That this interpretation is the correct one, is confirmed by the second part of the treatise, in which the problem of the power of the Church is analysed into its ecclesiastical power in the absolute, material and executive senses. We shall return to this in another context. At any rate, the *potestas ecclesiastica* in this sense is described as the total of the *hierarchical* powers.

3. In the final chapter we shall see that Gerson distinguishes himself from Ockham, Conrad of Gelnhausen, Heinrich of Langenstein and d'Ailly by the fact that he makes no use of the concept of the *ecclesia universalis* as they do. He shunned the laicist implications hidden in this idea, and considered it unthinkable that the Church could ever be found in a single woman or in laymen.

All this makes it clear that he did not think of the Church in either the Marsilian or the Ockhamist sense. There is nothing to indicate that he based his theories on the idea of the Church as a *congregatio fidelium* or *ecclesia universalis*, still less that he opposed the Church in this sense to the Church as hierarchy. The simple alternative 'Church' or 'hierarchy', is completely inapplicable to the interpretation of his thought, for the no less simple reason that he could not imagine the Church except as a hierarchic entity. And how could this 'commentateur Dionysien' have thought differently, completely imbued as he was with the idea of the hierarchy of the Church as a reflection of the hierarchy of heaven?

1. *The hierarchy of the Church as totality*

The more we emphasise the hierarchic character of his ecclesiology, the more difficult it becomes to identify what was new and characteristic in it. For the traditional view of the Church had also been hierarchic. It seems to us that Gerson's theory broke relatively new ground by considering the hierarchy as a totality which, following Aristotle, he stated to have priority above the composing parts. These parts were: the papacy, the cardinalate, the patriarchate, archiepiscopate, episcopate and priesthood. Together they formed the totality of the 'Church', immutable because it was of divine origin.

Within the mystical body of the Church this hierarchical totality represented a sort of corporation, which was responsible for the transmission of salvation to all believers. Expressed in non-gersonian terms, one may say that he considered the totality of the hierarchy as *ecclesia docens*, by whose activity salvation was transmitted to the laity as *ecclesia audiens*.

The idea that the whole logically precedes the part or, to put it another way, that the part is dependent on the *totum integrale*, comes, as has been said, from Aristotle, for whom it was a central principle. Petrus Hispanus adopted the relevant texts from Aristotle in his *Summulae logicales*, and it seems certain that Gerson referred to this when, in the introduction to his second set of distinctions between the powers of the Church, he gave a survey of the various ways in which, according to Aristotle, one thing can be contained in another, the so-called *modi essendi in*;[1] the first way being *sicut pars integralis in suo toto*; the second *sicut totum integrale in suis partibus*.[2] We can infer from this that it was logical school learning which helped him to formulate his peculiar concept of the hierarchy in the sense of a hierarchical totality. Theologians before him had also employed the distinction *pars – totum*[3] but, so far as we can discover, Gerson was the first to apply it to the concept of the hierarchy in such a specific way, thereby giving a new form to a much older idea.

If we compare the hierarchical principle of his ecclesiology with the more detailed exposition given – the hierarchy in the sense of a totality – we find a certain contradiction. When we speak of a hierarchy we mean a pyramidal structure with a summit, a *summum* from which the lower organs are administered and from which they receive – *mediate* – their authority. It is inherent in the idea of a hierarchy that everything emanates from the top. But, if one describes the hierarchy as a totality in the Aristotelian sense, this implies that the summit, so to speak, is reduced to a mere part alongside the other parts, with which it must compete. This is a contradiction because the competitive position of a part cannot logically co-exist

---

[1] Peter of Spain, *Summule logicales*, III 3.2. (ed. De Rijk, 27-8), with reference to Aristotle, *Physica* IV 3 (210a 14-24). We fail to grasp why some authors consider the Aristotelian, common sense formula: 'totum est maius sua parte' typically nominalistic. See e.g. J. Hollnsteiner ('Die konziliare Idee', in: *Die Entwicklung des Konziliarismus*, 61): 'Es ist ein nominalistisches Axion: Das Ganze ist grösser als seine Teile.' Did Boniface VIII prove to be an adherent of nominalism by formulating the *regula iuris* (VI. (80): 'In toto partem non est dubium contineri?!'

[2] *De pot. eccl.* cons. 6 (Gl. 6, 220-1; Dupin II, 234B). Cf. Pierre d'Ailly (*De eccles. auct.*, pars III c. 1, Dupin II, 950D-951A), who distinguishes between the fullness of power 'proprie loquendo', 'tropologice' and 'equivoce' – referring, respectively, to the pope, the church and the general council. He connects this threefold distinction with the particular way in which a thing can be in another. 'Primo tanquam [in] subjecto, sicut virtus in anima; secundo modo, tanquam in objecto, sicut aliquis effectus dicitur esse in sua causa, vel in suo fine, quia in illum tendit, tanquam in suum objectum finale; tertio modo, tanquam in exemplo, ut res visa dicitur esse in speculo, vel aliqua doctrina in libro, quia ibi est repraesentative. Primo ergo modo, plenitudo potestatis est in papa, tanquam in subjecto ipsam recipiente, et ministerialiter exercente. Secundo, est in in universali ecclesia, tanquam in objecto ipsam causaliter et finaliter continente. Tertio, est in generale concilio, tanquam in exemplo ipsam repraesentante et regulariter dirigente.' For more details, see Oakley, *Political Thought*, 120ff.

[3] Pierre d'Ailly, *De materia concilii generalis* (ed. Oakley, 304): 'Et ad hoc probandum videtur esse ratio evidens, quia omne totum sua parte maius est. Sed papa est pars concilii, sicut caput pars corporis.' See also De Lagarde, *La naissance* II, index s.v. 'partie et tout'; Wilks, *The Problem of Sovereignty*, 479ff., & index s.v. 'part/whole.'

with the monopoly position of a summit. Expressed in scholastic terminology, the contradiction arises from the fact that one cannot consider a hierarchy in a distributive and collective sense *at the same time*. This is what Gerson did, and in our opinion this is why his ecclesiological views are not always satisfying in their logic.

When discussing the idea of plenitude of power he distinguishes two aspects: *supremitas* and *latitudo*. Plenitude of power seen from the first aspect, – in which the distributive principle is recognised, – implies that all authority in the Church depends on the office of the papacy, through which it is transmitted to the lower hierarchical organs. But seen from the aspect of *latitudo*, – in which the collective principle is recognised, – the authority is entrusted to the hierarchy as a whole, in which all parts participate directly. In the first case, the authority of the different hierarchical degrees is derived from the office of the papacy; in the second the priority belongs to the hierarchy as such, in which not only the office of the papacy participates directly, but all the other hierarchical offices as well.

> Haec enim latitudo potestatis complectitur in se alias potestates ecclesiasticas collective a summmo usque deorsum et est in eis plenitudo tamquam pars integralis in suo toto.[4]

A tendency towards equal rights for the parts is inherent in such a theory, but is in conflict with the vertical principle natural to the idea of a hierarchy.

Yet despite this fundamental contradiction, the logical flaws in Gerson's theory of the Church remain minor. This is because he allowed the collective principle to prevail, and as far as possible argued from the standpoint of the entire hierarchy. He imagined the hierarchy as a collective body, in which authority was not found only in the highest hierarchical regions but was distributed equitably among all its organs; for his argument was that these organs had received their authority not through the Pope as intermediary but *immediate* from God.[5] In his programme of reform he aimed at nothing less than the restoration of this order with the lower organs being given a say and allowed some responsibility. Their representatives were to respect one another and the Pope was in particular to

---

4 *De pot. eccl.* cons. 11 (Gl. 6, 233; Dupin II, 143D).

5 Alexander of St. Elpidio, *De pot. eccl.* I. c. 7 (ed. Rocaberti, 9b, 10) refuted this view, which he qualified as 'erronea', though not as 'haeretica'.

refrain from interfering in the competence of others without urgent reason. His intervention was to be regarded not as the rule but as the exception, only allowable when there was a clear necessity for a dispensation.

All this means that Gerson affirmed the *potestas indirecta* of the Pope not only with reference to the State but, *to a certain degree*, to the Church as well. In fact, he considered that the Pope only had the right to make use of his plenitude of power when the representatives of the lower organs of the hierarchy had failed in their duty or when it was in the interest of the Church in general, just as when, in the State, the princes had not understood their responsibility or when the well-being of the temporal realm demanded otherwise. The following citation from an appendix to his treatise summarises this clearly.

> Neque tamen plenitudo potestatis papalis sic intelligenda est immediate super omnes christianos, quod pro libito possit immediate iurisdictionem in omnes per se vel alios extraordinarios passim exercere, sic enim praeiudicaret ordinariis *qui ius habent immediatius immo immediatissimum* super plebes eis commissas actus hierarchicos exercendi. Extenditur ergo plenitudo potestatis papae super ommes inferiores *solum dum subest necessitas ex defectu ordinariorum inferiorum, vel dum apparet evidens utilitas ecclesiae.*[6]

It seems undeniable that this theory was developed in order to oppose the absolutist conception of papal plenitude of power, the disastrous consequences of which had been dramatically manifested in the outbreak and continuation of the Schism. To the literally top-heavy ecclesiology of the curialists–prepared by the canonists, and propagated by the Popes themselves–Gerson opposed his doctrine of a more broadly disseminated hierarchical responsibility. That was, if one likes, the negative pole of his ecclesiology. But he knew that his views of the hierarchy were supported by tradition and that he had forerunners. Who were they?

Above all, we think, the Augustinian theologian, Henry of Ghent, and in general those who had defended the interests of the secular clergy against the regulars. In our final chapter we shall try

[6] *De plenitudine pot. eccl.* (Gl. 6, 250-1; Dupin II, 256AD). He refers for this thesis to *Gl. ord.* ad C. 9 q.3 c. 20, and concludes: 'quod etsi papalis potestas extendatur ad omnes immediate, supple «in casu necessitatis vel evidentis utilitatis», non tamen vult alicuius ecclesiae privilegium infringere, supple «quia nec ita velle debet»' (Gl. 6, 251; Dupin II, 256D).

to show that the ideas of the *doctor solemnis* in particular pointed the way for Gerson. In him he found support for his opinion that the degrees of the hierarchy had been received *immediate* from God, that the ecclesiastical order was immutable and that the Pope could only deviate from this order in case of evident necessity and emergency.

In very complete article Yves M.-J. Congar gave an excellent description of the conflict between the seculars and the regulars, as it raged with varying intensity from the middle of the thirteenth century till the end of the next century, particularly in France. Congar summarised the position of the secular clergy as follows:

1. According to divine law there are only two *ordines* in the Church, that of the bishops and that of the simple priests. 2. Both *ordines* were instituted by Christ, which implies that bishops and priests received their pastoral jurisdiction directly from Him, and not from the Pope. 3. The Pope ought therefore to respect this order and not disturb it by granting powers and privileges to the regular clergy. 4. The universal Church consists of a community of local churches which, from their base to their apex, are built up of ever more comprehensive corporations. Congar concludes: 'It is in this context that the seculars considered the role of the Pope, his *plenitudo potestatis*, the role of the council, the powers of bishops and pastors, and finally the position of the ordinary believers.'[7]

If we compare Gerson's ideas of the hierarchy with Congar's summary of the position of the seculars, we are led unmistakably to the conclusion that there was a wide agreement. To make this clear we shall compare a number of Gerson's statements with the characteristics listed by Congar. The statements are taken 1. from his *quaestio disputa* entitled *De consiliis evangelicis et statu perfectionis*. This work is difficult to date but was presumably written about 1401-2.[8] Here he argues emphatically that the pastors (*curati*) belonged to the hierarchy, that they formed an independent hierarchical *gradus*, and

---

[7] Y. M.-J. Congar, 'Aspects ecclésiologiques de la querelle entre mendiants et séculiers', *AHDLMA* 36 (1961), 15-150 (63).

[8] Gl. 3, 10-26; Dupin II, 669-81. The opening words of the disputation ('investigare libet in quo stat, manet et perconsistit vita animae nostrae spiritualis et perfectio vitae christianae...') seem to us to foreshadow what Gerson was to work in out in more detail in his cycle of lectures *De vita spir. animae* of 1402. For a careful discussion of the disputation, see Luise Abramowski, 'Johann Gerson, De consiliis evangelicis et statu perfectionis', in: *Studien zur Geschichte und Theologie der Reformation. Festschrift für Ernst Bizer*, Neukirchen 1969, 63-78. The differences between Gerson and Thomas Aquinas, whom he cited many times, are well set out in this article.

could not be regarded as the prolonged arms of the bishops.[9] 2. He again discussed the position of the pastors and, in general the stucture of the hierarchy at the end of the year 1408, when the Franciscan Jean Gorrel in his *Vesperiae* had defended the thesis that the right of cure of souls, preaching and hearing confession did not belong to the pastors but to the mendicant orders, on the ground of privileges they had received from the supreme hierarch, the Pope. All the evidence point to the fact that Gerson wielded the full authority of his chancellorship to induce Jean Gorrel to recant and that it was at his instigation that the faculty of divinity pronounced that the pastors had received their office directly from Christ and therefore could not be ousted from it by the privileges of the mendicants.[10] 3. Not long after this affair he came out openly, in his sermon *Quomodo stabit regnum,* against the bull *Regnans in excelsis* of Alexander V, in which the Pope, perhaps defending Gorrel's assertions but at any rate following a curial tradition, granted the wishes of the mendicants and gave them far-reaching powers in the cure of souls etc.[11] 4. The results of his polemics with Jean Gorrel were incorporated in a detailed treatise *De statibus ecclesiasticis*, which dealt more with specific ecclesiastical practices.[12] In this work, in a series of brief considerations, Gerson discusses the *status* of the Pope, the cardinals, the bishops, the pastors, the mendicants (*privilegati*) and, finally, those who combined in themselves the status of pastor and mendicant friar.

---

9 *De consiliis evangelicis* (Gl. 3, 25; Dupin II, 681A): '... curati parochiales non se habent ad episcopos sicut ballivi vel praepositi ad regem vel principem. Patet quoniam ipsi curati habent ordinariam iurisdictionem... praepositi autem en ballivi non habent nisi subdelegatam iurisdictionem, non ordinariam... Si curati non haberent ordinariam iurisdictionem plus quam praepositi vel ballivi regum et principum, tunc episcopi possent pro libitu et mere gratis eos deponere absque culpa, sicut principes de suis praepositis et ballivis facere possunt.' In this view Gerson followed Henry of Ghent and Godefroy of Fontaines, and challenged Thomas Aquinas, and the papalists. Cf. Congar, 'Aspects ecclésiologiques', 68 n. 88; Abramowski, 'Johann Gerson', 76, and Hervaeus Natalis, *De iurisdictione* (ed. Hödl), 28, 34.

10 Denifle-Chatelain, *CUP* IV, 162-4. Gerson referred to this decision in *De pot. eccl.*, cons. 12 (Gl. 6, 242; Dupin II, 250AB): 'Facit ad hoc determinatio sacrae facultatis theologiae Parisiensis nuper edita contra temeritatem extollentium privilegiatos super curatos in praedicationibus et confessionibus.'

11 Gl. 7*, 978-92; Dupin II, 431-42 (Latin). For a survey of Gerson's polemics with the mendicant orders, see 'Dossier sur les pouvoirs des mendiants' (Gl. 10, 30-1).

12 Gl. 9, 25-35; Dupin II, 529-37. We have adopted Dupin's title because it describes the contents more accurately than Mgr. Glorieux's *De statu papae et minorum praelatorum*.

1. On Congar's first point, the passage in *De potestate ecclesiastica* dealing with the representation of the hierarchy at a council provides the clearest sign that Gerson was continuing the tradition of the seculars. Just as they had been accustomed to do, he distinguished between only two *ordines* in the hierarchy: that of the *praelati maiores* (the successors of the twelve apostles–Pope, cardinals, archbishops, bishops) and that of the *praelati minores* (the successors of the seventy two disciples–pastors).[13]

2. On the *status* of the higher prelates–and this brings us to Congar's second characteristic–he argued in the first place that it was of supernatural institution,[14] and continued that Christ had granted it *immediate* to the first apostles, just as he had granted the *status papalis* to Peter.

> Status praelationis episcopalis in Ecclesia quoad sui collationem primariam fuit immediate a Christo datus primis Apostolis, sicut status papalis Petro.[15]

Because the episcopate traced its origin to its institution by Christ, the Pope could not abolish it, just as the *status papalis* could never be abolished. The Pope was, however, thanks to his possession of the *plenitudo fontalis* (Bonaventure) of episcopal authority, within his rights to intervene in the way in which his subject bishops exercised their power (*usus, exercitium*), as the latter had the right to intervene in the actions of their subordinate pastors. In both cases this right could only be exercised for good reasons and if it were to the advantage of the Church; guidance on this point was to be sought

---

[13] See Chapter IX n. 129. Cf. *De statibus ecclesiasticis* (Gl. 9, 28-33; Dupin II, 532B-4A).

[14] *De statibus ecclesiasticis*, De statu praelatorum, cons. 1 (Gl. 9, 28; Dupin II, 532B): 'Status praelationis episcopalis in Ecclesia sic est de primaria et immediata ac supernaturali institutione Christi, quod naturali vel humana solum auctoritate non potuit institui, sicut potuit status dominationis temporalis...'

[15] *De statibus ecclesiasticis*, de statu praelatorum, cons. 2 (Gl. 9, 28; Dupin II, 532C); *Quomodo stabit* (Gl. 7*, 984; Dupin II, 436D): 'Les sires curés sont en l'eglise les mendres prelas hierarchiques, c'est à dire principaux ou dominans, par la premiere institucion de Jhesucrist.' Gerson added a couple of references to this statement, which were incorrectly interpreted by Mgr. Glorieux (Gl. 7*, 984 n. *b*: 'Decret. XXI, 68' does not exist). Following Dupin's reading, Gerson referred to: Luke 10 [: 1-6] with glosses; d.a. D. 21; D. 68 c. 5, and C. 13 q. 1. c. 1–D.a. D. 21 contains the famous words: 'Simpliciter vero maiorum et minorum sacerdotum discretio in novo Testamento ab ipso Christo sumpsit exordium, qui duodecim Apostolos tamquam maiores sacerdotes, et lxxij. discipulos quasi minores sacerdotes instituit. Petrum vero quasi in summum sacerdotem elegit, dum ei prae omnibus claves regni caelorum tribuit...'

above all in the decisions and rules laid down by previous councils.[16]

> Status curatorum succedit statui septuaginta duorum discipulorum Christi quoad legem novam, et figuratus est in antiqua lege per levitas. Ac proinde status curatorum est de institutione Christi et Apostolorum suorum a principio fundationis Ecclesiae, quae institutio per declarationes summorum pontificum et synodorum tam generalium quam specialium magis et magis innotuit.[17]

The *status* of the pastors was thus just as essentially hierarchical in its nature as that of the bishops. They were subject to the authority of the bishops, because their *status* was less complete. Pastors were called on to practise the cure of souls, to hear confession, to preach and in general to do everything that served to promote the faith of their parishioners.[18]

The *status* of the mendicants, on the other hand, had a different origin and differed in its importance in the hierarchy.[19] The mendicants had not belonged to the original institution of the Church. Gerson traced their origin primarily to the growth in the Church's temporal possessions. This had entailed so many new burdens that others had to be appointed to assist the hierarchical dignitaries.

---

[16] *De statibus ecclesiasticis*, de statu praelatorum, cons. 3 & 4 (Gl. 9, 28-9; Dupin II, 532BC): 'Status praelationis episcopalis habuit in Apostolis et in successoribus usum vel exercitium suae potestatis sub papa Petro et successoribus eius, tamquam sub habente vel habentibus plenitudinem fontalem episcopalis auctoritatis. Unde et quoad talia, minores praelati scilicet curati, subsunt episcopis a quibus usus suae potestatis quandoque limitatur vel arcetur; et sic a papa posse fieri circa praelatos maiores ex certis et rationabilibus causis non est ambigendum. [Cons. 4]. ... status episcopalis quoad acquisitionem isti personae et quoad exercitium, subest rationabili papae voluntati et utilitatem Ecclesiae... Haec autem rationabilitas videtur attendenda seu regulanda maxime per determinationes conciliorum generalium, praesertim iam factas de consensu et auctoritate summorum pontificum.' See also the epigraph of this Chapter, where Gerson seems to refer to Johannes Teutonicus's *Glossa ad* C. 25 q. 2. 17: 'Ex hoc patet quod papa non potest contra generale ecclesiae statutum dispensare nec contra articulos fidei...' For more details, see Tierney, *Foundations*, chapter 2: 'Pope and General Council', 47-67 (53).

[17] *De statibus ecclesiasticis*, de statu curatorum, cons. 1 (Gl. 9, 31; Dupin II, 534A).

[18] *De statibus ecclesiasticis*, de statu curatorum, cons. 1-5 (Gl. 9, 31; Dupin II, 534AB).

[19] *De statibus ecclesiasticis*, de statu curatorum, cons. 6 (Gl. 9, 31; Dupin II, 534C): 'Status curatorum superior est in ordine hierarchico Ecclesiae ad statum simplicium religiosorum.' *Quomodo stabit regnum* (Gl. 7*, 984; Dupin II, 437A): 'S'ensuit que l'estat des curés est plus principal que des simples religieus; je diz simples car es religieux sont des curez comme sont prieurs, abbez, prevost ou telz. C'est la determination [de] saint Denis in ecclesiastica iherarchia, et de saint Jerome a Heliodorus. *Sunt in statu perfectionis acquirende.*'

> Status privilegiatorum ad praedicandum et confessiones audiendum statutus est post primariam Ecclesiae institutionem, rationabiliter ordinatus ad sublevamen eorum qui hierarchicos in Ecclesia status habent, praesertim post talem et tantam in temporalibus dotationem quae secum attulit multam occupationem.[20]

3. Implicitly, this has already touched on Congar's third characteristic: the demand that the Pope ought to respect the original hierarchical order of the Church as far as possible. In several passages Gerson drew the conclusion from this that the mendicants as newcomers could only perform pastoral duties with the consent of the bishops and the pastors. His main thesis was always that the mendicants only had a right to preach and hear confessions if the prelates consented,[21] and if there was a manifest need to intervene in the local circumstances.[22]

4. Congar's fourth characteristic also recurs in Gerson. In full conformity with the tradition of the seculars–and in a notable deviation from Ockham, whose concept of the *ecclesia universalis* he used in other sense–Gerson equated it with the total of the local churches.[23]

---

[20] *De statibus ecclesiasticis*, de statu privilegiatorum, cons. 1 (Gl. 9, 33; Dupin II, 536A). Cf. his exclamation in *De vita spir. animae*, lect.4 (Gl. 3, 164; Dupin III, 43C): 'Miratus sum aliquando qua ratione ipsi ecclesiastici, praesertim ordinati et religiosi, prohibentur a scientia medicinae, et non removentur de facto a studio traditionis humanae, nam corpus longe melius est quam terrena substantia cui traditiones istae deserviunt. Quod si per alios potest corpus curari, nonne similiter per vicarios et alios de Ecclesia contemptibiles, prout iubet Apostolus [1 Cor. 6: 4], possent temporalia ministrari?'

[21] *Contra bullam 'Regnans in excelsis'* (Gl. 10, 38; Dupin II, 445B): 'Putamus, immo certe scimus, Fratres Mendicantes non sic institutos per beatos Dominicum et Franciscum, qui nihil agendum invitis dominis suis,–ita enim episcopos et curatos appellabant,–nihil in praeiudicium eorum attentandum dixerunt et iusserunt. Juste quidem. Alioquin non coadiutores humiles praelatorum et plebis, sed fures et latrones aliunde quam per ostium in ovile dominicum induxissent [cf. Ioh. 10: 1].' *Quomodo stabit regnum* (Gl. 7*, 988; Dupin II, 439D): 'Aux mendiants n'appartient pas prescher ou confesser si non accidentellement et par privilege, c'est par commission et du bon plaisir des prelats... S'ensuit que les freres n'ont point estat iherarchique en sainte eglise si non comme autres religieux ou autres clercs et crestiens.'

[22] *Quomodo stabit regnum* (Gl. 7*, 989; Dupin II, 440A): 'Et s'aucun dit que le pape les envoie, il faut scavoir s'il est necessité. Car on ne doit mie bailler curateur ou coadjuteur à ung prelat ou aultre maulgré luy sans son deffault ou son insuffisance; autrement on le grave.'

[23] *De auctoritate concilii*, art. 5, concl. 4 (Gl. 6, 116): 'Ecclesiae consilium, quo papa in definiendo magistraliter et obligative veritates fidei aut veritates fidei aut necessarias pro regimine Ecclesiae tenetur uti, est *universalis ecclesiae et ecclesiae Romanae et ecclesiae Parisiensis et omnium singularium Christi vere ecclesiarum consilium, coniunctim et divisim.*' Cf. Chapter XII n. 67.

We believe that the above offers sufficient proof that Gerson's ideas about the hierarchy continued the tradition of the seculars. Apart from Henry of Ghent, he also owed a great deal in this respect to Richard FitzRalph.[24]

2. *The Cosmos and the State as mystical bodies*

More markedly than any of his contemporaries, Gerson developed his ecclesiological ideas on the basis of the 'mystical body'. This idea was as central to his ecclesiology as it was characteristic of it. Before we explain and analyse it more fully, we point out that he did not apply the term 'mystical body' exclusively to the Church but also used it in other contexts. The striking point in these non-ecclesiological connexions is that he always referred to the same texts of Paul. This shows that he believed that when the apostle used the term 'mystical body', he was not thinking merely of the Church but had also in mind other ontological entities and structures which could be distinguished in the cosmic order. In this Gerson was in conformity with a long tradition dating from antiquity.[25] In a sermon of 1409, for instance, he says:

> ... disons que les hommes sont ordonnés de Dieu comme *un corps mistique* à l'exemple du corps naturel qui doibt avoir paix et union entre ses membres. C'est la determination de l'Apostre en plusieurs lieux, ad Rom 12 [:4-5], ad 1 Cor. 12 [:12-28] et ad Eph. 4[:4-16].[26]

Elaborating this point, he argues that to belong to 'le corps mystique des hommes' implied that human beings were naturally disposed to support one another, avoid division and strive for peace and unity. He called this a universal law of nature and here too, he did not fail to refer to the University of Paris which, with its mem-

---

[24] See *Quomodo stabit regnum* (Gl. 7*, 989; Dupin II, 440B).

[25] *Ambulate* (Gl. 5, 44; Dupin II, 204A): 'Haec autem comparatio veri corporis ad mysticum, multum luminis affert inquisitoribus veritatis, nedum apud philosophos sicut Aristotelem et Plutarcum, sed apud theologos, Paulum praecipue.' For abundant details about the use of the term 'body' in antiquity and in Paul, see G. Kittel, *Theologisches Wörterbuch zum Neuen Testament* 7, 1024-91 (1035-42) s.v. 'σῶμα' (E. Schweizer), and Arnold Ehrhardt, 'Das corpus Christi und die Korporationen im spät-römischen Recht', *ZRG Rom. Abt.* (70) 1953, 299-347.

[26] *Pax hominibus* (Gl. 7*, 766; Dupin II, 144C).

bers who came from all corners of the earth, always seeks to obtain unity within the 'corps mystique des hommes'.

> Et car en la fille du Roy, en l'Université, sont membres de toutes les parties du monde pour soy espandre par tout, n'est pas merveille s'elle quiert union en tout *le corps mistique des hommes.*[27]

In the second place Gerson used the term 'corps mystique' when dealing with the structure of the State. In that context too, he referred to the same passages in Paul.[28] This is well expressed in his famous sermon *Vivat Rex*. We cite this at some length, not because we wish to go into his view of the State in depth,[29] but merely for comparison.

> Tout mon propoz... est que le roy vive; vive, dy je, de vie non seulement corporelle..., mais *civile et mistique*, laquelle se tient a garde par unité de luy comme d'ung chef avecques ses subietz, qui sont comme le corps aians divers membrez selon divers estas et officez qui sont ou royaulme. Pour tant ung roy n'est pas une personne singuliere, maiz est une puissance publique ordonnée pour le salut de tout le commun, ainsi comme de chief descent et despand la vie par tout le corps; et ad ce furent ordonnés les roys et les princes du commencement par un commun accort... Selon ce que par l'enseignement de nature tous les membrez en ung vray corps se exposent pour le salut du chief, pareillement estre doit ou *corps mistique* des vrayz subgetz à leur seigneur.[30]

His reason for using the term 'mystique' in this context must, we think, be explained as follows. Just as a natural body forms a visible unit of head and members, veins and sinews, which as equally important components support one another and keep the whole body in being, so Gerson was convinced that humanity, the State and the Church formed invisible units and structures, which he also regar-

---

27 *Pax hominibus* (Gl. 7*, 767, Dupin II, 144C).

28 Cf. *Vivat rex* (Gl. 7*, 1144; Dupin IV, 583): 'La vie civile se maintient en la conionction et unité du Seigneur et du peuple en une loy et juste ordonnance; de hoc Philosophus in Politicis ponit quod in legibus est vita civitatis; et Apostolus comparat corpus misticum ad verum, eadem ratione, Rom. 12 [:4-5] et I^mo ad Cor. 12 [:12-28], et Eph. 4 [:4-16].' See also Chapter VI, epigraph (*'corpus mysticum civile'*).

29 For this see Carl Schäfer, *Die Staatslehre des Johannes Gerson* (dissertation Cologne), Bielefeld 1935; and also, though it does not discuss Gerson in detail, the fundamental work of Ernst H. Kantorowicz, *The King's Two Bodies. A Study in Mediaeval Political Theory*, Princeton N.J. 1970, 207ff.

30 *Vivat rex* (Gl. 7*, 1155; Dupin IV, 597AB). In his sermon *Rex in sempiternum* (Gl. 7* 1030; Dupin IV, 676C), he uses the term 'l'ordre du *corps mystique de la chose publique.*' For more details, see Kantorowicz, *Two Bodies*, 218ff.

ded as bodies. Because these bodies were invisible and hidden, he described them as 'mystical', for 'mystical' means 'hidden' or 'secret'.[31]

We add that Gerson's metaphorical use of the idea of a body in this connection did not prevent him regarding as wholly real and active the organs and forces which, as in a natural body, he knew to be present in the invisible bodies of humanity, State and Church. He was convinced that there was a continuous flow (*influxus*) of immaterial, hidden forces from the mystical bodies into visible reality; and that, provided they were adequately received and applied by the organs intended for the purpose, these forces guaranteed the maintenance of form and order in visible reality.

All this was supported by the idea of a *generalis influentia Dei* which Gerson, like other scholastics, regarded as the force underlying all events, both in creation and its sustaining and in human actions.[32] Here we may pass over the way in which the scholastics distinguished in this force between the *causa prima* and *causa secunda*, God's providential guidance and human free will and responsibility. We merely wish to emphasise that Gerson was deeply convinced that these hidden forces exerted an actual, effective influence on visible reality, regardless of whether or not they formed part of the 'corps mystique des hommes', the 'corps civile et mystique', or the *corpus mysticum ecclesiae.*

Something of this was apparent in the above passage from the sermon *Vivat Rex*, especially where Gerson argued that the King was not a private person but, as he put it, 'represents a public power which was instituted for the benefit of the general welfare, and that therefore life flows downwards from the head ('chief') and is spread throughout the whole body' (of the State). The immaterial term 'life' is obviously used here to mean the concrete influence from above on the ordinances and decisions taken by the various organs and representatives of the 'corps civile et mistique' for the benefit of the social order.

A more eloquent example of his conviction that there was a di-

---

[31] Gerson, *De elucidatione scholastica* (ed. Combes, 222^{20-3}; Gl. 8, 155; Dupin III, 423A): 'et hoc est misticum et absconditum, quod nemo seculi sapientum capit [2 Cor. 2: 12]', with reference to Bonaventure, *Itinerarium* VII [4]: 'Hoc est mysticum et secretissimum, quod nemo novit, nisi qui accipit.'

[32] See Chapter VIII n. 86.

rect causal link between the visible and the invisible world – between the force which he saw as emanating from the mystical bodies and everyday reality – is offered by the sermon *Diligite iustitiam*, which he gave before the *parlement* of Paris, at the opening of its session, probably on 12 November 1405.[33]

The background to this sermon was a violation of University privileges committed by servants of the State. The University had responded to this scandal in its usual way, the only one at its disposal: a strike. Disputations, the granting of degrees, preaching by the University's clergy, all came to a standstill until it had been given satisfaction. After Gerson had informed the members of the highest legal college of this measure, he drew their attention to its consequences, crying:

> on cesse de leçons et de sermons en toute l'Université de Paris et à Paris. Entendez ycy quel meschief c'est; par non recevoir les biens qui viennent des leçons et de sermons, mil et mil pechies se laisseront à faire, mil et mil biens pour les vifz et pour les mors s'en faroient, mil et mil ames se partiront plus tôt du purgatoire...[34]

This neatly demonstrates the way in which he saw a direct connection between a strike of teachers and preachers on the one hand, and an interruption to the flow of salvation from above, on the other. In general one can say that such a direct causal link between the higher and lower spheres, and vice versa as in this case, must always be assumed when he uses the term 'mystical body', regardless of whether or not it referred to the cosmos, the State or the Church.[35]

---

[33] See the present author's *Jean Gerson et l'Assemblée de Vincennes*, 34-53.

[34] *Diligite iustitiam* (Gl. 7*, 613; Dupin IV, 652D-3A). The sermon *Veniat pax* (Gl. 7*, 1111-12; Dupin; IV, 633B-4B) gives another example of influence on the fate of the souls in purgatory by actions 'from below'. Cf. the treatise *Complainte des âmes au purgatoire* (Gl. 7, 363-7).

[35] In this connection one can also think of the numerous passages in which Gerson regards the Schism as God's punishment for the degeneracy of the Church and the sins of the faithful, a punishment that can only be averted by reformation of the Church, by penance and devotional practices. See n. 37.

3. *The Church as a mystical body*

More than once Gerson used the term mystical body (*corpus mysticum*) to indicate the Church.[36] Although he had already done so, if only rarely and always in more general terms, in his earlier years,[37] one has to wait till 1408, i.e. till the Council of Pisa had been announced, before we find the idea of the Church as a mystical body more fully worked out in the many treatises he composed in defence of this assembly. On the other hand it can be observed that his later writings do not contain any further developments or changes in this idea. The best proof of this is that in the sermons he gave at Constance and in *De potestate ecclesiastica*, he only repeated himself on this point by referring explicitly to his Pisan treatises. We may, therefore, conclude that his ideas on this subject had remained the same from 1408 and represented a constant factor in his thought since then. As he himself shows more than once, his newly won insights cannot be separated from ideas that he had found in two works written in 1379 and 1380 by Henry of Langenstein and Conrad of Gelnhausen.

Earlier we have seen that Gerson, like most of his fellow-scholastics, drew a clear distinction between the 'true body of Christ' and the 'mystical body of Christ'.[38] The French scholar Henri de Lubac, who investigated the historical and semantic developments of these terms, showed that in the early middle ages the term *corpus mysticum* was always used to denote the host in the eucharist, while the Church was usually indicated by the term 'body of Christ' (*corpus Christi*). Around the middle of the twelfth century, however, by a curious semantic shift, the eucharistic body ceased to be identified by the usual appellation 'mystical body', and now regularly came

---

36 A somewhat exalted interpretation of Gerson's ideas on the Church as mystical body is given by Mgr. Combes (*La théologie mystique* I, 256-72 (262-6)). For Pierre d'Ailly, see Oakley (*Political Thought*, 55-61, 261-2); for Ockham, Miethke, *Ockham's Weg*, 544ff.; for the canonists, Tierney, *Foundations*, 132-41.

37 See Chapter III n. 88, and, in the same vein, the sermon *Poenitemini* (Gl. 5, 456; Dupin II, 582C): 'Quoniam facta est scissio ita universalis in corpore mystico ex peccatis singularium personarum et eorum perversis moribus quomodo fit in corpore vero dissolutio eius ex vitio morbido partium et corruptis humoribus, consequens est ut medicina poenitentialis primum reparet in membris sanitatem, praesertim cum videatur esse hic digitus Dei cui humanum auxilium quasi penitus deesse sentitur.'

38 See Chapter IX n. 28.

to be referred to as the 'true body' (*corpus verum*). At the same time the traditional term used for the eucharist was transferred to the Church, which now came to be identified by the term *corpus mysticum*.[39]

This terminological change was linked, on the one hand, with the development of the doctrine of the eucharist towards the dogma of transubstantiation (IVth Lateran Council 1215), and, on the other, with the Gregorian reform in the eleventh century followed by the rediscovery of Roman law, both of which brought about an enormous change in the nature of the Church, causing it to develop more and more into a universal-juridical entity.

The outcome of this development was that 'the former liturgical concept of *corpus mysticum* faded away only to be transformed into a relatively colorless sociological, organological, or juristic notion.'[40] The traditional, patristic and Carolingian view, in which the eucharist held pride of place, since it was by participating in this sacrament that the connection with the Church was brought about, gradually changed into a juridical concept, according to which membership of the Church depended totally on the recognition which had to be given to its visible head, the Pope. De Lubac observed that this degeneration made itself felt very strongly in the circle of the curialist theologians around Boniface VIII.[41] Their writings depicted the Church as a *regnum ecclesiasticum*, in which the accent was shifted away from Christ as the head of his own body, to his *vicarius* as the head of the mystical body of the Church.[42] This led some curialists to go so far as to consider the Church as the *corpus mysticum papae*, and even to identify the Pope and the Church—*papa qui potest dici ecclesia*.[43]

---

[39] Henri de Lubac, *Corpus Mysticum. L'Eucharistie et l'Eglise au Moyen Age*,[2] Paris 1949, 89-135; Kantorowicz, *Two Bodies*, 194-218.

[40] Kantorowicz, *Two Bodies*, 202.

[41] De Lubac, *Corpus mysticum*, 130ff.

[42] Kantorowicz, *Two Bodies*, 202ff.

[43] See e.g. *Libellus articulorum* (Gl. 6, 277; Dupin II, 302B): 'Haec assertio Petri de Luna quod Christus et papa sunt unum caput Ecclesiae, est haereticalis nisi reducatur ad aliquem sensum sanum, satis improprium.' Perhaps he meant by 'sensus sanus, satis improprius' what was stated by d'Ailly in his *De eccl. pot.* (Dupin II, 953B): '... dico quod concilium, praesente papa, a quo ipsum concilium vocatum est, est velut corpus mysticum, cuius papa est caput, et alii sunt membra.'

Bearing these developments in mind, we turn now to Gerson, to investigate his ideas on the Church as a mystical body. At least three different elements are to be distinguished, which, apart from the Pauline background and inspiration,[44] can be traced back to 1. pseudo-Dionysius; 2. Aristotle; and 3. the law of nature and the law of corporations.

1. Fundamental to him, as we have repeatedly seen, is the pseudo-Dionysian idea of the Church as a *hierarchia subcelestis*,[45] i.e. as the reflexion on earth of the celestial hierarchy of the angels: the Seraphim, the Cherubim and the Thrones. He refers to pseudo-Dionysius more than once, notably in *De potestate ecclesiastica*, where, in a paragraph about the exercise of the ecclesiastical power, he summarises his ideas as follows:

> ... quoad exercitium actuum hierarchicorum, qui sunt purgare, illuminare et perficere, tres primi ordines [= Seraphim] hierarchizant non hierarchizati ab aliis; tres medii (= Cherubim] hierarchizantur et hierarchizant; tres infimi [= Thrones] hierarchizantur et non angelos hierarchizant.

Adapting this angelic order to the *hierarchia subcelestis* of the Church, he continues:

> Papalis auctoritas suo modo cum suis cardinalibus imitatur triplicitatem primam; alteram vero mediam imitatur patriarchalis, archiepiscopalis, episcopalis et sacerdotalis auctoritas in habentibus subiectos sibi, quod dicitur propter curatos, vel etiam propter solum titulares episcopos carentes plebe. Ultimi sunt instar tertiae hierarchiae qui hierarchizantur in Ecclesia sed non alios auctoritative hierarchizant, quemadmodum sunt populi et simplices religiosi secundum Dionysium.[46]

---

[44] For this, see especially his sermon *Ambulate* (Chapter VII n. 57).

[45] See Congar, 'Aspects ecclésiologiques', 58ff., 114-51 ('Le Pseudo-Denys dans l'ecclésiologie du XIIIe siècle'); *DSp* III 365-75, 'Denys l'Aréopagite. V. Influence du Pseudo-Denys en occident. 4. Gerson' (A. Combes); and Pascoe, *Jean Gerson*, 17-38 ('The Church: Order, Hierarchy, and Reform').

[46] *De pot. eccl.*, cons. 9 (Gl. 6, 227; Dupin II, 239AB). More than once Gerson expressed the same thought by making use of Aristotle's famous tripartition in monarchy, aristocracy, and democracy. See *De pot. eccl.*, cons. 8 (Gl. 6, 225; Dupin II, 237C): '... maneat ecclesiastica politia optimo regimine quale fuit sub Moyse gubernata, quoniam mixta fuit ex triplici politia: regali in Moyse, aristocratica in lxxii senioribus, et timocratica dum de populo et singulis tribubus sub Moyse rectores sumebantur.' Cf. Chapter VII n. 79, and XII § 4. John of Paris.

This summary reaffirms that in the controversy between regulars and seculars Gerson clearly took the side of the latter. Since the regulars did not belong to the authentic members of the ecclesiastical hierarchy, they played a less active role in the mediation of salvation within the mystical body of the Church.

2. The essence of the Church, created by God and therefore perfect – *Dei perfecta sunt opera*[47] – is described in more detail as a potential, a *semen*, which over time had developed and achieved its full realisation. This unmistakeably adds Aristotle to pseudo-Dionysius, in the form of the former's well known theory of potential and act.

> ... sunt enim gradus omnes seminati a Christo in ecclesia primitiva quamquam parvula, in qua nondum erant sic explicati gradus ecclesiasticae hierarchiae ut nunc inspicimus, quemadmodum spica totos numeros suos habet in grano, et nux arbor virtualiter continetur; has vocant philosophi 'inchoationes formarum in materia'.[48]

He went on to describe this *semen* as a spiritual force which was operative in the mystical body of the Church and which would preserve it in its unalterable hierarchical form until the end of time.

> Hoc autem semen quid aliud debet intellegi quam vis insita spiritualis et ars quaedam vivifica per universum corpus ecclesiae, per quam hierarchicus ordo potest usque in finem subsistere.[49]

Elaborating this idea, he goes on to state that it is just as impossible for a mystical body to exist without a head as it is for a natural body.

> ... nemo concesserit quod absque capite valeat permanere corpus aliquod, sive vere sive mysticum. Sed ecclesiae corpus mysticum manere semper usque ad consummationem saeculi necesse est, lege stante. Mt. ultimo [28:20]. Hoc ergo fiet per vivificum influxum capitis in ipsum.[50]

3. Gerson argued from the perfection of its structure that in this dispensation, *lege stante*,[51] the Church and its hierarchy would remain in being for all time; he also argued, on the same grounds, that the

---

47 See Chapter VIII n. 66.

48 *Propositio facta coram Anglicis*, ver. 10 (Gl. 6, 133; Dupin II, 129A). See also Chapter VI n. 48.

49 *De auferibilitate*, cons. 6 (Gl. 3, 397; Dupin II, 212A).

50 *De auferibilitate*, cons. 1 (Gl. 3, 294; Dupin II, 210AC).

51 See Chapter VII n. 13.

Church was not doomed to remain passive and powerless when it faced a crisis over its earthly head, the *caput secundarium*, as it had during the Schism. For then God, who watches over his perfect creation, would come to its aid in the form of Christ, the *caput primarium*, who by sending down the Holy Spirit *supplied* whatever the Church lacked when its Vicar was absent or incapable of his duties.[52]

Gerson's explanation of the above clearly reveals that his conception of the Church as a *corpus mysticum* was also nourished by ideas that were part of current legal thought; in particular that he was inspired by ideas drawn from the law of nature and the law of corporations. From the fact that the Church, as God's creation, was a perfect community (*congregatio perfecta*), he deduced that it had the same right to assemble on its own authority and to defend itself that belonged to every corporation.

> Quaelibet congregatio libera, non subiecta tyrannidi, habet facultatem se ipsam congregandi. Patet in confraternitatibus et aliis multis conventionibus.[53]

Hence, if its unity was threatened, the Church was entitled to take action and free to take the law into its own hands through a general council, to restore its unity.

> In talibus et similibus casibus congregatio ecclesiastica sumit auctoritatem et virtutes seipsam uniendi ex divino semine per universum corpus suum diffuso.[54]

In that case the unity of the *corpus mysticum* formed a sufficient reason to depose a lawful elected Pope.[55]

---

[52] *Nuptiae factae sunt* (Gl. 5, 384; Dupin II, 355A): '... habet ecclesia synodaliter congregata plenitudinem potestatis etiam super papam ordinative, regulative et *suppletive*.' *De pot. eccl.*, cons. 11 (Gl. 6, 235; Dupin II, 245B): '[generale concilium] potest tamen *supplere* dum necessitas urget vel suadet evidens utilitas... Et hoc modo dicitur esse plenitudo potestatis ecclesiasticae in Ecclesia *suppletive*.' Cf. Henry of Langenstein, *Epistola concilii pacis*, cap. XV (Dupin II, 832C): 'Cuius [sc. papae] defectum, vel cum illud non est, vel cum est et non constat quis est,... *supplet* Christus, caput Ecclesiae suae inseparabile et primarium, cuius gratia et meritis Ecclesia, corpus suum mysticum, suscipit incessanter sensum, motum et spiritum vitalem.'

[53] Chapter VI n. 56, and n. 100. See also Oakley, *Political Thought*, 58ff.

[54] *Propositio coram Anglicis*, ver. 12 (Gl. 6, 134; Dupin II, 129D).

[55] *De auferibilitate*, cons. 16 (Gl. 3, 309; Dupin II, 221B): '... multae sunt connexiones membrorum in corpore mystico Ecclesiae, sicut diversae sunt in eodem corpore unitates. Una est enim unitas charitatis, et ita soli habentes charitatem dicuntur membra vera Ecclesiae... Alia est unitas in donis naturae, sicut omnes homines connectuntur in intel-

To the objection that a council could only assemble lawfully if it was convoked by the supreme hierarch, Gerson countered that the situation of the Schism made it impossible to fulfil this condition, and that in a situation for which positive law made no provision, the Church had to resort to the rules of natural and divine law. *Epikie* and *aequitas* both indicated that in such a situation positive law might be set aside, and consequently that a council could lawfully be called, without being convoked by the supreme hierarch.[56]

This opinion was reinforced by arguments from the law of corporations. As we have seen, Gerson regarded the mystical body of the Church as a collective, a *totum*, which, with Christ as its head, comprised all degrees of the hierarchy. Building on the idea that this *totum* did not cease to exist when the papal see was vacant, but remained in being thanks to the never-failing *influxus* which emanated down to it from Christ, its *caput primarium*, he came at length to the conviction that the distress to which the Church had been reduced by the Schism in fact meant that it faced a vacancy. And this put the Schism in a very different light.

From an intractable case, scarcely or not at all foreseen by canon law, it was reduced to a much simpler affair of more manageable proportions, a case of vacancy. Unlike schism such cases occurred almost daily in the numerous medieval corporations, both church and lay, and there was a detailed body of case law on them. These laws were in Gerson's mind when he concluded his apologia for the council, both for the way in which it had assembled and for its powers, with the words: *sicut de capitulo et decano vel de universitate et rectore suo modo diceretur.*[57] That is an important statement, because it allows us to see that Gerson was also using an argument drawn from the law of corporations.

---

lectu et ratione... Alia est unitas in simili participatione sacramentorum... *Et haec unio videtur absolute sufficere ad hoc quod aliquis rite prius in papam electus maneat caput Ecclesiae quousque fuerit per sententiam definitivam depositus.*'

[56] The fact that Conrad of Gelnhausen and Henry of Langenstein also operated with the current concept of epikie is not, in our opinion, proof that Gerson borrowed it from them. See Chapter VIII n. 111. The same applies to his use of the distinction between *caput primarium* and *caput secundarium*, which is found in Conrad of Gelnhausen. Gerson first used this distinction, which was no less current, in 1402; but there is nothing to show that he was already under Conrad's influence at that time. See Chapter VI n. 43.

[57] *De pot. eccl.*, cons. 11 (Gl. 6, 233, Dupin II, 244A).

> One of the central problems of medieval jurists was the question, vital during a vacancy, of where the legal powers of a corporation were located: in the corporation as a whole, or only in its head. Innocent IV (d. 1254) upheld, at least as far as the relationship of a university and its rector was concerned, the latter, typically authoritarian standpoint: 'Et est notandum quod rectores assumpti ab universitatibus habent iurisdictionem et non ipsae universitates. Aliqui tamen dicunt quod universitates deficientibus rectoribus, possunt exercitare iurisdictionem, quod non credo.'[58] Hostiensis (d. 1271), a younger contemporary of Innocent IV, took another view, and claimed that the rights of a corporation were located in its members. This became the general opinion which, as we have seen, was shared by Gerson.

It has been pointed out that the development of the canonist theory of corporations during the thirteenth century displayed a gradual extension and systematisation of the rights of members of a corporation relative to their head.[59] If this opened the door for the members to exercise the powers of the head during a vacancy, it did not result in the head coming to be regarded as superfluous. Vacancy remained an exceptional case, in the general opinion. One could get by, but that was all. A head was indispensable for the actual exercise of authority.

Gerson thought of the Council of Constance in a similar spirit. For him, it was undoubtedly an exceptional council, but not, therefore, illegitimate, for just like other corporations the Church possessed the power to act in default of its head and to take measures necessary for its welfare and continued existence.

When we survey Gerson's views on the Church as a mystical body, we conclude that there were two essential components: a hierarchical, and a collective-corporative component. The hierarchical component went back in the first instance to pseudo-Dionysius and was in harmony with the views customarily defended by the secular clergy and the Paris *magistri* in their long and ever-recurring struggle against the regulars. The other component, the collective-corporative, derived largely from Aristotelian principles, particularly the idea that the *totum* preceded the *pars* and prevailed over it. At the same time this component was supported and articulated by considerations drawn from the law of nature and of corporations.

---

58 Cited by Tierney, *Foundations*, 107.
59 Tierney, *Foundations*, 106, 130.

Although Gerson had long had the treaties of Conrad of Gelnhausen and Henry of Langenstein in his hands,[60] there is nothing to show that he was deeply influenced by them before 1408. That was to change when the Council of Pisa was announced and he felt called to write in its defence. Comparison of the texts shows that he owed a great deal to the two German writers; there are fairly numerous parallel pronouncements and reasonings – in particular on the seminal nature of the hierarchy, the *influxus* that radiated from Christ to the mystical body of the Church and its 'supplementing' consequences[61] – to prove this indebtedness. We add at once, however, that this influence did not cause him to lose his theological independence, for – as will appear – on a very central point of their view of the Church, Gerson was eager to distance himself from them.

4. *General Council and infallibility*

We need say only a few words on Gerson's opinions concerning the general council, for they are entirely in accordance with the fundamental hierarchical premise of his ecclesiology. He saw the council as the reflection and the representation of the Church in the absolute sense, of the Church as hierarchy. The council shared in the invariability which belonged to the hierarchy, i.e. it included in itself all the parts from which the immutable hierarchy had been built up. It was, so to speak, the microcosm of the hierarchical macrocosm. Because the latter was of divine origin, the decisions of the former, the council, were indefectible.[62]

Brian Tierney developed a sort of typology based on three different kinds of representation that one encounters in medieval thought and practice: personification, delegation, and mimesis. He explains:

---

[60] BN lat. 14643 contains a dossier of texts and documents on the Schism, collected and sometimes annotated by Gerson. Mgr. Glorieux had the happy idea of printing a list of them in his edition of Gerson's works (Gl. 10, 436-42, 492-3). The list shows that Gerson had a copy of Conrad's *Epistola concordiae* and of Henry's *Epistola concilii pacis* (439, 440). He also owned Conrad's treatise *Super conclusione et probatione vie cessionis* (493), which has already been published by DuBoulay (*Historia* IV, 785-97). We became aware of the existence of this highly interesting dossier too late to be able to make thorough use of it.

[61] See above n. 52.

[62] See Chapter IX n. 70, and Chapter IV n. 57.

> We have representation by personification when a community is conceived of as symbolized by its head; delegation is when a community confers its authority on a representative by an act of election or consent; by mimesis when an assembly can represent a community as a kind of microcosmos of it, by including in its composition members of all classes and groups that make up the large-scale community. These kinds of representation can occur in any human community. In addition, for the medieval Church in particular, an adequate attendance of bishops seemed especially important, since they were held to bear the authority of Christ originally conferred on the apostles.[63].

It is clear from this that Gerson is to be ranked among the convinced adherents of the concept of representation by *mimesis*. He took it as an axiom, even with the force of a religious conviction, that a general council as a microcosm reflected and represented the Church hierarchy as the macrocosm. In that conviction he distinguished himself from most of his contemporary theologians, for when they concerned themselves with ecclesiology, they never failed to deal, often in great detail, with questions of conciliar representation, making lavish use of theories and considerations of a canonist nature and origin. We do not wish to assert that these were entirely lacking in Gerson, but that in comparison with his contemporaries, he made remarkably sparing use of them.

If we search for an explanation of this, we may think of his generally critical attitude to canon law and its practitioners, and assume that that was the reason why he distanced himself from the results of their thinking on questions of representation. It may have played some part, but we are more inclined to look in quite a different direction. We believe that his view of the mimetic character of hierarchy and council, and the axiomatic way in which he always assumed their indefectibility and inerrancy, must be connected above all with Bonaventure, whom he admired immensely and with whose all-embracing mystical-hierarchical world-concept he was thoroughly familiar.[64]

It therefore appears acceptable that it must have been above all

---

[63] Brian Tierney, 'The idea of representation in the medieval councils of the West', *Concilium* 19 (1983), no. 8/9, 25-30. We cite from the summary given in his 'Canon law and church institutions', in: *Proceedings of the seventh international congress of medieval canon law* (Cambridge, 23-27 July 1984), *Monumenta Iuris Canonici*, series C: subsidia vol. 8, Città del Vaticano 1988, 49-69 (55-6).

[64] See Chapter XII § 5.

the *doctor seraphicus* who reinforced his conviction that the ecclesiastical hierarchy on earth would never disappear altogether or, to put it more strongly, that it *could* never disappear *lege stante*. And this was not simply because Bonaventure also maintained that the earthly hierarchy reflected and represented the hierarchy in heaven but above all that it owed its existence directly and continuously to it.[65] In Bonaventure he could find that the earthly hierarchy reflected its heavenly example, thanks to a causal power which the latter radiated to it. For Bonaventure thought of the heavenly hierarchy not only as the immobile 'exemplum' of the hierarchy on earth, but as its 'exemplar',[66] that is as its active, effective example which was continuously transferring and giving form and life to the earthly hierarchy as its formative cause. In this respect too, God would not let the works of his hands perish. The divine forces from above, provided they were adequately received and applied, were in other words present in and continued through the organs of the earthly hierarchy and that was what gave them their indestructible character. We assume that it was on the grounds of the same conviction that Gerson firmly believed in the infallibility of the decisions of a hierarchically represented council.

Be this as it may, it is certain that in this view he was clearly distancing himself from the ideas expressed by other theologians who, the more Ockhamist they were in their thinking, the less they were convinced of the inerrancy of conciliar decisions. But the differences between Gerson's conciliar theory and that of Marsilius of Padua are even more striking. Marsilius transposed the idea of the sovereignty of the people to the Church, and developed an ecclesiology with a democratic appeal, in which the general council was given the function of a representative body. In this conception, the hierarchy possessed no more than a derived authority. It derived it

---

[65] See in particular the sermon *Ambulate* (Gl. 5, 41-2; Dupin II, 203B-4A), which clearly seems to point to Bonaventure.

[66] Cf. J.-M. Bissen, *L'exemplarisme divin selon Saint Bonaventure*, Paris 1929, (3-4), who refers to Bonaventure, *Comm. in l.s.* I, d. 31, p. II a. 1 q. 1 concl.: 'Exemplar dicitur ad cuius imitationem fit aliquid'. And on the quality of an exemplar (I, d. 6 a. unic. q. 3 concl.): 'Per modum exemplaritatis est procedere dupliciter. Uno modo sicut in exemplatum proprie; et sic creatura procedit a Deo tamquam exemplatum ab exemplari, et sic *exemplar importat causalitatem formalem respectu exemplati*'; ... exemplar secundum proprietatem vocabuli dicit expressionem per modum activi.' See also Altensteig, *Lexicon*, 310 s.v. 'exemplar'.

from the sovereign Christian people (*congregatio fidelium*), which exercised its legislative authority through the general council.

No trace of such a concept is to be found in Gerson. Far from letting the power of the council flow from the base upwards, he interpreted it in the light of his hierarchical views. The representatives of the entire hierarchy were entitled to appear at a council. True, ordinary believers might also attend, by which, we think, he had particularly kings and princes in mind, and in general higher representatives of the temporal sphere. Besides these authorities, 'consultants' could also be invited, scholars whose specialised knowledge, notably in law, philosophy and ethics, might be useful when the council was called upon to formulate complicated questions of that nature. All these had a *vox consultativa*.[67] The *vox declarativa*, however, was reserved to the members of the hierarchy only. Their representation at a general council guaranteed the inerrancy of its decisions.

That we must think chiefly of representation by the *praelati maiores* is confirmed in several passages. This view is most clearly stated in the theses contained in the *De auctoritate concilii* of 1408, where Gerson argued that it was unthinkable that the order of bishops should ever disappear or fall into heresy. Stronger still: he regarded it as an article of faith that the episcopate as a whole could never err or fall into schism.

> Collegium omnium episcoporum christianorum non posse errare in fide et schismate maculari, est certa fide credendum.[68]

Although, of course, he did not deny that the ordinary faithful formed part of the mystical body of the Church, he never allotted them any but a passive role in it. As laymen they belonged to the *ecclesia audiens*; they were *perficiendi*, and as such dependent for grace on the mediation of the representatives of the hierarchy–according to the rule of pseudo-Dionysius: '*ut infima reducantur ad suprema per media.*' But as members of the Church they participated in the *influxus* of the Spirit which inspired this mystical body at all times.

---

[67] See Chapter IX n. 133.

[68] See Chapter VI notes 14–16, and *Propositio facta coram Anglicis*, cons. 4 (6) (Gl. 6, 132; Dupin II, 128C): 'congregatio ecclesiastica ad unum caput Christum lege stante non remanebit in sola muliere, immo nec in solis laicis sed *erunt usque ad consummationem saeculi episcopi et sacerdotes aliqui fideles*.'

That same Spirit also ensured that ordinary believers were brought to accept the infallible decisions of the councils.

> Sicut ecclesia universalis congregata habet singulare privilegium in tradendo fidelibus credenda explicita aut necessaria pro ecclesiae regimine, et hoc indicative vel obligative, ita multitudo fidelium singulariter *trahitur* a Spiritu Sancto ad assentiendum determinative aut auctoritative per ecclesiam congregatam.[69]

Gerson's argument for a relatively wide measure of representation at the council was by no means a novelty. Many years ago, Hauck already showed that the idea of the representation of the universal Church in a general council, in the sense in which the conciliarists understood it, was of an earlier date and went back in particular to Innocent III. 'The conception of a universal council which is at the basis of the so-called conciliar theory of the fifteenth century, does not stem from Conrad of Gelnhausen or Ockham, but its roots reach back to the greatest Pope of the middle ages.'[70]

Gerson distinguished himself from both Conrad and Ockham by limiting universal representation strictly to the members of the hierarchy and making no use of the idea of the *ecclesia universalis* which underlay Ockham's conception of a general council and that of all those who followed him in this. Even when Gerson appealed to arguments drawn from the law of corporations, to defend the exceptional summoning of the Council of Constance, he did not imagine the corporation of the Church other than as being made up of the members of the hierarchy. Once again, this time as a defender of a conciliar solution of the Schism, Gerson showed himself a loyal disciple of pseudo-Dionysius Areopagita.

---

[69] *De auctoritate concilii*, art. 5 concl. 10 (Gl. 6, 116). He uses the same characteristic verb 'trahere' in his sermon *Ambulate* (Gl. 5, 42; Dupin II, 204A): 'Deus magnus et terribilis *trahit* et allicit omnes in commune christianos ad unius veri capitis unitatem, tamquam causa formans et exemplans.'

[70] A. Hauck, 'Die Rezeption und Umbildung der allgemeinen Synode im Mittelalter,' *HV* X (1907), 465-82 (470).

CHAPTER ELEVEN

CHURCH, SCRIPTURES, AND TRADITION

> *Sensus litteralis sacrae Scripturae fuit primo per Christum et apostolos revelatus et miraculis elucidatus; deinde fuit per sanguinem martyrum confirmatus, postmodum sacri doctores per rationes suas diligentes contra haereticos diffusius elicuerunt praedictum sensum litteralem et conclusiones ex illo clarius vel probabilius consequentes; postea successit determinatio sacrorum conciliorum, ut quod erat erat doctrinaliter discussum per doctores fieret per Ecclesiam sententialiter definitum.*
>
> Gerson, *De sensu litterali* (Gl. 3, 335; Dupin I, 3C)

In the preceding chapters we have shown that Gerson's ecclesiology may be seen partly as moderately juridical – so far as it is based on a protest against the extreme juridical views of the Church held by the canonists –, and partly as dispersed-hierarchical – so far as it regards not only the head but also the members as of importance. Both characteristics explain why Gerson's ecclesiology could develop into a conciliar direction. His ecclesiology, however, was not confined to the problem of the proper structure of the Church; it also raised the question of the Church in the dogmatic sense. In other words: the complex of Church, Scriptures and tradition also forms an aspect of his ecclesiology. What does this mean?

Gerson accused the canonists of applying the concept of *ius divinum* in an uncritical, and actually in a positivistic way, by intolerably multiplying the number of absolute legislative enactments. His criticism assumed that there was within the Church a more or less clearly definable body of absolute truth and absolute law. We have seen how he attempted to define the limits of this body of truth by drawing up a catalogue of the faith, in which he arranged the Catholic truths in an hierarchical order. In this catalogue he spoke of 'laws revealed directly by Christ or which could be derived logically from this revelation; or which have reached us through the tradition of the apostles and others, and which now possess an authority equal to that of the holy Scripture.' This formula immediately raises questions of the sources of the revelation, Scripture and tradition, and their relationship to one another. But this in turn leads to the question, for example, of how these sources of revelation are to be recognised and authorised; and this automatically involves the doctrinal and magisterial authority of the Church.

The title of this chapter is to some extent anachronistic, for in Gerson's time doctrinal development had not yet advanced so far that a clear distinction was made between the Church, the Scriptures and tradition as different entities. This does not mean that the distinction was unknown, but that it was much more blurred than it later became. The complex of Church, Scriptures and tradition was left largely undisturbed during the middle ages and had not yet become an independent subject for theological reflection. The boundaries between the three were still fluid, while the terminology used was far from exact. This would not change until the sixteenth century, when the reformers dared to demand the Church's credentials. Even then it is clear from the answer which the Council of Trent drew up, with particular reference to the relationship of the Church and tradition, that the time was still not ripe for an unambiguous statement on the relationship between the sources of revelation.[1] *A fortiori*, one can scarcely expect it to have been clearly defined a century and half earlier.

We no longer possess Gerson's commentary on the sentences, in which he would surely have made some pronouncement on the nature, essence and limits of theology and thus on the question which concerns us here. In its absence we shall base our exposition on 1. the lecture *De duplici logica* of 1401,[2] and 2. a pair of antiheretical works of 1414 and 1417 entitled *De sensu litterali sacrae scripturae*[3] (also given as a lecture) and *De necessaria communione laicorum sub utraque specie*.[4] We shall begin with the first work, which will give us a general insight into his attitude to the Scriptures. We shall then discuss the relationship of Church, Scripture and tradition, with particular reference to the antiheretical works and also to the socal-

[1] J.N. Bakhuizen van den Brink, 'Traditio in de reformatie en het katholicisme in de zestiende eeuw,' *MKNAW* afd. letterkunde, NR 15, 2, Amsterdam 1952, 26ff; Y. M.-J. Congar, *La Tradition et les Traditions. Essai historique*, Paris [1960], 207-32.

[2] Gl. 3, 57-63; Dupin IV, 213-18.

[3] Gl. 3, 333-40; Dupin I, 1-7.

[4] Gl. 10, 55-68; Dupin I, 457-67.

led *Declaratio compendiosa quae veritates sint de necessitate salutis credendae* of 1416.[5]

1. *The general interpretation of the Scriptures*

In *De duplici logica*, a lecture which must be studied in conjunction with *Contra curiositatem studentium*,[6] Gerson again shows himself to be a cautious and moderate theologian, who does his utmost to give their appropriate encyclopaedic role to the various sciences that make up theology, and to reconcile them with one another. He warns against a one-sided emphasis on one aspect of theology and against the hegemonic ambitions of some practitioners of logic and metaphysics. Such a one-sided approach soon leads to transgression of the limits and causes catastrophic confusion in theology.[7] In his eyes this was *hubris*, and wherever possible he attempts to recall the representatives of these sciences from their haughty isolation and to remind them of their place in the whole. Just as he accused the canonists of thinking of themselves as autonomous, so he opposes the opinion of some who believe that in the interpretation of the Scriptures the highest place is to be allotted to formal logic, and that only logical questions are actually theological questions. The analogy goes further, for just as his criticism of the canonists did not lead him to reject canon law as such, so he does not exclude formal logic from theology altogether. He only marks out the frontiers of the two sciences, but does not surrender them.[8]

He makes it vividly clear to his students that the interpretation of the Scriptures may not be determined by formal logic, but must be approached by another path. 'When Mark says that the whole land of Israel and all the inhabitants of Jerusalem went out to hear John the Baptist (Mark 1: 5), then a logician will take offence at this statement, for it cannot be believed that even the children, the idiots and the babes in arms – that is literally *all* – really went out to see John.' The logician will be inclined to accuse the evangelist of an

---

5 Gl. 6, 181-9; Dupin I, 22-8.

6 Gl. 3, 224-49; Dupin I, 86-106.

7 *De duplici logica* (Gl. 3, 59; Dupin IV, 214D-15A).

8 *De duplici logica* (Gl. 3, 59; Dupin IV 215A): 'Neque tamen nego quin vicissim logica una alterius opem quandoque requirat et quin pari quodam sensu ad veritatis unius inquisitionem plerumque occurrant.'

untruth, because of his absolute use of language. But this is not an isolated example; there are innumerable passages which defy logic and which therefore could compel the conclusion that the Scriptures do not possess any absolute authority. This impossible consequence proves that the Scriptures are not to be interpreted in accordance with formal logic, but by another method. Such a method was provided by rhetoric, which is by its nature of more use in the practical sciences.

> (Rhetorica) principaliter ancillatur, servit et adminiculum praestat scientiis moralibus, politicis et civilibus.[9]

Unlike formal logic, rhetoric is directed towards the *intellectus practicus*, the affects and action. As the science of speech, it is at the service of morality and tries to influence and persuade its audience by using style and figures of speech.[10] Rhetoric may also explain the typical expressions of the Scriptures. It makes it clear that Mark was not aiming at precise exactitude when he said that *all* the inhabitants of Jerusalem went out to see John the Baptist, but was simply trying to indicate the greatness of the event.[11] One may therefore rightly say:

> quod theologia suam habet logicam et modum loquendi proprium.[12]

2. *Church, Scriptures, and Tradition in the anti-heretical writings*

Both the works with which we deal here date from Gerson's later life, the period of the Council of Constance. Both are polemical by nature, their chief target being the Hussite heresy. In the *De sensu literali* he discusses the question of what is to be understood by the literal sense of the Scriptures; in the second work, *Contra haeresim de communione sub utraque specie*, he speaks first in general terms of the rules that must be obeyed in the exegesis and interpretation of the Scriptures before turning to the actual theme, the administration of the chalice to the laity. Only the first part of this treatise will concern us here.

It is worth remarking that Gerson, in these works, is attacking

---

9 *De duplici logica* (Gl. 3, 58; Dupin IV, 214A).
10 *De duplici logica* (Gl. 3 58-9; Dupin IV, 214BC).
11 *De duplici logica* (Gl. 3, 60; Dupin IV, 215C).
12 *De duplici logica* (Gl. 3, 59; Dupin IV, 215B).

not only the Hussite heresy but also such completely different movements as the Beghards, the Turlepins and the Poor Men of Lyons.[13] Sometimes he depicts the heretics with the characteristics of Wyclif and Hus, sometimes those of the pure spiritualists. We may conclude that it was self-evident to him, just as it was to the later opponents of Luther, that anyone who came into conflict with the Church, for whatever motive, was *eo facto* to be included indiscriminately among the adherents of the spiritualist error. Seen from this standpoint, birds of a very different feather may indeed be lumped together. Huss and the spiritualists had in common their protest against the Church as they found it. Wyclif and Marsilius of Padua–whom Gerson also names in the same breath[14]–belong to one and the same revolutionary group. It is obvious that this dogmatic view is open to historical objections. We shall pass over this, however, and merely stress that for Gerson the answer to the question, how far a particular tendency was heretical, was determined by its attitude to the Church.

> Sacra scriptura est fidei regula contra quam bene intellectam non est admittanda auctoritas, ratio hominis cuiuscunque; nec aliqua consuetudo, nec constitutio, nec observatio valet si contra sacram scripturam militare convincatur. Haec regula fundamentum est commune nobis et haereticis quos impugnare conamur.[15]

The argument which Gerson states here leads him to conclude that the Scriptures are to be regarded as a single entity, a unity which, by virtue of the authorship of the Holy Spirit, is infallible in all its parts. He agrees with Augustine's pronouncement that if a single sentence of the Scriptures were to be considered false, the authority of the Scriptures as a whole would be shaken.[16] He expresses himself rather unusually, employing a term borrowed from logic, but his meaning is clear:

> Sacra scriptura debet considerari quasi sit una propositio copulativa, connectens singulas partes, et unam confirmans per alteram, elucidans et exponens.[17]

---

[13] *De necessaria communione*, 8 (Gl. 10, 58; Dupin I, 459B).

[14] *Pax hominibus* (Gl. 7*, 770; Dupin II, 147A).

[15] *De necessaria communione*, 1 (Gl. 10, 55; Dupin I, 457BC).

[16] Augustine, *ep.* 67 c.3, included in *Decr. Grat.* D. 9 c. 7; cf. *Declaratio compendiosa* (Gl. 6, 185; Dupin I, 24D).

[17] *De necessaria communione*, 1 (Gl. 10, 55; Dupin I, 457C). For the term 'propositio copulativa', see Chapter VIII n. 102.

Thus the Scriptures must be regarded as a whole, as a single chain of argument, the weaker links connected to the stronger, that is the more obscure passages must be interpreted and elucidated by reference to the clearer ones.

Gerson develops this classic hermeneutic rule further, explaining that a bible text may not be isolated and considered *per se et nude*, but must always be compared with other texts and harmonised with them.[18] Whoever omits to do this, and for example concerns himself exclusively with such a text as 'Whoever believes and is baptised, he shall be saved' (Mark 16: 16) cannot but fall into heresy; in this case the heresy that faith alone is sufficient for salvation. If one fails to compare the biblical texts with one another and thus to reveal their actual intention, one lays the Scriptures open to confusion, and they appear to contain more contradiction than truth.[19]

After pointing out that not everyone is called to explain the Bible, and that the interpreters of Scripture must be intelligent, well-versed in their subject, moderate and free from passion, Gerson asks what assistance is available to them.

> Scriptura sacra in sui primaria expositione habuit homines eruditos, non solum humana ratiocinatione vel studio, sed divina revelatione et inspiratione Spiritus sancti.[20]

Among the earliest interpreters who enjoyed such gifts were the apostles and also the doctors of the Church at Antioch (Acts 8: 4ff. & 13: 1). Paul spoke of the different gifts of grace bestowed by the Spirit, among them that of *interpretatio sermonum* (1 Cor. 12: 4-11). The post-apostolic Church too had its interpreters of the Scriptures, some of them to be preferred to others. One should always follow the doctor who is most competent and who gives the clearest evidences of the qualities mentioned above. In other words, Gerson is saying that the Church has never lacked qualified exegetes, and that the modern interpreter can draw on its tradition.

He goes a step further and argues that the Scriptures are not to be regarded as so unassailable – *nude et in solidum* – that everything else must be rejected as *traditiones hominum*. To penetrate to the true meaning of the Scriptures it is also permissible to make use of hu-

---

18 *De necessaria communione*, 2 (Gl. 10, 56; Dupin I, 457CD).
19 *De necessaria communione*, 2 & 3 (Gl. 10, 56; Dupin I, 458A).
20 *De necessaria communione*, 5 (Gl. 10, 56; Dupin I, 458BC).

man and canon law, of decrees and the glosses of the Fathers.[21] The heretics do this too, indeed they choose their authorities and buttress their assertions with the support of theologians and canonists. Only they are not usually authorities of the first rank, nor is their number very impressive. But that does not affect the principle: the heretics too adduce authorities. They may therefore be accused of arbitrariness and illogicality, for on the one hand they seem to value the support of the authorities they can cite, while on the other they do not want to know about those witnesses who oppose their views. Through this arbitrariness they entangle themselves in contradiction and may be rightly accused of an even more excessive literalism than the Jews.[22]

It may be positively stated that the Scriptures are not to be interpreted by reference to themselves alone, but that there is a place for the commentators as well.

> Scriptura sacra recipit interpretationem et expositionem nedum in suis verbis originalibus, sed etiam in suis expositionibus.[23]

The heretics err in omitting to compare the exegetical remarks of the commentators, just as they fail to compare and where necessary to harmonise the scriptural texts themselves.

Without actually using the word, Gerson's argument was a plea for the Scriptures to be interpreted by reference to tradition. But the targets of his polemic by no means rejected tradition en bloc. On the contrary, the heretics too felt the need to cite their authorities and consequently they too were guided by tradition in the interpretation of the Scriptures. The great difference was that the heretics appealed to a tradition which differed in quantity and quality. That fact raised the question: which tradition was to be taken as the norm?

The answer is given by reference to the Church. According to Gerson, not only the determination of the canon but also the authentic interpretation of the Scriptures belonged in the final analy-

---

[21] *De necessaria communione*, (Gl. 10, 57; Dupin I, 458C): 'Scriptura sacra non ita recipienda est nude et in solidum, contemptis aliis traditionibus hominum, quin debeat ad intelligentiam veram ipsius habendam, iuribus humanis et canonibus et decretis et glossis sanctorum doctorum frequenter humiliter uti.'

[22] *De necessaria communione*, 8 (Gl. 10, 57-8; Dupin I, 459B). The reference to Rabbi Salomo and Rabbi Moyses must have been borrowed from Nicholas of Lyra, *Postilla super Bibliam*, prol. II (Paul of Burgos).

[23] *De necessaria communione*, 7 (Gl. 10, 57; Dupin I, 459A).

sis to the universal Church. This is especially true of the primitive Church because at Pentecost it had received both the Scriptures and the revelation of their true meaning directly from Christ himself, through the Holy Spirit.

> Scriptura sacra in sui receptione et expositione authentica finaliter resolvitur in auctoritatem, receptionem et approbationem universalis ecclesiae, praesertim primitivae, quae recepit eam et eius intellectum immediate a Christo, revelante Spiritu sancto in die Pentecostes, et alias pluries.[24]

The Scriptures and their interpretation were thus entrusted to the Church; it determines their extent and their content. It is only on the word of the Church that we know that Matthew and not Nicodemus was the author of the true gospel, as Augustine said: '*Ego vero evangelio non crederem, nisi me catholicae ecclesiae moveret auctoritas.*'[25] This emphasis on the authority of the Church could give the impression that Gerson regarded it as autonomous. But in his opinion this was far from the case. The Church did not derive its authority from within itself, but had been endowed with it by the Holy Spirit; the authority of the Church was founded on the infallibility of the Spirit. For Gerson this unity and identity of Church and Spirit was such a fundamental principle of the faith that he did not feel obliged to provide any further evidence of it, and explicitly said that any discussion with those who denied it was completely futile.

> Haec enim est infallibilis regula a Spiritu sancto directa, qui in his quae fidei sunt, nec fallere potest nec falli. Probationes omitto. Et quia hoc est primum principium in fide tenendum, quo non credito non superest arguere contra sic negantem, sicut nec contra negantem prima principia in moralibus et speculabilibus arguendum esse tradit Aristoteles.[26]

If we review his argument, Gerson started by saying that he could agree on some common ground with the heretics, but ended by being so far removed from them that he no longer even wished to enter into argument with them. At first, when it was a question of interpreting the Scriptures by reference to the scriptural texts themselves, there was agreement. After that their paths diverged. The

---

[24] *De necessaria communione*, 9 (Gl. 10, 58; Dupin I, 459C). For the meaning of 'authenticus' see M.-D. Chenu, *Introduction à l'étude de Saint Thomas d'Aquin*, 2nd ed., Montreal/Paris 1954, 109ff., and *DThC* I 2, 2584-98 s.v. 'authenticité' (E. Mangenot).

[25] Augustine, *Contra ep. Manichaei* 5, 6 (*ML* 42, 76).

[26] *De necessaria communione*, 9 (Gl. 10, 58; Dupin I, 459C).

first divergence came on the point of tradition: the heretics adhered to a tradition which was both qualitatively and quantitatively inferior to that of the Church. Gerson could see in this only arbitrariness and subjectivism. He accused the heretics of being slaves to the letter because they would not accept the fact that the Scriptures had been entrusted to the Church by the Holy Spirit. The Church, with the aid of the Spirit, had established the canon and it was the Church, under the same exalted guidance, which had the right to pass a final judgement on the meaning of the Scriptures. Loyalty to the Scriptures therefore meant for Gerson above all loyalty to the Church.

In this conception there is a very close relationship between the Spirit and the Church, on the one hand, and the Church and the Scriptures, on the other. Reduced to its essentials, this is based on the idea that the Spirit is above the Church, and the Church above the Scriptures. There is no Scripture or interpretation without the Church; and the Church has no authority without the Spirit. This order of precedence: Spirit – Church – Scriptures, poses the question of how far the Church, which in logical terms is closer to the Spirit than the Scriptures are, can be bound by the Scriptures. In other words, how far does the Church, by virtue of its more intimate relationship with the Spirit, 'know' more than the Scriptures? Did Gerson regard the Church as a second source of revelation?

To answer this question, we turn to the tract *De sensu litterali sacrae scripturae.*[27] The point of departure of this work is that the heretics not only call themselves 'Catholic', but always claim to found their beliefs on a literal interpretation of the Scriptures, which, completely rejecting the socalled apocryphal constitutions, decrees and decretals, are the only foundation for the faith and theology which they allow to be valid.[28] This opinion gave Gerson the occasion to ask what must be understood by the literal sense of the Scriptures.

[27] Gl. 3, 333-40; Dupin I, 1-7. A rather critical judgement on Gerson's exegetical method is given by H. de Lubac, *Exégèse médiévale. Les quatres sens de l'écriture*, sec. partie II, 491-4: 'Exégèse, construction dogmatique et organisation de l'expérience intérieure sont bien pour lui trois disciplines, qui sans doute communiquent entre elles, mais sans se compénétrer, ou à peine... Lorsqu'il commente l'Ecriture au cours de ses prédications, Gerson ne tire la plupart du temps de la lettre qu'un symbolisme moral assez pauvre, par un procédé pédagogique souvent très artificielle... Il recourt constamment à l'allégorie: mais il s'agit de l'allégorie littéraire ou rhétorique, sans aucun rapport avec celle du quadruple sens.' Cf. however Combes, *La théologie mystique* II, 262 n. 128 (263).

[28] *De sensu litterali* (Gl. 3, 334; Dupin I, 2A).

In marshalling his arguments he makes use of Augustine's *De doctrina christiana*, the *Postillae super bibliam* of Nicholas of Lyra and, finally, of the *quaestiones* from the prologue of a commentary on the sentences by Henry Totting of Oyta (d. 1397),[29] a theologian who had been a professor at Paris from 1377 till 1381, and later taught at Prague.[30] Gerson borrowed a great deal from Henry, – who in his turn was especially indebted to Thomas. A critical edition of the *quaestio* concerned has been produced by the German scholar Albert Lang.[31]

In his *Summa*, Thomas, who adopted the hermeneutical views of his time but used Aristotelian philosophy to classify them more exactly,[32] asks: '*Utrum sacra scriptura sub una litera habet plures sensus?*'[33] He answers that it does; the Scriptures have a fourfold meaning: literal, allegorical, moral and anagogical. The last three are grouped together by Thomas under the heading of *sensus spiritualis*, so that we have a literal and a spiritual sense of Scripture. The difference between them is, briefly, that we may speak of the literal sense whenever the words stand for certain realities, while we speak of the spiritual sense whenever these realities represent other realities.[34] According to Thomas, we may rule out the risk that the distinction between literal and spiritual senses will cause the Scriptures to be

---

29 *De sensu litterali* (Gl. 3, 334-5; Dupin I, 3A). See also *Responsio ad quaestionem*, inc. *Ego, Joannes de Gersono* (Gl. 10, 241; Dupin V, 928A): '... hanc materiam de sensu literali sacrae scripturae declaravit pulchre Magister H. de Heuta in suo Prologo super Sententias. Videatur illic, si habeatur. Ponit enim tria ad cognoscendum sensum literalem. Unum est circumstantia litterae praecedentis et sequentis. Alium, consideratio modorum loquendi per figuras et tropos et colores rhetoricos. Tertium est usus loquendi sanctorum doctorum et expositorum scripturae, sicut docet Augustinus *De doctrina christiana* per totum; ubi ponit inter cetera septem regulas Tichonii quasi totidem claves ad intelligendum sacram Scripturam. Unde patet quod perniciosissimum est dicere sensum litteralem sacrae Scripturae quoquo modo falsum esse, quia est infirmare totam sacram Scripturam et invalidam reddere ad aliquid concludendum et irrisione audientium exponere.'

30 Cf. *LThK* 5, 193 s.v. 'Heinrich Totting v. Oyta' (A. Lang).

31 Henrici Totting de Oyta *Quaestio de sacra scriptura*, ed. Albertus Lang, Monasterii 1932. This *quaestio* contains more than a discussion of the nature and extent of the *sensus litteralis*.

32 Beryl Smalley, *The Study of the Bible in the Middle Ages*, Oxford 1952, 292ff.

33 *S.th.* Ia q.1 a.10. See also *Quodlib.* VII q. 6 a. 14 & 15 (ed. Mandonnet, 273-8).

34 *S.th.* Ia q.1 a.10 c: 'Illa ergo prima significatio qua voces significant res, pertinet ad primum sensum, qui est sensus historicus vel literalis. Illa vero significatio qua res significatae, per voces, iterum res alias significant, dicitur sensus spiritualis, qui super literalem fundatur et eum supponit.'

abandoned to confusion or *multiplicitas*. The plurality of senses is not founded on the circumstance that the words of the Scriptures have more than one meaning, but on the fact that the realities meant by these words '*aliarum rerum possunt esse signa.*' In other words there is only one literal sense, and that is primary. It forms the basis of and the assumptions behind the spiritual sense. Confusion is ruled out, for only the the single literal sense can have any force in theological arguments. It is also clear that there are no essential points of the faith which are not revealed *per literalem sensum* somewhere in the Scriptures.[35] Thomas defines the literal sense of the Scriptures as that which agrees with the intention of the author,[36] a common opinion which was shared by Gerson.[37]

Henry of Oyta also argued that the fourfold sense of the Scriptures can be reduced to two genera: the literal and the spiritual, which he preferred to call the mystical.[38] Both senses are inspired by the Holy Spirit. The difference is that the literal sense, the *sensus primarius*, is plain from the Scriptures, while the mediation of an expositor is required to unveil the mystical sense.[39] Like Thomas, he states that only the literal sense can be used to supply an *argumentum efficax*, although the mystical sense may also be invoked as proof, among believers.[40]

---

35 *S.th.* Ia q.1 a.10 ad primum.

36 *S.th.* Ia q.1 a.10 c.: 'Sensus litteralis est quem auctor intendit; auctor autem sacrae scripturae Deus est.' For a detailed exposition of Thomas's exegetical principles, see C. Spicq, *Esquisse d'une histoire de l'exégèse latine au moyen âge*, Paris 1944, 273-88.

37 *Responsio ad quaestionem* (Gl. 10, 239; Dupin V, 926D): '... sensus literalis cuiuscumque locutionis est ille sensus quem principaliter et de directo intendit ipse loquens; unde idem est dicere: «non est tenendus sensus literalis», et dicere: «non est capienda intentio loquentis». Cum igitur Spiritus Sanctus sit ille qui in sacra Scriptura loquitur, erroneum est dicere quod sensus literalis non sit verus aliquando et non semper tenendus. Propter hoc dicit Augustinus quod semper est verus, sic quod non est efficax argumentum nisi in sensu litterali fundatum.' See also below n. 40.

38 Henry of Oyta, *Quaestio* (ed. Lang, 50^{25-6}): 'Et manifestum est quod primus istorum sensuum est literalis, quilibet vero aliorum trium misticus seu spiritualis.'

39 Henry of Oyta, *Quaestio* (ed. Lang. 47^{29}-8^{7}).

40 Henry of Oyta, *Quaestio* (ed. Lang, 51^{17-22}). Pseudo-Dionysius (*ep.* 9, *MG* 3, 1103): 'Theologia symbolica non est argumentativa.' See also Augustin *ep.* 93 c. 8, 25 (*ML* 33, 334): 'allegoria non sufficit ad probationem alicuius, nisi cum habeatur aliunde auctoritas manifesta.' Through Nicolas of Lyra these two authorities were constantly referred to in exegetical treatises. Cf. Gerson, *Responsio ad quaestionem* (Gl. 10, 241; Dupin V, 927D-8A): 'Sensus literalis sacrae Scripturae est sensus qui concluditur ex circumstantia litterae, esse primarius et principalis intellectus eius, *ex quo solo potest trahi efficax argumentum secundum auctoritatem*. Et recitat diffuse magister Nicolaus de Lyra in primo prologo suae Postillae super Bibliam.'

It is remarkable that Henry of Oyta, although he goes into detail on the hermeneutic question, differs from Thomas in that he never says that the essential truths of the faith are always indicated in the literal sense of the Scriptures. He relates the truths of the faith not only to the Scriptures but also to the infallibility of the Church. Something similar can be observed in Gerson:

> Sensus scripturae litteralis iudicandus est prout Ecclesia Spiritu Sancto inspirata et gubernata determinavit, et non ad cuiuslibet arbitrium vel interpretationem.[41]

This thesis, whose negative argument is directed against heretical subjectivism, can hardly be called anything but traditional, all the more so when we hear his assurance that the literal sense:

> ex circumstantiis scripturae sacrae trahi potest et debet.[42]

The literal sense is thus established by the Church but bound by the Scriptures. Which fact carried more weight? That the literal sense is scriptural, or that the Church has established it? We believe it was the latter, and find support for this in the fact that the concept of *sensus literalis* is also used by Gerson independently of the Scriptures, and outside the scriptural context. Originally, he argues, the literal sense was revealed by Christ to the apostles. Then it was confirmed by the blood of the martyrs, later the doctors of the Church elaborated the literal sense and made its meaning, implications and conclusions appear more clearly. Finally, it was confirmed by the councils:

> ut quod erat doctrinaliter discussum per doctores fieret per ecclesiam sententialiter definitum.[43]

This development allows us to see that for Gerson the literal sense of the Scriptures coincided with what we call doctrine, theology—in the last analysis with dogma. Starting from the irrefragable unity of the Scriptures and the Church, he has no need, whenever he wishes to establish what belongs to the literal sense of the Scriptures, to appeal to the texts themselves for guidance; he can rest content with pointing to the doctrinal decisions of the Church. The literal sense of the Scriptures is identical with whatever is already

---

41 *De sensu litterali*, cons. 1, prop. 6 (Gl. 3, 335; Dupin I, 3A).
42 *Declaratio compendiosa* (Gl. 6, 185; Dupin I, 24B).
43 *De sensu litterali*, cons. 1, 6 (see above, device).

dogma, or is yet to be adopted as dogma. From this it follows that, in a manner of speaking, his theological speculations are made with the Scriptures behind him and his gaze fixed firmly on the Church in front of him. But does this imply that he thought the Church was free and independent with respect to the Scriptures? Could the Church add anything to them?

> Sensus litteralis sacrae scripturae, si reperitur determinatus et decisus in decretis et decretalibus et codicibus conciliorum, iudicandus est ad theologiam et sacram scripturam non minus pertinere quam symbolum apostolorum. Propterea non est spernendus tamquam humana seu positiva constitutione fundatus.[44]

In his previous theses it was not possible to find conclusive proof that Gerson did in fact regard the Church as a second source of revelation alongside, and up to a point independent of, the Scriptures. At any rate he expressly stated that the literal sense must be plain from the Scriptures, and for that reason one might conclude, despite the remarkable emphasis which he placed on the concept of the Church, that ultimately it was only a matter of interpretation and that the function of the Church was not to supplement the Scriptures but merely to explain them. But if one reads the last thesis carefully this can no longer be maintained: the distinction between Scripture and interpretation can no longer be applied, for the simple reason that they are considered to be identical. For Gerson, the Scriptures and their authentic interpretation by the Church are one and the same. Hence, he can speak of a *sensus literalis* outside the Scriptures and can identify the doctrinal decisions of the Church, its dogma, with the literal sense of the Scriptures. This means that he did in fact regard the Church as a second source of revelation. For whenever dogma is identified with the Scriptures, then it no longer makes sense to speak of interpretation, and 'supplementing' the Scriptures is the only appropriate description.[45] Ultimately Gerson seems to be untrue to his principle that the literal sense of the Scriptures must be taken from the scriptural texts themselves.

---

44 *De sensu litterali*, cons. 1, prop. 8 (Gl. 3, 336; Dupin I, 3D).

45 We agree with Oberman (*Harvest*, 385ff.) who, identifying Gerson as an adherent of what he called the 'Tradition II' position (a 'spirit-guided Church'), concluded that 'through the ongoing definition of truth by the Church, the canonical boundaries are enlarged and Holy Scripture is materially extended.'

3. *Church, Scriptures, and Tradition in the catalogue of the faith*

Gerson remarks somewhere that when we judge a doctrine, we must ask '*si doctrina sit conformis sacrae scriptura tam in se quam in modo traditionis.*' [46] He says that sacred Scripture is an infallible and sufficient rule for the organisation of the Church; hence, if a particular theological pronouncement does not appear to be in accordance with the Scriptures, it is for that reason suspect and heretical. But he counters his own argument by asking if there are not many doctrines which have been elaborated in the course of time, and which are not to be found in the Scriptures. His answer is: they certainly are to be found in them, but '*secundum aliquem gradum veritatum catholicarum.*'[47] That leads us to the truths of the faith.

Gerson summarised these truths on more than one occasion.[48] The most detailed example is in his *Declaratio compendiosa quae veritates sint de necessitate salutis credendae.*[49] This work is a socalled 'catalogue of the faith', that is a list in which the *veritates catholicae*[50] are arranged in their hierarchical order, and a formal description of the Church's faith is given. Ockham was the first to compile such a catalogue of the faith. He was followed by countless others, among them Henry of Oyta, Marsilius of Inghen, Pierre d'Ailly, Jean Courtecuisse, Torquemada, and others.[51] We may remark in passing that catalogues were also compiled in later times by both Catholic and Protestant theologians.

Because we have already seen, in the chapter on the Church and the law, what subjects are dealt with in a catalogue of the faith, we

---

[46] *De examinatione doctrinarum*, pars 2, 1(Gl. 9, 465; Dupin I, 12D): 'Declaratur ex auctoritate beati Dionysii dicentis in sententia: «Nihil audendum dicere de divinis, nisi quae nobis a Scriptura sacra tradita sunt». Cuius ratio est, quoniam Scriptura nobis tradita est tanquam regula sufficiens et infallibilis pro regimine totius ecclesiastici corporis et membrorum usque in finem saeculi.'

[47] *De examinatione doctrinarum* (Gl. 9, 465; Dupin I, 13A).

[48] *De iurisdictione*, see Chapter I n. 77. *De vita spir. animae*, corr. 7 (Gl. 3, 137-41; Dupin III, 23B-5D); *Dominus his opus*, cons. 11 (Gl. 5, 224-5; Dupin IV, 691AC). The lists are not identical.

[49] *Declaratio compendiosa* (Gl. 6, 181-9; Dupin I, 22-7).

[50] *Declaratio compendiosa* (Gl. 6, 189; Dupin I, 27B): 'Veritas catholica potest describi quod est veritas habita per divinam revelationem immediate vel mediate, explicite in propria [forma] verborum, vel implicite in bona et certa consequentia.'

[51] See De Vooght, *Les sources de la doctrine chrétienne*, s.v., and G.H. Tavard, *Holy Writ or Holy Church*, New York [1959], 22-66.

can be content with a summary here. In his *Declaratio* Gerson distinguishes six kinds of Catholic truth:

1. the canon of the Scriptures and all the truths which are contained in them;
2. the truth of the apostolic tradition;
3. the special, post-apostolic revelations;
4. the truths that can be deduced from the first three with the aid of *ratio*, e.g. the canons of the Church;
5. the truths that are only probable and rest on a premise which has not been revealed;
6. the truths which merely serve piety.[52]

For our purpose the first three kinds of truth are the most important. Gerson takes them together and argues that one must accept that they have been directly and explicitly revealed by God.

> Primus gradus veritatum credendarum est canon totius scripturae sacrae et singularum quae in ea litteraliter asserta sunt, sic videlicet quod non stat cum fide ut aliquis dissentiat pertinaciter aluicui contento in eadem scriptura ad intellectum Spiritus Sancti, qui est vere et proprie sensus litteralis.[53]

After our previous remarks on the *sensus literalis*, we do not need to go into more detail on this formulation. It may merely be pointed out that Gerson cited Matt. 5: 18 and 24: 35 to prove that the Scriptures in all their parts were revealed by God and therefore true and imperishable.

The second category of truths was that which the Church had laid down and

> ab indubitata relatione apostolorum per successionem continuam devenerunt.[54]

Even though he does not use the term it is clear that Gerson refers to the apostolic tradition. It is striking that his demonstration of the existence of this tradition is much less subtle than that of Henry of

52 *Declaratio compendiosa* (Gl. 6, 181-3; Dupin I, 22A-4B).
53 *Declaratio compendiosa* (Gl. 6, 181-2; Dupin I, 22B).
54 *Declaratio compensiosa* (Gl. 6, 181-2; Dupin I, 22BC).

Oyta (d. 1396), for example,[55] who not only cited pronouncements of Innocent III[56] and Basil the Great[57] to prove its existence but also such a text as John 16: 12. Gerson confined himself to the well-known statement of Augustine, '*Ego vero evangelio non crederem* ...'. This shows that the idea of tradition was largely hidden behind that of the Church. It was such an inseparable part of it that in fact one can say that in his theology the complex of Church, Scriptures and tradition was reduced to Church and Scriptures. The idea of tradition was present, but in such an indefinite form that it barely had a name of its own. Compared to Henry of Oyta, therefore, Gerson was taking a step backwards. How are we to explain this?

It seems most probable that where the word *traditio* was used largely in a negative sense in the Scriptures, Gerson was reluctant to apply it in a positive sense. The number of times when he spoke of *traditio* pejoratively is legion. He always uses the words 'human tradition' and consistently refers to such a text as Matt. 15: 6, 'You have made God's law null and void out of respect for your tradition'. We have already seen that he regarded tradition as the special domain of canon law. In view of his rather critical attitude to this science and its practitioners in particular, it is not surprising that he speaks of human tradition for the most part in legal contexts. Sometimes it is the inappropriate emphasis on the temporal power of the Church; sometimes the numerous excommunications which give him the occasion to fulminate against the human traditions; sometimes it is the excessive power of positive law in general which makes him reach for this term. His sermons to licentiates in canon law, and above all the *De vita spirituali animae*, are full of criticism of human traditions in the Church.[58] The last work especially was eagerly read in Reformation circles, and Lutherans in particular were very ready to agree with it.[59] But this should not blind us to the fact

---

[55] Heinrich von Oyta, *Quaestio de veritatibus catholicis*, ed. Albert Lang, Monasterii 1933, 2-13.

[56] Letter *inc*. 'Cum Marthae', incorporated in X 3.41.6.: 'Sane multa tam de verbis quam de factis dominicis invenimus ab evangelistis omissa, quae apostoli vel supplesse facto vel expressisse verbo leguntur... Credimus igitur formam verborum, sicut in canone ponitur et a Christo apostoli et ab ipsis corum acceperunt successores.'

[57] D.11 c.5. (= Basilius, *Liber de Spiritu*, cap. 27, 66 (*SC* 17, 232-3). Cf. Congar, *La Tradition et les Traditions*, 61.

[58] Chapter VIII n. 49 and n. 65.

[59] See Adolf Sperl, *Melanchthon zwischen Humanismus und Reformation*, München 1959, 30 n. 21.

that Gerson did pass some positive judgements on tradition, although he preferred not to use the term.

In his *Declaratio* he observed that not everything which the Church had handed down was part of the necessary truths of the faith.

> Attendendum tamen est quod non omnia quae tradit vel tolerat ecclesia publice legenda, sunt de necessitate salutis credenda...; sed dumtaxat illa quae sub definitione iudiciali tradit esse credenda, vel opposita reprobanda, concurrente totius universalis ecclesiae consensu implicite, vel explicite, vere vel interpretative.[60]

Just as the Church judged the Scriptures, so it judged tradition. It is the Church which determined the canon; it is the Church which determines those parts of the tradition of the universal Church which belong to the *credenda*.

The third category of truths of the faith includes the revelations received in post-apostolic times. In principle, Gerson argues, these are only binding on those who received them. He continues:

> Ceteri vero quibus non est huiusmodi revelatio facta, non obligantur credere nisi vel per miraculum vel per scripturam sacram et praecipue per Ecclesiam detur certitudo.[61]

The last words of this passage may serve as a pregnant summary of this section, which allows us to see how Gerson used the concept of tradition and how the authority of the Church was paramount for him.

4. *The Church and the doctors*

In this section we shall attempt to show exactly what Gerson had in mind when he argued that it was up to the Church to decide on the sense of the Scriptures. Which bodies were involved in making pronouncements on doctrine, and to whom did he allow the highest authority–the doctors of theology or the representatives of the hierarchy?[62] Louis Salembier thought that it was the former. He as-

---

[60] *Declaratio compendiosa* (Gl. 6, 182; Dupin I, 22C).

[61] *Declaratio compensiosa* (Gl. 6, 82; Dupin I, 22CD): 'Tertius gradus est veritatum specialiter aliquibus revelatarum, quae ab illis quibus revelatio facta est absque ulla dubitatione credendae sunt; alioquin non esset revelatio, de cuius ratione est ut sit certa.'

[62] For more details, see the present author's 'Het gezag van de theologische doctor

serted that the doctors were granted an authority at the Council of Constance which they had never possessed before. He related this to the influence of the Universities, which was so strongly felt at Constance. 'D'Ailly, Gerson et les premiers gallicans ont souvent exalté, sans mesure comme sans raison, cette sorte d'omnipotence magistrale.'[63] That is a harsh verdict; whether it was just, we shall see below.

It was the task of the doctors to teach and defend the revealed doctrine in Church and society. They formed a corporation of professional interpreters, who did not have a hierarchical status in the strict sense but whose legal title was dependent on their corporation. The *doctores theologiae* or *magistri*, Chenu argues, 'ont qualité officielle pour parler foi et doctrine, ils déterminent après la question disputée, et leur solution est autorisée. Ils ne sont pas des autorités, *auctoritates*, au sens décisif, du magistère ecclésiastique, car ni leur situation hiérarchique, ni la matière de leur travail propre ne le comportent; mais enfin ils ont un lieu théologique, L'Ecole existe dans l'Eglise en dessous des Pères de la foi.'[64] This refers to their relationship with the hierarchy in general terms.

To bring out Chenu's definition in more detail, we turn to Gratian. His *Decretum* lays down more than once that the Holy See is the highest instance in matters of faith, and that doctrinal disputes ought to be resolved by the Pope. Gratian himself, however, emphasised that papal pronouncements could only be valid if they agreed with the existing tradition of the faith; and he added that the Pope's authority in the interpretation of the Scriptures was less than that of the doctors. There was a manifest contradiction between this statement and the first, in which he acknowledged the Holy See as the highest instance in doctrine. Gratian tried to reconcile it by analysing the power of the keys. He distinguished between the *clavis scientiae* and the *clavis potestatis*, and pointed out that both knowledge and authority were required for a decision in law, but that *potestas* held pride of place. The doctors might have more

---

in de kerk der middeleeuwen–Gratianus, Augustinus Triumphus, Ockham en Gerson,' *NAKG.N.S.* 63 (1984), 102-28; and 'Quasi stellae fulgebunt: the Doctor of Divinity in Mediaeval Society and Church.' in: D.W.D. Shaw (ed.), *In Divers Manners. A St Mary's Miscellany to commemorate the 450th anniversary of the founding of St Mary's College, 7th March 1539*, (St Andrews 1990), 11-28. Cf. below n. 74.

63 Salembier, *Le grand schisme d'Occident*, 299.

64 Chenu, *Introduction à l'étude de St. Thomas d'Aquin*, 18-19.

knowledge than the Pope, but they lacked the jurisdictional authority and thus the power to give authentic interpretations.

> apparet, quod divinarum tractatores scripturarum, etsi scientiam pontificibus praeemineant, quia dignitatis eorum apicem non sunt adepti, in sacrarum quidem scripturarum expositionibus eis praeponuntur; in causis vero definiendis secundum post eos locum merentur.[65]

Because they did not belong to the hierarchy, the doctors had no power of jurisdiction. They fell outside the hierarchical succession and could not invoke any authority other than that which belonged to them by virtue of their knowledge of *sacra doctrina*. But they did not derive that knowledge from themselves; it had been handed down to them generation after generation. Beginning in the age of the apostles, with Paul, doctrine had been transmitted by the saints – Ambrose, Augustine, Jerome and Gregory – and others, to later ages. Hence, besides the hierarchical succession symbolised in Peter, there was a specifically doctrinal succession, symbolised in Paul. Gerson was probably referring to this in one of his earliest sermons, when he said:

> Non pour quant chascun de ces deux apostres a eu aucunes excellances et dignités sur terre: l'un en une maniere et l'autre en une autre, comme saint Pierre ot dignité de universal prelacion, et saint Pol de generale predicacion: *Petrus preest principatu, Paulus pollet magistratu tocius Ecclesie.* En signe de ces deux excellences on les met ou seel de la bulle du pape.[66]

---

[65] Gratian, d.a. D. 20. In our text we followed Tierney, 'Ockham, the Conciliar Theory, and the Canonists, *JHI* 15 (1954), 47-8. Cf. also the same author's *Origins of papal infallibility, 1150-1350*, 39-45.

[66] We follow the text as given by Mourin in his *Six sermons français inédits de Jean Gerson*, 486[69-70] (= Sermon *Nimis honorati sunt*, Gl. 7*, 722). The Latin sentence which Mourin was unable to identify, stems from the *Sequentia in festo Petri et Pauli apostolorum*, vs. 5: 'Laus communis est amborum / cum sint tamen singulorum / dignitates propriae./ Petrus praeest principatu,/ Paulus pollet magistratu/ totius Ecclesiae.' See W. Moll, 'Hymnen en sequentiën uit handschriften en oude drukwerken van Nederlandsche oorsprong', *Studiën en bijdragen op 't gebied der historische theologie* (edd. W. Moll and J.G. de Hoop Scheffer), I (1870), 385. We are indebted to Dr. J. Trapman for this reference. – An analogous statement can be found in *An liceat* (Gl. 6, 284; Dupin II, 304B): 'Constat autem quod Petrus erat summus pontifex et secundum doctores confirmatus in fide et gratia post Pentecosten. Propterea dicunt quod Petrus non errabat in fide nec haereticabat circa observationem legalium. Dicebat ideo Paulus quod non recte ambulabat ad veritatem evangelii et quod represensiblis erat [Gal. 2: 11ff.]. Ex quibus palam elicitur quod *Summus Pontifex qui succedit Petro in apostolatu, reprehendi potest publice per doctorem theologum, qui in officio praedicationis succedit Paulo.*' Cf. our art. 'Iconografie en primaat. Petrus en Paulus op het pauselijk zegel', *NAKG* N.S. 49 (1968), 4-36.

The *magistri* knew that they stood in the succession of Paul.

As the highest representatives of the hierarchy oriented themselves more and more to canon law, the natural result was a widening gulf between them and the university *magistri* who, though far from disputing the power of jurisdiction of the Popes, had grave objections to the way in which they wielded it without limits. Papal absolutism provoked protests from the *magistri*, because they felt it failed to do them justice in their capacity as interpreters of doctrine. They reasoned that there was a rightful distinction between *scientia* and *potestas*, but that the two might not be so far removed from each other that they were entirely separated, for then *potestas* became arbitrary and *scientia* futile.

In their criticism of absolutism the *magistri* readily cited the controversy between Peter and Paul, described in Galatians 2: 11.[67] They recognised themselves in Paul, and just as Paul had corrected Peter, they felt entitled to ask the Pope: 'Cur ita facis?' (Job 9: 12). This formula, as we have seen, is very often met with in Gerson,[68] but in itself this means little, for Petrus Cantor (d. 1197) had already used it in his *Verbum abbreviatum*.[69] And in the fourteenth century it would be more difficult to find theologians who did not use it than those who did.[70]

Be this as it may, if Gerson and the theologians felt that they had a right to call the Pope to account, this does not prove that they belittled his dignity. They used the formula: 'Cur ita facis'? only to protest, in the name of the *doctrina sacra* which was entrusted to their care, against the excessively large claims made for the idea of papal plenitude of power, claims of which we can find an example in the following passage from the canonist Tancredus (d. c. 1235):

> in iis gerit vicem Dei quia sedet in loco Iesu Christi qui est verus Deus et verus homo... item de nichilo facit aliquid ... item in iis gerit vicem Dei quia plenitudinem potestatis habet in rebus ecclesiasticis... item quia

---

67 See Chapter IV n. 31.

68 E.g. *De vita spir. animae* (Gl. 3, 152-3; Dupin III, 34C): 'Quod si quis in oppositum mille decretales vel decreta produxerit tamquam papae in nullo casu dicere licet: «Cur ita facis?»... respondemus quod potestas superioris nihil potest statuere adversus veritatem legis naturalis et divinae.' Other examples in *Trilogus in materia schismatis* (Gl. 6, 75; Dupin II, 88A); *Apparuit* (Gl. 5, 71, 85; Dupin II, 59D, 70A); *De unitate* (Gl. 6, 136; Dupin II, 114A); *Nova positio* (Gl. 6, 154; Dupin V, 412B).

69 Petrus Cantor, *Verbum abbreviatum*, c. 44 (*ML* 205, 139-40), cited by d'Ailly in his *De materia concilii generalis* (ed. Oakley, 260).

70 See Leclerc, *Jean de Paris*, 129.

> potest dispensare supra ius et contra ius... item quia de iusticia potest iniusticiam corrigendo ius et mutando... nec est qui dicat ei: 'Cur ita facis?'[71]

Now the question is: what of the verdict of Salembier? Did Gerson claim for the doctors an authority that they had never possessed before? What kind of authority they had? Gerson handed down the formula in which the Chancellor granted the degree of licentiate:

> Ego auctoritate apostolica, do tibi licentiam legendi, regendi, disputandi, docendi in sacra theologiae facultate hic et ubique terrarum, in nomine Patris et Filii et Spirit us Sancti. Amen.[72]

On papal authority therefore, the Chancellor granted the licentiate the right to practise theology in the fullest sense. But–and this is the point–did Gerson claim the term 'apostolic' for this work of the licentiates; and did he, in other words, also claim the power of jurisdiction for the doctors? No, as we can see from the following statement:

> Doceant nos exempla posita: licentiando in theologia et decretis, datur a papa auctoritas. Qualis auctoritas? Exponendi et interpretandi sacram scripturam. Non tamen ut expositio illa sit auctoritas apostolica, sed est declaratio quaedam magistralis et scholastica.[73]

This passage shows that Gerson was certainly aware of the distinction between the socalled 'scholastic' or 'magisterial' interpretation of the Scriptures by the doctors, and the dogmatic fixing of a certain interpretation by the hierarchy, for which the terms 'authentic'

---

[71] Cited by Tierney, *Foundations*, 89 and 147 (Innocent IV). Other examples in Klaus Ganser, 'Päpstliche Gesetzgebungsgewalt und kirchlicher Konsens', in: *Von Konstanz bis Trient*, 171-88 (177). Both canonists and curialists defended the thesis that the Pope's plenitude of power was beyond discussion, especially on the grounds of C. 17 q. 4 c. 30. Alvarez Pelayo, *De planctu*, lib. I, art. 45 (ed. Venetiis 1560, fol 26^{b}): '... in omnibus et per omnia potest [papa] facere et dicere quicquid placet, auferendo etiam ius suum cui vult, quia non est qui dicit ei: «Cur ita facis?» [with ref. to D. 19 c. 3].'

[72] In *De examinatione doctrinarum* (Gl. 9, 462; Dupin I, 10BC) Gerson explains the difference between the pastoral and the doctoral office as follows: '... doctores theologici non obligantur praecise ex potestate sibi tradita praedictos actus omnes, legendi scilicet, regendi, praedicandi etc. passim exercere. Secus de praelatis ordinariis, quorum officio pastorali annexum est debitum vel obligatio docendi, praedicandi etc. subdito sibi gregi, sicut iungit Apostolus haec duo: pastores et doctores; quod ratio manifesta convincit. Oportet enim esse quosdam in Ecclesia, qui sint ex officio constituti tales actus exercere; aliquin non fuisset perfecte instituta, contra illud: «Dei perfecta sunt opera» [Deut. 32: 4].' Cf. Denifle, *CUP* II nr 185, Appendix (25), 684.

[73] *De vita spir. animae*, lect. 6 (Gl. 3, 201; Dupin III, 7A).

and 'apostolic' were reserved. This shows that he did not confuse *scientia* and *potestas*, University and Church, but that he fully respected the traditional boundaries defined by Gratian. It is true that he was zealous in his efforts to give the doctors a greater say in the Church, but that stemmed not from disdain for the hierarchy – Peter – but from the conviction that the Church could not survive without solid doctrine – Paul.[74]

5. *Scriptures and theology*

The scholastics did not draw a sharp distinction between Scriptures, tradition, and theology; the three concepts overlapped.[75] Divine revelation, laid down in Scriptures and tradition, and human reason, which – not without divine assistance – explained and interpreted this revelation, were regarded as a single organic unity. The terminology of the scholastics is revealing in this context. Whichever mediaeval theologian one chooses, they all use the terms *sacra scriptura* and *sacra doctrina* and their equivalents indiscriminately.

---

[74] According to a tradition going back to patristic times, Gerson states that bishops, as successors of the apostles, were doctors *ex officio.* As such they were entitled to decide 'auctoritative' in matters of faith and, consequently, they could bind the consciences of the faithful entrusted to their care. This consideration played a great role in Gerson's vain efforts at the Council of Constance to bring about a condemnation of Jean Petit's theses on tyrannicide, which had already been condemned by the Bishop of Paris in 1414. Cardinal Antoine de Chalant contested the competence of the Bishop in this matter. See Brandmüller, *Das Konzil von Konstanz* II ('Burgund und Orléans im Streit um den Tyrannenmord', 95-115 (113 n. 220)). Cf. *Oportet haereses esse* (Gl. 5, 430; Dupin II, 345D-6A) and *Nova positio* (Gl. 6, 149; Dupin V, 409C), where Gerson cites from a treatise – at that time in the hands of Antoine de Chalant – which was prepared by the faculty of theology and sent to Clement VII in 1388, probably in connection with the Monzon affair: '... si doctores possunt *doctrinaliter* tractare materias fidei, quia datur eis in licentia potestas determinandi et interpretandi Scripturam sacram, constat quod episcopi ex officio sunt doctores et possunt docere populum *auctoritative*, poenas scilicet apponendo.' See also *Conclusiones octo de iure episcoporum* (Gl. 6, 175-8; Dupin II, 287-90), and the end of the sermon *Suscepimus* (Gl. 5, 545; Dupin II, 286) which was given, according to Finke, *Acta* II, 429 at Constance on Febr. 2. 1416, and not two years later as stated by Mgr. Glorieux (Gl. 5, xv).

[75] J. de Ghellinck, ' "Pagina" et "Sacra Pagina". Histoire d'un mot et transformation de l'objet primitivement désigné', in: *Mélanges Aug. Pelzer*, Louvain 1947, 23-59; De Vooght, *Les sources*, 27-8, and Congar, *La tradition et les traditions*, 127 (171 n. 25): Since the Decretum Gelasianum (sixth century) it was usual 'd'englober les Pères, les canons conciliaires, voire les décrets pontificaux et (plus rarement) les traités les plus honorés des théologiens, dans la *Scriptura sacra.'*

Thomas, for example, after establishing that God is the *auctor scripturae*, continues his argument in the words: '*ista scientia*'.[76] Bonaventure in his *Breviloquium* says:

> Ratio autem huius veritatis haec est, quia cum *sacra scriptura sive theologia* sit scientia.[77]

Gerson did not differ from the older scholastics in this respect either. Arguing for the art of rhetoric to be applied to Scripture, he says on one occasion:

> *theologia* suam habet logicam et modum loquendi proprium.[78]

and elsewhere:

> habet enim *scriptura sacra* ... suam logicam propriam.[79]

The statement that *sacra scriptura* must acknowledge a greater role in interpretation to the custom of the universal Church than to the opinion of a single doctor,[80] which sounds rather odd to our ears, points in the same direction.

This background helps to explain why Gerson had such objections to vernacular translations of the Bible.[81] For that would break the organic unity of the Church and Scriptures, theology and Scriptures, and would detach the Bible from its proper interpretation. He warned of such dangers more than once in his sermons and treatises, and as he grew older these warnings became even more emphatic.

---

76 *S.Th.* I^a q. 1 a. 10 c.

77 *Breviloquium*, cap. I.

78 *De duplici logica* (Gl. 3, 59; Dupin IV, 25B). Cf. *Prosperum iter* (Gl. 5, 476-7; Dupin II, 277D).

79 *De sensu litterali* (Gl. 3, 334; Dupin I, 3).

80 This rule is used against Ockham in *De schismate* (Gl. 6, 48; Dupin II, 21B): '... ipse Ockham videtur oppositum in Dialogo suo suasisse, contra quod est usus et lex Ecclesiae.' Cf. *De necessaria communione*, 9 (Gl. 10, 58; Dupin I, 459CD): 'Sacra scriptura in expositione sua habet et habere debet in reverentia et auctoritate maiori consuetudinem universalis Ecclesiae circa ea quae fidei sacramenta respiciunt et dispensationem ipsorum, quam auctoritatem doctoris unius particularis, etiam sancti.' *De distinctione revelationum*, 4 (Gl. 3, 47; Dupin I, 51B): 'Est namque sacra scriptura locus vel officina ubi cunus regius monetae spiritualis reconditur; quod si in aliquo vel minimo puncto denarius discrepat in sua figuratione et superscriptione ab hoc cuno regio, absque ulla dubitatione falsatus est.'

81 See Schwab, *Gerson*, 317. For vernacular translations of the Bible in general, see *The Cambridge History of the Bible*, vol. 2 (ed. G.W.H. Lampe), Cambridge 1969, 338-491. *Le Moyen Age et la Bible* (ed. Pierre Riché and Guy Lobrichon), [Paris 1984] contains only a section on 'La prédication en langues vernaculaires' (489-516).

While he was able, in one passage, to admit that some good might come of a translation of the Bible into the vernacular,[82] elsewhere he expressly urged that such translations be forbidden, especially of those portions of the Bible that were not of a historical or moral character.[83] His argument was always that Scripture required qualified interpreters, and that an uninstructed layman who lacked deeper knowledge of theology could not perform this role. If he tried to do so, he would fall easily into heresy, as history showed.

> Il ne souffit pas d'entendre la sainte Escripture que on sache la significacion grammaticale et vulgaire des moz, mais est requise grande et longue estude tant es aultres sciencez de philosophie et de logique comme es sainctz docteurs qui ont exposé la sainte escripture par inspiration divine, et par comparer l'ung a l'autre; aultrement chascun grammairien simple seroit tantost bon theologien; d'ou scaroit par soy toute science escripte en latin, ce qui n'est pas, maiz est occasion tres grande de cheoir en heresie, comme Julien l'Apostat, Elvidius, Jovinien et les Turelupins fierent, et ung darrenierement vers Cambrai, qui se nommoit Vespertilien. Et presquez toutez heresiez sont venuez de ceste presumption, car les mos sont souvent equivoquez et se prennent aultrement en ung lieu que en ung aultre et que en commune grammaire...[84]

In his treatise *De necessaria communione* of 1417 he remarks that the errors of the Beghards, the Poor Men of Lyons and their like were on the increase, and that the followers of these movements had access to vernacular translations of the Bible, '*in grande praeiudicium et scandalum catholicae veritatis*'.[85] He felt that measures ought to be taken against this. Later he described such translations as the most effective means of the devil to lead people, especially the *vulgares idiotae*, astray from the path of truth. 'We demand the pure text as

---

[82] *Contre les fausses assertions des flatteurs* (Gl. 7, 361; Dupin IV, 623AB): 'Ainsi comme il peust venir aucun bien se la Bible est bien et au vray translatee en francoyz et entendue sobrement, ainsi par le contraire en peuvent venir maulz et erreurs sans nombre s'elle est mal translatee, ou s'elle est presumptueusement estudiee et entendue, en refusant lez sens et expositions des sainctz docteurs.' Cf. *Puer natus est* (Gl. 7*, 952; Dupin III, 940B): 'Et pour tant je prens icy un enseignement que c'est une tres perilleuse chose de bailler aux simples gens qui ne sont pas grans clercs, livres de la saincte escripture translatez en francoys, car par mauvais entendement ilz puent tantost cheoir en erreurs.'

[83] See below, n. 86.

[84] *Contre les fausses assertions des flatteurs* (Gl. 7, 361; Dupin IV, 623AB). Nearly the same text in *Vivat Rex* (Gl. 7*, 1157; Dupin IV, 598D).

[85] *De necessaria communione* (Gl. 10, 58; Dupin I, 459B)

the Holy Spirit handed it down to us,' they cry, 'but in the end they have become self-willed and despise all authority.'[86]

But it would be a mistake to think that Gerson's emphatic rejection of Bible translations in the vernacular was the product of intellectual pride, of a university academic's scorn for the *vulgares idiotae*. That played no part at all, as we see from the fact that he was zealous to improve the religious education of the common people. As Chancellor of the University of Paris, he did not think himself too exalted to compose brief popular works on diverse religious subjects, in which he used a variety of literary genres to make them more attractive to the reader. The popularity of these works is shown by the wide circulation that they continued to enjoy in later times.[87]

We cannot know for certain whether d'Ailly's extreme views on the authenticity of the Vulgate text had any influence on Gerson. In his *Epistola ad novos Hebraeos* d'Ailly attempted to show that, in spite of mistakes and copyists' errors, Jerome's translation ought to be regarded as authentic, because it was approved by the Church:

> firmiter de necessitate salutis ... credendum est beatum Hieronymum in translatione scripturarum non errasse, aliquid in iis vel addendo vel subtrahendo vel immutando a sensu literali hebraicae veritatis. Nam auctoritas ecclesiae catholicae dictam translationem nequaquam recepisset, tamquam scripturam canonicam seu divinam, nec approbasset, tamquam firmiter credendam de necessitate salutis, si ipsa esset tali errore vitiata.[88]

There is no passage, we think, in which Gerson speaks in the same sense, but it seems acceptable to assume that he would have shared his master's views on this subject, for d'Ailly's view not only coincided entirely with Gerson's ideas on the authority of the Church but also with the ideal of unity hat he had in mind. There was one faith, one spiritual head and so there must be one textual basis for

[86] *Collectorium super magnificat* (Gl. 8, 350; Dupin IV, 372C).

[87] Cf. Connolly, *John Gerson*, 113-38, and in particular Burger, *Aedificatio*, 71-110. For more recent studies in this field, see Giovanni Matteo Roccati, 'Forschungsbericht Gersoniana', in: *Wolfenbütteler Renaissance Mitteilungen* IX (1985), 41 n. 12 (44).

[88] Tschackert, *Peter von Ailli*, Appendix: *Epistola ad novos Hebraeos*, [12]. We have been unable to consult the essay of L. Salembier, *Une page inédite de l'histoire de la Vulgate*, 1889, which contains a better edition of the *Epistola*. See also *DThC* I 2, 2584-98 s.v. 'authenticité' (E. Mangenot).

the theology of the Church. Translations of the Bible into the vernacular would endanger this unity:

> ... sicut est una fides et unum caput in spiritualibus, sic sit unicus et praecipuus studii theologiae fons incorruptus, a quo caetera theologiae studia velut rivuli deriventur. Rursus sequitur ex praemissis prohibendam esse vulgarem translationem librorum sacrorum nostrae Bibliae praesertim extra moralitates et historias.[89]

[89] *Contra vanam curiositatem* (Gl. 3, 248-9; Dupin I, 105D).

CHAPTER TWELVE

THE SOURCES OF GERSON'S ECCLESIOLOGY

> *Intolerabile siquidem est confestim existimare de sanctis sapientibus et tanta sedulitate scrutantibus, eos in rebus non usquequaque difficilibus tum dissonis assertionibus erravisse.*
>
> Gerson, *De vita spirituali animae* (Gl. 3, 183; Dupin III, 57A).

'Perhaps we are really lacking a branch in the intellectual family tree of d'Ailly, Gerson and their contemporaries. Who were their teachers? We do not know them.' It was the German historian Johannes Haller who wrote these words in the beginning of this century, once again revealing his great historical intuition.[1] Though he had never made a special study of Gerson, Haller felt that something in the background of Gerson's theory of the Church eluded his grasp. And by admitting this so frankly he set a chastening example to many an interpreter of Gerson, old and new, who instead of answering the question of sources with a *non liquet* had been led, sometimes by indolence, sometimes by a dogmatic parti pris, without further investigation, to name a number of names, often open to objection and damaging to Gerson, who deserved better.

Now the question of Gerson's ecclesiological sources is rather complicated. The first difficulty we face is that he was generally rather sparing in explicit references to his authorities. This was not because he wanted to appear better or more independent than he was, but because he was mostly writing for insiders who knew these authorities and for whom a vague allusion – mostly to the commentaries on the sentences – or a mere name was enough. Moreover, he was averse to a parade of erudition. Unlike d'Ailly, for example, he knew there was no need to prove his mastery, his intellect or his knowledge by citing an array of witnesses and engaging them in brilliant discussion or polemic. Because he was guided by the conviction – another proof of his humility and his conservatism – that others had already said it all, and mostly better, he saw it as his task

[1] *Papsttum und Kirchenreform* I, 1903, 344.

to compile whatever of value he had found in them and make it accessible to his contemporaries in a convenient form.[2] It is not by chance that we find in his greatest works such statements as this:

> non quidem alia dicturus quam alii, quamquam forte aliter.[3]

> Nihil quoque novi allaturus sum quod nequaeat in aliis sanctorum libris inveniri: ab eis nimirum quid obmissum est? Sed eorum sententias meo ordine ac verbis explicabo.[4]

> Satis est si ex bene inventis et doctrinis aliorum ego meis verbis, meo ordine, favum aliquem veritatis, instar apum, propria arte compingam.[5]

The humble view of his task which Gerson took does not make it easier for those who would trace his sources, for it is not immediately clear whom he meant by 'others'. Those, on the other hand, who feel that the above expressions are part of the typical jargon of a revolutionary who wishes to claim that his assertions are not new, may reflect that his great example, Bonaventure, expressed himself in exactly the same way:

> Non enim intendo novas opiniones adversare, sed communes et approbatas retexere.[6]

A further complication – which goes with his anti-intellectualistic attitude – is that Gerson reworked his sources very intensively and integrated them so completely into his own argument that they are sometimes very difficult to distinguish. In him we very rarely find the long, almost verbatim citations common in other authors, such as the passages which Pierre d'Ailly transcribed, often literally, from Roger Bacon, John of Paris or Ockham. Quite often, after naming an authority once, Gerson did not cite him again when he took up the same subject later. Examples of this are legion and they forbid

---

[2] His great respect for tradition is shown above all in *Contra vanam curiositatem* (Gl. 3, 224-34; 234-49; Dupin I, 86-93; 94-106).

[3] *De vita spir. animae*, lect. 3 (Gl. 3, 143; Dupin III, 27B).

[4] *Mystica theologia* (ed. Combes, 6[95-8]).

[5] *De pot. eccl.* (Gl. 6, 211; Dupin II, 227A). Cf. also *De vita spir. animae* (Gl. 3, 137; Dupin III, 23B): 'Nihil hic novum fingo. Distinxerunt itaque in simili doctores ante nos...'; or letter inc. *Jocundum est* (Gl. 2, 32): 'Sufficiant interim mihi meique similibus sobria humilitate uti bene inventis...'

[6] *Comm. in lib. sent.*, IV, 1, II praeloc. – Morrall, *Gerson*, 10: 'Gerson himself was unwilling to face the fact of his new radicalism. Like most innovators, he saw himself as a conservative.'

the researcher to confine himself to the study of a single work; one treatise always proves to be indispensable for the interpretation of another.

The publications of Brian Tierney are very important, albeit chiefly indirectly, for the question that concerns us. Tierney, especially in his *Foundations of Conciliar Theory*, has shown that fifteenth century conciliar thought drew on a much broader and longer stream of specifically canonist tradition than was once assumed.[7] Whereas in the past it was believed that John of Paris, Marsilius of Padua and Ockham were chiefly to be held responsible for the development of a conciliar theory of the Church, Tierney's study has shown that both older and more recent commentators on the decrees and decretals supplied the conciliarists with many an argument. Although we cannot expect any direct support from these new insights, for, as we saw earlier, Gerson was not greatly concerned with canonist arguments, Tierney's book does offer a challenge to take up the struggle against a misconception: the current view of Gerson's ecclesiological sources.

In this chapter we shall first examine current opinion on the sources of Gerson's ecclesiology a little more closely, and then try to go rather deeper and make some new suggestions on the influences that may have affected him. To anticipate, we hope to show that we must rule out any influence from Marsilius of Padua, while the importance of Ockham and the Ockhamists must certainly not be exaggerated. We wish to show that the core of Gerson's ecclesiology may not be described as Ockhamist, but must be linked to the teachings of the great scholastics or their direct successors, especially Bonaventure, Durand of St Pourçain and Henry of Ghent.

1. *Marsilius of Padua and Dietrich of Niem*

The interpretation of Gerson's ecclesiology still suffers today from the consequences of a whim of the German scholar Von der Hardt, who in 1696 attributed the *De modis uniendi ac reformandi ecclesiam in*

---

[7] Besides this work see also Tierney's, 'Ockham, the Conciliar Theory and the Canonists', in *JHI* 15 (1954), 40-70.

concilio universali to the Chancellor.[8] Before we illustrate this thesis further we wish to analyse the theory of the Church that is found in this treatise, now generally ascribed to the German conciliarist Dietrich of Niem.[9]

> Dietrich's ecclesiology is entirely built on the distinction between two kinds of Church: the *ecclesia particularis*, identical with the clergy, on the one hand; and the *ecclesia universalis*, or *congregatio fidelium*, on the other hand. The Head of the Church in the first sense is the Pope, the head of the universal Church is Christ. This *ecclesia universalis* comprises all believers, regardless of their position in the Church or the world: emperors and princes, Pope and cardinals, with the whole of the laity, constitute the Church in this sense. The usual qualifications: infallibility, continuity of the faith, sacramentality and the power of the keys, are not attributed to the institutional Church but to this *congregatio fidelium*. The hierarchy fulfils a merely instrumental function; it is the executive power of the community of believers, which possesses the legislative power.
> Denying the divine institution of the primacy of Peter, Dietrich explains its origin historically, partly as the voluntary acknowledgement by the principal apostles who were equal in their rights, partly as the result of imperial donations. The Pope is not the Head of the Church but its chief member, not its lord but its ruler, and this only as long as he does not abuse his power, for it was the intention of the divine legislator to secure the welfare of the whole Christian commonwealth, and its maintenance was more important than the maintenance of particular rights. All apostolic constitutions, all laws issued in favour of the Popes, cardinals or prelates, are therefore subject to a permanent reservation, that they do not harm the interests of the Christian commonwealth.[10]

Closely following Marsilius of Padua, whom he calls a *magnus theologus*, but also Ockham, Dietrich developed his theory of the Church. It is dominated by the idea of popular sovereignty, which Dietrich, in the footsteps of Marsilius, transposed to the Church. Although it is difficult to deny that this results in a coherent ecclesiology, this advantage is gained at rather a high price, for Dietrich broke radically with tradition, that is with ideas of an hierarchical Church, and fell instead into the arms of Aristotle. From a theolog-

---

[8] H. von der Hardt, *Magnum Oecumenicum Constantiniense Concilium* I, Frankfurt/Leipzig 1700, 30, 68-142, 255-69.

[9] H. Heimpel, *Dietrich von Niem*, Münster i.W. 1932, 77ff.

[10] See Martin, *Gallicanisme* II, 126ff.

ical point of view, moreover, it betrays not a little naivety to identify the Church of the Creed with the visible Church.[11]

It is hardly necessary to explain that Von der Hardt did Gerson's reputation no good by attributing such a radical work to him. Following Von der Hardt's arbitary ascription, Dupin also regarded *De modis* as Gerson's and thus opened the way to a Marsilian interpretation of his ecclesiology. He included the work in the second volume of his edition of Gerson's *Opera Omnia* of 1706[12] and thus took it as the basis for the influential exposition of Gerson's theology with which his first volume opened. Lenfant, although he remarked that the *De modis* was not included in older editions of Gerson's works, did not draw the consequences of this observation, but followed Von der Hardt and Dupin in his *Histoire du Concile de Constance* of 1727.[13] After Döllinger had thrown some doubt on the authorship in 1843[14] Johannes Schwab produced conclusive arguments to prove that Gerson could not possibly have been the author of this radical work.[15] Schwab's discovery has never been contradicted, but it was a long time before it was generally accepted and longer still before the full consequences were drawn from it.

In a very defective study published in 1868, Louis Girardez appeared unaware of Schwab's discovery and included the *De modis* in his study of Gerson's ecclesiology.[16] Friedrich von Bezold did likewise in an influential article 'Die Lehre von der Volkssouveränität während des Mittelalters', in 1876.[17] Ten years later Louis Salembier, an expert on d'Ailly and the whole period of the Western Schism, failed to take Schwab's discovery into account.[18] Later he corrected his error but found no occasion to reconsider his verdict on Gerson. In his much read and often reprinted *Le grand*

---

[11] Heimpel, *Dietrich von Niem*, 106, 124ff.

[12] *Tractatus de modis uniendi ac reformandi Ecclesiam in Concilio universali* (Dupin II, 161-200).

[13] *Histoire du Concile de Constance* II, 286 n. 2: 'Ce Traité [sc. *De modis uniendi*] n'est point dans les anciennes Editions de Gerson. M. Von der Hardt l'a donné au public pour la premiere fois en 1696, & ensuite Mr. Dupin dans sa derniere Edition des Oeuvres de Gerson.'

[14] I. Döllinger, *Lehrbuch der Kirchengeschichte*, IIB, I. Abt., [2] Regensburg 1843, 298, cited by Schwab, *Gerson*, 482 n. 3.

[15] Schwab, *Gerson*, 482-7.

[16] *Exposé de la doctrine de Gerson sur l'Église*, Strasbourg 1868.

[17] Originally published in *HZ* 36 (1876); later included in Fr. von Bezold, *Aus Mittelalter und Renaissance. Kulturgeschichtliche Studien*, Munich/Berlin 1918, 1-48.

[18] *Petrus de Alliaco*, Insulis 1896.

schisme d'occident at least, he describes Gerson, as if he were Dietrich of Niem or Marsilius of Padua himself, as an adherent of absolute democracy, also called 'multitudinism'.

> D'après eux le pouvoir spirituel réside tout entier dans le corps mystique de l'Eglise, qui le communique au pape et aux évêques. Ce système, on le voit, correspond à celui de l'origine démocratique du pouvoir en politique. Les chefs des deux sociétés ne recevraient l'investiture de leur autorité que par l'intermédiaire du peuple.[19]

A crasser misrepresentation of Gerson's intentions is hardly possible!

Georges de Lagarde argued that although Gerson could hardly resist the temptations of Marsilius's *Defensor pacis*, and praised it as one of the best of books, he probably never took the trouble to read it.[20] This is undoubtedly true, and as for the rest of his remark the suspicion has often been voiced that de Lagarde regarded Gerson as the author of *De modis*, for it was Dietrich of Niem who praised Marsilius and not Gerson.

More recently, Gerson and Marsilius have been brought into contact with each other by Marcel Pacaut and Paul de Vooght. Pacaut did so in a work of more general scope;[21] De Vooght in a highly controversial article on Gerson and Hus[22] as well as in his contribution to the symposium *Le concile et les conciles* of 1960.[23] De Vooght made it appear as if Gerson's ecclesiological ideas, like

---

[19] *Le grand schisme d'occident*, 121, 118 n. l, 299. Cf. Combes, *Jean de Montreuil*, 468ff.

[20] G. De Lagarde, *La naissance de l'esprit laïque au déclin du Moyen Age II. Marsile de Padoue ou le premier théoréticien de l'esprit laïque*, 1934, 328: 'Lorsque l'on voit un Gerson céder à cet engouement [pour le *Defensor pacis*] et reconnaître l'oeuvre comme une des meilleures qui soient, on se demande si l'impulsif chancelier de l'université de Paris avait bien pris la peine de lire son auteur.' (Cited by Martin, *Gallicanisme* II, 126 n.1). Although De Lagarde in the second ed. of his work (*La naissance* III, Louvain 1970, chap. XII 'Influence du Defensor', 358-77 (367)) is less outspoken about a supposed influence of Marsilius on Gerson, he concludes nevertheless: 'En somme, si, pour l'essentielle, Gerson rejette expressément les thèses marsiliennes, il a lu attentivement le *Defensor* et cette lecture a laissé quelques traces dans son ecclésiologie.' A really acrobatic 'tour de force': while De Lagarde declares in 1934 that Gerson – whom he calls, purely gratuitously, 'impulsive' – had not taken the trouble to read the *Defensor pacis*, he says in 1970 that he had studied it with care, which in both cases led to the same conclusion, namely that he was indebted to Marsilius!

[21] Marcel Pacaut, *La théocratie, L'église et le pouvoir au moyen âge*, Paris 1957, 200ff.

[22] 'L'ecclésiologie des adversaires de Huss au concile de Constance', *ETL* xxxv (1959), 5-24.

[23] 'Le conciliarisme à Constance et à Bâle', in: B. Botte, [e.a.], *Le concile et les conciles. Contribution à l'histoire de la vie conciliaire de l'église*, [s.l.] 1960, 143-81 (144 n. 2).

those of d'Ailly and Zabarella, differed in no way from those of Dietrich of Niem and Marsilius of Padua. Like Salembier, he regarded them as apologists of the doctrine of popular sovereignty in the Church, but he went even further by arguing:

> ... je ne crois pas que l'apport de Marsile de Padoue au conciliarisme puisse etre nié. On retrouve ses arguments chez Conrad de Gelnhausen, Henri de Langenstein, Gerson, d'Ailly, etc.[24]

This statement is impressive only in so far as it shows what we must understand by traditionalism in scholarship!

Yet it would be inaccurate to assume that no attempts have ever been made to free Gerson from the taint of Marsilianism. Victor Martin, for example, in his well known work *Les origines du Gallicanisme* of 1939, not only openly acknowledged that if Gerson had ever shown any sign of admiring Marsilius, it had escaped his, Martin's, notice, but he also pointed out that the Chancellor had implicitly denied Marsilian doctrines in several of his writings.[25] André Combes supported Martin[26] while John B. Morrall also denied any influence of the *Defensor Pacis* on Gerson.[27] Taking our cue from the arguments put forward by these scholars – almost all of which are based on indirect data – we wish to show that Gerson did in fact make explicit statements about Marsilius and formulated a verdict on him that left nothing to be desired in clarity.

The most important evidence about Marsilius is to be found in the *De iurisdictione spirituali et temporali*,[28] which we have tried to show must have been composed shortly before the sermon *Diligite iustitiam*. To a certain extent this curious work, to which we shall come back later, must be regarded as a continuous refutation of Marsilius

---

[24] *A.c.*, 144 n. 2. Cf. also De Vooght's global statement (152): '... l'essentiel de la doctrine conciliaire qui, d'une part, a été formulée avec une clarté croissante par les canonistes de Gratien à Zabarella et, d'autre part, descend de Marsile de Padoue par Conrad de Gelnhausen et Henri de Langenstein jusqu'à Gerson, d'Ailly et Théodore de Niem...' – Even in Delaruelle's fine work *L'Eglise au temps du grand schisme* I, 338 n. 12, ('Les débuts du Gallicanisme', 329-44), *De modis* is still attributed to Gerson, with farreaching consequences! See Bernstein, *D'Ailly and the Blanchard affair*, 182 n. 2!

[25] See above n. 22. Earlier, J.I. Sullivan, 'Marsiglio of Padua and William of Ockham', in *AHR* II, (1896-97), 409-26, 593-610: 'No work seems to have been used so much as the *Defensor Pacis*. On Gerson its influence cannot be traced.'

[26] Combes, *Jean de Montreuil*, 359 n. 1.

[27] Morrall, *Gerson*, 120: 'Still less can Gerson be accused of influence from Marsiglio of Padua'.

[28] Critical ed. in our *Jean Gerson et l'assemblée de Vincennes*, 121-36.

of Padua. True, Gerson was not directing his argument primarily against this heretic but against the socalled royalists, and their thesis of the relationship of Church and State, but that thesis agreed with Marsilius on so many points that it is hardly surprising to find his name cited explicitly:

> Notetur condemnatio in Padua specialiter in quinque articulis per Ioannem vicesimum secundum.[29]

This was not all, for Gerson also cited the condemnation of Marsilius and John of Jandun pronounced in the bull *Licet iuxta doctrinam* of 23 October 1327, *in pleno*.[30] That this was not merely a casual reference, but that he saw this judgement as having a normative value, is clear from the following passage taken from the *De auferibilitate sponsi* of 1408:

> Et oppositum sentientes de ecclesia quod scilicet fas est esse plures papas aut quod quilibet episcopus est in sua diocesi papa, vel pastor supremus aequalis papae romano, errant in fide et unitate ecclesiae, contra articulum illum *Et in unam sanctam* etc. Et si pertinaces maneant, iudicandi sunt haeretici, sicut Marsilius de Padua et quidam aliorum.[31]

Though this is enough to show that Gerson emphatically rejected Marsilius's view of the papal dignity, he made more than one protest against his thesis that Church and State were completely separate spheres, and that the Church ought to confine itself exclusively to spiritual matters – the soul and salvation – because everything else, such as law, power and property, belonged to the domain of the State. Gerson regarded this thesis as spiritualist; hence he was able to couple Marsilius's name with that of such heterogeneous figures as Wyclif or the Waldensians. We give an example:

> Ycy sont deux erreurs extremes; les ungs dient que gens d'Esglise, Pape ou autre, ne peuvent tenir quelconque temporalité ou juridiccion, sicut Padua et Wiclef. Les autres dient que les seigneurs terriens n'ont quelconque droit en temporalité...[32]

[29] *De iurisdictione spirituali et temporali* (ed. Posthumus Meyjes, 127).

[30] *De iurisdictione spirituali et temporali* (ed. Posthumus Meyjes, 128). Denzinger-Schönmetzer, *Enchiridion symbolorum*,[33] Friburgi Brisg. 1965, 941-6, p. 289-90.

[31] Gl. 3, 298-9; Dupin II, 213BC.

[32] *Pax hominibus* (Gl. 7*, 770; Dupin II 147A); cf. *Pax vobis* (Gl.5, 442; Dupin IV, 708A). See also Chapter VIII n. 68.

Apart from the conclusions at which we arrived in the previous chapters, we feel that the above is sufficient proof that any influence of Marsilius of Padua has to be ruled out.

2. *Ockham*

Much more complicated than the question of his alleged dependence on Marsilius of Padua is that of how far Gerson was influenced by Ockham (d. 1349). The greatest difficulty is that no received opinion of the theology, still less of the ecclesiology, of the *venerabilis inceptor* has yet been arrived at, and in all probability it will be long before it is; above all because the problems that this extremely acute Franciscan presents are numerous and often very intricate; secondly because the necessary basis for research, a critical edition, is still largely absent. For his chief ecclesiological work, the *Dialogus*, we are still dependent on the seventeenth century edition of Goldast, which was recently reprinted. The lack of a critical edition of this work is only very inadequately compensated for by recent editions of his *Breviloquium de principatu tyrannico*,[33] a much more accessible and concise work than the *Dialogus*, but one which, it seems, was unknown at the time with which we are concerned.[34] Gerson never made a single reference to it; nor did Pierre d'Ailly or Conrad of Gelnhausen, whose library is fortunately known to us.[35] Because Ockham's other writings on Church policy were much less widely known in France at this time than his *Dialogus*, it is with this work that we must begin.

As the title indicates, this book recounts a fictitious conversation between a *magister* and a *discipulus*, whose discussion was, to say the least, rather lengthy, since 500 folio pages were barely enough to record it. The *discipulus* put the questions, raised objections, and thus gave his master the opportunity to pronounce on the most various questions concerning the Church, its organisation and pol-

---

33 R. Scholz, *Wilhelm von Ockham als politischer Denker und sein Breviloquium de principatu tyrannico*, Stuttgart 1952.

34 Only one ms is known; cf. Ockham, *Breviloquium* (ed. Scholz), 29.

35 Conrad left his library to the young University of Heidelberg. G. Toepke, *Die Matrikel der Universität Heidelberg I*, Heidelberg 1884, 655ff., mentions the list of his books, which are now in the Vatican Library.

icy, its deeper nature and its relation to the State. The prologue explains the method of the work.[36] There the pupil asks his master to summarise as many different opinions as possible, but not to reveal his own opinion, nor to name the authorities he cites. The reason for this surprising request is that the pupil wishes to form his own opinion, and fears that he will be unable to do so if he has been given a hint of the preferences of his respected teacher. This method is also recommended to prevent the quest for truth being disturbed by passions of friend or foe. Anonymity is the way to stick to the point and the point alone.

The *Dialogus* is therefore in its plan a compilation, a sort of encyclopaedia of ecclesiology. Just as one may not hold the editors of an encyclopaedia responsible for the views of their contributors, one cannot simply assume that the views put forward by Ockham in the *Dialogus* were his own. How to identify his own views is a question in itself, which has to be answered in each case by comparison with other sources, e.g. the *Breviloquium*. Be this as it may, the fact is that not everything in the *Dialogus* can be regarded as Ockhamist *per se*. This also means that when the theologians of the conciliar epoch refer to this work, this does not necessarily imply that they were Ockhamists.

That they consulted this work frequently is as well known as it is understandable. No other work offered such an overwhelming wealth of views; no other work was better fitted to give advice in the perplexity to which the Schism had reduced the Church. But it was not only fourteenth and fifteenth century theologians who sought support in it. Modern scholars who have studied these theologians have exploited the work. For however obscure a pronouncement of one of their heroes might be, the *Dialogus* always offered a way out; and however strange a reasoning, it was found in Ockham too. Hence the name of Ockham appeared in the scholarly apparatus of many a publication, more often than it deserved, thus giving the impression not only that the *venerabilis inceptor* bestrode the field during the conciliar period, but that the conciliarists were all *homines unius libri*, incapable of practising theology on their own, that they spent their days poring over the *Dialogus* and then did no more than

---

[36] *Dialogus*, prol. (ed. Goldast, 398).

mechanically reproduce its arguments. This was certainly not the case, as Gerson can prove to us.

How far did Ockham influence Gerson? And may we say that Gerson's ecclesiology was 'Ockhamist'? The influence of the *venerabilis inceptor* was twofold: firstly direct, through Ockham's own works, and secondly indirect, via such Ockhamists as Pierre d'Ailly, Henry of Langenstein and Conrad of Gelnhausen. Confining ourselves for the moment to the direct influence, we can state that the explicit references to Ockham in Gerson's writings on ecclesiology and Church policy, in the broadest sense, are very few, not more than about fifteen. In itself this figure says little, for, as we have already said, Gerson was rather sparing in naming his authorities. On the other hand, it is remarkable that he should have named Bonaventure about fifty times.

What are we to make of these references? Firstly that, in all probability, Gerson only knew the following works of Ockham: the commentary on the sentences, the *Dialogus* and the treatise that was once regarded as part of it, *De dogmatibus Ioannis XXII*.[37] Leaving aside the commentary on the sentences, which is not cited in an ecclesiological context,[38] it seems that the *Dialogus* is the most frequently cited work, with seven references. Gerson first cited it, twice, in his *Resumpta* (1392),[39] then in his *De substractione oboedientiae* (1395)[40] and after that in the lecture *De vita spirituali animae* (1402),[41] at about the same time in the *De schismate*[42] and *De protestatione circa materiam fidei*,[43] and finally in the treatise *An liceat in causis fidei a papa appellare*.[44] It is not entirely certain, but it appears probable, that he also appealed to Ockham's *De dogmatibus Ioannis XXII* in the work known as *Replicationes*[45] and in his *Oportet haereses esse*.[46]

37 See L. Baudry, *Guillaume d'Ockham I, L'homme et l'oeuvre*, Paris 1950, 174ff.

38 *De vita spir. animae* (Gl. 3, 125-6; Dupin III, 14C). Cf. A. Combes, *Jean Gerson commentateur dionysien*, Paris 1940, 319 n. 5 (320).

39 Gl. 3, 4, 6; Dupin II, 263C, 265A; cf. *Dialogus* (ed. Goldast, 411-12).

40 Gl. 6, 22-3; Dupin II, 8. Cf. *Dialogus* (ed. Goldast, 456).

41 Gl. 3, 134-5; Dupin III, 21B. Cf. *Dialogus* (ed. Goldast, 411-12).

42 Gl. 6, 48; Dupin II, 21B. Cf. *Dialogus* (ed. Goldast, 439). Here he refers to Ockham but does not agree with him.

43 Gl. 6, 167; Dupin I, 37B. Cf. *Dialogus* (ed. Goldast, 456-7).

44 Gl. 6, 285; Dupin II, 305A. Cf. *Dialogus* (ed. Goldast, 521).

45 Gl. 6, 41-2; Dupin II, 13B. Cf. *De dogmatibus Ioannis XXII* (ed. Goldast, 752-60).

46 Gl. 5, 426, 434; Dupin II, 342D, 348C. Cf. *De dogmatibus Ioannis XXII* (ed. Goldast, 752-60, 755[22-31]).

The references show that in the first place he was aware of and emphatically agreed with Ockham's hierarchical classification of the truths of the faith. As we have seen, he took over this socalled catalogue of the faith and even devoted a whole treatise to it.[47] Secondly, he found support in Ockham for his initial view that a council was not the appropriate means to restore the unity of the Church. For the conflict was one about facts—in particular the conduct of elections—on which a council could not make an infallible pronouncement: '*in iis quae sunt facti fallere potest.*'[48] In the third place Ockham's expositions of the concepts of *determinatio, revocatio* and *protestatio* were significant for him. His *De protestatione circa materiam fidei* even seems to have been greatly inspired by Ockham's insights in this respect. Finally, Gerson tells us that he consulted Ockham's exposition of the question of whether an appeal to the council was lawful.[49]

If we survey all this, the harvest can only be described as scant, for except on the first and last points Gerson seems to have chosen Ockham as his guide chiefly in questions which were not of central importance for ecclesiology. This conclusion must be considered tentative, as long as we have not determined his relationship with the Ockhamists. Before we turn to them we wish to pause to consider one passage cited.

In a discussion of the right of appeal to a general council, Gerson says of Ockham:

> Hanc autem materiam latissime et studiosissime prosecutus est, et fundavit Ockham in Dialogo suo, cuius solius auctoritate non oportet inniti, quamvis fuerit egregius theologus, sed innitendum est rationibus suis, pro quanto robur et auctoritatem accipiunt a sacra scriptura, cuius contemptus, cum suis professoribus saepe duxit, et ducit in errores.[50]

Far from wishing to follow Ockham slavishly, this passage admirably proves that Gerson was well aware of his independence from him. Certainly he considered him an outstanding theologian, but that was by no means a reason to accept his word as law without putting it to the test. We can detect in this passage a protest against following Ockham exclusively. We know that Gerson had grave

---

[47] Gl. 6, 181-9; Dupin I, 22-8.
[48] Gl. 3, 6; Dupin II, 265A.
[49] *An liceat* (Gl. 6, 285; Dupin II, 305A).
[50] *An liceat* (Gl. 6, 285; Dupin II, 305A).

objections to such epigonism, and often warned his pupils against it; see his *Contra vanam curiositatem*, where he says in so many words that a theologian who stubbornly follows a single authority merely proves his own obstinacy.[51] And this warning applied even when the authority was no less than Ockham, so that we may conclude that he revered the *venerabilis inceptor*, but not blindly: *amicus Plato sed magis amica veritas.*

3. *The Ockhamists*

For convenience we include Pierre d'Ailly, Conrad of Gelnhausen and Henry of Langenstein under the heading of Ockhamists in this section, although it seems to us to be less certain than is often assumed that they can all be described as such in the strict sense. At any rate, as for Gerson, Ockham was by no means their only inspiration nor were they his uncritical admirers. Yet if one consults Salembier, Tschackert, Haller or Martin, one has the impression that d'Ailly in his *Resumpta* was already entirely following in the footsteps of the *venerabilis inceptor.* That is as inaccurate as the view that Conrad of Gelnhausen and Henry of Langenstein would not have had a leg to stand on without Ockham. We do not wish to deny that these authors had read Ockham and sometimes made intensive use of him, but to describe them as Ockhamists on those grounds alone would be to deny the eclecticism which is much more characteristic of their theology.

a. *Pierre d'Ailly*

The previous chapters have made it abundantly clear that Gerson kept up a very close and warm relationship with Pierre d'Ailly, his former teacher, throughout his life. In Church policy they shared many of the same views, although it seems that d'Ailly was able to retain his trust in Benedict XIII longer than Gerson, and also went

[51] Gl. 3, 239; Dupin I, 97D-98: 'Signum curiosae singularitatis est indebita doctorum et doctrinarum appropriatio. Si unus Dominus, una fides, una lex; si rursus veritas communis est, et a quocumque dicatur, a Spiritu sancto est, quorsum tendit haec animosa contentio apud diversos status et ordines christianorum, quod iste plus quam ille doctor ab istis et non illis defenditur, colitur, antefertur?' Cf. Chapter XI n. 80.

over to the *via concilii* before his pupil; the close intellectual bond between them is also shown by their numerous joint initiatives.

But Gerson's great respect for his former teacher did not prevent his taking a stand of his own, or mean that d'Ailly set the tone in everything. This holds true only, we think, for the domain of canon law. In that respect d'Ailly remained Gerson's teacher over the years. André Combes has shown that Gerson went his own way in his mystical views.[52] To a certain extent the same was true of his Church policy, indeed at times the relationship of master and pupil seems to be turned on its head, and it was Gerson who led and d'Ailly who followed. The finest example of this is offered by the *De concilio unius oboedientiae* of 1402. The authorship of this treatise was long in doubt. Dupin included it among Gerson's works but it appeared to be incorporated in one of d'Ailly's writings, so that it was assumed that he must be regarded as its author. However reasonable this assumption, it was incorrect for d'Ailly himself tells us that the work was by Gerson, while he also explains that he made use of it in composing the first part of his *De materia concilii generalis.* This solved the riddle of the authorship but at the same time proved a much more important fact, namely that the initiative was not always with the master but sometimes with his pupil. When we recall that Gerson's *De concilio unius oboedientiae* was a plea for nothing less than the ending of substraction and a return to obedience, this brings his independence of d'Ailly into even sharper relief.[53] Although this example chiefly concerns Church policy, we shall see that Gerson went his own way in ecclesiology as well.

b. *Conrad of Gelnhausen and Henry of Langenstein*

In previous chapters we made several references to Conrad of Gelnhausen and Henry of Langenstein, the earliest proponents of a conciliar solution to the Schism in France. Henry's treatise, the *Epistola concilii pacis*, seems to have been known to Gerson at quite an early stage, at least if we assume that a vague allusion in his

[52] *Jean Gerson commentateur dionysien*, 424-7. For the relationship between both, see in particular Max Lieberman, Chronologie gersonienne V., 'Gerson et d'Ailly', *Rom.* 78 (1957), 433-62; VI., 'Gerson ou d'Ailly', *Rom.* 79 (1958), 339-75; VII. 'Gerson et d'Ailly (II)', *Rom.* 80 (1959), 289-336; VIII., 'Gerson et d'Ailly (III)', *Rom.* 81 (1960), 44-98; also F. Oakley, 'Gerson and d'Ailly', *Speculum* 40 (1965), 74-83.

[53] See Appendix I.

Resumpta of 1392 refers to it.[54] That is all for the time being, for his other works before 1408 contain not a single hint that he had made any intensive study of Henry. This changed in 1408, when he came to look exclusively to the *via concilii* and composed no fewer than four works in defence of the Council of Pisa. After that date he referred to the two Germans several times[55] and we find evident traces of their works in his writings, as we have seen above.[56] We saw that he was particularly influenced by Conrad of Gelnhausen's *Epistola concordiae*, not only in its content but in its form as well. This lasted until 1409; after that the name of Conrad disappears from Gerson's works completely. The same applied to Henry of Langenstein, who is only named once more, and then in a non-ecclesiological context.[57]

This is not the place to go into Conrad's treatise in detail, but we must express our conviction that it would do him an injustice to represent him as if his secret intention was to overthrow the existing form of Church government and plead for a structure that was in conflict with the established tradition. He was convinced that the Schism was no mere quarrel about incidentals but nothing less than a *casus fidei*; and his intention was to return as quickly and efficiently as possible to the established and sanctified Church order, by way of a general council. There seems to us to be every reason to interpret his *Epistola concordiae* in this conservative sense.[58]

The idea of the *ecclesia universalis* was at the heart of Conrad's ecclesiology. What did he understand by it? It is the Church which finds in

---

[54] *De iurisdictione spirituali* (Gl. 3, 9; Dupin II, 267B). Here Gerson deals with the question of the legal validity of ordinations in the schismatic party. He refers to the view of 'Hassia', and says: 'Ita videtur tenere [Henricus de] Hassia' (= Henry of Langenstein). Cf. Henry's *Epistola concilii pacis*, c. 14 (Dupin II, 826-9).

[55] *Pro convocatione concilii Pisani* (Gl. 6, 124; Dupin II, 122C): 'Videatur tractatus praepositi Wormacensis (Conrad of Gelnhausen was provost of the chapter of Worms, and as such chancellor of the Heidelberg university) et tres considerationes suae. Item tractatus magistri de Hassia'. See also *Propositio facta coram Anglicis* (Gl. 6, 130; Dupin II, 126C) cited above, Chapter VI n. 51.

[56] See Chapter VI *passim*, and Chapter X, § 2.

[57] *De probatione spirituum* (Gl 9. 181; Dupin I, 40A): 'Hinc clarae memoriae magister Henricus de Hassia comprimendam esse tot hominum canonizationem scripsit'. Probably a reference to Henry's *De probatione spirituum*. From an historical point of view the study by Paschal Boland, *The Concept of Discretio Spirituum in Gerson's 'De Probatione Spirituum' and 'De Distinctione Verarum Visionum a Falsis'*, Washington 1959, is of no importance.

[58] *Epistola concordiae*, c.1 (ed. Bliemetzrieder, $116^{20\text{-}21}$; $119^{19\text{-}20}$)): 'adversus sacrosancta catholicae ecclesiae unitatem scisma a saeculo inauditum et perniciosissimum insurrexit... casus hodiernus est maximum casus fidei, eo quod tangit caput fidei in terris.'

> Christ its foundation, its head and its inspirer, and which as such is infallible and indestructible. This universal Church possesses and must possess, besides its *caput principale*, a *caput secundarium*, the Pope, who acts as *vicarius primi capitis Christi*.[59] The Vicar is head of the *ecclesia romana*, which is the head and symbol of the universal Church.[60] Distinguishing between the papacy and the Pope, the office and the person, Conrad argues that the first, which was instituted by Christ, – unlike the second, which is based on human election, – will never disappear. The papacy is indestructible but a Pope can be absent for a shorter or longer period, either by natural death or because he sins and falls from grace.[61] The Church is then led by Christ alone. It is even imaginable that the whole hierarchy could lapse and the Church would continue to exist in a single believer. This was the case of Mary after Jesus's death, when all the disciples had fled. Then the faith continued in her alone, just as the rights of a corporation can survive in an individual: *Ius universitatis in uno salvari potest*.[62]

What we have said about Conrad's ecclesiology applies equally to Henry of Langenstein, and Pierre d'Ailly. All three, like many others, drew a similar distinction between the *ecclesia universalis* and the *ecclesia romana*, and drew the same conclusions from it.[63] Leaving aside their indebtedness to one another, we can say categorically that these theories were not developed without the influence of Ockham. At various places in his *Dialogus* the *venerabilis inceptor's* thinking seems to have led him in this direction, in fact we may say that this distinction was an essential element of his ecclesiology. Let us examine it more closely.

---

59 *Epistola concordiae*, c. 3 (ed. Bliemetzrieder, 129^{10-41}).

60 *Epistola concordiae*, c. 3 (ed. Bliemetzrieder, 122^{19-26}).

61 *Epistola concordiae*, c. 3 (ed. Bliemetzrieder, $129^{20-2,39-42}$): 'sed illud caput potest quandoque simpliciter non esse, scilicet per mortem, quandoque secundum quid, scilicet a gratia deficiendo, licet papatus non moriatur ...; Papa vero est caput minus principale et secundarium quo deficiente, sive in esse naturae sive in esse gratiae, nihilominus corpus et membra vivunt, quamvis ex ordinatione divinam, eo cedente vel decedente, protinus de alio debet provideri.'

62 *Epistola concordiae*, c. 3 (ed. Bliemetzrieder, 129^{6-9}): 'unde fides Christi, cum omnes discipuli eo relicto fugerunt (Mc. 14), in sola virgine Maria salva creditur remansisse; nam et ius universitatis in uno salvari potest, ut notatur, de postu. prela. c. *Gratum* [= X 1.29.20].'

63 Henry of Langenstein, *Epistola concilii pacis*, c. 13 (Dupin II, 822C-6B); Pierre d'Ailly, *Utrum Petri ecclesia lege reguletur* (Dupin I, 666C). Cf. also Jean Courtecuisse, *Tractatus de fide* (Dupin II, 886C), and Dietrich of Niem, *De modis uniendi* (Dupin II, 189A): '... sicut enim universalis ecclesia potest salvari in minima vetula, sicut factum est tempore passionis Christi, quia est salva facta in virgine beata, sic ad salvationem universalis ecclesiae posset convocatio concilii fieri per minimam vetulam...'

In his youth Ockham did not distinguish between the *ecclesia romana* and the *ecclesia universalis*. Like some of the decretists, he regarded the latter as synonymous with the *universitas fidelium*, and the *ecclesia romana* as its head and infallible mouthpiece.[64] It had not yet occurred to him that there might be a discrepancy between the two or that the *ecclesia romana* could prove fallible and that he might live to see a Pope utter heretical doctrines.

The case was altered once there was a breach with the Pope, and Ockham put himself entirely at the service of the Franciscan ideal of poverty. He could no longer believe that the body which represented infallibility must self-evidently be identified with the Pope of Rome. Why not? In the first place because John XXII had deviated from the traditional line taken by his predecessors on a point which was vital for the Franciscan order, in the new constitutions he had proclaimed. Ockham felt that this had been a case of vanity, lack of theological skill and a false appeal to the Pope's plenitude of power, all signs that the Pope was to be regarded as a heretic.[65]

The consequence of all this was that Ockham now applied the promise of infallibility to the *ecclesia universalis* exclusively. By this he understood the Church at all times and places, both clergy and laity. This universal Church was led by the Holy Spirit, and therefore it could never lack the necessary means to salvation. It was to this Church that he applied the promise given to Peter: '... for you I have prayed that your faith may not fail' (Luke 22: 32), a text which he interpreted, following Augustine, in the sense that the faith of Peter stood for the faith of the Church.

He incorporated this idea in characteristic fashion by arguing that in the *ecclesia universalis* as a whole there was no office, no institution, no group or person which was exempt from the possibility of apostasy or guaranteed against the danger of heresy; Pope, cardinals, bishops, even councils could betray the faith. In fact it was even imaginable that they might all fall into heresy, apart from one person in whom the true faith would be maintained. The Spirit would then rest on that one person, and the infallibility of the Church would be embodied in him or her. History had given an example of this, for during Christ's passion on the cross, when all the disciples had fled, the faith had been embodied in one woman alone, Mary.[66]

---

[64] For the meaning of the term *ecclesia romana* in the canonists, see Tierney, *Foundations*, 36-46. For Ockham's use of the term, see J. Miethke, *Ockhams Weg zur Sozialphilosophie*, Berlin 1969, 289ff.

[65] For references see the present author's, 'Het gezag van de theologische doctor in de kerk der middeleeuwen – Gratianus, Augustinus Triumphus, Ockham, Gerson', *NAKG* 63 (1984), 102-28 (115 n. 21).

[66] Ockham voiced this idea in many places. See Miethke, *Ockhams Weg*, 539, n. 386. Cf. Y.M.-J. Congar, 'Incidence ecclésiologique d'un thème de dévotion mariale', *MSR*

Our interest is in how this concept of the Church is related to that of Gerson. It is striking, first of all, that he never used the idea of the *ecclesia universalis* in its specifically Ockhamist sense, but understood it in the purely traditional sense, as the Church spread throughout the whole world, that is as synonymous with the *ecclesia catholica*.[67] Secondly, he several times flatly rejected the consequences which Henry of Langenstein, Conrad of Gelnhausen, Pierre d'Ailly and others, following Ockham, had drawn from the concept of the *ecclesia universalis*. Repeatedly and emphatically he denied the idea that the rights of the community could be preserved in one person – *ius universitatis in uno salvari potest* – and the Mariological application of this principle, because of the laicist implications which were threatened by it. He called it an unthinkable idea that the Church might ever be found in a single woman, all women or in the laity alone.[68] Why? Because that would mean that the Church could do without the hierarchy and consequently without the sacraments.

In so many words he says that a Church which was not built on the hierarchy and the sacraments could only exist if God were to revoke his original decision and resolve on a completely new dispensation. For him that was a purely speculative assumption, which could only be imagined *de potentia Dei absoluta*. His central conviction, however, was and remained that God, in the present dispensation – *de potentia ordinata, lege stante* – had called the Church into being as an hierarchical body and that Christ continued to lead it through his Spirit, by exercising an influence on it through the hierarchical offices and dignities which had been established at the same time

8 (1951) 277-92, and K. Binder, *Wesen und Eigenschaften der Kirche bei Kardinal Juan de Torquemada, O.P.*, Innsbruck 1955, 116-9.

[67] Cf. *De auctoritate concilii*, art. 5, concl. 4 and art. 10, concl. 6 (Gl. 6, 120): 'Ecclesia catholica et universalis per totum orbem diffusa'. See also Chapter X n. 23.

[68] *De auferib.*, cons. 7 (Gl. 3, 297; Dupin II, 213): 'Auferibilis non est sponsus Ecclesiae Christus ab Ecclesia sponsa sua et filius eius, sic quod remaneat Ecclesia in sola muliere, immo nec in solis mulieribus omnibus, immo nec in laicis solis, *lege stante et non facta divinitus nova institutione*.' In the context of the Jean Petit affair, Gerson fell into a vehement argument with the Bishop of Arras, Martin Porrée. In his treatise against Gerson (Gl. 10, 220-5 (221); Dupin V, 439-44 (440B), Porrée reproached him for this statement as follows: 'Haec assertio videtur temeraria et erronea ac scandalosa fidei pietati qua creditur in sola beatissima Virgine triduo remansisse passionis et per consequens Ecclesia'. In his *Summaria responsio* (Gl. 10, 227; Dupin V, 447B) Gerson repeated his assertion and called it 'vera et catholica'.

as the Church. For that reason it would continue to exist in its hierarchical form until the end of time, and would never be reduced to a single believer.

> Congregatio ecclesiastica ad unum caput Christum, lege stante, non remanebit in sola muliere, immo nec in solis laicis, sed erunt usque ad consummationem saeculi episcopi et sacerdotes aliqui fideles.[69]

Another point on which Gerson distanced himself from the Ockhamists, especially from Henry of Langenstein, concerned the origin of the primacy. In his *Epistola concilii pacis* Henry had argued that although Christ, according to the Scriptures, had chosen one of the apostles, Peter, as Vicar-General of the militant Church, the various ways in which Peter's successors had been elected justified the conclusion that if Christ had not done so himself, the Church would have been entitled to choose an earthly Head for itself.[70] From the very beginning of his academic career Gerson was fascinated by this pronouncement of Henry, and though he passed varying judgments on it at various times, some mild, some strict, he ended by rejecting it absolutely:

> Falsa est assertio de Hassia in qua dicit, quod esto Christum nullum discipulorum constituisset sibi generale vicarium, ecclesia catholica habuisset potestatem talem constituendi.[71]

What Gerson had in mind here was that the primacy, like the entire hierarchical order of the Church, went back to a supernatural institution and therefore could never have been instituted by the Church itself. He knew that he was supported by the judgement of the doctors of the Church on this point.[72]

To resume, we can say that the explicit references to theologians described as Ockhamists show that Gerson was unwilling to go all the way with them, and that he sometimes took a different view on fundamental issues. In spite of his esteem for them, he was always aware of his independence from them, an independence which came to the fore whenever he felt that the idea of the hierarchy was

---

69 *Propositio coram Anglicis*, ver. 6 (Gl. 6, 132; Dupin II, 128B).
70 *Epistola concilii pacis*, c. 14, II 826BC.
71 See above note 56. Also *De auferibilitate* (Gl. 3, 298-9; Dupin II, 213-13A).
72 *De auferibilitate* (Gl. 3, 298; Dupin II, 213A): 'Nec opinor quod aliquis doctorum theologorum senserit in hac contrarie.'

being depreciated. Precisely because d'Ailly and Gerson are so often named in the same breath and almost regarded as interchangeable, it is worth pointing out explicitly that Gerson distinguished himself from his teacher in his strictly hierarchical view of the Church.

4. *John of Paris*

Although Gerson never mentions John of Paris by name, there are two reasons to assume that he knew his work *De regia potestate et papali*:[73] firstly because John of Paris played an important role in the history of conciliar thought; secondly because a contemporary and friend of Gerson, the Viennese theologian Nicolas of Dinkelsbühl (1360-1433), tells us that he had heard Gerson was greatly influenced by John of Paris. In a Viennese manuscript collection of ecclesiological works, one of many known from the time, Nicolas wrote after Gerson's *De potestate ecclesiastica* and before the treatise of John of Paris, the following remark:

> Sequitur tractatus bonus de sacerdotio et regno et multa bona circa ista tractantur in sequentibus, quem composuit, ut audivi, quidam magister Parysiensis et ex quo precedens tractatus in magna parte est tractus.[74]

We must doubt the accuracy of this verdict, even though it was passed by a contemporary, and wish to defend the thesis that if there was a connection between Gerson and John of Paris, it was not direct but indirect and came about through Pierre d'Ailly.

That d'Ailly made extensive—one is inclined to say even plagiaristic—use of the *De regia potestate et papali*, without acknowledging his source, was first shown by Tschackert in the last century, and has only been confirmed by others since.[75] In his *De materia concilii*

---

[73] Fritz Bleienstein, *Johannes Quidort von Paris. Ueber königliche und papstliche Gewalt (De regia potestate et papali)*, Stuttgart [1969].

[74] Bibl. Vienna lat. 3954, fol. 290vo, cited by H. Finke, *Aus den Tagen Bonifaz VIII*, Münster i.W. 1902, 172 n. 1. See also the marginal annotation in BN lat. 4364, fol. 18vo. col. 2, cited by Scholz, *Publizistik*, 309 n. 101, and 332: 'Die engen Beziehungen zwischen den Traktate Johannes von Paris und den Werken Gersons ... sind bereits den Zeitgenossen wiederholt aufgefallen.'

[75] Tschackert, *Peter von Ailli*, Beilage VI: 'Ailli's Verhältnis zu Johann von Paris,' 376; J. Leclercq, *Jean de Paris et l'ecclésiologie du XIIIe siècle*, Paris 1942, 154-5; Oakley, *Political*

generalis of 1403 and in his *De ecclesiae auctoritate*, written during the Council of Constance, long passages are taken from John of Paris, often verbatim. As we saw repeatedly in previous chapters, Gerson was very familiar with both works of his teacher.

But if we compare Gerson's own works with the *De regia potestate*, we arrive at a different conclusion. There is no question of verbatim quotations, while agreements in the treatment of important concepts and ideas such as *dominium*[76] and *regnum*,[77] or the idea of the Pope as the *dispensator*, are as absent as any obvious link between their views on the nature and composition of a council.[78] In fact, if we look at it aright there is only one point on which we might hesitate, and that is the distinction of monarchy, aristocracy and democracy which both apply to the Church.

This distinction was developed by Aristotle in the third chapter of his *Politics*. In view of the enormous popularity of this work since 1250 and the increasing tendency to apply Aristotelian principles in theology, it is not surprising that the threefold distinction should be found in many political treatises. Most of these authors followed Aristotle in recommending a mixed polity as the most ideal.

That was the case of Aquinas, for example. He felt that the best form of (secular) government was a combination—*regnum mixtum*—of monarchy, aristocracy and democracy.[79] Giles of Rome urged the same argument in his very influential *De regimine principum*,[80] which Gerson praised.[81] We find the threefold distinction in John of Paris

Thought, 49-51 and index s.v. 'John of Paris'. Oakley's account of the influence of John of Paris on Pierre d'Ailly is incomplete.

76 See below n. 97.

77 Unlike John of Paris, who in his definition of the term *regnum* followed Aquinas very closely (cf. Congar, *Die Lehre von der Kirche*, 183ff.), Gerson was much closer to Augustine, as is shown, for example, in his sermon *Dedit illi gloriam* (Gl. 5, 184-5; Dupin III, 1453C-4C).

78 John of Paris, *De reg. pot.*, cap. 25 (ed. Bleienstein, 192-5). He says nothing about the composition of a council. Cf. Bleienstein, Introduction, 31: '... die Frage der Stellung des Generalkonzils [wird] nicht systematisch und ausdrücklich behandelt, sondern mehr nebenher aufgeworfen.'

79 *S.Th.* I^{a}, 2^{ae} q. 105 a. 1. in corp.

80 Scholz in his introduction to Giles of Rome's *De ecclesiastica potestate*, xii, n. 5 : 'Welches fast kanonische Ansehen Aegidius im 14. Jh. als politischer Denker genoss, zeigt besonders deutlich, dass der grösste Jurist der Zeit, Bartolus von Sassoferrato, der Untersuchung über die beste Regierungsform nicht Aristoteles, sondern der Traktat des Aegidius De Regimine Principum zugrunde legt, weil er klarer sei; Bartolus, De Regimine Civitatis, § 7.'

81 Giles's treatise is mentioned in the sermon *Ave Maria—Je te salue Marie* (Gl. 7, 546;

as well. Directly following his fellow-Dominican Thomas Aquinas, he defends the mixed form of government as the best and applies the idea to the Church (was he the first to do so?).[82] D'Ailly and Gerson did so too, which raises the question: did they owe it to John of Paris? D'Ailly certainly did, but what of Gerson?

Gerson repeatedly applied Aristotle's threefold classification both to the State and the Church. To confine ourselves to the latter, the first point that strikes us is that his statements, although they do not excel in clarity, agree with one another to the extent that they always emphasise two points: 1. the strict necessity that the Church should be under the monarchical rule of the Pope; but 2. that the Pope should not exercise his power at the expense of the responsibility borne by the other hierarchical representatives for the welfare of the Church.[83] In other words, Gerson puts this triple distinction at the service of his view on the disseminated responsibility of the hierarchy – *latitudo* –, thus giving it an anti-absolutist point.

This is most clearly expressed in his statements referring to a general council.[84] In these the point is always that the Pope must not

---

Dupin III, 1370B); *Vivat Rex* (Gl. 7*, 1168; Dupin IV, 608A), and in the letter inc. *Claro eruditori* (Gl. 2, 213; Dupin III, 23B). Cf. Schäfer, *Die Staatslehre des Johannes Gerson*, 87-8.

[82] John of Paris, *De regia potestate*, c. 19 (ed. Bleienstein, 175[8-19]): 'Et tale erat regimen a Deo optime institutum, in populo illo, quia erat regale in quantum unus singulariter praeerat omnibus, ut Moyses vel Josue; erat etiam alioquid de aristocratia, quae est principatus aliquorum optimorum principantium secundum virtutem, in quantum sub illo uno septuaginta duo eligebantur seniores (Deut. 1: 15); erat etiam aliquid de democratia, id est principatu populi, in quantum omnes in regimine illo aliquam habebant partem. Sic certe esset optimum regimen ecclesiae, si sub uno papae eligerentur plures ab omni provincia et de omni provincia, ut sic in regimine ecclesiae omnes aliquo modo haberent partem suam.'

[83] *De pot.eccl.*, cons. 8 (Gl. 6, 225; Dupin II, 237C). 'Teneatur ergo suum iudicium et maneat ecclesiastica politia optimo regimine quale fuit sub Moyse gubernata; quoniam mixta fuit ex triplice politia: regali sub Moyse, aristocratica in lxxii senioribus, et timocratica dum de populo et singulis tribubus sub Moyse rectores sumebantur.'

[84] *De statibus ecclesiasticis*, super statu summi pont. cons. 2 (Gl. 9, 26; Dupin II, 530B): '... praesideat assidue unicus et certus summus pontifex quantum fieri potest ...; sic quod non est licitum scienter impedire quominus sit unus talis ecclesiasticae potestatis plenitudo; et quod non sint plures ex aequo, tamquam ecclesiasticum regimen desinere esse posset monarchicum, et in aliam politiae speciem, ut in aristocraticam aut in tymocratiam verteretur, quamvis papatus has politiarum species non excludat, sed assumat, quemadmodum de sacro dominorum cardinalium collegio, et de generali concilio videre est.' *De pot. eccles*, cons. 13 (Gl. 6, 246; Dupin II, 254D): 'Possumus conformiter ad praedictam Philosophi politiam tripliciter distinctam in naturali regimine, politiam ecclesiasticam dividere, quod alia est papalis, alia collegialis, alia synodalis seu concilii generalis. Papalis imitatur regalem; collegialis dominorum cardinalium imitatur aristo-

exercise his power autocratically, but in discussion and collaboration with all the hierarchical dignitaries represented at the council. Behind this lies the conviction that not the highest hierarch alone but the hierarchy as a whole, is under the direct inspiration of the Holy Spirit.

> Esset verum omnium optima et saluberrima politia quae triplicem hanc bonam complecteretur, regalem, aristocratiam et timocratiam. Est enim concilium generale politia talis composita, habens suam directionem magis ex assistentia speciali Spiritus Sancti et promissione Iesu Christi (Mt. 28: 20), quam ex natura vel sola humana industria.

Gerson introduces this statement by an analogy, in which he compares the relationship of Pope and hierarchy (or council) with that between the King of France and his *parlement*:

> Esset autem inter istas politias illa melior quam aliqua singularis, quae ex regali et aristocratia componeretur, ut in regno Franciae, ubi rex instituit parlamentum a quo iudicari non refugit.[85]

It is because of this analogy in particular that we believe that Gerson borrowed his application of Aristotle's triple classification to the Church from Pierre d'Ailly rather than from John of Paris. For John does not connect the distinction with the composition of a general council, nor does he use this analogy with the King of France and his *parlement*, as d'Ailly does. D'Ailly in fact urges the same analogy twice, in identical terms, in his writings.[86] On both occasions the context is an argument that in certain cases a general council can act against a Pope.

To grasp the meaning of the analogy it should be realised that the *parlement* at the time was not the body which represented the three estates (clergy, nobility, third estate), for France possessed the Estates General for that. The *parlement* in Gerson's day was France's supreme Law Court, and the analogy is to be regarded as an *exemplum*. Its sense is that just as the King of France is called on to bear

---

cratiam; synodalis imitatur politiam seu timocratiam; vel potius est perfecta politia quae resultat ex omnibus.'

[85] *Prosperum iter* (Gl. 5, 478-9; Dupin II, 279B).

[86] D'Ailly, *De materia* (ed. Oakley, 304): 'Nam rex Franciae qui est maior et superior in toto regno, saepe in aliquibus casibus iudicatur, et contra eum fertur sententia in suo parlamento. Similiter papa in foro conscientiae a simplici sacerdote iudicatur. Etiam in foro exteriori potest iudicari ab inferiori suo, si se et sponte subiiciat ...'. Cf. d'Ailly, *De eccl. auct.* (Dupin II, 957B), and Oakley, *Political Thought*, 53 and 123.

responsibility, together with the members of his *parlement*,[87] for the maintenance of justice in his realm, so the Pope *together with the other members of the hierarchy*, is responsible for the protection of the divine truth in the world. If the King or the Pope should refuse to listen to the *parlement* or to the general council, respectively, and this is to the detriment of State or Church, then it is lawful to correct them and take action against them. It is against the same 'parlementary' background that both decrees *Haec sancta* and *Frequens* should be considered.[88]

To summarise, we conclude that if is still maintained that Gerson was dependent on John of Paris, this influence was not very deep. The fact that both men used Aristotle's threefold distinction of forms of government and applied it to the Church, is no proof of direct dependence. It is much more likely that the agreement came about indirectly via the works of Pierre d'Ailly.[89]

***

Our results so far have been rather negative, for we found that a direct influence of Marsilius of Padua had to be ruled out completely, a direct influence of John of Paris was very unlikely, and the significance of Ockham and his followers was no more than limited. Gerson differed from Marsilius and Ockham in his deep-

---

[87] The members of the *parlement* were called 'pars corporis Regis.' Cf. F. Aubert, *Le Parlement de Paris de Philippe-le-Bel à Charles VII (1314-1422. Son organisation)*, Paris 1886, 141 n. 3.

[88] Cf. Brandmüller, *Das Konzil von Konstanz*, 353 n. 118. Cf. Jedin, 'Bischöfliches Konzil oder Kirchenparlement?', in: *Die Entwicklung des Konziliarismus*, 221: 'Wenn man mit der ersten Aussage des Dekrets «Haec sancta», dass das allgemeine Konzil die universale Kirche gegenwärtig setzt, ernst macht, dann wäre auch die Periodizität der Konzilien durchaus denkbar, ohne dass durch sie die hierarchische Struktur der Kirche und das ordentliche Lehramt des Papstes in Frage gestellt würde; in Gegenteil: regelmässige Versammlungen des Episkopates ... unter Leitung seines Hauptes könnten die innere Konsistenz der kirchlichen Ordnung festigen, den Austausch zwischen Haupt und Gliedern fördern und der Gesetzgebung wie der Verwaltung grössere Elastizität verleihen...' See also Chapter IX n. 127.

[89] The same holds true, we think, for the question if Gerson was influenced by William Durant the Younger. He never cites Durant's *Tractatus de modo generalis concilii celebrandi*, but it might be that certain proposals uttered in this work have reached him through d'Ailly. Cf. Constantin Fasolt, *Council and Hierarchy. The Political Thought of William Durant the Younger*, Cambridge [1991], index s.v. 'Ailly, Pierre d''.

rooted hierarchical conviction, a conviction which cannot be separated from his pseudo-Dionysian preferences. This explains why, even when the Schism was most desperate, he never felt any enthusiasm for a solution which would have weakened the idea of the hierarchy and thus of the sacramental essence of the Church. Now we must trace the way in which he developed his ecclesiological thought, while remaining loyal to his pseudo-Dionysian idea of the Church; how he gave concrete form to it; and in particular, who helped him in this.

To answer these questions we start with a letter which Gerson wrote on 29 April 1400, from Bruges, to his younger friends at the College of Navarre. Speaking of theological studies, he advised them to consult in the first place the commentaries on the sentences, above all those of the doctors who had been the purest and most solid compilers of such works. He continued:

> inter quales, meo iudicio, dominus Bonaventura et sanctus Thomas et Durandus videntur numerandi, excellit quibus in suis quodlibetis Henricus de Gandavo.[90]

Passing over Thomas, whose influence on Gerson was considerable chiefly in the field of moral theology,[91] we shall now attempt to identify the contributions of Bonaventure, Durand of St Pourçain and Henry of Ghent to his ecclesiology.

5. *Bonaventure*

No theologian meant more to Gerson than the *doctor seraphicus*, Bonaventure; for no other did he feel such an affinity. The great reverence for tradition which he found in Bonaventure, the balanced mildness of his judgement, his ideas about poverty, and the affective tendency of his mystical and hierarchical thought,[92] were in complete harmony with his own aspirations. Bonaventure was his ideal; his *Breviloquium* and *Itinerarium mentis in Deum* were among his

---

90 Letter inc. *Jucundum est* (Gl. 2, 33; Dupin I, 108B).

91 In his letter inc. *Scriptum est* (Gl. 2, 112; not in Dupin) he recommends Thomas's *Summa* II^a II^{ae}.

92 J.G. Bougerol, 'Saint Bonaventure et la hiérarchie Dionysienne', *AHDLM* 36 (1969), 131-67.

best loved books.[93] He considered these two short works excellent introductions to theology, comparable to Petrus Hispanus's textbook of logic and Donatus' grammar.[94] He found the *Itinerarium* above all praise and was astonished that his Franciscan contemporaries–Jean de Ripa!–should pass over the author of this work, for, he asked, 'had the University of Paris ever had a greater teacher?'[95]

Now it is a remarkable fact that in spite of his deep admiration for the 'divine' Bonaventure, – an eloquent sign of which is to be found in about fifty references to his works – Gerson named him rather infrequently in an ecclesiological context. This is surprising but explicable. Gerson found little in Bonaventure – or in Thomas – which he could use to solve the problem that faced him and his contemporaries: the Schism. This was not because the two scholastics had said nothing about the *casus schismaticus*, but because their arguments were not sufficiently developed to offer a way out of the highly complicated Western Schism. This was no reproach to Bonaventure or Thomas, for how could they have foreseen that around a hundred years after their death the Church would be faced by such a crisis, a crisis which contemporaries rightly saw as a *casus novus et inauditus*? In our opinion the specific case of the Western Schism explains why Gerson referred so rarely to them in questions of church politics. He simply could not find a point of contact in them; his guides failed him in this and their influence therefore had to remain in the background.

This is neatly confirmed by a statement he made in one of his sermons preached at Constance. Dealing with the *plenitudo potestatis* of the Pope, Gerson cited both Thomas and Bonaventure, pointing

---

[93] For Gerson's verdict on Bonaventure see *Contra curiositatem* (Gl. 3, 231, 240-1; Dupin I 91D, 99C); *De examinatione doctrinarum* (Gl. 9, 475; Dupin I, 21B): 'Porro si quaeratur a me, quis inter caeteros doctores plus videatur idoneus, respondeo sine praeiudicio, quod dominus Bonaventura, quoniam in docendo solidius et securius, pius insuper, iustus et devotus... recedit a curiositate quantum potest;... dum studet illuminationi intellectus, totum refert ad pietatem et religiositatem...'; and, above all, his letter inc. *Ignem veni mittere* to a Franciscan (1426) (Gl. 2, 276-80): a hymn of praise to the theology of Bonaventure. Cf. P. Glorieux, 'Gerson et S. Bonaventure', in: *S. Bonaventura. 1274-1974* IV, Grottaferrata / Rome 1974, 773-91.

[94] *De examinatione doctrinarum* (Gl. 9, 475; Dupin I, 21C).

[95] *Contra curiositatem* (Gl. 3, 231; Dupin I, 91D): '... qui libellus [sc. *Itinerarium*] omni laude superior est. Nec admirari sufficio qualiter patres et fratres minores dimisso tanto doctore, qualem nescio si umquam Studium Parisiense habuerit, converterunt se ad nescio quos novellos, pro quibus parati sunt pedibus et manibus decertare; tandem quantum in aliis proficiant, ipsi viderint...'

out that they had quite rightly attributed the highest authority in the Church to the Pope. In his opinion they had been led to this view because they had compared the position of the Pope with that of the faithful, or the local churches. But, he continues, if Thomas and Bonaventure had compared the papal *potestas* with the assembled Church, they would have reached another conclusion:

> Dum autem comparatio facienda fuisset ad auctoritatem ecclesiae synodaliter congregatae, subiecissent [sc. Thomas et Bonaventura] papam et usum potestatis suae eidem ecclesiae, tamquam matri suae.[96]

The *modus hypotheticus* which Gerson employs here proves that the men by whom he preferred to set his course had not addressed the central question of the Schism, the relationship of Pope and hierarchy, clearly enough for him to find in them the support he needed. Hence, he could hardly do anything but resort to conjecture.

In his ecclesiological works Gerson appealed to Bonaventure's commentary on the sentences more than once, or chose the distinctions elaborated there as the starting point of his own reasoning. For example in his *De vita spirituali animae*, he took up Bonaventure's argument when he came to explain the crucial conception of *dominium*. Gerson borrowed the distinction of *natura instituta, destituta, restituta* and *glorificata* from Bonaventure and used it to form the basis of his fourfold division of the idea of *dominium*.[97]

In the same work he appealed to the *Itinerarium* to substantiate his view on the relationship of divine and human reason.[98] He cited Bonaventure again in his *De auferibilitate sponsi* and in the closely related work, the *De potestate ecclesiastica*,[99] to confirm his thesis that the episcopate did not form a special *ordo* above the priesthood.

> Bonaventura ... quaerit si episcopatus sit ordo supra sacerdotium, et ponit quod neque episicopatus neque papatus dicit nisi plenitudinem aliquam vel dignitatem in ordine, et ordinem novum nullum addit.[100]

---

96 *Nuptiae factae sunt* (Gl. 5, 385; Dupin II, 355CD).

97 Cf. *De vita spir. animae*, lect. 3 (Gl. 3, 145-6; Dupin III, 29A) and Bonaventure, *Comm. in l.s.*, II d. 44 a. 2 q. 2 n. 4.

98 *De vita spir. animae*, lect. 2 (Gl. 3, 136-7; Dupin III, 22CD); cf. Bonaventure, *Itinerarium*, c. III 4.

99 *De pot. eccl.*, cons. 3 (Gl. 6, 214; Dupin II, 227D).

100 *De auferibilitate*, cons. 15 (Gl. 3, 306; Dupin II, 219C, 220B). Cf. Bonaventure, *Comm. in lib. sent.*, IV d. 25.

Moreover he appealed to Bonaventure when he turned to challenge Wyclif, who had upheld the Donatist view that the validity of the exercise of an office depended on the personal sanctity of the office holder.

Passing over less important references, we can state that the special circumstances of the Schism explain why the *doctor seraphicus* was cited less often than we might expect, given Gerson's tremendous admiration for him. The scanty references are, however, sufficient to show that he always had Bonaventure in mind, if not on his desk, and as far as possible continued to set his course by him.

6. *Durand of St Pourçain*

Gerson recommended the commentary on the sentences by Durand of St Pourçain to his young friends at the College of Navarre because it was his opinion that this Dominican, the *doctor modernus*, had been a solid theologian. One could build on him. For Gerson, this meant that Durand was clear and impartial in his judgements and did not defend extreme theses. Before we examine whether and how far he made use of Durand's ecclesiology in his own work, we must first ask who Durand was.

Born around 1270, Durand belonged to the second generation of Dominicans after Thomas.[101] He is first heard of in 1303 at the monastery of St Jacques in Paris, where he gained the degree of *magister theologiae* at the University in 1312. He rose in the hierarchy of the Church; after successfully completing a diplomatic mission for Pope John XXII he was rewarded with the bishopric of Limoux, which he exchanged later the same year for that of Le Puy-en-Velay and then again for Meaux, where he died in 1334. He was a member of the commission which censured fifty one articles taken from Ockham's commentary on the sentences. In his ecclesiology he was a defender of the papalist standpoint.

Though Durand was highly regarded by the curia, he caused some commotion in his order. He was an independent thinker who was inclined to believe that – where an article of faith was not in question – one must rely on reason rather than on the authority of

---

[101] On Durand: J. Koch, *Durandus a S. Porciano*, Münster 1927.

even the most distinguished doctor. That was not welcome to the order. 'Le seul tort de Durand aux yeux de son ordre semble de n'avoir pas été thomiste, et de l'avoir manifesté à une époque où Saint Thomas en était déjà le Docteur officiel'.[102] The result of this discontent with his order was that three redactions of his commentary on the sentences were published. We choose to start with the last of them.

We have been able to find about twenty direct references to Durand's commentary in Gerson's whole oeuvre, fourteen of them in his ecclesiological works alone. These figures are given with great reservations, because passages may have been overlooked. What can we make of them? In the first place, that since 1394 Gerson had studied Durand intensively; and secondly that he consulted, for preference, above all the third and fourth books of the commentary, and was therefore interested chiefly in Durand's doctrine of the incarnation and the sacraments, and related questions.

Gerson referred to Durand on many and varied points, some central, others marginal. We cannot go into all of them in detail but we may remark in passing that he let himself be guided by Durand in questions of christology,[103] angelology,[104] the doctrine of sin,[105] the nature of the *praecepta*,[106] and the right of reservation,[107] among other topics. We can say that his influence was broad; confining ourselves to ecclesiology, we must now examine its depth.

On both the right of reservation and the doctrine of the *praecepta* – both points of only incidental importance for ecclesiology – Gerson appears to have shared many of Durand's views. He re-

---

[102] E. Gilson, *La philosophie au moyen âge*², Paris 1952, 623.

[103] *Pax vobis* (Gl. 7*, 786; Dupin III, 1209B) – cf. Durand, *Comm. in lib. sent. III*, d.3 q.4 (?) (fol. 225vo-6ro); *Puer natus est* (Gl. 7*, 959; Dupin III, 944C) – cf. Durand, *Comm.in lib. sent. III*, d.12 q.3 (fol. 234vo-5ro); *Vade in domum tuam* (Gl. 5, 565; Dupin III, 1294A) – cf. Durand, *Comm. in lib.sent. III*, d. 9 q.5 ad sec. (fol. 269vob).

[104] *Factum est proelium* (Gl. 5, 315; Dupin III, 1484D) – cf. Durand, *Comm.in l.s. II*, d.7 q.3 (5) (fol. 146ro).

[105] *De vita spir. animae* (Gl. 3, 132; Dupin III, 19B) – cf. Durand, *Comm. in l.s.* III, d.25 q.1. ad 1 (fol. 258ro).

[106] *De vita contemplativa* (Gl. 3, 65; Dupin IV, 219B), and *De vita spir. animae*, lect.4, corr.1 (Gl. 3, 158; Dupin III, 8D-9) – cf. Durand, *Comm. in l.s. IV*, d.17 q.8 (fol. 342ro). See L. Vereecke, 'Droit et morale chez Jean Gerson', *RHDF* 4 série 32 (1954), 413-27, and by the same author, *Conscience morale et loi humaine selon Gabriel Vazquez S.J.*, [Paris etc. 1957], 9-32; 111-25.

[107] See also his letter-treatise to an unknown bishop inc. *Pastoralis auctoritas*, *Super moderatione casuum reservandorum* (Gl. 2, b 90-3; Dupin II, 415-17).

garded him as an expert in matters of reservation, recognising his own limits in Durand's inability to solve certain problems in this connection. He fully agreed with Durand that the right of reservation had to be kept for irregular cases, and hence that the papal plenitude of power could only exceptionally be used to the detriment of the lower organs in the hierarchy.[108] Just as this betrays clear signs of an anti-absolutist tendency, so we find indications that in the doctrine of the *praecepta* too, it was thanks to Durand that Gerson steered well clear of an absolutist extremism in which the boundaries between *forum internum* and *forum externum* were erased.[109]

Much more important than these points, it appears from passages in his *De vita spirituali animae* that he also followed Durand in his view of the greater authority value that had belonged to the primitive Church. Dealing with the concept of *lex divina*, and using Ockham's catalogue of the faith to give it meaning, he identified as the fourth class of divine laws those which had been specially revealed and divulged to particular people for their own benefit or that of a limited number of the elect. Exactly who he had in mind – the great names of sacred history the great names in the history of the Church – is not clear, but it is a fact that he he made no mention of the history of the Church in his exposition but spoke only of the age of the apostles, that is of sacred history. The direct contact of the apostles with Christ; the fact that they had been eye-witnesses of his acts; that Peter had received the keys from his hands and had been instructed in the truths of the faith by the Holy Spirit at Pentecost – all these unrepeated events gave the apostles, that is the primitive Church, a higher authority than their successors in the later Church.

---

[108] *Si non lavero te* (Gl. 5, 506-7; Dupin II, 511A), and *De vita contemplativa* (Gl. 3, 65; Dupin IV, 219A): 'Obiecitur iterum de illo quem in mortis articulo absolvit simplex sacerdos super casibus papae reservatis ... Fateor hic cum Durando... involutissimam et vix enodabilem tangi materiam.' – cf. Durand, *Comm. in l.s. IV*, d.18 q.15 (13) (fol. 345[ro]).

[109] *De vita contemplativa* (Gl. 3, 65; Dupin IV, 219B): 'Aliud fundamentum tangit Durandus... Supponit itaque pro regula, quod numquam praelatus ecclesiae vel alius iudex potest circa illud praeceptum iubere nisi circa illud quod ad forum suum publicum potest deduci si non fiat; alioquin potest praelatus ferre praecepta super occultissimis cogitationibus sibi remediandis ...' – cf. Durand, *Comm. in lib. sent. IV*, d.17 q.8 (7) (fol. 348[ro]).

'*Hanc materiam tractat Durandus*'[110] Gerson concludes in his exposition, referring to the third book of Durand's commentary on the sentences, dist. 24 q. 1: '*Utrum Deus sit obiectum fidei.*'[111] Durand's argument here was curious. Starting from the well known words of Augustine: '*Ego vero evangelio non crederem ...*' he argued that the idea of the Church in this passage stood for the

> primitiva congregatio fidelium eorum qui Christum viderunt, audierunt et sui testes extiterunt.

That this was an incorrect interpretation of Augustine's words needs no demonstration; the main point is that for Gerson the extra authority of the primitive Church was an established fact, thanks to Durand. But why is this so important? Because Gerson attached very important consequences to it. He deduced from the greater authority of the primitive Church

> quod non est in potestate papae aut concilii aut ecclesiae immutare traditiones datas ab evangelistis et a Paulo, sicut quidam delirant. Nec habent quoad hoc quod est facere aliquid esse pure de fide, parem auctoritatis firmitatem.[112]

Once and for all, in other words, the apostles and the primitive Church had set bounds to dogma which were to be respected by everybody, even by the successors of the apostles, those who bore the highest authority in the present day Church. If we assume that 'quidam' in this passage means the canonists, which appears acceptable, it is once again clear that Gerson found support in Durand for his attack on ecclesiastical absolutism. Dogma, so the *doctor modernus* had emphasised, was not arbitrarily whatever the Pope, the council or the Church as such had laid down, but only what was in

---

[110] *De vita spir. animae*, lect. 2 (Gl. 3, 139; Dupin III, 24BC).

[111] *Comm. in l.s. III*, d.24 q.1 (fol. 257[ro]): 'Ergo ... primum inter credibilia, quod est ratio credendi alia et ad quod sit ultima resolutio credibilium, est credere ecclesiam regi a Spiritu Sancto. Hoc autem quod dictum est de approbatione scripturae per ecclesiam intelligitur solum de ecclesia quae fuit tempore Apostolorum, qui fuerint repleti Spiritu Sancto, et nihilominus viderunt miracula Christi et audierunt eius doctrina, et ob hoc fuerunt convenientes testes omnium quae Christus fecit aut docuit, ut per eorum testimonium scriptura continens facta et dicta Christi approbaretur.'

[112] *De vita spir. animae*, lect. 2 (Gl. 3, 139; Dupin III, 24B). Cf. Chapter IX n. 66, and Petrus de Palude, *De potestate papae* (ed. Stella, 128[22-4]); 'Unde papa nihil potest contra Evangelium aut Apostolorum dicta in his quae tangunt fidem et Ecclesie sacramenta, 25, q. 1. *Sunt*, et quatuor c. sequentia [= C. 25 q. 1 c. 6-10].' Here one observes once again that canonistic thought reached Gerson not directly, but indirectly through theological channels.

harmony with the teaching of the apostles, what complied with the norms fixed by the primitive Church.[113] It goes without saying that this view was not just of theoretical importance, but mattered for Church policy as well.

All our references above are to Durand's commentary on the sentences, but that was not the only work of the *doctor modernus* that Gerson knew, for he must also have consulted Durand's brief and very clear *De origine iurisdictionum*. In this Durand dealt with the relationship of Church and State, which he approached by answering the following three questions: 1. does secular power originate from God? 2. Is there another jurisdiction *ad bonum regimen populi* besides the secular power? If not, ought there to be such a jurisdiction? 3. Can the clerical and secular powers be united in one person?[114]

The Bishop of Autun, Pierre Bertrand, a contemporary of Durand and famous jurist, was so impressed with this work that he proceeded to incorporate it in his own. Leaving the thrust of Durand's argument unchallenged, he reinforced it by adding passages from the canonists as evidence, while expanding the work by adding a fourth question: must the spiritual power exercise rule over the secular power? In 1329 Pierre Bertrand appeared at a meeting in Paris and Vincennes, where he and Pierre Roger, the later Pope Clement VI, acting as joint spokesmen for the clergy, defended the Church's power of jurisdiction in temporal matters against encroachments and attacks from the royalist side. He used this work, expanded by him but originally by Durand, as the basis of his argument.

Armed with these details we can return to Gerson's *De iurisdictione*

---

113 Though his name is not mentioned – 'probationes omitto' –, Durandus' argument returns in *De necessaria communione*, 9 (Gl. 10, 58; Dupin I, 459C).

114 For what follows we refer to our *Jean Gerson et l'Assemblée de Vincennes*, 67ff. The genealogy of Durand's work is especially interesting; there appears to be a connexion between the *De origine iurisdictionum* on the one hand and his *Comm. in l.s. II*, d.44 qq. 2 and 3, on the other. The arguments pro and contra which are urged in the commentary recur in part, adapted to the different questions, in *De orig. iur.* This is remarkable because we see in it a demonstration of how such a treatise came into being. When a particular problem became acute, as in this case the relationship of Church and State, the theologian reached for his *Liber sententiarum*, looked for the most suitable distinction and tried to use it to solve the new problem. In this way the distinction concerned was detached from its original context, which naturally resulted in the emergence of a new and independent treatise.

spirituali et temporali.[115] The greater part of this work is devoted to an attack on a thesis that was defended, though from different points of view, by spiritualists, royalists and the followers of Marsilius: namely, that Church and State were completely separate spheres with their own tasks and rights, which might never be confused. For the Church to exercise temporal power was against Christ's command, and donations from the princes could never form a lawful title. So far as the Church possessed *temporalia*, it could not dispose of them freely; it remained subordinate to the State, to which Christ had been willing to pay taxes.

To this extremist standpoint, which favoured the prince, i.e. the State, at the expense of the Church, Gerson opposed the other extreme: that the Pope was not only the ruler of the Church but of the whole world. He concluded his treatise by rejecting this absolutist standpoint, and tried to find a *via media* between the two extremes.

What is noteworthy about his rejection of the spiritualist-royalist thesis? That he founded his whole argument on the Vincennes dossier, that is, he made intensive use of the theses defended by Pierre Roger, the later Pope. Gerson made excerpts form Roger's balanced discourse, sometimes changing the order, and recast it in simpler form. He did not omit to refer to the works of Pierre Bertrand and his precursor Durand.

All this reveals that although he has become known as a 'Gallican', Gerson by no means followed a royalist course, but on the contrary was inspired by a trio of undeniable papalists. In particular he followed Pierre Roger, whose views, like those of Pierre Bertrand, were fully in harmony with and indeed largely derived from the ideas that Durand had developed in his *De origine iurisdictionum.*

Summarising, we can state that Durand was of great importance for Gerson's ecclesiology. Gerson took up and developed, in particular, the ideas of the *doctor modernus* on the right of reservation, the doctrine of *praecepta*, the greater authority of the primitive Church and the legitimacy of the Church's temporal possessions.

---

[115] Gl. 6, 259-64; Dupin II, 267-71. For a critical text, see our *Jean Gerson et l'Assemblée de Vincennes*, 121-31.

7. *Henry of Ghent*

Besides Durand and Bonaventure Gerson urged his friends at the College of Navarre to read the *Quodlibeta* of the *doctor solemnis*, Henry of Ghent. Henry was a secular cleric, greatly influenced by Augustine. His theology found little echo in later times and has been little studied. He was born about 1245, appointed canon of Tournai in 1267, Archdeacon of Bruges in 1276, and then of Tournai two years later. In 1276 he earned the degree of *magister theologiae* at the University of Paris. As such he must have attended the well known meeting called the following year by Etienne Tempier, which resolved to condemn Averroism and some Thomist theses. His *Quodlibeta* reflect the theological discussions at the University of Paris in the last quarter of the thirteenth century. Henry chaired these discussions each year between 1277 and 1292. He died in 1293.[116]

Gerson's references to the *doctor solemnis* are about as frequent as those to Ockham. But that was the only resemblance, for though Gerson admired Ockham greatly, the emphasis which Henry laid on ethics, and in general the Augustinian tendency of his theology, must have appealed to him far more. His affinity with the south Netherlander was much greater than with Ockham, and for this reason we are not inclined to attach too much importance to the statistical coincidence.

As with Durand, Gerson first mentioned Henry by name in a sermon preached in 1394,[117] while the references grew much less frequent in his later works after 1410.[118] Examining the ecclesiological contexts in which Gerson referred to 'Gandensis', as he preferred to call him, he first cited him in the tract of early 1402, which attacks the immoderate luxury of the prelates. Besides Bernard of Clairvaux and some others, he names Henry of Ghent, who had

[116] For the philosophy of Henry of Ghent see Gilson, *La philosophie au moyen age*, 427-32, 435. Much useful information for our purpose is supplied by De Lagarde, *La naissance de l'esprit laïque* II, 161-212.

[117] *Pax vobis* (Gl. 7*, 786; Dupin III, 1209C): 'La seconde question de curiosité est assavoir se le corps Nostre Seigneur eust point esté pourry s'il eust longuement demouré? Respondent les docteurs, specialiter Gandavensis in quodlibetis, que nennil, car les deffaulx de nature humaine qui furent en Jhesucrist furent plus par miracle et dispensacion especiale que par nature entiere...'

[118] *Collectorium super magnificat* (Gl. 8, 206; Dupin IV, 266B).

devoted a separate *quaestio* to this problem. Gerson could subscribe wholeheartedly to Henry's view

> quod de bonis ecclesiae viri ecclesiastici nihil possunt sumere ad superfluitatem, sed solum quod pertinet ad victus et vestitus necessitatem.[119]

Besides this agreement on a certain aspect of the outward form of the Church, Gerson found support if not direct inspiration in Henry on two other points, both of fundamental ecclesiological importance. The first was in his view of the law, in particular the relativity of positive law, which he developed in detail in the *De vita spirituali animae*; the second was his conception of the hierarchy, and especially the position of the *curati* in it, as expressed in his writings on the Gorrel affair of 1409-10.

In an earlier chapter we saw how Gerson's insight into Church policy developed in the years after 1400. Until that date he had assumed that the Schism could and must be resolved within the positive legal order; after 1400 it began to dawn on him that this way was a blind alley, and that another means had to be found to reach the desired goal. Passing over positive law, he now took his stand on the natural or divine law and was willing to accept any solution which was not in conflict with it. In his *De vita spirituali animae* he provided the theoretical basis for this new insight.

It was no small step to bid farewell to positive law, and we may be sure that he would never have taken it if he had not found a precedent in an earlier theological *casus*. Which was this? Dispensation. It is no coincidence that he explicitly tells us that he chose his starting point in Bernard's *De praecepto et dispensatione*,[120] and his four references to Bernard's work in this tract[121] show how serious he was. But he went to Henry of Ghent for guidance as well.

It is certain that he studied Henry's *Quodlibeta* deeply at this time. We are also convinced that Henry's influence on Gerson was greater than one might suspect from the scanty references. We have been struck by the fact that the passage from Augustine which

---

119 *Super victu et pompa praelatorum* (Gl. 3, 103; Dupin II, 640B), with a reference to Henry's *Quod.* II q. 19 (fol. 46vo) in which Bernard is also named, as in Gl. 3, 101; Dupin II, 639A. This text forms the background of *De pot. eccl.*, cons. 12 (Gl. 6, 236-7; 239; Dupin II, 246B; 248A).

120 *De vita spir. animae*, lect. 2 (Gl. 3, 129; Dupin III, 17B).

121 *De vita spir. animae*, (Gl. 3, 159-60; 181; 182; 194; Dupin III, 39C; 56B; 56D; 65D).

Gerson cited at the beginning of his second *lectio*[122] also appeared in Henry's *Quodlib.* V q. 36, which asks: *Utrum per ecclesiam potest fieri dispensatio aut immutatio circa ea quae sunt essentialia sacramenti.*[123] The agreement is striking and we consider that Gerson–even if he omitted to name his source–must have borrowed this reference to Augustine from Henry, since the *quaestio* in which it appears deals with dispensation, a topic of unusually acute interest to Gerson at the time.

Together with Thomas, he cited the *doctor solemnis* in support of his assertion that a superior authority must revoke a law whenever he detected that it was being broken and was unwilling to take steps to stop this.[124] Gerson found in this view the occasion to criticise the fact that many canons of canon law were not honoured, although they had been enacted by general councils. This turned into a criticism of canonists, who did not sufficiently realise that they existed to build up the body of Christ and not destroy it.

Passing over the reference to the doctrine of sin,[125] we remark finally that Gerson's theory of law as a whole was very similar to that of Henry. The simplest way to grasp this similarity is to compare Gerson's theory with the fine chapter that Georges de Lagarde devoted to Henry's legal views.[126] This reveals that both men were inspired by the same reverence for divine and natural law, and therefore looked at the human law of the Church with a degree of relativity. For them it was an accidental, and as such could be amended, adapted and even, if necessary, temporarily suspended. And that was precisely what Gerson put forward as the solution to the Schism. He must have agreed wholeheartedly when he read Henry's words:

---

[122] *De vita spir. animae* (Gl. 3, 129-30; Dupin III, 17AB).

[123] (fol. 212ro). Augustine, *ep.* 54, 2, 2 ad Ianuarium (CSEL 34, 160, 9sq.); *ep.* 55, 19, 35 (*CSEL* 34, 209, 18sq.). In the *Confessio Augustana* art. XXVI, there is a reference to this letter of Augustine and Gerson is also named, so that one may assume that he must have drawn the attention of the framers of this confession to this passage. But he himself took it from Henry of Ghent, so that it was in fact Henry who did the framers of the confession this service.

[124] *De vita spir. animae* (Gl. 3, 169-70; Dupin III, 47BC). Thomas, *S. Th.*, I^{a} II^{ae} q. 97. a. 4; Henry of Ghent, *Quodl.*?

[125] *De vita spir. animae* (Gl. 3, 181-2; Dupin III, 56B); cf. Henry of Ghent, *Quodl.*, III q.21 (fol. 81vo-2vo).

[126] See note 116 above.

> ... cavendum est ... multum ecclesiae, ne potestate sibi concessa abutatur quoquo modo in praeiudicium scientiae Dei, ponentem falcem suam in messem alienam.[127] Etenim etsi liberam habet potestatem in omnibus quae sunt iuris positivi ab homine instituti cuiuscumque auctoritatis, etiam ut ecclesia contra instituta apostolorum et concilia generalia in eis quae non statuerunt secundum praecepta evangelica vel scripta, vel secundum quod ea a Christo audierunt observata, possit dispensare et addere vel subtrahere et immutare, nihil tamen horum potest contra instituta legis naturae et divinae.[128]

The other point on which we can detect Henry's influence concerns the structure of the hierarchy in general and the function of the *curati* in it in particular. We have already seen what Gerson's views were[129] and now we have to establish how far he was dependent for them on Henry of Ghent.

If one reads the works that Gerson devoted to the Gorrel affair and the bull *Regnans in excelsis* of Alexander V, one is struck by more than one reference to Henry.[130] Apart from his personal preference, this is not surprising because Henry had played a central role in the controversy between the mendicant orders, which the Pope favoured, and the secular clergy, who had the support of the University of Paris. He had ranged himself decisively alongside the University and had justified his choice in many of his quodlibets.[131] Gerson could second him without hesitation.

> Christ, so Henry argued, had instituted the twelve apostles and the seventy two disciples, thus indicating that the Church order, which reflected the threefold hierarchy of the angels, would immutably consist of three *status*, represented respectively by the Pope, the bishops and the *curati*. The Pope had no right to modify this essential *ordo ecclesiasticus*. He could intervene in the field of Church organisation by creating a new diocese or bringing a particular abbey under the authority of another bishop, but even these minor changes ought always to be inspired by *necessitas, ratio* and *utilitas communis*.
>
> It follows from this assumption that according to the *doctor solemnis* not only the Pope but also the bishops and the *curati* had received their authority immediately from Christ. The vicar of Christ could not there-

---

[127] Deut. 23: 26: 'Non mittere falcem in messem alienam.' As pointed out by Congar ('Aspects ecclésiologiques', 57 n. 38) this is a classical topos.

[128] *Quodl.* V q. 36 (fol. 212vo).

[129] See above Chapter X § 1.

[130] *De consiliis evangelicis* (Gl. 3, 19; Dupin II, 676D); *Quomodo stabit regnum* (Gl. 7* 989; Dupin II, 440B).

[131] De Lagarde, *La naissance* I, 75.

fore, without compelling reason, withdraw the faithful from the authority of their pastors, nor had he the authority to encroach on the rights of the lower clergy. In other words, the divine order of the Church and thereby the competences of others had to be respected.
One may guess how our author replied to the mendicant friars. They argued that their authority to preach and hear confessions took precedence over that of the *curati*, because their privileges were bestowed by the Head of the Church, that is the hierarchical superior of the bishops to whom the pastors owed their authority. Henry denied this pretension because it mocked the divine order of the Church, pointing out that there had to be a distinction between the *potestas delegata* and the *potestas ordinaria*. 'La puissance déleguée doit toute sa vertu à la délégation éphémère dont elle bénéficie ... la puissance ordinaire découle de l'ordre essentiel de l'église. Celle-ci est supérieure à toute puissance déléguée parce qu'elle remonte directement à Dieu.[132]

Referring to what we said above about Gerson's ideas of the hierarchy, we conclude that they were very much in agreement with those of Henry of Ghent. Altogether we feel we can say that the *doctor solemnis* had a considerable influence on Gerson and that Gerson was especially indebted to him for his ideas on the boundaries of positive law in the Church and the structure of the hierarchy. Less certain is whether Gerson also drew on Henry of Ghent in his thought on the papal power with regard to the State, but on this point too one can observe some agreement between them.[133]

8. *The Curialists*

Walter Ullmann has pointed out that the importance of the defenders of the hierocratic ideology, the so-called curialists or papal publicists, for the growth and development of papal power must not be overestimated. In this respect they were far less important than the canonists, who must be regarded as the true creators of the doctrine of papal absolutism. Even though the curialists tried to outdo the absolutism of their legal colleagues they never succeeded in winning such a prominent place in the Church order. 'The publicists did not rely on the law, and therefore had far less influence than the canonists. It was all very well to derive the plenitude of papal power from

[132] In the above we have followed De Lagarde, *La naissance* II, 202-13 (207).
[133] See Chapter IX n. 109.

extra-legal sources, mainly from 'articles of faith' and other speculations, but all these taken together could not possibly command the same respect as one decretal of an Innocent III or one saying of an Hostiensis commanded.'[134]

What it comes down to is that one may not conclude from the ideological agreement between curialists and canonists that Gerson, whose objections to the canonists and their absolutist creed are sufficiently familiar to us, passed the same negative verdict on the curialists.[135] The contrary is the case. He nowhere gives any sign of regarding the curialists as a separate group of theologians who distinguished themselves from their predecessors and successors by their extreme emphasis on the papal plenitude of power. Rather, one must assume that he regarded them as fully worthy representatives of the scholastic tradition and therefore did not feel compelled to issue a warning against them as he did with the canonists. It is impossible to find a single negative statement about the curialists anywhere in his writings, and we therefore feel that there is more reason to assume his attitude to them was positive than negative.

Referring to what we have said earlier about Gerson's indebtness to the curialist literature,[136] we notice that he called Giles of Rome *venerabilis*,[137] and not only commended his mirror for princes, the *De regimine principum*,[138] but also enthusiastically recommended his *Contra exemptos*.[139] We could mention more points in support of our thesis that Gerson was not ill-disposed towards the curialists, in spite of the absolutism that they professed.

This is a curious fact, for why was he such a keen critic of the canonists while the curialists were certainly no less absolutistic in their thinking? Did Gerson know that the latter were not the actual

---

134 *Medieval Papalism*, 17-18.

135 Cf. Tierney, *Foundations*, 11: 'The widespread assumption that there was one single canonistic theory of Church government which was adequately reflected in the works as such publicists as Giles of Rome or Augustinus Triumphus does scant justice to the richness and diversity of canonistic speculations in this field. The theories of the more extreme papal publicists do indeed reflect one trend of canonistic thought, but the conciliar arguments in favour of a limitation op papal authority by Council and cardinals reflect another; both parties alike drew their weapons from the canonists' armoury.'

136 See Chapter IX notes 13ff. For Gerson's use of Giles's *De renunciatione papae*, see Chapter VI n. 84.

137 *Oportet haereses esse* (Gl. 5, 425; Dupin II, 342B).

138 See above n. 81.

139 *Quomodo stabit regnum* (Gl. 7*, 981; Dupin II, 434D).

creators of papal absolutism?[140] This may have played some part, but it seems much more probable that he never criticised the curialists, and never could do so, because they were theologians and as such were in the same line of succession as he was himself. One should not underestimate the solidarity that Gerson felt with the *doctores*. He told his students:

> Signum curiositatis et singularitatis poenitentiam atque credulitatem impedientis apud scholasticos est gaudere plus in impugnatione doctorum aut in defensione unius pertinaci quam ad eorum dicta concordanda operam dare. Intolerabile itaque esse dicit Guillelmus Parisiensis confestim iudicare sapientissimos inquisitores veritatis erravisse.[141]

Against the background of such a pronouncement, it becomes understandable why Gerson in his *De potestate ecclesiastica* and elsewhere never entered into an open polemic with the curialists, although he differed from them on many points. We have tried to show that he was following a custom of the curialists when he gave his most important ecclesiological work this title.[142] One may assume that he chose it deliberately, tacitly indicating that his work was intended to supplement and correct the curialist treatises of former times, on the grounds of the recent decisions of the Council of Constance, on the one hand, and the bitter experience of a long Schism on the other, a Schism whose origin and continuation, he was firmly convinced, was to be blamed above all on the obstinate adherence of the highest leaders of the Church—and their 'flatterers'—to the doctrine of papal absolutism.

---

[140] Cf. Ullmann, *Medieval Papalism*, 18: 'Contemporaries, like Dante, quite correctly saw in the canonists, and not in the publicists, the ideological framers of the papalist system of government: the former, and not the latter, were made the target of imperialist attacks.'

[141] *Contra vanam curiositatem*, cons. 5 (Gl. 3, 240; Dupin I, 99B).

[142] Chapter IX n. 14ff.

CONCLUSION

Diutius spe nostra tenuit nos sermo de hac potestate summi pontificis, quoniam tempestas praesens ad hoc impulit, pro qua magis necesse est potestatem hanc ad clarum dignoscere atque secernere quam olim antea.

Gerson, *De vita spirituali animae* (Gl. 3, 155; Dupin III, 36B)

It was with good reason that we called Gerson an 'apostle of unity' in the title of this book. We were led to do so, not merely because he himself regarded it as his distinguishing characteristic, but chiefly because, objectively, the views which he championed as Chancellor in the ecclesiastical politics of his time were largely determined by the question of how the unity of the Church would best be served.

From his youth, Gerson revealed the primacy of this yearning for unity in the way in which he consistently tried to sympathise with his opponents and take account of their views. He believed the legal question of who was to be regarded as the lawfully elected Pope, the Pope of Rome or the Pope of Avignon, was insoluble; and so instead of concentrating on it, he always asked himself what would be the effect of particular decisions in church policy on the Roman obedience, and above all if and how far they would bring the unity of the Church any nearer.

This characteristic is all the more remarkable because Gerson himself was convinced that the Pope of Rome must be regarded as an 'intrusus' and that the true successor of Peter reigned at Avignon. But that did not lead him to argue for the expulsion of the 'intrusus' in Rome or for another forcible solution to the Schism, in a Gallican sense or in any other. On the contrary, from his youth he defended the thesis that it was possible to imagine that the true believers were to be found among the followers of the Pope of Rome, and the schismatics among those of Avignon!

Resignation, the voluntary withdrawal of both pretenders to the papal throne, was his preferred solution from the beginning, and not merely because he felt that it offered the best chances of a solution, but because it was an eminently Christian solution. Resignation would offer an example of humility, for what could be more Christian than to surrender one's own rights for the general good? He expected that if both obediences were willing to settle on the basis of resignation, the way would be cleared for a joint election which would end the Schism and reunite the Church.

As Chancellor, he long continued to argue for resignation as the best solution. But when it became clearer and clearer that in spite of repeated promises, neither of the rival Popes was willing to withdraw voluntarily, more drastic measures were prepared; France adopted a policy of forcing Benedict to resign by withdrawing its obedience to him (1398). This Gallican decision for substraction was taken in Gerson's absence and did not command his support. He regretted it but could hardly do anything but submit. But when, a couple of years later, even more far-reaching proposals surfaced and, in University circles above all, voices were raised urging that a unilateral council should declare Benedict a heretic, Gerson opposed them vigorously. He was delighted when these proposals failed and not long afterwards even the decision for substraction was revoked and France returned to its obedience to Benedict (1403).

It was characteristic of his attitude in the following years that he continued to hope for great things from a policy of resignation but did not rely on it exclusively. In personal conversations he tried to induce Benedict to adopt it, but did not rule out other solutions to the Schism. He did not give up his preference for a policy of resignation until France had gone over to neutrality and shortly afterwards the cardinals of both obediences took the decision to reunite the Church by holding a general council (1408).

Gerson immediately approved this decision and from that date defended the conciliar solution with conviction. This can be explained by the fact that both parties had willed this solution *equally*. That was precisely what he had always hoped and striven for: that the parties should *jointly* agree on how unity was to be restored. Once the cardinals of the two parties had reached agreement, he exerted every effort to bring about the restoration of unity by the conciliar path – first at Pisa, then at Constance.

We recall all this to show that Gerson did not allow himself to be tossed helplessly to and fro on the waves of France's chaotic church politics, but that he steered a relatively consistent course. That course was influenced by his personal conception of unity, deeply rooted in the ideas of Augustine, Boethius and pseudo-Dionysius; and to a great extent it was also determined by his office as Chancellor of the University of Paris. He cherished a deep and lifelong respect for this institution, which, as he said, 'could not lightly err in the field of faith and morals'. One may say that his consciousness of his office was entirely in harmony with this. He was profoundly convinced that the University of Paris was a beacon of wisdom for the whole of Christendom and for France in particular. And that entailed obligations which were not to be assumed lightly. As Chancellor it was his duty to watch over the University and ensure that it remained faithful to its vocation and did not step beyond the bounds of orthodoxy. The beacon of orthodoxy itself could not be allowed to drift! That raises the question of how he, as Chancellor, interpreted the content of that orthodoxy in terms of ecclesiastical policy. What boundaries had to be respected, if orthodoxy was not to be endangered?

In general, he tried to protect the orthodoxy of the University by holding fast to the three paths which the University itself had suggested as solutions to the Schism (resignation, compromise, council) in its famous letter to the King in 1394, and with which the other party had agreed. That led him to dismiss all suggestions which differed from these three proposals as 'radical', i.e. as the product of *pertinacia*. That had to be prevented at all costs, for it carried the threat that the Schism would harden into heresy. After all, schism and heresy were near neighbours, in fact there was only one step between them: *pertinacia*, the obstinate adherence to a wrong-headed point of view. There was very little that inspired greater fear in Gerson; indeed, he was fully convinced that only one would rejoice at it: the Devil!

Hence he always attempted to prevent France isolating and alienating itself from the rest of Christendom by taking unusual and extreme measures which would only make negotiations with the other obedience even more difficult. Maintaining orthodoxy in the sense of remaining within the context of resignation, compromise or a council, and remaining continuously in sympathy with the obedience of Rome as to how unity was to be restored, in other words, were the main principles which guided his ecclesiastical policy.

Gerson's ultimate choice of a conciliar solution to the Schism was, as we saw, the direct expression of his desire for unity. But that is not the whole story. For years his mind had been prepared for this choice by his desire for a reformation, a restructuring of the Church according to the pattern of the primitive Church. And that was not without influence on his judgement of the Schism itself.

In his younger years Gerson regarded the Schism as a more or less casual disaster that had befallen the Church, a disaster which could be averted by relatively modest measures. But the long continuance of the Schism and the painful experiences with Benedict and his Roman rival awoke Gerson to a realisation that the Schism was not just a fortuitous event, but much rather a sign that there was something wrong with the structure of the Church. This put the phenomenon of the Schism in a new perspective; it was impossible to detach it from the need for a reformation, and the old cry for reformation in head and members was raised again, with new urgency, in the current distress of the Church.

This new insight was prepared and its theological foundations laid in his influential course of lectures *De vita spirituali animae* of 1402, the main ideas of which he presented to Benedict in the sermon *Apparuit gratia Dei* (1 January 1404). About this time Gerson came to see that if the responsible leaders of the Church had heeded earlier calls for a reformation, the Schism would never have come about; or to put it another way, that the origin and continuance of the Schism showed that they had paid too little attention to the call for reformation.

In a word, his new insight represented a critical attitude towards the current papalist form of the Church, to an ecclesiology which was virtually absorbed into the doctrine of papal *potestas*. He vehemently criticised the extreme legalistic thinking which had captured the highest offices in the Church, and which found its chief expression in a boundless exaggeration of the idea of papal plenitude of power. Gerson held the canonists responsible for the development of this doctrine. They were the ones who had deformed the papal office in an absolutist sense. They had disregarded its sacramental character and defined it primarily in terms of power and legal rights, both from a spiritual point of view in the sense of power and rights over the Church, and from a temporal point of view in terms of power and rights over the world.

Gerson coupled this criticism with a theory of law in which he sharply defined the boundaries of divine law, natural law and positive law. He did so because he believed that the canonists had been insufficiently critical, notably in their treatment of the concept of divine law. They had misused it by confusing it with positive legal rules and enactments, thus endangering the good order of the Church and obscuring its essential core, its divine origin and spiritual purpose.

In his view power, rights and possessions of a temporal nature were not essential for the Church, for it had been created as a purely spiritual entity by God, and was therefore perfect. 'Not essential', however, is not the same as 'incompatible'; Gerson rejected the second statement because of its spiritualist tendency, and adopted the first as his opinion. He was thus able, up to a point, to approve of the historical process which had led to the enormous accumulation of wealth and worldly power in the hands of the Church. Yet this did not prevent him from addressing serious criticism to the holders of the highest offices in the Church, if he suspected them of being concerned solely with the increase of their power and legal pretensions. In such cases he accused them of being concerned entirely with secondary matters, and urged them to realise that the Church could well manage without worldly possessions, indeed it had reached its healthiest state when it had lived in poverty. In this respect Gerson was clearly in tune with Franciscan theology, which also explains why, albeit hesitantly, he could express himself in later years in more positive terms about a politic of substraction.

His objections to the absolutist form of the Church grew from his conviction that it was God's will that not only the supreme hierarch but all the hierarchical dignitaries should share in in the government of the Church. In his defence of this thesis he echoed the view upheld by the secular clergy in their long struggle with the regulars around a century and a half earlier. In his conciliar theory he gave that doctrine of a disseminated hierarchical responsibility a new form. He incorporated in his theory the lesson that the times had taught him, the bitter experience of a long Schism which he believed would never have come about but for papal absolutism.

His ecclesiology was therefore anti-absolutist to a great degree, but that does not mean that it was in any way democratic. Neither Ockham's notion of the *ecclesia universalis* nor Marsilius's views on the *congregatio fidelium* played any part in his ecclesiology. Throughout his life Gerson remained a follower of pseudo-Dionysius the Areopagite, and even when, after many years, his ecclesiology took a conciliar turn, he never gave up the idea of a hierarchical

Church. For him ordinary believers were never more than the *ecclesia audiens*, and it was for the hierarchy alone to take doctrinal decisions.

The qualification 'anti-absolutist' does not mean that he regarded the office and the primacy of the Pope as negligible quantities or wished to replace the papal supremacy by the supremacy of the bishops. He was no episcopalist, but dreamt of a Church in which high and low – Pope, bishops and pastors – would respect one another and grant one another the freedom to exercise their authority, in the knowledge that the hierarchical function which each of them fulfilled went back directly to a divine institution.

He did not deny that the Pope possessed plenitude of power, but he set his face firmly against the autocratic, absolutist application of that doctrine as it was expressed, for example, in the practice of papal reservation and *non-obstante*, in particular in the annulment of the decisions and rules adopted by former councils after wise deliberation between the head and the members. Here as elsewhere he was always concerned to ensure that the right to a say and the collegial structure of the whole hierarchy should be respected. Though he never mentioned his name in this context, Gerson's view of the papal office often reminds us of Cyprian: the Pope as *primus inter pares*. That was a direct corollary of the normative authority of the primitive Church.

Thus his conciliar views were entirely in accordance with the fundamental hierarchical premise of his ecclesiology. Far from considering the general council as a 'democratic' controle of the Church, he saw it exclusively as the reflection and representation of the Church as hierarchy, i.e. of the Church from on high, not from below. The council shared in the 'invariability' which belonged to the hierarchy, for it included in itself all the parts from which the immutable hierarchy had been built up. It was, so to speak, the microcosm of the hierarchical macrocosm (Tierney). Because the latter was of divine origin, and moreover was kept in being and inspired by a never-failing *influxus* of grace from above, the decisions of the former, the council, were infallible. Gerson was so convinced of the direct causal force implicit in Christ's promise (Matt. 28: 20) that it was self-evident to him that just as the hierarchical Church could never disappear, so a hierarchically represented council could never err.

How are we finally to appreciate Gerson's ecclesiology? Here, everything depends on the view one takes of papal absolutism. Those who believe that this ideology must be considered normative and correct for the age will have little understanding, let alone sympathy, for Gerson's intentions. Those, on the other hand, who feel that this ideology did more harm than good to the Church since it was detrimental to its primarily spiritual and sacramental nature, will take a much more positive view of them. Indeed, as a careful reaction against a puffed up theory of power, they will appreciate Gerson's efforts and not deny them a justification.

APPENDIX ONE

THE AUTHOR OF THE TREATISE *DE CONCILIO UNIUS OBOEDIENTIAE*

(Gl. 6, 51-8; Dupin II, 24-29c)

L. Salembier in his *Petrus de Alliaco*, 265, 266, as well as V. Martin, *Les origines du Gallicanisme*, t. II, 78, n. 4, regarded Pierre d'Ailly as the author of the work *De concilio unius oboedientiae*. Mgr. Glorieux (*La vie et les oeuvres de Gerson*, 164), attributed it to Gerson, while André Combes (*Jean de Montreuil*, 359 n. 5), and B. Meller (*Studien zur Erkenntnislehre des Peter von Ailly*, 289), left the question of authorship undecided.

That Mgr. Glorieux was right appears from a statement made by d'Ailly in his *Apologia concilii Pisani* of 1412 (ed. P. Tschackert, *Peter von Ailly*, Appendix XII [31]-[41]). In this he points out that in the first part of his *Tractatus de concilio generalis* (= *Tractatus) de materia concilii generalis* (ed. B. Meller, *op. cit.*, 290-336), he had taken over a number of theses from Gerson. In so many words d'Ailly says (*Apologia*, [41]):

> In cuius prima parte septem considerationes satis utiles, ex scriptis praememorati Iohannis cancellarii Parisiensis recepi, aliqua in iis non inutiliter superaddens.

This can only refer to Gerson's *De concilio unius oboedientiae*, which indeed consists of seven theses. D'Ailly's statement, from which, oddly enough, neither Tschackert nor Salembier drew the consequences, is confirmed, if confirmation is needed, by BN lat. 3124 (cited in ed. Meller, *op. cit.*, 290 d) and 299 d): 'Praemissas considerationes pro maiori parte posuit Johannes cancellarius ecclesiae Parisiensis ...

It may be stated as a fact that *De concilio unius oboedientiae* is a work of Gerson, which was expanded by d'Ailly, who added biblical and canonistic references and thus laid the basis for his *Tractatus de materia concilii generalis* of 1402-3.

We wrote the above in the first version of this book (1963). These words provoked Mgr. Combes to take issue with our conclusion in a very detailed passage (*La théologie mystique* I, 405-12). He tried to make the case:

1. that Gerson's authorship of *De concilio unius oboedientiae* must be denied;
2. that this work drew on d'Ailly's *De materia concilii generalis*, and was not to be regarded as its source;
3. that d'Ailly's statement in his *Apologia*, that he owed his seven considerations to Gerson, was contradicted by his own text.

To rule out any misunderstanding, we quote Mgr. Combes' conclusion verbatim (*op. cit.*, 411-2):

> Cela dit, le *De concilio* paraît un opuscule factice, artificiellement constitué de deux parties hétérogènes, dont la première se présente plutôt comme un abrégé destiné à en effacer les hésitations et l'équilibre, du *De materia concilii generalis* de Pierre d'Ailly, que comme sa source. L'hypothèse que Pierre d'Ailly devrait à ce traité même les sept considérations dont son *Apologia* nous affirme qu'il les a reçues à Gerson est donc, ce semble, condamnée par le texte. Comme on doit convenir qu'il devient difficile d'attribuer à Gerson ce traité, tel qu'il a eté dite, c'est ailleurs qu'il faudra dorénavant chercher.

What is one to say of this? We are happy to be instructed, but we can only regard what Mgr. Combes asserts in these pages as yet another example of his remarkable tendency, detectable elsewhere in his works, to reject the natural explanation and make simple matters highly problematical in order to develop very far-fetched and speculative 'solutions', which are completely unconvincing, because they show such lofty disregard for the evidence. As far as the authorship of the *De concilio unius oboedientiae* is concerned, we therefore reaffirm our opinion and continue to ascribe this work to Gerson.

We are supported in our obstinacy by the fact that in 1964 the American scholar Francis Oakley–completely independently of our proposal – reached the same conclusion on precisely the same grounds. In his *The Political Thought of Pierre d'Ailly* Oakley offered a new edition of d'Ailly's *De materia concilii generalis*, more complete than that of Meller. Naturally, he also went into the question of its authorship (246). Referring to d'Ailly's own testimony in the *Apologia concilii Pisani*, and to the marginal annotations in BN lat. 3124 he came to the same conclusion as we had, namely that d'Ailly had used Gerson's *De concilio unius oboedientiae* in compiling the first part of his *De materia*.

We feel we are released from the obligation to refute Mgr. Combes' thesis in detail. We only wish to pause to consider one of his arguments, which is central to his whole speculative edifice.

Mgr. Combes lays great weight on a statement made towards the end of the first consideration in *De concilio*. We read 'sed tales materias non expedit in hoc Concilio ventilare ad determinandum hic, *prout statim dictum est*' (Gl. 6, 52; Dupin II, 25B). Given the order in which the considerations are arranged in *De concilio*, the concluding sentence, in Mgr. Combes' opinion, ought to have read differently.

> 'Ce n'est pas *statim dictum est*, mais *statim dicendum est*, qu'il eût fallu écrire.' This is directly followed by the rhetorical question: 'Ce lapsus ne suffit-il pas à prouver que ce n'est pas Pierre d'Ailly qui utilise le *De concilio* mais l'auteur du *De concilio* qui abrège et remanie Pierre d'Ailly?' (411)

We feel that there can be absolutely no question of a scribal lapse, but that Mgr. Combes committed an error of translation by overlooking the conjunction *prout*. The phrase *prout statim dictum est* means 'just as it is said immediately after'. And that occurs eight lines further on, where 'the author' (i.e. in our opinion: Gerson) defends the thesis that 'neque expedit fieri concilium ad tractandum determinative materiam fidei'. In other words, there is no reason at all to draw such far-reaching conclusions from this brief phrase. We could find more far-fetched arguments to remove; but what purpose would it serve? We prefer to stick to the evidence!

APPENDIX TWO

THE DATING OF THE *LIBER DE VITA SPIRITUALI ANIMAE*

(Gl. 3, 113-202; Dupin III, 5-72)

The dating of the *Liber de vita spirituali animae* is a controversial question, well set out by Morrall (*Gerson*, 46, with references to the literature). While Schwab assumed that this treatise had originated while Gerson was living in Bruges, 1399-1400, André Combes put it a little earlier, in 1398-9; Mgr. Glorieux, on the other hand, a few years later, in the first half of 1402. It is not our intention to go into the sometimes very complicated evidence produced by these and other scholars who occupied themselves with this problem; we merely wish to adduce a single argument which supports the dating given by Mgr. Glorieux.

If the work in question was written in the first half of 1402, one might expect that in all probability it would have left traces in other works of the same period. This seems to us to be the case. In the fourth *lectio* of the *Liber de vita spirituali animae*, (Gl. 3, 169; Dupin III, 47B) Gerson argues that, just as a law is sometimes set aside because of human sinfulness, a prelate ought to bear in mind the wickedness of his subjects. He clarifies this abstract statement by citing an example from the politics of the church. Let us look at the passage in full:

> Et si per peccatum etiam possit aliqua lex abrogari aut per malitiam subditorum. Puto enim quod sic et quod ad multa agenda vel omittenda praelatus aliquis potest obligari propter generalem malitiam aut errorem subditorum, quorum opposita aliquando agere vel omittere tenetur, *sicut in materia nunc currente dixisse et scripsisse memini*: quod etiam ubi via cessionis fuisset minus bona, tamen acceptare eam debebat dominus Benedictus, attenta deliberatione regni Franciae et aliorum subditorum suae oboedientiae.

Gerson thus recalled that he had both said and written that Benedict ought to resign, as soon as he learned that his subjects desired this. Now we know nothing about what he said, but we do know what he wrote. Where did he write that the Pope, in view of the wishes of the faithful, ought to resign? We can give a clear answer to this question: he argued in this sense in almost identical words, first in *De schismate*, (not in Glorieux's edition; Dupin II 24C), and later in *De restitutione oboedientiae* (Gl. 6, 63; Dupin II 30C), both of which were composed in the spring of 1402. In the latter we read:

> Sicut regulariter verum est, quod praelatus non solum potest, immo debet aliqua agere vel omittere, propter generalem inclinationem subditorum, ubi etiam quandoque mala esset, quae alias agere vel omittere in grave delictum sibi verteretur. Iuxta quod inferunt aliqui quod etiam ubi via cessionis minus bona fuisset, tamen attentis deliberationibus omnium subditorum super postulatione huius viae dominus Benedictus illam acceptare tenebatur, sicut nunc acceptavit, quantumcumque alias ad eam acceptandam non fuisset arctatus vel arctandus.

Unless one were to accept that the pronouncement in the *Liber de vita spirituali animae* was interpolated later–which cannot be proven –we feel that the above shows that this work cannot in any case have been written before 1402.

APPENDIX THREE

WHOM DID GERSON HOLD UP TO BENEDICT XIII AS A WARNING EXAMPLE IN HIS SERMON *APPARUIT GRATIA DEI*?

In his famous sermon at Tarascon on 1 January 1404, Gerson admonished Benedict XIII by holding up to him the following example (Gl. 5, 76; Dupin II 63A):

> Mentior si non tempore meo apparuit et verborum copia et iurium scientia et abstinentia famatus, corpore vegeto et forti; quem usque ad hoc insanum reddidit ambitio coeca, contemptrix alieni omnis consilii laudibusque suis credula, ut putaverit post illusiones plurimas esse verus papa concorditer electus. Et cum ita desiperet, nihilominus affirmabat se per multos annos nihil tentationis a vana gloria sensisse. Cum praeterea moneretur ut sapientorum crederet consiliis: «non», inquit, «quia factum meum tale tantumque est, ut alius a me nemo illud intelligat».

Schwab, *(Gerson*, 174 n. 1) called this example 'anzüglich' and 'verletzend' for Benedict, while André Combes (*Jean de Montreuil et le chancelier Gerson*, 356 n. (357)) said of it: 'Tout ce qu'on peut voir en cette anecdote c'est une maladresse.' That is too hasty a judgement, for one must ask to whom this anecdote actually referred. Not to Benedict himself, argue the two gersonisants, and that is crystal clear; but who was it then? Who was this ascetic Vicar of Christ, this famous jurist, who would not listen to the advice of others? Neither author names him, but that is the crux of the whole matter.

To be brief, it seems to us that there can be no doubt but that it must refer to Urban VI, the man whose election had been the immediate cause of the Schism. What is the evidence? Gerson, born in 1363, tells us that he was a contemporary of the Pope in question, who was wrongly convinced that he had been unanimously elected; for he speaks of him as appearing in 'tempore meo'. In the first place, therefore, the *terminus post quem* must be fixed at 1363. But because neither the scholarly Urban V (1362-70) nor Gregory XI (1370-78), nor their respective elections, are said to have caused any problem for their contemporaries, the *terminus post quem* can be brought forward to 1378, the year in which Gregory XI died. That brings us to the period of the Schism, and the example must therefore refer to one of the Popes who reigned between 1378 and 1404 – the *terminus ante quem* – either in Rome or in Avignon.

So far as the Popes of Avignon were concerned, since Benedict XIII himself is not eligible, we can only think of Clement VII (1378-94). But, apart from the extreme improbability of Gerson criticising Benedict's predecessor and the head of his own obedience to Benedict's face, this assumption cannot be reconciled with the verdict which Gerson had passed on Clement in the past (see e.g. Chapter I n. 52 and Chapter III n. 32, where he calls Urban VI 'an intruder'.) Nor is Clement VII said to have had ascetic leanings or to have been distinguished as a jurist. That leaves only the Popes of Rome.

Leaving aside Urban VI for the moment, the only candidate is Boniface IX (1389-1404). Dietrich of Niem said of this Neapolitan that he could write no better than he could sing. This sounds rather legendary, but it is certain that Boniface IX was not a distinguished scholar, or even a graduate – 'non habuit in aliqua scientia praeeminentiam sive gradum (*De schismate*, ed. Schardius, Basil., 1566, lib. II c. 6, 59-60). Thus this possibility also fails and only Urban VI remains.

The same Dietrich was in close relations with this Pope for many years, and recorded his experiences in detail in the same work (*De schismate*, lib. I c. 1, 1-2). Here we find what is generally assumed to be an accurate portrait of Urban (Heimpel, *Dietrich von Niem*, 207ff.). Dietrich tells us that Urban was an outstanding jurist – 'egregius decretorum doctor' – and, at least before he became Pope, a humble and devout man and a sworn enemy of simony. His only fault was that he trusted too much to himself and was too ready to listen to flatterers: '... nimis suae prudentiae innitendo, et credens adulatoribus libenter aures praebuit ipsis'. He faithfully kept the fasts prescribed by the Church and valued those who followed the same pattern of conduct.

All this fits in perfectly with the picture that Gerson held up to Benedict. As for the physical likeness, Gerson speaks of a 'corpus vegetum et forte', that is a well-built and powerful physique, while Dietrich described Urban as short and stocky: 'erat brevis staturae et spissus'. Although this likeness is less striking, we cannot say that the two descriptions are at odds, for short stature can be found with a well built frame and strength and stockiness are also found together. Expressed in modern psychological terms, Urban VI was a pronounced 'pyknic' type.

Thus everything suggests that the anonymous example whom Gerson depicted to Benedict was Pope Urban VI. If we accept this, it was by no means a 'maladresse' to hold up this mirror to him, but much rather a tactical manoeuvre, for Gerson could be quite sure that Benedict, who had not broken with Urban for nothing, would give a very warm welcome to any unfriendly story about his former master (see Chapter IV n. 40).

APPENDIX FOUR

THE DATING OF THE SERMON *VADE IN PACE*

(Gl. 7*, 1093-100; Dupin IV, 565-71)

The editor of Gerson's works, Dupin, dated the sermon *Vade in pace* to 1394 or 1395. 'Habita est ista oratio in tempore quo nuntiatum est Bonifatium et Benedictum contendentes de papatu, viam cessionis admisisse.' (Dupin, IV 565). Schwab (*Gerson*, 194 n. 3), disagreed: 'Von dem Herausgeber der Werke Gersons ist sie irrigerweise auf 1394 (aut) 95 ... verlegt, was schon die Worte des Textes (567B) «depuis de *trente* ans avons nous demandé paix» hätten hindern sollen, abgesehen von dem gänzlichen Mangel eines geschichtlichen Anhaltspunktes für 1394 oder 1395!' Valois (*Schisme*, III, 479 n. 2) agreed with Schwab, although he dated the sermon not to Palm Sunday but to 16 January 1407. '... J.B. Schwab assigne bien à ce discours la date de 1407, mais le suppose, je ne sais pourquoi, prononcé le dimanche des Rameaux.' André Combes (*Jean de Montreuil*, 569 n. 3), again took up the supposition of Dupin and believed the sermon to have been given in 1394 or 1395 'car l'orateur célèbre la paix obtenue par les bonnes dispositions des deux rivaux à l'égard de la voie de cession, ce qui serait d'une ironie assez cruelle, et fort peu gersonienne, en janvier 1407.'

One may rub one's eyes in amazement at this, for was the author unaware that Gerson had from the very beginning always regarded cession as the best and most Christian solution? Was he ignorant of the fact that Gerson had repeatedly expressed the hope that Benedict in the first place, but the Pope of Rome as well, would declare themselves willing to adopt it? And now, in early 1407, it seemed that the long cherished expectations were about to be fulfilled. The language of Gerson's sermon was exalted, the more so because the leaders of the Church seemed at last to have reached agreement on a basis which he had always recommended, most recently in his *Disputatio de schismate tollendo* (Gl. 6, 100; Dupin II 79A).

In the absence of other arguments for his thesis that this sermon would not fit the context of 1407, and although he had to admit that 'trente ans' '... inviterait normalement à raisonner comme Noël Valois' – and Schwab (PM) – A. Combes tried to weaken the force of this last argument by observing that 'trente ans' appears in BN fr. 24841 fol. 320vo as XXX, a method of writing which, he argues, can easily lead to error. 'Il est moins invraisemblable qu'un de ces X ait été ajouté par distraction de copiste. Près de XX ans, voilà qui n'irait pas mal en 1395.' Leaving aside the fact that 'près de XX ans' would point to 1396 or 1397 rather than 1395, and that Schwab was right to point out the absence of a suitable occasion in those years, it will be clear to everyone that Combes's argument is very far-fetched and a proof of his embarrassment. One can make matters more difficult than they really are.

To eliminate any remaining doubt about the dating, however unlikely, we refer to the following passage in the sermon *Vade in pace* (Gl. 7*, 1096; Dupin IV 568A):

> Je vous pry, que chascun à présent considere, et avise la difficulté qui est a surmonter temptacion quelconque, tant soit petite; et par especial quant ce vient que son honneur, ou sa gloire, ou sa renommée y perit, et lors nous verrons, que ce n'est pas si legiere chose de renuncier à l'estat papal, comme aucuns pensent, et que à ce convient que la grace divine y oeuvre: je ne dy pas que à ce ne soit obligié ung pape, ou ung pasteur, en temps, et en lieu, *sicut deduxi pluries coram papa* ...

It comes down to these last words, in which Gerson asserts that he had repeatedly reminded the Pope of his duty to resign. Now we think there can be no doubt that this refers to the end of 1403 and early in 1404 when he was in attendance on the curia; and this explanation tallies exactly with what we know of this period. In his sermon at Tarascon on 1 January 1404 he had urged the Pope to resign. He did so by holding up to Benedict the Pope's own statements which he, Gerson, said he had often – *pluries* – heard from the Pope's lips (Gl. 5, 86; Dupin II, 70C).

> ... dictum illud memorabile et vere dignum a summo pontifice, quod his auribus *pluries accepi ab ore domini nostri*, – hoc sine adulationis spiritu refero. «Paratus sum», inquit, «etiam usque ad mortem vel immolationem proprii corporis, si ita res exigat, ecclesiasticam unionem procurare.» Quanto amplius usque ad proprii status abdicationem. Nam quando daret vitam, qui non desereret vestem aut vitam, coronam seu mitram?

By linking the first fact with the second, not only is the dating suggested by Schwab and Valois confirmed and that of Dupin and Combes ruled out but more light is shed on the content of the conversations that Gerson had with the Pope while he was present in the curia. He must have urged Benedict more than once to take the matter of resignation seriously. The discovery of this new fact, which in our opinion is not unimportant, may justify going into such detail on a problem which, far from being raised by the text itself, only existed in the mind of a learned but sometimes hypercritical gersonisant: Mgr. André Combes.

By adding the first and with the second, [illegible] is the [illegible] [illegible] and [illegible] and [illegible] and that of [illegible] and [illegible] question [illegible] of the co[illegible] that [illegible] had with the [illegible] which was present in the [illegible] [illegible] that he [illegible] [illegible] [illegible] [illegible] in a [illegible] point [illegible] the first [illegible] [illegible] [illegible] [illegible].

ABBREVIATIONS

a.c.	*articulus citatus*
AHC	*Archivum Historiae Conciliorum*
AHDLM	*Archives d'Histoire Doctrinale et Littéraire du Moyen Age*
AHR	*American Historical Review*
AKG	*Archiv für Kulturgeschichte*
ALKGM	*Archiv für Literatur und Kirchengeschichte des Mittelalters*
BCRH	*Bulletin de la Commission Royale d'Histoire*
BN	*Bibliothèque Nationale*
CH	*Church History*
COD	*Conciliorum Oecumenicorum Decreta*, 3d. ed., ed. J. Alberigo [e.a.]
CSEL	*Corpus Scriptorum Ecclesiasticorum Latinorum*
CUP	Denifle-Chatelain, *Chartularium Universitatis Parisiensis*
DAEM	*Deutsches Archiv für die Erforschung des Mittelalters*
DDC	*Dictionnaire de Droit Canonique*
DS	*Dictionnaire de la Spiritualité*
DThC	*Dictionnaire de Théologie Catholique*
ETL	*Ephemerides Theologicae Lovanienses*
ep.	*epistola*
Hinschius	P. Hinschius, *Decretales Pseudo-Isidoriani*
HLF	*Histoire Littéraire de la France*
HV	*Historische Vierteljahrschrift*
HZ	*Historische Zeitschrift*
JHI	*Journal of the History of Ideas*
JTS	*Journal of Theological Studies*
L	*Luthertum*
l.s.	*liber (libri) sententiarum*
LThK	*Lexikon für Theologie und Kirche* (2d. ed.)
Mansi	J. Mansi, *Sacrorum conciliorum nova et amplissima collectio*
MKNAW	*Mededelingen der Koninklijke Nederlandse Akademie van Wetenschappen*
MG	*Migne, Patrologia, series Graeca*
MHE	*Miscellanea Historiae Ecclesiasticae*
MM	*Miscellanea Medievalia*
ML	*Migne, Patrologia, series Latina*
MS	*Medieval Studies*
MSR	*Mélanges de Sciences Religieuses*
MTZ	*Münchener Theologische Zeitschrift*
NAKG	*Nederlands Archief voor Kerkgeschiedenis*
PRE	*Realencyklopädie für protestantische Theologie und Kirche* (3d. ed.)
RHE	*Revue d'Histoire Ecclésiastique*
RHDF	*Revue Historique de droit français et étranger*
RHF	*Revue d'Histoire de l'Église de France*
RMAL	*Revue du Moyen-âge Latin*

RHPR	*Revue d'Histoire et de Philosophie Religieuses*
Rom.	*Romania*
RQ	*Römische Quartalschrift für christliche Altertumskunde und für Kirchengeschichte*
RSR	*Revue des Sciences Religieuses*
RTAM	*Recherches de Théologie Ancienne et Médiévale*
SC	*Sources Chrétiennes*
S.th.	*Summa theologica*
TRE	*Theologische Realenzyklopädie*

BIBLIOGRAPHY

Primary Sources

Acta concilii Constanciensis: ed. H. Finke et al., I-IV, Münster 1896-1928.
Alexander a Sancto Elpidio: *De potestate ecclesiastica*, ed. Rocaberti II, 1-40.
Alvarez Pelayo: *De planctu ecclesiae*, Venetiis 1560.
Augustinus Triumphus: *Summa de potestate ecclesiastica*, Augsburg 1473.
–, *De potestate praelatorum*, ed. Duynstee, *'s Pausen primaat* II, 331-45.
Basilius, *Liber de Spiritu*, *SC* 17.
Bernard of Clairvaux: *De consideratione*, *ML* 183, 727-808.
–, *De praecepto et dispensatione*, *ML* 183, 859-95.
–, *In Cant. homiliae*, *ML* 184, 11-252.
Boethius, *De consolatione philosophiae* (Loeb ed., 1953).
Bonaventura: *Opera omnia*, I-X, Ad Claras Aquas (Quaracchi) 1882-1902.
Conciliorum oecumenicorum decreta: ed. J. Alberigo, 3 Bologna 1973.
Conrad of Gelnhausen: *Epistola concordiae*, ed. Bliemetzrieder, *Literarische Polemik*, 111-40.
–, *Epistola brevis*, ed. Kaiser, *HV* III (1900), 381-86.
Decretales Pseudo-Isidoriani: ed. P. Hinschius, Leipzig 1863.
Denifle, H. & Chatelain, E.: *Chartularium universitatis Parisiensis*, III-IV, Paris 1894-97.
–, *Auctarium chartularium universitatis Parisiensis*, I-II, Paris 1894-97.
Dietrich of Niem: *De modis uniendi ac reformandi ecclesiam in concilio universali*, ed. Dupin, *Gersonii Opera omnia* II, 161-201 (Modern ed.: Dietrich von Nieheim. ed. Hermann Heimpel, Leipzig 1933).
–, *De schismate*, ed. S. Schardius, Basel 1566.
Dionysius Areopagita: *Opera*, *MG* 3.
–, *Dionysiaca*, I-II, ed. Ph. Chevalier, Paris 1937-50.
DuBoulay, C.E.: *Historia universitatis Parisiensis*, IV-V, Paris 1668-70.
Durand of St Pourçain: *Commentaria in IV libros sententiarum*, Paris 1508.
–, *De origine iurisdictionum*, Paris 1516.
Enchiridion Symbolorum: ed. H. Denzinger & A. Schönmetzer, 33 Barcinone [etc.] 1975.
Giles of Rome: *De ecclesiastica sive de summi pontificis potestate*, ed. Scholz, Weimar 1929.
–, *De renunciatione papae*, ed. Rocaberti II, 1-64.
–, *Contra exemptos*, ed. Duynstee, *'s Pausen primaat* II, 345-49.
Hardouin, J.: *Acta conciliorum et epistolae decretales et constitutiones summorum pontificum*, VIII, Paris 1714.
Hardt, Hermann von der: *Magnum oecumenicum Constanciense concilium*, I-VI, Frankfurt / Leipzig 1692-1700.
Henry of Langenstein: *Epistola concilii pacis*, cap. I, ed. Hartwig, Marburg 1858, 28-33; cap. II ff. ed. Dupin, *Gersonii Opera omnia* II, 809-40.

Henry Totting of Oyta: *Quaestio de sacra scriptura*, ed. A. Lang, Münster i.W. 1932.
–, *Quaestio de veritatibus catholicis*, ed. A. Lang, Münster i.W. 1933.
Henry of Ghent: *Quodlibeta*, Paris 1518.
Henricus of Cremona: *Non ponant laici os in celum*, ed. Scholz, *Publizistik*, 471-84.
–, *De potestate papae*, ed. Scholz, *Publizistik*, 459-71.
Hervaeus Natalis: *De iurisdictione*, ed. Hödl, München 1959.
Jacob of Viterbo: *De regimine christiano*, ed. Arquillière, Paris 1926.
Jean Courtecuisse: *Tractatus de fide et ecclesia, romano pontifice et concilio generalis*, ed. Dupin, *Gersonii Opera omnia* I, 805-904.
Jean Gerson: *Opera omnia*, ed. E. Richer, I-IV, Paris 1606.
–, *Opera Omnia*, ed. Lud. Ellies Dupin, I-V, Antwerpiae 1706.
–, *Oeuvres complètes*, ed. Mgr. P. Glorieux, I-X, Paris 1960-73.
–, *Six sermons français inédits de Jean Gerson*. ed. L. Mourin, Paris 1946.
–, *De mystica theologia*, ed. A. Combes, Lugano [1958].
–, *De iurisdictione spirituali et temporali*, ed. G.H.M. Posthumus Meyjes, Leiden 1978.
John of Paris: *De regia potestate et papali*, ed. F. Bleienstein, Stuttgart [1969].
Johannes Teutonicus: *Glossa ordinaria*, Romae 1584.
Mansi, J.D.: *Sacrorum conciliorum nova et amplissima collectio*, 26 & 27, Venetiis 1784.
Marsilius of Padua: *Defensor pacis*, ed. Scholz, Hannover 1932-33.
Martène, E. & U. Durand: *Thesaurus novus anecdotorum*, II, Paris 1717.
–, *Veterum scriptorum... amplissima collectio*, II, Paris 1624.
Martin de Alpartils, *Chronica actitarum temporibus Benedicti XIII*, ed. F. Ehrle, I, Paderborn 1906.
Nicolas of Lyra: *Postilla super Bibliam*, [Norimbergae] 1481.
Nicolas of Clémanges: *De corrupto Ecclesiae status*, ed. J. Lydius, *Opera omnia* I, Leiden 1613, 4-28.
Pierre d'Ailly: *Apologia concilii Pisani*, ed. Tschackert, Gotha 1877, [31-41].
–, *Commentaria in IV libros sententiarum*, Brussels 1484.
–, *Radix omnium malorum est cupiditas*, ed. Bernstein, Leiden 1978, 197-236 (= *Tractatus I adversus Cancellarium Parisiensem*, ed. Dupin, *Gersonii Opera Omnia* I, 723-44).
–, *Super omnia vincit veritas*, ed. Bernstein, 237-98 (= *Tractatus II adversus Cancellarium Parisiensem*, ed. Dupin I, 745-78).
–, *Epistola diaboli Leviathan*, ed. Tschackert, [5-21].
–, *Epistola ad novos Hebraeos*, ed. Tschackert, [7-12].
–, *Utrum indoctus in iure divino possit iuste praeesse in ecclesiae regno*, ed. Dupin I, 646-62.
–, *Utrum Petri ecclesia rege gubernetur*, ed. Dupin I, 672-93.
–, *De legitimo dominio*, ed. Dupin I, 641-46.
–, *De materia concilii generalis*, ed. Oakley, New Haven (Conn.) 1964.
–, *Propositiones utiles*, ed. Dupin II, 112-13.
–, *Octo conclusiones per plures doctores in Italiae partibus approbatae*, ed. Dupin II, 110-11.
–, *De potestate ecclesiastica seu de ecclesiae, concilii generalis, romani pontificis et cardinalium auctoritate*, ed. Dupin II, 925-60.
Petrus Aureoli: *Commentarium in secundum librum sententiarum* II, Rome 1605.
Petrus Hispanus: *Summule logicales*, ed. L.M. De Rijk, Assen 1972.
Petrus Lombardus: *Libri IV sententiarum*, I-II, Ad Claras Aquas (Quaracchi) 1916.
Petrus de Palude: *De potestate papae*, ed. P.T. Stella, Zürich 1966.
–, *Tractatus de causa immediata ecclesiasticae potestatis*, Paris 1506.

Religieux de Saint-Denis, *Chronique contenant le règne de Charles VI de 1390 à 1422*, ed. L. Bellaguet, I-VI, Paris 1839-52.
Rocaberti, J.Th. de: *Bibliotheca maxima pontificia* II, Roma 1695.
Richard of Bury: *Philobiblon*, ed. by Michael Maclagan, Oxford [1960].
Richard of Middletown, *Super quatuor libros Sententiarum*, Brescia 1591.
Richental, Ulrich von: *Chronik des Constanzer Conzils 1414-1418*, ed. Michael Buck, Stuttgart 1882.
Robert Holcot: *Commentaria in IV libros sententiarum*, Lugduni 1518.
–, *Sapientia Salomonis*, (ed. 1586).
Thomas Aquinas: *Scriptum super libros sententiarum magistri Petri Lombardi Episcopi Parisiensis*, ed. R.P. Mandonnet, I-III, Paris. 1929.
–, *Contra pestiferam doctrinam retrahentium homines a religionis ingressu*, in: *Opuscula* IV, ed. R.P. Mandonnet, Paris. 1927, 265-323.
Thomas de Vio cardinalis Caietanus: *De comparatione auctoritatis papae et concilii cum Apologia eiusdem tractatus*, ed. Vincentius M.J. Pollet, Romae 1935.
William of Ockham: *Dialogus*, ed. Goldast, *Monarchia* II, 398-957.
–, *De dogmatibus Ioannis XXII*, ed. Goldast, *Monarchia* II, 740-70.
–, *Breviloquium de principatu tyrannico*, ed. Scholz, Stuttgart 1952.
–, *Tractatus contra Ioannem*, in: *Opera Politica* III, ed. H.S. Offler, Manchester 1956, 20-156.

Secondary Sources

Abramowski, Luise: 'Johann Gerson, De consiliis evangelicis et statu perfectionis,' in: *Studien zur Geschichte und Theologie der Reformation (Festschrift für Ernst Bizer)*, Neukirchen 1969 63-78.
Adam, Paul: *La vie paroissiale en France au XIVe siècle*, [Paris] 1964.
Alberigo, Giuseppe: *Chiesa conciliare: Identità e significato del conciliarismo*, Brescia 1981.
Altensteig, J.: *Lexicon Theologicum*, Cologne 1619 (reprint 1974).
Amann, E.: art. 'Pierre de Luna,' in: *DThC* XII, 2020-9.
Arquillière, H.-X.: *Le plus ancien traité de l'Eglise, Jacques de Viterbe, De regimine christiano (1301-1302). Etude des sources et édition critique*, Paris 1926.
Asseldonk, G. van: *De Nederlanden en het Westers Schisma (tot 1398)*, Utrecht/Nijmegen 1955
Aubert, Félix: *Le Parlement de Paris de Philippe-le-Bel à Charles VII (1314-1422). Son organisation*, Paris 1886.
Bakhuizen van den Brink, J.N.: 'Traditio in de Reformatie en het Katholicisme in de zestiende eeuw,' *MKNAW* afd. Lett. NR 15, 2, Amsterdam 1952,
–, 'La tradition dans l'église primitive,' *RHPR* 36 (1956) 271-81.
Barker, John W.: *Manuel II Palaeologus (1391-1425). A Study on late Byzantine Statesmanship*, New Brunswick 1969.
Baudry, L.: *Guillaume d'Occam. Sa vie, ses oeuvres, ses idées sociales et politiques*, I. L'homme et l'oeuvre, Paris 1950.
–, *Lexique philosophique de Guillaume d'Ockham*, Paris [1958].
Bauer, Clemens: 'Diskussionen um die Zins- und Wucherfrage auf dem Kon-

stanzer Konzil,' in: August Franzen & Wolfgang Müller [edd.], *Das Konzil von Konstanz*, 174-86.

Bäumer, Remigius [ed.]: *Von Konstanz nach Trient. Beiträge zur Kirchengeschichte von den Reformkonzilien bis zum Tridentinum (Festschrift A. Franzen)*, München 1972.

–, 'Das Verbot der Konzilsappellation Martins V. in Konstanz,' in: *Das Konzil von Konstanz*, 187-213.

–, [ed.]: *Die Entwicklung des Konziliarismus. Werden und Nachwirken der konziliaren Idee*, Darmstadt 1976.

–, 'Die Erforschung des Konziliarismus', in: *Die Entwicklung des Konziliarismus*, 3-56.

Bernstein, Alan E.: *Pierre d'Ailly and the Blanchard Affair. University and Chancellor of Paris at the Beginning of the Great Schism*, Leiden 1978.

Bess, B.: *Johannes Gerson und die kirchenpolitischen Parteien Frankreichs vor dem Konzil zu Pisa*, Marburg 1890.

Bezold, Friedrich von: 'Die Lehre von der Volkssouveränität während des Mittelalters,' in: *Aus Mittelalter und Renaissance. Kulturgeschichtliche Studien*, München/-Berlin 1918, 1-48.

Binder, Karl: *Wesen und Eigenschaften der Kirche bei Kardinal Juan de Torquemada O.P.*, Insbruck 1955.

Bissen, J.-M.: *L'exemplarisme divin selon Saint Bonaventure*, Paris 1929.

Bliemetzrieder, Franz: *Das Generalkonzil im grossen abendländischen Schisma*, Paderborn 1904.

–, *Literarische Polemik zu Beginn des grossen abendländischen Schismas*, Wien/Leipzig 1909.

Böhner, Philotheus: William Ockham, *Philosophical Writings. A selection*, s.l. 1957.

Boland, Paschal, *The Concept of Discretio Spirituum in Gerson's 'De Probatione Spirituum' and 'De Distinctione Verarum Visionum a Falsis*,' Washington 1959.

Botte, B. & H. Marot [edd.]: *Le Concile et les Conciles. Contribution à l'histoire de la vie conciliaire de l'Eglise*, s.l. [1960].

Bougerol, J.G.: 'Saint Bonaventure et la hiérarchie Dionysienne,' *AHDLM* 36 (1969) 131-67.

Bourgeois du Chastenet, L.: *Nouvelle histoire du concile de Constance*, Paris 1718.

Brandmüller, Walter: 'Besitzt das Konstanzer Dekret «Haec Sancta» dogmatische Verbindlichkeit?', *AHC* 1 (1969) 96-113. (Reprinted in: *Die Entwicklung des Konziliarismus*, ed. R. Bäumer, 247-71).

–, 'Das Konzil, demokratisches Kontrollorgan über den Papst?', *AHC* 16 (1984) 328-47

–, *Das Konzil von Konstanz (1414-1418)*, I-II, Paderborn 1991-7.

Brown, D. Catherine: *Pastor and Laity in the Theology of Jean Gerson*, London [etc.] [1987].

Buisson, L.: *Potestas und Caritas*, Cologne/Graz 1958.

Burger, Christoph-Peter: art. 'Gerson, Jean' in: *TRE* 12, 532-8.

–, *Aedificatio, Fructus, Utilitas. Johannes Gerson als Professor der Theologie und Kanzler der Universität Paris*, Tübingen 1986.

Burrows, Mark Stephen: *Jean Gerson and De Consolatione Theologiae (1418). The consolation of a Biblical and Reforming Theology for a Disordered Age*, Tübingen [1991].

Chenu, M.-D.: *Introduction à l'étude de Saint Thomas d'Aquin*, [2] Montréal/Paris 1954.

–, *La théologie au XIIIe siècle*, [3] Paris 1957.

–, 'Officium. Théologiens et canonistes,' in: *Etudes d'Histoire du Droit Canonique, dédiées à Gabriel LeBras* II, Paris 1965, 835-39.

Combes, André: 'Etudes gersoniennes I. L'authenticité gersonienne de l'«Annotatio doctorum aliquorum qui de contemplatione locuti sunt», *AHDLM* 14 (1939) 291-364.

–, 'Etudes gersoniennes II. Note sur les «Sententiae magistri Joannis Gerson» du manuscrit B.N. lat. 15156,' *AHDLM* 14 (1939) 365-85.

–, *Jean Gerson commentateur dionysien. Pour l'histoire des courants doctrinaux à l'Université de Paris à la fin du XIVe siècle*, Paris 1940.

–, *Jean de Montreuil et le chancelier Gerson. Contribution à l'histoire des rapports de l'humanisme et de la théologie en France au début du XVe siècle*, Paris 1942.

–, 'Gerson et la naissance de l'humanisme. Notes sur les rapports de l'histoire doctrinale et de l'histoire littéraire,' *RMAL* 1 (1945) 259-84.

–, *Essai sur la critique de Ruysbroeck par Gerson*, I-IV, Paris 1945-72.

–, art. 'Denys l'Aréopagite V.' Influence du Ps.-Denys en occident, 4 Gerson (d. 1429), *DS* III, 365-75.

–, *La théologie mystique de Gerson. Profil de son évolution*, I-II, Rome 1963-64.

Congar, Yves M.-J.: Incidence ecclésiologique d'un thème de dévotion mariale', *MSR* VIII (1951) 277-92

–, *La Tradition et les tradition. Essai historique*, Paris [1960].

–, 'Aspects ecclésiologiques de la querelle entre mendiants et séculiers dans la seconde moitié du XIIIe siècle et le début du XIVe,' *AHDLM* 36 (1961) 35-151.

–, 'Un témoignage des désaccords entre canonistes et théologiens,' in: *Etude d'histoire du droit canonique, dédiées à Gabriel LeBras* II, Paris 1965, 861-84.

–, *Die Lehre von der Kirche. Von Augustinus bis zum abendländischen Schisma*, in: *Handbuch der Dogmengeschichte* III, fasc 3c, Freiburg 1971.

Connolly, James. L.: *John Gerson. Reformer and Mystic*, Louvain 1928.

Coville, Alfred: *Jean Petit: La question du tyrannicide au commencement du XVe siècle*, Paris 1935.

–, *Le traité de la ruine de l'église de Nicolas de Clamanges*, Paris 1936.

Crowder, C.M.D.: 'Le concile de Constance et l'édition de Von der Hardt', *RHE* 57 (1962) 409-15.

–, *Unity, Heresy, and Reform, 1379-1460: The Conciliar Response to the Great Schism*, London 1977.

Davy, M.-M,: *Les sermons universitaires Parisiens de 1230-31*, Paris 1931.

Delaruelle, Etienne, E.R. Labande & Paul Ourliac: *L'Eglise au temps du Grand Schisme et la crise conciliaire, 1378-1449*, Paris 1962-64, (A. Fliche & V. Martin, *Histoire de l'Eglise*, XIV)

Döllinger, J.J.I.: *Papstfabeln des Mittelalters* I, München 1863.

Duynstee, X.P.D.: *'s Pausen primaat in de latere middeleeuwen en de Aegidiaanse school*, I-II, Hilversum/ Amsterdam 1935-36.

Ehrle, F.: 'Neue Materialien zur Geschichte Peters de Luna,' *ALKGM* VI (1892) 139-302; VII (1900) 1-306

–, 'Aus den Akten des Afterconcils von Perpignan,' *ALKGM* V (1891) 387-465; VII (1900) 576-693.

–, *Der Sentenzenkommentar Peters von Candia des Pisaner Papstes Alexander V. Ein Beitrag zur*

Scheidung der Schulen in der Scholastik des 14. Jhdts und zur Geschichte des Wegestreites, Münster i.W. 1925.

Fabricius, J.A.: *Bibliotheca latina mediae et infimae aetatis*, I, Florentiae 1858.

Fasolt, Constantin. *Council and Hierarchy: The Political Thought of William Durant the Younger*, Cambridge [1991].

Feine, Hans Erich: *Kirchliche Rechtsgeschichte auf der Grundlage der Grundlage des Kirchenrechts von Ulrich Stutz, I: Die katholische Kirche*, Weimar 1950.

Féret, Pierre: *La faculté de théologie de Paris au 14e et 15e siècles. A. Moyen Age*, I-IV, Paris 1894-97.

Finke, Heinrich: *Aus den Tagen Bonifaz' VIII*, Münster 1902.

Franzen, August & Wolfgang Müller [edd.]: *Das Konzil von Konstanz. Beiträge zu seiner Geschichte und Theologie*, Freiburg [etc.] 1964.

–, 'Zur Vorgeschichte des Konstanzer Konzils', in: *Das Konzil von Konstanz*, 3-35.

–, 'Konziliarismus', in: Remigius Bäumer [ed.], *Die Entwicklung des Konziliarismus*, 75-81.

–, 'Das Konzil der Einheit. Einigungsbemühungen und konziliare Gedanken auf dem Konstanzer Konzil. Die Dekrete «Haec sancta» und «Frequens»,' in: *Das Konzil von Konstanz*, 69-112.

Gabriel, Astrik L.: '«Via antiqua» and «via moderna» and the migration of Paris students and masters to the German universities in the fifteenth century,' *MM* 9 (1974) 439-83.

Ganzer, Claus: 'Päpstliche Gesetzgebuggewalt und kirchlicher Konsens. Zur Verwendung eines Diktum Gratians in der Concordia Catholica des Nikolaus von Kues,' in: Remigius Bäumer [ed.], *Von Konstanz nach Trient* (Festschrift A. Franzen), 171-88.

Ghellinck, Joseph de: 'Un évêque bibliophile au XIVe siècle. Richard Aungerville de Bury (1345),' *RHE* XVIII (1922) 271-312; 482-508; XIX (1923) 157-200.

–, 'Magister Vacarius. Un juriste théologien peu aimable pour les canonistes,' *RHE* XLIV (1943) 173-8.

–, '«Pagina» et «Sacra Pagina». Histoire d'un mot et transformation de l'objet primitivement désigné,' in: *Mélanges August Pelzer*, Louvain 1947, 23-59.

Gierke, Otto von: *Das Deutsche Genossenschaftsrecht* III, Darmstadt 1954.

Gilson, E.: *La philosophie au moyen âge des origines patristiques à la fin du XIVe siècle*, [2] Paris 1952.

Girardez, L.: *Exposé de la doctrine de Gerson sur l'Eglise*, thèse Strasbourg, Strasbourg 1868.

Glorieux, Palémon: *Répertoire des maîtres en théologie à Paris au XIIIe*, I-II, Paris 1933-34.

–, 'L'année universitaire 1392-1393 à la Sorbonne à travers les notes d'un étudiant', *RSR* 19 (1939) 429-82.

–, 'La vie et les oeuvres de Gerson,' *AHDLM* 25-26 (1950-51) 149-92.

–, 'Le Commentaire des Sentences attribué à Jean Gerson,' *RTAM* 18 (1951) 128-39.

–, 'Autour de la liste des oeuvres de Gerson,' *RTAM* 22 (1955) 95-105.

–, 'L'enseignement universitaire de Gerson,' *RTAM* 23 (1956) 88-113.

–, 'Les «Lectiones duae super Marcum» de Gerson,' *RTAM* 27 (1960) 344-56.

–, 'Gerson et S. Bonaventure,' in: *S. Bonaventure 1274-1974* IV, Grottaferrata / Rome 1974, 773-91

–, art. 'Gerson (Jean), théologien et auteur spirituel', *DS* VI, 314-31.

Grabmann, Martin: *Die Lehre des hl. Thomas von Aquin von der Kirche als Gotteswerk*, Regensburg 1903.

–, *Die Geschichte der katholischen Theologie seit dem Ausgang der Väterzeit*, Freiburg i.B. 1933.

–, art. 'Nikolaus von Dinkelsbühl', *LThK* 7, 577.

–, 'Die Erörterung der Frage ob die Kirche besser durch einen guten Juristen oder durch einen Theologen regiert werde, bei Gottfried von Fontaines (d. nach 1306) und Augustinus Triumphus von Ancona (d. 1328)', in: *Festschrift Eduard Eichmann*, Paderborn 1940, 1-19.

Grundmann, H.: 'Sacerdotium-Regnum-Studium. Zur Wertung der Wissenschaft im 13 Jhdt.,' *AKG* 34 (1952) 5-21.

Haller, Johannes: *Papsttum und Kirchenreform. Vier Kapitel zur Geschichte des ausgehenden Mittelalters*, Berlin 1903.

Hartwig, O.: *Leben und Schriften Heinrichs von Langenstein*, Marburg 1858.

Hauck, A.: 'Die Rezeption und Umbildung der allgemeinen Synode im Mittelalter,' *HV* X (1907) 465-82

–, 'Gegensätze im Kirchenbegriff des späteren Mittelalters,' *L* XLIX (1938) 225-40.

Hefele-Leclercq: *Histoire des conciles*, VI 1 & 2, Paris 1915.

Heimpel, Hermann. *Dietrich von Niem*, Münster 1932.

Hinschius, P.: *System des katholischen Kirchenrechts mit besonderer Rücksicht auf Deutschland* I, Berlin 1869.

–, art. 'Dispensation,', *PRE* IV, 708-10.

Hochstetter, E.: '«Viator mundi». Einige Bemerkungen zur Situation des Menschen bei Wilhelm von Ockham,' in: *Wilhelm Ockham (1349-1949). Aufsätze zu seiner Philosophie und Theologie*, Münster i.W. 1950, 1-21.

Hödl, L.: 'Kirchengewalt und Kirchenverfassung nach dem Liber de ecclesiastica potestate des Laurentius von Arezzo,' in: *Theologie in Geschichte und Gegenwart*, (Festschrift Michael Schmaus), ed. J. Auer & H. Volk, München 1959.

–, *De iurisdictione. Ein unveröffentliches Traktat des Hervaeus Natalis O.P. (1323) über die Kirchengewalt*, München 1959.

Hoffmanns J.: 'Le dixième Quodlibet de Godefroid de Fontaines (texte inédit), in: *Les philosophes Belges* IV, fasc. III, Louvain 1931, 395-98.

Holl, Karl: 'Der Streit zwischen Petrus und Paulus zu Antiochien in seiner Bedeutung für Luthers innere Entwicklung,' in: *Gesammelte Aufsätze* III, Tübingen 1928, 134-46.

Hollnsteiner, J.: 'Die konziliare Idee,' in: Remigius Bäumer [ed.], *Die Entwicklung des Konziliarismus*, 59-74.

Horst, Ulrich: 'Das Wesen der «potestas clavium» nach Thomas von Aquin,' *MTZ* IX (1960), 191-201.

Hove, A. von: *Commentarium Lovaniense in codicem iuris canonici*, vol. I, I Prolegomena, Mechliniae [etc.] 1928.

Hübler, B.: *Die Constanzer Reformation und die Concordate von 1418*, Leipzig 1867.

Iung, N.: *Un Franciscain, théologien du pouvoir pontifical au XIVe siècle, Alvaro Pelayo, évêque et pénitencier de Jean XXII*, Paris 1931.

Jadart, H.: *Jean Gerson, 1363-1429, recherches sur son origine, son village natal et sa famille*, Rheims 1882

Jedin, Hubert: *Geschichte des Konzils von Trient I*, Freiburg 1951.

–, art. 'Konziliarismus' in: *LThK* 6, 532-3.

–, 'Bischöfliches Konzil oder Kirchenparlement?' in: Remigius Bäumer [ed.], *Die Entwicklung des Konziliarismus*, 198-228.

Kantorowicz, Ernst H.: *The King's Two Bodies. A Study in Mediaeval Political Theology*, Princeton 1957

Kerken, L. van der: art. 'Exemplarursächlichkeit' in: *LThK* 3, 1294-5.

Kibre, Pearl: Scholarly Privileges in the Middle Ages. *The Rights, Privileges and Immunities of Scholars and Universities at Bologna, Padua, Paris and Oxford*, Cambridge (Mass.) 1961.

Kneer, August. *Die Entstehung der konziliaren Theorie: Zur Geschichte des Schismas und der kirchenpolitischen Schriftsteller, Konrad von Gelnhausen (d. 1390) und Heinrich von Langenstein (d. 1397)*, *RQ*, Erstes Supplementsheft, 1893, 48-60 (Reprinted in: Remigius Bäumer [ed.], *Die Entwicklung des Konziliarismus*, 103-12.

Koch, J.: 'Durandus a S. Porciano O.P. Forschungen zum Streit um Thomas von Aquin zu Beginn des 14. Jhdt, I,' in: *Beiträge zur Geschichte der Philosophie des Mittelalters*, XXVI, Münster 1927.

Kreuzer, Georg: *Heinrich von Langenstein. Studien zur Biographie und zu den Schismatraktaten unter besonderer Berücksichtigung der Epistola pacis und der Epistola concilii pacis*, Paderborn [etc.] 1987.

Küng, Hans: *Strukturen der Kirche*, Freiburg 1962.

Kuiters, R.: *De ecclesiastica sive de summi pontificis potestate secundum Aegidium Romanum*, Vatic. 1949.

Kuttner, Stephan G.: *Harmony from Dissonance. An Interpretation of Medieval Canon Law* (Wimmer Lecture, X), Latrope (Pa.) 1960

Lagarde, Georges de: *La naissance laïque au déclin du moyen age*, I-V, [2] Louvain 1956-63.

Lampe, G.W.H. ed.: *The Cambridge History of the Bible*, II, Cambridge 1969.

Landau, P.: 'Vorgratianische Kanonessammlungen bei Dekretisten und in frühen Dekretalensammlungen,' in: *Proceedings of the Eight Internat. Congress of Med. Canon Law*, Città del Vaticano 1992, 93-116.

LeBras, Gabriel: *Institutions ecclésiastiques de la Chrétienté médiévale*, I-II, Paris 1962-64.

–, & Ch. Lefebvre, J. Rambaud: *Histoire du Droit et des Institutions de l'Eglise en Occident VII: L'age classique 1140-1378, Sources et théorie du droit*, Paris [1965].

Leclercq, J.: 'La rénonciation de Célestin V et l'opinion théologique en France du vivant de Boniface VIII,' *RHF* 25 (1939) 173-92

–, *Jean de Paris et l'ecclésiologie du XIIIe siècle*, Paris 1942.

–, 'Le magistère du prédicateur au XIIIe siècle,' *AHDLM* 15 (1946) 105-47.

Lefebvre, Ch.: art. 'épikie' in: *DDC* V, 364-75.

Lehmann, Paul: 'Konstanz und Basel als Büchermarkte während der grossen Kirchenversammlungen', in: *Erforschung des Mittelalters. Ausgewählte Abhandlungen und Aufsätze*, Leipzig 1941, 253-68.

Lemarignier, J.-F., J. Gaudemet & Mgr. Guillaume Mollat: *Histoire des Institutions Françaises au Moyen Age* III, Institutions Ecclésiastiques, Paris 1962.
Lenzenweger, 'Von Pisa nach Konstanz,' in: August Franzen & Wolfgang Müller [edd.], *Das Konzil von Konstanz*, 36-54.
Lieberman, Max: Chronologie gersonienne I, *Rom.* 70 (1948) 51-67; II., *Rom.* 73 (1952) 480-96; III., *Rom.* 74 (1953) 289-337; V. 'Gerson et d'Ailly', *Rom.* 78 (1957) 433-62; VI. 'Gerson ou d'Ailly': «Annotatio doctorum aliquorum qui de contemplatione locuti sunt» *Rom.* 79 (1958) 339-75; VII. 'Gerson et d'Ailly' (II), *Rom.* 80 (1959) 289-336; VIII. 'Gerson et d'Ailly' (III), *Rom.* 81 (1960) 338-79; X. 'Le sermon Memento finis,' *Rom.* 83 (1962) 52-89; 'Autour de l'iconographie gersonienne', *Rom.* 84 (1963) 307-53; 'Autour de l'iconographie gersonienne' (II), 'Le tombeau de Philippe le Hardi', *Rom.* 85 (1964) 49-100; 230-68.
–, art. 'Ailly, Peter von', *LThK* 8, 329.
Long, R. James: '«Utrum iurista vel theologus plus proficiat ad regimen ecclesiae». A Questio disputata of Francis Caraccioli. Edition and study,' *MS* 30 (1968) 134-62.
Lubac, Henri de: *Corpus Mysticum. L'Eucharistie et l'Eglise au Moyen Age*, [2] Paris 1949.
–, *Exégèse médiévale. Les quatre sens de l'Ecriture*, sec. partie II, [Paris 1964].
Maccarone, M.: 'Teologia e diritto canonico nella Monarchia III 3,' *Rivista di storia della Chiesa in Italia*, 5 (1951) 7-42.
Mangenot E.: art. 'authenticité' in *DThC* I 2, 2584-98.
Martimort, Aimé-Georges: *Le Gallicanisme de Bossuet*, Paris 1953,
Martin, J.: art. 'Vigilius' in: *LThK* 10, 788-9.
Marlot, G.: *Histoire de la ville de Rheims* IV, Rheims 1846.
Martin, V.: *Les origines du Gallicanisme*, I-II, [Paris] 1939.
Matteo, Giovanni: 'Forschungsbericht: Gersoniana,' *Wolfenbütteler Renaissance Mitteilungen* XI (1985) 40-6.
Meller, B.: *Studien zur Erkenntnislehre des Peter von Ailly.* Anhang: Aillys Traktat De materia concilii generalis, Freiburg 1954.
Michel, A.: art. 'ordre' in *DThC* XI 2, 1193-1405.
Miethke, Jürgen: *Ockhams Weg zur Sozialphilosophie*, Berlin 1969.
–, 'Die Kirche und die Universitäten im Spätmittelalter und in der Zeit der Reformation.' in: *The Church in a Changing Society*, (CIHEC-Conference in Uppsala 1977), Publications of the Swedish Society of Church History NS 30 [Uppsala 1978], 240-4.
–, 'Marsilius und Ockham. Publikum und Leser ihrer politischen Schriften im späteren Mittelalter,'in: *Medioevo. Rivista di Storia della filosofia medievale* 5 (1979) 543-68.
–, 'Das Konsistorialmemorandum «De potestate papae» des Heinrich von Crèmona von 1302 und seine handschriftliche Ueberlieferung,' in: *Studi sul XIV seculo in memoria di Anneliese Maier*, edd. A. Maierù & A. Paravicini Bagliani, Romae 1981 (*Storia e Letteratura*, 151) 421-51.
–, 'Die Konzilien als Forum öffentlicher Meinung,' *DAEM* 37 (1981) 736-73.
–, 'Die Traktate "De potestate papae". Ein Typus politiktheoretischer Literatur im späten Mittelalter,' in: *Les genres littéraires dans les sources théologiques et philosophique médiévales*, (Actes du Colloque internat. de Louvain-la-Neuve, 25-27 mai 1981), Louvain-la-Neuve 1982, 193-211.

–, Wilhelm von Ockham, *Dialogus. Auszüge zur politischen Theorie*, ed. Jürgen Miethke, Darmstadt [1994].

–, & Lorenz Weinrich (edd.): *Quellen zur Kirchenreform im Zeitalter des grossen Konzilien des 15. Jahrhunderts* I, Darmstadt [1995].

Mollat, G.: 'L'application en France de la soustraction d'obédience à Benoît XIII jusqu'au concile de Pise.' *RMAL*, I (1945) 149-63.

Morrall, John B.: *Gerson and the Great Schism*, [Manchester 1960].

Mourin, Louis: *Six sermons français inédits de Gerson. Etude doctrinale et littéraire suivie de l'édition critique et de remarques linguistiques*, Paris 1946.

–, 'L'oeuvre oratoire française de Jean Gerson et les manuscrits qui la contiennent,' *AHDLM* 21 (1946) 225-61.

–, *Jean Gerson. Prédicateur français*, Brugge 1952.

–, 'Sur la date de quelques sermons français de Gerson,' *RTAM* 20 (1953) 120-28.

Nörr, Knut Wolfgang: *Kirche und Konzil bei Nicolaus de Tudeschis (Panormitanus)*, Köln/Graz 1964

Oakley, F.: 'The Propositiones utiles of Pierre d'Ailly: an epitome of conciliar theory,' *CH* 29 (1960), 399-403.

–, *The Political Thought of Pierre d'Ailly. The Voluntarist Tradition*, New Haven 1964.

–, 'Gerson and d'Ailly', *Speculum* 40 (1965) 74-83.

Oberman, Heiko Augustinus: *The Harvest of Medieval Theology*, Cambridge (Mass.) 1963.

–, *Forerunners of the Reformation. The Shape of Late Medieval Thought. Illustrated by Key Documents*, New York [etc.] [1966].

–, ' "Et tibi dabo claves regni caelorum". Kirche und Konzil von Augustin bis Luther. Tendenzen und Ergebnisse,' II, *Nederlands Theologisch Tijdschrift* 29 (1975) 97-118.

Olsen, Glenn: 'The Idea of the Ecclesia Primitiva in the Writings of the Twelf-Century Canonists,' *Traditio* XXV (1969) 61-89.

Ott, Ludwig, Erich Naab: *Eschatologie in der Scholastik*, in: *Handbuch der Dogmengeschichte* IV, fasc. 7b, Freiburg 1990.

Ouy, Gilbert: 'La plus ancienne oeuvre de Gerson retrouvée: le brouillion inachevé d'un traité contre Jean de Monzon (1389-90),' *Rom.* 83 (1962) 433-92.

–, 'Le receuil épistolaire autographe de Pierre d'Ailly et les notes d'Italie de Jean de Montreuil,' in: *Umbrae codicum occidentalium* 9, Amsterdam 1966.

–, 'Le Collège de Navarre, berceau de l'humanisme français,' in: *Actes du 95e Congrès National des Sociétés Savantes. Section de philologie et d'histoire jusqu'à 1610* I, Bibliothèque Nationale, Paris 1975, 275-99.

–, 'Gerson et Angleterre. A propos d'un texte polémique retrouvé du Chancelier de Paris contre l'Université d'Oxford,' in: *Humanism in France at the end of the Middle Ages and in early Renaissance*, ed. A.H.T. Levi, Manchester 1970, 43-81.

Ozment, S.E.: 'The University and the Church: patterns of reform in Gerson,' *Mediaevalia et Humanistica*, NS 1 (1970) 111-26.

Pacaut, Marcel: *La théocratie. L'Eglise et le pouvoir au moyen âge*, Paris 1957.

Pascoe, Louis B.: *Jean Gerson: Principles of Church Reform*, Leiden 1973.

–, 'Gerson and the Donation of Constantine,' in: *Growth and Development within the Church. Viator. Medieval and Renaissance Studies* 5, Berkeley/Los Angeles/London 1974.

Pastor, Ludwig von: *Geschichte der Päpste* I, Freiburg 1886.
Pauw, N. de: 'L'adhésion du clergé de Flandre au pape Urbain VI et les évêques de Gand, 1379-1395,' *Bulletin de la Commission Royale d'Histoire*, II (1904) 692-702.
Pelster, F.: 'Die indirekte Gewalt der Kirche über den Staat nach Ockham und Petrus de Palude,' *Scholastik* 28 (1953) 78-82.
Post, Gaines: *Studies in Medieval Legal Thought*, Princeton New Jersey 1964
Posthumus Meyjes, G.H.M.: *De controverse tussen Petrus en Paulus. Galaten 2: 11 in de historie*, 's-Gravenhage 1967.
–, 'Iconografie en Primaat. Petrus en Paulus op het pauselijk zegel,' *NAKG* NS 49 (1968) 4-36.
–, 'Nicolas de Dinkelsbühl à propos des auréoles des docteurs. Recherche fondée sur Melk, Stiftsbibliothek, cod. lat 504 (autographe),' in: *Texts & Manuscripts*, 47-55. Essays presented to G.I. Lieftinck II, ed. J.P. Gumbert & M.J.M. de Haan. *Literae textuales*, Amsterdam 1972.
–, *Jean Gerson et l'Assemblée de Vincennes (1329). Ses conceptions de la juridiction temporelle de l'Eglise. Accompagné d'une édition critique du De iurisdictione spirituali et temporali*, Leiden 1978.
–, 'De editie van Nicolaas van Clémanges, Opera Omnia, bezorgd door Johannes Lydius (Leiden 1613),' in: *Boeken Verzamelen*, ed. J.A.A.M. Biemans [e.a.], Leiden 1983, 231-48.
–, 'Jean Gerson,' in: *Gestalten der Kirchengeschichte. Mittelalter* II, ed. M. Greschat, Stuttgart 1983, 267-85.
–, 'Het gezag van de theologische doctor in de kerk der middeleeuwen – Gratianus, Augustinus Triumphus, Ockham en Gerson.' *NAKG* NS 63 (1984) 102-28.
–, 'Quasi stellae fulgebunt: the Doctor of Divinity in Mediaeval Society and Church,' in: *In Divers Manners. A St Mary's Miscellany to commemorate the 450th anniversary of the founding of St Mary's College, 7th March 1539*, ed. D.W.D. Shaw, University of St Andrews 1990, 11-28.
–, 'Pierre d'Ailly's verhandeling *Utrum indoctus in iure divino possit iuste praeesse in ecclesiae regno*,' in: *Kerk in Beraad. Opstellen aangeboden aan J.C.P.A. van Laarhoven*, ed. Gian Ackermans [e.a.], Katholieke Universiteit Nijmegen 1991, 87-101.
–, 'Exponents of Sovereignty: Canonists as seen by Theologians in the Late Middle Ages,' in: *The Church and Sovereignty c 590-1918. Essays in Honour of Michael Wilks*, ed. Diana Wood, Oxford 1991, 299-312.
–, 'Quel exemple avertisseur Jean Gerson présente-t-il au pape Benoît XIII dans son sermon *Apparuit gratia Dei*?', in: *Christianitas et Cultura Europae [Essays in Honour of J. Kloczowsky]* I, Lublin 1998, 112-6.
Powicke, F.M.: 'Alexander of St Albans: A Litarary Muddle,' in: *Essays presented to Reginald Lane Poole*, Oxford 1927, 246-60.
Rahsdall, Hastings: *The Universities of Europe in the Middle Ages*, rev. ed. ed. by F.M. Powicke & A.B. Emden, I-III, 1936-64.
Raymond, I.W.: 'D'Ailly's «Epistola Diaboli Leviathan»,' *CH* 22 (1953) 181-91.
Riché, Pierre & Guy Lobrichon (edd.), *Le Moyen Age et la Bible*, [Paris 1984].
Rivière, J.: *Le problème de l'Eglise et de l'Etat au temps de Philippe le Bel*, Louvain/Paris 1926.
Ritter, G.: *Studien zur Spätscholastik, II: Via antiqua und via moderna auf den deutschen Universitäten des XV. Jhdts.*, Heidelberg 1922.

Rueger, Z.: 'Le «De auctoritate concilii» de Gerson', *RHE* LIII (1958) 775-95.
Salembier, L.: *Petrus de Alliaco*, Insulis 1886.
–, 'Deux conciles inconnus de Cambrai et de Lille durant le grand schisme,' in: Hefele-Leclercq, *Histoire des Conciles* VI², 1481-1544.
–, art. 'd'Ailly, Pierre' in: *DThC* I, 642-54.
–, art. 'Gerson, Jean' in: *DThC* VI, 1313-30.
–, *Le grand schisme d'occident*, ⁵ Paris 1921.
–, *Le Cardinal Pierre d'Ailly*, Tourcoing 1932.
Schmiel, David: *Via Propria and Via Mystica in the Theology of Jean Charlier de Gerson*, St Louis (Miss) [1969].
Schwab, Johann Baptist: *Johannes Gerson. Professor der Theologie und Kanzler der Universität Paris. Eine Monographie*, Würzburg 1858.
Schäfer, C.: *Die Staatslehre des Johannes Gerson*, (Thesis Cologne), Bielefeld 1935.
Scholz, R.: *Die Publizistik zur Zeit des Philipps des Schönen und Bonifaz VIII*, Stuttgart 1903.
–, *Wilhelm von Ockham als politischer Denker und sein Breviloquium de principatu tyrannico*, Stuttgart 1942.
Schulte, J.F. von: *Geschichte der Quellen und Literatur des kanonischen Rechts von Gratian bis auf die Gegenwart* II, Stuttgart 1873.
Seeberg, Reinold, *Lehrbuch der Dogmengeschichte* III, ⁵ Darmstadt 1953.
Smalley, Beryl: *The Study of the Bible in the Middle Ages*, Oxford 1952.
Sohm, Rudolph: *Das altkatholische Kirchenrecht*, München/Leipzig 1908.
Sperl, A.: *Melanchthon zwischen Humanismus und Reformation*, München 1959.
Spicq, C.: *Esquisse d'une histoire de l'exégèse latine au moyen âge*, Paris 1944.
Steinbüchel, Th.: *Der Zweckgedanke in der Philosophie des Thomas von Aquino nach den Quellen dargestellt*, Münster i.W. 1912.
Stickler, A.M.: *Historia Iuris Canonici Latini* I, Augustae Taurinorum 1950.
Stump, Phillip H.: *The Reforms of the Council of Constance (1414-1418)*, Leiden [etc.] 1994.
Sullivan, J.I.: 'Marsiglio of Padua and William of Ockham,' *AHR* II (1896-97), 409-26; 593-610.
Swanson, R.N.: *Universities, Academics and the Great Schism*, London [etc.] [1979].
Tavard, G.H.: *Holy Writ or Holy Church. The Crisis of the Protestant Reformation*, New York [1959].
Tessier, Georges: 'Jean de Mirecourt. Philosophe et théologien,' *HLF* XL (1966) 1-52.
Thiersch, H., (A. Hauck): art. 'Bellarmin,' *PRE* II, 549-55.
Thorndike, Lynn: *University records and life in the middle ages*, (Norton paperback ed.) New York [1975].
Thurot, Ch.: *De l'organisation de l'enseignement dans l'université de Paris au moyen âge*, Paris 1850.
Tierney, Brian: 'Ockham, the Conciliar Theory, and the Canonists,' *JHI* 15 (1954) 40-70.
–, *Foundations of the Conciliar Theory. The contribution of the medieval canonists from Gratian to the Great Schism*, Cambridge 1955.
–, 'Pope and Council,' *MS* 19 (1957) 197-218.

–, 'Hermeneutics and History: The Problem of Haec Sancta,' in: *Essays in Honour of Bertie Wilkinson*, Toronto 1969, 355-70.
–, *Origins of papal infallibility 1150-1350*, Leiden 1972.
–, 'The Idea of Representation in the Medieval Councils of the West,' *Concilium* 19 (1983) 25-30.
–, 'Canon Law and Church Institutions,' in: *Proceedings of the Seventh International Congress of Medieval Canon Law* (Cambridge, 23–27 July 1984). *Monumenta Iuris Canonici*, series C: subsidia vol. 8, Città del Vaticano 1988, 49-69.
Toepke, G.: *Die Matrikel der Universität Heidelberg* I, Heidelberg 1884.
Tschackert, Paul: *Peter von Ailli (Petrus de Alliaco). Zur Geschichte des grossen abendländischen Schisma und der Reformconcilien von Pisa und Constanz*, Gotha 1877.
Ullmann, W.: *The Origins of the Great Schism*, London 1948.
–, *Mediaeval Papalism*, London [1949].
–, *The Growth of Papal Government in the Middle Ages*, London [1955].
Valois, Noël: *La France et le Grand Schisme d'Occident*, I-IV, Paris 1896-1902.
–, 'Gerson, curé de Saint-Jean-en-Grève,' *Bulletin de la Société de l'Histoire de Paris et de l'Ile de France*, XXVIII (1901) 49-57.
–, 'Pierre Auriol, Frère Mineur,' *HLF*, XXXIII (1906) 479-528.
Vansteenberghe, E.: 'Gerson à Bruges', *RHE* XXXI (1935) 5-52.
–, art. 'Schisme d'Occident, Grand' in: *DThC* XIV, 1468-92.
Vereecke, Louis: 'Droit et Morale chez Jean Gerson,' *RHDF* 4e série 32 (1954) 413-27.
–, *Conscience morale et loi humaine selon Gabriel Vazquez S.J.*, Paris [etc.] [1957].
Viollet, P.: *Histoire des Institutions politiques et administratives de la France*, II, Paris 1898.
Vooght, P. de: *Les sources de la doctrine chrétienne*, s.l. [1954].
–, 'L'ecclésiologie des adversaires de Huss au concile de Constance,' *ETL* 35 (1959) 5-24.
–, 'Le conciliarisme aux conciles de Constance et de Bâle,' in: B. Botte & H. Marot [edd.], *Le concile et les conciles*, 143-81.
Walsh, Katharine: *A fourteenth century Scholar and Primate. Richard FitzRalph, Avignon and Armagh*, Oxford 1981.
Wilks, M.J.: '*Papa est nomen iurisdictionis.* Augustinus Triumphus and the Papal Vicariate of Christ,' *JTS* NS VIII (1957) 71-91; 256-71.
–, 'The Idea of the Church as «Unus homo perfectus» and its bearing on the Medieval Theory of Sovereignty, in: *MHE* (Congrès de Stockholm, Août 1960) Louvain 1961, 32-50.
–, *The Problem of Sovereignty in the later Middle Ages. The Papal Monarchy with Augustinus Triumphus and the Publicists*, Cambridge 1963.
Williams, Georges H.: *Wilderness and Paradise in Christian Thought. The Biblical Theme of the Desert in the History of Christianity and the Paradise Theme in the Theological Idea of the University*, New York 1962.

INDEX OF BIBLICAL TEXTS

INDEX OF LEGAL TEXTS

d.a. = dictum ante
d.p. = dictum post

INDEX OF WORKS OF GERSON

The following list contains all the works of Gerson mentioned in this book according to the order of the edition of Mgr. Glorieux. In the references the texts concerned are also indicated according to the edition of Dupin.

INDEX OF PERSONS

INDEX OF SUBJECTS, TERMS, AND EXPRESSIONS

Studies in the History of Christian Thought

EDITED BY HEIKO A. OBERMAN

3. BAUMAN, Cl. *Gewaltlosigkeit im Täufertum.* 1968. ISBN 90 04 02181 7
6. TIERNEY, B. *Origins of Papal Infallibility, 1150-1350.* 2nd ed. 1988. ISBN 90 04 08884 9
10. FARR, W. *John Wyclif as Legal Reformer.* 1974. ISBN 90 04 04027 7
12. BALL, B. W. *A Great Expectation.* Eschatological Thought in English Protestantism. 1975. ISBN 90 04 04315 2
21. NIJENHUIS, W. *Adrianus Saravia (c. 1532-1613).* Dutch Calvinist. 1980. ISBN 90 04 06194 0
22. PARKER, T. H. L. (ed.). *Iohannis Calvini Commentarius in Epistolam Pauli ad Romanos.* 1981. ISBN 90 04 06408 7
25. LOCHER, G. W. *Zwingli's Thought.* New Perspectives. 1981. ISBN 90 04 06420 6
26. GOGAN, B. *The Common Corps of Christendom.* Ecclesiological Themes in Thomas More. 1982. ISBN 90 04 06508 3
27. STOCK, U. *Die Bedeutung der Sakramente in Luthers Sermonen von 1519.* 1982. ISBN 90 04 06536 9
28. YARDENI, M. (ed.). *Modernité et nonconformisme en France à travers les âges.* 1983. ISBN 90 04 07087 7
29. PLATT, J. *Reformed Thought and Scholasticism.* 1982. ISBN 90 04 06593 8
31. SPRUNGER, K. L. *Dutch Puritanism.* 1982. ISBN 90 04 06793 0
32. MEIJERING, E. P. *Melanchthon and Patristic Thought.* 1983. ISBN 90 04 06974 7
34-35. COLISH, M. L. *The Stoic Tradition from Antiquity to the Early Middle Ages.* Vols. 1-2. 2nd ed. 1991. ISBN 90 04 09330 3
36. GUY, B. *Domestic Correspondence of Dominique-Marie Varlet, Bishop of Babylon, 1678-1742.* 1986. ISBN 90 04 07671 9
37-38. CLARK, F. *The Pseudo-Gregorian Dialogues.* 2 pts. 1987. ISBN 90 04 07773 1
39. PARENTE, Jr. J. A. *Religious Drama and the Humanist Tradition.* 1987. ISBN 90 04 08094 5
40. POSTHUMUS MEYJES, G. H. M. *Hugo Grotius, Meletius.* 1988. ISBN 90 04 08356 1
41. FELD, H. *Der Ikonoklasmus des Westens.* 1990. ISBN 90 04 09243 9
42. REEVE, A. and SCREECH, M. A. (eds.). *Erasmus' Annotations on the New Testament.* Acts—Romans — I and II Corinthians. 1990. ISBN 90 04 09124 6
43. KIRBY, W.J.T. *Richard Hooker's Doctrine of the Royal Supremacy.* 1990. ISBN 90 04 08851 2
44. GERSTNER, J.N. *The Thousand Generation Covenant.* Reformed Covenant Theology. 1990. ISBN 90 04 09361 3
46. GARSTEIN, O. *Rome and the Counter-Reformation in Scandinavia.* 1553-1622. 1992. ISBN 90 04 09393 1
47. GARSTEIN, O. *Rome and the Counter-Reformation in Scandinavia.* 1622-1656. 1992. ISBN 90 04 09395 8
48. PERRONE COMPAGNI, V. (ed.). *Cornelius Agrippa, De occulta philosophia Libri tres.* 1992. ISBN 90 04 09421 0
49. MARTIN, D. D. *Fifteenth-Century Carthusian Reform.* The World of Nicholas Kempf. 1992. ISBN 90 04 09636 1
50. HOENEN, M. J. F. M. *Marsilius of Inghen.* Divine Knowledge in Late Medieval Thought. 1993. ISBN 90 04 09563 2
51. O'MALLEY, J. W., IZBICKI, T. M. and CHRISTIANSON, G. (eds.). *Humanity and Divinity in Renaissance and Reformation.* Essays in Honor of Charles Trinkaus. 1993. ISBN 90 04 09804 6
52. REEVE, A. (ed.) and SCREECH, M. A. (introd.). *Erasmus' Annotations on the New Testament.* Galatians to the Apocalypse. 1993. ISBN 90 04 09906 9
53. STUMP, Ph. H. *The Reforms of the Council of Constance (1414-1418).* 1994. ISBN 90 04 09930 1

54. GIAKALIS, A. *Images of the Divine.* The Theology of Icons at the Seventh Ecumenical Council. With a Foreword by Henry Chadwick. 1994. ISBN 90 04 09946 8
55. NELLEN, H. J. M. and RABBIE, E. (eds.). *Hugo Grotius – Theologian.* Essays in Honour of G. H. M. Posthumus Meyjes. 1994. ISBN 90 04 10000 8
56. TRIGG, J. D. *Baptism in the Theology of Martin Luther.* 1994. ISBN 90 04 10016 4
57. JANSE, W. *Albert Hardenberg als Theologe.* Profil eines Bucer-Schülers. 1994. ISBN 90 04 10071 7
59. SCHOOR, R.J.M. VAN DE. *The Irenical Theology of Théophile Brachet de La Milletière (1588-1665).* 1995. ISBN 90 04 09961 1
60. STREHLE, S. *The Catholic Roots of the Protestant Gospel.* Encounter between the Middle Ages and the Reformation. 1995. ISBN 90 04 10203 5
61. BROWN, M.L. *Donne and the Politics of Conscience in Early Modern England.* 1995. ISBN 90 04 10157 8
62. SCREECH, M.A. (ed.). *Richard Mocket, Warden of All Souls College, Oxford, Doctrina et Politia Ecclesiae Anglicanae.* An Anglican Summa. Facsimile with Variants of the Text of 1617. Edited with an Introduction. 1995. ISBN 90 04 10040 7
63. SNOEK, G.J.C. *Medieval Piety from Relics to the Eucharist.* A Process of Mutual Interaction. 1995. ISBN 90 04 10263 9
64. PIXTON, P.B. *The German Episcopacy and the Implementation of the Decrees of the Fourth Lateran Council, 1216-1245.* Watchmen on the Tower. 1995. ISBN 90 04 10262 0
65. DOLNIKOWSKI, E.W. *Thomas Bradwardine: A View of Time and a Vision of Eternity in Fourteenth-Century Thought.* 1995. ISBN 90 04 10226 4
66. RABBIE, E. (ed.). *Hugo Grotius, Ordinum Hollandiae ac Westfrisiae Pietas (1613).* Critical Edition with Translation and Commentary. 1995. ISBN 90 04 10385 6
67. HIRSH, J.C. *The Boundaries of Faith.* The Development and Transmission of Medieval Spirituality. 1996. ISBN 90 04 10428 3
68. BURNETT, S.G. *From Christian Hebraism to Jewish Studies.* Johannes Buxtorf (1564-1629) and Hebrew Learning in the Seventeenth Century. 1996. ISBN 90 04 10346 5
69. BOLAND O.P., V. *Ideas in God according to Saint Thomas Aquinas.* Sources and Synthesis. 1996. ISBN 90 04 10392 9
70. LANGE, M.E. *Telling Tears in the English Renaissance.* 1996. ISBN 90 04 10517 4
71. CHRISTIANSON, G. and T.M. IZBICKI (eds.). *Nicholas of Cusa on Christ and the Church.* Essays in Memory of Chandler McCuskey Brooks for the American Cusanus Society. 1996. ISBN 90 04 10519 0
72. MALI, A. *Mystic in the New World.* Marie de l'Incarnation (1599-1672). 1996. ISBN 90 04 10606 5
73. VISSER, D. *Apocalypse as Utopian Expectation (800-1500).* The Apocalypse Commentary of Berengaudus of Ferrières and the Relationship between Exegesis, Liturgy and Iconography. 1996. ISBN 90 04 10621 9
74. O'ROURKE BOYLE, M. *Divine Domesticity.* Augustine of Thagaste to Teresa of Avila. 1997. ISBN 90 04 10675 8
75. PFIZENMAIER, T.C. *The Trinitarian Theology of Dr. Samuel Clarke (1675-1729).* Context, Sources, and Controversy. 1997. ISBN 90 04 10719 3
76. BERKVENS-STEVELINCK, C., J. ISRAEL and G.H.M. POSTHUMUS MEYJES (eds.). *The Emergence of Tolerance in the Dutch Republic.* 1997. ISBN 90 04 10768 1
77. HAYKIN, M.A.G. (ed.). *The Life and Thought of John Gill (1697-1771).* A Tercentennial Appreciation. 1997. ISBN 90 04 10744 4
78. KAISER, C.B. *Creational Theology and the History of Physical Science.* The Creationist Tradition from Basil to Bohr. 1997. ISBN 90 04 10669 3
79. LEES, J.T. *Anselm of Havelberg.* Deeds into Words in the Twelfth Century. 1997. ISBN 90 04 10906 4
80. WINTER, J.M. VAN. *Sources Concerning the Hospitallers of St John in the Netherlands, 14th-18th Centuries.* 1998. ISBN 90 04 10803 3
81. TIERNEY, B. *Foundations of the Conciliar Theory.* The Contribution of the Medieval Canonists from Gratian to the Great Schism. Enlarged New Edition. 1998. ISBN 90 04 10924 2
82. MIERNOWSKI, J. *Le Dieu Néant.* Théologies négatives à l'aube des temps modernes. 1998. ISBN 90 04 10915 3

83. HALVERSON, J.L. *Peter Aureol on Predestination.* A Challenge to Late Medieval Thought. 1998. ISBN 90 04 10945 5
84. HOULISTON, V. (ed.). *Robert Persons, S.J.: The Christian Directory (1582).* The First Booke of the Christian Exercise, appertayning to Resolution. 1998. ISBN 90 04 11009 7
85. GRELL, O.P. (ed.). *Paracelsus.* The Man and His Reputation, His Ideas and Their Reputation. 1998. ISBN 90 04 11177 8
86. MAZZOLA, E. *The Pathology of the English Renaissance.* Sacred Remains and Holy Ghosts. 1998. ISBN 90 04 11195 6

Prospectus available on request

BRILL — P.O.B. 9000 — 2300 PA LEIDEN — THE NETHERLANDS